The **Rough Guide** to

Norway

written and researched by

Phil Lee

with additional contributions by

Belinda Dixon and Emma Rose Rees

This book is dedicated to my dear Mother, Lois Mary Lee, whose wonderful stories I will always remember.

NEW YORK • LONDON • DELHI

www.roughguides.com

N-57MS

Contents

Colour section 1–24

Introduction 6
Where to go 9
When to go 14
Things not to miss 17

Basics 25–70

Getting there 27
Red tape and visas 40
Information, maps and websites 41
Health 42
Insurance 43
Costs, money and banks 44
Getting around 48
Accommodation 54
Food and drink 58
Opening hours, public holidays and festivals 60
Mail and telecommunications 62
Media 64
Crime and personal safety 64
Outdoor pursuits 65
Travellers with disabilities 67
Gay Norway 69
Directory 69

Guide 71–380

1 Oslo 73
2 The South 137
3 Central Norway 163
4 Bergen & the western fjords 197
5 Trondheim to the Lofoten islands 273
6 North Norway 339

Contexts 381–456

History 383
Legends and folklore 403
Viking customs and rituals 408
Flora and fauna 412
Cinema 415
Books 417
Literary extracts 427

Language 457–466

Words and phrases 459
Menu reader 462
Glossaries 465

Travel store 467–474

Small print & Index 475–488

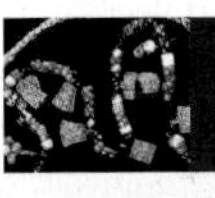

The Vikings insert following p.216

Hiking insert following p.392

◀◀ Lyngenfjord ◀ Hamnøy

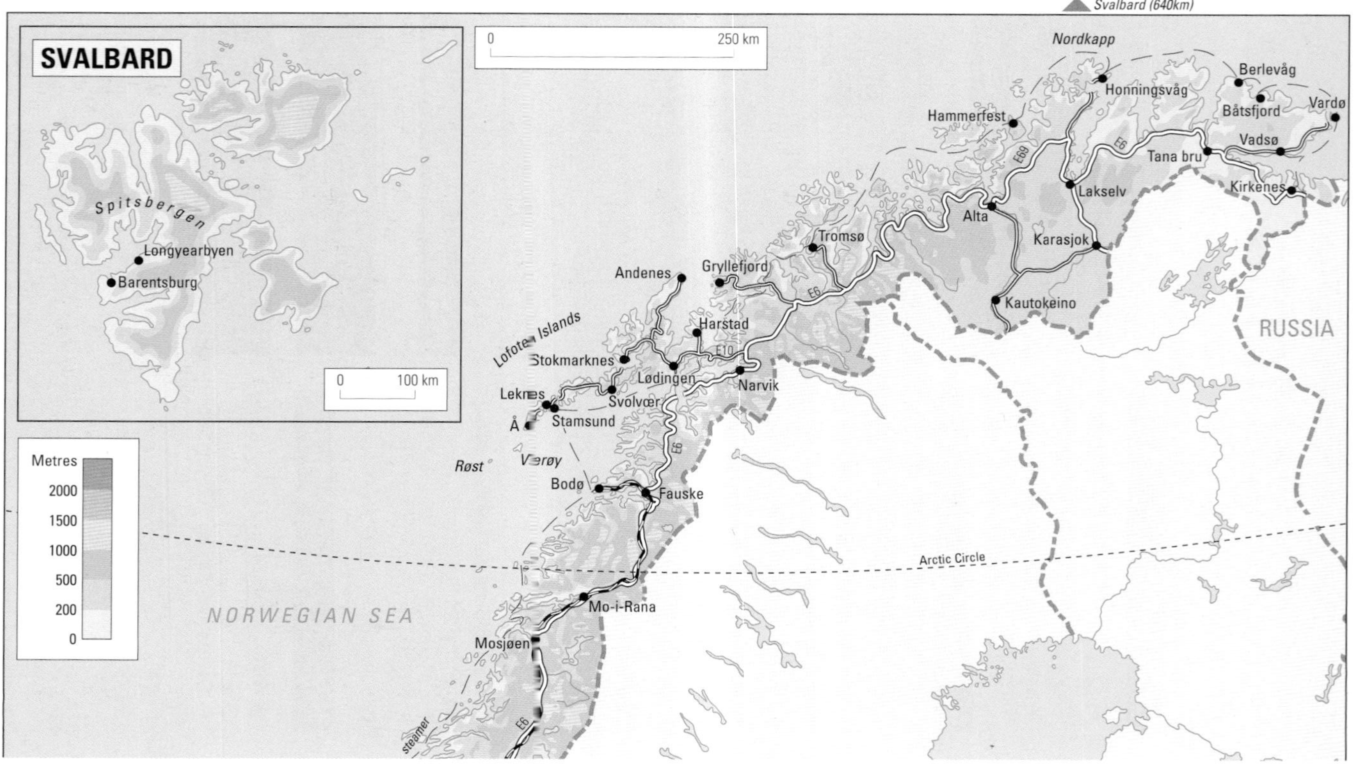
Svalbard (640km)
SVALBARD
Spitsbergen
Longyearbyen
Barentsburg
0
100 km
0
250 km
Metres
2000
1500
1000
500
200
0
Nordkapp
Honningsvåg
Berlevåg
Båtsfjord
Vardø
Vadsø
Tana bru
Kirkenes
Hammerfest
Lakselv
Alta
Karasjok
Kautokeino
E6
E69
RUSSIA
Tromsø
Gryllefjord
Andenes
Harstad
E10
Narvik
Lødingen
Stokmarknes
Svolvær
Stamsund
Lofoten Islands
Leknes
Å
Værøy
Røst
Bodø
Fauske
Arctic Circle
Mo-i-Rana
Mosjøen
NORWEGIAN SEA
steamer

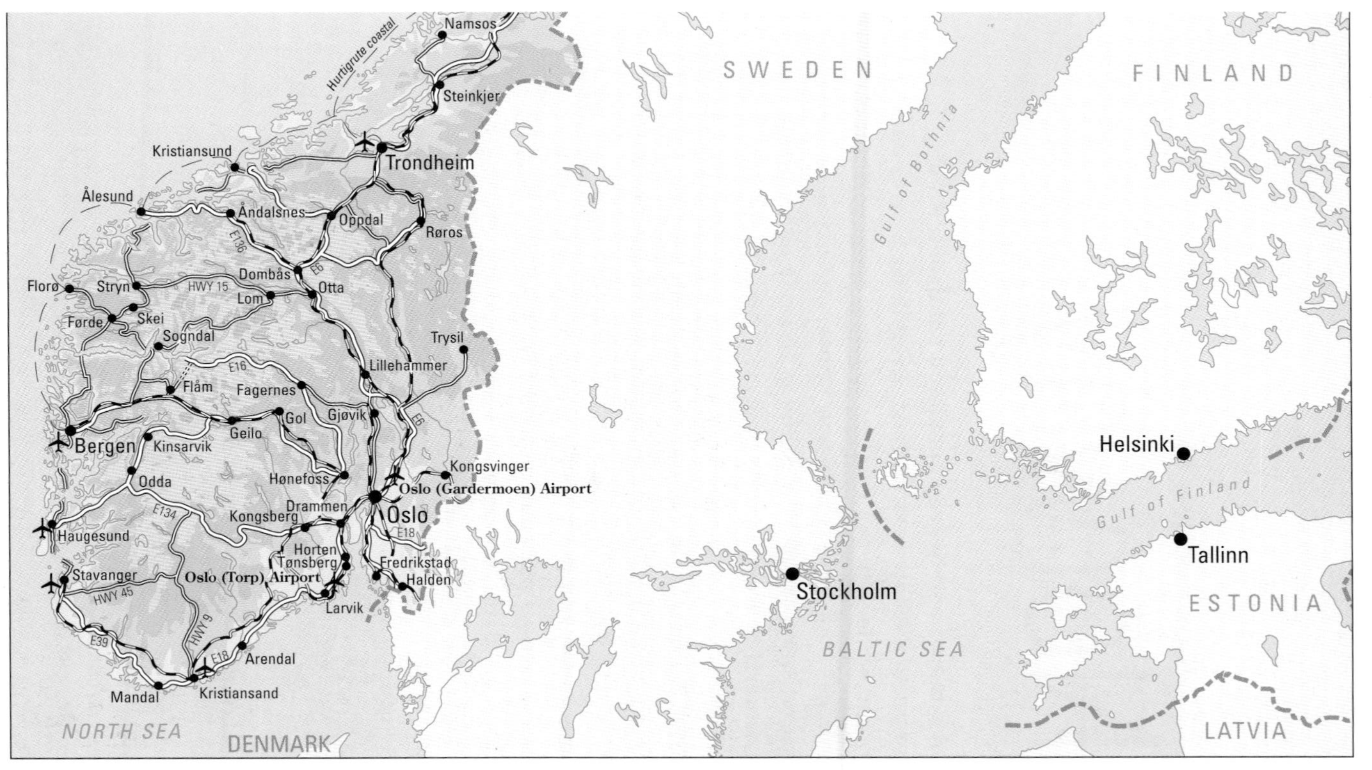
SWEDEN
FINLAND
ESTONIA
LATVIA
DENMARK
NORTH SEA
BALTIC SEA
Gulf of Bothnia
Gulf of Finland
Helsinki
Tallinn
Stockholm
Hurtigrute coastal
Namsos
Steinkjer
Trondheim
Kristiansund
Ålesund
Åndalsnes
Oppdal
Røros
E136
Dombås
E6
Otta
Florø
Stryn
HWY 15
Lom
Førde
Skei
Sogndal
Trysil
E16
Lillehammer
Flåm
Fagernes
Gol
Gjøvik
Geilo
Bergen
Kinsarvik
Kongsvinger
Hønefoss
Oslo (Gardermoen) Airport
Odda
Drammen
Oslo
E134
Kongsberg
E18
Haugesund
Horten
Tønsberg
Fredrikstad
Halden
Stavanger
Oslo (Torp) Airport
HWY 45
Larvik
HWY 9
E39
Arendal
Mandal
Kristiansand

Introduction to Norway

In a tamed and heavily populated continent, Norway remains a wilderness outpost. Everything here is on a grand scale with the country boasting some of Europe's wildest land- and seascapes, whose vast expanses are merely pinpricked by a clutch of likeable cities, most memorably Trondheim, Bergen and Oslo. From the Skagerrak – the choppy channel that separates the country from Denmark – Norway stretches north in a long, slender band along the Atlantic seaboard, up across the Arctic Circle to the Barents Sea and the Russian border. Behind this rough and rocky coast are great mountain ranges, harsh upland plateaux, plunging river valleys, rippling glaciers, deep forests and, most famously, the mighty fjords that gash deep inland.

The **fjords** are the apple of the tourist industry's eye, and they are indeed magnificent, but with the exception of Oslo, the capital city, and Bergen, its nearest rival, the rest of the country might as well be blank for all that many visitors know. Few seem aware of the sheer variety of the landscape or the lovely little towns that are sprinkled over it. Neither are the Norwegians given enough credit for their careful construction of one of the most civilized, educated and **tolerant societies** in the world – one whose even-handed internationalism has set standards that few other European nations can approach. With every justification, the bulk of the population have a deep loyalty for – and pride in – their country, partly at least because independence was so long in coming: after the heady days of the Vikings, Norway was governed by the Danes for four centuries and was then passed to the Swedes, who only left in 1905.

It is the **Vikings** who continue to grab the historical headlines, prompting book after book and film upon (foreign) film. These formidable warriors burst upon an unsuspecting Europe from the remoteness of Scandinavia in the ninth century. The Norwegian Vikings sailed west, raiding every seaboard from the Shetlands to Sicily, even venturing as far as Greenland and Newfoundland. Wherever they settled, the speed of their assimilation into the indigenous population was extraordinary – William the Conqueror, the archetypal Norman baron, was only a few generations removed from his Viking ancestors – but in the unpopulated Faroes and Iceland, the settlers could begin from scratch, creating societies which then developed in a similar fashion to that of their original homeland.

Norway's so-called "period of greatness" came to an abrupt end: in 1349, an English ship unwittingly brought the **Black Death** to the country,

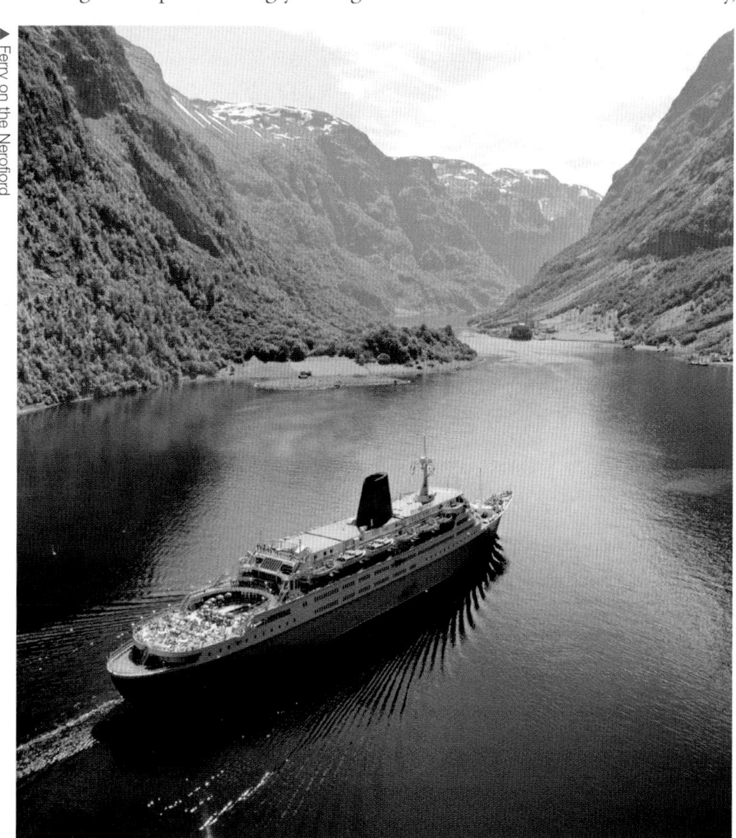

▲ Ferry on the Nerofiord

Fact file

- Norway is one of the five **Nordic nations**, along with Denmark, Sweden, Finland and Iceland. It is bordered to the east by Sweden, Finland and Russia, but otherwise is flanked by the sea – the Atlantic to the west, the Barents Sea to the north and the Skagerrak, which leads off the North Sea, to the south. Extremely long and thin, Norway has a surface area of 386,000 square kilometres, of which half is mountain and a further third forest, lake and river.
- The country's **population** numbers about 4.5 million, of which more than ten percent (half a million) live in the capital, Oslo. Norway's second city, Bergen, clocks up about 240,000 residents, while around 30,000 indigenous Sami (Lapps) live mostly in the north of the country.
- Norway is a **constitutional monarchy** and the present king, Harald V, came to the throne in 1001. The parliament – the *Storting* – sits in Oslo, but many functions are devolved to a complex network of local authorities. The Lutheran **Church of Norway** is the official state church and over eighty percent of the population belong to it, however nominally. Norway is not a member of the EU, but has signed up to the EEA (European Economic Agreement) free-trade deal.
- The **economy** of Norway is highly dependent on the oil industry, with crude oil accounting for forty percent of the country's total exports. Natural gas, metals and fish products come a distant second, at about eight percent each.

▲ The northern lights

and in the next two years somewhere between half and two-thirds of the population was wiped out. The enfeebled country was easy meat for the **Danes**, who took control at the end of the fourteenth century and remained in command until 1814. As colonial powers go, the Danes were comparatively benign, but everything specifically "Norwegian" – from language to dress – became associated with the primitive and uncouth. To redress this state of affairs, Norway's bourgeois nationalists of the mid- to late nineteenth century sought to rediscover – and sometimes to reinvent – a national identity. This ambitious enterprise, enthusiastically undertaken, fuelled a cultural renaissance which formed the backdrop to the work of acclaimed painters, writers and musicians, most notably Munch, Ibsen and Grieg, and the endeavours of explorers like Amundsen and Nansen. Its reverberations can be felt to this day, for example in Norway's "No" vote on EU membership.

Where to go

Norway is one of Europe's most sparsely inhabited countries, and for the most part its people live in small towns and villages, but the country's five largest cities are the obvious – and the most popular - initial targets for a visit. The five begin with urbane, vivacious **Oslo**, one of the world's most prettily sited capitals, with a flourishing café scene and a clutch of outstanding museums. Beyond Oslo, in roughly descending order of interest, are **Trondheim**, with its superb cathedral and charming, antique centre; the beguiling port of **Bergen**, gateway to the western fjords; gritty, bustling **Stavanger** in the southwest; and northern **Tromsø**. All are likeable, walkable cities worthy of time in themselves, as well as being within comfortable reach of some startlingly handsome scenery. Indeed, each can serve as either a base or a starting point for further explorations: the trains, buses and ferries of Norway's finely tuned public transport system will take you almost anywhere you want to go, although services are curtailed in winter.

Outside of the cities, the perennial draw remains the **western fjords** – a must, and every

The Puffin (Fratercula arctica)

Some 30cm tall, with a triangular, red, blue and yellow striped bill, the puffin is the most distinctive of the many seabirds that congregate along the Norwegian coast. It feeds on small fish, and breeds in holes it excavates in turf on cliffs or grassy flatlands, sometimes even adapting former rabbit burrows. When hunting, puffins use their wings to propel themselves underwater and, indeed, are much better at swimming than flying, finding it difficult both to get airborne and to land – collisions of one sort or another are commonplace. Their nesting habits and repetitive flight paths make them easy to catch, and puffin has long been a west-coast delicacy, though hunting them is now severely restricted. In the summer, puffins nest along the whole of the Atlantic coast from Stavanger to Nordkapp, with Værøy (see p.336) and Runde (see p.287) being the most likely places for a sighting. In the autumn the puffins move south, though residual winter populations remain on the southerly part of the west coast between Stavanger and Ålesund.

Roald Amundsen

One of Norway's best-known sons, Roald Amundsen (1872–1928) was intent on becoming a polar explorer from his early teens. He read everything there was to read on the subject, even training as a sea captain in preparation and, in 1897, embarked upon his first trip to Antarctica, with a Belgian expedition. Undeterred by a winter on the ice after the ship broke up, he was soon planning his own expedition, the first ever crossing of the Northwest Passage, from the Atlantic to the Pacific round the north of the American continent. He left in the *Gjøa* in June 1903 and finally reached Alaskan waters three years later.

His next target was the North Pole, but during his preparations, in 1909, the American Robert Peary got there first. Amundsen immediately switched his attention to the South Pole, which he reached on December 14, 1911, famously beating the British expedition of Captain Scott. Neither did Amundsen's ambitions end there: in 1926, he became one of the first men to fly over the North Pole in the airship of the Italian Umberto Nobile. It was, however, the Italian who was to do for Amundsen: in 1928, the Norwegian flew north out of Tromsø in a bid to rescue a stranded Nobile and was never seen again.

bit as scenically stunning as the publicity suggests. Dip into the region from Bergen or **Åndalsnes**, both accessible by direct train from Oslo, or take more time to appreciate the subtle charms of the tiny, fjordside villages, among which **Balestrand** and **Mundal** are especially appealing. This is great hiking country too, with a network of cairned trails and lodges (maintained by the nationwide hiking association DNT) threading along the valleys and over the hills. However, many of the country's finest hikes are to be had further inland, within the confines of a trio of marvellous **national parks**: the **Hardangervidda**, a vast mountain plateau of lunar-like appearance, the **Rondane**, with its bulging mountains; and the **Jotunheimen**, famous for its jagged peaks. Of these three, the first is most easily approached from Finse, Rjukan or Kinsarvik, the others from small-town Otta. Nudging the Skagerrak, the **south coast** is different again. This island-

"Few seem aware of the sheer variety of the landscape or the lovely little towns that are sprinkled over it."

▲ Wooden houses in Bergen

strewn shoreline is best appreciated from the sea, though its pretty, old whitewashed ports are popular with holidaying Norwegians; the pick of these towns are **Arendal** and **Mandal**, the proud possessor of the country's finest sandy beach.

Away to the **north**, beyond Trondheim, Norway grows increasingly wild and inhospitable as it sprawls across the Arctic Circle on the way to the modern, workaday port of **Bodø**. From here, ferries shuttle over to the rugged **Lofoten** islands, which hold some of the most ravishing scenery in the whole of Europe – tiny fishing villages of ochre- and red-painted houses tucked in between the swell of the deep blue sea and the severest of grey-green mountains. Back on the mainland, it's a long haul north from Bodø to the iron-ore town of **Narvik**, and on to **Tromsø**. These towns are, however, merely the froth of a vast wilderness that extends up to **Nordkapp** (North Cape), the northernmost

▼ Liberty Day Parade, Oslo

▲ Dog-sledging

accessible point of mainland Europe, and the spot where the tourist trail peters out. Yet Norway continues east for several hundred kilometres, round to remote **Kirkenes** near the Russian border, while inland stretches an immense and hostile upland plateau, the **Finnmarksvidda**, one of the last haunts of the Sami (formerly Lapp) reindeer-herders.

Stokfisk and klippfisk

The Vikings were able to sail long distances without starving to death because they had learnt how to dry white fish, mostly cod, in the open air. This dried fish, stokfisk, remained edible for years and was eaten either raw or after soaking in water – chewy and smelly no doubt, but very nutritious. In time, stokfisk became the staple diet of western Norway and remained so until the early twentieth century, with every fishing port festooned with wooden A-frames carrying hundreds of drying white fish, headless and paired for size.

It wasn't until the 1690s that the Dutch introduced to Norway the idea of salting and drying white fish, again usually cod. The fish was decapitated, cleaned and split before being heavily salted and left for several weeks. Then it was dried for a further four to six weeks, by being left outside on rocky drying grounds, klipper in Norwegian, hence klippfisk. The Norwegians never really took to eating klippfisk, but they (or rather their merchants) made fortunes by exporting it to Spain, Portugal, Africa and the Caribbean, where salted cod remains extremely popular to this day.

NORWAY: DISTANCE CHART (Distance in kilometres)

	Bergen	Bodø	Hamar	Hammerfest	Kirkenes	Kristiansand	Lillehammer	Narvik	Nordkapp	Oslo	Røros	Stavanger	Tromsø	Trondheim	Ålesund
Bergen	0	1380	471	2214	2588	492	439	1561	2283	478	637	170	1844	657	378
Bodø	1380	0	1108	956	1331	1534	1065	304	1025	1217	936	1560	562	723	1010
Hamar	471	1108	0	1942	2316	443	59	1279	2011	123	289	575	1606	385	441
Hammerfest	2214	956	1942	0	494	2368	1899	652	181	2051	1810	2394	549	1567	1844
Kirkenes	2588	1331	2316	494	0	2742	2273	1027	517	2425	2185	2768	944	1931	2218
Kristiansand	492	1534	443	2368	2742	0	471	1715	2437	320	753	245	2054	811	811
Lillehammer	439	1065	59	1899	2273	471	0	1246	1968	167	282	587	1562	342	382
Narvik	1561	304	1279	652	1027	1715	1246	0	721	1398	1123	1741	251	904	1191
Nordkapp	2283	1025	2011	181	517	2437	1968	721	0	2120	1869	2463	609	1626	1913
Oslo	478	1217	123	2051	2425	320	167	1398	2120	0	423	452	1733	494	533
Røros	637	936	289	1810	2185	753	282	1123	1869	423	0	740	1352	166	430
Stavanger	170	1560	575	2394	2768	245	587	1741	2463	452	740	0	1852	837	621
Tromsø	1844	562	1606	549	944	2054	1562	251	609	1733	1352	1852	0	1205	1519
Trondheim	657	723	385	1567	1931	811	342	904	1626	494	166	837	1205	0	287
Ålesund	378	1010	441	1844	2218	811	382	1191	1913	533	430	621	1519	287	0

Ferry crossings not included in distances quoted.

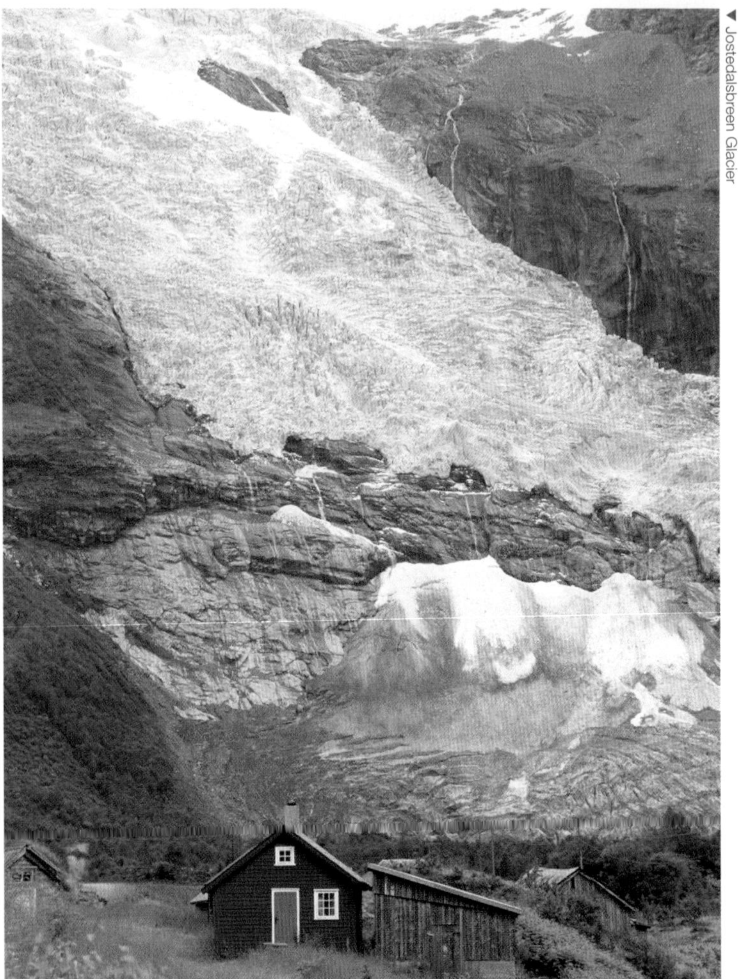

▲ Jostedalsbreen Glacier

When to go

Norway is widely regarded as a remote, cold country – spectacular enough but climatically inhospitable. There is some truth in this, of course, but **when to go** is not, perhaps, as clear-cut a choice as you might imagine. There are advantages to travelling during the long, dark **winters** with their reduced everything: daylight, opening times and transport services. If you are equipped and hardy enough to reach the north, seeing the phenomenal **northern**

The midnight sun

The **midnight sun** is visible at the following places on the following dates, though climbing the nearest hill can – trees and clouds permitting – extend this by a day or two either way:

Bodø: June 2–July 10
Hammerfest: May 14–July 28
Longyearbyen April 19–Aug 23
Nordkapp: May 12–July 29
Tromsø: May 20–July 21

lights (aurora borealis) is a distinct possibility and later, once the days begin to lighten, the **skiing** – and for that matter the dog sledging and ice fishing – is excellent. There are skiing packages to Norway from abroad, but perhaps more appealing – and certainly less expensive – is the ease with which you can arrange a few days' skiing wherever you happen to be. As the year advances, **Easter** is the time of the colourful Sami festivals, and **mid-May** can be absolutely delightful if your visit coincides with the brief Norwegian **spring**, though this is difficult to gauge. Springtime is particularly beguiling in the fjords, with myriad cascading waterfalls fed by the melting snow, and wildflowers in abundance. **Autumn** can be exquisite too, with **September** often bathed in the soft sunshine of an Indian summer, but – especially in the far north – it is frequently cold, often bitterly so, from late September to mid- to late-May and this guide has been deliberately weighted towards the **summer** season, when most people travel and when bus, ferry and train connections are at their most frequent. This is the time of the **midnight sun**: the further north you go, the longer the day becomes, until at Nordkapp the sun is continually visible from mid-May to the end of July. Something worth noting, however, is that the **summer season** in Norway is relatively short, stretching roughly from the beginning of June to the end of August. Come in September and you'll find that many tourist offices, museums and other sights cut back their

◀ Fresh seafood

Oslo

hours and buses, ferries and trains often switch to reduced schedules.

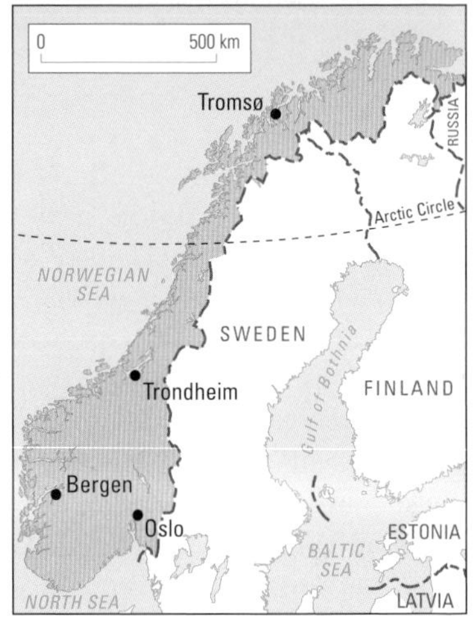

As regards **climate**, the Gulf Stream keeps all of coastal Norway temperate throughout the year. Inland, the climate is more extreme – bitterly cold in winter and hot in summer, when temperatures can soar to surprising heights. January and February are normally the coldest months in all regions, July and August the warmest. Rain is a regular occurrence throughout the year, particularly on the west coast, though there are significant local variations in precipitation.

Average daytime temperatures (°C) and rainfall

	Oslo		Bergen		Trondheim		Tromsø	
	°C	mm	°C	mm	°C	mm	°C	mm
January	-3.7	49	1.5	190	-3.3	63	-4.7	95
February	-2.8	36	1.6	152	-1.8	52	-4.1	87
March	1.3	47	3.3	170	1.9	54	-1.9	72
April	6.3	41	5.9	114	5.4	49	1.1	64
May	12.6	53	10.5	106	10.9	53	5.6	48
June	17.0	65	13.5	132	13.8	68	10.1	59
July	18.2	81	14.5	148	15.1	84	12.7	77
August	17.2	89	14.4	190	14.8	87	11.8	82
September	12.8	90	11.5	283	11.2	113	7.7	102
October	7.5	84	8.7	271	7.0	104	2.9	131
November	1.5	73	4.6	259	1.1	71	-1.5	108
December	-2.6	55	1.6	235	-1.8	84	-3.7	106

25

things not to miss

It's not possible to see everything Norway has to offer in one trip – and we don't suggest you try. What follows is a selective taste of the country's highlights: outstanding scenery, picturesque villages and dramatic wildlife. They're arranged in five colour-coded categories, which you should browse through to find the very best things to see and experience. All highlights have a page reference to take you straight into the guide, where you can find out more.

01 **Walking in the Jotunheimen mountains** Page **181** • Norway's most celebrated hiking area, the Jotunheimen National Park, is criss-crossed with trails and includes Northern Europe's two highest peaks.

02 The midnight sun Page **384** • North of the Arctic Circle, visitors can experience the midnight sun. The further you go, the longer it lasts: at Nordkapp, at the northern tip of the mainland, the phenomenon lasts from mid-May to the end of July.

03 Wildlife safaris Page **377** • From whalewatching through to polar-bear spotting, Norway offers an extravagant range of wildlife safaris, nowhere more so than among the icy wastes of Svalbard.

04 Vigelandsparken Page **108** • Before his death in 1943, Gustav Vigeland populated Oslo's favourite park with his fantastical, phantasmagorical sculptures.

05 The Flåmsbana Page **232** • A trip on the Flåm railway from the mountains to the fjords below is one of the most dramatic train rides in the world.

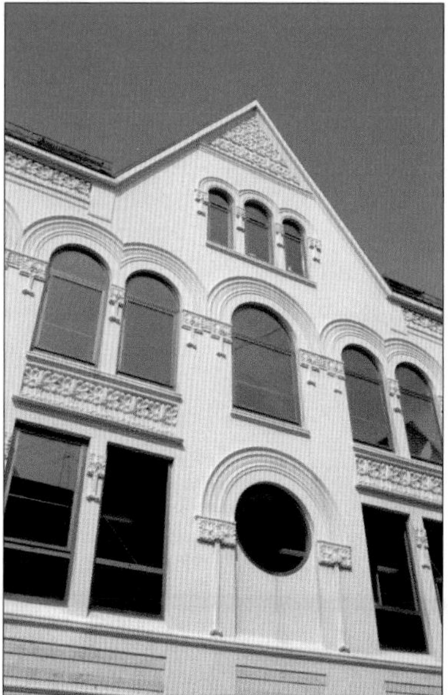

06 Ålesund Page **284** • The small, west-coast fishing port of Ålesund boasts a bevy of handsome Art Nouveau buildings dating from 1904.

07 The Oslofjord Page **114** • The islands of the Oslofjord – Hovedøya and Langøyene – are great for swimming, sunbathing and walking, and lie just a short ferry ride from the city centre.

08 Hørundfjord Page **258** • A wild and remote fjord, whose deep, dark waters and icy peaks make it one of Norway's most elegiac.

09 The Norsk Fiskevaersmuseum in Å Page **334** • Hanging on for dear life between the mountains and the sea, the tiny village of Å has preserved its nineteenth-century buildings as the Norwegian Fishing Village Museum.

10 Troldhaugen Page **214** • The one-time home of Norway's most famous composer, Edvard Grieg, has been preserved pretty much as he left it.

11 Union Hotel, Øye Page **259** • Bend your budget to stay in one of fjordland's most original hotels. Sited in the remote village of Øye, it offers charming views over the Norangsfjord.

12 Bergen Page **201** • Eminently appealing, Bergen, Norway's second city, nudges its way along a rough and craggy shoreline.

13 **Whalewatching** Page **319** • Take a whalewatching safari from Andenes between late May and mid-September, and you're virtually assured of a sighting.

14 **Urnes stave church** Page **246** • Perhaps the finest of Norway's stave churches, Urnes is distinguished by the frenzied intricacy of its Viking woodcarving.

15 **The Jostedalsbreen glacier** Page **246** • Take a guided walk out onto this mighty ice plateau that grinds and groans, slips and slithers its way across the mountains of the fjordland.

16 The Oseberg ship Page **105** • This superbly preserved Viking longboat can be seen at Oslo's Viking Ships Museum.

18 Geirangerfjord Page **255** • Shadowed by bulging mountains, the S-shaped Geirangerfjord is one of Norway's most beautiful fjords.

19 Alta rock carvings Page **353** • Simple in design but complex in their symbolism, the prehistoric rock carvings of Alta provide an intriguing insight into the lives and beliefs of the region's earliest inhabitants.

17 Trondheim cathedral Page **282** • Scandinavia's largest medieval building is a stirring – and sterling – edifice built of blue and green-grey soapstone.

20 Seabird colonies on Værøy Page **336** • This remote Lofoten island is renowned for its birdlife, including puffins, cormorants, kittiwakes, guillemots and rare sea eagles.

21 Svalbard archipelago Page **375** • Glaciers cover two-thirds of the surface of Norway's wild and chilly Svalbard archipelago, which enjoys continuous daylight from April to August.

22 Henningsvær Page **350** • The Lofoten islands are confettied with picture-postcard fishing villages, but Henningsvær is perhaps the most beguiling of all.

23 **Mandal** Page **150** • This pretty south-coast resort boasts the country's finest sandy beach.

24 **Edvard Munch** Page **111** • Munch's unsettling, highly charged paintings appear in several of the country's museums, most memorably at the National Gallery in Oslo.

25 **Kjerringøy** Page **305** • A visit to this extraordinarily well-preserved trading station gives a real insight into the hardships of nineteenth-century life in a remote Arctic outpost.

Basics

Basics

Getting there ... 27

Red tape and visas ... 40

Information, maps and websites ... 41

Health ... 42

Insurance ... 43

Costs, money and banks ... 44

Getting around ... 46

Accommodation ... 54

Food and drink ... 58

Opening hours, public holidays and festivals ... 60

Mail and telecommunications ... 62

Media ... 64

Cime and personal safety ... 64

Outdoor pursuits ... 65

Travellers with disabilities ... 67

Gay Norway ... 69

Directory ... 69

Getting there

From the UK and Ireland, the most convenient way of getting to Norway is by air – there's a good selection of flights and the cheapest fares are often less expensive than the long and arduous journey by train or coach. There are a couple of ferry services from Britain to Norway, but these can be pretty costly in high season and are really only worth considering if you're taking your car. From North America, a handful of airlines fly direct to Oslo, though it may be cheaper to route via London, picking up a budget flight onwards from there. There are no direct flights from Canada, South Africa, Australia or New Zealand. Finally, getting to Norway from the rest of Scandinavia (Denmark, Sweden and Finland) is quick, easy and relatively inexpensive, whether you travel by plane, bus or train.

Though the waters have been muddied by the arrival of budget airlines, airfares still tend to depend on the **season**, with the highest from (roughly) early June to mid-September, when the weather is best; fares drop during the "shoulder" seasons – mid-September to early November and mid-April to early June – and you'll get the best prices during the low season, November through to April (excluding Christmas and New Year, when prices are hiked up and seats are at a premium). Bear in mind, though, that ticket prices from the UK are not subject to seasonal changes to the extent that they are in North America. Note also that flying on weekends is generally more expensive; price ranges quoted below assume midweek travel.

Budget airlines aside, you can often cut costs by going through a **specialist flight agent** – either a consolidator, who buys up blocks of tickets from the airlines and sells them at a discount, or a **discount agent**, who in addition to dealing with discounted flights may also offer special student and youth fares and a range of other travel-related services such as insurance, rail passes, car rentals, tours and the like. Bear in mind, though, that penalties for changing your plans on discounted tickets can be stiff. Don't automatically assume that tickets purchased through a travel specialist will be cheapest – once you get a quote, check with the airlines and you may turn up an even better deal.

Students might be able to find cheaper flights through the major student travel agencies, such as Council Travel, STA Travel or, for Canadian students, Travel CUTS.

Booking flights online

Many airlines and discount travel websites offer you the opportunity to **book tickets online**, so cutting out the costs of agents and middlemen.

Online booking agents and general travel sites

Ⓦ**www.cheapflights.com** (UK, Ireland & US); Ⓦwww.cheapflights.ca (Canada); Ⓦwww.cheapflights.com.au (Australia). Comprehensive sites providing details of bargain flights to anywhere in the world, including Scandinavia.

Ⓦ**www.ebookers.com** (UK) Efficient, easy to use flight finder, with competitive fares.

Ⓦ**www.expedia.com** (US); Ⓦwww.expedia.co.uk (UK); Ⓦwww.expedia.ca (Canada). Discount airfares, all-airline search engine and daily deals.

Ⓦ**www.flynow.com** (UK). Simple to use independent travel site offering good-value fares.

Ⓦ**www.hotwire.com** (US). Last-minute savings of up to forty percent on regular published fares. Travellers must be at least 18 and there are no refunds, transfers or changes allowed. Log-in required. If you're looking for the cheapest possible scheduled flight, this is probably your best bet.

Ⓦ**www.kelkoo.co.uk** (UK) Useful price-comparison site, checking several sources of low-cost flights (and other goods & services) according to specific criteria.

Ⓦ**www.lastminute.com** (UK); Ⓦwww.lastminute.com.au (Australia). Good last-minute holiday package and flight-only deals.

Fly less – stay longer! Travel and climate change

Climate change is a serious threat to the ecosystems that humans rely upon, and air travel is among the fastest-growing contributors to the problem. Rough Guides regard travel, overall, as a global benefit, and feel strongly that the advantages to developing economies are important, as is the opportunity for greater contact and awareness among peoples. But we all have a responsibility to limit our personal impact on global warming, and that means giving thought to how often we fly, and what we can do to redress the harm that our trips create.

Flying and climate change

Pretty much every form of motorized travel generates CO_2 – the main cause of human-induced climate change – but planes also generate climate-warming contrails and cirrus clouds and emit oxides of nitrogen, which create ozone (another greenhouse gas) at flight levels. Furthermore, flying simply allows us to travel much further than we otherwise would do. The figures are frightening: one person taking a return flight between Europe and California produces the equivalent impact of 2.5 tonnes of CO_2 – similar to the yearly output of the average UK car.

Fuel-cell and other less harmful types of plane may emerge eventually. But until then, there are really just two options for concerned travellers: to reduce the amount we travel by air (take fewer trips – stay for longer!), and to make the trips we do take "climate neutral" via a carbon offset scheme.

Carbon offset schemes

Offset schemes run by climatecare.org, carbonneutral.com and others allow you to make up for some or all of the greenhouse gases that you are responsible for releasing. To do this, they provide "carbon calculators" for working out the global-warming contribution of a specific flight (or even your entire existence), and then let you contribute an appropriate amount of money to fund offsetting measures. These include rainforest reforestation and initiatives to reduce future energy demand – often run in conjunction with sustainable development schemes.

Rough Guides, together with Lonely Planet and other concerned partners in the travel industry, are supporting a **carbon offset scheme** run by climatecare.org. Please take the time to view our website and see how you can help to make your trip climate neutral.

Ⓦ**www.opodo.co.uk** (UK) Popular and reliable source of low airfares. Owned by, and run in conjunction with, nine major European airlines.
Ⓦ**www.orbitz.com** (US) Comprehensive travel resource, with the usual flight, car hire and hotel deals but also great follow-up customer service.
Ⓦ**www.qixo.com** A comparison search that trawls through other ticket sites – including agencies and airlines – to find the best deals from any country.
Ⓦ**www.travelocity.com** (US) and Ⓦ**www.travelocity.co.uk** (UK) Destination guides, hot web fares and best deals for car hire, accommodation and lodging.
Ⓦ**www.zuji.com.au** (Australia). Destination guides, hot fares and great deals for car rental, accommodation and lodging.

Flights from Britain

There's a good choice of direct flights **from London** to Oslo's Gardermoen airport plus a scattering of flights there from the UK's **regional airports** too. Other Norwegian cities and towns are less well served, though there are a handful of direct flights to Sandefjord, Bergen and Stavanger, but you may well end up flying to Oslo and catching a connecting flight from there, not necessarily for much more money. Scandinavian Airlines (SAS) is the main local carrier, but has recently come under intense pressure from several budget airlines, most notably Ryanair and Norwegian Air Shuttle. Airlines and principal routings are given on p.30.

As for **ticket prices**, the intensity of the competition between the airlines means that there's a plethora of special deals. The best starting point is the **Internet**. Airline websites give up-to-the-minute information about

Air passes in Scandinavia

The SAS **Visit Scandinavia Air Pass** comes in the form of discount coupons for air travel within Norway, Sweden, Denmark and Finland. It can only be purchased in conjunction with an international flight on SAS in your home country. The coupons are valid for three months from arrival and cost £50–80 depending on the distance and route. The main advantage of the pass is that you're guaranteed a low fare. Although you may be able to get a cheaper flight once you're in Scandinavia, this can't be relied upon, and the £50–80 tariff is very reasonable.

timetables, fares and special offers, while online booking agents (see p.27) can cut costs, as can flight and travel agents (see below). As examples, Ryanair have charged as little as £20 (not including taxes) for a return from London Stansted to Sandejord's Oslo Torp airport, though £130 is the more usual price, while SAS currently charge around £120 for the return flight from Birmingham to Oslo via Copenhagen.

Flight times are insignificant – it's just one hour from Aberdeen to Stavanger, about two hours fifteen minutes from London to Oslo. The only thing to watch is the **location of the airport** – Oslo (Torp), for example, is 110km from Oslo itself in Sandefjord.

For air travel within Norway, you might consider buying an **air pass**, usually sold only in conjunction with SAS tickets from Britain; for details, see the box above.

Airlines and flight routings from Britain

British Airways ⓣ0870/850 9850, ⓦwww.britishairways.com. London Heathrow and Manchester to Oslo.
Finnair ⓣ0870/241 4411, ⓦwww.finnair.com. London Heathrow to Oslo.
KLM ⓣ0870/507 4074, ⓦwww.klm.com. Aberdeen, Birmingham International, Bristol, Cardiff, Durham Tees Valley, Edinburgh, Glasgow, Humberside, Leeds/Bradford, London City, London Heathrow, Manchester, Newcastle and Norwich direct to Amsterdam Schiphol, from where there are onward flights and connections to Bergen, Kristiansand, Oslo, Stavanger, Sandefjord and Trondheim.
Norwegian Air ⓣ0047/21 49 00 15 (in Norway), ⓦwww.norwegian.no. London Stansted to Bergen, Oslo and Trondheim.
Ryanair ⓣ0906/270 5656 (25p per minute), ⓦwww.ryanair.com. Glasgow Prestwick and Liverpool to Oslo Torp; London Stansted to Haugesund and Oslo Torp; Newcastle to Oslo Torp.
SAS Scandinavian Airlines ⓣ0870/607 27727, ⓦwww.scandinavian.net. Aberdeen to Stavanger; Manchester to Bergen and Oslo; London Heathrow to Bergen, Oslo and Stavanger.
SN (Brussels Airlines) ⓣ0870/735 2345, ⓦwww.flysn.com. Birmingham, Bristol, London Gatwick, London Heathrow, Manchester and Southampton to Brussels International, from where there are onward flights and connections to Oslo.
Sterling ⓣ0870/787 8038, ⓦwww.sterlingticket.com. Edinburgh to Oslo.

Discount flight and travel agents in Britain and Northern Ireland

Bridge the World ⓣ0870/814 4400, ⓦwww.bridgetheworld.com. Specializing in round-the-world tickets, with good deals aimed at the backpacker market.
ebookers ⓣ0870/010 7000, ⓦwww.ebookers.com. Low fares on an extensive selection of scheduled flights and package deals.
Flightcentre ⓣ0870/890 8099, ⓦwww.flightcentre.co.uk. Rock-bottom fares.
Flights4Less ⓣ0871/222 3423, ⓦwww.flights4less.co.uk. Good discount airfares. Part of Lastminute.com.
Holidays4Less ⓣ0871/222 3423, ⓦwww.holidays4less.co.uk. Offshoot of Lastminute.com, offering discounted package deals.
North South Travel ⓣ01245/608 291, ⓦwww.northsouthtravel.co.uk. Friendly, competitive travel agency, offering discounted fares. Profits are used to support projects in the developing world, especially the promotion of sustainable tourism.
Premier Travel ⓣ028/7126 3333, ⓦwww.premiertravel.uk.com. Discount flight specialists.
Rosetta Travel ⓣ028/9064 4996, ⓦwww.rosettatravel.com. Flight and holiday agent, specializing in deals direct from Belfast.
STA Travel ⓣ0870/160 0599, ⓦwww.statravel.co.uk. Specialists in low-cost flights and tours for students and under-26s, though other customers welcome.

Top Deck ⓣ020/8879 6789, ⓦwww.topdecktravel.co.uk. Long-established agent dealing in discount flights.
Trailfinders ⓣ0845/058 5858, ⓦwww.trailfinders.co.uk. One of the UK's best-informed and most efficient agents for independent travellers.
Travel Care ⓣ0870/112 0085, ⓦwww.travelcare.co.uk. Flights, holiday deals and city breaks around the world.

Flights from Ireland

From the Republic of Ireland, the only supplier of direct flights to Norway is SAS, who fly direct **from Dublin** to Oslo. **Fares** are very reasonable, with the cost of a return working out at €150–200 depending on seat availability. SAS passengers flying from Ireland can also purchase the Visit Scandinavia Air Pass (see box opposite).

Airlines and flight routings from Ireland

bmi ⓣ01/407 3036, ⓦwww.flybmi.com. Belfast, Dublin and Cork to London Heathrow.
British Airways ⓣ1-890/626 747, ⓦwww.britishairways.com. Cork, Dublin and Shannon to London or Manchester.
Ryanair ⓣ1530/787 787 at 33c per minute, ⓦwww.ryanair.com. Cork, Derry, Dublin, Kerry, Knock and Shannon to London Stansted.
SAS Scandinavian Airlines ⓣ01/844 5440, ⓦwww.scandinavian.net. Dublin to Oslo.

Discount flight and travel agents in Ireland

CIE Tours International ⓣ01/703 1888, ⓦwww.cietours.ie. General flight and tour agent.
ebookers ⓣ01/241 5689, ⓦwww.ebookers.ie. Low fares on an extensive selection of scheduled flights and package deals.
Go Holidays ⓣ01/874 4126, ⓦwww.goholidays.ie. City breaks and package tours.
Joe Walsh Tours ⓣ01/676 0991, ⓦwww.joewalshtours.ie. Long-established general budget fares and holidays agent.
Lee Travel ⓣ021/427 7111, ⓦwww.leetravel.ie. Flights and holidays worldwide.
Neenan Travel ⓣ01/607 9900, ⓦwww.neenantrav.ie. Specialists in city breaks.
Trailfinders ⓣ01/677 7888, ⓦwww.trailfinders.ie. One of the best-informed and most efficient agents for independent travellers.
usit NOW Republic of Ireland ⓣ01/602 1600, Northern Ireland ⓣ028/9032 7111; ⓦwww.usitnow.ie. Student and youth specialists for flights and trains.
World Travel Centre ⓣ01/416 7007, ⓦwww.worldtravel.ie. Excellent fares to Europe and worldwide.

Flights from the US and Canada

From **North America**, Norway is reasonably well served by numerous American and European airlines, though the vast majority of flights involve **changing planes** either in one of the Scandinavian capitals – primarily Copenhagen – or in a European hub city such as London or Amsterdam (for onward flights from the UK to Norway, see opposite); and if you don't live in a US hub city you may well have to change planes more than once. **Direct flights** are obviously preferable, and if you can be fairly flexible with your departure dates you'll be able to take advantage of the special promotional fares offered regularly by the airline concerned, Continental. However, the difference in price between nonstop and stopover flights is, in general terms at least, surprisingly small. The **flying time** on a direct, nonstop flight from the east coast of North America to Norway is just over seven hours.

Fares from North America to Oslo are fairly similar whichever carrier you choose, but it's still worth shopping around for the fastest routings and the best deals. If you're planning to hop around by plane, an **air pass** (see opposite) might be a good way of reducing costs. As sample summertime fares, an economy return on Continental's nonstop flight from New York to Oslo will cost in the region of US$1800, whilst SAS will charge in the region of US$1500 for a return from Seattle to Oslo. Special deals, flight agents (see p.32) and online booking (see p.27) can often halve these prices.

Airlines and flight routings from North America

Air Canada ⓣ1-888/247-2262, ⓦwww.aircanada.ca. Daily from Toronto (with connections from Vancouver) to Frankfurt, London and Zurich, from where there are onward connections to Norway.
Air France US ⓣ1-800/237-2747, ⓦwww.airfrance.com, Canada ⓣ1-800/667-2747, ⓦwww.airfrance.ca. Daily flights from many North

American cities to Paris, from where there are connecting flights to Oslo.

British Airways ⓣ1-800/AIRWAYS, ⓦwww.british-airways.com. Daily flights from 22 North American cities to London Heathrow.

Continental Airlines domestic ⓣ1-800/523-3273, international ⓣ1-800/231-0856, ⓦwww.continental.com. Daily flights between various major North American and European cities, from where there are connections to Norway. Also direct daily flights from New York to Oslo.

Delta Air Lines domestic ⓣ1-800/221-1212, international ⓣ1-800/241-4141, ⓦwww.delta.com. Frequent flights from all the major North American hub cities to London and Amsterdam, and onward flights to Norway

Icelandair ⓣ1-800/223-5500, ⓦwww.icelandair.com. Direct flights from New York, Baltimore, Boston, Minneapolis, Orlando and San Francisco to Reykjavik, from where there are onward connections to Oslo. Some flights allow a three-night stopover in Reykjavik.

Lufthansa US ⓣ1-800/645-3880, Canada ⓣ1-800/563-5954, ⓦwww.lufthansa-usa.com. Daily flights from major North American cities to Frankfurt, from where there are onward flights to Norway.

Northwest/KLM Airlines domestic ⓣ1-800/225-2525, international ⓣ1-800/447-4747, ⓦwww.nwa.com, ⓦwww.klm.com. Frequent flights from all the major North American hub cities, either direct or via Amsterdam, to Oslo.

SAS (Scandinavian Airlines) ⓣ1-800/221-2350, ⓦwww.scandinavian.net. Direct flights from Chicago, New York (Newark), Seattle and Washington DC to Copenhagen, onward flights from Copenhagen to a bevy of Norwegian towns and cities.

Virgin Atlantic Airways ⓣ1-800/862-8621, ⓦwww.virgin-atlantic.com. Daily flights from various US cities to London, with onward connections to Norway.

Discount flight and travel agents in North America

Educational Travel Center ⓣ1-800/747-5551 or 608/256-5551, ⓦwww.edtrav.com. Low-cost fares worldwide, student/youth discount offers, Eurail passes, car rental and tours.

Flightcentre US ⓣ1-866/WORLD-51, ⓦwww.flightcentre.us, Canada ⓣ1-888/WORLD-55, ⓦwww.flightcentre.ca. Rock-bottom fares from North America to Scandinavia.

STA Travel US ⓣ1-800/329-9537, Canada ⓣ1-888/427-5639; ⓦwww.statravel.com. Worldwide specialists in independent travel; also student IDs, travel insurance, car rental, rail passes and more.

Student Flights ⓣ1-800/255-8000 or 480/951-1177, ⓦwww.isecard.com/studentflights. Student/youth fares from North America to Scandinavia, plus student IDs and European rail and bus passes.

Travel Cuts US ⓣ1-800/592-CUTS, Canada ⓣ1-888/246-9762, ⓦwww.travelcuts.com. Popular, long-established student-travel organization, with worldwide offers.

Travelers Advantage ⓣ1-877/259-2691, ⓦwww.travelersadvantage.com. Discount travel club, with cashback deals and discounted car rental. Membership required ($1 for three months' trial).

Travelosophy US ⓣ1-800/332-2687, ⓦwww.itravelosophy.com. Good range of discounted and student fares.

Flights from Australia and New Zealand

There's no shortage of flights to the four Scandinavian capitals of Oslo, Copenhagen, Helsinki and Stockholm **from Australia and New Zealand**, but all of them involve at least one stop; of the quartet, Oslo is much more poorly served than Copenhagen, which is the most easily reached. Airlines flying out of Australia and New Zealand often use SAS for connecting services on to Oslo and Copenhagen, and SAS itself flies from Tokyo, Singapore and Bangkok to Copenhagen and Oslo. Otherwise, Singapore and Thai Airways offer two of the more direct routes out of Sydney to Copenhagen (stopping in Singapore and Bangkok respectively). If you end up in Copenhagen or Stockholm, it's just a short hop to Oslo and there are lots of SAS flights from here to other parts of Norway too. One other option is to pick up a cheap ticket to London, and then continue your journey on to Norway (see p.30). If you intend to take in a number of European countries on your trip, it might be worth buying a Eurail or ScanRail pass before you go (see p.34); train passes are available from most travel agents, or from branches of CIT or Bentours (see p.34; an SAS air pass (see p.30) is another money-saving option.

Tickets purchased direct from the airlines tend to be expensive, with published fares to Europe ranging from A$2000/NZ$2200 in low season to A$3500/NZ$3800 in high season. Travel agents can offer better deals on **fares**, and have the latest information on special promotions, such as free stopovers en route and fly-drive-accommodation packages. Flight Centre and STA generally offer the best discounts, especially for students and those under 26.

For extended trips, visiting Norway as part of a **round-the-world** (RTW) ticket can be good value. Fares are based either on the number of continents you visit, or the number of miles you travel, and tickets are usually cheapest through travel agents. The lowest-priced tickets usually involve three to four stopovers, with prices rising the further you travel or the more stops you add.

Airlines in and flight routings from Australia and New Zealand

Air New Zealand Australia ⓣ13 24 76, ⓦwww.airnz.com.au, New Zealand ⓣ0800/737 000, ⓦwww.airnz.co.nz. Frequent flights from Auckland to Singapore, Hong Kong and Taipei, from where partner airlines carry passengers to Frankfurt and Munich for onward flights to the capitals of Scandinavia. Also frequent flights from Auckland to Los Angeles and London.

British Airways Australia ⓣ1300/767 177, New Zealand ⓣ0800/274 847 or 09/356 8690; ⓦwww.britishairways.com. Frequent one-stop flights to London (in conjunction with Qantas), from Adelaide, Auckland, Brisbane, Melbourne, Perth and Sydney, with onward flights to Norway.

Cathay Pacific Australia ⓣ13 17 47, New Zealand ⓣ0508/800 454 or 09/379 0861; ⓦwww.cathaypacific.com. Frequent flights from Perth, Adelaide, Melbourne, Sydney, Brisbane, Cairns and Auckland to Hong Kong, with onward connections to Amsterdam, London, Paris and Frankfurt, and partner airlines services on from London to Oslo.

Qantas Australia ⓣ13 13 13, New Zealand ⓣ0800/808 767 or 09/357 8900; ⓦwww.qantas.com. Frequent one-stop flights, in conjunction with British Airways, from Adelaide, Auckland, Brisbane, Melbourne, Perth and Sydney to London, for onward flights to Norway.

SAS Scandinavian Airlines Australia ⓣ1300/727 707, ⓦwww.scandinavian.net. Sydney to Copenhagen via Bangkok, Singapore or Tokyo; and Sydney to Oslo via Bangkok, Singapore or Tokyo and Copenhagen.

Singapore Airlines Australia ⓣ13 10 11, New Zealand ⓣ0800/808 909;ⓦwww.singaporeair.com. Adelaide, Brisbane, Melbourne, Perth, Sydney and Auckland to Copenhagen and London, via Singapore.

Thai Airways Australia ⓣ1300/651 960, New Zealand ⓣ09/377 3886; ⓦwww.thaiair.com. Brisbane, Melbourne, Perth, Sydney and Auckland to Stockholm and Copenhagen, via Bangkok.

Discount flight and travel agents in Australia and New Zealand

CIT Australia ⓣ02/9267 1255, ⓦwww.cittravel.com.au. Europe-wide rail passes.

Flight Centre Australia ⓣ13 31 33, ⓦwww.flightcentre.com.au, New Zealand ⓣ0800 243 544, ⓦwww.flightcentre.co.nz. Rock-bottom air fares worldwide.

Holiday Shoppe New Zealand ⓣ0800/808 480, ⓦwww.holidayshoppe.co.nz. Great deals on flights, hotels and holidays.

OTC Australia ⓣ1300/855 118, ⓦwww.otctravel.com.au. Deals on flights, hotels and holidays.

STA Travel Australia ⓣ1300/733 035, New Zealand ⓣ0508/782 872; ⓦwww.statravel.com. Specialists in low-cost flights and holiday deals. Good discounts for students and under-26s. Great deals for students.

Trailfinders Australia ⓣ02/9247 7666, ⓦwww.trailfinders.com.au. One of the best-informed and most efficient agents for independent travellers.

travel.com Australia ⓣ1300/130 482 or 02/9249 5444, ⓦwww.travel.com.au; New Zealand ⓣ0800/468 332, ⓦwww.travel.co.nz. Comprehensive online travel company, with discounted fares and good flight and hotel deals.

Flights from South Africa

From **South Africa**'s two main international airports, Johannesburg and Cape Town, Norway is easy enough to reach by air, but this always involves **changing planes** in a European hub city such as London or Amsterdam (for onward flights from the UK to Norway, see p.30). The **flying time** on a direct, nonstop flight from South Africa to London is just over eleven hours. **Fares** from South Africa to London start at around R5000 for a return trip in low season, sometimes less on charter flights and smaller airlines.

Airlines

British Airways ⓣ011 441 8600, ⓦwww.ba.com. Cape Town and Johannesburg nonstop to London Heathrow.

Lufthansa ⓣ0861 842 538, ⓦwww.lufthansa.com. Flights from Jo'burg and Cape Town to Scandinavian airports via Amsterdam.

Nationwide Airlines ⓣ 0861 777 777, ⓦ www.flynationwide.co.za. Johannesburg to London Gatwick.
South African Airways (SAA) ⓣ 0861 359 722, ⓦ www.flysaa.com. Cape Town and Johannesburg nonstop to London Heathrow, with onward connections available.
Swiss ⓣ 0860 0400 506, ⓦ www.swiss.com. Flights from Jo'burg to Zurich for onward connections.
Virgin Atlantic ⓣ 011 340 3400, ⓦ www.virgin-atlantic.com. Cape Town and Jo'burg nonstop to London Heathrow.

By rail from the UK

Taking a **train** can be a relaxing, if long-winded, way of getting from the UK to Norway, though it is likely to work out much more expensive than flying, especially if you're over 26. A number of deals involving rail passes (see below) make it possible to cut costs, however, and there's the added advantage of being able to break your journey – travelling to Oslo from London, for instance, you could stop off at Brussels, Hamburg, Copenhagen and Gothenburg.

The largest UK company dealing with train travel within Europe is **Rail Europe** (see below). They sell all the rail passes available, and will through-ticket you from London Waterloo as far as Copenhagen on the fastest and most convenient routing, normally via Brussels (on Eurostar) and Hamburg. To get the cheapest **fares** with Rail Europe, you'll need to book around fourteen days in advance, and include one Saturday night in your time away. With this type of ticket, the adult return fare from **London to Copenhagen** is currently £300–350, more if you have a sleeper berth, and the journey takes around twenty hours. Getting to Norway by train from Britain involves first travelling to Copenhagen, as described above, and then taking one of the daily services onward at the cost of another £50 or so return.

Rail contacts

In the UK and Ireland

Eurostar ⓣ 08705/186 186, ⓦ www.eurostar.co.uk. Timetables and online booking for Eurostar trains.
Rail Europe UK ⓣ 08708/371 371, ⓦ www.raileurope.co.uk. Pan-European train bookings, including discounted rail fares for under-26s on a variety of routes; also sells every sort of European rail pass (though for Eurail consult ⓦ www.raileurope.com), and is an agent for Eurostar.

In North America

Eurorail International Canada ⓣ 1-888/667-9734, ⓦ www.europrail.net. Eurail and Norway passes.
Rail Europe US ⓣ 1-877/257-2887, Canada ⓣ 1-800/361-7245; ⓦ www.raileurope.com/us. Official North American Eurail agent; also sells multinational passes and most Norway passes.
ScanTours US ⓣ 1-800/223-7226 or 310/636-4656, ⓦ www.scantours.com. Eurail and Norway passes.

In Australia and New Zealand

CIT Australia ⓣ 02/9267 1255, ⓦ www.cittravel.com.au. Europe-wide rail passes.
Bentours Australia ⓣ 02/9241 1353, ⓦ www.bentours.com.au. Scandinavian rail passes.
Rail Plus Australia ⓣ 613/9642 8644, New Zealand ⓣ 649/377 5415; ⓦ www.railplus.com.au. Most European rail passes and tickets.
Trailfinders Australia ⓣ 02/9247 7666, ⓦ www.trailfinders.com.au. All European rail passes.

Rail passes

Rail passes can reduce the cost of train travel significantly, especially if you plan to travel extensively around Norway or visit the country as part of a wider tour of Europe. There's a huge array of passes available, covering regions of Europe as well as individual countries. Some have to be bought before leaving home, while others can only be purchased in the country itself. **Rail Europe** is the umbrella company for all national and international rail tickets, and its comprehensive website (see above) is the most useful source of information on available passes; it also gives all current prices.

ScanRail pass

If you're planning to travel around Scandinavia by train, it's well worth considering a **ScanRail pass** (ⓦ www.scanrail.com), which covers all four Scandinavian countries (Norway, Sweden, Denmark and Finland) and is available to all, although you do have to buy it before you leave home. The ScanRail pass is available for travel on

Useful timetable publications

The red-covered **Thomas Cook European Timetable** details schedules of over 50,000 trains in Europe, as well as timings of over 200 ferry routes and rail-connecting bus services. It's updated and issued every month; main changes are in the June edition (published end of May), which has details of the summer European schedules, and the October one (published end of September), which includes winter schedules; some have advance summer/winter timings also. The book can be purchased online at ⓦwww.thomascookpublishing.com or from branches of Thomas Cook, and costs around £11. Their useful *Rail Map of Europe* can also be purchased online for £6.

any five days in a two-month period (adult £171/US$291); any ten days in two months (adult £229/US$390) and 21 consecutive days (adult £266/US$453). Over-60s get a discount of about twelve percent on the full price of the pass, children fifty percent and people under 26 and over 12 get thirty percent. There's also an eight-day **Scan-Rail Drive Pass**, which allows five days of train travel and two days of car rental, with the option of adding additional car days. Note that a small supplement is charged for certain inter-city express trains.

For details of rail passes for use specifically within Norway, see "Getting Around", p.46.

Inter-Rail pass

If you have no clear itinerary, the **Inter-Rail pass** (ⓦwww.raileurope.co.uk/inter-rail) might be your best bet. These are only available to European residents, and you will be asked to provide proof of residency before being allowed to purchase one. They come in over-26 and (cheaper) under-26 versions, and cover 29 European countries grouped together in **zones**. These zones include **A**: UK and the Republic of Ireland **B**: Norway, Sweden, Finland; **C**: Germany, Austria, Switzerland, Denmark; and **E**: France, Belgium, Netherlands, Luxembourg. The passes are available for 16 days (one zone only; £215), 22 days (two zones only; £295), and one month (all zones; £405); those aged 12 to 26 years get a thirty percent discount on the above prices. Inter-Rail passes do not include travel between Britain and the continent, although holders are eligible for discounts on cross-Channel ferries and Eurostar trains.

Eurail Pass

The **Eurail pass** (only available to non-Europeans) is not likely to pay for itself if you're planning just to stick to Norway. The pass, which must be purchased before arrival in Europe, allows unlimited free first-class train travel in seventeen European countries, including Norway, and is available in increments of 15 days, 21 days, one month, two months and three months. If you're under 26, you can save money with a **Eurail pass Youth**, which is valid for second-class travel; the same applies if you're travelling with between one and four companions on a joint **Eurail pass Saver**; both of these are available in the same increments as the standard Eurail pass. You stand a better chance of getting your money's worth out of a **Eurail pass Flexi**, which is good for ten or fifteen days' first-class travel within a two-month period. This, too, comes in under-26/second-class (**Eurail pass Youth Flexi**) and group (**Eurail pass Saver Flexi**) versions. A standard Eurail pass currently costs US$588 for 15 days, US$762 for 21 days, US$946 for one month, US$1338 for two months and US$1654 three months.

Details of prices for all these passes can be found on ⓦwww.raileurope.com; they can be purchased from the agents listed opposite.

By coach from Britain

A **coach journey** to Norway from Britain can be an endurance test, and with airfares falling so dramatically it can actually prove more expensive than flying. It's only worth taking the bus if time is no object and price all-important, or if you specifically do not want to fly.

The major UK operator of international coach routes is **Eurolines** (UK ⓣ0870/514 3219), whose tickets are bookable online at ⓦwww.nationalexpress.com, though most major travel agents will oblige too. Eurolines run eight services weekly to **Copenhagen**, either via Brussels (20hr) or Amsterdam (26hr), with connections on to **Oslo** (five weekly; 30hr 35min). **Fares** to Norwegian destinations start at £120 return, though advance booking – seven days or more – can provide a substantial discount; there are also discounts for the over-60s and those under 26.

Another option is the **Euroline Pass**, which offers unlimited coach travel throughout much of Europe, including southern Norway but not the north. The pass is valid either for fifteen days (£169 mid-Sept to late June, £235 late June to mid-Sept); thirty days (£230/£315) or forty days (£255/£355). Once again, seniors and the under-26s are entitled to discounts of around ten percent.

There are no through services from anywhere in Britain outside London, though **National Express** buses connect with Eurolines buses in London from all over the British Isles.

By car and ferry from Britain

Car ferries departing from Aberdeen and Newcastle link Britain with Norway. The shortest sea route is on DFDS Seaways' twice-weekly service from Newcastle to Kristiansand (18hr), which continues on to Gothenburg in Sweden (26hr). **Fares** aren't cheap – prices vary enormously according to the season, number of passengers and type of cabin accommodation – but discounts and special deals, such as DFDS Seaways' discounted midweek returns, can reduce costs greatly. Not surprisingly, fares are usually at their lowest during the winter months. As an example, DFDS Seaways charge from as little as £35 per person for a low-season midweek return from Newcastle to Kristiansand, plus £50 each way for a car; in summer prices per person begin at around £50, plus £60 or so for the car; these fares include a berth in a sleeping cabin. Fjord Line sailings from Newcastle to Stavanger (20hr), Haugesund (23hr) and Bergen (27hr) offer a minimum fare in winter of £90 return for one or two passengers and car (plus £10 extra for a cabin berth), rising to around £330 for the same deal in summer (plus £20 extra for a cabin berth). There is no difference in prices between the three ports. The crossing from Aberdeen to Norway involves a Northlink ferry to Lerwick in Shetland, and then a Smyril Line ferry on to Bergen; the whole journey takes about three days in all, including a stopover in Lerwick – altogether a sea voyage of almost epic proportions.

Ferry companies and routings to Norway

DFDS Seaways ⓣ0870/252 0524, ⓦwww.dfdsseaways.co.uk. Newcastle to Kristiansand (18hrs). Also Copenhagen and Helsingborg to Oslo (16hrs/14hrs).

Fjord Line ⓣ0191/296 1313, ⓦwww.fjordline.com. Newcastle to Stavanger (20hrs), Haugesund (23hrs) and Bergen (27hrs). Also Hantsholm in Denmark to Egersund (19hrs), Haugesund (25hrs) and Bergen (29hrs) in Norway.

Northlink Ferries ⓣ0845/600 0449, ⓦwww.northlinkferries.co.uk. Aberdeen and usually Kirkwall (Orkneys) to Lerwick (Shetland) – for onward ferries with Smyril Line to Bergen. The Aberdeen to Lerwick ferry takes 14hrs.

Smyril Line UK ⓣ01595/690 845, ⓦwww.smyril–line.com. Smyril ferries shuttle around the north Atlantic, linking Iceland, the Faroe Islands, Lerwick in the Shetlands, Bergen in Norway and Hantsholm in Denmark. See Northlink Ferries above for services to the Shetlands. Journey time from Lerwick to Bergen is 21hrs.

Packages and organized tours

Don't be put off by the idea of visiting Norway on an **inclusive package**. In such an expensive part of Europe, it can be the cheapest way to do things, and may also be the only way to reach remote parts of the region at inhospitable times of year; if you just want to see one city and its environs, then **city break** packages often work out cheaper than arranging the same trip independently. Prices usually include return travel and accommodation (with breakfast), with most operators offering a range from hostel to luxury-class hotel.

There are also an increasing number of operators offering **special-interest holidays** to Norway, ranging from birdwatching and fjord camping trips to Arctic cruises and both midnight sun and northern lights viewing expeditions. Inevitably, prices vary enormously, largely depending on the quality of the accommodation and the type of activity, but they are often very good value.

Finally, the staggering beauty of the Norwegian coastline attracts **cruise ships** by the shoal. These holidays aren't cheap, starting at around £2000 per person on sailings from the UK, but in terms of comfort and luxury, you almost always get what you pay for. Routes vary considerably, some concentrating on the fjord coastline, others trawling up to the North Cape (Nordkapp), and yet more including Norway on a wider Baltic itinerary. Frequency also varies, with some cruises leaving weekly, but with the more exotic weighing anchor only once or twice a year. We've detailed four cruise companies below, but any good travel agent will have the details of many more. The most celebrated Norwegian sea voyage is, however, the journey up the coast from Bergen to Kirkenes on the **Hurtigrute coastal boat** (see p.49).

Britain

British tour operators offer a wide gamut of Norwegian holidays catering for the mildly inert to the full-blooded athlete; there is something to suit every size of wallet too.

Tour operators in Britain

Anglers' World Holidays ⓣ01246/221 717, ⓦwww.anglers-world.co.uk. Sea and river fishing holidays in Norway.

Arctic Experience/Discover the World ⓣ01737/218 800, ⓦwww.discover-the-world.co.uk. Specialist adventure tours including whale-watching in Norway, wildlife in Spitsbergen and dog-sledging in Lapland.

Crystal Holidays ⓣ0870/402 0291, ⓦwww.crystalholidays.co.uk. Country tours and Norwegian skiing holidays.

DFDS Seaways ⓣ0870 5333 000, ⓦwww.dfdsseaways.co.uk. This ferry company offers a variety of breaks in Norway, including two nights on board ship and two or three nights at the destination concerned; especially good deals out of season.

Fred Olsen Cruise Lines ⓣ01473/746 175, ⓦwww.fredolsencruises.com. Over a dozen Baltic and Norwegian cruises a year.

Headwater Holidays ⓣ08700/662 650, ⓦwww.headwater.com. Guided walking holidays in the Rondane national park and the Gudbrandsdal valley in the summer, cross-country skiing on the Hardangervidda in winter. Canoeing and cycling holidays too.

Inntravel ⓣ01653/617 788, ⓦwww.inntravel.co.uk. Outdoor holidays in Norway including skiing, walking, dog-sledging, fjord cruises, and whale- and reindeer-watching.

Insight ⓣ01475/741 203, ⓦwww.insighttours.com. City tours and "Spectacular Scandinavia and its fjords" – a 15-day trip for £1450.

Norwegian Coastal Voyage ⓣ0208/846 2666, ⓦwww.norwegiancoastalvoyage.com. UK agent for the Hurtigrute coastal boat (see p.49), Norway's most famous cruise. Extremely helpful and efficient.

Norwegian Cruise Line ⓣ0845/658 8010, ⓦwww.ncl.com. Among other sailings, this company operates a twelve-night Baltic capitals cruise and a fjord cruise.

P&O Cruises ⓣ0845/355 5333, ⓦwww.pocruises.com. P&O offer a variety of Baltic, fjord and Nordkapp cruises.

Scantours ⓣ020/7839 2927, ⓦwww.scantoursuk.com. Huge range of packages and tailor-made holidays to every Scandinavian nook and cranny.

Saddle Skedaddle ⓣ0191/265 1110, ⓦwww.skedaddle.co.uk. Highly recommended company organizing a couple of cycling tours of Norway each year, usually one to the Lofoten islands and another round the western fjords.

Specialised Tours ⓣ01342/712 785, ⓦwww.specialisedtours.com. Specialists in Scandinavia offering independent, tailor-made or group city breaks and holidays.

Taber Holidays ⓣ01274/594 656, ⓦwww.taberhols.co.uk. Scandinavian specialists with dozens of options, including self-catering holidays, fjord cruises, motoring tours and guided coach trips.

Waymark Holidays ⓣ01753/516 477, ⓦwww.waymarkholidays.com. Winter sports specialist offering an excellent range of cross-country skiing holidays. Most are based in the mountains between Oslo and Bergen, in the south of Norway, but there are also holidays further north, in the Rondane, and further west on the Hardangervidda. Waymark cater for everyone from the novice through to the experienced skier, and do summer walking packages too. Reckon on £700 per week for skiing, all-inclusive. Highly recommended.

Ireland

Not many operators run **package tours** to Norway from Ireland and it's often easier to use a UK company. There are, however, a couple of city-break specialists in Ireland and their offerings may well work out cheaper than arranging the same trip independently.

Tour operators in Ireland

Arrow Tours ⓣ041 983 1177, ⓦwww.arrowtours.ie. Short and city-break specialist with several Oslo options.
Crystal Holidays Dublin ⓣ01/433 1043, ⓦwww.crystalholidays.ie. City breaks and skiing holidays.
Go Holidays Dublin ⓣ01/874 4126, ⓦwww.goholidays.ie. Package tour specialists with one- or two-centre city breaks to Scandinavia.

North America

A substantial number of companies in North America operate **organized tours** around Scandinavia in general and Norway in particular, ranging from city breaks to deluxe cruises and cycling holidays. Group tours can be very expensive, however, and sometimes don't include the airfare, so check what you're getting. If your visit is focused on cities, you could simply book a hotel-plus-flight package (which can work out cheaper than booking the two separately).

Tour operators in North America

Adventures Abroad ⓣ1-800/665-3998, ⓦwww.adventures-abroad.com. Specializing in small-group tours, and offering a variety of Norwegian packages.
Adventure Center ⓣ1-800/228-4747, ⓦwww.adventurecenter.com. This operator offers an imaginative programme of distinctive escorted holidays, from snow mobile and reindeer sleigh trips in winter, through to train and hiking tours of the fjords in the summer.
Backroads ⓣ1-800/462-2848, ⓦwww.backroads.com. Specializing in activity holidays, including seven-day cycle tours of the Lofoten and a six-day hiking tour of the Norwegian mountains, glaciers and fjords.
Borton Overseas ⓣ1-800/843-0602, ⓦwww.bortonoverseas.com. Adventure-vacation specialists, with a large selection of biking, hiking, rafting, birdwatching, dog-sledging and cross-country skiing tours, plus farm and cabin stays and city packages.
Brekke Tours – Spirit of Scandinavia ⓣ1-800/437-5302, ⓦwww.brekketours.com. A well-established company offering a host of sightseeing and cultural tours in Scandinavia.
Nordic Saga Tours ⓣ1-800/848 6449, ⓦwww.nordicsaga.com. Packages, flights and information on air passes within Scandinavia.
Norwegian Coastal Voyage Inc ⓣ1-800/323-7436, ⓦwww.coastalvoyage.com. A mixture of escorted and independent cruises along the Norwegian coastline, to Svalbard and round the Lofoten.
Passage Tours ⓣ1-800/548-5960, ⓦwww.passagetours.com. Scandinavian specialist offering an extensive range of Norwegian tours, for example the "Nordfjord Crescendo" and the "Fjord Duet", which mix time in the city with time in the sticks. Also coastal cruises, dog-sledging, whale-watching and ski packages.
Picasso Travel ⓣ1-800/995-7997, ⓦwww.nordiquetours.com. A wide range of Scandinavian packages including the Norwegian fjords and "Scandinavian capitals".
Scanam World Tours ⓣ1-800/545-2204, ⓦwww.scanamtours.com. Scandinavian specialist offering an extensive programme of group and individual tours and cruises within Norway.
Scand-America Tours ⓣ1-800/886-8428, ⓦwww.scandamerica.com. A wide variety of packages – everything from dog-sledging to garden tours – throughout Scandinavia.
Scantours ⓣ1-800/223-7226, ⓦwww.scantours.com. Major Scandinavian holiday specialists offering vacation packages, hotel bookings and customized itineraries, including cruises and city sightseeing tours.

Australia and New Zealand

There are very few **package holidays** to Norway originating in Australia and New Zealand. Your best bet is probably Bentours, who can put together a package for you, and are about the only agents who offer skiing holidays. Alternatively, you can go with one of the UK agents (see p.37), which offer a greater choice of holidays and prices.

Tour operators

Adventures Abroad New Zealand ⓣ0800/800 434, ⓦwww.adventures-abroad.com. Escorted tours of Oslo and fjord Norway for anything up to two weeks.
Bentours Australia ⓣ02/9241 1353, ⓦwww.bentours.com.au. Much-lauded agency providing Hurtigrute excursions, Spitsbergen cruises and fjord tours.
Explore Holidays Australia ⓦwww.exploreholidays.com.au. Escorted two- and three-week tours through coastal Norway. Bookings through travel agents or STA travel (see p.33).

Getting there from the rest of Scandinavia

There's no problem in reaching Norway from the rest of **Scandinavia**. There are regular train services from Sweden, year-round ferry connections from Denmark and frequent flights from Denmark, Sweden and Finland.

By train

By train you can reach **Oslo** from both Stockholm (3 daily; 8–9hr) and Copenhagen (2–3 daily; 8hr 30min). There are also regular services from Stockholm to **Trondheim** (2 daily; 11hr) and **Narvik** (2 daily; 19hr). Inter-Rail, ScanRail and Eurail passes are valid – for train pass details see p.34; for timetable details, consult RESPLUS, who bring all the international timetables together at Ⓦwww.resplus.se. Note that there are no direct train services from Finland to Norway.

By bus

Two main **bus** companies provide a regular daily service to Oslo from **Copenhagen**, **Gothenburg** and **Malmo**. They are Eurolines Scandinavia (Ⓦwww.eurolines-travel.com) and Safflebussen (Ⓦwww.safflebussen.se). The main difference between the two is price: Safflebussen are almost always less expensive, but there again the Eurolines buses link into a much larger network of international and pan-Scandinavian bus routes; both are cheaper than the train. Safflebussen also operates a fast and frequent service from **Stockholm** to Oslo; there are no direct long-distance express buses to Norway from **Finland**, not even in the far north where the two countries share a common border.

By ferry

Of the several **car ferry** services shuttling across the Skagerrak **from Denmark** to Norway, one of the most useful is DFDS Seaways' ferry (Ⓦwww.dfdsseaways.com) from Copenhagen to Oslo (1 daily; 16hr). Alternatively, Stena Line (Ⓦwww.stenaline.com) links Frederikshavn with Oslo (1–2 daily; 8hr 30min–12hr), while Color Line (Ⓦwww.colorline.com) ferries depart Hirtshals for Oslo (6–7 weekly; 8hr), Kristiansand (1–2 daily; 4hr 30min), and Stavanger and Bergen (3 weekly; 11hr/18hr). There's also a Color Line ferry service to Norway **from Sweden**, linking Strömstad, north of Gothenburg, with Sandefjord, 120km or so from Oslo (2–6 daily; 2hr 30min).

Details of sailings and costs can be had via the company websites or from any major travel agent. Prices tend to rise sharply in summer, though this is partly offset by all sorts of special deals; rail-pass holders get discounts on some routes, too.

By plane

Norway has international **airports** at Oslo (Gardermoen), Bergen, Kristiansand, Sandefjord (Torp), Stavanger and Trondheim; most flights from elsewhere in Scandinavia are with SAS (Ⓦwww.sas.no) or one of its subsidiaries, primarily Braathens (same website). Standard unrestricted tickets are very expensive, but discounts are legion, mostly with caveats about the length of stay and so forth. As examples of standard one-way fares, Stockholm to Oslo costs about 900kr, Copenhagen to Oslo up to 1200kr. SAS is also being pressured by a number of new Budget airlines – primarily Snowflake (Ⓣ0046/8797 4000, Ⓦwww.flysnowflake.com), Sterling (Ⓣ0870/787 8038, Ⓦwww.sterlingticket.com) and Norwegian (see Norwegian Air, p.30). The latter, for example, charge as little as 400kr for a single fare from either Stockholm or Copenhagen to Oslo. For details of pan-Scandinavian air passes, see p.30.

Red tape and visas

Citizens of the EU/EEA, US, Canada, Australia and New Zealand need only a valid passport to enter Norway for up to three months. All other nationals should consult the relevant embassy or consulate about visa requirements.

For **longer stays**, EU/EEA nationals can apply for a residence permit while in the country, which, if it's granted, may be valid for up to five years. In most cases, the permit is renewable, and also grants the holder the right to work (though EU/EEA nationals can start work before the residence permit has been obtained) and to reside anywhere in Norway. Non-EU/EEA nationals can only apply for residence permits before leaving home, and must be able to prove they can support themselves without working. If the application is successful, a residence permit issued to a non-EU/EEA national is rarely for longer than one year, takes time to renew, and does not include the right to work, for that a work permit is required. The applicant is also required to have a fixed address for the period concerned. Contact the relevant embassy in your country of origin.

In spite of the lack of restrictions, **checks** are frequently made on travellers at the major points of entry. If you're young and are carrying a rucksack, be prepared to prove that you have enough money to support yourself during your stay. You may also be asked how long you intend to stay and why. **Border controls** between the Scandinavian countries are patchy – sometimes no-one seems very bothered, while at other times you might have your car searched and have to answer endless questions.

Norwegian embassies and consulates

In Australia

Embassy in Canberra ⓣ02/6273 3444, ⓔemb .canberra@mfa.no.

In Canada

Embassy in Ottawa ⓣ613/238-6571, ⓔemb .ottawa@mfa.no. There are also consulates in Calgary, Edmonton, Halifax, Montréal, Québec, Regina, Saint John, St John's, Toronto, Vancouver, Ville de la Baie and Winnipeg; for contact details, go to ⓦwww.emb-norway.ca.

In New Zealand

See Australia

In the Republic of Ireland

Embassy in Dublin ⓣ01/662 1800, ⓔemb .dublin@mfa.no.

In South Africa

Embassies in Pretoria (ⓣ12 342 6100, ⓔemb .pretoria@mfa.no) and Cape Town (ⓣ21 425 1687, ⓔembctn@noramb.co.za). Also consulates in Johannesburg, Cape Town and Durban; see ⓦwww.norway.org.za for contact details.

In UK

Norway Embassy in London ⓣ020/7591 5500, ⓔemb.london@mfa.no. Consulate in Edinburgh ⓣ0131/226 5701, ecgedi@mfa.no.

In the US

Embassy in Washington, DC ⓣ202/333-6000; Consulate General in New York ⓣ212/421–7333, ⓔcg.newyork@mfa.no; other consulates in Houston, Minneapolis and San Francisco, contact the Washington embassy.

Information, maps and websites

Before you leave for Norway, it may be worth contacting the Norwegian Tourist Board for free maps, timetables, accommodation listings and brochures – though don't go mad, since much of what you'll need can easily be obtained in Norway itself. Three of the board's most useful publications, which are hard to find in Norway, are their Camping booklet, listing several hundred campsites, their Norway: Facts and Information brochure, containing several general maps of the country and contact details for most tourist offices, and the very detailed NRI Guide to Transport and Accommodation.

Once inside the country, information is very easy to come by too, as every town and most of the larger villages have their own **tourist office**; we've given their addresses, opening hours, websites and telephone numbers throughout the Guide. **Maps** are widely available in Norwegian bookshops and sometimes at the tourist offices as well, but buying one before you go helps in planning – and if you're driving you will, of course, need a good road map. There's also a wealth of information available **online** – Norway is spectacularly well represented on the Internet in terms of everything from activity holidays through to bus timetables, and we've listed a few general websites below.

The Norwegian Tourist Board

Australia Contact the embassy in Canberra (see opposite), or check ⓦwww.scandinavia.com.au.
Canada Contact the embassy or consulate (see opposite), or check ⓦwww.goscandinavia.com
Ireland Contact the embassy (see opposite), which handles tourist information.
New Zealand See Australia
South Africa Contact the embassy (see opposite), or check ⓦwww.norway.org.za.
UK Norwegian Tourist Board 5th floor, Charles House, 5 Lower Regent St, London SW1Y 4LR ⓣ0906/302 2003 (premium-rate line), ⓦwww.visitnorway.com. No walk-in service.
USA Norwegian Tourist Board, 655 Third Ave, New York, NY 10022 ⓣ1-212/885-9700, ⓦwww.norway.org.

Some useful websites

ⓦ**www.goscandinavia.com** The official website of the Scandinavian Tourist Board in North America, offering a general introduction to Scandinavia, latest travel deals and links to the Norwegian Tourist Board website.

ⓦ**www.gulesider.no** Norway's yellow pages – either business (ⓦwww.gulesider.no/eng) or private (ⓦwww.gulesider.no/gsi/whitesearchfront.do).

ⓦ**www.itv.se/boreale/Sámieng.htm** Comprehensive introduction to the Sámi people and their culture, with features on history, music, art and reindeer.

ⓦ**www.kulturnett.no** Comprehensive information on the country's museums and current exhibitions, but only in Norwegian.

ⓦ**www.odin.dep.no** Government site of ODIN (Official Documentation and Information from Norway); despite the plain presentation, this has everything you ever wanted to know about Norway and then some. Especially good on politics.

ⓦ**www.scandinavia.com.au** Excellent source of info with useful sections on current events and exhibitions, plus helpful advice on where to go for best flight deals. Australia-orientated, as you might expect from the domain name.

ⓦ**www.visitnorway.com** The official site of the Norwegian Tourist Board, with links to all things Norwegian and good sections on outdoor activities and events.

Maps

The **maps** in this book should be adequate for most purposes, and Norwegian tourist offices often give out reasonably useful local road maps and town plans too, but drivers, cyclists and hikers will require something more detailed. For **Scandinavia** as a whole, Cappelen (@www.cappelen.no) produces a good-quality road map on a scale of 1:800,000, though this can be hard to get hold of outside the region, in which case plump for the more readily available Freytag & Berndt version (@www.freytagberndt.com). For an excellent map of Norway, complete with index, it's Cappelen again – their **Norway** (1:325,000) is the best on the market – as is their first-rate map of **Oslo** (1:10,000).

The best **book of Norwegian road maps** is the *Veiatlas Norge*, produced by the state-run Statens Kartverk (@www.statkart.no), an arm of the highways department. This consists of 57 two-page maps (1:300,000) and 80 city and town maps (1:20,000); it is widely available both within Norway and abroad for about £30/US$52. The only drawback is that the city maps are not nearly as accurate as the road maps. Amongst the regional, **single-sheet road maps**, the best and most widely available is the series produced by Freytag & Berndt (1:400,000). These cover the country in four maps, have an index and are easy to follow except in the most congested parts of the country – around Oslo and Bergen and so forth – where the scale is insufficient to pick out many of the roads.

Statens Kartverk also publishes authoritative **hiking maps** at a scale of 1:50,000. This series covers every part of the country and is extremely accurate. In addition, the same people publish maps to all the more popular hiking areas at a scale of 1:100,000, which gives the hiking trails greater prominence. Statens Kartverk maps are available abroad at any good map shop, though there's usually a significant mark-up on the domestic price of 65–75kr. For more on hiking, see the Hiking colour section. Cycling maps, with route suggestions, are usually on sale at tourist offices in the more popular cycling areas; for more on cycling see p.53.

Health

Under reciprocal health arrangements, all citizens of EU and EEA (European Economic Area) countries are entitled to discounted medical treatment within Norway's public health-care system. Non-EU/EEA nationals are not entitled to discounted treatment and should, therefore, take out their own medical insurance to cover them while travelling in Norway. EU/EEA citizens may want to consider private health insurance too, in order to cover the cost of the discounted treatment as well as items not within the EU/EEA's scheme, such as dental treatment and repatriation on medical grounds.

Note also that the more worthwhile policies promise to sort matters out before you pay (rather than after) in the case of major expense; if you do have to pay upfront, get and keep the receipts. For more on insurance policies and what they cover, see opposite.

Seeking medical treatment

Health care in Norway is of a very high standard and widely available: even the remotest communities are within relatively easy – or well-organized – reach of medical attention. Rarely will **English speakers** encounter language problems – if the doctor or nurse can't speak English themselves (which is unlikely) there will almost certainly be someone at hand who can. Your local pharmacy, tourist office or hotel should be able to provide the address of an English-speaking doctor or dentist. For **medical emergencies**, call ⓣ113.

If you're seeking treatment under EU/EEA **reciprocal public health agreements**, double-check that the doctor/dentist is working within (and seeing you as) a patient of the relevant public health-care system. This being the case, you'll receive reduced-cost/government–subsidized treatment just as the locals do; any fees must be paid upfront, or at least at the end of your treatment, and are non-refundable. Sometimes you will be asked to produce documentation to prove you are eligible for EU/EEA health care, sometimes no-one bothers, but technically at least you should have your passport and your **European Health Insurance Card** (**EHIC**) to hand. The EHIC, the successor to the old E111 form, is issued in Britain at post offices, or online at ⓦwww.dh.gov.uk; in Ireland from local Health Boards or online at ⓦwww.ehic.ie. Allow a couple of weeks for your application to be processed. If, on the other hand, you have a travel insurance policy covering medical expenses, you can seek treatment in either the public or private health sectors, the main issue being whether – at least in major cases – you have to pay the costs upfront and then wait for reimbursement or not.

Insurance

Most people will want to take out some kind of travel insurance before they travel. A typical policy usually provides cover for loss of baggage, tickets and – up to a certain limit – cash or cheques, as well as cancellation or curtailment of your journey.

Before paying for a new policy, however, it's worth checking whether you are already covered. Some all-risks home insurance policies may cover your possessions when overseas, and many private medical schemes include cover when

Rough Guides travel insurance

Rough Guides has teamed up with Columbus Direct to offer you travel insurance that can be tailored to suit your needs.

Readers can choose from many different travel insurance products, including a low-cost backpacker option for long stays; a short-break option for city getaways; a typical holiday package option; and many others. There are also annual multi-trip policies for those who travel regularly, with variable levels of cover available. Different sports and activities (trekking, skiing, etc) can be covered if required on most policies.

Rough Guides travel insurance is available to the residents of 36 different countries, with different language options to choose from via our website – ⓦwww.roughguidesinsurance.com – where you can also purchase the insurance.

Alternatively, UK residents should call ⓣ0800 083 9507; US citizens should call ⓣ1-800 749-4922; Australians should call ⓣ1 300 669 999. All other nationalities should call ⓣ+44 870 890 2843.

abroad. In Canada, provincial health plans usually provide partial cover for medical mishaps overseas, while holders of official student/teacher/youth cards in Canada and the US are entitled to meagre accident coverage and hospital in-patient benefits. Students will often find that their student health coverage extends during the vacations and for one term beyond the date of last enrolment.

After exhausting the possibilities above, you might want to contact a specialist travel insurance company, or consider the travel insurance deal we offer (see box on p.43). Most travel insurance policies exclude so-called dangerous sports unless an extra premium is paid: in Norway this can mean **hiking**, **whitewater rafting**, **climbing** and **skiing**, though probably not kayaking. Check carefully that any insurance policy you are considering will cover all of the activities you'll be undertaking. Many policies can be chopped and changed to exclude coverage you don't need – for example, sickness and accident benefits can often be excluded or included at will. If you do take medical coverage, ascertain whether benefits will be paid as treatment proceeds or only after return home, and whether there is a 24-hour medical emergency number. When securing baggage cover, make sure that the per-article limit – typically under £500 – will cover your most valuable possession. If you need to make a **claim**, you should keep receipts for medicines and medical treatment, and in the event you have anything stolen, you must obtain an official statement from the local police.

Costs, money and banks

Norway has a reputation as one of the most expensive of European holiday destinations, and in some ways (but only some) this is entirely justified. Most of what you're likely to need – from a cup of coffee to a bottle of beer – is costly, but on the other hand certain major items are reasonably priced, most notably accommodation which, compared with other north European countries, can be remarkably inexpensive: Norway's (usually) first-rate youth hostels, almost all of which have family, double and dormitory rooms, are particularly good value. Getting around is good news, too. Most travellers use some kind of rail pass, there are myriad discounts and deals, and the state subsidizes the more remote and longer bus hauls. Furthermore, concessions are almost universally available at attractions and on public transport, with infants (under 4) going everywhere free, children and seniors (over 67, sometimes 60) paying – on average at least – half the standard rate. Food is, however, a different matter. With few exceptions – such as tinned fish – it's expensive, while the cost of alcohol is enough to make even a heavy drinker contemplate abstinence.

Average costs, if you're prepared to buy your own picnic lunch, stay in youth hostels and stick to the less expensive cafés and restaurants, are around £30/$52 a day excluding the cost of public transport. Staying in three-star hotels, eating out in medium-range restaurants most nights (but avoiding drinking in a bar), you'll get through at least £50/$90 a day – with the main variable being the cost of your room. As always, if you're travelling alone you'll spend much more on accommodation than you would in a group of two or more: most hotels do have single rooms, but they're usually around sixty to eighty percent of the price of a double.

Currency and exchange rates

Norwegian currency consists of **kroner**, one of which, a krone (literally "crown"; abbreviated **kr** or **NOK**), is divided into 100 **øre**. Coins in circulation are 50 øre, 1kr, 5kr and 10kr; notes are for 50kr, 100kr, 200kr, 500kr and 1000kr.

At the time of writing the **exchange rate** was 11.45kr to one pound sterling; 6.50kr to one US dollar; 5.50kr to one Canadian dollar; 4.90kr to one Australian dollar; 4.55kr to one New Zealand dollar and 7.80kr to one euro.

Changing money

ATMs are commonplace in Norway, especially in the cities, and are undoubtedly the quickest and easiest way of getting money. Most ATMs give instructions in a variety of languages, and accept a host of **debit cards.** If in doubt, check with your bank to find out whether the card you wish to use will be accepted – and if you need a new (international) PIN. You'll rarely be charged a transaction fee as the banks make their profits from applying different exchange rates. **Credit cards** can be used in ATMs too, but in this case transactions are treated as loans, with interest accruing daily from the date of withdrawal. All major credit cards, including American Express, Visa and Mastercard, are widely accepted in Norway.

All but the tiniest of settlements in Norway have a **bank** or **savings bank**, and the vast majority will change foreign currency and travellers' cheques. **Banking hours** in Norway are usually Monday to Friday 8.15am–3.30pm, though they usually close thirty minutes earlier during the summer (June–Aug) and are open till 5pm, sometimes 6pm, on Thursday all year. All major **post offices** change foreign currency and travellers' cheques at rates that are competitive with those of the banks, and they have longer opening hours too, generally Monday to Friday 8am–4/5pm and Saturday 9am–1pm. Almost every bank and post office charges a small commission for changing currency and cheques; if commission is waived, it probably means you're getting a lower exchange rate instead. Outside banking and post office hours, most major hotels, many travel agents and some hostels and campsites will change money at less generous rates and with variable commissions, as will the **exchange kiosks** to be found in Oslo.

Tax-free shopping

Taking advantage of their decision not to join the EU, the Norwegians run a **tax-free shopping scheme** for tourists. If you spend more than 308kr at any of the three thousand outlets in the tax-free shopping scheme, you'll get a voucher for the amount of VAT you paid. On departure at an airport, ferry terminal or frontier crossing, present the goods, the voucher and your passport and – provided you haven't used the item – you'll get an 11–18 percent refund, depending on the price of the item. There isn't a reclaim point at every exit from the country, however – pick up a leaflet at any participating shop to find out where they are – and note that many of the smaller reclaim points keep normal shop hours, closing for the weekend at 2pm on Saturday.

Wiring money

Having **money wired** from home using one of the companies listed below is never convenient or cheap, and should be considered as a last resort – indeed it can actually be cheaper to have **your own bank** send the money through. For the latter, you need to nominate a receiving bank in Norway and confirm the arrangement with them before you set the wheels in motion back home. The sending bank's fees are geared to the amount being transferred and the urgency of the service you require – for example standard transfers, taking five working days, start at around £20/US$40 for the first £2,000/US$3780 or so.

Money-wiring companies

Travelers Express/MoneyGram ⓦ www.moneygram.com US ⓣ 1-800/444-3010; Canada ⓣ 1-800/933-3278; UK, Ireland and New Zealand ⓣ 00800/6663 9472; Australia ⓣ 0011800/6663 9472.

Western Union ⓦwww.westernunion.com US and Canada ⓣ1-800/CALL-CASH; Australia ⓣ1800/501 500; New Zealand ⓣ0800/005 253; Republic of Ireland ⓣ66/947 5603; UK ⓣ0800/833 833.

Getting around

Norway's public transport system – a huge mesh of trains, buses, car ferries and passenger express ferries – is comprehensive and reliable. In the winter (especially in the north) services can be cut back severely, but no part of the country is unreachable for long. Bear in mind, however, that Norwegian villages and towns usually spread over a large distance, so don't be surprised if you end up walking a kilometre or two from the bus stop, ferry terminal or train station to get where you want to go. It's this sprawling nature of the country's towns and, more especially, the remoteness of many of the sights, that encourages visitors to rent a car. This is a very expensive business, but costs are manageable if you hire locally for a day or two rather than for the whole trip.

Timetables for most of the principal air, train, bus and ferry services are detailed in the NRI Guide to Transport and Accommodation, a free and easy-to-use booklet available in your home country from the Norwegian Tourist Board. In Norway itself, almost every tourist office carries a comprehensive range of free local and regional public transport timetables. In addition, all major train stations carry the NSB Togruter, a brochure detailing Norway's principal train timetables, whilst long-distance bus routes operated by the national carrier, Nor-Way Bussekspress, are listed in the free Rutehefte (timetable), available at principal bus stations. Norwegian public transport timetables are also widely available on the Internet, but although the major carriers are easy enough to track down, other companies are more elusive in English, less so if you can read Norwegian; we have provided public transport websites throughout the Guide.

Trains

With the exception of the Narvik line into Sweden, operated by Connex (Narvik train station: ⓣ47 76 92 31 21, ⓦwww.connex.se), all Norwegian **train** services are run by the state railway company, Norges Statsbaner (NSB; within Norway dial ⓣ81 50 08 88, then 4 for English, ⓦwww.nsb.no). Apart from a sprinkling of branch lines, NSB services operate on three main domestic routes, linking Oslo to Stavanger in the southwest, to Bergen in the west and to Trondheim and on to Bodø in the north. In places, the rail system is extended by a *TogBuss* (literally train-bus) service, with connecting coaches continuing on from train terminals. The nature of the country has made several of the routes engineering feats of some magnitude, worth the trip in their own right – the tiny **Flåm line** and the sweeping **Rauma line** from Dombås to Åndalsnes are exciting examples.

Prices are bearable with the popular Oslo–Bergen run, for example, costing around 700kr one-way, Oslo–Trondheim 770kr. Both journeys take around six and a half to seven hours. Costs can be reduced by purchasing a **rail pass** in advance (see p.34 & p.48) or, in the case of the Norway Rail Pass (see p.48), either in advance or within Norway – though even in this case you're probably best off buying in advance too, as

sorting things out can be surprisingly time-consuming. Inside Norway, NSB offers a variety of **discount fares**. The main discount ticket scheme is the **Minipris** (mini-price), under which you can cut up to fifty percent off the price of long-distance journeys. In general, the further you travel, the more economic they become. The drawback is that Minipris tickets must be purchased at least one day in advance, are not available at peak periods and on certain trains, and stopovers are not permitted. In addition, NSB offers a variety of special deals and discounts – inquire locally (and ahead of time) for details on any specific route.

In terms of **concessionary fares**, there are group and family reductions; children under 4 travel free provided they don't take up a seat; under-16s pay half-fare, and so do senior citizens (67+). It's worth noting that on many intercity trains and on all overnight and international services, an advance **seat reservation** (30kr) is **compulsory** whether you have a rail pass or not. In high season it's wise to reserve a seat on main routes anyway, as trains can be packed. **Sleepers** are reasonably priced if you consider you'll save a night's hotel accommodation: a bed in a three-berth cabin costs around 175kr, two-berth from 270kr.

NSB have two main sorts of train – local (Lokaltog) and regional (Regiontog). There is one standard class on both, but certain regional trains have a "Komfort" (read more luxurious, spacious) carriage, for which you pay a supplement of 75kr. NSB **timetables** are available free at every train station: there is a general timetable, the *NSB Togruter*, and this is supplemented by individual timetables and, in the case of the more scenic routes, by leaflets describing the sights as you go.

For further advance advice about passes, discounts and tickets, either contact NSB or the specialist agents listed in "Getting there" (p.34).

Rail passes

Both the **Inter-Rail** and **Eurail** passes (see p.35) are valid for the Norwegian railway system, as is the **ScanRail** pass (see p.34). The other alternative is the **Norway Rail Pass**, which allows unlimited travel on the NSB railways of Norway (except the Oslo Airport Express) on a specified number of days within a specific period. Three days in one month costs 1370kr, with additional days costing 230kr each. The Norway Rail Pass can be bought from major train stations inside Norway (in theory at least) and from agents abroad (see p.34). Children under 4 travel free, under-16s get a fifty percent discount and seniors (60-plus) twenty percent.

All rail-pass holders have to shell out a small additional surcharge on certain trains on certain routes, and also have to pay the compulsory seat reservation fee on most intercity trains and all overnight and international services. On the plus side, rail passes are good for travel on connecting Togbuss services, while two of them (ScanRail and Inter-Rail) give a fifty-percent discount on scores of intercity bus and boat routes.

Buses

Where the train network won't take you, **buses** will – and at no great cost, either: a substantial fjord journey, like the ten-hour bus ride between Ålesund and Bergen, is, for instance, a reasonable 548kr; even better, many of the long-distance express buses have a discounted maximum price – Oslo to Bergen, for example, costs a maximum of 290k. All tolls and ferry costs are included in the price of a ticket, which can represent a significant saving. You'll need to use buses principally in the western fjords and the far north, though there are also lots of long-distance express services between major towns. Most long-distance buses are operated by the national carrier, **Nor-Way Bussekspress** (from abroad ⓣ+47/75 54 80 20; inside Norway, ⓣ81 54 44 44, ⓦwww.nor-way.no), whose principal information office is at Oslo's main bus station. Their services are supplemented by a dense network of local buses, whose timetables are available at most tourist offices and bus stations as well as on the Internet. In general, most longer-distance routes tend to operate once or twice daily, with one bus leaving early in the morning, while shorter hauls, although more frequent, often tail off in the late afternoon. **Tickets** are usually bought on board, but bus stations and travel agents sell advance tickets on the more popular long-distance routes; be sure to keep your ticket till the journey is completed.

In terms of **concessionary fares**, there are group and family reductions, children under 3 travel free provided they don't take up a seat, youngsters under 16 pay half fare, and senior citizens over 67 get a 33 percent discount. Nor-Way Bussekspress offers Inter-Rail and ScanRail pass holders a fifty percent reduction on certain services – for instance on the Nord–Norgeekspressen (Bodø–Fauske–Narvik–Tromsø–Alta) – and some local bus companies have comparable deals. Indeed, rail-pass and student-card holders should always ask about discounts when purchasing a ticket.

Ferries

Using a **ferry** is one of the highlights of any visit to Norway – indeed, among the western fjords and around the Lofotens they are all but impossible to avoid. The majority are roll-on, roll-off **car ferries**. These represent an economical means of transport, with **prices** fixed on a nationwide sliding scale: short journeys (10–15min) cost foot passengers 20–30kr, whereas car and driver will pay 50–70kr. Ferry procedures are straightforward: foot passengers walk on and pay the conductor, car drivers usually wait in line with their vehicles on the jetty till the conductor comes to the car window to collect the money – although some busier routes have a drive-by ticket office. One or two of the longer car ferries – in particular Bodø–Moskenes – take advance reservations, but the rest operate on a first-come, first-served basis. In the off season, there's no real need to arrive more than twenty minutes before departure – with the possible exception of the Lofoten Island ferries – but in the summer allow two hours, two-and-a-half to be really safe.

Hurtigbåt passenger express boats

Norway's **Hurtigbåt passenger express boats** are catamarans that make up in speed what they lack in enjoyment: unlike the ordinary ferries, you're cooped up and have to view the passing landscape through a window, and in choppy seas the ride can be disconcertingly bumpy. Nonetheless, they're a convenient time-saving option: it takes just four hours on the Hurtigbåt service from Bergen to Balestrand, for instance, the same from Narvik to Svolvær, and a mere two-and-a-half hours from Harstad to Tromsø. Hurtigbåt services are concentrated on the west coast around Bergen and the neighbouring fjords; the majority operate all year. There's no fixed tariff table, so **rates** vary considerably, though Hurtigbåt boats are significantly more expensive per kilometre than car ferries – Bergen–Flåm, for instance, costs 560kr for the five-and-a-half-hour journey, 630kr for the four-hour trip from Bergen to Stavanger. There are **concessionary fares** on all routes, with infants up to the age of 3 travelling free, and children (4–15) and senior citizens (over 67) getting a fifty percent discount. In addition, rail-pass holders and students are often eligible for a fifty percent reduction on the full adult rate, for example on the Narvik–Svolvaer and Bergen–Flåm routes.

The Hurtigrute

Norway's most celebrated ferry journey is the long and beautiful haul up the coast from Bergen to Kirkenes on the **Hurtigrute** (literally "rapid route") **coastal boat** – or "coastal steamer", in honour of its past rather than present means of locomotion. To many, the Hurtigrute remains the quintessential Norwegian experience, and it's certainly the best way to observe the drama of the country's extraordinary coastline. Fourteen ships combine to provide one daily service in each direction, and the boats stop off at over thirty ports on the way.

The whole trip lasts eleven days, and in the summer (mid–April to mid–Sept) the one-way "port-to-port" **fare** from Bergen to end-of-the-line Kirkenes is 5500kr, 3800kr the rest of the year. These fares do not, however, include meals or accommodation and there is a host of all-inclusive deals on offer with tickets going for anything from 10,000kr to 25,000kr depending on whether you're sailing on one of the old or new vessels, where your cabin is on the boat and when you sail. There are also **concessionary fares** offering fifty percent discounts for senior citizens (over 67), families, groups of ten or more, students and children (4–15). Infants up to 3 years old travel free providing they do not occupy a separate berth. Note that in the summertime these discounts are only valid for a limited number of cabins, which makes pre-booking pretty much essential. Further details are available from authorized travel agencies back home, whom you can also make bookings with – there's a list of agents on the Hurtigrute website (ⓦwww.hurtigruten.com). Making a Hurtigrute booking once you've got to Norway is easy too, though some of the special deals may not be available. In Norway, the general Hurtigrute number is ⓣ81 03 00 00. Most city and west-coast tourist offices have sailing schedules.

A **short or medium-sized hop** along the coast on a portion of the Hurtigrute route is also well worth considering. **Port-to-port fares** are not particularly cheap, especially in comparison with the bus, but they are affordable. The standard, high-season (mid-April to mid-Sept), one-way passenger fare from Bergen to Trondheim (40hr), for example, costs 1700kr; from Svolvær to Stokmarknes (3hr) 230kr. Last-minute bargains, however, can bring the rates down to amazingly low levels and there are substantial discounts of around 35 percent in winter. All the tourist offices in the Hurtigrute ports have the latest details and should be willing to telephone the captain of the nearest ship to make a reservation on your behalf. Note that prices for port-to-port trips don't include meals.

As for specifics, you don't need to have a cabin, as sleeping in the lounges or on deck is allowed (though you would of course be nuts to sleep on deck in winter), and bikes travel free. There are luggage racks and laundry as well as a restaurant and a 24-hour cafeteria supplying coffee and snacks on all Hurtigrute boats; the restaurant is very popular, so book as soon as you board.

Planes

Internal flights can prove a surprisingly inexpensive way of hopping about the country, and are especially useful if you're short on time and want to reach, say, the far north: Tromsø to Kirkenes takes the best part of two days by bus, but it's just an hour

Hurtigrute sailing schedule

Northbound departure times from principal ports:

Summer schedule (mid-April to mid-Sept)

Bergen 8pm
Florø 2.15am
Ålesund 9.30am
Geiranger 1.30pm
Ålesund 6.45pm
Trondheim noon
Bodø 3pm
Stamsund 7.30pm
Svolvær 10pm
Harstad 8am
Tromsø 6.30pm
Hammerfest 6.45am
Honningsvåg 3.15pm
Arrive Kirkenes 10am

Winter schedule (mid-Sept to mid-April)

Bergen 10.30pm
Florø 4.45am
Ålesund 3pm
(No service to Geiranger)
Trondheim noon
Bodø 3pm
Stamsund 7.30pm
Svolvær 10pm
Harstad 8am
Tromsø 6.30pm
Hammerfest 6.45am
Honningsvåg 3.15pm
Arrive Kirkenes 10am

Southbound: year-round departure times from principal ports:

Kirkenes 12.45pm
Honningsvåg 6.15am
Hammerfest 12.45pm
Tromsø 1.30am
Harstad 8.30am
Svolvær 7.30pm
Stamsund 9.30pm
Bodø 4am
Trondheim 10am
Kristiansund 5pm
Ålesund 00.45am
Doesn't stop at Geiranger southbound
Florø 8.15am
Arrives Bergen 2.30pm

by plane. Domestic air routes are serviced by several companies, but the only big player is **SAS Braathens** (ⓦwww.sas.no), a conglomerate with many (airline) subsidiaries, the most useful of which, for domestic flights, is Widerøe (ⓦwww.wideroe.no). You might also want to check out one up-and-coming budget airline, **Norwegian Airlines** (see Norwegian Air Shuttle, p.30). Regular standard fares with SAS Braathens are around 650kr one-way from Oslo to Bergen, 1000kr from Oslo to Tromsø, and 1100kr from Bergen to Trondheim. SAS/Braathens also offer all sorts of deals and discounts, especially on return fares, which often cost just ten percent more than single tickets, but these bargains usually come with restrictions, regarding, for example, advance booking and including a Saturday night away. In terms of **concessionary fares**, SAS/Braathens permit infants under 2 to travel free on most flights, while on others ten percent of the regular fare is charged. In addition, people over 65, and children under 16 travelling in a family group including at least one full-fare-paying adult, receive a 33 percent discount on most flights. The details of these various discounts vary from year to year, so it's always worth checking them out.

With fares tumbling in recent years, **air passes** are much less tempting than they used to be, but SAS/Braathens do offer a reasonably economic **Visit Scandinavia AirPass** (see p.30) and **Widerøe** (outside of Norway, contact SAS, within Norway ⓣ81 00 12 00, ⓦwww.wideroe.no), an SAS subsidiary, offer two competitively priced Norway-only passes – Explore Norway and Fly Norway. **Explore Norway** provides two weeks unlimited travel between 35 Widerøe destinations during the summer (from late June to mid–Aug) at a cost of 3750kr; destinations include all of the country's cities. You can also opt for a southern, central or northern Explore Norway pass, with travel within one area (or zone) costing 2600kr, or 3330kr for two zones; the zonal boundaries are drawn through Tromsø and Trondheim, both of which are counted in two zones – thus Tromsø is in the north as well as the central zones. Alternatively, the all-year **Fly Norway** pass offers heavily discounted fares for non-Scandinavians to all 35 Widerøe destinations. Under the scheme, there is a standard charge for any direct flight of between 470kr and 640kr, with some shorter routes costing even less.

Driving

Norway's **main roads** are excellent, especially when you consider the rigours of the climate, and nowadays, with most of the more hazardous sections either ironed out or tunnelled through, driving is comparatively straightforward. Nonetheless, you still have to be careful on some of the higher sections and in the longer, fume-filled tunnels. Once you leave the main roads for the narrow mountain byroads, however, you'll be in for some nail-biting experiences – and that's in the summertime. In winter the Norwegians close many roads and concentrate their efforts on keeping the main highways open, but obviously blizzards and ice can make driving difficult to dangerous anywhere, even with winter tyres, studs and chains. At any time of the year, the more adventurous the drive, the better equipped you need to be: on remote drives you should pack provisions, have proper hiking gear, check the car thoroughly before departure, carry a spare can of petrol and take a mobile phone.

Norway's main highways have an **E prefix** – E6, E18 etc; all the country's other significant roads (*riksvei*, or *rv*) are assigned a number and, as a general rule, the lower the number, the busier the road. In our guide, we've used the E prefix, but designated other roads as Highways, or "Hwy" (followed by the number). **Tolls** are imposed on certain roads to pay for construction projects such as bridges and tunnels. Once the costs are covered the toll is normally removed. The older projects levy a fee of around 20–30kr, but the toll for some of the newer works (like the tunnel near Fjaerland) runs to well over 100kr per vehicle. There's also a modest toll on entering the country's larger cities (15–20kr), but whether this is an environmental measure or a means of boosting city coffers is a moot point. On most toll-roads, you simply pay at the toll booth, but at the busiest – for example, on the way into Oslo – drivers are presented with three lanes and choices: the "Abonnement" lanes are for passholders only and are always on

Opening dates of major mountain passes

Obviously enough, there's no preordained date for the opening of **mountain roads** in the springtime – it depends on the weather, and the threat of avalanches is often much more of a limitation than actual snowfalls. The dates below should therefore be treated with caution; if in doubt, seek advice from a local tourist office. If you do head along a mountain road that's closed, sooner or later you'll come to a barrier and have to turn round.

E6: Dovrefjell (Oslo–Trondheim). Usually open all year.

E69: Skarsvåg–Nordkapp. Closed late Oct to April.

E134: Haukelifjell (Oslo–Bergen/Stavanger). Usually open all year.

Hwy 7: Hardangervidda (Oslo–Bergen). Usually open all year.

Hwy 51: Valdresflya. Closed Dec to early May.

Hwy 55: Sognefjellet. Closed Nov to early May.

Hwy 63: Grotli–Geiranger–Åndalsnes (Trollstigen). Closed late Oct to May.

the left; the "Mynt/Coin" lanes are for exact cash payments only and usually have a bucket-shaped receptacle where you throw your money; and the "Manuell" lanes are also used for cash payments, but provide change. To avoid getting flustered at a toll booth, Norwegians carry a supply of coins ready to hand. Finally, there's often a modest toll of 10–20kr on privately maintained country roads; drivers are expected to deposit their money in a roadside **honesty box**, and these are easy to spot.

Fuel is readily available, even in the north, though here the settlements are so widely separated that you'll need to keep your tank pretty full; if you're using the byroads extensively, remember to carry an extra can. Current fuel prices are 11–13kr a litre, and there are four main grades: unleaded (*blyfri*) 95 octane; unleaded 98 octane; super 98 octane; and diesel (the cheapest). It's worth remembering that some petrol stations don't accept credit cards, so be sure to double-check before filling up.

Documentation and rules of the road

EU **driving licences** are honoured in Norway, but other nationals will need – or are recommended to have – an **International Driver's Licence** (available at minimal cost from your home motoring organization). No form of provisional licence is accepted. If you're bringing your own car, you must have vehicle registration papers, adequate insurance, a first-aid kit, a warning triangle and a green card (available from your insurers or motoring organization). Extra insurance coverage for unforeseen legal costs is also well worth having, as is an appropriate **breakdown policy** from a motoring organization. In Britain, for example, the RAC and AA charge members and non-members about £110 for a month's Europe-wide breakdown cover, with all the appropriate documentation, including green card, provided.

Rules of the road are strict: you drive on the right, with dipped headlights required at all times; seat belts are compulsory for drivers and front-seat passengers, and for back-seat passengers too, if fitted. There's a speed limit of 30kph in residential areas, 50kph in built-up areas, 80kph on open roads and 90kph on motorways and some other main roads. Cameras monitor hundreds of kilometres of road – watch out for the *Automatisk Trafikk Kontroll* warning signs – and they are far from popular with the locals: there are all sorts of folkloric (and largely apocryphal) tales of men in masks appearing at night with chain saws to chop them down. **Speeding fines** are so heavy that local drivers stick religiously within the speed limit. If you're filmed breaking the limit in a hire car, expect your credit card to be stung by the car hire company to the tune of at least 700kr. If you're stopped for speeding, large spot fines (1000–3000kr) are payable; rarely is any leniency shown to unwitting foreigners. **Drunken driving** is also severely frowned upon. You can be asked to take a breath test on a routine traffic-check; if you're over the limit, you will have your licence confiscated and may face 28 days in prison.

If you **break down** in a hire car, you'll get roadside assistance from the particular repair company the car hire firm has contracted. The same principle works with your own vehicle's breakdown policy (see opposite). Two major **breakdown companies** in Norway are Norges Automobil-Forbund and Viking Redningstjeneste, who combine to operate a 24hr emergency assistance line on ⓣ81 00 05 05. There are emergency telephones along some motorways, and NAF patrols on all mountain passes between mid-June and mid-August.

Car rental

All the major international **car rental** companies are represented in Norway – see below and in the "Listings" sections of larger cities for contact details.

To rent a car, you'll need to be 21 or over (and have been driving for at least a year), and you'll need a credit card. Rental **charges** are fairly high, beginning at around 3500kr per week for unlimited mileage in the smallest vehicle, but include collision damage waiver and vehicle (but not personal) insurance. To cut costs, watch for special local deals – a Friday to Monday weekend rental might, for example, cost you as little as 800kr. If you go to a local company, rather than one of the big names – and there are lots of them, listed in the telephone directory under *Bilutleie* – you should proceed with care. In particular, check the policy for the excess applied to claims and ensure that it includes collision damage waiver (applicable if an accident is your fault). Bear in mind, too, that one-way car rental **drop-off charges** are almost always wallet-searing, from 1000kr and up.

Car rental agencies

In North America

Alamo US ⓣ1-800/462-5266, ⓦwww.alamo.com.
Auto Europe US and Canada ⓣ1-888/223-5555, ⓦwww.autoeurope.com.
Europcar US and Canada ⓣ1-877/940 6900, ⓦwww.europcar.com.
Europe by Car US ⓣ1-800/223-1516, ⓦwww.europebycar.com.
Hertz US ⓣ1-800/654-3131, Canada ⓣ1-800/263-0600; ⓦwww.hertz.com.
National US and Canada ⓣ1-800/962-7070, ⓦwww.nationalcar.com.

In Britain

Europcar ⓣ0870/607 5000, ⓦwww.europcar.co.uk.
National ⓣ0870/536 5365, ⓦwww.nationalcar.co.uk.
Hertz ⓣ0870/844 8844, ⓦwww.hertz.co.uk.
Holiday Autos ⓣ0870/400 0099, ⓦwww.holidayautos.co.uk.

In Ireland

Europcar Northern Ireland ⓣ028/9442 3444, Republic of Ireland ⓣ01/614 2888, ⓦwww.europcar.ie.
Hertz Republic of Ireland ⓣ01/676 7476, ⓦwww.hertz.ie.
Holiday Autos Republic of Ireland ⓣ01/872 9366, ⓦwww.holidayautos.ie.
Thrifty Republic of Ireland ⓣ1800/515 800, ⓦwww.thrifty.ie.

In Australia

Europcar ⓣ1300/131 390, ⓦwww.deltaeuropcar.com.au.
Hertz ⓣ13 30 39 or 03/9698 2555, ⓦwww.hertz.com.au.
Holiday Autos ⓣ1300/554 432, ⓦwww.holidayautos.com.au.
National ⓣ13 10 45, ⓦwww.nationalcar.com.au.
Thrifty ⓣ1300/367 227, ⓦwww.thrifty.com.au.

In New Zealand

Hertz ⓣ0800/654 321, ⓦwww.hertz.co.nz.
Holiday Autos ⓣ0800/144 040, ⓦwww.holidayautos.co.nz.
National ⓣ0800/800 115 or 03/366 5574, ⓦwww.nationalcar.co.nz.
Thrifty ⓣ09/309 0111, ⓦwww.thrifty.co.nz.

Cycling

Cycling is a great way to enjoy Norway's scenery – just be sure to wrap up warm and dry, and don't be overambitious in the distances you expect to cover. Cycle tracks as such are few and far between, and are mainly confined to the larger towns, but there's precious little traffic on most of the minor roads and cycling along them is a popular pastime. Furthermore, whenever a road is improved or rerouted, the old highway is usually redesigned as a cycle route. At almost every place you're likely to stay in, you can anticipate that someone will **rent bikes** – either the tourist office, a sports shop, youth hostel or campsite. Costs are pretty uniform: reckon on paying between 120kr and 200kr a day for a seven-speed bike, plus a refundable deposit of up to 1000kr; mountain bikes are about thirty percent more.

A few tourist offices have maps of recommended **cycling routes**, but this is a rarity. It is, however, important to check your itinerary thoroughly, especially in the more mountainous areas. Cyclists aren't allowed through the longer tunnels for their own protection (the fumes can be life-threatening), so discuss your plans with whoever you hire the bike from. Bikes mostly go free on car ferries and attract a nominal charge on passenger express boats, but buses vary. National carrier Nor-Way Bussekspress accepts bikes only when there is space and charges a child fare, whilst local rural buses sometimes take them free, sometimes charge and sometimes do not take them at all. There's a fee of 50–180kr to take bikes on NSB trains.

If you're planning a **cycling holiday**, your first port of call should be the Norwegian Tourist Board (see p.41), where you can get general cycling advice, a map showing roads and tunnels inaccessible to cyclists and a list of companies offering all-inclusive cycling tours. Obviously enough, tour costs vary enormously, but as a baseline reckon on about 5000kr per week all-inclusive.

The Norwegian Cyclist Association Syklistenes Landsforening, Storgata 23D, Oslo (Ⓣ22 47 30 30, Norwegian-language only: Ⓦwww.slf.no) has an excellent range of specific cycling **books** and **maps**, some of which are in English. Finally, the website Sykkelturisme i Norge (Ⓦwww.bike-norway.com) has ideas for a dozen routes around the country from 100km to 400km, plus useful practical information about road conditions, repair facilities and places of interest en route.

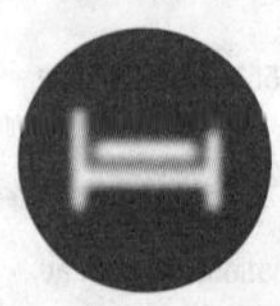

Accommodation

Inevitably, hotel accommodation is one of the major expenses you will incur on a trip to Norway – indeed, if you're after a degree of comfort, it's going to be the costliest item by far. There are, however, budget alternatives, principally private rooms (broadly Bed & Breakfast arranged via the local tourist office), campsites and cabins, and last but certainly not least, an abundance of HI-registered hostels. Also bear in mind that most hotels offer 25–40 percent discounts in summer and often give substantial year-round weekend discounts too.

Hotels

Almost universally, Norwegian **hotels** are of a high standard: neat, clean and efficient. Summer prices and impromptu weekend deals also make many of them, by European standards at least, comparatively economical. Another plus is that the price of a hotel room always includes a buffet breakfast – in mid- to top-range hotels especially, these can be sumptuous banquets. The only negatives are the sizes of rooms, which tend to be small – singles especially – and their sameness: Norway abounds in mundanely modern concrete and glass sky-rise chain hotels. In addition to the places we've detailed in the guide, most Norwegian hotels, along

Accommodation price codes

All the accommodation detailed in this guide has been graded according to the following price categories, based on the cost of the **least expensive double room during the high season** (usually June to mid-August). However, almost every hotel offers seasonal and/or weekend discounts, which can reduce the rate by one or even two grades. Wherever hotels have an **official summer or weekend rate** we've given two grades, covering both the regular and the discounted rate – the latter signified by **sp/r**. Single rooms, where available, usually cost between 60 and 80 percent of a double. At hostels, we have also given the price of a dormitory bed.

- ❶ under 350kr
- ❷ 350–600kr
- ❸ 600–800kr
- ❹ 800–1000kr
- ❺ 1000–1200kr
- ❻ 1200–1400kr
- ❼ 1400–1600kr
- ❽ 1600–2000kr
- ❾ Over 2000kr

with their room rates, summer discounts and facilities, are listed in the free booklet *Transport and Accommodation*, available from Norwegian tourist offices abroad (see p.41).

Summer is the best time to use one of the several **hotel discount and pass schemes** that operate throughout Norway. There are five main ones to choose from; each serves to cut costs, though often at the expense of a flexible itinerary – advance booking is the norm. Most Norwegian hotels are members of one discount/pass scheme or another, and you can usually join the scheme at one of the hotels, or at a tourist office; it's also worth checking what's available with your travel agent before leaving home. Amongst the options, perhaps the best is the **Fjord Pass** (Ⓦwww.fjord-pass.com), which offers discounts of around 30 percent at over 200 hotels with the Fjord Pass discount card; the card costs just 100kr and is valid for two adults and children under the age of fifteen. A second option is the **Rica Holiday Pass** (*Rica Feriepass*, Ⓦwww.rica-hotels.com), basically a free loyalty card that promises the bearer the best rate available and every fifth night free; it's available at any of Rica's seventy Norwegian hotels.

Pensions, guesthouses and inns

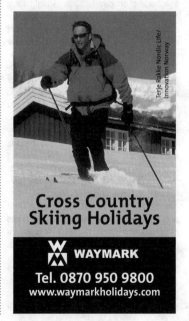

For something a little less formal and anonymous than the average hotel, **pensions** (*pensjonater*) are your best bet – small, sometimes intimate boarding houses, which can usually be found in the larger cities and more touristy towns. Rooms go for 450–550kr single, 500–650kr double; breakfast is generally extra. Broadly comparable in price and character is a *gjestgiveri* or *gjestehus*, a **guesthouse** or **inn**, though some of these offer superb lodgings in historic premises with prices to match. Facilities in all of these establishments are usually adequate and homely without being overwhelmingly comfortable; at the cheaper places you'll share a bathroom with others. Some pensions and guesthouses also have kitchens available for the use of guests, which means you're very likely to meet other residents – a real boon (perhaps) if you're travelling alone.

Hostels and private rooms

For many budget travellers, as well as hikers, climbers and skiers, the country's **HI hostels** (vandrerhjem; Ⓦwww.vandrerhjem.no) are the accommodation mainstay. There are almost a hundred in total, with handy concentrations in the western fjords, the central hiking and skiing regions and in Oslo. The Norwegian hostelling association, **Norske Vandrerhjem**, has its headquarters in Oslo, at Torggata 1 (Ⓣ23 13 93 00). They maintain an excellent website – where you can make bookings at any hostel – and prepare a free booklet, *Norske Vandrerhjem*, which details locations, opening dates, prices and telephone numbers; the booklet is available at most hostels. The hostels themselves are invariably excellent – the only quibble, at the risk of being churlish, is that those occupying schools tend to be rather drab and institutional.

Prices per night vary from 120kr to 200kr, although the more expensive hostels nearly always include a grand breakfast. On average, reckon on paying 130kr a night for a bed, 50kr for breakfast and 80–100kr for a hot evening meal. Bear in mind also that almost all hostels have at least a few regular double and family rooms on offer: at 300–700kr a double, these are among the cheapest rooms you'll find in Norway..If you're not a member of Hostelling International (HI) you can still use the hostels, though it will cost you an extra 25kr or so a night – better to join up at the first Norwegian hostel you stay at or before you leave home (see below), especially considering the low cost of annual membership. If you don't have your own sheet sleeping bag, you'll mostly have to rent one for around 40–50kr a time.

It cannot be stressed too strongly that **pre-booking** a hostel bed will save you lots of unnecessary legwork. Many hostels are only open from mid-June to mid-August and most close between 11am and 4pm. There's sometimes an 11pm or midnight curfew, though this isn't a huge drawback in a country where carousing is so expensive. Where breakfast is included – as it usually is – ask for a breakfast packet if you have to leave early to catch transport; otherwise note that hostel **meals** are nearly always excellent value, though of variable quality, ranging from the bland and filling to the delicious. Most, though not all, hostels have small **kitchens**, but often no pots, pans, cutlery or crockery, so self-caterers should take their own.

Tourist offices in the larger towns and amongst the more touristy settlements can often fix you up with a **private room** in someone's house, possibly including kitchen facilities. Prices are competitive – from 250–350kr per single, 350–400kr per double – though there's usually a booking fee (20–30kr) on top, and the rooms themselves are frequently some way out of the centre. Nonetheless, they're often the best bargain available and, in certain instances, an improvement on the local hostel. Where this is the case, we've said so in the Guide. If you don't have a sleeping bag, check the room comes with bedding – not all of them do; and if you're cooking for yourself, a few basic utensils may not go amiss.

Youth hostel associations

In Australia

Australia Youth Hostels Association
Ⓣ02/9261 1111, Ⓦwww.yha.com.au.

In Canada

Hostelling International Canada Ⓣ1-800/663 5777 or 613/237 7884, Ⓦwww.hihostels.ca.

In England and Wales

Youth Hostel Association (YHA) Ⓣ0870/770 8868, Ⓦwww.yha.org.uk.

In Ireland

Irish Youth Hostel Association Ⓣ01/830 4555, Ⓦwww.irelandyha.org.

In New Zealand

Youth Hostelling Association New Zealand Ⓣ0800/278 299 or 03/379 9970, Ⓦwww.yha.co.nz.

In Northern Ireland

Hostelling International Northern Ireland Ⓣ028/9032 4733, Ⓦwww.hini.org.uk.

In Scotland

Scottish Youth Hostel Association ⓣ0870/155 3255, ⓦwww.syha.org.uk.

In the US

Hostelling International-American Youth Hostels ⓣ301/495-1240, ⓦwww.hiayh.org.

Campsites, cabins and mountain huts

Camping is a popular pastime in Norway, and there are literally hundreds of sites to choose from – anything from a field with a few tent pitches to extensive complexes with all mod cons. The Norwegian tourist authorities detail several hundred campsites in their free *Norway Camping* brochure (also online at ⓦwww.camping.no), classifying them on a one- to five-star grading depending on the facilities offered (and not on the aesthetics of the location). Most sites are situated with the motorist (rather than the cyclist or walker) in mind, and a good few occupy key locations beside the main roads, though in summer these prime sites can be inundated by seasonal workers. The majority of campsites are two- and three-star establishments, where prices are usually per tent, plus a small charge per person and then for vehicles; on average expect to pay around 100kr for two people using a tent, 40kr more with a car, though four- and five-star sites average around twenty percent more. During peak season it can be a good idea to **reserve ahead** if you have a car and a large tent or trailer; contact details are listed in the free camping booklet and throughout the Guide. The Scandinavia **Camping Card** (*Campingkort*) brings faster registration at many campsites across Scandinavia and occasionally entitles the bearer to special camping rates. It is valid for one year, costs 100kr and can be purchased from participating campsites or online at ⓦwww.camping.no.

Camping rough in Norway is a tradition enshrined in law. You can camp anywhere in open areas as long as you are at least 150m away from any houses or cabins. As a courtesy, ask farmers for permission to use their land – it is rarely refused. Fires are not permitted in woodland areas or in fields between April 15 and September 15, and camper vans are not allowed (ever) to overnight in lay-bys. A good sleeping bag is essential, since even in summer it can get very cold, and, in the north at least, mosquito repellent is vital.

The Norwegian countryside is dotted with thousands of timber **cabins/chalets** (called *hytter*), ranging from simple wooden huts through to comfortable lodges. They are usually two- or four-bedded affairs, with full kitchen facilities and sometimes a bathroom, even TV, but not necessarily **bed linen**. Some hostels have them on their grounds, there are nearly always at least a handful at every campsite, and in the Lofoten islands they are the most popular form of accommodation, many occupying refurbished fishermen's huts called *rorbuer*. **Costs** vary enormously, depending on location, size and amenities, and there are significant seasonal variations, too. However, a four-bed *hytter* will rarely cost more than 800kr per night – a more usual average would be about 600kr. If you're travelling in a group, they are easily the cheapest way to see the countryside – and in some comfort. Hundreds of *hytter* are also rented out as holiday cottages by the week.

One further option for hikers is the **mountain huts** (again called *hytter*), which are strategically positioned on every major hiking route. Some are privately run, but the majority are operated by **Den Norske Turistforening** (DNT; see The Hiking colour section), and although you don't have to be a member of DNT to use their huts, you'll soon recoup your outlay through reduced hut charges for members. For members staying in staffed huts, a bunk in a dormitory costs 160kr, a family or double room 200kr per person; meals start at 80kr for breakfast, 195kr for a three-course dinner. At unstaffed huts, where you leave the money for your stay in a box provided, an overnight stay costs 160kr.

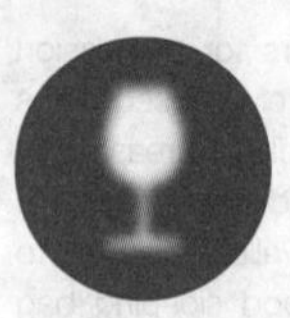

Food and drink

At its best, Norwegian food can be excellent: fish is plentiful, and carnivores can have a field day trying meats like reindeer and elk or even, conscience permitting, seal and whale. Admittedly it's not inexpensive, and those on a tight budget may have problems varying their diet, but by exercising a little prudence in the face of the average menu (which is almost always in Norwegian and English), you can keep costs down to reasonable levels. Vegetarians, however, will have slim pickings (except in Oslo), and drinkers will have to dig very deep into their pockets to maintain much of an intake. Indeed, most drinkers end up visiting the supermarkets and state off-licences (Vinmonopolet) so that they can sup away at home (in true Norwegian style) before setting out for the evening.

Food

Many travellers to Norway exist almost entirely on a mixture of picnic food and by cooking their own meals, with the odd café meal thrown in to boost morale. Frankly, this isn't really necessary (except on the tightest of budgets), as there are a number of ways to eat out inexpensively. To begin with, a good self-service buffet breakfast, served in almost every hostel and hotel, goes some way to solving the problem, whilst special lunch deals will get you a tasty hot meal for 70–90kr. Finally, alongside the regular restaurants – which are expensive – there's the usual array of budget pizzerias, cafeterias and café-bars in most towns.

Breakfast, picnics and snacks

More often than not, **breakfast** (*frokost*) in Norway is a substantial self-service affair of bread, crackers, cheese, eggs, preserves, cold meat and fresh and pickled fish, washed down with tea and ground coffee. It's usually first-rate at youth hostels, and often memorable in hotels, filling you up for the day for 70–100kr when and wherever it's not thrown in with the price of your room as it mostly is.

If you're buying your own **picnic food**, bread, cheese, yoghurt and local fruit are all relatively good value, but other staple foodstuffs – rice, pasta, meat, cereals and vegetables – can be way above the European average. Anything tinned is particularly dear (with the exception of fish), but coffee and tea are quite reasonably priced. **Supermarkets** are ten-a-penny.

As ever, **fast food** offers the best chance of a hot, bargain-basement takeaway snack. The indigenous Norwegian stuff, served up from street kiosks or stalls – **gatekjøkken** – in every town, consists mainly of rubbery hot dogs (*varm pølse*), while pizza slices and chicken pieces and chips are much in evidence too. American burger bars are also creeping in – both at motorway service stations and in the towns and cities. A better choice, and usually not much more expensive, is simply to get a sandwich, normally a huge open affair called a **smørbrød** (pronounced "smurrbrur"), heaped with a variety of garnishes. You'll see them groaning with meat or shrimps, salad and mayonnaise in the windows of bakeries and cafés, or in the newer, trendier sandwich bars in the cities.

Good **coffee** is available everywhere, rich and strong, and served black or with cream. **Tea**, too, is ubiquitous, but the local preference is for lemon tea or a variety of flavoured infusions; if you want milk, ask for it. All the familiar **soft drinks** are also available.

Lunch and dinner

For the best deals, you're going to have to eat your main meal of the day at lunch or possibly tea time, when **kafeterias** (often self-service restaurants) lay on daily specials, the *dagens rett*. This is a fish or meat dish served with potatoes and a vegetable or salad, often including a drink, sometimes bread, and occasionally coffee, too; it should go for 80–100kr. Dipping into the menu is more expensive, but not cripplingly so if you stick to omelettes and suchlike. You'll find *kafeterias* hidden above shops and offices and adjoining hotels in larger towns, where they might be called *kaffistovas*. Most close at around 6pm, and many don't open at all on Sunday. As a general rule, the food these places serve is plain-verging-on-the-ordinary (though there are many exceptions), but the same cannot be said of the continental-style **café-bars** which abound in Oslo and, increasingly, in all of Norway's larger towns and cities. These eminently affordable establishments offer much tastier and much more adventurous meals like pasta dishes, salads and vegetarian options with main courses in the region of 90–120kr.

In all of the cities, but especially in Oslo, there are first-class **restaurants**, serving dinner (*middag*) in quite formal – and/or smart and chic – surroundings. Apart from exotica such as reindeer and elk, the one real speciality is the seafood, simply prepared and wonderfully fresh – whatever you do, don't go home without treating yourself at least once. In the smaller towns and villages, gourmets will be harder pressed – many of the restaurants are pretty mundane, though the general standard is improving rapidly. Main courses begin at around 150kr, starters and desserts at around 90kr. If in doubt, smoked salmon comes highly recommended, as does catfish and monkfish. Again, the best deals are at lunchtime, though some restaurants don't open till the evening. In the western fjords, look out also for the help-yourself, all-you-can-eat **buffets** available in many of the larger hotels from around 6pm; go early to get the best choice and expect to pay around 250kr to be confronted by mounds of pickled herring, salmon (*laks*), cold cuts of meat, a feast of breads and crackers, and usually a few hot dishes too – meatballs, soup and scrambled eggs.

In the towns, and again especially in Oslo, there is also a sprinkling of **non-Scandinavian restaurants**, mostly Italian with a good helping of Chinese and Indian places. Other cuisines pop up here and there, too – Japanese, Moroccan and Persian to name but three.

Most restaurants have bilingual menus (in Norwegian and English), but we have provided a **menu reader**, on pp.462–464

Vegetarians

Vegetarians are in for a hard time. Apart from a handful of specialist restaurants in the big cities, there's little option other than to make do with salads, look out for egg dishes in *kafeterias* and supplement your diet from supermarkets. If you are a **vegan** the problem is greater: when the Norwegians are not eating meat and fish, they are attacking a fantastic selection of milks, cheeses and yoghurts. At least you'll know what's in every dish you eat, since everyone speaks English. If you're self-catering, look for **health food shops** (*helsekost*), found in some of the larger towns and cities.

Drink

One of the less savoury sights in Norway – and especially common in the north – is the fall-over drunk: you can spot them at any time of the day or night zigzagging along the street, a strangely disconcerting counter to the usual stereotype of the Norwegian as a healthy, hearty figure in a wholesome woolly jumper. For reasons that remain obscure – or at least culturally complex – many Norwegians can't just have a drink or two, but have to get absolutely wasted. The majority of their compatriots deplore such behaviour and have consequently imposed what amounts to alcoholic rationing: thus, although booze is readily available in the bars and restaurants, it's taxed up to the eyeballs and the distribution of wines and spirits is strictly controlled by a state-run monopoly, **Vinmonopolet**. Whether this paternalistic type of control makes matters better or worse is a moot point, but the majority of Norwegians support it.

What to drink

If you decide to splash out on a few drinks, you'll find Norwegian **beer** is lager-like and characteristically uninspiring; popular brands include Hansa and Ringsnes. There's no domestically produced **wine** to speak of and most **spirits** are imported, too, but one local brew worth experimenting with at least once is **aquavit** (*akevitt*), a bitter concoction served ice-cold in little glasses and, at forty percent proof or more, real headache material – though it's more palatable with beer chasers: Linie aquavit is one of the more popular brands.

Where to buy alcohol

Beer is sold in supermarkets and shops all over Norway, though some local communities, particularly in the west, have their own rules and restrictions; at around 21kr per third of a litre, the supermarket price is about half what you'd pay in a bar. The strongest beers, along with **wines and spirits**, can only be purchased from the state-run **Vinmonopolet** shops. There's generally one branch in each medium-size town and many more in each of Norway's cities. Opening hours are characteristically Monday to Wednesday 10am–4/5pm, Thursday 10am–5/6pm, Friday 9am–4/6pm, Saturday 9am–1pm, though these times can vary depending on the location, and they all close on public holidays. At Vinmonopolet stores, wine is quite a bargain, from around 80kr a bottle, and there's generally a wide choice.

Where to drink

Wherever you **go for a drink**, a third-litre of beer should cost between 35kr and 45kr, and a glass of wine from 30kr. You can get a drink at most outdoor cafés, in restaurants and at bars, pubs and cocktail bars, but only in the towns and cities is there any kind of "European" bar life: in Oslo, Bergen, Stavanger, Trondheim and Tromsø you will be able to keep drinking in bars until at least 1am, 4am in some places.

Opening hours, public holidays and festivals

Although there's recently been some movement towards greater flexibility, opening hours for shops and businesses remain fairly restrictive. Tourist attractions and leisure amenities, on the other hand, tend to have extended opening hours in the summer, but close down early (or completely) in winter especially outside the cities. On public holidays, most things close – though not, of course, restaurants, bars and hotels – and public transport is reduced to a limited (Sunday) timetable.

Opening hours

Normal **shopping hours** are Monday through Friday 10am to 5pm, with late opening on Thursdays till 6pm or 7pm, plus Saturdays 10am to 1pm or 3pm. Most supermarkets stay open much longer – from 9am until 8pm in the week and from 9am to 6pm on Saturdays, but close on Sundays. In addition, the majority of kiosks-cum-newsstands stay open till 9pm or 10pm every night of the week (including Sundays), but much more so in the cities and towns than in the villages. Many petrol stations sell a basic range of groceries and stay open till 11pm daily. Vinmonopolet, the state-run liquor store chain, has limited opening hours that vary between stores. **Office hours** are normally Monday to Friday 8.30am or 9am to 5pm or 5.30pm.

Public holidays

National **public holidays** are a noticeable feature of the Norwegian calendar and act as a further unifying force in what remains an extremely homogeneous society. There are thirteen national public holidays per year, most of which are keenly observed, though the tourist industry carries on pretty much regardless. Incidentally, some state-run museums adopt Sunday hours on public holidays, except on Christmas Day and New Year's Day (and often December 26) when they close. Otherwise most businesses and shops close, and the public transport system operates a skeleton or Sunday service. Some of these public holidays are also **official flag-flying days**, but there are additional flag days as well – for example on Queen Sonja's birthday (July 4). Most Norwegians take their holidays in the summer season, between mid-June and mid-August.

National public holidays

New Year's Day
Palm Sunday (week before Easter)
Maundy Thursday (Thursday before Easter)
Good Friday
Easter Sunday
Easter Monday
Labour Day (May 1)
Ascension Day (early to mid-May)
National Day (May 17)
Whit Sunday (the seventh Sunday after Easter)
Whit Monday
Christmas Day
Boxing Day (day after Christmas Day)

Note that when a public holiday falls on a Sunday, then the next day becomes a holiday as well.

Festivals and events

Almost every town in Norway has some sort of summer shindig and there are winter celebrations too. For the most part, these are worth attending if you are already in the area rather than meriting a special journey. There are two main sorts of **festival**, one being celebrations of historical or folkloric events, the other more contemporary-based jazz and pop music binges and the like. As you might expect, most tourist-oriented events take place in summer and, as always, national and local tourist offices can supply details of exact dates, which tend to vary from year to year. Below we have listed the more important festivals, some of which are detailed in the Guide.

A festival calendar

January
The three- to four-day **Nordlysfestivalen** (Northern Lights Festival) of classical and contemporary music takes place in Tromsø, and features everything from jazz to chamber music. It coincides with the return of the sun, hence its name. For information and tickets contact ⓣ77 66 33 66 or ⓦwww.nordlysfestivalen.no.

February
Ski events at Oslo's Holmenkollen run from early February to late March. All sorts of races take place in all sorts of disciplines, from ski marathons to the Nordic World Cup, ending with a massively popular ski jumping competition. Information ⓦwww.skiforeningen.no.

March
In late March, Lillehammer stages the **Birkebeinerrennet**, a famous, 58km cross-country ski race from Rena to Lillehammer that celebrates the dramatic events of 1206, when the young prince Haakon Håakonsson was rushed over the mountains to safety. The race follows what is thought to have been the original route. Information and tickets on ⓣ41 77 29 00 and ⓦwww.birkebeiner.no.

May
Constitution or **National Day** sees processions and flag-waving all over the country to celebrate the signing of the Norwegian constitution on May 17, 1814. There's also the first-rate and diverse **Festspillene i Bergen** (Bergen International Festival) of contemporary music, which takes place from late May until early June. Information and tickets on ⓣ55 21 06 30 and ⓦwww.fib.no.

June
Held in late June in Voss, the **Ekstremsportveko** (Extreme Sport Week) features adventure sports from paragliding and base jumping through to rafting. Information and tickets on ⓦwww.ekstremsportveko.com, or contact Voss tourist office (see p.231).
The three-day **Norwegian Wood** open-air rock festival takes place in Oslo's Frogner Park amphitheatre, showcasing big-name international artists as well as up-and-coming local bands. Information on ⓦwww.norwegianwood.no; tickets on ⓣ81 53 31 33 and ⓦwww.billettservice.no.

July
Held over a five-day period in the middle of the month, the **Molde Jazz Festival** is one of the best of its type, attracting big international names as well as Scandinavian artists. Information and tickets on ⓣ71 20 31 50 and ⓦwww.moldejazz.no.

Olavsfestdagene takes place at the end of the month, with historical pageants and plays honouring Olav, Norway's first Christian king, being staged at Stiklestad, where he was killed in battle in 1030. The events are spread over several days leading up to the main attractions on St Olav's Day. Information on ⓣ73 84 14 50 and ⓦwww.olavsfestdagene.no; tickets on ⓣ81 53 31 33 and ⓦwww.billettservice.no.

August

The **Oslo Jazz Festival** is held around the middle of the month, a five-day event attracting some big international names. Information and tickets on ⓣ22 42 91 20 and ⓦwww.oslojazz.no.

October

The ten-day **Ultimafestivalen** (Ultima Contemporary Music Festival) features performances by international and Scandinavian talent at various venues across Oslo. Information and tickets on ⓣ22 42 99 99 and ⓦwww.ultima.no.

Mail and telecommunications

Both postal and telephone systems are very efficient in Norway, and most of the staff speak at least some English.

Mail

Post offices are plentiful; usual opening hours are Monday to Friday 8am/8.30am–4/5pm and Saturday 9am–1pm, though some urban post offices open longer hours. **Postage** costs are currently 5.5kr for either a postcard or a letter under 20g sent within Norway (7kr within Scandinavia, 9kr to the EU), and 10kr to countries outside. Mail to the USA takes a week to ten days, two to three days within Europe. You can have letters sent **poste restante** to any post office in Norway by addressing them "Poste Restante", followed by the name of the town and country. When picking mail up you'll need to take your passport; make sure to check under middle names and initials, as letters can get misfiled.

Telephones

Domestic and international calls are easy to make from **public telephones**, which are plentiful and almost invariably work. They are of the usual Western European kind, where you deposit the money before you make your call. They take 1kr, 5kr, 10kr and 20kr coins, though the minimum charge for a call is 5kr. Most public telephones also accept **phonecards** (*TeleKorts*). These can be purchased at newsstands, Narvesen kiosks, post offices and some supermarkets, and come in a variety of denominations from 40kr to 140kr. An increasing number of public phones also accept major credit cards. Phone booths have English instructions displayed inside. Most hotel rooms have phones too, but note that they nearly always attract an exorbitant surcharge.

Domestic telephone calls **cost** a minimum of 5kr, while 10kr is enough to start an international telephone call, but not much more. Discounted rates on domestic and international calls (of around thirty percent) apply from 5pm to 8am on weekdays and all weekend. All Norwegian telephone numbers have eight digits and there's no area code.

Useful numbers and international dialling codes

Directory enquiries: domestic ⓣ1881; international ⓣ1882
Collect and reverse-call operator ⓣ115
Emergencies: ambulance ⓣ113; fire ⓣ110; police ⓣ112

Phoning Norway from abroad

Dial your country's international access code, then ⓣ47 + number

Phoning abroad from Norway:

To **Australia**: ⓣ0061 + area code minus zero + number.
To **Canada**: ⓣ001 + area code + number.
To the **Republic of Ireland**: ⓣ00353 + area code minus zero + number.
To **New Zealand**: ⓣ0064 + area code minus zero + number.
To **South Africa**: ⓣ0027 + area code minus zero + number
To the **UK**: ⓣ0044 + area code minus zero + number.
To the **US**: ⓣ001 + area code + number.

Telephone charge cards

Various telephone companies, including British Telecom, issue **telephone charge cards** to their subscribers for use abroad. These cards can be used on any phone line and the subsequent call is automatically billed to your home telephone number. To use them, you first dial a code for Norway, which accesses your own company's lines, and then you tap in your account number and PIN – and away you go. In most cases, there is no local charge, but some hotels apply a connection or access fee. For further details, ask your phone company.

Mobile phones

Most of Norway is on the **mobile phone network**, which means hikers, skiers, climbers and other outdoor enthusiasts can contact someone by phone almost no matter where they are – invaluable if things go wrong. The region's mobile network is on the **GSM 900/1800** band common to the rest of Europe, Australia and New Zealand. This means that the vast majority of mobile phones from these countries will work here, although, if you haven't used your mobile abroad before, you should check with your phone company: some mobiles are, for example, barred from international use. It's also a good idea to check **call charges** as costs can be excruciating – particularly irritating is the supplementary charge that you pay on incoming calls.

Things are more complicated (and expensive) for Canadians and Americans. The **North American mobile network** is not compatible with the GSM system, so you'll need a **tri-band phone** which is able to switch from one band to the other.

Internet access

You can access the **Internet** either at one of the country's growing number of Internet cafés (all major cities have at least a couple), most of the smarter hotels and at public libraries. Library access is free, but Internet café charges vary wildly – 30kr per thirty minutes is a reasonable average.

If you're **taking your own computer**, ⓦwww.kropla.com is a useful website which gives details of how to get connected when abroad. It also has a list of international access codes and information about electrical systems in different countries, including Norway.

Media

Most British and some American daily newspapers, plus the occasional periodical, are sold in every town and city from Narvesen kiosks, which are ubiquitous and always at train stations and airports. As for the Norwegian media, state advertising, loans and subsidized production costs sustain a wealth of smaller papers that would bite the dust elsewhere. Most are closely linked with political parties, although the bigger city-based titles tend to be independent. Highest circulations are claimed in Oslo by the independent Verdens Gang and the independent-conservative Aftenposten, and in Bergen by the liberal Bergens Tidende. There are no English-language titles.

Norway's **television** network has expanded over the last few years, in line with the rest of Europe. Alongside the state channels, NRK1, NRK2 and TV2, there are satellite channels like TV Norge, while TV3 is a channel common to Norway, Denmark and Sweden; you can also pick up Swedish TV – though pornographic programmes are jammed. Many of the programmes are English-language imports with Norwegian subtitles, so there's invariably something on that you'll understand, though much of it is pretty unadventurous stuff. The big global cable and satellite channels like MTV and CNN are commonly accessible in hotel rooms.

Local tourist **radio**, giving details of events and festivals, is broadcast during the summer months; watch for signposts by the roadside and tune in. The BBC World Service can be picked up right across Norway. Frequencies and schedules are listed on the BBC website (Ⓦwww.bbc.co.uk/worldservice). The same applies to Radio Canada (Ⓦwww.rcinet.ca) and Voice of America (Ⓦwww.voa.gov).

Crime and personal safety

There's little reason why you should ever come into contact with the Norwegian police. This is one of the least troublesome corners of Europe – indeed, in the whole of the country there's an average of only one murder per week. You will find that most public places are well lit and secure, most people genuinely friendly and helpful, and street crime and hassle relatively rare.

It would be foolish, however, to assume that problems don't exist. Oslo in particular has its share of **petty crime**, fuelled – as elsewhere – by drug addicts and alcoholics after easy money. But keep tabs on your possessions, use the same common sense that you would use at home and you should have little reason to visit the police. If you do, you'll find them courteous, concerned, and usually able to speak English. If you have something stolen, make sure you get a police report – essential if you are to make a claim against your insurance.

As for offences *you* might commit, drinking alcohol in public places is not permitted, and being drunk on the streets can get you arrested. Drinking and driving is treated especially rigorously. Drugs offences, too, are met with the same attitudes that prevail throughout most of Europe. Women won't, however, be cautioned for topless sunbathing, which is universally accepted in the resorts (elsewhere there probably won't be anyone around to care), and camping rough is a tradition enshrined in law. Should you be **arrested** on any charge, you have the right to **contact your embassy or consulate** (see p.40 for details). Unfortunately, consular officials are notoriously reluctant to get involved, though most are required to assist you to some degree if you have your passport stolen or lose all your money. If you've been detained for a drugs offence, don't expect any sympathy or help.

Sexual harassment

In the normal course of events, **women travellers** in almost any part of Norway are unlikely to feel threatened or attract unwanted attention. The main exception is in the seedier areas of Oslo, where the atmosphere may feel frightening especially late at night, but with common sense and circumspection you shouldn't have anything to worry about. In terms of nightclubs and bars, the men who hang around in them pose no greater or lesser threat than similar operators at home, though the language barrier (where it exists) makes it harder to know who to trust.

Outdoor pursuits

Norwegians have a deep and abiding love of the great outdoors. They enjoy many kinds of sports – from dog-sledging and downhill skiing in winter, through to mountaineering, angling and white-water rafting in the summer – but the two most popular activities are hiking and cross-country skiing.

Hiking

Norway boasts some of the most beautiful mountain landscapes in the world and substantial portions of these mountain ranges have been protected by the creation of a string of **national parks** (see the Hiking colour section). These parks attract thousands of hikers, who take full advantage of the excellent network of hiking trails and several hundred mountain cabins, which provide the most congenial of accommodation.

For more on hiking areas, mountain lodges and DNT (the Norwegian Mountain Touring Association), see the Hiking colour section.

Skiing

Norway has as good a claim as anywhere to be regarded as the home of **skiing**: a 4000-year-old rock carving found in Northern Norway is the oldest-known illustration of a person on skis; the first recorded ski competition was held in Norway in 1767; and Norwegians were the first to introduce skis to North America. Furthermore, one of the oldest cross-country ski races in the world, the 55km **Birkebeinerrennet**, is held annually in late March, attracting five thousand skiers to participate in the dash between Rena and Lillehammer. The race follows the route taken by Norwegian mountain men in 1206 when they rescued the two-year-old Prince Håkon. The rescuers wore birch bark leggings known as Birkebeiners, hence the name of the race.

Downhill skiing and **snowboarding** conditions in Norway are usually excellent from mid-November through to late April, though daylight hours are at a premium around the winter solstice. Otherwise, Norway scores well in comparison with the better-known skiing regions of southern Europe: temperatures tend to be a good bit colder and the country has, in general terms at least, a more consistent snowfall; Norway's resorts tend to be less crowded, have smaller class sizes, shorter lift queues, and are at a lower altitude. Three main centres for downhill skiing are Voss (see p.230), Oppdal (see p.183), and Geilo (see p.189).

Cross-country skiing is a major facet of winter life in Norway. Approximately half the population are active in the sport, and many Norwegians still use skis to get to work or school. Norwegian interest in the sport is such that in 1994 thousands waited overnight in temperatures of -25°C to see the final day of racing at the Lillehammer Winter Olympics. In the classic style of cross-country skiing, the whole body is angled forwards and the skis remain parallel except when braking or turning. For forward propulsion the skier transfers all weight to one ski, then straightens that leg while kicking downwards and backwards. At the same time, the arm on the opposite side of the body pushes down and back on the ski pole close to the line of the unweighted ski, which glides forward. At the finish of the kick, weight is transferred to what was the gliding ski, ready for the next kick. An unweighted cross-country ski is arc shaped, with the central section not touching the ground until the skier's down-kick flattens it on to the snow; the ends of the skis glide while the middle grips. Near major ski resorts, sets of parallel ski tracks called *Loipe* are cut in the snow by machine. They provide good gliding conditions and help keep the skis parallel; some *Loipe* are floodlit.

Skis can be **waxed** or **waxless**. Waxless skis have a rough tread in the middle called "fishscales", which grips adequately at temperatures around zero. Waxed skis work better at low temperatures and on new snow. Grip wax is rubbed onto the middle third of the ski's length, but a sticky substance called *klister* is used instead in icy conditions. All skis benefit from hard glide wax applied to the front and back thirds of the base.

In the Telemark region of Southern Norway a technique has been developed to enable skiers to descend steep slopes on free-heel touring skis. This technique, known as **"Telemarking"**, provides a stable and effective turning platform in powder snow. Essentially the skier traverses a slope in an upright position, but goes down on a right knee to execute a right turn and vice versa.

For companies specializing in downhill **ski packages** to Norway see p.37 and p.38; nearly all of them will also deal with cross-country skiing and other, more obscure winter activities such as frozen waterfall climbing and ice fishing. Several specialist operators organize **cross-country skiing tours** (see p.37 and p.38), and DNT (see the Hiking colour section) arranges a limited range of guided excursions too. Touring skiers should adopt the precautions taken by winter hill walkers: if going out for more than a couple of hours the skier should have emergency clothing, food and a vacuum flask with a hot drink. Detailed advice about coping with winter conditions is available from DNT (see the Hiking colour section).

Although you may be tempted to go on a ski package, remember that in most places you should find it easy (and comparatively inexpensive) to go skiing independently. Even in Oslo, there are downhill ski runs within the city boundaries, and plenty of places from which to **rent equipment**; cross-country skiers will also have few difficulties in renting skiing tackle by the day (or week). In terms of **preparation**, lessons on a dry slope are useful in so far as they develop confidence and balance, but cross-country skiing needs stamina and upper body as well as leg strength.

Finally, **summer skiing** on Norway's mountains and glaciers – both alpine and cross-country – is now very popular. Lots of places offer this, but one of the largest and most convenient spots is the **Folgefonn Sommar Skisenter** (late May to late Sept daily 10am–4pm; ⓣ53 66 80 28, ⓦwww.folgefonn.no), not far from Bergen, which has ski rental, a ski school, a café and a ski lift to the slopes; see p.225 for more details.

Fishing

Norway's myriad rivers and lakes offer some of Europe's finest **freshwater fishing** with common species including trout, char, pike and perch, not to mention the salmon that once brought English aristocrats here by the cartload. In the south of the country, the fishing is at its best from June to September,

July and August in the north. **Seawater fishing** is more the preserve of professionals, but (amateur) sea angling off the Lofoten islands is a popular pastime. Fresh- and seawater fishing are both tightly controlled. To do the first, you need two **licences** – a national licence, which is available at any post office for either 200kr or 100kr depending on the type of fish you are aiming to catch, and a local licence (*fiskekort*), available from sports shops, a few tourist offices, some hotels and most campsites. The cost of the local licence varies enormously from 50kr to 350kr per day. **Seawater fishing** only requires a national licence. If you take your own fishing tackle, you must have it disinfected before use.

A number of tour companies specialize in Norwegian fishing trips and holidays, but if you're just after a day or two's fishing, it's easy enough to get fixed up locally – start off by asking down at the nearest tourist office.

River-rafting

Norway has literally dozens of top-notch **whitewater river-rafting** runs. Two of the best places are Voss (see p.230) and Sjoa (see p.175). For a full list of **tour operators** offering rafting trips, contact Norges Padleforbund (the Norwegian Canoe Association), Service boks 1, Ullevål stadion, 0840 Oslo (Ⓣ21 02 98 35, Ⓦwww.padling.no).

Travellers with disabilities

As you might expect, the Norwegians have adopted a progressive and thoughtful approach to the issues surrounding disability and, as a result, there are decent facilities for travellers with disabilities across the whole country. An increasing number of hotels, hostels and campsites are equipped for disabled visitors, and are credited as such in the tourist literature by means of the standard wheelchair-in-a-box icon. Furthermore, on most main routes the trains have special carriages with wheelchair space, hydraulic lifts and disabled toilets; domestic flights either cater for or provide assistance to disabled customers; and new ships on all ferry routes have lifts and cabins designed for disabled people.

In the cities and larger towns, many **restaurants** and most **museums** and public places are wheelchair-accessible, and although facilities are not so advanced in the countryside, things are improving rapidly. Drivers will find that most motorway **service stations** are wheelchair-accessible and that, if you have a UK-registered vehicle, the disabled **car parking badge** is honoured. Note also that several of the larger car rental companies have modified vehicles available. On a less positive note, city pavements can be uneven and difficult to negotiate and, inevitably, winter snow and ice can make things much, much worse.

Getting to Norway should be relatively straightforward too. Most airlines and shipping companies provide assistance to disabled travellers, while some also have specific facilities, such as DFDS Scandinavian Seaways ferries' specially adapted cabins.

Contacts for travellers with disabilities

In Norway

Norwegian Association of the Disabled (Norges Handikapforbund) Schweigaardsgt 12, Oslo Ⓣ24 10 24 00, Ⓦwww.nhf.no; postal address Postboks 9217, Grønland, 0134 Oslo. This organization produces a wide range of useful information, from general guidance on accessibility across the whole of the country through to comments about the major hotel chains and transport. The website is particularly good, and has an English-language version.

In the UK and Ireland

Access Travel 6 The Hillock, Astley, Lancashire M29 7GW ⓣ01942/888 844, ⓦwww.access-travel.co.uk. Tour operator that can arrange flights, transfer and accommodation. This is a small business, personally checking out places before recommending.

Holiday Care 2nd floor, Imperial Building, Victoria Rd, Horley, Surrey RH6 7PZ ⓣ0845/124 9971 or 0208/760 0072, ⓦwww.holidaycare.org.uk. Provides free lists of accessible accommodation abroad – including Norway. Information on financial help for holidays available too.

Irish Wheelchair Association Blackheath Drive, Clontarf, Dublin 3 ⓣ01/818 6400, ⓦwww.iwa.ie. Useful information on travelling abroad with a wheelchair.

Tripscope The Vasapll Centre, Gill Ave, Bristol BS16 2QQ ⓣ0845/7 58 56 41 ⓦwww.tripscope.org.uk. This registered charity provides a national telephone information service offering free advice on UK and international transport for those with a mobility problem.

In the US and Canada

Access-Able ⓦwww.access-able.com. Online resource for travellers with disabilities.

Directions Unlimited 123 Green Lane, Bedford Hills, NY 10507 ⓣ1-800/533-5343 or 914/241-1700. Travel agency specializing in bookings for people with disabilities.

Mobility International USA 451 Broadway, Eugene, OR 97401 ⓣ541/343-1284, ⓦwww.miusa.org. Information and referral services, access guides, tours and exchange programmes.

Society for the Advancement of Travelers with Handicaps 347 5th Ave, New York, NY 10016 ⓣ212/447-7284, ⓦwww.sath.org. Non-profit educational organization that has actively represented travellers with disabilities since 1976. Annual membership $45; $30 for students and seniors.

Wheels Up! ⓣ1-888/38-WHEELS, ⓦwww.wheelsup.com. Provides discounted airfare, tour and cruise prices for disabled travellers, and publishes a free monthly newsletter. Comprehensive website.

In Australia and New Zealand

ACROD (Australian Council for Rehabilitation of the Disabled) PO Box 60, Curtin ACT 2605; ⓣ02/6282 4333 (also TTY), ⓦwww.acrod.org.au. Provides lists of travel agencies and tour operators for people with disabilities.

Disabled Persons Assembly 4/173–175 Victoria St, Wellington, New Zealand ⓣ04/801 9100 (also TTY), ⓦwww.dpa.org.nz. Resource centre with lists of travel agencies and tour operators for people with disabilities.

Gay Norway

Norway was one of the first countries in the world to pass a law (1981) making discrimination against homosexuals and lesbians illegal. In 1993, it followed this up by becoming only the second country to pass legislation giving lesbian and gay couples the same rights as married couples, while retaining a bar on church weddings and the right to adopt children. The church bar remains to this day, though many Norwegian clergy oppose it, but further legislation in 2002 and 2003 relaxed the restrictions on gay adoption. As further proof of this progressive pudding, a member of the government, the finance minister, married his gay partner in 2002 and few of his fellow Norwegians blinked an eye. All this progressiveness, however, has more to do with respect for the rights and freedoms of the individual than a positive attitude to homosexuality – Norway remains, in essence at least, very much a (heterosexual) family-oriented society. Nevertheless, the general attitude to gays is so tolerant that few feel the need to disguise their sexuality. The age of consent for both gays and straights is sixteen.

It's commonplace for bars and pubs to have a mixture of straights and gays in their clientele. There is something of a separate scene in Bergen, Trondheim and especially Oslo, but it's pretty low-key stuff and barely worth seeking out – and the same applies to the weekly gay and lesbian nights held in some small-town nightclubs. The best source of information on the **Oslo scene** is Unginfo or Use-it, a youth information shop near the main train station at Møllergata 3 (July–Aug Mon–Fri 9am–6pm; Sept–June Mon–Fri 11am–5pm; ⓣ24 14 98 20, ⓦwww.use-it.no). They produce a free annual booklet, *Streetwise*, which is also online, and this includes a 'gay guide' to the city. The main gay event in the Oslo calendar, the **Skeive Dager** (Queer Days; ⓦwww.skeivedager.no), takes place over nine days each June and includes the city's Gay Pride celebrations.

Landsforeningen for Lesbisk og Homofil frigjøing (LLH) Norway's strong and effective gay and lesbian organization has a national HQ in Oslo at Kongensgate 12 (ⓣ23 10 39 39, ⓦwww.llh.no organization). Their website is Norwegian-only, but there are links to other affiliated sites giving details of gay and lesbian events.

Directory

Addresses Norwegian addresses are always written with the number after the street name. In multi-floored buildings, the ground floor is always counted as the first floor, the first the second and so on.

Alphabet The letters Æ, Ø and Å come at the end of the alphabet, after Z (and in that order).

Borders There is (usually) little formality at either the Norway–Sweden or Norway–Finland borders, but the northern border with Russia is a different story. Despite the break-up of the Soviet Union, border patrols (on either side) won't be overjoyed at the prospect of you nosing around. If you have a genuine wish to visit Russia from Norway, it's best to sort out the paperwork – visas and so forth – before you leave home. Kirkenes (see p.373) is the main starting point for tours into Russia from Norway.

Glaciers These slow-moving masses of ice are in constant, if generally imperceptible, motion, and are therefore potentially dangerous. People, often tourists, die on them nearly every year. Never climb a glacier without a guide, never walk beneath one and always heed the instructions at the site. Guided crossings can be terrific – see the relevant accounts in the Guide.

Left Luggage There are coin-operated lockers in most railway and bus stations and at all major ferry terminals.

Mosquitoes Whatever you do, don't forget the insect repellent if you are venturing into the great outdoors during the summer.

Smoking Smoking has long been prohibited in all public buildings, including train stations, as well as on flights and bus services. In June 2004, these restrictions were widened and smoking is now banned in restaurants, bars and cafés. A pack of twenty costs £6/$11, but nevertheless – and perhaps rather surprisingly – one in four Norwegians still puff away.

Time Norway is one hour ahead of the UK and six to nine hours ahead of continental USA.

Tipping Hotels, cafés and restaurants often add a service charge to their bills and this is – or at least should be – clearly indicated. Otherwise, few people tip at hotels or bars, but restaurant waiters and taxi drivers will be disappointed not to get a tip of between 10 and 15 percent.

Guide

Guide

1 Oslo and the Oslofjord 73–135

2 The South 137–161

3 Central Norway 163–196

4 Bergen and the western fjords 197–272

5 Trondheim to the Lofoten islands 273–338

6 North Norway 339–380

Oslo and the Oslofjord

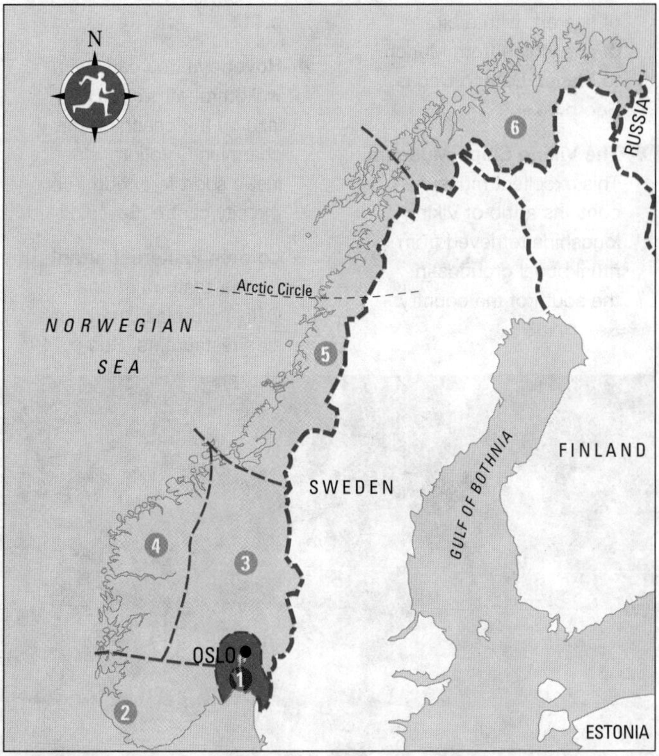

CHAPTER 1 Highlights

* **Cultural Heritage Museum** Often neglected, this museum boasts a superb, thirteenth-century painted and vaulted wooden room moved here from the stave church in Ål, near Geilo. See p.93
* **The National Gallery** Norway's largest collection of fine art, with a bit of everything from Munch to Manet, Dahl to Degas. See p.94
* **The Viking Ships Museum** This excellent museum contains a trio of Viking longships retrieved from ritual burial grounds in the south of the country. See p.105
* **The Vigelandsparken** Take a stroll round the fantastical creations of Gustav Vigeland in this open-air sculpture park. See p.109
* **The Munch Museum** Extraordinary collection of paintings, woodcuts and lithographs by Norway's most eminent artist. See p.111
* **Hovedøya** You can swim, walk through woods or laze on the beach on this charming Oslofjord island, just a short ferry ride from the city centre. See p.114
* **Lofoten Fiskerestaurant** Try the seafood at one of Oslo's top-class, harbourside restaurants. See p.119

△ Vigelandsparken

Oslo and the Oslofjord

OSLO is a vibrant, self-confident city whose urbane, easy-going air makes it one of Europe's most amenable capitals, though this was not always the case. Oslo was something of a poor relation to Stockholm until Norway's break for independence from Sweden at the beginning of the twentieth century and it remained dourly provincial until well into the 1950s, since when it has forged ahead to become today's enterprising and cosmopolitan commercial hub with a population of about half a million people. Oslo is also the only major metropolis in a country brimming with small towns and villages – its nearest rival, Bergen, being less than half its size. This gives Oslo a powerful – some say overweening – voice in the political, cultural and economic life of the nation and has pulled in all of Norway's big companies, as a rash of concrete and glass tower blocks testifies. Fortunately, these monoliths rarely interrupt the stately Neoclassical lines of the late nineteenth-century **city centre**, Oslo's most beguiling district, which boasts a lively restaurant and bar scene as well as a clutch of excellent museums. Indeed, Oslo's biggest single draw is its **museums**, which cover a hugely varied and stimulating range of topics: the fabulous Viking Ships Museum, the Munch Museum showcasing a good chunk of the painter's work, the sculpture park devoted to the bronze and granite works of Gustav Vigeland, and the moving historical documents of the Resistance Museum, are, to name just four, enough to keep even the most unenthusiastic of museum-goers busy for days. There's also a decent **outdoor life** with Oslo rustling up a good range of parks, pavement cafés, street entertainers and festivals, especially in summer when virtually the whole population seems to live outdoors – and visiting is a real delight. Winter is also a good time to be here, when Oslo's location amid hills and forests makes it a thriving, convenient and affordable ski centre.

Although Oslo's centre is itself compact, the **outer districts** spread over a vast 453 square kilometres, encompassing huge areas of forest, beach and water. Almost universally, the city's inhabitants have a deep and abiding affinity for these wide open spaces and, as a result, the waters of the Oslofjord to the south and the forested hills of the Nordmarka to the north are tremendously popular for everything from boating and swimming to hiking and skiing. For all but the shortest of stays, there's ample opportunity to join in – the open forest and **cross-country ski** routes of the Nordmarka and the

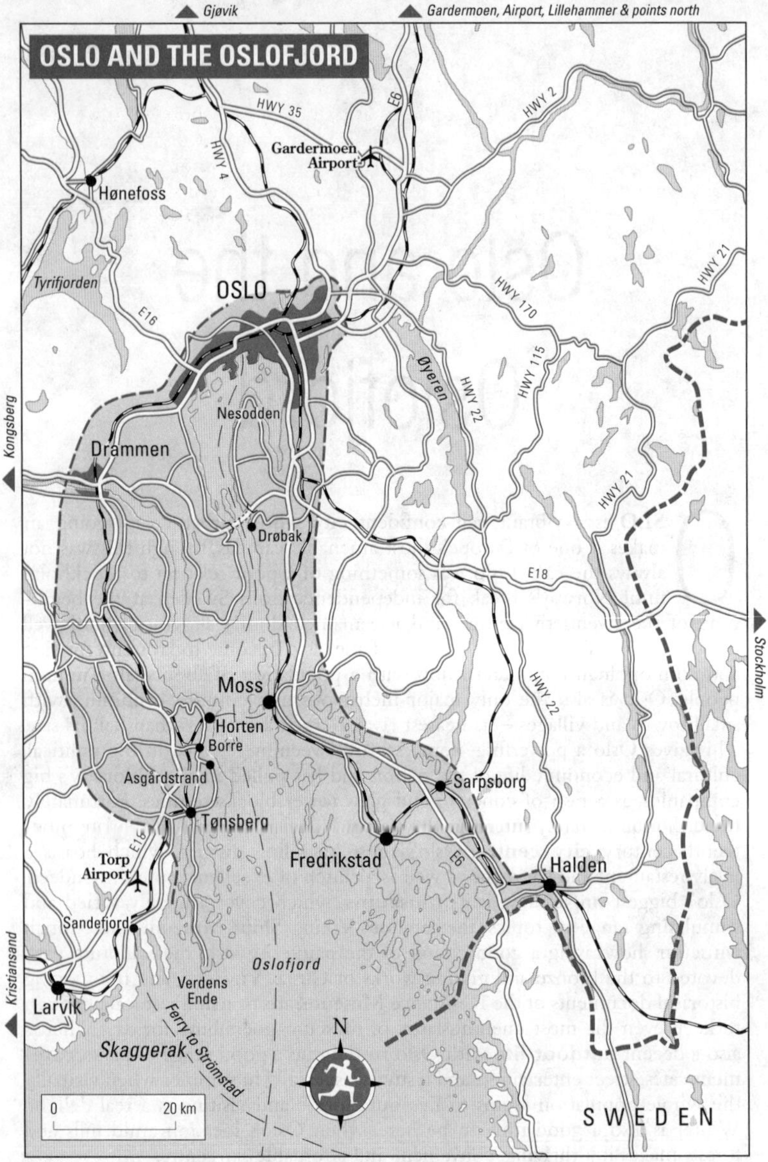

OSLO AND THE OSLOFJORD

island beaches just offshore in the Oslofjord are both easily reached by metro or ferry.

Oslo curves round the innermost shore of the **Oslofjord**, whose tapered waters extend for some 100km from the Skagerrak, the choppy channel separating Norway and Sweden from Denmark. As Norwegian fjords go, the Oslofjord is not particularly beautiful – the rocky shores are generally low and unprepossessing – but scores of pretty little islets diversify the seascape. Many of these forested bumps accommodate summer chalets, but several have been protected from development and one of them – Hovedøya – makes a lovely excursion. By comparison, the towns that trail along the shores of the Oslofjord are of little immediate appeal, being for the most part workaday industrial settlements. The few exceptions include, on the eastern shore, **Fredrikstad**, Norway's only surviving fortified town, and on the western shore, the Viking burial mounds of **Borre** and the popular holiday resort of **Tønsberg**.

Oslo

If Oslo is your first taste of Norway, you'll be struck by the light – soft and brilliantly clear in the summer and broodingly gloomy in winter. The grand late nineteenth- and early twentieth-century buildings of central Oslo suit the climate well, doughty structures that once gave a sense of security to the emergent nation, and still look reassuringly sturdy today. Largely as a result, most of **downtown Oslo** remains easy and pleasant to walk around, a humming, good-natured place whose airy streets and squares combine these appealing remnants of the city's early days with a clutch of good museums – in particular the Nasjonalgalleriet (National Gallery) and the Hjemmefrontmuseum (Resistence Museum) – and dozens of lively bars, cafés and restaurants.

The city's showpiece museums – most notably the remarkable Vikingskipshuset (Viking Ships Museum) – are located on the **Bygdøy peninsula**, to which ferries shuttle from the jetty behind the **Rådhus** (City Hall); other ferries head south from the Vippetangen quay behind the Akershus to the string of rusticated **islands**, such as the pretty, wooded Hovedøya, that necklace the inner waters of the Oslofjord. Back on the mainland, **east Oslo** is the least prepossessing part of town, a gritty sprawl housing the poorest of the city's inhabitants, though the newly revived district of **Grünerløkka** is now home to a slew of fashionable bars and clubs. The main sight on the east side of town is the **Munch Museum**, which boasts a superb collection of the artist's work. Afterwards, it's mildly tempting to pop along the eastern shore of Oslo's principal harbour for the views over the city and to look at the skimpy remains of the medieval town. **Northwest Oslo** is far more prosperous, with big old houses lining the avenues immediately to the west of the Slottsparken. Beyond is the **Frognerparken**, a chunk of parkland where the stunning open-air sculptures of Gustav Vigeland are displayed in the **Vigelandsparken**. Further west still, beyond the city limits in suburban Høvikodden, the **Henie-Onstad Kunstsenter** displays more prestigious modern art, enhanced by the museum's splendid setting on a headland overlooking the Oslofjord.

The city's enormous reach becomes apparent only to the north of the centre in the **Nordmarka**. This massive forested wilderness, stretching far inland, is patterned by hiking trails and cross-country ski routes. Two T-bane lines provide ready access, clanking their way up into the rocky hills that herald the region. The more westerly T-bane grinds on past **Holmenkollen**, a ski resort where the ski-jump makes a crooked finger on Oslo's skyline. The line terminates at

Frognerseteren – although the station is still within the municipal boundaries, the forested hills and lakes nearby feel anything but urban. The more easterly T-bane is perhaps even more appealing, ending up near **Sognsvannet**, a pretty little lake set amidst the woods and an ideal place for an easy stroll and/or a picnic.

Compared to other European capitals, Oslo is extremely safe. However, the usual cautions apply to walking around on your own late at night, when you should be particularly careful in the vicinity of Oslo S, the main train station, where the junkies gather.

Some history

Oslo is the oldest of the Scandinavian capital cities. Its name is derived from *Às*, a Norse word for God, and *Lo,* meaning field. The city was founded around 1048 by Harald Hardrada, but it wasn't until Harald's son, Olav Kyrre, established a bishopric and built a cathedral here, that the city really began to take off. Despite this, the kings of Norway continued to live in Bergen – an oddly inefficient division of state and church, considering the difficulty of communication. At the start of the fourteenth century, **Håkon V** rectified matters by moving to Oslo, where he built himself the Akershus fortress, and the town boomed until 1349, when bubonic plague wiped out almost half the population. The slow decline that followed this catastrophe accelerated when Norway came under Danish control in 1397. No longer the seat of power, Oslo became a neglected backwater until its fortunes were revived by the Danish king **Christian IV**. He moved Oslo lock, stock and barrel, shifting it west to its present site and modestly renaming it **Christiania** in 1624. The new city prospered, and continued to do so after 1814, when Norway broke away from Denmark and united with Sweden. In the event, this political realignment was a short-lived affair, and by the 1880s, Christiania – and the country as a whole – was clamouring for independence. This was eventually achieved in 1905, though the city didn't revert to its original name for another twenty years – and has hardly looked back since.

Arrival and information

Downtown Oslo is at the heart of a superb public transport system, which makes arriving and departing convenient and straightforward. The principal arrival hub is **Oslo Sentralstasjon** (usually shortened to **Oslo S**), a large complex that includes the main train and bus stations, city tram, metro and bus stops, a tourist office and exchange facilities; it is located at the eastern end of the main thoroughfare, **Karl Johans gate**. The other transport hub is **Nationaltheatret** at the west end of Karl Johans gate, handier for most city-centre sights and Oslo's main harbour. There's a **tourist information** office in Oslo S and another close to Nationaltheatret, at Fridtjof Nansens plass 5.

Arriving by air: Gardermoen airport

Opened in 1998, **Oslo Gardermoen airport** is a lavish affair designed in true pan-Scandinavian style, with acres of cool stone floor and lightly varnished pine, soft angles, slender concrete pillars and high ceilings. Departures is on the upper level, Arrivals on the lower, where there are also currency exchange facilities, car rental offices (see p.125 for details) and a visitor information desk.

Gardermoen is located 45km north of the city centre, at the end of a seven-kilometre spur road off the E6 motorway. There are three ways to get from the airport to the centre of Oslo by **public transport** – express train, local train, and airport bus. The fastest and most expensive option is the **FlyToget** (Express train; daily 5.30am–12.30pm every 10–15 min; 160kr single, 320kr return; Ⓦwww.flytoget.no), which takes twenty minutes to reach Oslo S, a couple more to Nationaltheatret. Alternatively, the once-hourly Eidsvoll–Kongsberg **local train** links Gardermoen with Oslo S and Nationaltheatret; it takes forty to forty-five minutes and costs a lot less than the Flytoget (77kr each way). Note also that there are express trains north from Gardermoen to a number of destinations, including Lillehammer, Røros and Trondheim; many of these services require a reservation – details and bookings at the train ticket office in Arrivals.

By bus, **SAS Flybussen** (daily 5.20am–1am, every 20–30min; 110kr single, 170kr return; Ⓦwww.flybussen.no) depart from outside the Arrivals concourse for the main downtown bus station, Oslo Bussterminalen, part of the Oslo S complex; the journey takes about 45 minutes, traffic depending. They then continue on to Jernbanetorget, Grensen and the *Radisson SAS Scandinavia Hotel*. **For Gardermoen departures**, the Flybussen follows the same route in the opposite direction. In addition, **Flybussekspressen** (Ⓣ177 from within Oslo, Ⓣ815 00 176 from without; Ⓦwww.flybussekspressen.no) operates a variety of bus services from the airport direct to the small towns surrounding Oslo at regular intervals and at reasonable rates.

The **taxi fare** from Gardermoen to the city centre is 490kr. Finally, note that if you're heading into Oslo from Gardermoen by **car**, there is a 15kr toll on all approach roads into the city – so have some kroner handy.

Arriving by air: Oslo (Torp) airport

Oslo's second airport, **Oslo (Torp)**, is located just outside the town of Sandefjord, about 110km southwest of Oslo. The **Torp-Ekspressen bus** (Ⓣ177 from within Oslo, Ⓣ815 00 176 from without; Ⓦwww.torpekspressen.no) links this airport with the main downtown bus station, Oslo Bussterminalen, part of the Oslo S complex, three to six times daily; the bus schedule, both to and from Torp, links with flight arrivals and departures. The bus journey takes a little under two hours and costs 130kr each way; you buy tickets from the driver.

Arriving by train

International and domestic **trains** use **Oslo Sentralstasjon**, known as Oslo S (train information and reservations Ⓣ815 00 888, Ⓦwww.nsb.no), sited on the Jernbanetorget, a square at the eastern end of the main drag, Karl Johans gate. There are money exchange facilities here, as well as a post office, a tourist office and two **train information** offices – one for enquiries, the other for tickets and seat reservations. (The latter are compulsory on many long-distance trains – see p.48). Many domestic trains also pass through the Nationaltheatret station, at the west end of Karl Johans gate, which is slightly more useful for the city centre.

Arriving by bus

The central **Bussterminalen** (bus terminal) is part of the Oslo S complex; it is handily placed a short, signposted walk to the northeast of the train station on Schweigårdsgate. International and domestic long-distance buses arrive at and depart from here, as do the SAS Flybussen (from Oslo Gardermoen airport) and the Torp-Ekspressen (from Oslo Torp airport). For all bus enquiries, consult the

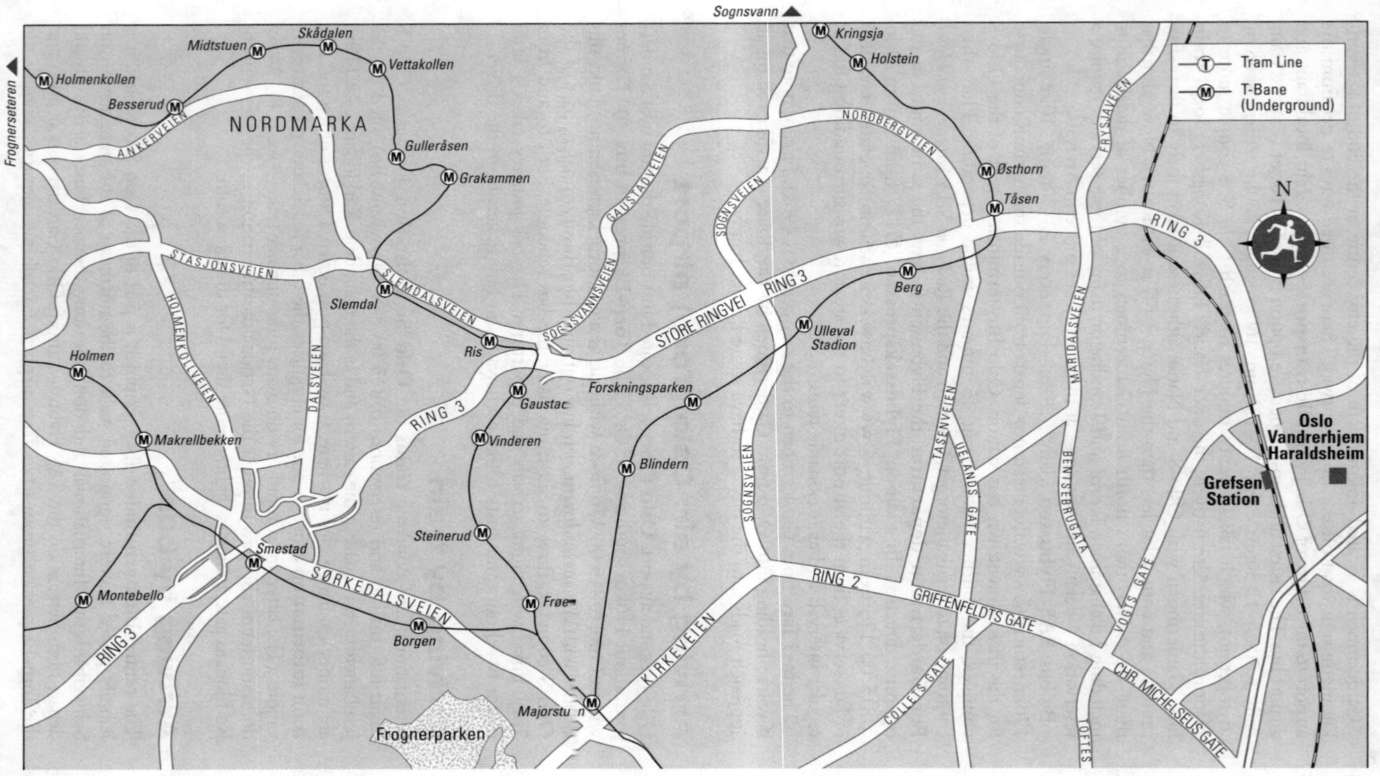
Sognsvann
Frognerseteren
Tram Line
T-Bane (Underground)
N
NORDMARKA
Holmenkollen
Besserud
Midtstuen
Skådalen
Vettakollen
Gulleråsen
Grakammen
Slemdal
Ris
Gaustac
Vinderen
Steinerud
Frøe
Borgen
Smestad
Montebello
Makrellbekken
Holmen
Majorstu n
Blindern
Forskningsparken
Ulleval Stadion
Berg
Tåsen
Østhorn
Holstein
Kringsja
Frognerparken
Oslo Vandrerhjem Haraldsheim
Grefsen Station
ANKERVEIEN
STASJONSVEIEN
HOLMENKOLLVEIEN
DALSVEIEN
SLEMDALSVEIEN
SØRKEDALSVEIEN
RING 3
STORE RINGVEI
GAUSTADVEIEN
SOGNSVANNSVEIEN
SOGNSVEIEN
NORDBERGVEIEN
TÅSENVEIEN
UELANDS GATE
MARIDALSVEIEN
BENTSEBRUGATA
FRYSJAVEIEN
VOGTS GATE
RING 2
GRIFFENFELDTS GATE
KIRKEVEIEN
COLLETS GATE
CHR. MICHELSEUS GATE
TOFTES

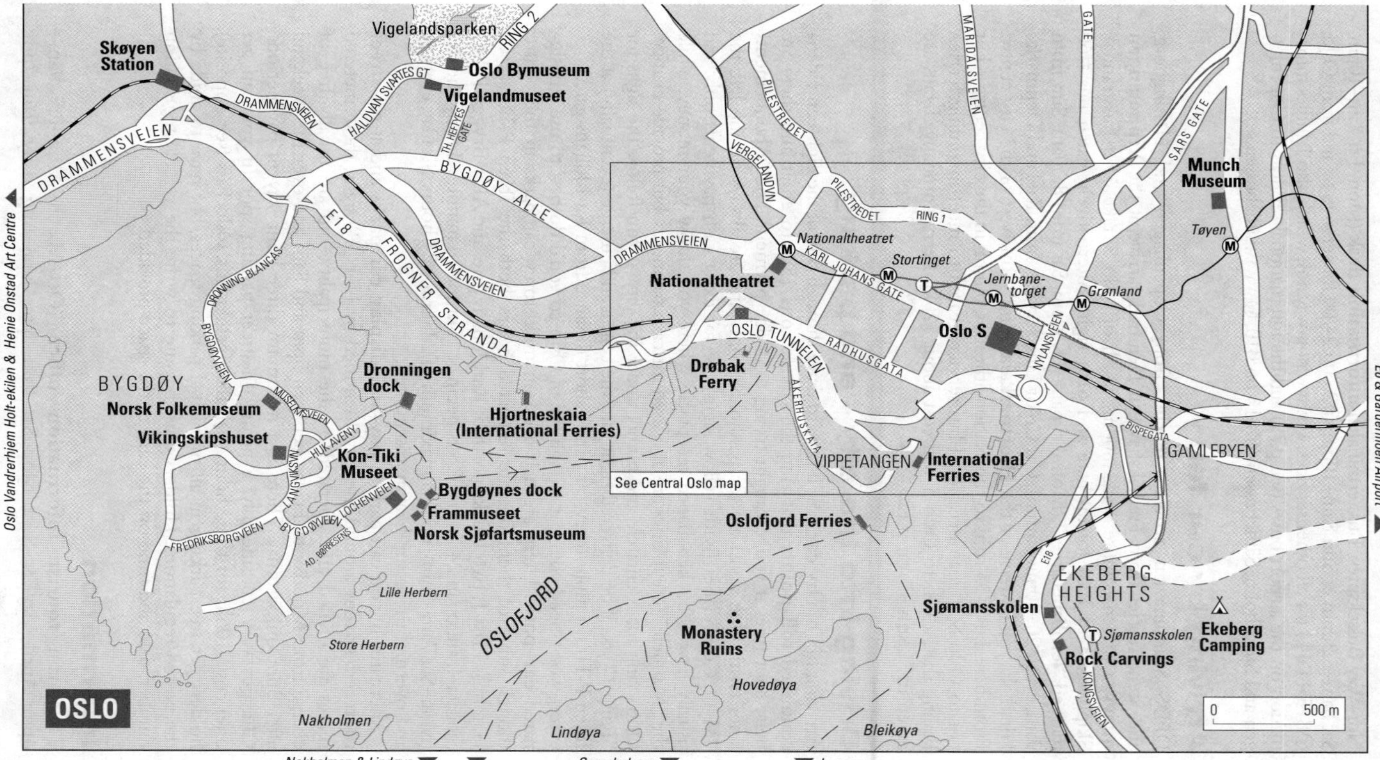
OSLO
Vigelandsparken
RING 2
Skøyen Station
Oslo Bymuseum
Vigelandmuseet
HALDVAN SVARTES GT
TH. HEFTYES GATE
DRAMMENSVEIEN
BYGDØY ALLE
E18
FROGNER STRANDA
DRONNING BLANCAS
BYGDØYVEIEN
BYGDØY
Norsk Folkemuseum
Vikingskipshuset
MUSEUMSVEIEN
HUK AVENY
LANGVIKSVN
Kon-Tiki Museet
LOCHENVEIEN
FREDRIKSBORGVEIEN
AD. BØRRESENS
Dronningen dock
Hjortneskaia (International Ferries)
Bygdøynes dock
Frammuseet
Norsk Sjøfartsmuseum
Lille Herbern
Store Herbern
OSLOFJORD
Nakholmen
Lindøya
Monastery Ruins
Hovedøya
Bleikøya
PILESTREDET
VERGELANDVN
MARIDALSVEIEN
GATE
RING 1
Nationaltheatret
KARL JOHANS GATE
Stortinget
Jernbane-torget
Grønland
Tøyen
Munch Museum
SARS GATE
Oslo S
NYLANSVEIEN
OSLO TUNNELEN
RÅDHUSGATA
Drøbak Ferry
AKERHUSKAIA
VIPPETANGEN
International Ferries
See Central Oslo map
Oslofjord Ferries
BISPEGATA
GAMLEBYEN
E18
EKEBERG HEIGHTS
Sjømansskolen
Rock Carvings
KONGSVEIEN
Ekeberg Camping
0
500 m
Oslo Vandrerhjem Holt-ekilen & Henie Onstad Art Centre
E6 & Gardermoen Airport
Nakholmen & Lindøya
Gressholmen
Langøyene

Nor-Way Bussekspress Bussterminalen **information desk** (Mon–Fri 7am–10pm, Sat 8am–5.30pm & Sun 8am–10pm; ⓣ23 00 24 00 for services to and from Oslo; ⓣ815 44 444 for all other services; ⓦwww.nor-way.no), which also handles information on the airport buses (see p.79) and the international services to Copenhagen and Stockholm, Säfflebussen (ⓣ815 66 010, ⓦwww.safflebussen.se).

Arriving by car ferry

DFDS Scandinavian Seaways **ferries** from Copenhagen and Helsingborg, and Stena ferries from Fredrikshavn in Denmark, arrive at the **Vippetangen quays**, a fifteen-minute walk (800m) south of Oslo S: take Akershusstranda/Skippergata to Karl Johans gate and turn right. Alternatively, catch bus #60 marked "Jernbanetorget" (Mon–Fri 6am–11.30pm, Sat from 8.30am, Sun from 9am, every 20–30min; 5min). On Color Line services from Kiel and Denmark's Hirsthals, you'll arrive at the **Hjortneskaia**, some 3km west of the city centre. From here, bus #33 runs to the Nationaltheatret, plumb in the city centre – but not to Oslo S; it is an occasional bus service geared to meet incoming ferries. Failing that, a taxi to Oslo S will cost about 120kr. Ferry company details are given in "Listings", on p.125.

Driving into the city – and parking

Arriving in Oslo **by car**, you'll have to drive through one of the eighteen video-controlled **toll-points** that ring the city; it costs 15kr to enter and there are hefty spot fines if you're caught trying to dodge payment. The "Abonnement" lanes (with blue signs) are for passholders only and are always on the left; the "Mynt/Coin" lanes (with yellow signs) are for exact cash payments only and usually have a bucket-shaped receptacle where you throw your money; while the "Manuell" (grey) lanes are also used for cash payments, but provide change. Oslo's ring roads encircle and tunnel under the city; if you follow the signs for "Ring 1" you'll be delivered right into the centre and emerge (eventually) at the Ibsen P-Hus, a multistorey car park a short distance from Karl Johans gate.

You won't need your car to sightsee in Oslo, so you'd do best to use a designated **car park**. There are half a dozen multistorey car parks in the centre, though some of them operate restricted hours: both the Ibsen P-hus at CJ Hambros Plass 1, two blocks north of Karl Johans gate, and Aker Brygge P-hus, Sjøgata 4, are open 24 hours. Costs begin at 15kr for 20 minutes during the day (Mon–Sat 7am–5pm), up to a maximum of 225kr for 24 hours; Sunday, evening and overnight rates are heavily discounted.

Alternatively, you can park in **pay-and-display car parks** and at **on-street metered spaces** around the city. Identified by blue "P" signs, these metered spaces are owned and operated by the municipality, and are usually free of charge from Monday to Friday between 5pm and 8am and over the weekend after 3pm on Saturday. There is a maximum three-hour stay in pay periods. **Charges** vary considerably: a prime on-street parking spot (if you can get one) costs 106kr for three hours, half that further out. Oslo Pass (see opposite) holders get free parking in all municipal parking spaces, but have to abide by the posted regulations. Holders must be sure to write the vehicle registration number, date and time on the card in the space provided.

Information

The main **tourist information office** (Oct–March Mon–Fri 9am–4pm; April–May & Sept Mon–Sat 9am–5pm; June–Aug daily 9am–7pm;

Oslo Pass

The useful and money-saving **Oslo Pass** gives free admission to almost every museum in the city, unlimited free travel on the whole municipal transport system, and free parking in municipal car parks. It also provides some discounts in shops, hotels and restaurants, though in winter, when opening hours for many sights and museums are reduced, you may have to work hard to make the card pay for itself. Valid for 24, 48 or 72 **hours**, it costs 210kr, 300kr or 390kr respectively, with children aged four to fifteen charged 90kr, 110kr or 140kr. It's available at the city's two tourist offices, most hotels and campsites in Oslo, the Trafikanten office (see below) and some of the larger downtown Narvesen convenience stores. The card is valid for a set number of hours (rather than days) starting from the moment it is first used, at which time it should either be presented and stamped, or you should fill in the date and time yourself. A booklet detailing every advantage the Oslo Pass brings is issued when you buy one.

Ⓣ815 30 555, Ⓦwww.visitoslo.com) is in front of the Rådhus, at Fridtjof Nansens plass 5. They have a full range of information about Oslo and its environs, and they issue both free city maps and maps of the transport system. They also sell the Oslo Pass (see above) and supply free copies of both the excellent and very thorough *Oslo Official Guide* and the listings brochure *What's On in Oslo*. They can also make reservations on guided tours and book accommodation (see p.85). There's a second tourist office inside **Oslo S** (Oct–April Mon–Sat 8am–5pm; May–Sept daily 8am–11pm) and this offers the same services. Oslo also has a youth information shop, **Unginfo** or **Use-it**, near Oslo S at **Møllergata** 3 (July–Aug Mon–Fri 9am–6pm; Sept–June Mon–Fri 11am–5pm; Ⓣ24 14 98 20, Ⓦwww.use-it.no). They produce a free annual booklet, *Streetwise*, which provides an excellent city roundup of everything from bars and clubs to museums and cafés; they also have public Internet access and fliers for gigs and concerts.

The **Trafikanten information office** (see below) provides information on Oslo's public transport system.

City transport

Oslo's safe and efficient public transport system consists of buses, trams, a small underground rail system (the Tunnelbanen) and local ferries. It's run by AS Oslo Sporveier, whose information office, **Trafikanten**, is beneath the distinctive, transparent clocktower outside Oslo S, on the Jernbanetorget (Mon–Fri 7am–8pm, Sat & Sun 8am–6pm; Ⓣ177, Ⓦwww.trafikanten.no). The office sells all the tickets and passes detailed below, has racks of free timetables and gives away a useful **visitor's transit map**, the *Sporveiens besøskart*, though this is also available at the tourist office. Route plans for the buses and trams are posted at every stop.

Fares and passes

Flat-fare **single tickets** for all forms of city transport cost 20kr if purchased before the journey (there are automatic ticket machines at all T-bane stations and ferry docks, most tram stops and many bus stops), or 30kr if purchased from a bus or tram driver. They are valid for unlimited travel within the city boundaries for one hour including transfers; seniors and children four to sixteen years old travel half price, babies and toddlers free.

There are several ways to cut costs. The best is to buy an **Oslo Pass** (see p.83), which is valid on the whole network and on certain routes into the surrounding *kommunes* – but not on trains or buses to the airport. If you're not into museums, however, a straight **travel pass** might be a better buy. A Dagskort (24hr pass) is valid for unlimited travel within the city limits and costs 60kr, a seven-day pass costs 210kr, while a monthly pass will set you back 700kr. Alternatively, there's the Flexikort which is valid for eight city trips and costs 150kr. As well as the Trafikanten office, all these passes and tickets can be bought at the automatic machines mentioned above.

All tickets and passes must be **stamped** when they are first used: buses, trams, ferries (except those to the Bygdøy) and T-bane stations all have automatic stamping machines. Ticket inspectors roam around in mufti and if you haven't got a valid, stamped pass or ticket, you will receive a hefty on-the-spot fine of 750kr.

Buses

Many city **bus** services originate at – or pass through – Jernbanetorget, the square in front of Oslo S, while most suburban services depart from the Bussterminalen nearby. A second common port of call is Nationaltheatret further to the west near the harbour. Most buses stop running at around midnight, though on Friday and Saturday nights **night buses** (*nattbussen*) take over on certain major routes (flat-rate fare 50kr; Oslo Pass and other passes not valid).

Trams

The city's **trams** run on eight routes through the city, crisscrossing the centre from east to west, and sometimes duplicating the bus routes. They are a bit slower than the buses, but are a rather more enjoyable and relaxing way of getting about. Major stops include Jernbanetorget, Nationaltheatret and Storgata. Most operate regularly – every ten or twenty minutes, from 6am to midnight.

Tunnelbanen and trains

The Tunnelbanen – **T-bane** – has five lines which converge to share a common slice of track crossing the city centre from Majorstua in the west to Tøyen in the east, with Nationaltheatret, Stortinget, Jernbanetorget and Grønland stations in between. From this central section, three lines run westbound (*Vest*) and two eastbound (*Øst*). The system mainly serves commuters from the suburbs, but you may find it useful for hopping around the centre and for trips out into the forested hills of the Nordmarka, or to Frognerseteren, Holmenkollen and Sognsvann. Apart from the central section, trains travel above ground. The system runs from around 6am until 12.30am.

A series of **local commuter trains**, run by NSB, links Oslo with Moss, Eidsvoll, Drammen and other outlying towns; departures are from Oslo S, with many also stopping at Nationaltheatret.

For details of services to and from the airport, see p.79.

Ferries

Numerous **ferries** shuttle across the northern reaches of the Oslofjord to connect the city centre with the outlying districts. As far as visitors are concerned, the most popular are the summertime ferries (April–Sept) leaving from Pier #3, immediately behind the Rådhus, bound for the museums of the Bygdøy peninsula. There are also all-year ferry services to a number of Oslofjord islets, including Hovedøya, and a June to August service to Langøyene, but these depart from the Vippetangen quay, 1300m south of Oslo S. To get to the Vippetangen quay by public transport, take bus #60 from Jernbanetorget. If you're venturing beyond the city limits, there are also boats to Nesodden (all year) and Drøbak (late June to early August; 5 weekly), leaving from the piers behind the Rådhus.

Taxis

The speed and efficiency of Oslo's public transport system means that you should rarely have to resort to a **taxi**, which is probably just as well as they are expensive. Taxi fares are regulated, with the tariff varying according to the time of day – night-times are about 25 percent more expensive than daytime – though on many longer routes there is a fixed tariff: central Oslo to Gardermoen airport, for instance, costs 490kr. Taxi ranks can be found round the city centre and outside all the big hotels. To call a cab, ring Oslo Taxi ⓣ02323 or Taxi2 ⓣ02202.

Bicycles

Renting a **bicycle** is a pleasant way to get around, particularly as Oslo has a reasonable range of cycle tracks and many roads have cycle lanes; what's more, central Oslo is not engulfed by traffic thanks to its network of motorway tunnels. Even better, there is a **municipal bike rental scheme** in which bikes are released like supermarket trolleys from racks all over the city. Visitors can join the scheme at the tourist office by paying 60kr for a 24hr cycling pass plus a refundable deposit of 500kr. Bikes can be used for up to three hours before they have to be dropped off (or swapped) at one of the bike racks; a map showing you the location of the racks is provided by the tourist office.

Accommodation

Oslo has the range of **hotels** you would expect of a capital city, as well as **B&Bs**, a smattering of **guesthouses** (*pensjonater*) and a quartet of **youth hostels**. To appreciate the full flavour of the city, you're best off staying on or near the western reaches of Karl Johans gate – between the Stortinget and the Nationaltheatret – though the well-heeled area to the north and west of the Royal Palace (Det Kongelige Slott) is enjoyable too. Many of the least expensive lodgings are, however, to be found in the vicinity of Oslo S, a somewhat grimy district which – along with the grey suburbs to the north and east of the station – hardly sets the pulse racing. That said, if money is tight and you're here in July and August, your choice of location may well be very limited as the scramble for **budget beds** becomes acute – or at least tight enough to make it well worth phoning ahead to check on space. For peace of mind, it is advisable to make an advance reservation, particularly for your first night.

If you don't want to book ahead, one way to cut the hassle after you arrive is to use the **accommodation service** provided by the tourist office either online (ⓦwww.visitoslo.com) or in person at either of their branches – in Oslo S train station (see p.83) and near the Rådhus (see p.83). Each office issues full accommodation lists and will make a booking on your behalf for a minimal fee, altogether a real bargain when you consider that they often get discounted rates; note also that the Oslo S office is especially good for B&Bs.

Hotels

In Oslo, 600–1000kr will get you a fairly small and simple en-suite room. You hit the comfort zone at about 1000kr, and luxury from around 1200kr. However, special offers and **seasonal deals** often make the smarter hotels more affordable than this. Most offer up to forty percent discounts at weekends, while in July and August – when many Norwegians leave town for their holidays – prices everywhere tend to drop radically. Also, most room rates are tempered by the inclusion of a good-to-excellent self-service buffet **breakfast**. The tourist office keeps lists of the day's best offers, or try the places in the following list – but always ring ahead first.

Central

Best Western Bondeheimen Rosenkrantz gate 8 ⓣ23 21 41 00, ⓦwww.bondeheimen.com. One of Oslo's most enjoyable hotels, handily located just two minutes' walk north of Karl Johans gate. Both the public areas and the comfortable bedrooms are tastefully decorated in a modern, pan-Scandinavian style, with polished pine everywhere. The inclusive buffet breakfast, served in the *Kaffistova* (see p.117) is substantial, and there's free coffee, soup and bread in the foyer throughout the evening. The rack rate for a double is 1045–1345kr (single 785–1145kr), but look out for weekend and summer discounts of up to forty percent. ❺, sp/r ❸

Bristol Kristian IV's gate 7 ⓣ22 82 60 00, ⓦwww.bristol.no. Plush establishment distinguished by its sumptuous public areas with ornate nineteenth century chandeliers, columns and fancifully carved arches. The 200-odd bedrooms are decorated in lavish period style. Rack rate ❾, sp/r ❻

City Skippergata 19 ⓣ22 41 36 10, ⓦwww.cityhotel.no. This modest but pleasant hotel, a long-time favourite with budget travellers, is located above shops and offices in a typical Oslo apartment block near Oslo S. The surroundings are a little seedy, but the hotel is cheerful enough, with small but perfectly adequate rooms. ❸

Continental Stortingsgata 24-26 ⓣ22 82 40 40, ⓦwww.hotel-continental.no. Arguably the classiest hotel in town, family-owned and with swish public areas that even boast some Munch paintings. The bedrooms beyond are extremely comfortable and decorated in a fetching, almost Georgian style – all soft colours and delicate patterned wallpaper. The hotel is also ideally located, a stone's throw from Karl Johans gate, and the breakfast is a veritable banquet. ❾, sp/r ❻

First Hotel Nobel House Kongens gate 5 ⓣ23 10 72 00, ⓦwww.firsthotels.com. Deluxe hotel with style – from the smart wooden floors to the cool, modernist decor. Close to the restaurants and art museums of Bankplassen, it's hard to beat. ❽, sp/r ❹

Grand Karl Johans gate 31 ⓣ23 21 20 00, ⓦwww.grand.no. Once Norway's most prestigious hotel, its café the haunt of Ibsen and his chums, the Grand remains one of Oslo's best hotels, its 300 guest rooms mostly decorated in a modern rendition of early twentieth-century style. Hefty weekend and summertime discounts make the Grand much more affordable than you might perhaps expect. Now a Rica hotel. ❾, sp/r ❻

Quality Savoy Universitetsgata 11 ⓣ23 35 42 00, ⓦwww.choicehotels.no/hotels/no060. Efficient chain hotel with one hundred guest rooms decorated in crisp, modern style. In an interesting area, near bookshops and cafés at the corner of Universitetsgata and Kristian Augusts gate. ❼, sp/r ❺

Rica Holberg Holbergs plass 1 ⓣ23 15 72 00, ⓦwww.rica.no. This grand, nineteenth-century building has recently been refurbished, both inside and out, but still retains some of its historic atmosphere. The public rooms are pleasant and appealing, while the bedrooms are spick, span and modern. Overlooks Holbergs plass, a pint-sized square about 500m to the north of the Slottsparken. ❻, sp/r ❹

Rica Victoria Rosenkrantz gate 13 ⓣ24 14 70 00, ⓦwww.rica.no. A large modern hotel, just south of Karl Johans gate. Its spacious rooms have every convenience, and it's justifiably popular with visiting business folk. ❼, sp/r ❹

Thon Hotel Europa St Olavs gate 31 ⓣ23 25 63 00, ⓦwww.thonhotels.no. Large, modern chain establishment that is perfectly proficient, even though it's in dreary surroundings near the west end of St Olavs gate. ❻, sp/r ❹

Thon Hotel Stefan Rosenkrantz gate 1 ⓣ23 31 55 00, ⓦwww.thonhotels.no. Unremarkable but spick-and-span modern hotel above the ground-floor shops in a five-storey building. Handy location, just a couple of minutes' walk north of Karl Johans gate. Near the bottom of its price range, it's one of the city's better deals. ❼, sp/r ❹

Westside

Best Western West Hotel Skovveien 15 ⓣ22 54 21 60, ⓦwww.bestwestern.com/no/west. Located in one of Oslo's ritziest neighbourhoods, this pleasant hotel occupies a revamped nineteenth-century townhouse. Each of the comfortable bedrooms is decorated in an attractive contemporary manner. One kilometre west of the centre off Frognerveien – take tram #12 from the centre. ❺

Clarion Collection Hotel Gabelshus Gabels gate 16 ⓣ23 27 65 00, ⓦwww.gabelshus.no. This attractive, medium-sized hotel occupies an old villa in a smart residential area a couple of kilometres west of the city centre, off Drammensveien. The public areas are kitted out with antique furnishings, while the bedrooms are smart, well-appointed and efficient. Tram #10 from the centre. ❼, sp/r ❹

Rica Bygdøy Allé Bygdøy allé 53 ⓣ23 08 58 00, ⓦwww.rica.no. With its forest of spiky, late nineteenth-century towers, this Rica possesses the most imposing hotel facade in the city. Inside, each of the rooms is individually decorated in tasteful modern style. On the first floor you'll also find the excellent *Restaurant Magma*, run by one of Norway's most high-profile chefs, Sonja Lee (see p.119). The hotel is situated in a busy residential area about 2km west of the centre; to get there from the city centre, take bus #30, #31 or #32 from Oslo S or the Nationaltheatret. ❻

Eastside

Best Western Anker Storgata 55 ⓣ22 99 75 00, ⓦwww.anker.oslo.no. A large budget hotel in a glum high-rise block beside the Akerselva river at the east end of Storgata. The clientele are mainly Norwegian, and the facilities are adequate, if somewhat frugal. Fifteen minutes' walk from Oslo S or five minutes by tram; the same block also houses the *Anker Hostel* (see below). ❺, sp/r ❹

Hostels, B&Bs and guesthouses

There are two very popular HI **hostels** in Oslo, though you'll need to be an HI member to get the lowest rate – non-members pay a small surcharge. Alternatively, the tourist office can book you into a **B&B**, which will cost in the region of 250kr for a single room, and 450–500kr for a double. This is something of a bargain especially as many B&Bs have cooking facilities, but they do tend to be out of the city centre, and there is often a minimum two-night stay; note also that the tourist office will only arrange them when you turn up at either of their offices (see p.82) in person. Another option is a **guesthouse**, or *pensjonater*, and these start at around 340kr for a single room, 450kr for a double. They offer basic but generally adequate accommodation, either with or without en-suite facilities, but breakfast is not included, and at some places you may need to supply your own sleeping bag. Unfortunately, there are very few in Oslo, and only one is near the city centre.

Anker Hostel Storgata 55 ⓣ22 99 72 10, ⓦwww.ankerhostel.no. This hostel occupies part of the same unattractive modern block as the *Anker Hotel* (see above), and it's in a cheerless neighbourhood at the east end of Storgata. More positively, the rooms are plain and simple, but perfectly adequate, with dorm beds at 175kr in a 4-bedded room, or 150kr in a 6-bedded room, and double rooms for 440kr; breakfast costs an extra 60kr. Bed linen and towels are for hire, or bring your own; sleeping bags are not allowed. The hostel is fifteen minutes' walk from Oslo S or five minutes by tram #11, #12, #13 or #17. ❷

Cochs Pensjonat Parkveien 25 ⓣ23 33 24 00, ⓦwww.cochspensjonat.no. Straightforward guesthouse occupying the third floor of an old apartment block, in a handy location behind Slottsparken at the foot of Hegdehaugsveien. There are three types of room: those with shared facilities cost 540kr for a double (390kr single), en suite 640kr (490kr) and those with a kitchen unit 700kr (530kr). Triples and quadruples are also available. ❷

MS Innvik Langkaia ⓣ22 41 95 00, ⓦwww.nordicblacktheatre.no. Owned by Nordic Black Theatre, MS Innvik is a 1980s boat that has been turned into – to quote the blurb – "a multi-cultural, cross-cultural, transcultural small ship." It is moored on Langkaia, in between Oslo S and the Vippetangen ferry terminal, and a dozen or so of their two-berth cabins are rented out for B&B. It's far from deluxe accommodation, but it's certainly different. ❸

Oslo Vandrerhjem Haraldsheim Haraldsheimveien 4, Grefsen ⓣ22 22 29 65, ⓦwww.haraldsheim.oslo.no. The best of Oslo's three HI youth hostels, 4km northeast of the centre, and open all year except Christmas week. The public areas are comfortable and attractively furnished and the bedrooms are frugal but clean. There are 270 beds in 70 rooms, most of which are four-bedded, and a good number have their own showers and WC. There are self-catering facilities, a restaurant, Internet access and washing machines. The only downside can be the presence of parties of noisy schoolchildren. It's a very popular spot, so advance booking is essential throughout the summer. To get there, take tram #17 from Storgata, near the Domkirke, to the Sinsenkrysset stop, from where it's a five-minute (signposted) walk. By road, the hostel is close to – and signed from – Ring 3. The basic dorm bed price is 175kr, which includes breakfast; doubles are 410–490kr.

Oslo Vandrerhjem Holtekilen Micheletsvei 55, Stabekk ⓣ67 51 80 40, ⓦwww.vandrerhjem.no. Much smaller than *Haraldsheim*, this HI hostel occupies part of a college building in its own grounds some 8km west of the city centre off the E18. There are kitchen facilities, a restaurant and a laundry. To get there from Oslo Bussterminalen, take bus #151, #153, #161, #162 or #252. The hostel is 200m from the Kveldsroveien bus stop. Open mid-May to Sept. Dorm beds cost 180kr, including breakfast, single rooms 280kr. ❷

Camping and cabins

Camping is a fairly easy proposition in an uncrowded city, and of the sixteen-odd sites dotted within a fifty-kilometre radius, the nearest to the centre is just 3km away. If you're out of luck with rooms in town, most sites also offer **cabins**, but ring ahead to check availability.

Ekeberg Camping Ekebergveien 65 ⓣ22 19 85 68, ⓦwww.ekebergcamping.no. Large, somewhat rudimentary but still popular campsite in a rocky, forested piece of parkland just 3km east of the city centre. To get there, take bus #34 from Jernbanetorget. Open June–Aug.

Langøyene Camping Langøyene island ⓣ22 36 37 98. Extremely popular, no-frills, semi-wilderness camping among the low forested hillocks of Langøyene, one of the most agreeable – and least developed – of the islands of the inner Oslofjord. Langøyene also has the city's best beach, but that's not a great boast – it's no more than a narrow sliver of brownish sand. To get there, take ferry #94 (late May to Aug hourly 9am–7/8pm; 15min) from the Vippetangen quay.

Central Oslo

Despite the mammoth proportions of the Oslo conurbation, the **city centre** has remained surprisingly compact, and is easy to navigate by remembering a few simple landmarks. From the Oslo S train station, at the eastern end of the centre, the main thoroughfare, **Karl Johans gate**, heads directly up the hill, passing the **Domkirke** (Cathedral) and cutting a pedestrianized course until it reaches the **Stortinget** (Parliament building). From here it sweeps down past the **University** to **Det Kongelige Slott**, or Royal Palace, situated in parkland – the **Slottsparken** – at the western end of the centre. South of the palace, on the waterfront, sits the harbourside **Aker Brygge** shopping complex, across from which lies the distinctive twin-towered **Rådhus** (City Hall). South of the Rådhus, on the lumpy peninsula overlooking the harbour, rises the severe-looking castle, Akershus **Slott**. The castle, the Stortinget and Oslo S form a triangle enclosing a tight, rather gloomy grid of streets and high tenement buildings that was originally laid out by Christian IV in the seventeenth century. For many years this was the city's commercial hub, and although Oslo's burgeoning suburbs undermined its position in the 1960s, the district is currently making a comeback, reinventing itself with specialist shops and smart restaurants.

The National Museum

Established in 2003, Norway's **Nasjonalmuseet** (National Museum) is the collective name for four separate collections, the Nasjonalgalleriet (National Gallery; see p.94); the Kunstindustrimuseet (Museum of Applied Art, see p.47); the Museet for Samtidskunst (Contemporary Art Museum, see p.100); and the Arkitekturmuseet (Museum of Architecture, see p.100).

Along Karl Johans gate to the Domkirke

Heading west and uphill from Oslo S train station, **Karl Johans gate** begins unpromisingly with a clutter of tacky shops and hang-about junkies. But things soon pick up at the corner of Dronningens gate, where the curious **Basarhallene** is a circular, two-tiered building whose brick cloisters once housed the city's food market, but now hold shops and cafés. The adjacent **Domkirke** (Cathedral; daily 10am–4pm; free) dates from the late seventeenth century, though its heavyweight tower was remodelled in 1850. From the outside the cathedral appears plain and dour, but the elegantly restored interior is a delightful surprise, its homely, low-ceilinged nave and transepts awash with maroon, green and gold paintwork. At the central crossing, the flashy Baroque **pulpit**, where cherubs frolic among the foliage, faces a **royal box** that would look more at home at the opera. The **high altar** is Baroque too, its relief of the Last Supper featuring a very Nordic-looking sacrificial lamb. To either side are stained-glass **windows** created by Emanuel Vigeland in 1910 (for more on the Vigelands, see p.109). The brightly coloured **ceiling paintings** are also modern, with representations of God the Father above the high altar, Jesus in the north transept and the Holy Spirit in the south. Down below, the **crypt** is sometimes used for temporary exhibitions of religious fine and applied art.

Outside the cathedral, **Stortorvet** was once the main city square, but it's no longer of much account, its nineteenth-century **statue** of a portly Christian IV merely the forlorn guardian of a second-rate flower market.

To the Stortinget and the Nationaltheatret

Returning to Karl Johans gate, it's a brief stroll up to the **Stortinget** (Parliament building), an imposing chunk of neo-Romanesque architecture whose stolid, sandy-coloured brickwork, dating from the 1860s, exudes bourgeois certainty. The Stortinget is open to the public during the summer (June–Sept Wed & Fri–Sun 11am–5pm, plus Tues & Thurs 11am–7pm; 45kr), but the interior is notably unexciting. In front of the Parliament, a narrow **park-piazza** runs west to the Nationaltheatret, filling in the gap between Karl Johans gate and Stortingsgata. In summer, the park brims with promenading city folk, who dodge between the jewellery hawkers, ice-cream kiosks and street performers; in winter the magnet are the dinky little open-air and floodlit ice-skating rinks – where skates can be rented at minimal cost.

Lurking at the western end of the park is the Neoclassical Nationaltheatret, built in 1899 and fronted by statues of Henrik Ibsen and Bjørnstjerne Bjørnson. Inside, the 800-seater red-and-gold main hall has been restored to its turn-of-the-twentieth-century glory and can be savoured during a performance – though these are usually in Norwegian – or by taking one of the occasional

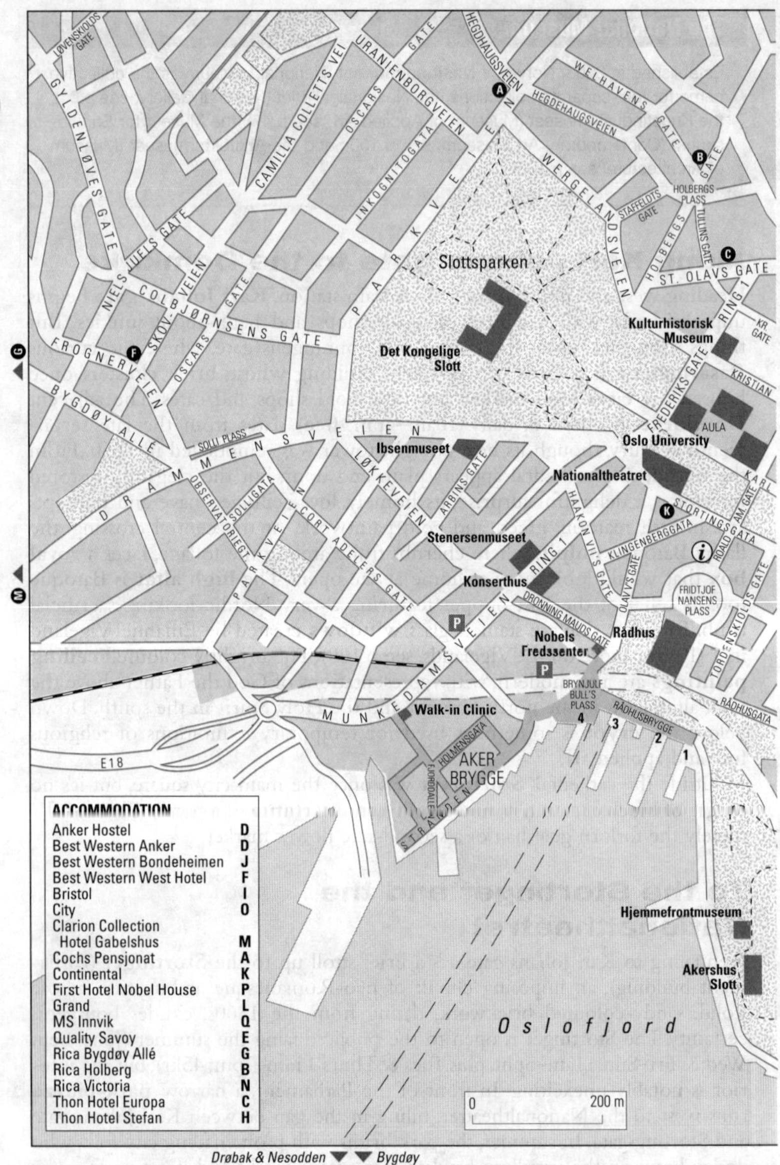

guided tours (ask for details at the box office or phone ☎22 00 14 00; theatre tickets on ☎815 00 811). The Nationaltheatret is also a useful transport interchange. A pair of tunnels round the back – one for points west, the other east – give access to NSB trains, the T-bane and the Flytoget, the airport express train. In addition, many city buses and trams as well as the Flybussen stop behind the Nationaltheatret, on Stortingsgata.

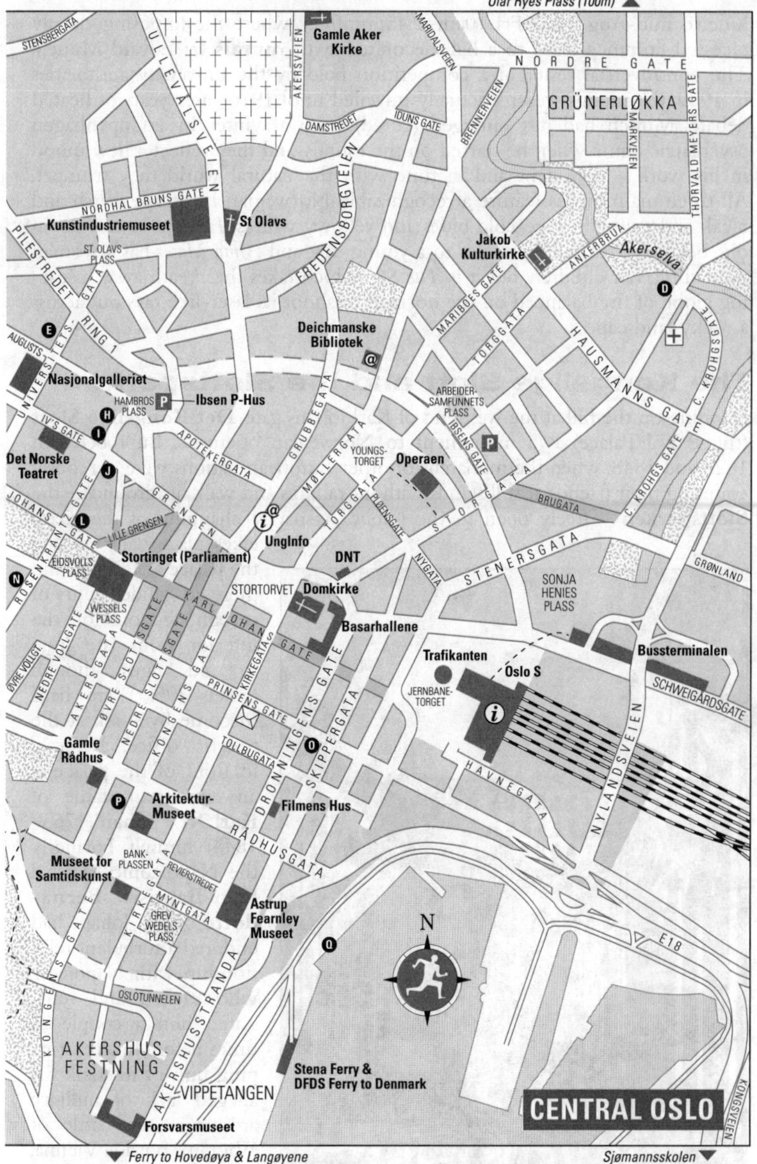

The University

Opposite the Nationaltheatret, at the western end of Karl Johans gate, stand three of the **University**'s main buildings, grand nineteenth-century structures whose classical columns and imperial pediments fit perfectly with this monumental part of the centre. The middle of the trio is the **Aula** (late

June to mid-Aug Mon–Fri 10am–2.45pm; free), where the imposing, deeply recessed entrance leads to a hall decorated with **murals** by Edvard Munch. The controversial result of a competition held by the university authorities in 1909, the murals weren't actually unveiled until 1916, after years of heated debate. Munch had just emerged (cured) from a winter in a Copenhagen psychiatric clinic when he started on the murals, and they reflect a new mood in his work – confident and in tune with the natural world they trumpet. All three main pieces feature a recognizably Norwegian landscape, harsh and bleak and painted in ice-cold blues and yellowy whites. *History* focuses on an old, bearded man telling stories to a young boy, and *Alma Mater* has a woman nourishing her children, but it is *The Sun* which takes the breath away, a searing globe of fire balanced on the horizon to shoot its laser-like rays out across a rocky landscape.

The Kongelige Slott and the Slottsparken

Standing on the hill at the west end of Karl Johans gate, **Det Kongelige Slott** (the Royal Palace) is a monument to Norwegian openness. Built between 1825 and 1848, when the monarchs of other European nations were nervously counting their friends, it still stands without railings and walls, its grounds – the **Slottsparken** – freely open to the public. A snappy changing of the guard takes place daily outside the palace at 1.30pm, and there are guided tours of certain sections of the interior from late June to mid-August, though tickets (95kr) are hard to come by – ask at the tourist office. Directly in front of the palace is an equestrian statue of **Karl XIV Johan** (1763–1844) himself. Formerly the Napoleonic Marshal **Jean-Baptiste Bernadotte**, Karl Johan had endured a turbulent relationship with Napoleon, who sacked and reinstated him a couple of times before finally stripping him of his rank for alleged lack of military ardour at the battle of Wagram, outside Vienna, in 1809. In a huff, Bernadotte stomped off back to Paris, where – much to his surprise – he was informed that the Swedish court had elected him

△ Constitution Day, Karl Johans gate

as the heir to their king, the childless Charles XIII. This was not, however a quixotic gesture by the Swedes, but rather a desire to ensure that their next king was a good soldier able to protect them from their enemies, especially Russia. In the event, it worked out well: Bernadotte successfully steered the Swedes through the tail end of the Napoleonic Wars and, as king from 1818, proved popular and efficient, adding Norway to his future kingdom in 1814. Not content, seemingly, with the terms of his motto (inscribed on the statue), "The people's love is my reward", Karl Johan had this whopping palace built for his further contentment, only to die before it was completed.

The Ibsen-museet

The grand old mansions bordering the southern perimeter of the Slottsparken once housed Oslo's social elite. Here, in a fourth-floor apartment at Arbins gate 1, **Henrik Ibsen** (1828–1906) spent the last ten years of his life, strolling down to the *Grand Café* (see p.86) every day to hold court – a tourist attraction in his own lifetime. His old quarters are now incorporated within the brand-new **Ibsen-museet**, whose entrance is round the corner on Drammensveien (Ibsen Museum; daily: May–Sept 11am–6pm; Oct–April 11am–4pm; 70kr; ⓦwww.ibsenmuseet.no). The museum provides a fascinating background to the great man's work, helping to explain the importance of the playwright to his emergent nation, and the apartment has been restored to its appearance in 1895. Both Ibsen and his wife died here: Ibsen paralyzed in bed, but his wife, unwilling to expire in an undignified pose, dressed herself to die sitting upright in a chair.

For more on Ibsen, see p.146.

Stenersenmuseet

From the Ibsen Museum, it's a five-minute walk south to the **Stenersenmuseet**, Munkedamsveien 15 (Stenersen Museum; Tues & Thurs 11am–7pm; Wed, Fri, Sat & Sun 11am–5pm; 45kr; ⓦwww.stenersen.museum.no), home to an eclectic collection of modern art, the bulk of which was gifted to the city in 1936 by the author and art collector Rolf Stenersen (the same man who gave a second collection to Bergen – see p.212). The first-floor entrance, across from the city's main concert hall, leads straight to the museum's pride and joy, its room of Munch paintings – Stenersen was a friend of Munch and bought many of his works. These include early paintings like *The Sick Room* and *Cabaret*, both dating from 1886, and disturbing later works, from the unnerving *Melancholy* to the forceful *Dance of Life*. Adjoining rooms hold an enjoyable sample of early- to mid-twentieth-century Scandinavian paintings, including the noteworthy *Small Girl on a Sofa* by **Alex Revold** and **Per Krohg**'s aloof but finely observed *Two Children*, *Actress* and *Dressmaker*. Other rooms are devoted to Munch sketches, the soft-hued Norwegian landscapes of **Amaldus Nielsen** (1838–1932), bright burlesques of Oslo life by **Ludvig Ravensberg** (1871–1958) and two portraits of Stenersen himself. There's also a lively programme of temporary exhibitions.

Kulturhistorisk Museum

Returning to the west end of Karl Johans gate, follow Frederiks gate to get to Oslo's **Kulturhistorisk Museum** (Cultural Heritage Museum; May–Aug daily 10am–6pm; Sept–April Tues–Sun 11am–4pm; 40kr), which holds within its capacious walls the university's hotch-potch historical and ethnographical collections. The highlight is the **Viking and early medieval** section, on the ground floor: in the rooms to the left of the entrance are several magnificent twelfth- and thirteenth-century stave-church porches and gateposts, alive with dragons and beasts emerging from swirling, intricately carved backgrounds; for more on stave churches, see p.188. Here also are weapons, coins, drinking horns, runic stones, religious bric-a-brac and bits of clothing as well as a superb **vaulted room** dating from the late thirteenth century and retrieved from the stave church in Ål, near Geilo. The room's brightly coloured wood planks are painted in tempera – a technique where each pigment was mixed with glue, egg white and ground chalk – and feature a complicated biblical iconography, beginning at the apex with the Creation, followed by depictions of Christ's childhood and ultimately his death and resurrection. An English-language leaflet, available in the room, gives the full lowdown, but it's the dynamic forcefulness of these naive paintings, as well as the individuality of some of the detail, that really impresses – look out, in particular, for the nasty-looking Judas at the Last Supper, and the pair of amenable donkeys peeping into the Christ's manger.

The rest of the ground floor is taken up by a pretty average **Viking Age** exhibition geared towards school parties. The tiny dioramas are downright silly, and detract from the exhibits, which attempt to illustrate various aspects of early Norwegian society, from religious beliefs and social structures through to military hardware, trade and craft. More positively, there is a fascinating sample of Viking decorative art, including the intensely flamboyant, ninth-century Oseberg and Borre styles and continuing into the Jellinge style, where greater emphasis was placed on line and composition. There's also a **skattkammeret** (treasure room) of precious objects – finger rings, crucifixes, pendants, brooches, buckles and suchlike – illustrating the sustained virtuosity of Norse goldsmiths and silversmiths.

On the first floor, the beginning of the **etnografiske utstillingene** (ethnographic exhibition; same times) is devoted to the Arctic peoples and features an illuminating section on the Sami, who inhabit the northern reaches of Scandinavia. Incongruously, there's a **myntkabinettet** (coin collection) here as well, while the top two floors contain a diverse collection of African and Asiatic art and culture, from Samurai suits to African masks and everything in between.

The Nasjonalgalleriet

From the Kulturhistorisk Museum, it's a couple of minutes' walk east to Norway's largest and most prestigious art gallery, the **Nasjonalgalleriet**, at Universitetsgata 13 (National Gallery; Tues, Wed & Fri 10am–6pm; Thurs 10am–8pm; Sat & Sun 10am–5pm; free; Ⓦ www.nationalmuseum.no). Housed in a grand nineteenth-century building, the collection may be short on internationally famous painters – apart from a fine body of work by Edvard Munch – but there's compensation in the oodles of Norwegian art, including work by all the leading figures up until the end of World War II. The only irritation is the way the museum is organized: the kernel of the collection is displayed on the **first floor** in three **colour-coded sections** – orange, green and blue. The orange section is subdivided by theme ("Landscape Painting" and so forth), but the green (1800–1910) and blue sections (1890–2005) are subdivided by both theme and chronology; as a result, the paintings of individual artists are usually displayed in several different rooms, which can be very frustrating. The **free plan** available at the reception sheds some light on matters, but it's too skimpy by half; the text below mentions room numbers where it's helpful, but note that locations are sometimes rotated.

Johan Christian Dahl and Thomas Fearnley

The five large rooms at the top of the main staircase comprise the **orange section** and here Room 17 features the work of the country's most important nineteenth-century landscape painters, **Johan Christian Dahl** (1788–1857) and his pupil **Thomas Fearnley** (1802–42). The Romantic Naturalism of their finely detailed canvases expressed Norway's growing sense of nationhood after the break-up of the Dano-Norwegian union in 1814. In a clear rejection of Danish lowland civil-servant culture, Dahl and Fearnley asserted the beauty (and moral virtue) of Norway's wild landscapes, which had previously been seen as uncouth and barbaric. This reassessment was clearly influenced by the ideas of the Swiss-born philosopher Jean Jacques Rousseau (1712–78), who believed that the peoples of mountain regions possessed an intrinsic nobility precisely because they were remote from the corrupting influences of (lowland) civilization. Dahl, who was a professor at the Academy of Art in Dresden for many years, wrote to a friend in 1841: "Like a true Poet, a Painter must not be led by the prevailing, often corrupt Taste, but attempt to create… a landscape [that]… exposes the characteristics of this Country and its Nature – often idyllic, often historical, melancholic – what they have been and are."

Dahl's large 1842 canvas *Stalheim* is typical of his work, a mountain landscape rendered in soft and dappled hues, dotted with tiny figures and a sleepy village. His *Hjelle in Valdres* (1851), in the green section – Room 20/21 – adopts the same approach, although here the artifice behind the apparent naturalism is easier to detect. Dahl had completed another painting of Hjelle the year before; returning to the subject, he widened the valley and heightened the mountains, sprinkling them with snow. Fearnley often lived and worked abroad, but he always returned to Norwegian themes, painting no fewer than five versions of the moody *Labrofossen ved Kongsberg* (The Labro Waterfall at Kongsberg); his 1837 version is displayed in Room 17.

Late nineteenth- and early twentieth-century Norwegian paintings

In the **green section** (Rooms 18–28), look out for the work of **Hans Frederik Gude** (1825–1903) and **Adolph Tidemand** (1814–76), not so much for the quality of the painting as for their content. Tidemand's absurdly romantic, folkloric scenes reflect the bourgeois nationalism that swept Norway in the middle of the nineteenth century. The two men were the leading lights of a generation of Norwegian artists, though they actually lived in Düsseldorf, where they lectured at the art academy. They collaborated on the creation of *Spearing Fish by Night* and the *Bridal Voyage on the Hardanger Fjord*, with Gude painting the landscape and Tidemand the figures.

In the 1880s, Norwegian landscape painting took on a mystical and spiritual dimension. Influenced by French painters such as Théodore Rousseau, Norwegian artists abandoned the naturalism of earlier painters for more symbolic representations. **Gerhard Munthe** (1849–1929) dipped into lyrical renditions of the Norwegian countryside, and his cosy, folksy scenes were echoed in the paintings of **Erik Werenskiold** (1855–1938), who is well represented by *Peasant Burial* in Room 22. Of a similar ilk was the work of **Christian Krohg** (1852–1925), whose highly stylized but distinctly tongue-in-cheek *Albertine to see the Police Surgeon* is Krohg at his best. During this period, **Theodor Kittelsen** (1857–1914) defined the appearance of the country's trolls, sprites and sirens in his illustrations for Asbjørnsen and Moe's *Norwegian Folk Tales*, published in 1883. Two modest examples of his other work – a self-portrait and a fairy-tale landscape – are displayed here in the green section.

Harald Sohlberg (1869–1935) clarified the rather hazy vision of many of his Norwegian contemporaries, painting a series of sharply observed Røros streetscapes and expanding into more elemental themes with such stunning works as *En blomstereng nordpå* (A Northern Flower Meadow) and *Sommernatt* (Summer Night). These are exhibited in Room 28, and are comparable with the paintings of **Halfdan Egedius** (1877–99), as in *Opptrekkende uvaer* (The Approaching Storm).

Edvard Munch

The Nasjonalgalleriet's star turn is, however, its **Munch** collection. Representative works from the 1880s up to 1916 are gathered together in Room 24 of the green section, with several lesser pieces displayed elsewhere. His early work is very much in the Naturalist tradition of his mentor Christian Krohg, though by 1885 Munch was already pushing back the boundaries in *The Sick Child* (Room 27), a heart-wrenching evocation of his sister Sophie's death from tuberculosis. Other works displaying this same sense of pain include *The Dance of Life*, *Madonna* and *The Scream*, a seminal canvas of 1893 whose swirling lines and rhythmic colours were to inspire the Expressionists. Munch painted several versions of *The Scream*, but this is the original, so it is hard to exaggerate the embarrassment felt by the museum when, in 1994, someone climbed in through the window and stole it. The painting was eventually recovered, but the thief was never caught. Consider Munch's words as you view it:

I was walking along a road with two friends. The sun set. I felt a tinge of melancholy. Suddenly the sky became blood red. I stopped and leaned against a railing feeling exhausted, and I looked at the flaming clouds that hung like blood and a sword over the blue-black fjord and the city. My friends walked on. I stood there trembling with fright. And I felt a loud unending scream piercing nature.

The gallery's sample of Munch's work serves as a good introduction to the artist, but for a more detailed appraisal – and a more comprehensive selection of his work – check out the Munch Museum (p.111).

Norwegian paintings from 1910

Munch aside, the general flow of Norwegian art was reinvigorated in the 1910s by a new band of artists who had trained in Paris under Henri Matisse, whose emancipation of colour from Naturalist constraints inspired his Norwegian students. The paintings of this group are displayed in the **blue section** (Rooms 32–42), and amongst them **Henrik Sørensen** (1882–1962) is the outstanding figure. Sørensen summed up the Frenchman's influence on him thirty years later: "From Matisse, I learned more in fifteen minutes than from all the other teachers I have listened to" – lessons that inspired Sørensen's surging, earthy landscapes of the lowlands of eastern Norway. **Axel Revold** (1887–1962) was trained by Matisse too, but also assimilated Cubist influences as in *The Fishing Fleet leaves the Harbour*, whilst **Erling Enger** (1899–1990) maintained a gently lyrical, slightly whimsical approach to the landscape and its seasons. Look out also for the work of **Arne Ekeland** (1908–94), whose various World War II paintings are bleak and powerful in equal measure – as evidenced by *The Occupation*.

Finally, the blue section holds an enjoyable sample of work by the **Impressionists** and **Post-Impressionists**, with assorted bursts of colour from Manet, Monet, Degas and Cézanne, as well as a distant, piercing Van Gogh self-portrait, while the early twentieth century is represented by works from the likes of Picasso, Gris and Braque. Nonetheless, it must be said that for a national gallery there are few works of international significance, reflecting Norway's past poverty and its lack of an earlier royal or aristocratic collection to build upon.

The Kunstindustrimuseet

The **Kunstindustrimuseet** (Museum of Applied Art; Tues, Wed & Fri 11am–5pm, Thurs 11am–8pm, Sat & Sun noon–4pm; free, but admission charged for exhibitions; ⓦwww.nationalmuseum.no), at St Olavs gate 1, occupies an imposing nineteenth-century building some five minutes' walk from the Nasjonalgalleriet – continue to the far end of Universitets gata, veer to the right and it's at the end of the street. Founded in 1876, it can lay claim to being one of the earliest applied art museums in Europe and its multifaceted permanent collection is particularly strong on **furniture**, with examples of all the major styles – both domestic and imported – that have been popular in Norway from the medieval period to the present day.

The museum spreads over four floors with the first floor devoted to a lively programme of temporary exhibitions. The next floor up focuses on the development of **Modernism**, casting a wide net to start in 1905 and end a century later. There are keynote displays on Art Nouveau and post-World War II Scandinavian design. The next floor up is devoted to the **History of Style 1100–1905**, and, in the first room to the right of the stairs, there's an engaging hotchpotch of **medieval** paraphernalia, from brooches and crosses through to portable altars. Here also is the museum's top exhibit, the intricate and brightly coloured **Baldishol Tapestry**, one of the finest and earliest examples of woven tapestry in Europe, plus a charming selection of **bedspreads** decorated with religious and folkloric motifs. Using skills distantly inherited from Flemish weavers, the Norwegians took to pictorial bedspreads in a big way, their main modification being the elimination of perspective in the attempt to cover the seams. Of ceremonial significance, these bedspreads were brought out on all major occasions – weddings and festivals in particular. The bedspreads began as fairly crude affairs at the start of the seventeenth century, but achieved greater precision and detail throughout the eighteenth century, after which the art went into a slow decline. The two most popular subjects were the arrival of the Magi, and the Wise and Foolish Virgins, a suitably didactic subject for any newlyweds. The next room boasts an enjoyable sample of tapestries and carved wooden furniture, of which the cheerily painted **chests** and **wardrobes** are especially fetching. Also on this floor is a sequence of **period interiors** illustrating foreign fashions from Renaissance and Baroque through to Rococo, Louis XVI, Jugendstil and Art Nouveau. There's also a curious little room kitted out in neo-Viking style, a medievalist fantasy dating from the late nineteenth century.

The top floor has ceramics and glassware from the early nineteenth century onwards, and displays on textiles and fashions. The highlight here is the collection of extravagant **costumes** worn by Norway's royal family at the turn of the twentieth century. Dresses is too prosaic a word for the fairy-tale affairs favoured by Queen Maud, daughter of England's Edward VII and wife of Haakon VII, not to mention Crown Princess Sonja's consecratory robe from the 1930s.

East from the Kunstindustrimuseet to Grünerløkka

Leaving the museum, walk round the dull, brown-brick pile of **St Olav Domkirke**, built for the city's Catholics in the middle of the nineteenth century, and follow Akersveien as far as the cemetery. There's a choice of routes here. If you keep straight, it's a short stroll up the slope to the **Gamle Aker Kirke** (May–Sept Tues–Fri noon–2pm; free), a sturdy stone building still in use as a Lutheran parish church. It dates from around 1100, which makes it the oldest stone church in Scandinavia, although most of what you see today is the result of a heavy-handed nineteenth-century refurbishment.

Alternatively, back at the cemetery, turn right down **Damstredet**, a steep cobbled lane flanked by early nineteenth-century clapboard houses built at all kinds of odd angles. These are some of the few wooden buildings to have survived Oslo's developers and they make the street a picturesque affair, a well-kept reminder of how the city once looked. At the bottom of Damstredet, there's another choice of routes. If you stroll south along **Fredensborgveien**, you'll thread your way past office blocks, regaining the city centre in around fifteen minutes. But if you head southeast for about five minutes along Iduns gate and then Hausmanns gate, you'll reach the **Jakob Kulturkirke**, a disused church now housing a cultural centre where concerts, art exhibitions and theatre are held (Ⓣ22 99 34 50, Ⓦwww.kkv.no for details).

Behind the church is the **Ankerbrua** (Anker bridge) across the **River Akerselva**. Sporting sculptures by Norwegian sculptor Per Ung – look out for Peer Gynt and his reindeer – the bridge marks the main approach to **Grünerløkka**. Formerly a run-down working-class district, Grünerløkka's recent regeneration has turned it into one of the most fashionable parts of the city, particularly amongst artists and students. Turn left just beyond the bridge, and you'll find yourself on **Markveien**, where there's a string of fashionable cafés, bars, restaurants and designer shops. At Olav Ryes Plass, the first splash of greenery, turn right to reach the liveliest part of Grünerløkka's other main drag, **Thorvald Meyers gate**, which runs north to **Birkelunden**, a grassy square that's especially popular for hanging out in the summer.

The quickest way to get back to the centre is on tram #11 or #12, which both run along Thorvald Meyers gate.

To the water: the Rådhus

Back in the city centre, just a couple of minutes' walk south of Karl Johans gate, the **Rådhus** (City hall; daily: May–Aug 8.30am–5pm; Sept–April 9am–4pm; free: guided tours June–Aug 3 daily, Sept–May Mon–Fri 3 daily; 40kr) rears high above the waterfront. Nearly twenty years in the making, Oslo's once controversial City Hall finally opened in 1950 to celebrate the city's nine-hundredth anniversary. Designed by Arnstein Arneberg and Manus Poulsson, this firmly Modernist, twin-towered building of dark brown brick was a grandiose statement of civic pride. At first, few people had a good word for what they saw as an ugly and strikingly un-Norwegian addition to the city, but with the passing of time the obloquy has fallen on more recent additions to the skyline – such as Oslo S – and the Rådhus has become one of the city's more popular buildings.

Initially at least, the ornamentation was equally contentious. Many leading Norwegian painters and sculptors contributed to the decorations, which were intended to celebrate all things Norwegian, but the pagan themes chosen for much of the work gave many of the country's Protestants the hump. The **main approach** to the Rådhus is up a wide ramp, whose side galleries are adorned by garish **wood panels** illustrating pagan Nordic myths with several featuring the Tree of the World, Yggdrasil or Yggdrask (see p.404). Inside, the principal hall – the **Rådhushallen** – is decorated with vast, stylized and very secular murals. On the north wall, Per Krohg's *From the Fishing Nets in the West to the Forests of* *the East* invokes the figures of polar explorer Fridtjof Nansen (on the left) and dramatist Bjørnstjerne Bjørnson (on the right) to symbolize, respectively, the nation's spirit of adventure and its intellectual development. On the south wall is the equally vivid *Work, Administration and Celebration*, which took Henrik Sørensen a decade to complete. The self-congratulatory nationalism of these murals is hardly attractive, although the effect is partly offset by the forceful fresco in honour of the Norwegian Resistance of World War II, running along the east wall.

Outside, at the back of the Rådhus, a line of six muscular **bronzes** represents the trades – builders, bricklayers and so on – who worked on the building. Behind them stand four massive granite female sculptures surrounding a fountain, and beyond is the busy central **harbour**, with the bumpy Akershus peninsula on the left and the islands of the Oslofjord filling out the backdrop. This is a delightful spot, one of the city's happiest moments, and a stone's throw away is the Nobels Fredssenter.

Nobels Fredssenter and Aker Brygge

The brand-new **Nobels Fredssenter** (Nobel Peace Centre; mid-June to Aug daily 9am–7pm; Sept to mid-June Tues-Sun 10am–6pm; 60kr; Ⓦ www.nobelpeacecenter.org) was founded to celebrate and publicize the Nobel Peace Prize. Born in Sweden, **Alfred Nobel** (1833–1896) invented dynamite in his thirties and went on to become extraordinarily rich with factories in over twenty countries. In his will, Nobel established a fund to reward good works in five categories – physics, chemistry, medicine, literature and peace. The awards were to be made annually, based on the recommendations of several Swedish institutions, with the exception of the Peace Prize, the recipient of which was to be selected by a committee of five, itself appointed by the Norwegian parliament.

Inside, the Peace Centre's ground floor features a series of widescreen displays designed to get visitors into thinking about conflict and peace with quotations from notorious thugs – Eichmann, Mussolini and so forth – set against those of the peaceable. Upstairs, there's a small display on the Nobel family, "wall papers" (broadly, information sheets) on all things to do with peace, and the so-called "Nobel Field", where each of the past holders of the Peace Prize is represented by a light bulb on a wispy stalk; taken together, and with the overhead lights dimmed down, the stalks make a sort of miniature electrical forest that really looks rather effective. As for the winners of the Peace Prize themselves, there are many outstanding individuals – Martin Luther King, Desmond Tutu, Nelson Mandela and Willy Brandt to name but four – but some real surprises too, especially Theodore Roosevelt, who was part of the American invasion of Cuba in the 1890s, and the USA's Henry Kissinger, who was widely blamed for destabilizing Cambodia in the 1970s. Indeed, despite its current exemplary image, the Nobel Prizes are in fact steeped in controversy: the writer and playwright Johan August Strindberg (1849–1912) was the pre-eminent literary figure in Sweden for several decades, but he was much too radical for the tastes of the prize givers and in 1911, after he had again failed to get one, the Swedish working class organized a whip-round and gave him a "Nobel Prize" themselves.

Behind the Peace Centre, the old Aker shipyard has been turned into the swish **Aker Brygge** shopping-cum-office complex, a gleaming concoction of walkways, circular staircases and glass lifts, all decked out with neon and plastic; the bars and restaurants here are some of the most popular in town.

East to Bankplassen and the Museet for Samtidskunst

Running east from the Rådhus, **Rådhusgata** cuts off the spur of land on which the Akershus Castle (see p.102) is built. For the most part the street is flanked by ponderous late nineteenth-century high-rises, reminders of the time when this was the commercial heart of the city, but at the foot of Akersgata it bisects an elegant cobbled square framed by a handful of much older pastel-painted buildings, including the pint-sized **Gamle Rådhus**, Oslo's old town hall, though this was heavily restored after fire damage in 1996. It was here, in 1667, that Oslo's first theatrical performance took place, as recalled on the building's second floor in the mildly diverting **Teatermuseet** (Theatre Museum; Wed 11am–3pm, Thurs & Sun noon–4pm; 30kr), with posters, puppets and costumes.

Bankplassen, arguably the city's most attractive square, lies one block south of Rådhusgata, between Kongens gate and Kirkegata. Framed by Gothic Revival and Second Empire buildings, the square is a perfect illustration of the grand tastes of the Dano-Norwegian elite who ran the country at the start of the twentieth century. The square's proudest building is the former Norges Bank headquarters of 1907, a redoubtable Art Nouveau edifice that has been refurbished to house the enterprising **Museet for Samtidskunst** (Contemporary Art Museum; Tues, Wed & Fri 10am–6pm, Thurs 10am–8pm, Sat & Sun 10am–5pm; free; Ⓦwww.nationalmuseum.no). The museum owns work by every major post-World War II Norwegian artist and many leading foreign figures too, and for the most part the **displays** take the form of a series of temporary, thematic exhibitions spread over three floors. The works, some of which are massive, are each allowed a generous amount of space, so – given that the museum also hosts prestigious international exhibitions of contemporary art – only a fraction of the permanent collection can be shown at any one time. Nonetheless, Norwegian names to look out for include Bjørn Carlsen, Frans Widerberg, Erik Killi Olsen, Knut Rose and Bjørn Ransve.

There are also two **permanent installations**, including the weird *Inner Space V*, the fifth in a series of angst-rattling rooms made from recycled industrial junk by the Norwegian Per Inge Bjørlo (b.1952), and, tucked away in a room of its own on the top floor, the peculiar – and peculiarly engaging – *The Man Who Never Threw Anything Away*. This is the work of the Russian Ilya Kabakov (b.1933), who spent over a decade from 1983 collecting hundreds of discarded items from the recesses of his house – bits of toenail, string etc, etc – to assemble them here, each precisely labelled and neatly displayed. The installation occupies a sort of parallel reality that was originally a retreat from the bureaucratic illogicalities of the Soviet system, but is now a tribute to the anally retentive.

The museum's exhibits hang from every wall and offset every corner and stairwell, but it's still difficult not to be just as impressed by the building itself, its polished, echoing halls resplendent with gilt and marble, ornamental columns and banisters. The museum also does a good line in T-shirts – a recent offering

The Arkitekturmuseet (Museum of Architecture)

One of Oslo's four national museums, the Arkitekturmuseet, is currently closed, but will move into new premises on Bankplassen sometime in 2007. It is a lavish redevelopment, costing millions of kroner, and will include a spanking new exhibition pavilion. Further details on Ⓦwww.nationalmuseum.no.

was inscribed "Welcome foreigners – don't leave us alone with the Danes" – and you can stop off in the first-floor *Café Sesam* for cakes and coffee.

Astrup Fearnley Museet for Moderne Kunst

Opened in 1993, the **Astrup Fearnley Museet for Moderne Kunst**, Dronningens gate 4 (Astrup Fearnley Modern Art Museum; Tues, Wed & Fri 11am–5pm, Thurs 11am–7pm, Sat & Sun noon–5pm; free; Ⓦ www.afmuseet.no), about 200m to the east of Bankplassen, occupies a sharp modern building of brick and glass, with six-metre-high steel entrance doors. It's meant to impress – a suitably posh setting for the display of several private collections and for prestigious temporary exhibitions. The latter often leave little space for the permanent collection, which includes examples of the work of most major postwar Norwegian artists, as well as a smattering of foreign works by such celebrated figures as Francis Bacon, Damien Hirst, Jeff Koons and Anselm Kiefer.

Norway has a well-organized, high-profile body of **professional artists** whose long-established commitment to encouraging artistic activity throughout the country has brought them respect, not to mention state subsidies. In the 1960s, abstract and conceptual artists dominated the scene, but at the end of the 1970s there was a renewed interest in older art styles, particularly Expressionism, Surrealism and Cubism, plus a new emphasis on technique and materials. To a large degree these opposing impulses fused, or at least overlapped, but by the late 1980s several definable movements had emerged. One of the more popular trends was for artists to use beautiful colours to portray disquieting visions, a dissonance favoured by the likes of **Knut Rose** (b. 1936) and **Bjørn Carlsen** (b.1945). The latter's ghoulish *Searching in a Dead Zebra* has been highly influential, and is now part of the museum's permanent collection. Other artists, the most distinguished of whom is Tore Hansen (b.1949), have developed a naive style. Their paintings, apparently clumsily drawn without thought for composition, are frequently reminiscent of Norwegian folk art, and constitute a highly personal response drawn from the artists' emotions and subconscious experiences.

Both of these trends embody a sincerity of expression that defines the bulk of contemporary Norwegian art. Whereas the prevailing mood in international art circles encourages detached irony, Norway's artists characteristically adhere to the view that their role is to interpret, or at least express, the poignant and personal for their audience. An important exception is Bjørn Ransve (b.1944), who creates sophisticated paintings in constantly changing styles, but always focused on the relationship between art and reality. Another exception is the small group of artists, such as **Bjørn Sigurd Tufta** (b.1956), who have returned to non-figurative modernism to create works that explore the possibilities of the material, while the content plays no decisive role. An interest in materials has sparked a variety of experiments, particularly among the country's sculptors, whose **installations** incorporate everyday utensils, natural objects and pictorial art. These installations have developed their own momentum, pushing back the traditional limits of the visual arts in their use of many different media including photography, video, textiles and furniture. Leading an opposing faction is the painter **Odd Nerdrum** (b.1944), who has long spearheaded the figurative rebellion against the modernists. The most prominent Norwegian sculptor today is Bergen's own **Bård Breivik** (b.1948), who explores the dialogue between nature and humankind.

The Akershus complex

Though very much part of central Oslo by location, the thumb of land that holds the sprawling fortifications of the **Akershus complex** (outdoor areas daily 6am–9pm; free) is quite separate from the city centre in feel. Built on a rocky knoll overlooking the harbour in around 1300, the original **Slott** (castle) was already the battered veteran of several unsuccessful sieges when Christian IV (1596–1648) took matters in hand. The king had a passion for building cities and took a keen interest in Norway – during his reign he visited the country about thirty times, more than all the other kings of the Dano-Norwegian union together. So, when Oslo was badly damaged by fire in 1624, he took his opportunity and simply ordered the town to be moved round the bay from its marshy location at the mouth of the River Alna beneath the Ekeberg heights. He had the town rebuilt in its present position, renamed it Christiania – a name which stuck until 1925 – and transformed the medieval castle into a Renaissance residence. Around the castle he also constructed a new fortress – the **Akershus Festning** – whose thick earth-and-stone walls and protruding bastions were designed to resist artillery bombardment. Refashioned and enlarged on several later occasions, and now bisected by Kongens gate, parts of the fortress have remained in military use until the present day.

There are several **entrances** to the Akershus complex, but the most appealing is at the west end of **Myntgata**, from where a footpath leads up to a side gate in the perimeter wall. Just beyond the gate is a dull museum-cum-information centre, which makes a strange attempt to tie in the history of the castle with modern environmental concerns. You're much better off keeping going along the signed **footpath** that twists its way up to the castle and the Resistance Museum, offering the possibility of heady views over the harbour on the way.

Hjemmefrontmuseum

The **Hjemmefrontmuseum** (Resistance Museum; mid-April to mid-June & Sept Mon–Sat 10am–4pm, Sun 11am–4pm; mid-June to Aug Mon, Wed, Fri & Sat 10am–5pm, Tues & Thurs 10am–6pm, Sun 11am–5pm; Oct to mid-April Mon–Fri 10am–3pm, Sat & Sun 11am–4pm; 30kr) occupies a separate building just outside the castle entrance, an apt location given that the Gestapo tortured and sometimes executed captured Resistance fighters in the castle. Labelled in English and Norwegian, the museum details the history of the war in Norway, from defeat and occupation through resistance to final victory. There are tales of extraordinary heroism here – notably the determined resistance of hundreds of the country's teachers to Nazi instructions and the sabotaging of German attempts to produce heavy water for an atomic bomb deep in southern Norway, at Rjukan (see p.194). There's also the moving story of a certain Petter Moen, who was arrested by the Germans and imprisoned in the Akershus, where he kept a diary by using a nail to pick out letters on toilet paper; the diary survived, but he didn't. Another section deals with Norway's Jews, who numbered 1800 in 1939; the Germans captured 760, of whom 24 survived. There's also an impressively honest account of Norwegian collaboration: fascism struck a chord with the country's petit bourgeois, and hundreds of volunteers joined the Wehrmacht. The most notorious collaborator was **Vidkun Quisling**, who was executed by firing squad for his treachery in 1945. When the German army invaded in April 1940, Quisling assumed he would govern the country and made a radio announcement proclaiming his seizure of power. In the event, the Germans soon sidelined him, opting for military control instead, but Quisling's proclamation can be heard at the touch of a button in the museum.

Akershus Slott

Next door to the Resistance Museum, the severe stone walls and twin spires of the medieval **Akershus Slott** (Akershus Castle; May to early Sept Mon–Sat 10am–4pm, Sun 12.30–4pm; 40kr including frequent guided tour; out of season 1 guided tour in English weekly – call ⓣ23 09 35 53 for details) perch on a rocky ridge high above the zigzag fortifications added by Christian IV. The castle is approached through a narrow tunnel-gateway, beyond which lies a stone-flagged courtyard and then the main gate. So far so good, but thereafter the interior is a bit of a disappointment, mostly comprising a string of sparsely furnished rooms linked by bare-brick passageways. Nevertheless, there are one or two items of interest, primarily the royal chapel and **mausoleum**, holding the sarcophagi of Norway's current dynasty – not that there have been many of them, just two in fact, Haakon VII (1872–1957) and Olav V (1903–1991). Amongst the castle's assorted halls, the pick is the **Romerikssalen**, worth a few moments for its grand fireplace, antique furniture and Flemish tapestries.

It's also a real surprise to find that the office of **Henrik Wergeland** (1808–1845), who worked in the castle as a royal archivist for the last four years of his life, has survived pretty much undisturbed. Wergeland was one of the most prominent Norwegian poets and dramatists of his day and also an ardent campaigner for greater Norwegian independence. He was, therefore, roundly mocked for accepting the archivist's job – and pension – from the regime he had disparaged and ended up a bitter man: he allegedly kept a (fang-less) adder in his office to disconcert the unwary visitor, a not-so-playful reminder of one of his last works, *Vinaegers Fjeldeventyr*, in which the cruelest critic of a poet is so poisonous that a snake dies after it has bit him.

Back outside, a **path** leads off the courtyard, running down the side of the castle with the walls pressing in on one side and views out over the harbour on the other. At the foot of the castle, the path swings across a narrow promontory and soon reaches the **footbridge** over Kongens gate. Cross the footbridge for the Forsvarsmuseet (see below), or keep straight for the string of ochre-coloured barrack blocks that lead back to Myntgata (see opposite).

Forsvarsmuseet

On the far side of the Kongens gate footbridge, head southeast across the army parade ground to reach the **Forsvarsmuseet** (Armed Forces Museum; May–Aug Mon–Fri 10am–5pm, Sat & Sun 11am–5pm; Sept–April Mon–Fri 11am–4pm, Sat & Sun 11am–5pm; free), which tracks through Norwegian military history from the Vikings to postwar peace-keeping. The most interesting section deals with World War II, but otherwise it's hard to get enthralled by the museum's assortment of uniforms, rifles and guns, doubly so since the wars fought between the Scandinavian countries are frequent and hard to disentangle.

From here, it's a short walk back to the main entrance of the Akershus complex at the foot of Kirkegata.

Southwest of the centre: the Bygdøy peninsula

Other than the centre, the place where you're likely to spend most time in Oslo is the **Bygdøy peninsula**, across the bay to the southwest of the main harbour, where **five museums** make for an absorbing cultural and historical trip. Indeed, it's well worth spending a full day or, less wearyingly, two half-days here. The most enjoyable way to reach Bygdøy is by **ferry**. These leave from the Rådhusbrygge (pier 3) behind the Rådhus every twenty to thirty minutes (late May to Aug daily 8.45am–8.45pm; April to late May & Sept daily 8.45am–6pm; 20kr), returning to a similar schedule. All the ferries to the peninsula perform a loop, calling first at the **Dronningen** dock (10min from Rådhusbrygge) and then the **Bygdøynes** dock (15min) before returning to the Rådhusbrygge; note that the ferries only go **one-way** – so there is no service from Bygdøynes to Dronningen. The two most popular attractions – the Viking Ships and Folk museums – are within easy walking distance of the Dronningen dock; the other three are a stone's throw from Bygdøynes. If you decide to walk between the two groups of museums, allow about fifteen minutes: the route is well signposted but dull. The alternative to the ferry is **bus** #30 (every 15–30min; 20min), which runs all year from Jernbanetorget and the Nationaltheatret to the Folk Museum and Viking Ships.

Norsk Folkemuseum

About 700m uphill from the Dronningen dock – just follow the signs – the **Norsk Folkemuseum**, at Museumsveien 10 (Norwegian Folk Museum; mid-May to mid-Sept daily 10am–6pm, 90kr: mid-Sept to mid-May daily 11am–3/4pm, 70kr; Ⓦwww.norskfolkemuseum.no), combines indoor collections on folk art, furniture, dress and customs with an extensive open-air display of reassembled buildings, mostly wooden barns, stables, storehouses and dwellings from the seventeenth to the nineteenth centuries. Look out also for the imaginative temporary exhibitions, for which the museum has a well-deserved reputation. Pick up a free **map** of the museum at the entrance.

The complex of buildings just beyond the entry turnstiles holds the museum's indoor collections, both permanent and temporary. Of the former, the **folk art** section on the lower level is delightful, exhibiting samples of quilted bedspreads and painted furniture from the sixteenth century onwards. It's here you'll spot the occasional fancily carved spoon and mangle board, whose significance is not at first apparent: these were in fact given by boys to girls as **love gifts** – though quite how a mangle board could be construed as romantic requires a leap of the imagination – and, if the attraction was mutual, the girls gave the boys mittens or gloves. In rural Norway, it was considered improper for courting couples to be seen together during the day, but acceptable (or at least tolerated) at night – and to assist the process parents usually moved girls of marrying age into one of the farm's outhouses, where tokens could be swapped without embarrassment. On the upper level, the **folk dress** section is excellent too. Rural customs specified the correct dress for every sort of social gathering, but it's the extravagant and brightly coloured bridal headdresses that grab the eye. The amount of work that went into the creation of the folk costumes was quite extraordinary, although perhaps it should be remembered that the exhibits were mostly owned by wealthier Norwegians – many others could barely avoid starvation, never mind indulge in fancy dress.

The **open-air collection** consists of more than 150 reconstructed buildings. Arranged geographically, they provide a marvellous sample of Norwegian rural architecture, somewhat marred by inadequate explanations. That said, it's still worth tracking down the **stave church** (see box on p.188), particularly if you don't plan to travel elsewhere in Norway. Dating from the early thirteenth century but extensively restored in the 1880s, when it was moved here from

Gol, near Geilo, the church is a good example of its type, with steep, shingle-covered roofs and dragon finials. The interior is cramped and gloomy, the nave preceding a tiny chancel painted with a floral design and sporting a striking *Last Supper* above and behind the altar. Elsewhere, the cluster of buildings from **Setesdal** in southern Norway holds some especially well-preserved dwellings and storehouses from the seventeenth century, while the **Numedal** section contains one of the museum's oldest buildings, a late thirteenth-century house from Rauland whose door posts are embellished with Romanesque vine decoration.

In **summer**, many of the buildings are open for viewing, and costumed guides roam the site to both explain the vagaries of Norwegian rural life and demonstrate traditional skills, from spinning and carving to dancing and horn blowing.

Vikingskipshuset

A five-minute walk south along the main road is the **Vikingskipshuset** (Viking Ships Museum; daily: May–Sept 9am–6pm; Oct–April 11am–4pm; 40kr; Ⓦwww.khm.uio.no), a large hall specially constructed to house a trio of ninth-century Viking ships, with viewing platforms to enable you to see inside the hulls. The three oak vessels were retrieved from ritual burial mounds in southern Norway around the turn of the twentieth century, each embalmed in a subsoil of clay, which accounts for their excellent state of preservation. The size of a Viking **burial mound** denoted the dead person's rank and wealth, while the possessions buried with the body were designed to make the afterlife as comfortable as possible. Implicit was the assumption that a chieftain in this world would be a chieftain in the next – slaves, for example, were frequently killed and buried with their master or mistress – a belief that would subsequently give Christianity, with its alternative, less fatalistic vision, an immediate appeal to those at the bottom of the Viking pile. Quite how the Vikings saw the transfer to the afterlife taking place is less certain. The evidence is contradictory: sometimes the Vikings stuck the anchor on board the burial ship in preparation for the spiritual journey, but at other times the vessels were moored to large stones before burial. Neither was ship burial the only type of Viking funeral – far from it. The Vikings buried their dead in mounds and on level ground, with and without grave goods, in large and small coffins, both with and without boats – and they practised cremation too.

The museum's star exhibits are the Oseberg and Gokstad ships, named after the places on the west side of the Oslofjord where they were discovered in 1904 and 1880 respectively. The **Oseberg ship** is 22m long and 5m wide, and is probably representative of the type of vessel the Vikings used to navigate fjords and coastal waters. It has an ornately carved prow and stern, both of which rise high above the hull, where thirty oar-holes indicate the size of the crew. It is thought to be the burial ship of a Viking chieftain's wife and much of the treasure buried with it was retrieved and is displayed behind it. The grave goods reveal an attention to detail and a level of domestic sophistication not traditionally associated with the Vikings. There are marvellous decorative items like the fierce-looking animal-head posts and exuberantly carved ceremonial items, including a sled and a cart, plus a host of smaller, more mundane household items such as shoes, rattles, agricultural tools and cooking pots.

Here also are finds from the **Gokstad ship**, most memorably an ornate bridle and two dragonhead bedposts, though the Gokstad burial chamber was ransacked by grave robbers long ago and precious little has survived. The

Gokstad ship itself is slightly longer and wider than the Oseberg vessel, and quite a bit sturdier. Its seaworthiness was demonstrated in 1893 when a replica sailed across the Atlantic to the USA. The third vessel, the **Tune ship**, is the smallest of the nautical trio and only fragments survive; these are displayed unrestored, much as they were discovered in 1867 on the eastern side of the Oslofjord.

The Frammuseet

Just up from the Bygdøynes dock stands the **Gjøa**, the one-time sealing ship in which **Roald Amundsen** (1872–1928) made the first complete sailing of the Northwest Passage in 1906. By any measure, this was a remarkable achievement and the fulfilment of a nautical mission that had preoccupied sailors for several centuries. It took three years, with Amundsen and his crew surviving two ice-bound winters deep in the Arctic, but this epic journey was soon eclipsed when, in 1912, the Norwegian dashed to the South Pole famously just ahead of the ill-starred Captain Scott. The ship that carried Amundsen to within striking distance of the South Pole, the *Fram*, is displayed inside the mammoth triangular display hall that is the **Frammuseet** (Fram Museum; daily: May to mid-June 10am–5.45pm; mid-June to Aug 9am–6.45pm; Sept 10am–4.45pm; Oct–April 10am–3.45pm; 40kr; Ⓦwww.fram.museum.no). Designed by Colin Archer, a Norwegian shipbuilder of Scots ancestry, and launched in 1892, the *Fram*'s design was unique, its sides made smooth to prevent ice from getting a firm grip on the hull, while inside a veritable maze of beams, braces and stanchions held it all together. Living quarters inside the ship were necessarily cramped, but – in true Edwardian style – the Norwegians found space for a piano. Look out also for the assorted knick-knacks the explorers took with them, exhibited in the display cases on the uppermost of the **three galleries** that run along the museum's walls. There are playing cards, maps, notebooks, snowshoes and surgical instruments – but this was as nothing to the equipment carted around by Scott, one of the reasons for his failure. Scott's main mistake, however, was to rely on Siberian ponies to transport his tackle. The animals were useless in Antarctic conditions and Scott and his men ended up pulling the sledges themselves, whereas Amundsen wisely brought a team of huskies.

△ The Gjøa

The Kon-Tiki Museet

Across from the Frammuseet, the **Kon-Tiki Museet** (Kon-Tiki Museum; daily: April–May & Sept 10.30am–5pm; June–Aug 9.30am–5.30pm; Oct–March 10.30am–4pm; 40kr; Ⓦwww.kon-tiki.no) displays the eponymous balsawood raft on which, in 1947, the Norwegian **Thor Heyerdahl** (1914–2002) made his famous journey across the Pacific from Peru to Polynesia. Heyerdahl wanted to prove the trip could be done: he was convinced that the first Polynesian settlers had sailed from pre-Inca Peru, and rejected prevailing opinions that South American balsa rafts were unseaworthy. Looking at the flimsy raft, you could be forgiven for agreeing with Heyerdahl's doubters – and for wondering how the crew didn't murder each other after a day, never mind several weeks in such a confined space. Heyerdahl's later investigations of Easter Island statues and cave graves lent further weight to his ethnological theory, which has now received a degree of acceptance. The whole saga is outlined here in the museum, and if you're especially interested, the story is also told in his book *The Kon-Tiki Expedition*. Preoccupied with transoceanic contact between prehistoric peoples, Heyerdahl went on to attempt several other voyages, sailing across the Atlantic in a papyrus boat, *Ra II*, in 1970, to prove that there could have been contact between Egypt and South America. *Ra II* is also displayed here and the exploit recorded in another of Heyerdahl's books, *The Ra Expeditions*.

Norsk Sjøfartsmuseum

Across from the Kon-Tiki Museet, the **Norsk Sjøfartsmuseum** (Norwegian Maritime Museum; mid-May to Aug daily 10am–6pm; Sept to mid-May Mon–Wed & Fri–Sun 10.30am–4pm, Thurs 10.30am–6pm; 40kr; Ⓦwww.norsk-sjofartsmuseum.no) occupies two buildings, the larger of which is a well-appointed, modern brick structure holding a varied collection of all things nautical. The museum's ground floor is given over to temporary exhibitions and the bulk of the permanent collection is shown on the floor above. Here, among much else, there are pinpoint-accurate ship models, a peculiar-looking fog cannon dating to 1900, a section on shipwrecks, old passenger ferry cabins, and even part of the deck of an old sailing ship from 1893. There's also the so-called **Gibraltar boat**, a perilously fragile, canvas-and-board home-made craft on which a bunch of Norwegian sailors fled Morocco for British Gibraltar after their ship had been impounded by the Vichy French authorities, and what is reputed to be the oldest surviving Norwegian boat, a **carved-out tree trunk** about two thousand years old.

The museum's second building, the **Båthallen** (boat hall), holds an extensive collection of small and medium-sized wooden boats from all over Norway, mostly inshore sailing and fishing craft from the nineteenth century. Non-sailors may find it of limited interest – and head straight for the museum's fjordside café instead.

West of the centre: the Henie-Onstad Kunstsenter

Overlooking the Oslofjord just beyond the city boundary in Høvikodden, some 15km west of the city centre, the **Henie-Onstad Kunstsenter** (Henie-Onstad Art Centre; Tues–Thurs 11am–7pm & Fri–Sun 11am–6pm; 80kr but free after 3pm on Wed; Ⓣ67 80 48 80; Ⓦwww.hok.no) is one of Norway's more prestigious modern art centres. There's no false modesty here – it's all about art as an expression of wealth – and the low-slung, modernistic building is a glossy affair on a pretty, wooded headland landscaped to accommodate a smattering of sculptures. The centre was founded by the ice-skater-cum-movie-star **Sonja Henie** (1910–69) and her shipowner-cum-art-collector husband Niels Onstad in the 1960s. Henie won three Olympic gold medals (1928, 1932 and 1936) and went on to appear in a string of lightweight Hollywood musicals. Many of her accumulated cups and medals are displayed in a room of their own, and once prompted a critic to remark: "Sonja, you'll never go broke. All you have to do is hock your trophies." In the basement are the autographed photos of many of the leading celebrities of Sonja's day – though the good wishes of a youthful-looking Richard Milhous Nixon hardly inspire empathy.

The wealthy couple accumulated an extensive collection of twentieth-century painting and sculpture. Matisse, Miró and Picasso, postwar French abstract painters, Expressionists and modern Norwegians all feature, but these now compete for gallery space with temporary exhibitions of contemporary art. It is, therefore, impossible to predict what will be on display at any one time – so call ahead for exhibition details. The centre also hosts regular concert and theatre performances.

After the museum, be sure to spend a little time wandering the surrounding sculpture park, where you'll see work by the likes of Henry Moore and Arnold Haukeland: plans of the park are available at reception.

Getting there is easy by public transport: bus #151 leaves Oslo S bus terminal every fifteen minutes or so and the journey takes about 25 minutes; you will, however, need to ask the driver to let you off – at the Høvikodden bus stop – or else you'll go whistling past. The Høvikodden stop is beside the main road about five minutes' walk from the Centre. By car, the Kunstsenter is close to – and signposted from – the **E18** road to Drammen.

Northwest of the centre: Frognerparken

The green expanse of **Frognerparken** (Frogner Park), to the northwest of the city centre, incorporates one of Oslo's most celebrated and popular cultural targets, the open-air **Vigelandsparken** which, along with the nearby museum, commemorates a modern Norwegian sculptor of world renown, **Gustav Vigeland** (1869–1943). Between them, the park and the museum display a good proportion of his work, presented to the city in return for favours received by way of a studio and apartment during the years 1921–30. The park is also home to Frogner Manor, now housing the **Oslo Bymuseum**.

Frogner Park is readily reached from the centre (two of the central tram stops are Jernbanetorget and Aker Brygge) on **tram #12**; get off at Vigelandsparken, the stop after Frogner plass.

The Vigelandsparken

A country boy, raised on a farm just outside Mandal, on the south coast, **Gustav Vigeland** began his career as a woodcarver but later, when studying in Paris, he fell under the influence of Rodin, and switched to stone and bronze. He started work on the open-air **Vigelandsparken** (daylight hours; free) in 1924, and was still working on it when he died almost twenty years later. It's a literally fantastic concoction, medieval in spirit and complexity, and it was here that Vigeland had the chance to let his imagination run riot. Indeed, when the place was unveiled, many city folk were simply overwhelmed – and no wonder. From the

Emanuel Vigeland

Gustav Vigeland enthusiasts may be interested in the work of the great man's younger and lesser-known brother, Emanuel Vigeland (1875–1948), a respected artist in his own right. His stained-glass windows can be seen in Oslo's Domkirke (see p.89), while the Emanuel Vigeland Museum (Sun only noon–4pm; 30kr; Ⓦwww.emanuelvigeland.museum.no), northwest of the city centre at Grimelundsveien 8 (T-bane #1 to Slemdal), has a collection of his frescoes, sculptures, paintings and drawings.

monumental wrought-iron gates on Kirkeveien, the central path takes you to the footbridge over the river and a world of frowning, fighting and posturing bronze figures – the local favourite is *Sinnataggen* (the angry child). Beyond, the **central fountain** is an enormous bowl representing the burden of life, supported by straining, sinewy bronze Goliaths, while underneath, water tumbles out around figures engaged in play or talk, or simply resting or standing.

Yet it's the twenty-metre-high **obelisk** up on the stepped embankment just beyond that really takes the breath away. It's a deeply humanistic work, a writhing mass of sculpture which depicts the cycle of life as Vigeland saw it: a vision of humanity playing, fighting, teaching, loving, eating and sleeping – and clambering on and over each other to reach the top. The granite sculptures grouped around the obelisk are exquisite too, especially the children, little pot-bellied figures who tumble over muscled adults, providing the perfect foil to the real Oslo toddlers who splash around in the fountain below.

The Vigeland-museet

From the obelisk, it's a ten-minute walk south across the lawns of the Frognerpark – and over the river by a second footbridge – to the **Vigeland-museet** (Vigeland Museum; June–Aug Tues–Sun 11am–5pm; Sept–May Tues–Sun noon–4pm; 45kr; Ⓦwww.vigeland.museum.no), on Halvdan Svartes gate. This was the artist's studio and home during the 1920s, built for him by the city, who let him live here rent free on condition that the building – and its contents – passed back to public ownership on his death. It's still stuffed with all sorts of items related to the sculpture park, including photographs of the workforce, discarded or unused sculptures, woodcuts, preparatory drawings, and scores of plaster casts. Vigeland was obsessed with his creations during his last decades, and you get the feeling that given half a chance he would have had himself cast and exhibited. As it is, his ashes were placed in the museum tower.

The Oslo Bymuseum

A couple of hundred metres north of the Vigeland-museet, the mildly diverting **Oslo Bymuseum** (City Museum; Tues noon–7pm & Wed–Sun noon–4pm; 50kr; Ⓦwww.oslobymuseum.no) is housed in the expansive, eighteenth-century **Frogner Manor**. The buildings are actually rather more interesting than the museum: a central courtyard is bounded on one side by the half-timbered Manor House, complete with its appealing clock tower, and by antique agricultural buildings on the other three. The **museum** is in one of the latter – the renovated old barn – and it holds a sequence of thematic displays exploring the history of the city. Amongst many, there are sections on prisons, kitchens, the fire brigade and the police, but it's the paintings and photos of old Oslo and its people that catch the eye.

The museum has its own **café**, but the park's *Frognerparkens Café*, between the Bymuseum and the Vigelandsparken, is much better.

North of the centre: the Nordmarka

Crisscrossed by **hiking trails** and **cross-country ski routes**, the forested hills and lakes that comprise the **Nordmarka** occupy a tract of land that extends deep inland from central Oslo – but is still within the city limits for some 30km. A network of byroads provides dozens of access points to this wilderness, which is extremely popular with the capital's outdoor-minded citizens. **Den Norske Turistforening** (DNT), the Norwegian hiking organization, maintains a handful of staffed and unstaffed huts here. Its Oslo branch, in the city centre at **Storgata 7** (Mon–Fri 10am–5pm, Thurs 10am–6pm, Sat 10am–2pm; Ⓣ22 82 28 22; Ⓦwww.dntoslo.no), has detailed **maps** and can sell a year's DNT membership for 545kr, which confers a substantial discount at its huts; see the Hiking colour section for more on DNT and hiking in general.

Frognerseteren and Holmenkollen

T-bane #1 delves deep into the Nordmarka, wriggling its way up into the hills to the **Frognerseteren terminus**, a thirty-minute ride north of the city centre. From the station, there's a choice of signposted trails across the surrounding countryside. The easiest is the squelchy 2.5-kilometre stroll to the **Tryvannstårnet TV Tower** (daily: May & Sept 10am–5pm; June 10am–6pm; July & Aug 10am–8pm; Oct–April 10am–4pm; 40kr), where a lift whisks you up to an observation platform. From here, there are panoramic views over to the Swedish border in the east, Oslo to the south and the forested hills of the Gudbrandsdal valley to the north. Labels inside the platform show where everything is, but it's not worth going up unless the weather is clear as even a light mist obscures the view. Alternatively, it's just a couple of hundred metres from the T-bane terminus to **Frognerseteren** (café: Mon–Sat 10.30am–10.30pm, Sun 10.30am–9pm; restaurant daily noon–9pm; Ⓣ22 92 40 40), a large and good-looking wooden lodge, where the views from the terrace out over Oslo and the Oslofjord are more enjoyable than the café food.

Forest footpaths link Frognerseteren with Sognsvannet to the east (see opposite), an arduous and not especially rewarding trek over the hills of about 5km. Locals mostly shun this route in summer, but it's really popular in winter with parents teaching their children to cross-country ski. There is a longer and more interesting hiking route to Sognsvannet via **Ullevålseter**, where the lodge (Tues–Fri 9am–4pm, Sat & Sun 9am–5pm; Ⓣ22 14 35 58) has a very good café serving excellent home-made applecake. The whole route is about 9km long, and takes about 3 hours.

Alternatively, you can hop back on the T-bane for the five-stop journey back down the line to the flashy chalets and hotels of the **Holmenkollen ski resort**, whose main claim to fame is its international **ski-jump** – a gargantuan affair that dwarfs its surroundings; it is located 1km or so from the T-bane station. At the base of the ski-jump, the diligent **Skimuseet** (Ski Museum; daily: Jan–April & Oct–Dec 10am–4pm; May & Sept 10am–5pm; June–Aug 9am–8pm; 60kr) exhibits skiing apparel and equipment through the ages, from the latest in competition wear to the seemingly makeshift garb of early polar explorers like Nansen and Amundsen. The museum also gives access to the mountain of metal steps that leads up the **ski-jump** for a peek straight down at what is, for most people, a horrifyingly steep, almost vertical, descent. It seems impossible that the tiny bowl at the bottom could pull the skier up in time – or that anyone could possibly want to jump off in the first place. The bowl is also the finishing point for the 8000-strong cross-country skiing race that forms part of the Holmenkollrennene ski festival every March.

From Holmenkollen T-bane station (line #1), it's a 20-minute ride back to central Oslo.

Sognsvannet

It takes fifteen minutes for T-bane #3 to reach its northerly **Sognsvann terminus** from central Oslo. It's not as pleasant a journey as the T-bane trip to Frognerseteren (see opposite) – the landscape is flatter and you never really leave the city behind – but from the T-bane station, it's just five minutes' walk straight ahead down the slope to **Sognsvannet**, an attractive loch flanked by forested hills and encircled by an easy four-kilometre hiking trail. The lake is iced over until the end of March or early April, but thereafter it's a perfect spot for swimming, though Norwegian assurances about the warmth of the water should be treated with caution. Forest footpaths link Sognsvannet with Frognerseteren (see opposite).

Northeast of the centre: the Munch-museet

Nearly everyone who visits Oslo makes time for the **Munch-museet** (Munch Museum) – and with good reason. In his will, Munch donated all the works in his possession to Oslo city council – a mighty bequest of several thousand

Edvard Munch

Born in 1863, Edvard Munch had a melancholy childhood in what was then Christiania (Oslo), overshadowed by the early deaths of both his mother and a sister from tuberculosis, not to mention the fierce Christian piety of his father. After some early works, including several self-portraits, he went on to study in Paris, a city he returned to again and again, and where he fell (fleetingly) under the sway of the Impressionists in general and Gauguin in particular, responding to his simplified forms and non-naturalistic colours. In 1892 he moved to Berlin, where his style developed and he produced some of his best and most famous work, though his first exhibition there was considered so outrageous it was closed after only a week – his painting was, a critic opined, "an insult to art": his recurrent themes, notably jealousy, sickness, alienation and the awakening of sexual desire, all of which he had extrapolated from his childhood, were simply too much for his early audience. Despite the initial criticism, Munch's work was subsequently exhibited in many of the leading galleries of the day. Generally considered the initiator of the Expressionist movement, Munch wandered Europe, painting and exhibiting prolifically. Meanwhile overwork, drink and problematic love affairs were fuelling an instability that culminated, in 1908, in a nervous breakdown. Munch spent six months in a Copenhagen clinic, after which his health improved greatly – and his paintings lost the hysterical edge characteristic of his most celebrated work – though he never dismissed the importance of his mental frailness to his art, writing, for example, "I would not cast off my illness, for there is much in my art that I owe to it". It wasn't until well into his career, however, that he was fully accepted in his own country, where he was based from 1909 until his death in 1944.

paintings, prints, drawings, engravings and photographs, which took nearly twenty years to catalogue and organize before being displayed in this purpose-built gallery. The museum has, however, had its problems: in August 2004, two armed **robbers** marched into the museum and, in full view of dozens of bemused visitors, lifted two Munch paintings – the *Madonna* and *The Scream*, his most famous work, though fortunately Munch painted several versions (the first is in the Nasjonalgalleriet, see p.96). As if this wasn't bad enough, further embarrassments followed: it turned out that the paintings were not alarmed and neither were they especially secure, only being attached to the wall by a cord. As of yet, the paintings have not been recovered – though arrests have been made – and, in a classic case of closing the stable door after the horse has bolted, the gallery has beefed up its security.

The museum itself (June–Aug daily 10am–6pm; Sept–May Tues–Fri 10am–4pm, Sat & Sun 11am–5pm; 65kr; Ⓦ www.munch.museum.no) is located to the northeast of the city centre in the workaday suburb of Tøyen, at Tøyengata 53. Getting there by public transport couldn't be easier: take the T-bane to Tøyen station and it's a signposted, five-minute walk.

The collection

The Munch-museet's **permanent collection** is huge, and only a small – but always significant – part can be shown at any one time. Consequently, the paintings are frequently rotated and the permanent collection also sources a lively programme of temporary exhibitions concentrating on various aspects of Munch's work. Naturally, all this means that you can't be certain what will be displayed and when, but the key paintings mentioned below are almost bound to be on view.

The landscapes and domestic scenes of Munch's **early paintings**, such as *Tête à Tête* and *At the Coffee Table*, reveal the perceptive if deeply pessimistic realism from which Munch's later work sprang. Even more riveting are the great works of the **1890s**, which form the core of the collection and are considered Munch's finest achievements. Among many there's *Dagny Juel*, a portrait of the Berlin socialite Ducha Przybyszewska, with whom both Munch and Strindberg were infatuated; the searing representations of *Despair* and *Anxiety*; the chilling *Red Virginia Creeper*, a house being consumed by the plant; and, of course, *The Scream* – of which the museum still holds several versions (see above).

Munch's style was never static, however. **Later paintings** such as *Workers On Their Way Home* (1913), produced after he had recovered from his breakdown and had withdrawn to the tranquillity of the Oslofjord, reflect his renewed interest in nature and physical work. His technique also changed: in works like the *Death of Marat II* (1907) he began to use streaks of colour to represent points of light. Later still, paintings such as *Winter in Kragerø* and *Model by the Wicker Chair*, with skin tones of pink, green and blue, begin to reveal a happier, if rather idealized, attitude to his surroundings, though this is most evident in works like *Spring Ploughing*, painted in 1919.

Look out also for Munch's **self-portraits**, which provide a graphic illustration of the artist's state of mind at various points in his career. There's a palpable sadness in his *Self-Portrait with Wine Bottle* (1906), along with obvious allusions to his heavy drinking, while the telling perturbation of *In Distress* (1919) and *The Night Wanderer* (1923) indicates that he remained a tormented, troubled man even in his later years. One of his last works, *Self-Portrait by the Window* (1940), shows a glum figure on the borderline between life and death, the strong red of his face and green of his clothing contrasted with the ice-white scene visible through the window.

Munch's **lithographs and woodcuts**, of which the museum owns several hundred, are a dark catalogue of swirls and fogs, technically brilliant pieces of work and often developments of his paintings rather than just simple copies. In these he pioneered a new medium of expression, experimenting with colour schemes and a huge variety of materials, which enhance the works' rawness: wood blocks show a heavy, distinct grain, while there are colours like rust and blue drawn from the Norwegian landscape. As well as the stark woodcuts on display, there are also sensuous, hand-coloured lithographs, many focusing on the theme of love (taking the form of a woman) bringing death.

East of the centre: medieval Oslo and prehistoric rock carvings

Founded in the middle of the eleventh century by Harald Hardrada, **medieval Oslo** lay tucked beneath the Ekeberg heights at the mouth of the River Alna, some 3km round the fjord to the east of today's city centre. The old town, which had a population of around 3000 by the early fourteenth century, had two palaces – one for the bishop and one for the king – reflecting the uneasy division of responsibility that dogged its history. The settlement was also plagued by fires, which ripped through the wooden buildings with depressing regularity. After one such conflagration in 1624, **Christian IV** moved the city to its modern location, widening the streets to combat the fire danger, and what remained of old Oslo became an insignificant outpost. In successive centuries the traces of the medieval town were almost entirely obliterated, and only recently has there been any attempt to identify the original layout of what is commonly called the **Gamlebyen** (Old Town). There are precious few fragments to see, but they're just about worth seeking out when combined with a peek at a group of nearby prehistoric **rock carvings**.

The rock carvings

From Jernbanetorget, it's a ten-minute tram ride (#18 or #19) east up to the old **Sjømannsskolen** (Merchant Marine Academy) – now a business school – housed in a large and conspicuous building perched high on a hill. The tram stops opposite the academy, whose fjord-facing terrace offers some of the most extensive views in Oslo, stretching all the way across the inner reaches of the Oslofjord to the Holmenkollen ski-jump. To the rear of the academy, a narrow drive – Karlsborgveien – leads downhill into a little dell. Here, a few metres down on the left-hand side, you'll spot a group of faded ochre **rock carvings** depicting elk, deer and matchstick people, around 6000 years old and the earliest evidence of settlement along the Oslofjord.

The Gamlebyen

Walking back down from the academy along Kongsveien and then Oslo gate, it takes about fifteen minutes to reach the junction of Bispegata at the heart of the **Gamlebyen**. On the corner, at Oslo gate 13, is the **Ladegård**, a comely eighteenth-century mansion built on the site of the thirteenth-century Bishop's Palace, whose foundations are underneath. On the other side of Oslo gate are the battered foundations of both St Hallvardskatedralen (St Halvard's Cathedral) and St Olavsklosteret (St Olav's Monastery) behind.

South of the centre: the islands and beaches of the inner Oslofjord

The compact archipelago of low-lying, lightly forested **islands** to the south of the city centre in the **inner Oslofjord** is the capital's summer playground, and makes going to the **beach** a viable option, especially on warm summer evenings when the less populated islands become favourite party venues for the city's youth. **Ferries** to the islands leave from the Vippetangen quay, at the foot of Akershusstranda – a twenty-minute walk or a five-minute ride on bus #60 from Jernbanetorget. Ferry tickets cost 20kr each way, though Oslo Pass and all other transport passes are valid and there's also a ferry day-pass allowing unlimited inter-island travel for 36kr.

Hovedøya and Langøyene

Conveniently, **Hovedøya** (ferry #92; daily mid-March to Sept 7.30am–6.30pm, every hour to ninety minutes; Oct to mid-March 4 daily; 10min), the nearest island, is also the most interesting. Its rolling hills comprise both farmland and deciduous woods as well as the overgrown ruins of a **Cistercian monastery** built by English monks in the twelfth century. There are also incidental remains from the days when the island was garrisoned and armed to protect Oslo's harbour. A map of the island at the jetty helps with orientation, but on an islet of this size – it's just ten minutes' walk from one end to the other – getting lost is pretty much impossible. There are plenty of footpaths to wander, you can swim at the shingle beaches on the south shore, and there's a seasonal café opposite the monastery ruins. Camping, however, is not permitted as Hovedøya is a protected area, which is also why there are no summer homes.

The pick of the other islands is **Langøyene**, a pint-sized, H-shaped islet, just ten minutes' walk or so from one side to the other, where a central meadow is flanked on either side by low, lightly forested rocky hills. There are no houses on the island and no roads to speak of, but there is a campsite (see p.88), a rudimentary café and a long and narrow sandy(ish) beach – though most visitors bring their supplies with them. To get to Langøyene, take ferry #94 (late May to Aug hourly 9am–7/8pm; 15min) from the Vippetangen quay.

Eating and drinking

There was a time when eating out in Oslo hardly set the pulse racing, but things are very different today. At the top end of the market, the city possesses dozens of fine **restaurants**, the pick of which feature Norwegian ingredients, especially fresh North Atlantic fish, but also more exotic dishes of elk, caribou and salted-and-dried cod – for centuries Norway's staple food. Many of these restaurants have also assimilated the tastes and **styles** of other cuisines and there is a reasonable selection of less expensive foreign restaurants too, everything from Italian to Vietnamese.

Even more affordable – and more casual – are the city's **cafés, coffee houses** and **café-bars**. These run the gamut from homely family places, offering traditional Norwegian stand-bys, to student haunts and ultra-trendy joints. Nearly all serve inexpensive lunches, and many offer excellent, competitively priced evening meals as well, though many cafés and coffee houses close. In addition,

△ Oslo café

downtown Oslo boasts a vibrant **bar** scene, boisterous but generally good-natured and at its most frenetic on summer weekends, when the city is crowded with visitors from all over Norway.

Finally, those carefully counting the kroner will find it easy to buy bread, fruit, snacks and sandwiches from stalls, supermarkets and kiosks across the city centre, while fast-food joints offering hamburgers and *pølser* (hot dogs) are legion. **Smoking** is forbidden in every Norwegian bar, café and restaurant.

Cafés, coffee houses and café-bars

For sit-down food, **cafés** represent the best value in town. Traditional *kafeterias* (often self-service) offer substantial portions of Norwegian food in pleasant surroundings as most are decorated in crisp, modern styles. Oslo also has a slew of **café-bars** dishing up salads, pasta and the like in attractive, often modish premises. The best deals are generally at lunchtime, when there's usually a dish of the day. In addition, Oslo now contains dozens of specialist **coffee houses**, both independent and chains – not that you should notice too much difference.

As for **opening hours**, most of the cafés listed below close between 5pm and 7pm, while the café-bars stay open much later, till midnight and often beyond. The coffee houses tend to close between 5pm and 7pm on weekdays, and around 5pm at weekends, though many are closed on Sundays altogether.

Central

Café Tekehtopa St Olavs plass 2. Known to all and sundry as *Apotheket*, this good-looking old building used to be a pharmacy, and has retained its high ceilings and old wooden fittings. It's now a very recommendable café-bar serving a wide range of food from omelettes and pizzas to tapas and meze, all washed down by a varied range of beers. Prices are very competitive, with omelettes, for example, costing 90kr, pizzas 100kr. Open Mon–Thurs 10am–1am, Fri 10am–3am, Sat noon–3am & Sun noon–1am; kitchen closes at 10pm.

Celsius Café Rådhusgata 19. Smashing café-bar occupying imaginatively

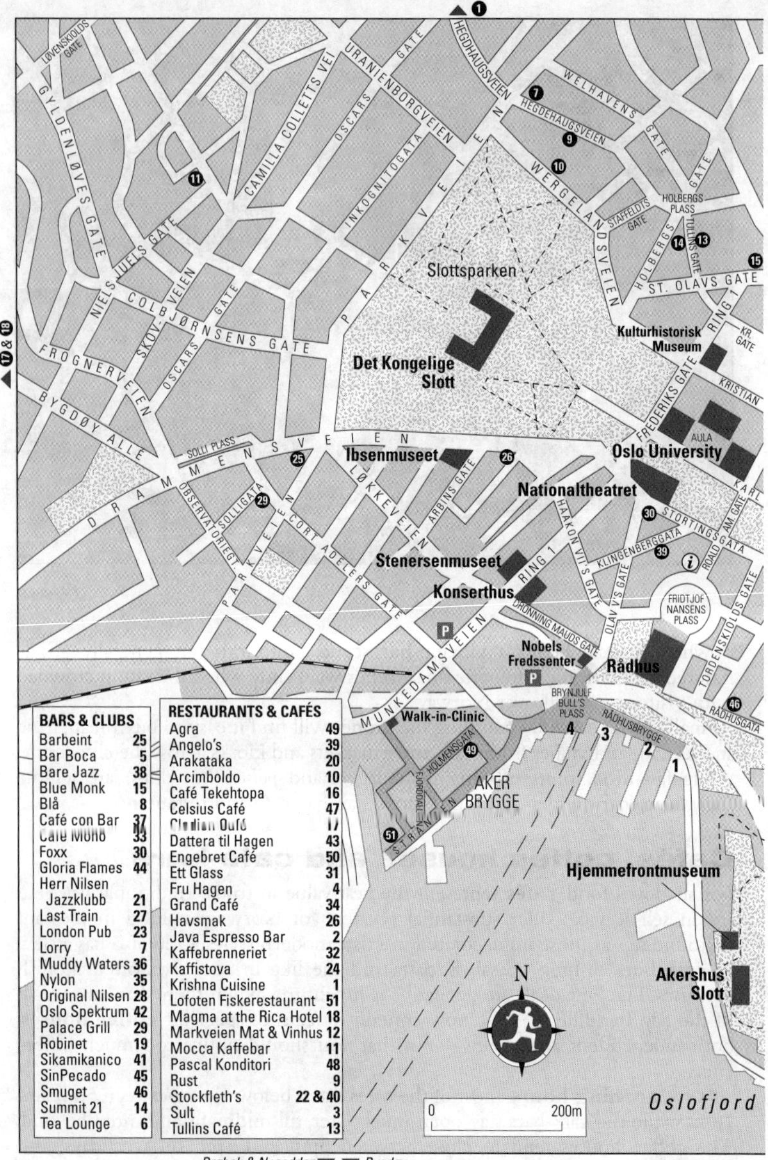

refurbished old premises just off the cobbled square at the junction of Rådhusgata and Nedre Slottsgate. Especially attractive courtyard seating too – for either a drink or a light meal: the menu is strong on chicken and seafood, with Caesar salad and chicken, for instance, costing 140kr. Daily 11am–midnight.

Ett Glass Karl Johans gate 33, but entrance round the corner on Rosenkrantz gate. Youthful, lively café-bar with an imaginative albeit short menu focusing on Mediterranean-influenced light meals and lunches with main courses around 90kr. Mon–Thurs & Sun 11.30am–12.30am, Fri–Sat noon–2.30am; kitchen closes at 10pm.

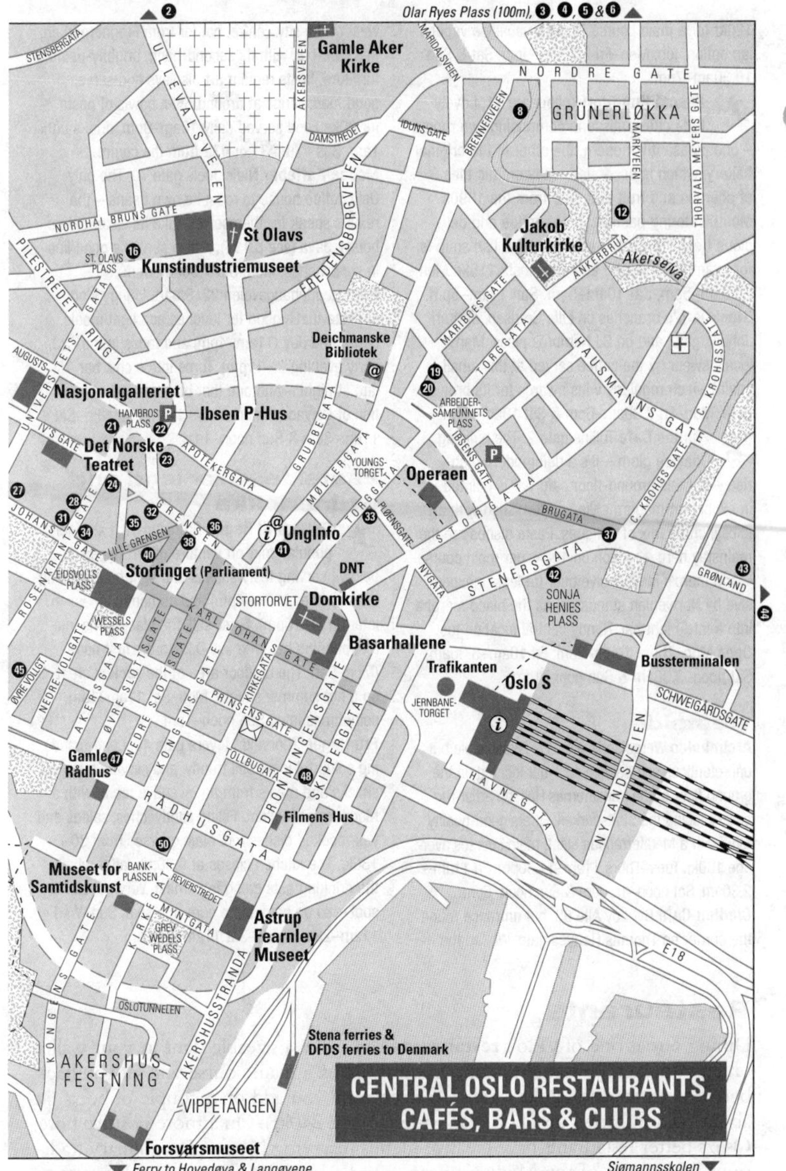

Java Espresso Bar Ullevålsveien 45B, St Hanshaugen district. Coffee connoisseur's paradise patronized by Norwegian royals, but without the corresponding pomp. Delicious sandwiches too. Mon–Fri 8am–6pm & Sat 9am–5pm.

Kaffebrenneriet 45 Grensen at Akersgata. One of the most central branches of the popular Norwegian coffee house chain. Serves particularly good espressos, as well as tasty snacks and great cakes. Bright, modern decor. Mon–Fri 7am–7pm, Sat 9am–5pm.

Kaffistova Rosenkrantz gate 8. Part of the *Hotell Bondeheimen* (see p.86), this spick-and-span self-service café serves quite tasty, traditional Norwegian cooking at very fair prices – reckon on

120kr for a main course. There's usually a vegetarian option, too. Mon–Fri 9.30am–9pm, Sat & Sun 10.30am–7pm.

Pascal Konditori Tollbugata 11. Lovely little café-patisserie comprising two rooms – one pleasantly modern, the other in the original bakery, which is decorated with ceramic tiles of cherubs and fruit that date from the 1890s. Mouthwatering pastries, great coffee and delicious freshly prepared lunches – the fish soup is, for example, first-rate and only costs 115kr. Mon–Fri 9am–5pm, Sat 10am–5pm, Sun 11am–5pm.

Stockfleth's branches on Lille Grensen, off Karl Johans gate, and on CJ Hambros plass. Many locals swear by the coffee served at this small chain, which regularly wins awards for its brews. Both: Mon–Fri 7.30am–6pm & Sat 10am–5pm.

Tullins Café Tullins gate 2. The building may be glum – it's a dull modern high-rise – but this ground-floor café-bar is painted in exuberant modern style and furnished with an idiosyncratic mix of antiques. Pasta dishes are the mainstay here – reckon on 100kr per main course – and there's inexpensive beer (at least inexpensive by Norwegian standards) as the place morphs into a late-night bar. Handy central location too. Open Mon–Thurs 10am–2am, Fri 10am–3.30am, Sat noon–3.30am & Sun noon–1am.

Westside

Arcimboldo Wergelandsveien 17. Fashionable but unpretentious self-service café-bar located on the ground floor of the Kunstnernes Hus, an artist-run gallery facing the Slottsparken. Offers good-quality food with a Mediterranean slant; main courses average 160kr. Tues–Thurs 11am–11.30pm, Fri 11am–2.30am, Sat noon–1.30am & Sun noon–5pm.

Clodion Café Bygdøy Allé 63, but entrance round the corner on Thomas Heftyes gate. Well to the west of the city centre, not far from Frognerparken, this café-bar, with its second-hand, brightly-painted furniture, hosts regular art displays and serves good food: soups at around 55kr, bowls of pasta for 80kr. Food served daily 10am–9pm, drinks until 1am. Bus #30, #31 or #32 from the centre.

Mocca Kaffebar Niels Juels gate 70. The only Oslo coffee house to roast its own beans – the results speak for themselves. Like its sister coffee house, Java (see p.117), it also serves a good line in sandwiches. Mon–Sat 7.30am–5pm.

Rust Hegdehaugsveien 22. Smart, loungy kind of place that's good for lunches and light meals during the day (11am–4pm) and tapas in the early evening (4–11pm). Turns into a chic bar late at night – and one that boasts a fine selection of Calvados. Mon–Thurs 11am–1am, Fri–Sat 11am–3am & Sun noon–1am.

Eastside: Grønland and Grünerløkka

Dattera til Hagen Grønland 10. Extremely popular spin-off venture of *Fru Hagen* (see below), serving tasty snacks and light meals during the daytime (11am–4pm) and authentic tapas later on (4–10pm). Later still, the place turns into a happening bar with live DJs on the first floor (Mon–Sat). The outdoor area at the back is great on a hot summer's night. Mon–Sat 11am–1am, sometimes later. Sun noon–1am.

Fru Hagen Thorvald Meyers gate 40. Long-standing colourful joint; still trendy, and serving tasty snacks and meals from an inventive menu with a Mediterranean slant. Filling sandwiches, salads and wok-cooked dishes too. Main courses from 80–130kr. The kitchen closes at 9.30pm, after which the drinking gets going in earnest. Very popular spot – so go early to be sure of a seat. Sun–Wed 11am–2am, Thurs–Sat 11am–3.30am.

Restaurants

Dining out at one of Oslo's **restaurants** can make a sizeable dent in your wallet unless you exercise some restraint. In most places, a main course will set you back between 150kr and 220kr – not too steep until you add on a couple of beers (at about 50kr a throw) or a bottle of wine (at least 240kr). On a more positive note, Oslo's better restaurants have creative menus marrying Norwegian culinary traditions with those of the Mediterranean – and a lousy meal is a rarity. Restaurant decor is often a real feature too, ranging from fishing photos and nets to sharp modernist styles, all pastel walls and angular furnishings and fittings. Advance **reservations** are a good idea almost everywhere, especially at the weekend.

Central

Agra Stranden 3, Aker Brygge ⓣ22 83 07 12. Smart north Indian restaurant serving all the classics – chicken tikka and so forth – with main courses averaging 210–250kr. Decorated in traditional style, from the Moghul decorative arches to the deep-red tiles of the ceiling. The only problem is that it is a little difficult to find: take the first right – Grundigen – off the Aker Brygge boardwalk, take a left at the end and you are there. Mon–Sat 4–11pm, Sun 2–10pm.

Angelo's Klingenberggaten 4 ⓣ22 82 86 50. Mon–Sat noon–11pm & Sun 3–11pm. Pleasingly old-fashioned Italian joint with rustic beams and artificial ivy on the ceiling. The food is not especially inspiring, but the service is fast and the food very competently prepared with a wide range of large and tasty shallow-crust pizzas for 110–130kr – something of a snip in central Oslo.

Arakataka Mariboes gate 7 ⓣ23 32 83 00. This smart, modern bar and restaurant serves outstanding food, mostly fish, at unbeatable prices, both à la carte (mains average 180kr) and with a set three-course menu for just 280kr. Highly recommended, though the service can be a tad patchy. A 15-minute walk north of the Domkirke on the way to Grünerløkka. Sun–Thurs 4pm to midnight, Fri–Sat 4pm–3am.

Engebret Café Bankplassen 1 ⓣ22 82 25 25. Across from the Museum of Contemporary Art, this smart and fairly formal restaurant occupies a fetching old building with oodles of wood panelling and old oil paintings on the wall. Specializes in Norwegian delicacies such as reindeer and fish, with mouthwatering main courses in the region of 250–350kr, less at lunchtime. Reservations advised. In summer, there's seating outside on the pretty cobbled square. Mon–Fri 11am–11pm, Sat noon–11pm.

Havsmak Drammensveien 4 ⓣ24 13 38 00. Smart, specialist seafood restaurant kitted out in cool modern style – and oodles of blue paint. First-rate range of fresh fish, albeit of minimalist portions, with main courses averaging 200kr. Mon–Thurs 11am–1am, Fri & Sat 11am–2am & Sun noon–10pm.

Lofoten Fiskerestaurant Stranden 75, Aker Brygge ⓣ22 83 08 08. This smart, modern restaurant offers an outstanding selection of fish and shellfish, all immaculately prepared and served. It's located beside the harbour at the far end of the Aker Bryyge jetty, which makes it popular with locals and tourists alike. Mains kick off at around 170kr, but some of the more unusual fish – including the wonderfully textured cat fish (steinbit) cost another 90kr or so. Mon–Sat 11am–1am & Sun noon–midnight.

Westside

Krishna Cuisine Kirkeveien 59B ⓣ22 60 62 50. Always tasty and filling, the dagens rett (daily special) here at what is generally considered the best vegetarian joint in the city costs 90kr. Just east of Bogstadveien and the briefest of walks from the Majorstuen T-bane station. Mon–Sat noon–8pm.

Magma at the Rica Hotel Bygdøy Allé Bygdøy allé 53 ⓣ23 08 58 10. Chic and expensive first-floor restaurant, run by one of Norway's most high-profile chefs, Sonja Lee. The restaurant's inventive international menu is based on French and north Italian cuisine. Main courses come in at around 200–250kr in the evening, 50kr or so less at lunchtimes, and are worth every kroner. To get there from the city centre, take bus #30, #31 or #32 from Oslo S or the Nationaltheatret. Open Mon–Sat 11am–2.30pm & 6–10.30pm; Sun 11am–5pm & 6–9.30pm. There is a bar too, open daily from 11am.

Grønland and Grünerløkka

Markveien Mat & Vinhus Torvbakkgata 12, Grünerløkka ⓣ22 37 22 97. This popular, top-quality restaurant and wine bar serves up Mediterranean-inspired dishes as well as traditional Norwegian favourites. Main courses average 220–250kr in the restaurant, half that in the wine bar, and the service is excellent. Also boasts one of the best wine cellars in the city. The entrance is on Markveien. Restaurant: Mon–Sat 5pm–12.30am, but kitchen closes at 11pm; wine bar Mon–Sat 4pm–1am.

Sult Thorvald Meyers gate 26, Grünerløkka ⓣ22 87 04 67. One of the city's most popular restaurants – called "Hunger" after the novel by Knut Hamsun – the informal and very relaxed *Sult* features a short but inventive menu using only the freshest of (local) ingredients. Main courses cost 170–200kr and star such delights as Hardanger trout and chicken from Stange. If that wasn't enough attraction, the adjacent bar *Tørst* (Thirst) serves mouthwatering margaritas. *Sult* kitchen open Tues–Thurs 4–10pm, Fri 4–11pm, Sat 1–11pm & Sun 1–10pm.

Bars

Bar-hopping in Oslo is an enjoyable affair. The more mainstream (meat-market) bars are in the centre along and around Karl Johans gate, while the sharper, more alternative spots are concentrated to the east in the Grønland and Grünerløkka districts. The westside of the city has its chic spots too, mostly along and around Hegdehaugsveien and Bogstadveien. Most city bars stay **open**

until around 1am on weekdays, often 3–4am on the weekend, and almost all of them are open daily. Drinks are uniformly expensive, so if you're after a big night out, it's a good idea to follow Norwegian custom and have a few warm-up drinks at home before you set out (*vorspiel* in Norwegian). A number of bars feature **live music**, blurring the lines between the "bars" listed here and the "clubs" listed opposite.

Central

Foxx Olavs gate 2. Owned by the Hotel Continental (see p.86), this bright and lively sidewalk bar is popular with the young(ish) and well-heeled. Mon–Fri 7.30am–midnight, Sat 10am–midnight & Sun noon–midnight.

Nylon Arbeidergata 2. Small and crowded basement bar with rock the musical big deal. Daily 9pm–3am.

Summit 21 Holbergs gate 30. On top of the *Radisson SAS Scandinavia Hotel*, this bar-lounge looks like the interior of a cruiseship in a groovy sort of way – and you can't fault the panoramic views over the city. Open daily until 3am.

Westside

Barbeint Drammensveien 20, close to Parkveien. If you're familiar with Scandinavian bands and films, you may recognize a few faces in this jam-packed, infinitely groovy bar with heavy drapes and mystery-making decor. Loud sounds – everything from rap to rock. Daily 8pm–3.30am.

Lorry Parkveien 12. Popular and enjoyable bar with old-fashioned fittings and attracting a mixed crowd. There's a wide choice of beers – well over one hundred – and outdoor seating in the summer. At the corner of Hegdehaugsveien. Mon–Sat 11am–3.30am, Sun noon–1.30am.

Palace Grill Solligata 2. Popular New Age-meets-alternative café-bar with a roots, rock and jazz soundtrack. Good food too. Mon 5pm–12.30am, Tues–Sat 5pm–3am & Sun 5pm–12.30am. In summertime, there's an outside bar, *Skaugum*, in the yard behind and beside the Palace – and it heaves.

Eastside: Grønland and Grünerløkka

Bar Boca Thorvald Meyers gate 30. Tiny 1950s retro-style bar serving the best cocktails in town. The bartenders take their work very seriously, and you need to get there early to avoid the crush. Live jazz once or twice weekly. Daily noon–3am.

Café con Bar Brugata 11. Hip-as-you-like with retro interior and a long bar that can make buying a drink hard work. Good atmosphere, loungy decor and unisex toilets for those surprise meetings. Mon–Sat 11am–3.30am.

Gloria Flames Grønland 18 ⓣ22 17 16 00, ⓦwww.gloriaflames.no. Not the easiest bar-cum-club to find – there's just a small sign on the door – but worth searching out if you're into rock and rockabilly. Regular live acts and a summer rooftop bar. Daily 4pm–3am.

Robinet Mariboes gate 7. Possibly the smallest bar in Oslo – 1950s retro kitsch combined with excellent drinks and an intellectual crowd. Daily noon–2am.

Tea Lounge Thorvald Meyers gate 33B. Lounge-type café-bar with velvety red couches and big windows. As you might guess from the name, tea is a big deal here – all sorts and served to a soft house backtrack. Cocktails also. Mon–Wed 11am–1am, Thurs–Sat 11am–3pm & Sun noon–1am.

Entertainment and nightlife

With the city's bars staying open till the wee hours, Oslo's **nightclubs** struggle to make themselves heard – indeed there's often little distinction between the two – though there is still a reasonably good and varied nightclub scene. **Live music** is not perhaps Oslo's forte, and the domestic **rock** scene is far from inspiring, but **jazz** fans are well served, with several first-rate venues dotted round the city centre, and **classical music** enthusiasts benefit from an ambitious concert programme. Most **theatre** productions are in Norwegian, but English-language theatre companies visit often, and at the **cinema** films are shown in the original language with Norwegian subtitles.

For **entertainment listings** it's worth checking out *Natt & Dag* (ⓦwww.nattogdag.no), a Norwegian-language, bi-monthly broadsheet that carries thorough listings and reviews; it's available free from downtown cafés, bars, some shops and the tourist office. The main alternative is *What's On in Oslo*, a monthly English-language freebie produced by the tourist office. One other useful free publication is *Streetwise*, which is produced annually by Use-It, the city's youth information shop (see p.83); it carries descriptions of – amongst much else – the city's best bars and clubs.

For **tickets**, contact the venue direct or try Billettservice (Ⓣ815 33 133, Ⓦwww.billettservice.no), who have an outlet in the Oslo Konserthus, Munkedamsveien 14, and employ the city's larger post offices as agents.

Nightclubs and live music

Oslo's hippest bars and **nightclubs** are located on the east side of the city, away from the centre in or near the Grønland and Grünerløkka districts, but there are also several clubs in the centre. Generally speaking, entry will set you back in the region of 100kr, and, surprisingly enough, drink prices are the same as anywhere else. Nothing gets going much before 11pm; closing times are generally around 3.30am. Many of the clubs also host a variety of **live music**, ranging from local home-grown talent to the big-name bands – check *Natt & Dag* (see opposite) for gigs.

Blå Brenneriveien 9C Ⓣ22 20 91 81, Ⓦwww.blx.no. Creative, cultural nightspot in Grünerløkka, featuring everything from live jazz and cabaret through to poetry readings. Also features some of the best DJs in town, keeping the crowd moving until 3.30am at the weekend. In summer, there's a pleasant riverside terrace too.

Blue Monk St Olavs gate 23 Ⓦwww.clubbluemonk.no. Crowded, earthy nightspot noted for its eclectic programme of live music, from blues through to Estonian funk. In the centre at the corner of Pilestredet.

Café Mono Pløens gate 4 Ⓣ22 41 41 66, Ⓦwww.cafemono.no. Darkly lit bar with retro fixtures and fittings that attracts a student crowd, who appreciate the live, mainly indie acts on several nights a week; diverse DJ sounds, too. Pløens gate is off Torggata, north of Oslo S. Mon–Sat 3pm–3am, Sun 6pm–3am.

Last Train Karl Johans Gate 45 Ⓣ22 41 52 93, Ⓦwww.lasttrain.no. The best rock-pub/club in town. Good old-style rock played at volume to a leather and jeans clientele. Entrance downtown on Universitetsgata. Mon–Fri 3pm–3.30am, Sat 6pm–3.30am.

Muddy Waters Grensen 13 Ⓣ22 40 33 70, Ⓦwww.muddywaters.no. Deep and dark bar with a (mostly) older clientele attracted by an excellent range of blues and R&B acts – the best in town – both imported and domestic. Fantabulous

Music festivals

Big-name rock bands often include Oslo on their tours, leavening what would otherwise be a pretty dull scene. The most prestigious annual event is Norwegian Wood (Ⓣ815 33 133, Ⓦwww.norwegianwood.no), a four-day open-air rock festival held in June in the outdoor amphitheatre at Frogner Park, a ten-minute ride from the city centre on tram #12. Previous years have attracted the likes of Iggy Pop, Lou Reed, the Kinks and Van Morrison, and the festival continues to pull in some of the best international artists, supported by a variety of Norwegian acts. The arena holds around six thousand people, but tickets, costing around 400kr per day, sell out well in advance.

Oslo also hosts the more contemporary Øyafestivalen (Ⓦwww.oyafestivalen.com), a four-day event that showcases a wide range of artists, mostly Norwegian but with some imports too – 2005, for example, included Babyshambles and Diskaholics Anonymous. A club night traditionally kicks the whole thing off in style. The festival takes place in the middle of August in the open air in Middelalderparken – about 10min by tram #18 from Jernbanetorget.

collection of blues and R&B CDs too. Daily 2pm–1am.

Oslo Spektrum Sonja Henies plass 2 ⓣ815 11 211, ⓦwww.oslospektrum.no. Major venue, close to Olso S, showcasing big international acts, as well as small-fry local bands.

Sikamikanico Møllergata 2 ⓣ22 41 44 09. ⓦwww.sikamikanico. Hip hop, drum and bass, jazz and house in heaving club near Oslo S. Great DJ nights too. Wed–Sun from 9pm.

Smuget Rosenkrantz gate 22 ⓣ22 42 52 62, ⓦwww.smuget.no. Large, long-established and still popular city-centre nightclub with bars, a disco and regular live acts, mostly by home-grown rock or blues bands.

Jazz venues

Oslo has a strong **jazz** tradition, and in early or mid-August its week-long **Jazz Festival** attracts internationally renowned artists as well as showcasing local talent. The Festival Office, at Tollbugata 28 (ⓣ22 42 91 20 ⓦwww.oslojazz.no), has full programme details of all the gigs, including those where there's an admission charge as well as the many free outdoor performances. At other times of the year, try one of the following for regular jazz acts.

Bare Jazz Grensen 8 ⓣ22 33 20 80, ⓦwww.barejazz.no. Split-level joint with a superb selection of jazz CDs for sale on the ground floor and a jazz café up above with frequent live sounds, both homegrown and imported. Mon–Wed 10am–10pm, Thurs–Sun 10am–midnight.

Herr Nilsen Jazzklubb CJ Hambros plass 5 ⓣ22 33 54 05, ⓦwww.herrnilsen.no. Small and intimate bar whose brick walls are decorated with jazz memorabilia. Live jazz – often traditional and bebop – most nights. Air-conditioned; central location. Daily 1pm–2.30am.

Original Nilsen Rosenkrantz gate 11 ⓦwww.original-nilsen.no. Popular bar featuring regular live jazz. Daily 1pm–3am.

Classical music and opera

Oslo's major orchestra, the **Oslo Filharmonien** (ⓣ22 01 49 02, ⓦwww.oslophil.com), gives regular concerts in the city's Konserthus, at Munkedamsveien 14. As you might expect, programmes often include works by Norwegian and other Scandinavian composers. Tickets for most performances cost around 300kr. In August and September, the orchestra traditionally gives a couple of free evening concerts in the Vigeland sculpture park, as part of the city's summer entertainment programme, which also sees classical performances at a variety of other venues, including the Domkirke, the Munch Museum and the University Aula; for details of the summer programme, contact the tourist office (see p.82).

In October, the ten-day **Ultima Contemporary Music Festival** (ⓦwww.ultima.no, ⓣ22 42 99 99) gathers together more Scandinavian and international talent in an ambitious programme of concerts featuring everything from modern contemporary music to opera, ballet, classical and folk. The performances take place in a variety of venues throughout the city; for full details check Ultima's website or contact the tourist office.

Finally, **Den Norske Opera**, Norway's prolific opera company, offers a popular repertoire – Mozart, R. Strauss and the Italians – but also undertakes a number of contemporary works each year. Performances are usually held at the Opera House, Storgata 23 (information ⓣ23 31 50 00; booking office ⓣ815 444 88; ⓦwww.operaen.no) – and will be until the new, super-modern opera house, currently under construction just to the east of the city centre, is opened in 2008.

Cinema

The facility with which most Norwegians tackle other languages is best demonstrated at the **cinema**, where films are shown in their original language with Norwegian subtitles. Given that American (and British) films are the most popular, this has obvious advantages for visiting English speakers. Oslo has its share of mainstream multi-screens, as well as a good art-house cinema. Prices are surprisingly reasonable with tickets averaging 80–90kr.

Cinema listings – including information on late-night screenings – appear daily in the local press, and the tourist office has details too. All the main cinemas share the **same telephone number** and website (Ⓣ820 30 001; Ⓦwww.oslokino.no). The following is a selection of central screens.

Eldorado Torggata 9. Mainstream cinema showing the usual blockbusters.

Filmens Hus Dronningens gate 16 at Tollbugata Ⓣ22 47 45 00, Ⓦwww.nfi.no. Art-house cinema with a varied programme mixing mainstream and alternative films. Tickets 70kr.

Filmteatret Stortingsgata 16. Old theatre converted into a cinema with wonderful decor. Shows mainstream and classic films.

Gimle Bygdøy allé 39. A sympathetically revamped old cinema with the most comfortable seats in town. A wine bar in the entrance adds a nice touch. Varied programme, mostly mainstream.

Saga Stortingsgata 28 at Olav V's gate. Mainstream cinema with six screens.

Theatre

Nearly all of Oslo's theatre productions are in Norwegian, making them of limited interest to (most) tourists, though there are occasional English-language performances by touring theatre companies. The principal venue is the **Nationaltheatret**, Stortingsgata 15 (Ⓣ815 00 811; Ⓦwww.nationaltheatret.no), which hosts the prestigious, annual Ibsen Festival. Touring companies may also appear at the more adventurous **Det Norske Teatret**, Kristian IV's gate 8 (Ⓣ22 47 38 00, Ⓦwww.detnorsketeatret.no).

Sports

Surrounded by forest and fjord, Oslo is very much an outdoor city, offering a wide range of **sports** and outdoor pursuits. In **summer**, locals take to the hills to hike the network of trails that lattice the forests and lakes of the Nordmarka (see p.110), where many also try their hand at a little freshwater fishing, while others head out to the offshore islets of the Oslofjord (see p.127) to sunbathe and swim. In **winter**, the cross-country ski routes of the Nordmarka are especially popular, as is downhill skiing at Holmenkollen. Indeed skiing is such an integral part of winter life here that the T-bane carriages all have ski racks. Sleigh-riding is possible too, and so is ice skating, with the handiest rinks right in the middle of the city in front of the Stortinget (see p.89).

Fishing

As regards **fishing**, the freshwater lakes of the Nordmarka are reasonably well stocked with such common species as trout, char, pike and perch. The Oslomarkas Fiskeadministrasjon, Sørkedalen 914 (Ⓣ22 49 90 04, Ⓦwww.ofa.no) provides all the background information you need. In particular they will advise about fishing areas and have lists of where local licences can be bought; see p.66

for general information about fishing in Norway. **Ice fishing** is another popular option, but follow what the locals do (or even better, keep them company) as it can be dangerous.

Skiing

Skiing is extremely popular throughout Norway, and here in Oslo both cross-country and downhill enthusiasts might begin by calling in at the **Skiforeningen** (Ski Association) office, at Kongeveien 5 (Ⓣ22 92 32 00; Ⓦwww.skiforeningen.no), near the Holmenkollen ski-jump, on T-bane #1. They have lots of information on Oslo's floodlit trails, cross-country routes, downhill and slalom slopes, ski schools (including one for children) and excursions to the nearest mountain resorts. Most Norwegians have their own skiing gear, but **equipment hire** is available from Skiservice Tomm Murstad, beside the Voksenkollen T-bane station (Ⓣ22 13 95 00, Ⓦwww.skiservice.no). For spectators, March sees the annual Holmenkollen Ski Festival: tickets and information from the Skiforeningen or the tourist office.

Ice-skating and horse-drawn sleigh rides

Every winter, from November to March, a floodlit **skating rink**, Narvisen, is created in front of the Stortinget, beside Karl Johans gate. Admission is free and you can hire skates on the spot at reasonable rates. In addition, **horse-drawn sleigh** rides in the Nordmarka can be arranged through Helge Torp, Sørbråten Gård, Maridalen, Oslo (Ⓣ22 23 22 21).

Oslo with children

There's no shortage of things to do with young (pre-teen) children in Oslo, beginning with the enchanting, open-air **Vigelandsparken** (see p.108) and, if the weather is good, the **beaches** of the Oslofjord islands (see p.127). In wintertime, ice-skating and horse-drawn sleigh rides (see above) are bound to appeal.

Few children will want to be dragged round Oslo's main museums, except perhaps for the **Frammuseet** (see p.106), but there are several museums geared up for youngsters. The most popular is the **Norsk Teknisk Museum**, at Kjelsåsveien 143 (Technology Museum; late June to late Aug daily 10am–6pm; late Aug to late June Tues–Fri 10am–4pm, Sat & Sun 10am–5pm; 75kr, children 35kr; Ⓦwww.tekniskmuseum.no). Out to the north of the city, this is an interactive museum par excellence, equipped with working models and a galaxy of things to push and touch, as well as a café and picnic area. To get there from the city centre, take bus #54 from the Aker Brygge to Kjelsås station alongside the museum.

Alternatively, there's the rather more creative **Barnekunstmuseet** at Lille Frøens vei 4 (Children's Art Museum; mid-Jan to late June Tues–Thurs 9.30am–2pm, Sun 11am–4pm; late June to early Aug Tues–Thurs & Sun 11am–4pm; mid-Sept to early Dec Tues–Thurs 9.30am–2pm, Sun 11am–4pm; closed mid-Aug to mid-Sept; 50kr, children 30kr; T-bane to Frøen station). This has an international collection of children's art – drawings, paintings, sculpture and handicrafts – along with a children's workshop where painting, music and dancing are frequent activities; call ahead for details on Ⓣ22 46 85 73 or check out the website Ⓦwww.childrensart.com.

One bit of good news is that **discounts** for children are commonplace. Almost all sites and attractions let babies and toddlers in free, and charge half of the adult tariff for children between 4 and 16 years of age. It's the same on public transport, and hotels are usually very obliging too, adding camp beds of some description to their rooms with the minimum of fuss and expense.

Listings

Airlines Air Lingus ⓣ24 14 87 50; British Airways ⓣ815 33 142; Finnair ⓣ810 01 100; KLM ⓣ22 64 37 52; Norwegian Air Shuttle ⓣ815 21 815; SAS/Braathens ⓣ05400; SN Brussels ⓣ23 16 25 68; Widerøe's ⓣ810 01 200.

Banks and exchange ATMs are liberally distributed across the city centre and there are also ATMs at Gardermoen airport. Among Oslo's plethora of banks, Den Norske Bank (DnB) has downtown branches at Stranden 21, Aker Brygge, Stortingsgate 30 and Grensen 17. Normal banking hours are mid-May to mid-Sept Mon–Fri 8.30am–3pm, Thurs till 5pm; mid-Sept to mid-May Mon–Fri 8.30am–3.30pm, Thurs till 5pm. You can also change money and travellers' cheques at major post offices, where the rates are especially competitive. There are late-opening bureaux de change at the airport in Arrivals (daily 8am–10.30pm) and Departures (daily 5.30am–8pm). The money exchange company Forex has several outlets dotted across the city centre with one branch at Oslo S (Mon–Fri 9am–7pm), another at Øvre Slottsgate 12 (same hours).

Books and maps Tanum, inside the Paleet shopping complex at Karl Johans gate 37 and Universitetsgata (Mon–Fri 10am–8pm, Sat 10am–6pm; ⓣ22 41 11 00), has the city's widest selection of English fiction, though Norli runs it a close second: Norli have several branches, but the largest is at Universitetsgata 20–24 (ⓣ22 00 43 00). This particular branch has a separate section devoted to English translations of Norwegian writers. Tronsmo, Kristian Augusts gate 19 (ⓣ22 99 03 99), has long been the city's best-stocked leftist bookshop with many of its titles in English. Norlis Antikvariat, opposite the National Gallery at Universitetsgata 18 (ⓣ22 20 01 40), sells second-hand and some new English-language books, as does J.W. Cappelens Antikvariat, Akersgata 18 (ⓣ23 31 02 80), which is particularly good on Arctic explorers and their tales of derring-do. Nomaden, Uranienborgveien 4 (ⓣ23 13 14 15), just behind the Slottsparken, is Oslo's best shop for travel guides and maps, though maps of Oslo in particular and Norway in general are to be found in dozens of locations – the best are produced by Cappelen. In addition, the shop of the Norwegian hiking organization, Den Norske Turistforening (DNT) Oslo, Storgata 7 (Mon–Fri 10am–5pm, Thurs till 6pm, Sat 10am–2pm; ⓣ22 82 28 22), has a comprehensive collection of Norwegian hiking maps.

Buses For information on all long-distance domestic and most international bus services, contact Nor-Way Bussekspress, at the Bussterminalen information desk, Schweigaardsgate (Mon–Fri 7am–10pm, Sat 8am–5.30pm, Sun 8am–10pm; ⓣ23 00 24 00 for services to and from Oslo; ⓣ815 44 444 for all other services; ⓦwww.nor-way.no). The information desk also has information on Säfflebussen (ⓣ815 66 010, ⓦwww.safflebussen.se) international buses to Copenhagen and Stockholm; and on the Torp-Ekspressen linking Oslo Bussterminalen with Oslo (Torp) airport (ⓦwww.torpekspressen.no; ⓣ23 00 24 00). For city and airport buses, see p.79.

Car breakdown Each of the two major national breakdown companies has a 24hr helpline. They are Falken Redningskorps (ⓣ02222) and Viking Redningstjeneste (ⓣ06000).

Car rental Bislet Bilutleie, Pilestredet 70 (ⓣ22 60 00 00, ⓦwww.bislet.no); Europcar, Haakon VII's gate 9 (ⓣ22 83 12 42); Hertz, Jernbanetorget 1 (ⓣ67 16 80 00), Holbergs gate 30 (ⓣ67 16 80 00), and at the airport (ⓣ67 16 80 00); National, at the airport (ⓣ64 81 06 60, ⓦwww.nationalcar.no). See also under "Bilutleie" in the Yellow Pages.

Crafts For traditional and authentic Norwegian handicrafts, one good bet is Heimen Husflid, Rosenkrantz gate 8 (Mon–Fri 10am–5pm, Thurs till 6pm, Sat 10am–3pm, ⓣ23 21 42 00, ⓦwww.heimen.net). For more modern, pan-Scandinavian gear, try Norway Designs, Stortingsgata 28 (Mon–Fri 9am–5pm, Thurs till 7pm, Sat 10am–3pm; ⓣ23 11 45 10, ⓦwww.norwaydesigns.no), which features an amazing glass castle every Christmas.

Cycling The Syklistenes Landsforening, Storgata 23c (Norwegian Cyclist Association; Mon–Fri 10am–4pm & Sat 10am–2pm; ⓣ22 47 30 30, ⓦwww.slf.no), gives advice and information on route planning and sells cycling maps. For bike hire in Oslo, see p.85.

Dentist Municipal dental information on ⓣ22 67 30 00. Otherwise, see under Tannleger in the Yellow Pages.

Embassies and consulates Canada, Wergelandveien 7 (ⓣ22 99 53 00); Ireland, Haakon VII's gate, 15 etg. (ⓣ22 01 72 00); Netherlands, Oscars gate 29 (ⓣ23 33 36 00); Poland, Olav Kyrres plass 1 (ⓣ22 43 00 15); South Africa, Drammensveien 88c (ⓣ23 27 32 20); UK, Thomas Heftyes gate 8 (ⓣ23 13 27 00); USA, Drammensveien 18 (ⓣ22 44 85 50). For others, look under Ambassadeur og Legasjoner in the Yellow Pages. There is no Australian consulate or embassy.

Emergencies Ambulance & medical assistance ⓣ113; Police ⓣ112; Fire brigade ⓣ110.

Ferries DFDS Seaways (from Helsingborg & Copenhagen), Vippetangen Utstikker (dock) #2, beside Akershusstranda (☎22 41 90 90, ⓦwww.dfds.no); Stena Line (from Frederikshavn in Denmark), also from Vippetangen Utstikker #2 (☎02 010, ⓦwww.stenaline.no); and Color Line (from Kiel and Hirtshals, Denmark), Hjortneskaia (☎810 00 811, ⓦwww.colorline.no). Tickets from the companies direct or travel agents.

Gay Oslo There's not much of a scene as such, primarily because Oslo's gays and lesbians are mostly content to share pubs and clubs with heteros. That said, gay men congregate at the *London Pub*, CJ Hambros plass 5 (daily 3pm–3am; ⓦwww.londonpub.no), with a pub/bar on one floor and a disco downstairs, and *SinPecado*, Øvre Vollgate 13 (Tues & Wed 6pm–1am, Thurs–Sat 8pm–3am; ⓦwww.sinpecado.no), is a popular lesbian bar. The main gay event is the *Skeive Dager* (Queer Days; ⓦwww.gaysir.no) festival usually held over ten days in late June with parties, parades, political meetings, a film festival and incorporating Gay Pride. Norway's national gay and lesbian organization is LLH (Landsforeningen for lesbisk og homofil frigjøring; ⓦwww.llh.no).

Internet Almost all city hotels and hostels provide Internet access for their guests at (fairly) reasonable rates. Internet access is also available for free at the main city library, the Deichmanske bibliotek, at Henrik Ibsen gate 1 (June–Aug Mon–Fri 10am–6pm, Sat 9am–2pm; Sept–May Mon–Fri 10am–8pm, Sat 9am–3pm; ⓦwww.deichman.no), and at Oslo's youth information shop, Use-it, Møllergata 3 (July–Aug Mon–Fri 9am–6pm; Sept–June Mon–Fri 11am–5pm; ☎24 14 98 20, ⓦwww.use-it.no.).

Lost credit cards American Express ☎800 68 100; Diners Club ☎21 01 50 00; Mastercard ☎21 01 52 22; Visa ☎08989.

Hiking Den Norske Turistforening (DNT) Oslo, Storgata 7 (Mon–Fri 10am–5pm, Thurs till 6pm, Sat 10am–2pm; ☎22 82 28 22, ⓦwww.dntoslo.no), sells a full range of Norwegian hiking maps, books and equipment. They are affiliated to the national organization, DNT (ⓦwww.turistforeningen.no), and you can become a member of DNT here. The annual subscription fee is 545kr per adult and there are concessions for Seniors, the Under-26s and families. DNT members can use a nationwide network of mountain huts at special rates, some operated by DNT itself, but the majority by its local affiliates.

Jewellery Juhl's Silver Gallery, Roald Amundsens gate 6 (☎22 42 77 99, ⓦwww.juhls.no), is the Oslo outlet for the jewellers and silversmiths of national repute, who established their first workshop in remote Kautokeino (see p.358) forty years ago. Many of the designs are Sami-inspired. Mon–Fri 10am–6pm & Sat 10am–4pm.

Laundry Majorstua Myntvaskeri, Vibes gate 15 (☎22 69 43 17); Snarvask, Thorvald Meyers gate 18, Grünerløkka (☎22 37 57 70). See under Vaskerier in the Yellow Pages.

Left luggage Coin-operated lockers (24hr) and luggage office at Oslo S.

Lost property (*hittegods*) Trams, buses and T-bane ☎22 08 53 61; NSB railways ☎23 15 40 47; police ☎22 66 98 65.

Medical treatment For emergencies, call ☎113. For lesser problems, either head for the nearest pharmacy (see "Pharmacy" below) or the Walk-In Clinic, to the rear of the Aker Brygge complex at the corner of Munkedamsveien and Sjøgata (☎22 83 10 83; ⓦwww.walk-in-clinic.com). The clinic is fast, efficient, friendly – and expensive. For cheaper treatment, stick to the A&E department of the nearest hospital, at the north end of Storgata, beside the river.

Newspapers Many English and American newspapers and magazines are available in downtown Oslo's Narvesen kiosks and there's an especially wide selection at the newsagents in Oslo S train station. They don't come cheap: a British daily broadsheet costs 35kr, 65kr for weekend editions.

Pharmacy A 24hr pharmacy – Vitusapotek Jernbanetorvet – is located across the street from Oslo Sentralstasjon, at Jernbanetorget 4b (☎23 35 81 00). See also "Medical Treatment".

Police In an emergency, ring ☎112.

Post offices The main post office is at the corner of Kirkegata and Prinsens gate (Mon–Fri 9am–5pm, Sat 10am–3pm). There are lots of other post offices dotted across the city, including a branch in Oslo S – for full details consult ⓦwww.posten.no. All post offices exchange currency and cash travellers' cheques at very reasonable rates.

Supermarkets There are lots of small supermarkets in central Oslo – Rimi, ICA and Kiwi are three of the larger chains. All of them sell at least a small selection of fresh fruit and veg. Rimi has a branch in Oslo S, ICA has one on Grensen near the corner with Akersgata 45. Opening hours are mostly Mon–Sat 9am–9pm, Sat 9am–6pm.

Taxis There are taxi ranks dotted all over the city centre. You can also telephone Oslo Taxi on ☎02323 or Taxi 2 on ☎02202.

Trains NSB (Norwegian State Railways) has two stations in Oslo – Oslo S and the Nationaltheatret. Enquiries and bookings on ☎815 00 888, ⓦwww.nsb.no.

Travel agents For discounted flights, train and bus tickets, try KILROY travels, Nedre Slotts gate 23 (☎02633, ⓦwww.kilroytravels.com). Tourbroker Reisebyrå, Drammensveien 4 (☎22 83 27 15), specializes in Eurolines bus tickets. For the full list of Oslo travel agents, see under Reisebyråer in the Yellow Pages.

Vinmonopolet There are lots of branches of this state-run liquor and wine store in Oslo, including one in Oslo S (Mon–Fri 10am–6pm, Sat 9am–6pm & Sun 9am–3pm).

Youth information Oslo's youth information shop, Use-it, Møllergata 3 (Ⓣ24 14 98 20, Ⓦwww.use-it.no), operates an advisory service on everything from sexual health to careers for the under-26s. It's also a good place to find out about live music and events, and offers a free Internet service (for everyone irrespective of age). They also produce a free annual booklet, Streetwise, which provides a review and round-up of all things Oslo, from bars and clubs to museums and cafés. Open July–Aug Mon–Fri 9am–6pm; Sept–June Mon–Fri 11am–5pm.

Around Oslo: the Oslofjord

Around 100km from top to bottom, the narrow straits and podgy basins of the Oslofjord link the capital with the open sea. This waterway has long been Norway's busiest, an islet-studded channel whose sheltered waters were once crowded with steamers shuttling passengers along the Norwegian coast. The young Roald Dahl, who spent his summer holidays here from 1920 to 1932, loved the area. In his autobiographical *Boy* he wrote: "Unless you have sailed down the Oslofjord…on a tranquil summer's day, you cannot imagine the sensation of absolute peace and beauty that surrounds you." Even now, though industry has blighted the shoreline and cars have replaced the steamers, the Oslofjord makes for delightful sailing, and on a summer's day you can spy dozens of tiny craft scuttling round its nooks and crannies. The ferry ride from Oslo to Drøbak, a pretty village on the fjord's east shore, does provide a pleasant introduction, though it's not quite the same as having your own boat.

Both sides of the fjord are dotted with humdrum industrial towns, and frankly there's not much to tempt you out of Oslo if your time is limited – especially as several of the major city sights are half-day excursions in themselves. But if you have more time, there are several places on the train and bus routes out of the city that do warrant a stop. The pick of the crop is the town of **Fredrikstad**, down the fjord's eastern side on the train route to Sweden. The old part of Fredrikstad consists of a riverside fortress whose gridiron streets and earthen bastions, dating from the late sixteenth century, have survived in remarkably good condition. The fortress was built to defend the country from the Swedes, as was the imposing hilltop stronghold that rears up above **Halden**, an otherwise innocuous town further southeast, hard by the Swedish border. Highlight of the fjord's western shore is the cluster of Viking burial mounds at **Borre**, just outside the ferry port of **Horten**, while the breezy town of **Tønsberg** gives easy access to the shredded archipelago that pokes a rural finger out into the Skagerrak.

Motorways leave Oslo to strip along both sides of the Oslofjord – the E6 in the east, the E18 to the west – and there's a regular **train** service from Oslo S serving both sides too. On the east side, the train stops at Fredrikstad and Halden, but not Drøbak, which is best reached from Oslo by ferry. On the western side, trains run to Drammen and Tønsberg, but not Horten. To cross the Oslofjord, you can either use the seven-kilometre tunnel that runs west from Drøbak, or catch the **car ferry** (Mon–Fri 5.30am–midnight, Sat & Sun 7.30am–midnight, every 30min; 30min; Ⓦwww.basto-fosen.no) between Horten and **Moss**, about 60km south of Oslo.

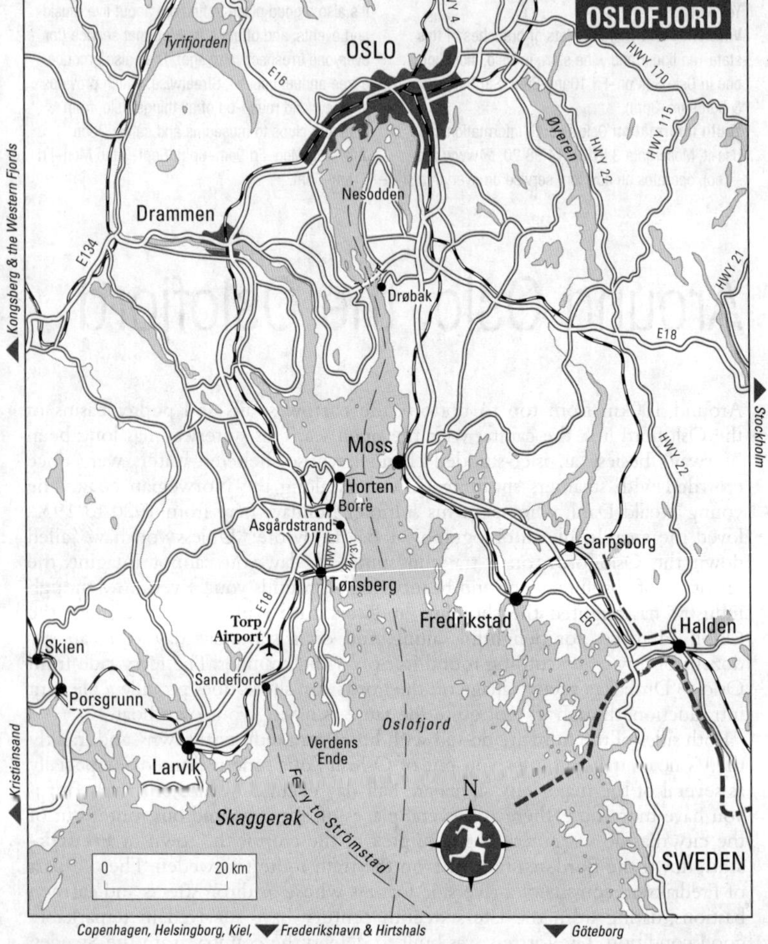

The east shore: Drøbak, Fredrikstad and Halden

The first place of any real interest on the Oslofjord's eastern shore is **DRØBAK**, a tiny port that slopes along the shoreline about 40km from the capital. It's at its prettiest round the old harbour, where a cluster of white clapboard houses covers the headland and straggles up towards a handsome timber church dating from the early eighteenth century. Drøbak witnessed one of the few Norwegian successes during the German invasion of 1940, when the cruiser *Blucher* was sunk by artillery as it steamed towards Oslo. The gunners had no way of realizing just how important this was – the delay to the German flotilla gave the Norwegian king, Haakon VII, just enough time to escape the capital and avoid capture. The village's only other claim to fame comes from its specialist Christmas shop, the *Julehuset* (March–May Mon–Fri 10am–5pm, Sat 10am–3pm; June–Oct Mon–Fri 10am–5pm, Sat 10am–3pm & Sun noon–4pm; Nov to Dec 23 Mon–Fri 10am–7pm, Sat 10am–3pm & Sun noon–4pm; Dec 24 9am–noon; Ⓦwww.julehus.no; Ⓣ64 93 41 78), whose popularity is such that many Norwegian kids believe that Father Christmas actually lives here: he doesn't, of course, because his reindeer prefer Lapland. As for **cafés**, *Det Gamle Bakeri* (daily 11am–11pm) serves tasty snacks and light meals in an attractive wooden building with an open log fire, while the *Skipperstuen*, in the wooden house on the knoll next to the harbour (same times), does excellent sandwiches.

The most enjoyable way to get to Drøbak from Oslo is by **boat**. From late June to early August, M/S Prinsessen (Ⓣ177; Ⓦwww.nbds.no) departs Oslo's Aker Brygge pier for Drøbak five times weekly, clipping out across the islet-studded fjord and stopping off at a couple of small islands on the way. The journey takes about an hour and costs 60kr each way. The boat's timetable makes it possible to complete the return trip on the same day – though this isn't crucial as there's also a fast and frequent bus service between Drøbak and Oslo (hourly to Jernbanetorget and several other downtown bus stops).

Fredrikstad

It's an hour-long, ninety-kilometre train journey south from Oslo to **FREDRIKSTAD**, named after the Danish king Frederick II, who had the original fortified town built here at the mouth of the River Glomma in 1567. Norway was ruled by Danish kings from 1387 to 1814 and, with rare exceptions, the country's interests were systematically neglected in favour of Copenhagen. A major consequence was Norway's involvement in the bitter rivalry between the Swedish and Danish monarchies, which prompted a seemingly endless and particularly pointless sequence of wars lasting from the early sixteenth century until 1720.

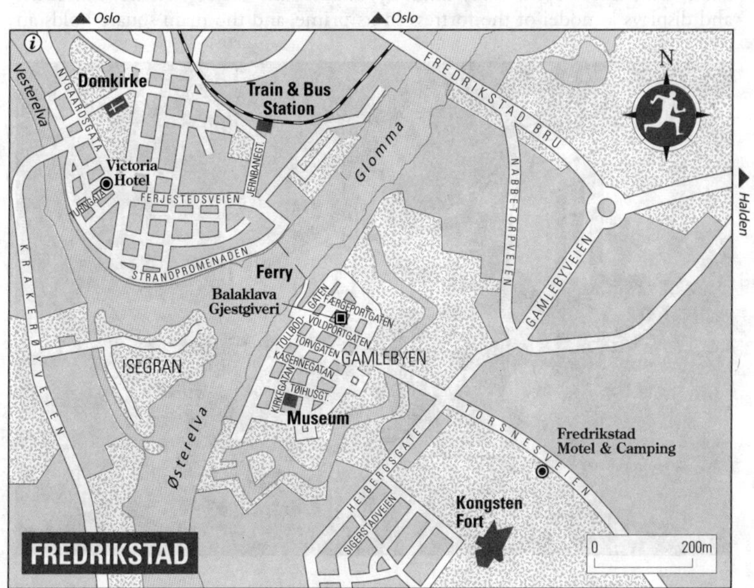

The eastern approaches to Oslo (then Christiania), along the Oslofjord, were especially vulnerable to attack from Sweden, and the area was ravaged by raiding parties on many occasions. Indeed, Frederick II's fortress only lasted three years before it was burnt to the ground, though it didn't take long for a replacement to be constructed – and for the whole process to be repeated again. Finally, in the middle of the seventeenth century, Fredrikstad's **fortifications** were considerably strengthened. The central gridiron of cobbled streets was encircled on three sides by zigzag bastions and these allowed the defenders to fire across and into any attacking force. In turn, these bastions were protected by a moat, concentric earthen banks and outlying redoubts. Armed with 130 cannon, Fredrikstad was, by 1685, the strongest fortress in all of Norway – and it has remained in military use to this day, which partly accounts for its excellent state of preservation. The fort was also unaffected by the development of modern Fredrikstad, which grew up as a result of the timber industry: the new town was built on the west bank of the Glomma while the old fort – now known as the **Gamlebyen** (Old Town; Ⓦ www.festningsbyen.no) – is on the east.

The town

From Fredrikstad's adjoining **train** and **bus** stations, located in the new part of town, it's a couple of minutes' walk to the river – head straight down Jernbanegata and take the first left along Ferjestedsveien. From the jetty, the **ferry** (Mon–Thurs 5.30am–11pm, Fri 5.30am–1am, Sat 7am–1am, Sun 9.30am–11pm; every 15–30min; 5min; 10kr) shuttles over to the gated back wall of the Gamlebyen. Inside, the pastel-painted timber and stone houses of the old town, just three blocks deep and six blocks wide, make for a delightful stroll, especially as surprisingly few tourists venture this way except at the height of the season. Indeed, on a drizzly day the streets echo only to the sound of your own footsteps plus the occasional army boot hitting the cobbles as the garrison goes about its duties. A **museum** (mid-June to Aug Mon–Fri 9am–4pm, Sat & Sun noon–5pm; 40kr) dutifully outlines the history of the Old Town and displays a model of the fortress in its prime, and the main square holds an

△ Fredrikstad

unfortunate **statue** of Frederick II, who appears to have a serious problem with his pantaloons, but it's the general appearance of the place that appeals rather than any specific sight.

Make sure also that you take in the most impressive of the town's outlying defences, the Kongsten **Fort**, about ten minutes' walk from the main fortress: go straight ahead from the main gate, take the first right along Heibergsgate and it's clearly visible on the left. Here, thick stone and earthen walls are moulded round a rocky knoll that offers wide views over the surrounding countryside – an agreeably quiet vantage point from where you can take in the lie of the land.

Back on the western side of the Glomma, a short walk along Ferjestedsveien away from the river brings you to a small park and the adjacent **Domkirke** (late June to mid-Aug Tues–Sat noon–3pm), a brown brick building with stained glass by Emanuel Vigeland (see p.109). Beyond the church is the centre of modern Fredrikstad, a humdrum place on a bend in the river.

Practicalities

Although it's best to visit Fredrikstad as a day-trip, there are a handful of **hotels**, among which the most recommendable is the *Victoria*, Turngata 3 (Ⓣ69 38 58 00, Ⓦwww.hotelvictoria.no; ❻, sp/r ❹), a comfortable, medium-sized and recently refurbished hotel that dates back to the 1880s; it overlooks the park next to the Domkirke. Alternatively, the bargain basement *Fredrikstad Motel & Camping*, Torsnesveien 16 (Ⓣ69 32 05 32; ❷), is located about 400m straight ahead outside the main gate of the Old Town; it provides tent space as well as inexpensive rooms. As for **food**, the Gamlebyen is dotted with cafés and patisseries, the pick of which is *Café Balaklava*, in antique premises and with an outdoor terrace at Færgeportgata 78; the adjacent **restaurant**, *Balaklava Gjestgiveri* (Ⓣ69 32 30 40; Mon–Sat 6–11pm), also occupies period premises and specializes in seafood; main courses average around 160kr.

Halden

Just 2km from the Swedish border and 35km from Fredrikstad, the workaday wood-processing town of **HALDEN** is bisected by the River Tista and hemmed in by steep forested hills, the closest of which is crowned by the commanding **Fredriksten Festning** (fortress). Work began on the stronghold in 1661 at the instigation of Frederick III, during a lull in the fighting between Sweden and Denmark. The stakes were high: the Swedes were determined to annihilate the Dano-Norwegian monarchy and had only just failed in their attempt to capture Oslo and Copenhagen. Consequently, Frederick was keen to build a fortress of immense strength to secure his northerly possessions. He called in Dutch engineers to design it and, after a decade, the result was a labyrinthine citadel whose thick perimeter walls, heavily protected gates, bastions and outlying forts were brilliantly designed to suit the contours of the two steep, parallel ridges on which they were built. The proof of the pudding was in the eating. The Swedes besieged Fredriksten on several occasions, but without success, though the town itself suffered badly. In 1716, the Norwegians razed it to the ground, a scorched earth policy that later prompted some nationalistic poppycock from the writer Bjørnstjerne Bjørnson: "We chose to burn our nation, ere we let it fall."

The town

Halden **train station** abuts the south bank of the Tista, while the **bus station** is a couple of minutes' walk away to the south on Tollbugata. The **fortress** (mid-May to Aug daily 10am–5pm & Sept Sun noon–3pm; 50kr) is on this side of the river too, its forested slopes climbed by several steep footpaths, the most enjoyable of which begins on **Peder Colbjørnsens gate** and leads up to the main gatehouse. Allow at least an hour for a thorough exploration of the fort, whose ingenuity and impregnability are its salient features. Although most of the buildings are labelled, only a handful are open to the public, most notably the **Krigshistorisk Utstilling** (Military History Exhibition) in the old prison in the eastern curtain wall. There are also hour-long guided tours (late June to mid-Aug 3 daily; 50kr), but you shouldn't require any help to absorb the obvious and powerful atmosphere. On the far side of the fortress, where the terrain is nowhere near as steep, you'll find a monument to the Swedish king Karl XII, who was killed by a bullet in the temple as he besieged the fort in 1718. An inveterate warmonger, Karl had exhausted the loyalty of his troops, and whether the bullet came from the fortress or one of his own men has been a matter of considerable Scandinavian speculation.

Practicalities

Despite its fortress, Halden is too routine a place to spend the night, but if you're marooned there's a reasonable range of accommodation. The **tourist office**, midway between the train and bus stations at Torget 2 (late Aug to mid-June Mon–Fri 9am–3.30pm; late June to mid-Aug Mon–Fri 9am–4.30pm; ⓣ69 19 09 80, ⓦwww.visithalden.com), has a full list, but the pick of the **hotels** is the *Park Hotel*, Marcus Thranes gate 30 (ⓣ69 21 15 00, ⓦwww.park-hotel.no; ❺, sp/r ❹), a neat, trim, modern place on the northwest edge of the town centre. Alternatively, Halden has a small, modern 32-bed HI **hostel** (late June to early Aug; ⓣ69 21 69 68, ⓦwww.vandrerhjem.no; dorm beds 125kr, doubles ❶), sited in a chalet-like school building on Flintveien, in the suburb of Gimle, 3km north of the train station and readily reached by several local buses.

The west shore: Drammen, Horten and Tønsberg

West of the city centre, Oslo's rangy suburbs curve round the final basin of the Oslofjord before bubbling up over the hills almost as far as **DRAMMEN**, a substantial industrial settlement some 40km southwest of the capital. Built on an arm of the Oslofjord and astride the fast-flowing River Drammenselva, the town handles most of the vehicles imported into Norway. This is hardly a reason to visit, however, and nor do the modern office blocks and stuffy late nineteenth-century buildings of its centre conjure up much interest. From here, there's a **choice of routes**, with the E134 wriggling west through Kongsberg (see p.190) bound for the western fjords (see p.220), while the E18 presses on south down the Oslofjord.

The **E18** soon slips past **HORTEN**, a small port and naval base from where a car ferry shuttles across the Oslofjord to Moss (Mon–Fri 5.30am–midnight, Sat & Sun 7.30am–midnight, every 30min; 30min; ⓦwww.basto-fosen.no), before scuttling on down to the old port of Tønsberg.

Tønsberg and around

The last town of any size on the Oslofjord's western shore, **TØNSBERG**, some 100km from Oslo, was founded by Harald Hårfagre in the ninth century, and rose to prominence in the Middle Ages as a major ecclesiastical and trading centre. The sheltered sound made a safe harbour, the plain behind it was ideal for settlement, and, once they were built, the town's palace and fortress assured it the patronage of successive monarchs. All of which sounds exciting, and you might expect Tønsberg to be one of the country's more important historical attractions. Sadly, though, precious little survives from the town's medieval heyday, the best of a decidedly poor hand being the renovated, nineteenth-century warehouses of the **Tønsberg Brygge**, a pedestrianized area whose narrow lanes, dotted with bars and restaurants, hug the waterfront in the centre of town.

As for the castle, the **Slottsfjellet**, only the foundations have survived, fragmentary ruins perched on a wooded hill immediately to the north of the centre, though it takes little imagination to appreciate the castle's strategic and defensive position. The Swedes burned it down in 1503 and the place was never rebuilt – today's watchtower, the inelegant Slottsfjelltårnet (mid-May to late June Mon–Fri 10am–3pm, Sat & Sun noon–5pm; late June to mid-Aug daily 11am–6pm; late Aug to mid-Sept Sat & Sun noon–5pm; late Sept Sun noon–3pm; 20kr), was plonked on top in the nineteenth century.

Its medieval importance aside, Tønsberg was known for whaling, an industry common to the whole coast, and the **Vestfold Fylkesmuseum** (Vestfold County Museum; mid-May to mid-Sept Mon–Sat 10am–5pm, Sun noon–5pm; mid-Sept to mid-May Mon–Fri 10am–2pm; 50kr), on Farmannsveien, on the east side of the Slottsfjellet, has a rather sad array of whale skeletons on show. Rather more cheery are the displays devoted to the town's history and the evolution of Vestfold shipping, while outside, on the hillside, the grazing livestock is actually part of the "Farming" section.

Practicalities

From Tønsberg **train station**, it's a five- to ten-minute walk south to the main square, Torvet. From here, it's just a couple of hundred metres along Rådhusgaten to the waterfront Tønsberg Brygge, where you'll find the **tourist office** (mid-June to July Mon–Sat 9am–7pm & Sun 9am–3pm; Aug to mid-June Mon–Fri 9.30am–3.30pm; Ⓣ33 35 45 20, Ⓦwww.visittonsberg.com), who issue free town maps and carry all sorts of local information. Tønsberg has several central **hotels**, including the waterfront *Rica Klubben*, Nedre Lang gate 49 (Ⓣ33 35 97 00, Ⓦwww.rica.no ❻, sp/r ❹), something of a brick-and-concrete monstrosity, but with comfortable rooms and fine views over the harbour. For frugal but well-kept rooms and a first-rate Norwegian breakfast, Tønsberg's HI **hostel**, at Dronning Blancasgate 22 (Ⓣ33 31 21 75, Ⓦwww.vandrerhjem.no; dorm beds 220/240kr, doubles ❷), is on a side street beneath (and to the east of) the Slottsfjellet: turn right out of the train station and follow the signs for the five-minute walk. For **food**, there is a medley of café-bars and restaurants in the Tønsberg Brygge with one of the better options being the *Esmeralda*, an Italian restaurant with a good line in pizzas; it's open daily.

South from Tønsberg: Verdens Ende

The low-lying islands and skerries that nudge out into the Skagerrak to the south of Tønsberg are a popular holiday destination. By and large, people come here for the peace and quiet, with a bit of fishing and swimming thrown in, and the whole coast is dotted with summer homes. To the outsider, this is not especially stimulating, but there is one wonderfully scenic spot, **Verdens Ende** – "World's End" – about thirty minutes' drive from Tønsberg, right at the southernmost tip of the southernmost island, **Tjöme**. In this blustery spot, rickety fishing jetties straggle across a cove whose blue-black waters are surrounded by bare, sea-smoothened rocks and miniature islets. It would be nice to think a wandering Viking gave the place its name, but in fact it was a romantic gesture by a visiting Victorian. To wet your whistle, pop along to the seashore restaurant.

Verdens Ende apart, the most enjoyable way to see the archipelago is by **boat**, and the Tønsberg tourist office has information about archipelago cruises. These include the *D/S Kysten I*, a 1909 tramp steamer that chugs round these waters in July (1 daily; 3hr 30min; 220kr; ⓣ33 35 45 20), departing from Honnørbryggen, the jetty just to the north of the tourist office.

North from Tønsberg: Åsgårdstrand and Borre's Viking burial mounds

Heading north from Tønsberg on Highway 311, it's a short drive to the seaside village of **ÅSGÅRDSTRAND**, where Edvard Munch spent many of his summers. The old fisherman's **cottage** (June–Aug Tues–Sun 11am–6pm; May & Sept Sat & Sun 11am–6pm) Munch purchased in 1897 has survived and has been returned to its appearance when the artist lived and painted here, but it's all really rather dull despite the fjordside setting: the cottage and the adjoining studio hold just a few Munch prints and bits and bobs of period furniture.

Just beyond Åsgårdstrand, Highway 311 intersects with Highway 19, which pushes on north to **BORRE**, a scattered hamlet that boasts one of the largest collections of extant **Viking burial mounds** in all of Scandinavia. There are seven large and twenty-one small mounds in total, with the best preserved being clustered together in the woods by the water's edge – follow the "Borrehaugene" sign. These grassy bumps date from the seventh to the tenth century, when Borre was a royal burial ground and one of the wealthiest districts in southern Norway. The mounds are quite interesting and well worth a wander, but the setting is even better – in springtime wild flowers carpet the woods and the sea gently laps the shoreline, making this a perfect spot for a picnic. The area has been designated a national park, and the neighbouring **Midgard Historisk Senter** (Historical Centre; May–Aug daily 11am–5pm, Sept–April Tues–Sun 10–4pm; 40kr; ⓦwww.midgardsenteret.org), in a brand-new, low-slung building by the village church, gives the historical lowdown. In a series of well-presented displays, the centre explores Borre's Viking history covering aspects such as Norse Religion and Mythology and Everyday Life in the Viking Era.

Borre is 5km south of Horten, 75km south of Oslo and 17km north of Tønsberg.

Travel details

Trains

Oslo to: Arendal (4 daily, change at Nelaug; 4hr 10min); Bergen (3–4 daily; 6hr 30min); Dombås (4–5 daily; 4hr); Drammen (4–5 daily; 40min); Fredrikstad (hourly; 1hr); Geilo (3–4 daily; 3hr); Halden (hourly; 1hr 45min); Hamar (7 daily; 1hr 20min); Hjerkinn (2–3 daily; 4hr 30min); Kongsberg (3–5 daily; 1hr 10min); Kristiansand (3–5 daily; 4hr 30min); Lillehammer (7 daily; 2hr); Myrdal (3–4 daily; 4hr 50min); Otta (2–3 daily; 3hr 30min); Røros (2–3 daily; 5hr); Stavanger (3–5 daily; 7hr 30min); Trondheim (2–3 daily; 6hr 40min); Tønsberg (every 2hr; 1hr 30min); Voss (3–4 daily; 5hr 30min); Åndalsnes (2–3 daily; 5hr 20min).

Principal Nor-Way Bussekspress (ⓦwww.nor-way.no) bus services

Oslo to: Balestrand (2–3 daily; 8hr 30min); Bergen (1 daily; 9hr); Dombås (2 daily; 6hr 15min); Drøbak (hourly; 40min); Flåm (1 daily;

6hr); Mundal, Fjaerland (3 daily; 7hr 50min); Grimstad (1–6 daily; 4hr 15min); Hamar (1 daily; 2hr); Haugesund (May–Oct 2–3 daily; 8hr 30min); Kongsberg (1–3 daily; 1hr 30min); Kristiansand (1–6 daily; 5hr 30min); Lillehammer (5 daily; 3hr); Lillesand (4–6 daily; 5hr); Lom (2–3 daily; 6hr 20min); Odda (1 daily; 8hr); Otta (2 daily; 5hr 30min); Rjukan (1–3 daily; 3hr 30min); Sogndal (3 daily; 7hr); Stavanger (2–3 daily; 10hr); Stryn (2–3 daily; 8hr 20min); Trondheim (1–3 daily; 8hr); Voss (1 daily; 7hr 30min); Ålesund (2 daily; 10hr): Åndalsnes (2 daily; 8hr).

Ferries

Horten to: Moss ((Mon–Fri 5.30am–midnight, Sat & Sun 7.30am–midnight, every 30min; 30min).

SAS domestic flights

SAS and its subsidiary Widerøe, link Oslo Gardermoen with over forty Norwegian cities and towns. **Oslo** to: Bergen (hourly; 1 hr); Bodø (6 daily; 1 hr); Harstad/Narvik (5 daily; 1hr 40min); Tromsø (8 daily; 2 hr); Trondheim (10 daily; 1 hr).

2

The South

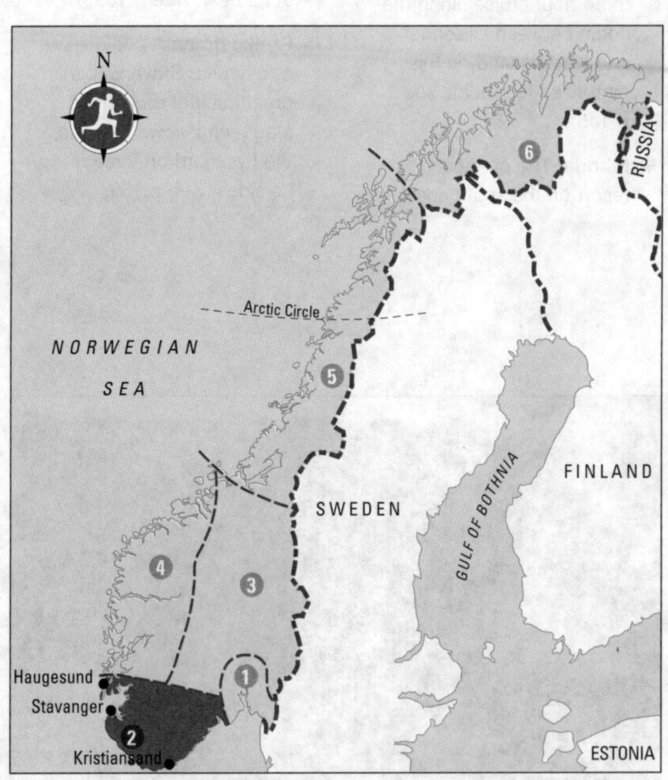

N
NORWEGIAN SEA
Arctic Circle
RUSSIA
FINLAND
SWEDEN
GULF OF BOTHNIA
ESTONIA
Haugesund
Stavanger
Kristiansand
1
2
3
4
5
6

CHAPTER 2

Highlights

* **The Clarion Hotel Tyholmen** Occupying a grand wooden building, Arendal's top-swank hotel is one of the finest places to stay on the south coast. See p.144
* **M/S Øya** Take a delightful three-hour cruise along the coast between Lillesand and Kristiansand on this pint-sized ferryboat. See p.145
* **Mandal** The prettiest resort on the south coast, with the country's finest sandy beach. See p.150
* **Norsk Hermetikkmuséet** Stavanger's Canning Museum displays a fascinating collection of sardine tin labels – commercial art at its best. See p.156
* **Preikestolen** A geological oddity near Stavanger, this great hunk of rock offers staggering views down to the Lysefjord on three of its sides. See p.159

△ Preikestolen rock

2

The South

Arcing out into the Skagerrak between the Oslofjord and Stavanger, Norway's **south coast** may have little of the imposing grandeur of other, wilder parts of the country, but its eastern half, running down to Kristiansand, is undeniably lovely. Speckled with islands and backed by forests, fells and lakes, it's this part of the coast that attracts Norwegians in droves, equipped not so much with bucket and spade as with boat and navigational aids – these waters, with their narrow inlets, islands and skerries, make for particularly enjoyable **sailing**. Camping on the offshore islands is easy too, with a few restrictions: you can't stay in one spot for more than 48 hours, nor light a fire either on bare rock or among vegetation, and you must steer clear of anyone's home. Leaflets detailing further coastal rules and regulations are available at any local tourist office.

If boats and tents aren't your thing, the white-painted clapboard houses of tiny towns like **Lillesand**, **Arendal** and – to a lesser degree – **Grimstad** have an appropriately nautical, almost jaunty, air. This portion of the coast is also important for Norway's international trade; it's just a short hop to Denmark from here, and larger towns such as Larvik and Porsgrunn have escaped their original roles as timber ports to become modern industrial centres in their own right. Most of these manufacturing towns are run-of-the-mill, except for the biggest of them, **Kristiansand**, a lively port and resort with enough sights, restaurants, bars and beaches to while away a night, maybe two, while **Sandefjord** may well be first up on your itinerary as it has its own international airport. Beyond Kristiansand lies **Mandal**, an especially fetching holiday spot with a great beach, but thereafter the coast becomes harsher and less absorbing, heralding a lightly populated region with precious little to detain you before **Stavanger**, a lively oil town and port within easy striking distance of some fine fjord and mountain scenery.

There are regular **trains** from Oslo to Kristiansand and Stavanger, but the rail line runs inland for most of its journey, only dipping down to the coast at the major resorts, which makes for a disappointing ride with the sea views mostly shielded behind the bony, forested hills. The same applies to the main **road and bus** route – the **E18/E39** – which also sticks stubbornly inland for most of the 330km from Oslo to Kristiansand (E18) and again for the 250km on to Stavanger (E39). Thanks to the E18/E39, even the tiniest of coastal villages is easy to reach, but you do need your own vehicle for most of the smaller places unless you are infinitely diligent with bus and rail timetables. Right along the south coast, **accommodation** of one sort or another is legion, with all the larger towns having at least a couple of hotels, but if you're after a bit of social bounce bear in mind the **season** is short, running from the middle of June to August; outside this period many attractions are closed and local boat trips curtailed.

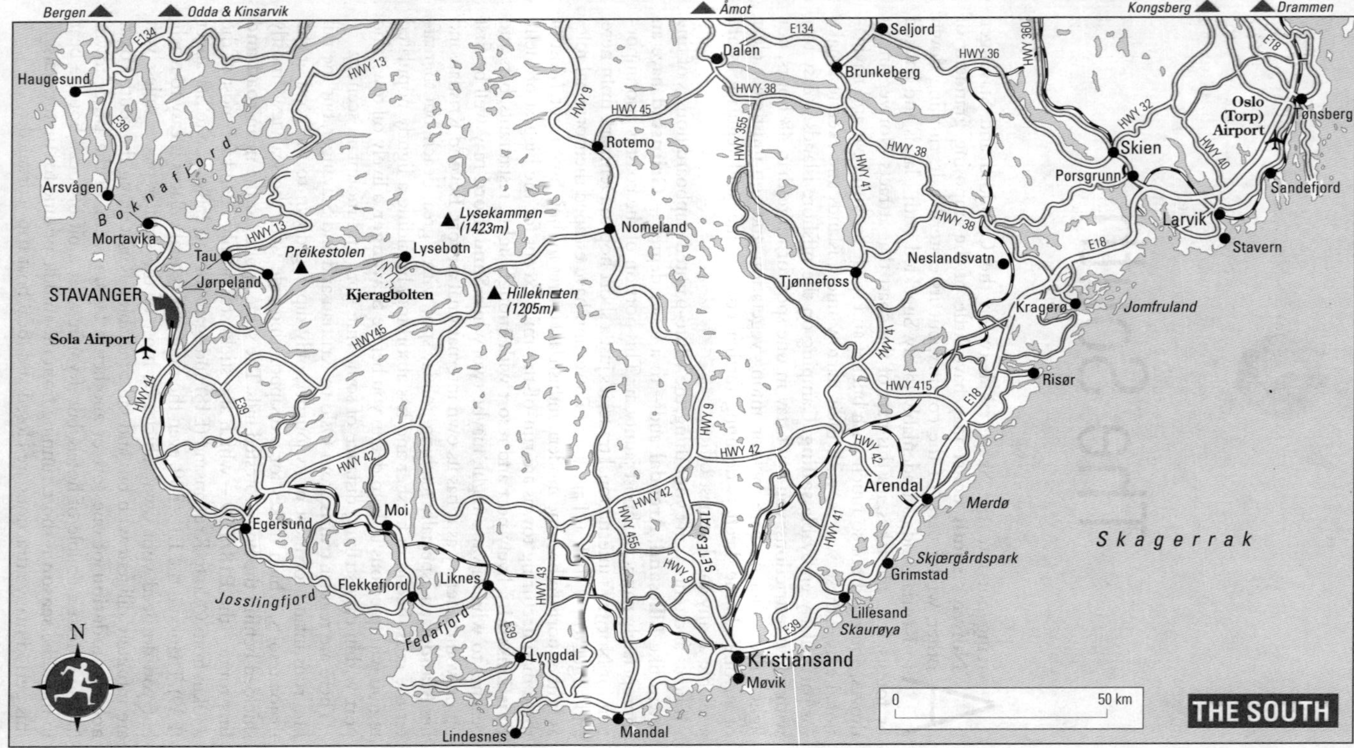
THE SOUTH
Bergen
Odda & Kinsarvik
Åmot
Kongsberg
Drammen
Haugesund
Arsvågen
Boknafjord
Mortavika
Tau
Jørpeland
STAVANGER
Sola Airport
Preikestolen
Lysebotn
Kjeragbolten
Lysekammen (1423m)
Hilleknuten (1205m)
Egersund
Moi
Flekkefjord
Liknes
Josslingfjord
Fedafjord
Lyngdal
Lindesnes
Mandal
Kristiansand
Møvik
Lillesand
Skaurøya
Grimstad
Skjærgårdspark
Arendal
Merdø
Skagerrak
Risør
Kragerø
Jomfruland
Neslandsvatn
Tjønnefoss
Nomeland
Rotemo
Dalen
Seljord
Brunkeberg
Skien
Porsgrunn
Larvik
Stavern
Sandefjord
Tønsberg
Oslo (Torp) Airport
Setesdal
E134
E39
E18
HWY 13
HWY 44
HWY 45
HWY 42
HWY 43
HWY 455
HWY 9
HWY 355
HWY 38
HWY 41
HWY 415
HWY 36
HWY 360
HWY 32
HWY 40
0
50 km
N

The E18 to Lillesand

The fretted shoreline that stretches the 200km southwest from Tønsberg (see p.132) to Lillesand is home to a series of small resorts that are particularly popular with weekenders from Oslo. The most interesting is **Grimstad**, with its Ibsen connections, the liveliest is **Arendal**, and the prettiest **Lillesand**. All three have decent places to stay, but only pint-sized **Kragerø** has an HI hostel. Many of the resorts, most notably Lillesand and Arendal, offer **boat trips** out to the myriad islets that dot this coast, with trippers bent on a spot of swimming and beach – or at least rock – combing. The islands were once owned by local farmers, but many are now in public ownership, and zealously protected from any development. In addition, most of the resorts offer longer cruises along the coast during the summer – the prettiest is probably the delightful three-hour trip from Lillesand to Kristiansand.

Fast and frequent express **buses** scuttle along the **E18** from Oslo and/or Tønsberg to Kristiansand, linking the key resorts, though you do have to change buses for Kragerø. A **train** line runs along the coast too, but it's not a particularly useful service – of the places described here only Arendal and Sandefjord have their own train stations. Kristiansand is also a major international port with **ferries** arriving from Denmark and Newcastle in the UK.

Sandefjord

The industrial town of **SANDEFJORD**, some 120km south of Oslo, is perhaps best known as the site of **Oslo (Torp) airport**, the capital's second airport, located just 8km north of the town. The airport has expanded dramatically in recent years and now picks up a slew of domestic and international flights with Ryanair leading the charge. The Torp-Ekspressen bus (see p.79; Ⓦwww.torpekspressen.no) links the airport with Oslo and there are also local buses to Sandefjord train station (Mon–Fri hourly; limited service at the weekend; 40kr; 20min).

As for Sandefjord itself, it may not be the most obvious tourist destination – or the brightest start to a Norwegian holiday – but this former whaling port does have a pleasant waterfront, where a strip of parks and gardens culminates in the former municipal baths, a grandiose complex built in 1899 in a splendid Viking-inspired dragon style; the baths closed at the beginning of World War II and now hold a civic centre.

Sandefjord's **train** and adjacent **bus station** are about 800m from the waterfront, straight down Jernbanealleen. The **tourist office** is also on the waterfont, at Thor Dahlsgate 7 (Ⓣ33 46 05 90, Ⓦwww.visitsandefjord.com), and a few metres from the Color Line quay (Ⓦwww.colorline.com), where **car ferries** to and from Strømstad in Sweden dock (4–6 daily; 2hr 30min). Of Sandefjord's several **hotels**, there's the large, plush *Rica Park Hotel Sandefjord*, in a big modern tower block on the waterfront at Strandpromenaden 9 (Ⓣ33 44 74 00, Ⓦwww.rica.no; ❺, sp/r ❹); or, more economically, try the straightforward *Sandefjord Pension* in a brightly painted house at Hystadveien 24b (Ⓣ33 46 40 79; ❷), a fifteen-minute walk northwest of the ferry terminal.

Kragerø

Pressing on down the E18, it's about 10km from Sandefjord to the turning for **Larvik**, where Color Line ferries arrive from Frederikshavn in Denmark, and then another 20km to **Porsgrunn**, with a rare view of the sea as you cross the massive bridge spanning the fjord. After another 40km or so, Highway 38 branches off for the thirteen-kilometre jaunt to **KRAGERØ**, whose narrow harbour is protected by a pair of bumpy little islets. One of the busiest resorts on the coast, Kragerø's tiny centre, with its cramped lanes and alleys rising steeply from the harbourfront, makes a good living as a supply depot for the surrounding coves and rocky islets, where the Norwegians have built themselves scores of summer cottages.

Founded as a timber port in the seventeenth century, Kragerø later boomed as a shipbuilding centre, its past importance recalled by the antique gun battery on the harbour islet of **Gunnarsholmen**. To take a closer look at this relic of the Napoleonic Wars, walk across the causeway on the south side of town. The port was also a fashionable watering hole in the late nineteenth and early twentieth century. It was here that Edvard Munch produced some of his jollier paintings and where **Theodor Kittelsen** (1857–1914), a native of Kragerø, spent his summers. A middling painter but superb illustrator, Kittelsen defined the popular appearance of the country's folkloric creatures – from trolls through to sirens – in his illustrations for Asbjørnsen and Moe's *Norwegian Folk Tales*, published in 1883. Kittelsen's family home, the **Kittelsenhuset**, at Theodor Kittelsens vei 5, in the town centre (late June to mid-Aug Tues–Sat noon–4pm; 30kr), is now a lively little museum celebrating the artist's life and times with a smattering of his paintings and a few family knick-knacks. Kragerø's only other sight of note is its **church**, an imposing brown-brick structure perched on a hill on the north side of the centre.

The most popular excursion from Kragerø is the **ferry to Jomfruland** (June to mid-Aug 3 daily; mid-Aug to late Sept Mon–Fri 2–3 daily, plus limited service the rest of the year; 1hr; 40kr each way; ⓣ40 00 58 58, ⓦwww.fjordbat.no), a long and slender island stuck out in the Skagerrak beyond the offshore skerries. Just 10km long and 600m wide, the island is popular for its easy walking trails which network the wooded interior, and its long rocky beaches. The ferry docks at **Tårnbrygga**, halfway along the north shore.

Practicalities

The main Oslo–Kristiansand **bus stops** in Tangen, where a connecting bus makes the twenty-minute journey to Kragerø. The nearest **train station** is at Neslandsvatn, where the *Togbuss* meets the Oslo–Kristiansand train for the 45-minute journey to Kragerø. In Kragerø itself, the **bus station** is next door to the **tourist office** at the northern tip of the main harbour (May to mid-June Mon–Fri 9am–4pm; mid- to late June & mid-Aug to early Sept Mon–Fri 9am–7pm, Sat 10am–2pm, Sun 11am–3pm; late June to mid-Aug Mon–Fri 9am–7pm, Sat 10am–6pm, Sun 10am–5pm; ⓣ35 98 88 82, ⓦwww.visitkragero.no).

Most holidaymakers shop and eat in Kragerø, but few actually **stay**. Nonetheless, if you are tempted, your best option is the comfortable *Victoria Hotel*, in a good-looking, brightly painted harbourside building at P.A. Heuchs gate 31 (ⓣ35 98 75 25, ⓦwww.aco.no; ❻, sp/r ❹). Much less expensive is the HI **hostel**, the *Kragerø Vandrerhjem*, at Lovisenbergveien 20, 2km out of town along Highway 38 (ⓣ35 98 57 00, ⓦwww.vandrerhjem.no; dorm beds 250kr, doubles ❷; late June to late Aug). The hostel occupies an expansive wooden building beside a pretty bay, rents out rowing boats, and serves tasty if simple evening **meals** and breakfasts; buses travelling into Kragerø on Highway 38 pass right by the hostel.

Arendal

Travelling west from the Kragerø turning along the E18, it's about 65km to small-town **ARENDAL**, one of the most appealing places on the coast, its

△ Arendal

sheltered harbour curling right into the centre, which is further crimped by the forested hills pushing in from behind. The town's heyday was in the eighteenth century when its shipyards churned out dozens of the sleek wooden sailing ships that then dominated international trade. There's an attractive reminder of these boom times in the elegant old merchants' buildings along the waterfront in the oldest part of town, known as **Tyholmen**. You can stroll these few blocks and then proceed north along the boardwalk flanking **Pollen**, the short rectangular inner harbour bordered by pavement cafés. For the architectural lowdown on the Tyholmen, call in at the tourist office (see below) and sign up for one of their **walking tours** (late June to early Aug 3 weekly; 1hr 30min; 50kr). Arendal's other key point of interest is the south coast's largest contemporary arts gallery, **Bomuldsfabriken**, Oddenveien 5 (Tues–Sun noon–4pm; 20kr; Ⓦwww.bomuldsfabriken.com), which hosts some excellent temporary exhibitions. It occupies an old lakeside factory a fifteen-minute walk north of the town centre – and is signposted off Highway 410, the main approach road from E18.

Also available at the tourist office are details of all sorts of **boat trips** leaving from Pollen. The most enjoyable excursion is to **Merdø** (hourly; 35kr), a low-lying, lightly wooded islet in the Skagerrak. Footpaths network the island, there's a beach, a café and the **Merdøgaard Museum** (late June to mid-Aug daily noon–4pm; 30kr); an eighteenth-century sea captain's house, complete with original fixtures and fittings.

Practicalities

From Arendal **train station**, it's a five- to ten-minute walk west to the main square, Torvet – either up and over the steep hill along Iuellsklev and then along Bendiksklev, or through the road tunnel. **Buses** stop in a large square across from the huge red-brick church with a copper-green steeple, about 150m northwest of the inner harbour, Pollen. Tyholmen is a few minutes' walk west of both, while Torvet is a similar distance east. Arendal's **tourist office** is sandwiched in the centre, alongside the bus station at Sam Eydes Plass, in the combined new Rådhus and concert hall (July Mon–Fri 9am–7pm, Sat & Sun 11am–6pm; Aug–June Mon–Fri 9am–7pm, Sat 11am–2pm; ⓣ37 00 55 44, ⓦwww.arendal.com).

The most luxurious place **to stay** is the first-rate *Clarion Hotel Tyholmen*, Teaterplassen 2 (ⓣ37 07 68 00, ⓦwww.choicehotels.no; ❽, sp/r ❹), which occupies a handsome wooden building in the style of an old warehouse on the Tyholmen quayside. The more modest *Thon Hotel Arendal*, Friergangen 1 (ⓣ37 05 21 50, ⓦwww.thonhotels.com/arendal; ❻, s/r ❹), is a straightforward modern hotel with well-appointed rooms, just off the west side of Pollen. Alternatively, 100m west of the *Clarion*, you can get a room with shared facilities in the pleasant *Høholthus Gjestehus*, Radhusgaten 6 (ⓣ92 83 63 90, ⓦwww.kulturkompasset.com/guesthouse; ❸). The price includes the use of the kitchen, garden and library with a tiny balcony overlooking the water.

For **food**, there are a couple of inexpensive cafés on Torvet and a string of more tempting places along and around Pollen, including *Madam Reiersen*, which offers delicious seafood and fresh pasta dishes from its harbourside premises at Nedre Tyholmsvei 3 (Mon–Fri 11.30am–2am, Sat 11am–2am & Sun 2pm–2am). Later on, the café-bars lining Pollen become lively **drinking** haunts till the wee hours, especially on a warm summer's night.

Grimstad

From Arendal, it's a short twenty-kilometre hop south on the E18 to **GRIMSTAD**, where a brisk huddle of white timber houses with orange-tiled roofs is stacked up behind the harbour. Nowadays scores of yachts are moored in the water, but at the beginning of the nineteenth century the town had no fewer than forty shipyards and carried on a lucrative import-export trade with France. It was not particularly surprising, therefore, that when **Henrik Ibsen** left his home in nearby Skien in 1844, aged sixteen, he should come to Grimstad, where he worked as an apprentice pharmacist for the next six years. The ill-judged financial dealings of Ibsen's father had impoverished the family, and Henrik's already jaundiced view of Norway's provincial bourgeoisie was confirmed here in the port, whose worthies Ibsen mocked in poems like *Resignation*, and *The Corpse's Ball*. It was here too that Ibsen picked up first-hand news of the Paris Revolution of 1848, an event that radicalized him and inspired his paean to the insurrectionists of Budapest, *To Hungary*, written in 1849. Nonetheless, Ibsen's stay on the south coast is more usually recalled as providing the setting for some of his better-known plays, particularly *Pillars of Society*. The pint-sized pharmacy where Ibsen lived and worked is now home to the **Ibsenhuset og Grimstad bymuseum** (Ibsen House and Grimstad Town Museum; June–Aug Mon–Fri 11am–5pm, Sat & Sun noon–5pm; Sept–May Mon–Fri 10am–2pm; 40kr), just up from the harbour in the centre of town on Henrik Ibsens gate. With its creaking wooden floors and narrow-beamed ceilings, the building has maintained its nineteenth-century appearance and houses a selection of Ibsen memorabilia – look out for the glass case displaying the playwright's hat, coat, umbrella and boots – as worn on his daily stroll down from his Oslo apartment to the *Grand Hotel*.

From the museum, it's a couple of minutes' walk south to the pedestrianized part of Storgata, once the town's main street. Signposted off it as you near the harbourfront is the **Reimanngården**, four uninspiring replica eighteenth-century buildings, one of which is a reconstruction of another pharmacy where Ibsen worked – the original building was demolished in the 1950s – and now home to the town's art society.

In the opposite direction from the Ibsen house, it's a short, steep hike north up to **Grimstad Kirke**, a large late nineteenth-century wooden church plonked on a hill above the harbour. Inside, many of the original fittings have survived, including some heavy-duty wrought-iron lamps and candelabras, and there's a tapestry of the Resurrection by the font.

Practicalities

With regular services from Oslo, Arendal and Kristiansand, Grimstad **bus station** is at the south end of the harbour, a couple of hundred metres along from the **tourist office** (June–Aug Mon–Fri 9am–6pm, Sat 10am–4pm, plus Sun in July 10am–4pm; Sept–May Mon–Fri 8.30am–4pm; ⓣ37 25 01 68, ⓦwww.grimstad.net). Here, you can pick up all the usual information as well as detailed maps of the islands that dot the seaward approaches to Grimstad harbour. Many of the islands are protected within the **Skjærgårdspark**, and have public access moorings, as well as picnic and bathing facilities: the tourist office can also advise on local **boat hire** companies. In addition, there are a handful of **boat cruises** to choose from, though these don't stop at any of the islands: the most popular is a two-hour coastal cruise on the M/S *Bibben* (July Tues, Thurs & Sun 1 daily; 150kr; ⓣ37 04 31 85, ⓦwww.bibben.com).

Grimstad has an attractive and central **hotel**, the *Grimstad Hotell*, Kirkegaten 3 (ⓣ37 25 25 25, ⓦwww.grimstadhotell.no; ❻), in an old and cleverly converted clapboard complex amongst the narrow lanes near the Ibsen house; the hotel also has the best **restaurant** in town. Wine buffs can check out the locally made fruit wines – Fuhr Rhubarb and Fuhr Vermouth are the two to try.

Lillesand

Bright, cheerful **LILLESAND**, just 20km south of Grimstad, is one of the most popular holiday spots on the coast, the white clapboard houses of its tiny centre draped prettily round the harbourfront. One or two of the buildings, notably the sturdy **Rådhus** (1734), are especially good-looking, but it's the general appearance of the place that appeals, best appreciated from the terrace of one of the town's waterfront café-restaurants: the *Sjøbua*, midway round the harbour, does very nicely.

To investigate Lillesand's architectural nooks and crannies, sign up at the tourist office (see p.146) for one of its hour-long **guided walks** (1 daily mid-June to Aug; 35kr). The tourist office also has information and sailing schedules for a wide variety of local **boat trips**, from fishing trips and cruises along the coast to the *badeboot* (bathing boat; July only 4 daily; 15min; 40kr return), which shuttles across to Hestholm bay on the island of **Skaurøya**, where swimmers don't seem to notice just how cold the Skagerrak is. Even better still is the three-hour cruise aboard **M/S Øya** (late June to mid-Aug Mon–Sat 1 daily; 200kr each way; ⓣ95 93 58 55), a dinky little passenger ferry which wiggles south to Kristiansand (see p.147) along a narrow channel separating the mainland from the offshore islets. Sheltered from the full force of the ocean, this channel – the **Blindleia** – was once a major trade route, but today it's trafficked by every sort of pleasure craft, from replica three-mast sailing ships to the sleekest of yachts. Other, faster, boats make the trip too, but the M/S *Øya* is the most charming.

Practicalities

Lillesand is not on the train line and long-distance buses drop passengers at the viadukten (viaduct); from there it's about a fifteen-minute walk southeast down

Ibsen

Henrik Johan Ibsen (1828–1906), Norway's most famous and influential playwright, is generally regarded as one of the greatest dramatists of all time, and certainly his central themes have powerful modern resonances. In essence, these concern the alienation of the individual from an ethically bankrupt society, loss of religious faith and the yearning of women to transcend the confines of their roles as wives and mothers. Ibsen's central characters often speak evasively, mirroring the repression of their society and their own sense of confusion and guilt. Venomous exchanges – a major characteristic of the playwright's dialogue – appear whenever the underlying tensions break through. Ibsen's protagonists do things which are less than heroic, often incompetent, even malicious. Nevertheless, they aspire to *dåd*, the act of the hero/heroine, arguably a throwback to the old Norse sagas. These themes run right through Ibsen's plays, the first of which, *Catalina* (1850), was written while he was employed as an apothecary's assistant at Grimstad.

The alienation the plays reveal was undoubtedly spawned by his troubled **childhood**: Ibsen's father had gone bankrupt in 1836, and the disgrace – and poverty – weighed heavily on the whole family. More humiliation followed at Grimstad, where the shy, young Ibsen worked for a pittance and was obliged to share a bed with his boss and two maids, which resulted in one of them bearing him a child in 1846. Ibsen **escaped provincial Norway** in 1850, settling first in Oslo and then Bergen. But he remained deeply dissatisfied with Norwegian society, which he repeatedly decried as illiberal and small-minded. In 1864, he **left the country** and spent the next 27 years living in Germany and Italy. It was during his exile that Ibsen established his literary reputation – at first with the rhyming couplets of *Peer Gynt*, featuring the antics of the eponymous hero, a shambolic opportunist in the mould of Don Quixote, and then by a vicious attack on small-town values in *Pillars of Society*. It was, however, *A Doll's House* (1879) which really put him on the map, its controversial protagonist, Nora, making unwise financial decisions before walking out not only on her patronizing husband, Torvald, but also on her loving children – all in her desire to control her own destiny. *Ghosts* followed two years later, and its exploration of moral contamination through the metaphor of syphilis created an even greater furore, which Ibsen rebutted in his next work, *An Enemy of the People* (1882). Afterwards, Ibsen changed tack (if not theme), firstly with *The Wild Duck* (1884), a mournful tale of the effects of compulsive truth-telling, and then *Hedda Gabler* (1890), where the heroine is denied the ability to make or influence decisions, and so becomes perverse, manipulative and ultimately self-destructive.

Ibsen **returned to Oslo** in 1891. He was treated as a hero, and ironically – considering the length of his exile and his comments on his compatriots – as a symbol of Norwegian virtuosity. Indeed, the daily stroll he took from his apartment to the *Grand Hotel* in Karl Johans gate became something of a tourist attraction. He was incapacitated by a heart attack in 1901 and died from the effects of another one five years later.

Jernbaneg to the centre. Local buses, shuttling between towns along the coast, often connect with this service before pulling in near the southern end of the harbour, a brief stroll from the **tourist office**, located in the old customs house (mid-June to mid-Aug Mon–Fri 10am–6pm, Sat 10am–4pm & Sun noon–4pm; mid-Aug to mid-June Mon–Fri 9am–4pm; ⓣ37 40 19 10, ⓦwww.lillesand.com). Lillesand has one central **hotel**, the first-rate *Hotel Norge*, Strandgata 3 (ⓣ37 27 01 44, ⓦwww.hotelnorge.no; ❼, sp/r ❻), which occupies a grand old wooden building metres from the harbour. Refurbished in attractive period style, the interior holds some charming stained-glass windows and the rooms are named after some of the famous people who have stayed here – the novelist Knut Hamsun and the Spanish king Alfonso XIII for starters. Alternatively, try *Tingsaker Familiecamping*, on Øvre Tingsaker (ⓣ37 27 04 21, ⓦwww.tingsakercamping.no;

May–Aug), a well-equipped waterfront campsite with cabins (❷). The campsite is about 1km north of the centre – take Storgata and keep going – and has self-catering facilities, canoe hire, a pool and a playground. The *Hotel Norge* has an excellent **restaurant**, but it's more expensive and formal than the harbourfront *Sjøbua* (☎37 27 03 66), where you can sample excellent fish dishes for around 180kr, in surroundings kitted out like an old sailing ship.

Kristiansand

With 75,000 inhabitants, **KRISTIANSAND**, some 30km west along the E18 from Lillesand, is Norway's fifth-largest town and a part-time holiday resort, a genial, energetic place which thrives on its ferry connections with Denmark, its busy marinas and passable sandy beaches. In summer, the seafront and adjoining streets are a frenetic bustle of cocktail bars, fast-food joints and flirting holiday-makers, and even in winter Norwegians come here to live it up.

Like so many other Scandinavian towns, Kristiansand was founded by and named after **Christian IV**, who saw an opportunity to strengthen his coastal defences here. Building started in 1641, and the town has retained the spacious quadrant plan that characterized all Christian's projects. There are few specific sights, but it's worth a quick look around, especially when everyone else has gone to the beach and left the central pedestrianized streets relatively empty. It's main attraction, however, is a few kilometres out of town at the **Kristiansand Kanonmuseum**, the forbidding remains of a large coastal gun battery built during the German occupation.

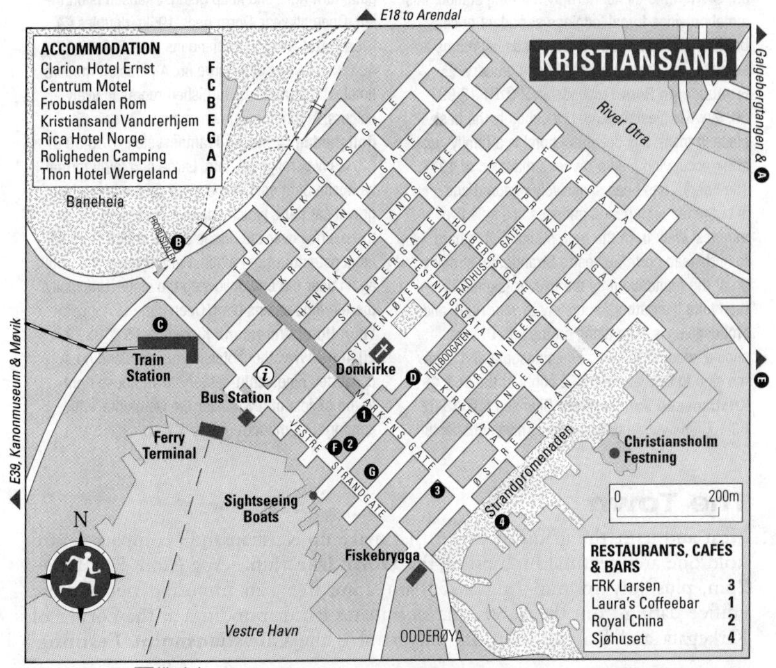

Arrival and information

Trains, **buses** and international **ferries** all arrive close to each other, by Vestre Strandgate, on the edge of the town grid. The main regional **tourist office** is here too, at Vestre Strandgate 32 (mid-June to mid-Aug Mon–Fri 8.30am–6pm, Sat 10am–6pm, Sun noon–6pm; mid-Aug to mid-June Mon–Fri 8.30am–3.30pm; ⓣ38 12 13 14, ⓦwww.sorlandet.com). Staff issue free town maps, public transport timetables and information on boat times, island bathing and beaches. **Parking** is easy throughout town, with car parks concentrated along Vestre Strandgate. The best way to explore the town centre is on **foot** – it only takes about ten minutes to walk from one side to the other – but for the more outlying attractions, including the best beaches, you might want to **rent a bike** at Kristiansand Sykkelsenter, about 800m north of the tourist office at Grim Torv 3 (ⓣ38 02 68 35).

Accommodation

Kristiansand has a reasonably good choice of **accommodation** with a fair sprinkling of hotels, a guesthouse or two, a youth hostel and a nearby campsite.

Clarion Hotel Ernst Rådhusgaten 2 ⓣ38 12 86 00, ⓦwww.ernst.no. Housed in a flashily modernized building, this hotel has large doubles with standard-issue modern furnishings. The air conditioning can be stuffy, so try to get a room where you can open a window and which doesn't face the covered courtyard. ❼, sp/r ❹

Centrum Motel Vestre Strandgate 49 ⓣ38 02 79 69, ⓦwww.motell.no. Hard by the train station, this motel provides frugal lodgings at budget prices. Doubles are in the form of bunkbeds, all rooms are en suite, and there's a kitchen and laundry. ❷

Frobusdalen Rom Frobusdalen 2 ⓣ91 12 99 06, ⓦwww.gjestehus.no. Undoubtedly the best place in town, this delightful hotel is a family-run affair occupying a ship-owner's mansion of 1917. The interior has been sensitively restored and is crammed with period antiques. It's only five minutes' walk from the train station but is hard to find: head north up Vestre Strandgate, straight on at the roundabout by the flyover (signed Evje), then take the path immediately to your right, and Frobusdalen is 10m along on the left. Drivers should head north along Festningsgata and follow the sign to Evje at the traffic lights at the end. ❷

Kristiansand Vandrerhjem Skansen 8 ⓣ38 02 83 10, ⓦwww.vandrerhjem.no. This youth hostel is in an odd location – a few hundred metres from the (busy) town beach, but also in a light industrial estate. It has cramped rooms in an ugly, prefabricated 1960s building, but the facilities are quite good with self-catering, a laundry and a café. The hostel is about fifteen minutes' walk east of the ferry terminal on the tiny peninsula – Tangen – edging the marina. Take any street up to Elvegata, turn right and keep going: Skansen is on the left. Open all year. Dorm beds 195kr, doubles ❷

Rica Hotel Norge Dronningens gate 5 ⓣ38 17 40 00, ⓦwww.hotel-norge.no. A pleasant modern hotel with attractively furnished rooms in lively colours. A good downtown choice. ❻, sp/r ❹

Roligheden Camping Framnesveien ⓣ38 09 67 22, ⓦwww.roligheden.no. Large and fairly formal campsite 3km east of the town centre behind a gravel car park, which edges a yacht jetty. To get there, drive over the bridge at the end of Dronningens gate, turn right along Marviksveien, then right again near the end, following the signs. Unusually, there are no cabins here. Open June to August.

Thon Hotel Wergeland Kirkegata 15 ⓣ38 17 20 40, ⓦwww.thonhotels.com/wergeland.no. A converted nineteenth-century town house right in the middle of town, near the Domkirke, with comfortable, modern rooms. ❺, sp/r ❸

The Town

Neat and trim, the gridiron streets that make up Kristiansand's compact centre hold one architectural high point, the **Domkirke** (June–Aug Mon–Fri 10am–2pm, plus July to mid-Aug Sat 10am–2pm; free), an imposing neo-Gothic edifice dating from the 1880s that dominates its surroundings at the corner of Kirkegata and Rådhusgaten. Its only rival is the **Christiansholm Festning**, on Strandpromenaden (mid-May to mid-Sept daily 9am–9pm; free), a squat fortress whose sturdy circular tower and zigzagging earth-and-stone ramparts overlook the marina in the east harbour. Built in 1672, the tower's walls are 5m thick, a defensive precaution that proved unnecessary since it never saw action. These days it houses various arts and crafts displays.

If you fancy a **swim**, one option is **Galgebergtangen** (Gallows' Point), an attractive rocky cove with a small sandy beach, 2km east of the town centre. To get there, go over the bridge at the end of Dronningens gate, take the first major right (at the lights) and follow the signs. Closer still, you can get a dose of Norwegian **wood** by visiting the **Odderøya**, a tiny peninsula and one-time quarantine station that juts out from the south end of Vestre Strandgate, just beyond the Fiskebrygga or fishmarket. About 3km long and half as wide, the peninsula is crisscrossed by footpaths and there's swimming off the rocks and beaches; the Norwegian armed forces controlled Odderøya until 2003, hence the scattering of military installations.

Kristiansand Kanonmuseum

Despite the inveigling of the German admiralty, who feared the British would occupy Norway and thus trap their fleet in the Baltic, **Hitler** was lukewarm about invading Norway until he met Vidkun Quisling in Berlin in late 1939. Hitler took Quisling's assurances about his ability to stage a coup d'état at face value, no doubt encouraged by the Norwegian's virulent anti-Semitism, and was thereafter keen to proceed. In the event, the invasion went smoothly enough – even if Quisling was soon discarded – but for the rest of the war Hitler overestimated both Norway's strategic importance and the likelihood of an Allied counterinvasion in the north. These two errors of judgement prompted him to garrison the country with nigh on half a million men and built several hundred artillery batteries round the coast – a huge waste of resources that were desperately needed elsewhere.

Work began on the coastal battery that is now conserved as the **Kristiansand Kanonmuseum** (mid-May to mid-June Mon–Wed 11am–3pm; mid-June to mid-Aug daily 11am–6pm; mid-Aug to Sept Mon–Wed 11am–3pm & Thurs–Sun 11am–5pm; Oct to mid-May Sun only noon–4pm; 60kr) in 1941, using – like all equivalent emplacements in Norway – the forced labour of POWs. Around 1400 men worked on the project, which involved the construction of protective housings for four big guns at the narrowest part of the Skagerrak. Guns on the Danish shore complemented those here, so that any enemy warship trying to slip through the straits could be shelled. Only a small zone in the middle was out of range, and this the Germans mined. The complex once covered 220 acres, but today the principal remains hog a narrow ridge, with a massive, empty artillery casement at one end, and a whopping 38cm-calibre **gun** in a concrete well at the other. The gun, which could fire a 500kg shell almost 55km, is in pristine condition, and visitors can explore the loading area, complete with the original ramrods, wedges, trolleys and pulleys. Below is the underground command post and soldiers' living quarters, again almost exactly as they were in the 1940s – including the odd bit of German graffiti.

The Kanonmuseum is situated an easy ten-kilometre drive south of Kristiansand, along the coast at **Møvik**: take Highway 456 out of Kristiansand, turning down Highway 457 for the last 3km of the journey.

Eating and drinking

There are lots of **restaurants** and **cafés** in the centre of Kristiansand, but the standard is very variable – we've given a few of the choicer places below. If you

Moving on from Kristiansand

When it comes to **moving on from Kristiansand**, the obvious choice – the 250-kilometre trip west to Stavanger – is also the best. It's a journey that can be made by train as well as by bus or car along the E39, though both the railway line and the highway only afford glimpses of the coast, travelling for the most part a few kilometres inland. It may not be a gripping journey, but it's certainly a lot more pleasant than the dreary 240-kilometre haul north up **Setesdal** on Highway 9 to the E134. If, on the other hand, you're travelling north towards Oslo between late June and mid-August, it might be worth considering the three-hour cruise up to Lillesand on the M/S *Øya* (see p.145).

want to buy ingredients for some alfresco dining, the fish market has a wonderful selection of raw and cooked seafood, or, more prosaically, there's a large supermarket (Mon–Fri 9am–10pm; Sun 9am–8pm) directly opposite the train station on Vestre Strandgate. There's also a fairly active nightlife based around a handful of downtown **bars**, which stay open until 2am.

Laura's Coffeebar Radhusgata 10. By the library in the heart of town, this mellow, friendly café serves excellent coffee, delicious cakes and tasty lunches.

FRK Larsen Markensgate 5. Near the corner of Kongensgate, this laid-back café-bar is an appealing, fashionable place. Also serves light meals and snacks.

Royal China Tollbodgaten 7 ☎38 07 02 77. Surprisingly plush Chinese restaurant offering tasty main courses from as little as 110kr. Open daily.

Sjøhuset Østre Strandgate 12a ☎38 02 62 60. In an old converted warehouse by the harbour at the east end of Markensgate, this excellent restaurant serves superb fish courses from 230kr (160kr at lunchtime). Nautical fittings and wooden beams set the scene. Daily 11am–11pm.

West from Kristiansand to Stavanger

West of Kristiansand lies a sparsely inhabited region, where the rough uplands and long valleys of the interior bounce down to a shoreline that is pierced by a string of inlets and fjords. The highlight is undoubtedly **Mandal**, a fetching seaside resort with probably the best sandy beach in the whole of Norway, but thereafter it's a struggle to find much inspiration. The best you'll do is the old harbour town of **Flekkefjord**, though frankly there's not much reason to pause anywhere between Mandal and Stavanger.

The **E39** weaves its way west for 240km from Kristiansand to Stavanger, staying inland for the most part and offering only the odd glimpse of the coast. The **train line** follows pretty much the same route, though it does avoid Flekkefjord, until it reaches **Egersund**, when it returns to the coast for the final 80km, slicing across long flat plains with the sea on one side and distant hills away to the east.

Mandal

MANDAL, just 40km from Kristiansand along the E39, is Norway's southernmost town. This old timber port reached its heyday in the eighteenth century, when pines and oaks from the surrounding countryside were much sought after by the Dutch to support their canal houses and build their trading fleet. Although it's now bordered by a modern mess, Mandal has preserved its quaint **old centre**, a narrow strip of white clapboard buildings spread along the north bank of the Mandalselva River just before it rolls into the sea. It's an attractive spot, well worth a stroll, and you can also drop by the municipal **museum** (late June to mid-Aug Mon–Fri 11am–5pm, Sat 11am–2pm & Sun noon–5pm; 20kr), whose rambling collection – from agricultural implements to seafaring tackle – occupies an old merchant's house overlooking the river. Its exhibits also include a small but enjoyable collection of nautical paintings, and outside by the front door is a statue of the town's most famous son, Gustav Vigeland (see p.109). It's not its antiquities that make Mandal a popular tourist spot, however, but its fine beach, **Sjøsanden**. An 800-metre stretch of golden sand backed by pine trees and framed by rocky headlands, it's touted as Norway's best beach – and although this isn't saying a lot, it's a very enjoyable place to unwind for a few hours. The beach is about 1.5km from the town centre: walk along the harbour, past the tourist office to the end of the road and turn left; keep going until you reach the car park at the beach's eastern end. You can also explore a tiny wooded peninsula directly to the west of the beach, where a network of paths winds through the trees and rocks to reveal hidden, sandy coves. Pick up a leaflet at the tourist office.

If you have your own transport, you should also consider an excursion to the windy headland of **Lindesnes** (literally "where the land curves round"), 40km away to the southwest – take the E39 and turn down Highway 460. This is Norway's most southerly point, a bare, lichen-stained promontory surmounted by a sturdy red-and-white lighthouse that is exposed to extraordinarily ferocious storms, especially when the warm westerly currents of the Skagerrak meet cold easterly winds.

Practicalities

There are no trains to Mandal, but buses from Kristiansand (2–4 daily; 40min) and Stavanger (1–3 daily; 3hr 30min) pull in at the ugly modern **bus station** by the bridge on the north bank of the Mandalselva River. From here it's a brief walk west to the old town centre, just beyond which is the **tourist office**, facing the river at Bryggegata 10 (June to Aug Mon–Fri 9am–7pm, Sat & Sun 10am–4pm; Sept to May Mon–Fri 9am–4pm; ⓣ38 27 83 00, ⓦwww.visitregionmandal.com). There are a couple of good places to **stay**, beginning with the handy and economical *Kjøbmandsgaarden Hotel*, which occupies an old timber house in a street of such buildings, across from the bus station at Store Elvegate 57 (ⓣ38 26 12 76, ⓦwww.kjobmandsgaarden.com; ❹). All the dozen or so rooms are spick and span and the decor is bright and cheerful. More upmarket is the *First Hotel Solborg*, Neseveien 1 (ⓣ38 27 21 00, ⓕ38 27 21 01; ❼, sp/r ❺), an odd-looking but somehow rather fetching modern structure with every mod con; it's on the west side of the town centre, a good ten-minute walk from the bus station, tight against a wooded escarpment. Alternatively, you can **camp** or rent a cabin (❷) very close to the western end of the beach at the *Sjøsanden Feriesenter*, Sjøsandvei 1 (ⓣ38 26 14 19, ⓦwww.sjosanden-feriesenter.no), a signposted two-kilometre walk from the town centre.

The *First Hotel Solborg* has the best **restaurant** in town, but for something less pricey and more informal, head into the centre where you'll find several places, including the lively pizzeria-restaurant, *Jonas B Gundersen*, at Store Elvegate 25. The café-restaurant of the *Kjøbmandsgaarden Hotel* comes highly recommended too, offering a tasty range of Norwegian dishes at inexpensive prices.

Flekkefjord

Moving on from Mandal, the **E39** hurries west, running past the turning for the Lindesnes lighthouse (see above) before proceeding over the hills to workaday **Lyngdal** and subsequently **LIKNES**, a fjordside village at the foot of Kvinesdal. Thereafter, the highway offers a rare glimpse of the ocean as it slips along the slender **Fedafjord** before turning inland again to snake over the hills to **FLEKKEFJORD**, 80km from Mandal. With a population of 6000, Flekkefjord is the big deal hereabouts, the old and picturesque timber houses of its tiny centre strung along the banks of a short (500m) channel that connects the Lafjord and the Grisefjord. Flekkefjord boomed in the sixteenth century on the back of its trade with the Dutch, who purchased the town's timber for their houses and its granite for their dykes and harbours. Later, in the 1750s, the herring industry was the main money spinner, along with shipbuilding and tanning, but the Flekkefjord economy had pretty much collapsed by the end of the nineteenth century when sailing ships gave way to steam. The oldest and prettiest part of Flekkefjord – known as **Hollenderbyen** after the town's Dutch connections – is on the west side of the channel, and only takes a few minutes to explore, though you can extend this pleasantly enough by visiting the nearby nineteenth-century period rooms of the **Flekkefjord Museum** (mid-June to Aug Mon–Fri noon–5pm, Sat & Sun noon–3pm; 25kr).

Buses pull in on Løvikgata, about 200m east of the central waterway, while the **tourist office** is on the west side of the same waterway at Elvegata 9 (mid-June to mid-Aug Mon–Fri 9am–5pm, Sat & Sun 10am–3pm; mid-Aug to mid-June Mon–Fri 9am–4pm; ⓣ38 32 69 95, ⓦwww.visitsydvest.no). There's no pressing reason to overnight here, but if you do want **to stay**, the unassuming *Maritim Fjordhotell* (ⓣ38 32 58 00, ⓦwww.fjordhotellene.no; ❺, sp/r ❹), overlooking the east side of the central waterway at Sundgata 9, is the best bet.

Egersund and the Jossingfjord

At Flekkefjord, the E39 turns inland, threading its way over the hills and down the dales bound for Stavanger, 120km away. Alternatively, you can take the more southerly, but slightly longer (30km or so), **Highway 44** which offers occasional glimpses of the sea, most memorably when it wiggles across the narrow **JOSSINGFJORD**, the scene of dramatic events in World War II. In February 1940, the German supply ship *Altmar* was transporting 300 Allied POWs to Germany, when it was spotted by a British destroyer, HMS *Cossack*. The destroyer gave chase, trapped the *Altmar* here in the Jossingfjord and freed the prisoners. At this time in the war, this was a rare British success and it prompted those Norwegians who were opposed to the Germans – the vast majority of the population – to call themselves "Jossings" throughout hostilities.

From the Jossingfjord, it's a further 35km or so to **EGERSUND**, a port and minor manufacturing centre that spreads over a jigsaw of bays and lakes at the end of a deep and sheltered ocean inlet. Apart from an assortment of old timber houses in the centre, along Strandgaten, Egersund's transport links are the main reason to visit: it's on the Kristiansand–Stavanger **train line** and has Fjord Line **ferry** connections with Bergen and Hantsholm in Denmark.

From Egersund, it's 10km north to the E39 and a further 65km to Stavanger.

Stavanger and around

STAVANGER is something of a survivor. While other Norwegian coastal towns have fallen foul of the precarious fortunes of fishing, Stavanger has grown

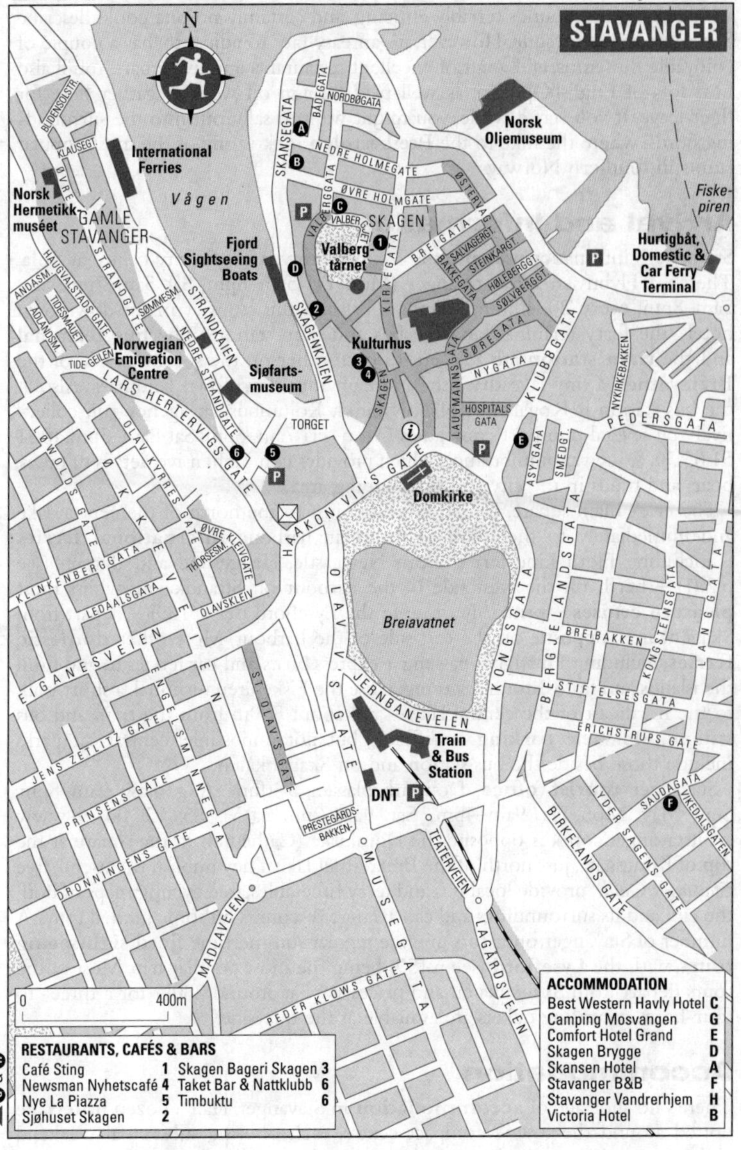

and flourished, and is now the proud possessor of a dynamic economy which has swelled the population to over 100,000. It was the herring fishery that first put money into the town, crowding its nineteenth-century wharves with coopers and smiths, net makers and menders. When the fishing failed, the town moved into shipbuilding and ultimately oil: today the port builds the rigs for Norway's offshore oilfields and refines the oil as well.

None of which sounds terribly enticing, and certainly no one could describe Stavanger as picturesque. However, it's an easy city to adjust to, has a couple of enjoyable museums, and a raft of excellent restaurants and lively bars. You'll also hear lots of English spoken, as well-paid foreign oil-workers gather here for their leave. If you stay a while, you might want to sally out into the surrounding fjords, where the hike to the **Preikestolen** rock is one of the most popular jaunts in southern Norway.

Arrival and information

Stavanger's international **airport** is 14km southwest of the city centre at **Sola**. There's a Flybussen into Stavanger (Mon–Fri 5am–8pm, Sat 5am–7pm, Sun 5am–8pm; every 20–40min; 40min; 60kr) and this stops at major downtown hotels, the ferry terminals and the bus and train stations. The **bus terminal** and the **train station** are adjacent to each other on the southern side of the **Breiavatnet**, a tiny lake that's the most obvious downtown landmark. Also at the bus station is Rogaland Kollektivtrafikk Kolumbus, an agency run collectively by several transport companies (Mon–Fri 7am–6pm, Sat 8am–3pm; ⓣ51 51 65 30, ⓦwww.kolumbus.no), which provides comprehensive details of buses, boats and trains in the city and surrounding area.

The city's main square, Torget, is located just to the north of the central lake and immediately to the south of the main harbour. **International ferries** – including Fjord Line ferries from Newcastle, Haugesund and Bergen (see p.201) – berth on the west side of the harbour on Strandkaien, whilst most **pleasure cruises** – primarily those to the Lysefjord (see p.159) – depart from Skagenkaien, opposite on the east side of the harbour. Most other **domestic ferries**, including Hurtigbåt passenger express boats and car ferries to and from the islands and fjords around Stavanger, use the Fiskepiren terminal, a short walk to the northeast of the central lake – and about 800m from the train and bus stations. On-street **parking** is difficult, but not impossible; central car parks include those beside the bus station and on Skagenkaien.

Stavanger **tourist office**, Domkirkeplassen 3 (June–Aug daily 9am–8pm; Sept–May Mon–Fri 9am–4pm, Sat 9am–2pm; ⓣ51 85 92 00, ⓦwww.visitstavanger.com), is opposite the Domkirke (Cathedral) in the square at the top of Kongsgata, just north of the Breiavatnet lake. They publish the useful, free *Stavanger Guide*, provide local bus and ferry timetables, free cycling maps of both the city and its surroundings and can arrange discounts on some guided tours. A number of Stavanger operators provide regular summertime **fjord sightseeing tours**, with the **Lysefjord** (see p.159) being the most popular trip. Most of the tours depart from Skagenkaien and prices start at around 280kr for a three- to four-hour excursion; tickets are available at the quayside.

Accommodation

There's no shortage of **accommodation** in Stavanger. Half a dozen **hotels** are dotted around the town's compact centre, each offering substantial weekend and summer discounts. Alternatively, there are a couple of convenient, no-frills **guesthouses** and, further afield, an HI **hostel** and **campsite**.

Hotels and guesthouses

Best Western Havly Hotel Valberggata 1 ⓣ51 93 90 00, ⓦwww.havly-hotell.no. Unassuming, quiet hotel in the narrow side streets off Skagenkaien. ❺, sp/r ❸

Comfort Hotel Grand Klubbgata 3 ⓣ51 20 14 00, ⓦwww.choicehotels.no. A good central choice, close to all the bars and restaurants. The rooms are smart, modern and spacious. The price includes a very good buffet breakfast and afternoon snacks. ❻, sp/r ❹

Skagen Brygge Hotell Skagenkaien 30 ⓣ51 85 00 00, ⓦwww.skagenbrygge hotell.no. A delightful quayside hotel, built in the style of an old warehouse but with lots of glass, and great views over the harbour. The rooms are modern and tastefully decorated, the buffet breakfast outstanding and delicious mid-afternoon nibbles are free. The only quibble concerns the noise from outside on summer weekends, when your best bet is probably to get a room at the back or on the top floor. ❼, sp/r ❹

Skansen Hotel Skansegata 7 ⓣ51 93 85 00, ⓦwww.skansenhotel.no. In a creatively revamped and remodelled old wooden building down by the main harbour, this attractive establishment has about thirty hotel rooms decorated in smart modern style plus sixteen guesthouse rooms that are somewhat plainer but still perfectly adequate. Guesthouse ❹, sp/r ❸; hotel ❺, sp/r ❹

Stavanger Bed and Breakfast Vikedalsgata 1a ⓣ51 56 25 00, ⓦwww.stavangerbedandbreakfast.no. This friendly, modern B&B in a residential area five minutes' walk southeast of the central lake has bright and cheerful rooms with showers and sinks – but shared toilets. A real snip at ❸

Victoria Hotel Skansegata 1 ⓣ51 86 70 00, ⓦwww.victoria-hotel.no. Part of the Rica chain, this large hotel occupies a big old building, with a fancy portico, that overlooks the east side of the main harbour. The foyer has kept much of its Victorian appearance, complete with wood panelling, leather sofas and ships' models, while the comfortable bedrooms beyond are also in a broadly period style. ❼, sp/r ❹

Hostels and campsites

Stavanger Camping Mosvangen Tjensvollveien 1b ⓣ51 53 29 71, ⓦwww.stavangercamping.no. On the south bank of lake Mosvatnet, a 3km walk from the centre and metres from the HI hostel (see below), this large campsite has cabins (❷) as well as areas for tents and caravans. To get there, take Kannikgata/Madlaveien west from near the station, continue along the north side of the lake and turn left just beyond it onto Tjensvollveien. Open mid-May to mid-Sept.

Stavanger Vandrerhjem Henrik Ibsens gate 19, ⓣ51 54 36 36, ⓦwww.vandrerhjem.no. This plain HI hostel stands on the south side of lake Mosvatnet, a 3km walk from the centre – directions are as for Stavanger Camping (see above), with Henrik Ibsens gate being a continuation of Tjensvollveien. The hostel has self-catering and laundry facilities; advance reservations are advised. Open early June to mid-Aug. Dorm beds 170kr, doubles ❶

The City

Built with oil money, much of **central Stavanger** is strikingly modern, a flashy but surprisingly likeable ensemble of mini tower blocks that spreads over the hilly ground that abuts the main harbour. The only relic of the medieval city is the twelfth-century **Domkirke** (June–Aug daily 11am–7pm; Sept–May Tues–Thurs & Sat 11am–4pm; free), whose pointed-hat towers signal a Romanesque church that has suffered from several poorly conceived renovations. The simple interior, originally the work of English craftsmen, has fared badly too, spoilt by ornate seventeenth-century additions, including an intricate pulpit and the five huge memorial tablets that adorn the walls of the aisles – a jumble of richly carved angels, crucifixes, death's-heads, animals and apostles.

A brief stroll to the northeast, beyond the fresh fish and flower stalls of **Torget**, the main square, is the **Skagen area**, built on the bumpy promontory that forms the eastern side of the main harbour. It's an oddly discordant district, a sometimes clumsy, sometimes charming mixture of the old and new, and it incorporates a busy shopping zone, whose mazy street plan is the only legacy of the original Viking settlement. The spiky **Valbergtårnet** (Valberg tower), sitting atop Skagen's highest point and guarded by three rusty cannons, is the one specific sight, a nineteenth-century firewatch offering sweeping views of the city and its industry.

Beside the waterfront on the far side of Skagen, the oil industry celebrates its achievements by way of the gleaming **Norsk Oljemuseum** (Norwegian Petroleum Museum; June–Aug daily 10am–7pm, Sept–May Mon–Sat 10am–4pm & Sun 10am–6pm; 80kr; ⓦwww.norskolje.museum.no). Housed in a hangar-like building, the museum has displays on North Sea geology, oil extraction and the like, complete with drill bits and other oil-rig paraphernalia. There are several hands-on exhibits too – including a diving bell – plus an honest account of the accidents and occasional disasters that have befallen the industry.

Gamle Stavanger (Old Stavanger)

The city's star turn is **Gamle Stavanger**, on the western side of the main harbour. Though very different in appearance from the modern structures back in the centre, the buildings here were also the product of a boom. From 1810 until around 1870, herring turned up just offshore in their millions, and Stavanger took advantage of this slice of luck. The town flourished and expanded, with the number of merchants and shipowners increasing dramatically. Huge profits were made from the exported fish, which were salted and later, as the technology improved, canned. Today, some of the wooden stores and warehouses flanking the western quayside hint at their nineteenth-century pedigree, but it's the succession of narrow, cobbled lanes behind them that shows Gamle Stavanger to best advantage. Formerly home to local seafarers, craftsmen and cannery workers, the area has been maintained as a residential quarter, mercifully free of tourist tat; the long rows of white-painted, clapboard houses are immaculately maintained, complete with gas lamps, picket fences and tiny terraced gardens. There's little architectural pretension, but here and there flashes of fancy wooden scrollwork must once have raised eyebrows among the Lutheran population.

The Norsk Hermetikkmuséet (Canning Museum)

Right in the heart of Gamle Stavanger at Øvre Strandgate 88, the **Norsk Hermetikkmuséet** (early June & late Aug Mon–Thurs 11am–3pm & Sun 11am–4pm; mid-June to mid-Aug daily 11am–4pm; Sept–May Sun only 11am–4pm; 50kr) occupies an old **sardine-canning factory** and gives a glimpse of the industry that saved Stavanger from collapse at the end of the nineteenth century. When the herring largely disappeared from local waters in

△ Gamle Stavanger

the 1870s, the canning factories switched to imported fish, thereby keeping the local economy afloat. They remained Stavanger's main source of employment until as late as 1960: in the 1920s there were seventy canneries in the town, and the last one only closed down in 1983.

A visit to an old canning factory may not seem too enticing, but the museum is actually very good, not least because of its collection of **sardine tin labels**, called *iddis* in these parts from the local pronunciation of *etikett*, the Norwegian for label. Hundreds of labels have survived, in part because they were avidly collected by the town's children, though this harmless hobby seems to have worried the town's adults no end – "Label thefts – an unfortunate collection craze", ran a 1915 headline in the *Stavanger Aftenblad* newspaper. The variety of label design is extraordinary – anything and everything from representations of the Norwegian royal family to surrealistic fish with human qualities. Spare a thought also for a Scottish seaman by the name of **William Anderson**: it was his face, copied from a photograph, that beamed out from millions of *Skippers'* sardine tins, a celebrity status so frowned upon by shipowners that Anderson couldn't find work, though fortunately the story ended happily: Anderson wrote to the cannery concerned to complain and they put him on the payroll for the remainder of his working life. You can watch the museum **smoking its own sardines** on the first Sunday of every month and every Tuesday and Thursday from mid-June to mid-August, and then nibble away to your heart's content.

The Sjøfartsmuseum (Maritime Museum) and the Norwegian Emigration Centre

Walk back through the old town towards the centre and you'll come to the **Sjøfartsmuseum** (same times as Canning Museum; 40kr), at Nedre Strandgate 17. Sited in a restored warehouse, this museum gives another insight into the history of Stavanger, with the exhibits mostly exploring the various trades that served the shipping industry. There are some nice touches like the old sailmakers' room, and some reconstructed shop and office interiors.

Just around the corner from the Sjøfartsmuseum, on the west side of the harbour at Strandkaien 31, the **Norwegian Emigration Centre** (Mon & Wed–Fri 9am–3pm, Tues 9am–7pm; Ⓣ51 53 88 60, Ⓦwww.utvandrersenteret.no) might be of interest if you have Norwegian ancestors. Among a wide portfolio of historical data, it holds parish registers, ship passenger lists and census records covering all of Norway, which enables people to trace Norwegian forebears. To stand a good chance of success, you really need to have the exact name, date of birth and year of emigration. The research is charged for by the hour, which can become very expensive, but if you want to do it yourself, you'll need to be able to read Danish and Norwegian, often in Gothic script.

Eating, drinking and nightlife

Although prices are marginally inflated by oil-industry expense accounts, Stavanger is a great place to **eat**, with several fine seafood restaurants clustered on the east side of the main harbour along Skagenkaien. For something less expensive, the best option is to stick to the more mundane cafés and restaurants near the Kulturhus in the heart of the Skagen shopping area.

Stavanger is lively at night, particularly at weekends when a rum assortment of oil workers, sailors, fishermen, executives, tourists and office workers gathers in the **bars and clubs** on and around Skagenkaien to live (or rather drink) it up. Most places stay open until 2am or later, with rowdy – but usually amiable – revellers lurching from one bar to the next.

For more subdued evenings, check out the programme at the **Stavanger Konserthus** (Concert Hall; ⓣ51 53 70 00, ⓦwww.stavanger-konserthus.no) in Bjergsted park, north of the centre beyond Gamle Stavanger, where there are regular concerts by the Stavanger Symphony Orchestra and visiting artists. There's an eight-screen **cinema**, Stavanger Kinematografer, inside the Kulturhus, on Sølvberggaten 2 (ⓣ820 00 100, premium line).

Cafés and restaurants

Café Sting Valbergjet 3 ⓣ51 89 38 78, ⓦwww.cafe-sting.no. Right next to the Valbergtårnet tower, this laid-back café-bar is probably the coolest place in town. The food is tasty and inexpensive, with mostly Mediterranean and Norwegian dishes. Also doubles as an art gallery and live music venue, hosting anything from indie through to rock. Daily from 11am to early in the morning.

Nye La Piazza Rosenkildetorget 1. By the main harbour, just off the Torget, this smart Italian restaurant serves delicious pizzas, pasta and more. Daily noon–midnight; mains from 125kr.

Sjøhuset Skagen Skagenkaien 16 ⓣ51 89 51 80. Excellent seafood restaurant in an attractive and brightly painted old harbourside building. Monkfish, every which way, is a house speciality. Main dishes are around 220kr. Mon–Fri 5pm–midnight, Sat 11.30am–midnight & Sun 1–10pm.

Skagen Bageri Skagen 18. This pleasant coffee house, with a finely carved antique door and lintel, occupies the prettiest of the old wooden buildings on Skagen, one block up from the quayside. Great pastries, cakes and snacks at reasonable prices. Mon–Fri 7am–5pm, Sat 8am–3pm & Sun noon–5pm.

Bars and clubs

Newsman Nyhetscafé Skagen 14. One block back from the east side of the harbour, this attractive and busy café-cum-bar has papers to read and a well-heeled clientele. Open Mon–Fri noon–1.30am, Sat 11am–1.30am & Sun 3pm–1.30am.

Taket Bar & Nattklubb Nedre Strandgate 15 ⓣ51 84 37 00, ⓦwww.herlige-restauranter.com. The best club in town, across the harbour from most of the bars, and strong on house music with special DJ nights; don't be surprised if you have to queue; above Timbuktu (see below). Open Wed–Sat 11pm–3.30am & Sun midnight–3.30am.

Timbuktu Nedre Strandgate 15. Flashy café-bar noted for its imaginative modern decor and trendy atmosphere; beneath Taket (see above). Open Mon–Wed 6pm–midnight, Thurs–Sat 6pm–1.30am.

Listings

Airlines Norwegian Air Shuttle (ⓣ815 21 815); SAS/Braathens (ⓣ05400); Widerøe's (ⓣ810 01 200).

Car rental Hertz, Olav V's gate 13 (ⓣ51 52 00 00).

Emergencies Fire ⓣ110; Police ⓣ112; Ambulance ⓣ113.

Exchange Competitive rates at the main post office (see below).

Ferries International: Fjord Line, Strandkaien (ⓣ81 53 35 00, ⓦwww.fjkordline.no). Domestic: Rogaland Kollektivtrafikk Kolumbus for regional bus, boat and train enquiries (ⓣ51 51 65 30, ⓦwww.kolumbus.no); Flaggruten (ⓣ51 86 87 80) for Hurtigbåt passenger express boat services to Haugesund and Bergen.

Hiking The DNT-affiliated Stavanger Turistforening, Olav V's gate 18 (Mon–Wed & Fri 10am–4pm, Thurs 10am–6pm, Sat 10am–2pm; ⓣ51 84 02 00, ⓦwww.stavanger-turistforening.no), will advise on local hiking routes and sells a comprehensive range of hiking maps. It maintains around 900km of hiking trails and runs more than thirty cabins in the mountains east of Stavanger, as well as organizing ski schools on winter weekends. It also offers general advice about local conditions, weather, etc, and you can obtain DNT membership here.

Internet Internet C@fe.com, Sølvberggata 15, just east of the Domkirke (Mon–Sat 11am–9pm, Sun noon–9pm; ⓣ51 55 41 20).

Laundry Renseriet, Kongsgata 40, by Breiavatnet. Coin-operated machines (Mon–Wed & Fri 8am–4pm, Thurs 8am–7pm, Sat 9am–2pm).

Left luggage At the Fiskepiren terminal (Mon–Fri 6.30am–11.15pm, Sat 6.30am–8pm, Sun 8am–10pm); and at the bus station (daily 7am–10pm).

Pharmacy Løveapoteket, Olav V's gate 11 (daily 9am–11pm; ⓣ51 52 06 07).

Post office The main post office is at Haakon VII's gate 9 (Mon–Fri 9am–6pm & Sat 10am–3pm).

Taxis Norgestaxi (ⓣ08000).

Vinmonopolet State-run liquor and wine outlet at Nytorget 5, a few minutes' walk northeast of the central lake (Mon–Wed 10am–5pm, Thurs 10am–6pm, Fri 9am–6pm & Sat 9am–3pm).

Around Stavanger: Lysefjord

Stavanger sits on a long promontory that pokes a knobbly head north towards the Boknafjord, whose wide waters form a deep indentation in the coast and lap against a confetti of islets and islands. To the east of Stavanger, longer, narrower fjords drill far inland, the most diverting being the blue-black **Lysefjord**, famous for its precipitous cliffs and an especially striking rock formation, the **Preikestolen**. This distinctive 25-metre-square table of rock boasts a sheer 600-metre drop to the fjord down below on three of its sides. There are regular summertime boat cruises to the Lysefjord, and Preikestolen can be reached by ferry and bus.

Along the Lysefjord

There are several ways to visit Lysefjord **by boat** from Stavanger. One option is a round trip halfway up the fjord with **Fjord Tours** (Ⓣ51 53 73 40, Ⓦwww.fjordpanorama.no), whose boats depart from the Skagenkaien (Sept to mid-May 1–3 weekly; mid-May to Aug 1–2 daily; 3hr 30min; 280kr). However, despite the gushing multilingual commentary, the fjord seems disappointingly gloomy when seen from the bottom of its cliffs, and from this angle the Preikestolen hardly makes any impression at all. A rather more dramatic trip, operated by – amongst others – **Veteran Fjordcruise** (Ⓣ51 86 87 88, Ⓦwww.vfc.no), takes you the full length of the fjord to **Lysebotn**, where a connecting bus heads up the mountainside, tackling no less than 26 switchbacks on its way to the minor road that leads back to Stavanger (mid-June to late Aug 1 daily; 7hr; 490kr). If you want to avoid the tours and cover the same ground on public transport, you'll need to be good at juggling timetables – check with the tourist information office to make sure you don't get stranded.

The **road from Lysebotn** offers spectacular views as it wiggles its way up the mountainside, but adventurous souls may prefer the very demanding **hiking trail** which leads west from the car park of the **Øygardstøl** café and information centre, just above the last hairpin, to a much-photographed boulder, the **Kjeragbolten**, wedged between two cliff faces high above the ground. It's a tough route, so allow between five and six hours for the round trip – and steel your nerves for the 1000-metre drop down to the fjord below.

Lysefjord's Preikestolen

Lysefjord's most celebrated vantage point, **Preikestolen** (Pulpit Rock), offers superlative views, though on sunny summer weekends you'll share them with lots of others. To get to the rock, take the **ferry** east from Stavanger to **Tau** (every 30min to 1hr; 40min; passengers 33kr, car & driver 100kr) and then drive south along Highway 13 until, after about 14km, you reach the signed side road leading to Preikestolen. A local **bus** covers the Tau–Preikestolen road too (4 daily; 25min), but you'll need to check with the tourist office as to which of the ferries connects with the bus. From the car park at the end of the road, it's a four-hour **hike** there and back to Preikestolen along a clearly marked trail. The first half is steep in parts and paved with uneven stones, while the second half – over bedrock – is a good bit easier. The change in elevation is 350m; take food and water.

Back at the Preikestolen car park, a short sharp hike leads down to **Refsvatn**, a small lake encircled by a footpath which takes three hours to negotiate, taking in birch and pine woods, marshes, narrow ridges and bare stretches of rock. It also threads through **Torsnes**, an isolated farm that was inhabited until 1962. The lake footpath connects with a rough path which careers down to the **Refsa**

From Stavanger to Bergen

With great ingenuity, Norway's road builders have cobbled together the **E39** coastal road, the **Kystvegen** (Ⓦwww.kystvegen.no), which traverses the west coast from Stavanger to Haugesund (see below), Bergen and ultimately Trondheim with eight ferry trips breaking up the journey. The first part of the trek, the 190-kilometre haul up to Bergen, includes two ferry trips and sees the highway slipping across a string of islands, which provide a pleasant introduction to the scenic charms of western Norway – and hint at the sterner beauty of the fjords beyond. Perhaps surprisingly, this region is primarily agricultural: the intricacies of the shoreline, together with the prevailing westerlies, made the seas so treacherous that locals mostly stuck to the land, eking out a precarious existence from the thin soils that had accumulated on the leeward sides of some of the islands.

By **car**, it takes between five and six hours to get from Stavanger to Bergen. The first of the two E39 **ferries** shuttles across the Boknafjord from Mortavika to Arsvågen, about 30km out of Stavanger (every 20–40min; 25min; car & passenger 153kr); the second, another 120km beyond, links Sandvikvåg with Halhjem (every 30min to 1hr; 50min; car & driver 162kr), 40km short of Bergen. A fast and frequent **bus** service – the **Kystbussen** – plies the E39 too, taking a little under six hours to get from Stavanger to Bergen (8–11 daily); it's slower, but more economical and offers much better views than the **Hurtigbåt** passenger express boat which plies the same route (2–3 daily; 4hr).

quay on the Lysefjord. For further details of these and other local hikes, consult the DNT-affiliated Stavanger Turistforening (see p.154), who sell an excellent English-language hiking guide to the area.

Also by the car park, a first-rate HI **hostel**, *Preikestolen Vandrerhjem* (Ⓣ97 16 55 51, Ⓦwww.vandrerhjem.no; dorm beds 210kr, doubles ❷; mid-May to mid-Sept) is perched high on the hillside, with great views over the surrounding mountains. Built on the site of an old mountain farm, the hostel comprises a small complex of turf-roofed lodges, each of which has a spick-and-span pine interior. There are self-catering facilities and boat rental, but no laundry; reservations are advised as the place is popular with school groups.

North to Haugesund

There is no strong reason to break your journey between Stavanger and Bergen, but **HAUGESUND**, a workaday industrial town 90km north of Stavanger via the E39 have their moments – and the Mortavika–Arsvågen ferry (see box above). A small but lively port that thrived on the herring fisheries in the nineteenth century, Haugesund now booms as a major player in the North Sea oil industry. It was here that the first ruler of a united Norway, **Harald Hårfagri** (Harald the Fair-Haired), was buried, and a granite obelisk, the **Haraldshaugen**, now marks his supposed resting place, by the seashore about 2km north of the centre. He gained sovereignty over these coastal districts following a decisive sea battle in 872, an achievement that, according to legend, released him from a ten-year vow not to cut his hair until he became king of all Norway. Haugesund's other claim to fame is as the town from where a local baker emigrated to the USA in an attempt to improve his fortunes; his daughter, Marilyn Monroe, was born in 1926.

Buses to Haugesund pull in on the east side of the centre, about 500m from the waterfront and the **Hurtigbåt** express passenger ferry terminal. The **tourist office** is about 200m south along the waterfront from the Hutigbåt jetty at Strandgata 171 (June–Aug Mon–Fri 10am–6pm, Sat 10am–4pm; Sept–May Mon–Fri 9am–3.30pm; ⓣ52 01 08 30, ⓦwww.visithaugesund.no). Although there's no strong reason **to stay** here, the *Rica Saga Hotel*, Skippergata 11 (ⓣ52 86 28 24, ⓦwww.rica.no; ❻), does have attractive, well-appointed guest rooms in a modern high-rise block; it's one of several straightforward chain hotels in the centre of town.

From Haugesund, you can either continue north on the E39 to Bergen (see box opposite), or branch off east along the **E134** towards Lofthus (see p.227) and Kinsarvik (see p.226), on the Hardangerfjord.

Travel details

Trains

Kristiansand to: Oslo (3–5 daily; 4hr 40min); Stavanger (3–5 daily; 3hr).

Oslo to: Arendal – change at Nelaug (3–5 daily; 4hr 40min); Egersund (3–5 daily; 6hr 40min); Kristiansand (3–5 daily; 4hr 40min); Neslandsvatn – for Kragerø (3–4 daily; 2hr 40min); Sandefjord (13–22 daily; 1hr 50min); Stavanger (3–5 daily; 7hr 30min).

Sandefjord to: Oslo (13–20 daily, fewer on Sun; 1hr 50min); Tønsberg (13–19 daily, fewer on Sun; 20min).

Stavanger to: Kristiansand (3–6 daily; 3hr); Oslo (3–5 daily; 7hr 30min).

Buses

Arendal to: Lillesand (6–7 daily; 45min); Oslo (6–9 daily; 4hr).

Grimstad to: Lillesand (6–7 daily; 15min); Oslo (6–9 daily; 4hr 30min).

Kristiansand to: Flekkefjord (2–4 daily; 2hr); Mandal (2–4 daily; 50min); Oslo (6–8 daily; 5hr 30min); Stavanger (2–4 daily; 4hr).

Oslo to: Arendal (7–8 daily; 4hr); Grimstad (6–7 daily; 4hr 30min); Kristiansand (7–8daily; 5hr 30min); Lillesand (6–7 daily; 4hr 45min).

Lillesand to: Arendal (6–7 daily; 45min); Kristiansand (6–7 daily; 45min); Grimstad (6–7 daily; 15min); Oslo (6–7 daily; 4hr 45min).

Mandal to: Kristiansand (2–4 daily; 50min); Stavanger (2–4 daily; 3hr 30min).

Stavanger to: Bergen (8–11 daily; 5hr 40min); Haugesund (8–11 daily; 2hr); Kristiansand (2–4 daily; 4hr); Mandal (2–4 daily; 3hr 30min).

Car ferries

Egersund to: Bergen (2–4 weekly; 8hr). With Fjord line; originates in Hantsholm, Denmark.

Stavanger to: Bergen (2–6 weekly; 7hr); Haugesund (2–6 weekly; 2hr 30min). With Fjord Line; originates in Newcastle, UK.

Hurtigbåt passenger express boats

Stavanger to: Bergen (2–4 daily; 4hr); Haugesund (2–4 daily; 1hr 15min).

3

Central Norway

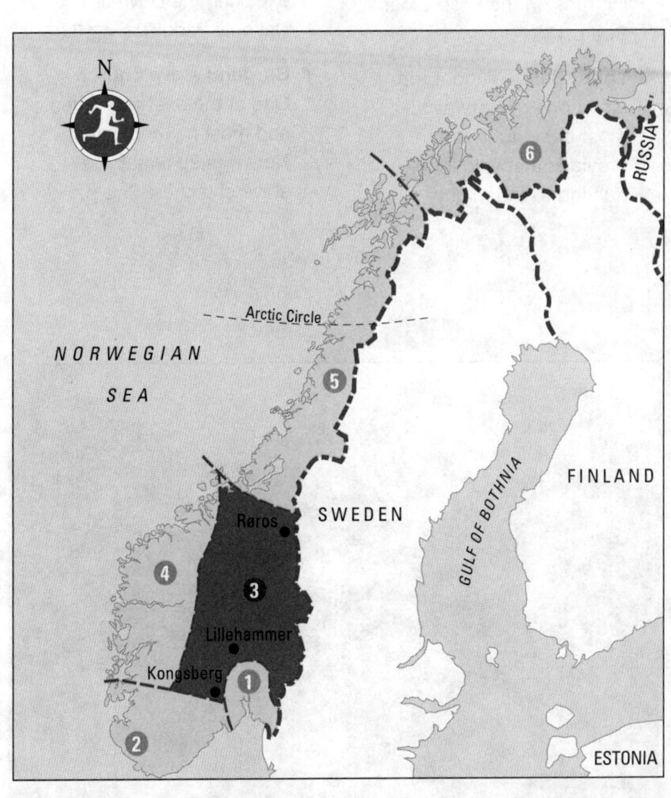

CHAPTER 3

Highlights

* **Sygard Grytting** Stay in a beautifully preserved eighteenth-century farmstead, near Hundorp. See p.174

* **Whitewater rafting** Brave some of Norway's most exciting whitewater rafting runs on the River Sjoa. See p.176

* **Lake Gjende** A boat trip along one of Norway's most beautiful lakes provides a scenic introduction to the mighty Jotunheimen mountains. See p.182

* **Kongsvold Fjeldstue** This lovely hotel occupies a tastefully restored complex of old timber buildings, and is convenient for exploring the Dovrefjell National Park. See p.183

* **Borgund stave church** One of the best-preserved and most harmonious of Norway's 29 remaining stave churches. See p.189

△ Lake Gjende, Jotunheimen National Park

3

Central Norway

Preoccupied by the fjords and the long road to Nordkapp, few tourists are tempted to explore **central Norway**. The Norwegians know better. Trapped between Sweden and the fjords, this great chunk of land boasts some of the country's finest scenery, with the forested dales that trail north and west from Oslo heralding the region's rearing peaks. It's here, within shouting distance of the country's principal train line and the E6 – long the main line of communication between Oslo, Trondheim and the north – that you'll find three of Norway's prime **hiking areas**. These comprise a trio of mountain ranges, each partly contained within a national park – from south to north, Jotunheimen, Rondane and the Dovrefjell. Of the three, **Jotunheimen** is the harshest and most stunning, with its string of icy, jagged peaks; the **Dovrefjell** is more varied with severe mountains in the west and open moors and rounded ridges in the east; whilst **Rondane**, a high alpine zone, has more accessible mountains and low vegetation. Each of the parks is equipped with well-maintained walking trails and DNT huts, and **Otta** and **Kongsvoll**, on both the E6 and the train line, make particularly good starting points for hiking expeditions.

Despite these attractions, it's easy to think of the whole region as little more than a **transport corridor** whose main highways rush from Oslo across the interior heading north and west. Of these, the **E6** is the most interesting, as it runs up the **Gudbrandsdal** valley past several historic sights en route to the Jotunheimen and Dovrefjell parks. The E6 also passes within comfortable striking distance of the intriguing old iron town of **Røros** and, even better, it's the starting point for **Highway 15** and the **E136**, two wonderful roads that thread through the mountains to the fjords: the first goes to Lom (see p.247) and Geiranger (see p.258), the second to Åndalsnes (see p.262). To the west of Oslo, the **E16** is the fastest of the three main roads to the fjords, as it bangs across to Lærdal and through the series of tunnels that enable it to fast track to Bergen. It has much to recommend it west of Flåm (see p.235), but its dull eastern reaches are enlivened only by the handsome **Borgund stave church**. Further south, the easterly sections of **Highway 7** to Flåm or Eidfjord (see p.227) and the **E134** to Lofthus (see p.227) are also pretty routine, though the latter does have the advantage of passing through the attractive former silver town of **Kongsberg**.

As you might expect, Nor-Way Bussekspress **bus** services along these main highways are excellent, although, once you get onto the minor roads, the bus system thins out and travelling becomes difficult without your own vehicle. **Trains** are fast and frequent too, shuttling along the two main railway lines that cross central Norway. The Oslo to Bergen line shadows Highway 7 until just

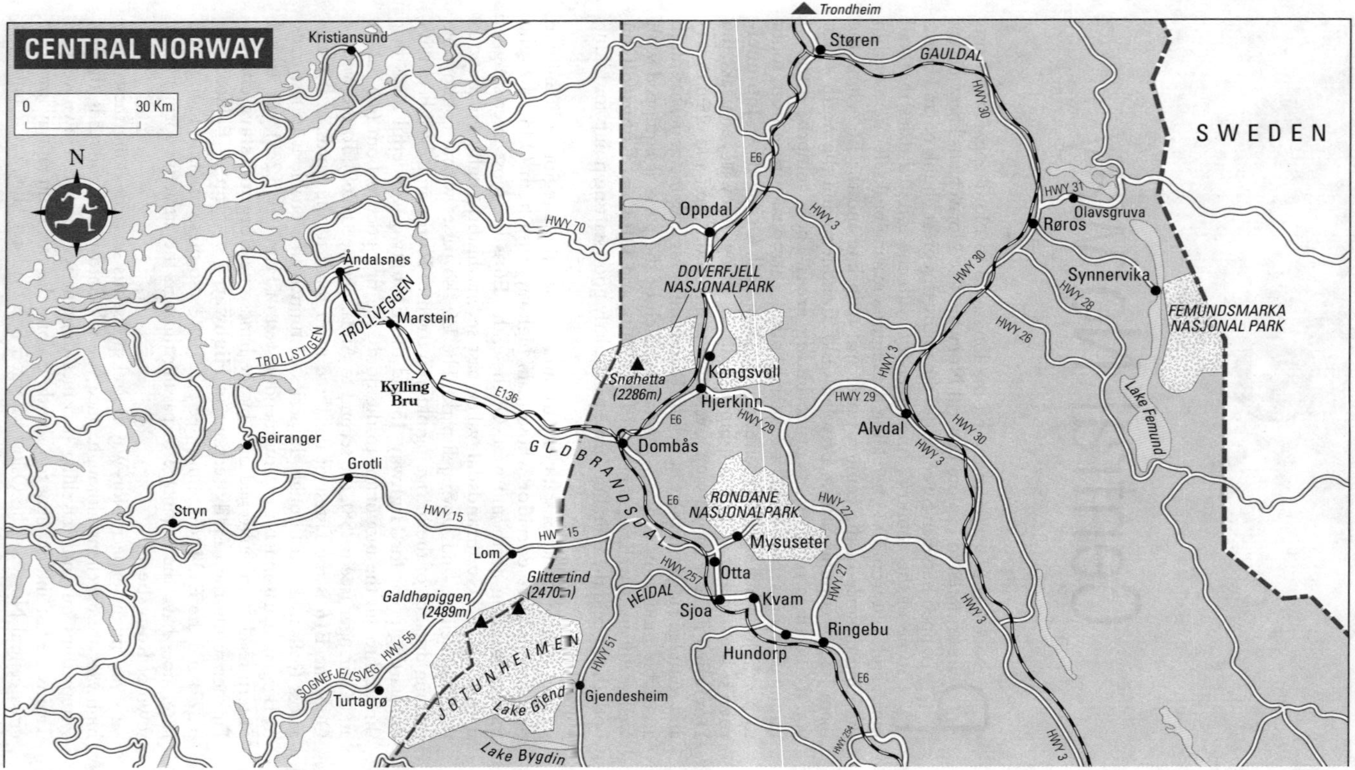

CENTRAL NORWAY

0 30 Km
N
Trondheim
SWEDEN
Kristiansund
Støren
GAULDAL
HWY 30
E6
Oppdal
HWY 3
HWY 31
Olavsgruva
Røros
HWY 70
Åndalsnes
DOVERFJELL NASJONALPARK
Synnervika
HWY 28
FEMUNDSMARKA NASJONAL PARK
HWY 26
TROLLVEGGEN
Marstein
TROLLSTIGEN
Kongsvoll
Snøhetta (2286m)
Hjerkinn
HWY 29
Alvdal
Lake Femund
Kylling Bru
E136
Dombås
GUDBRANDSDAL
Geiranger
Grotli
RONDANE NASJONALPARK
HWY 27
Stryn
HWY 15
Mysuseter
Lom
Otta
HWY 257
Glitte tind (2470m)
Galdhøpiggen (2489m)
HEIDAL
Sjoa
Kvam
Ringebu
Hundorp
JOTUNHEIMEN
HWY 51
HWY 55
SOGNEFJELLSVEG
Turtagrø
Gjendesheim
Lake Gjend
Lake Bygdin
HWY 254

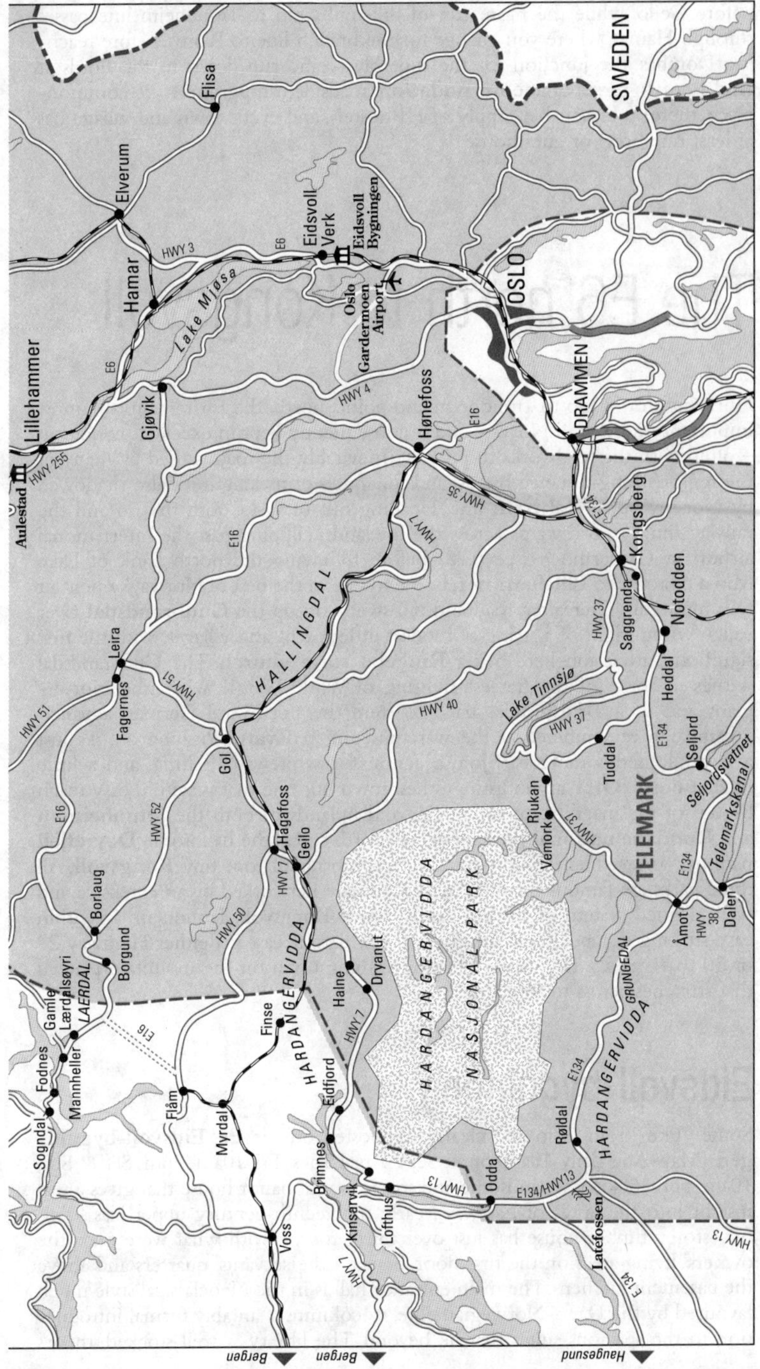

SWEDEN
Flisa
Elverum
Hamar
HWY 3
E6
Eidsvoll Verk
Eidsvoll Bygningen
Oslo Gardermoen Airport
OSLO
Lake Mjøsa
Lillehammer
Gjøvik
HWY 4
HWY 255
Aulestad
DRAMMEN
Hønefoss
E16
HWY 35
E134
Kongsberg
Notodden
Saggrenda
HWY 37
HWY 7
HALLINGDAL
Leira
Fagernes
HWY 51
Heddal
Lake Tinnsjø
HWY 40
Gol
HWY 52
Tuddal
Seljord
Seljordsvatnet
TELEMARK
Rjukan
Vemork
Hagafoss
Geilo
Telemarkskanal
Borlaug
HWY 50
HARDANGERVIDDA
NASJONAL PARK
Åmot
Dalen
HWY 38
Borgund
Dryanut
Halne
GRUNGEDAL
LAERDAL
Gamle Lærdalsøyri
Finse
Fodnes
Mannheller
Sogndal
Flåm
Myrdal
Eidfjord
Røldal
Brimnes
Kinsarvik
Lofthus
HWY 13
Odda
E134/HWY13
Latefossen
Voss
Bergen
Haugesund

before Geilo, while the more run-of-the-mill Oslo to Trondheim line passes through Hamar, where you change for the branch line to Røros, before reaching Dombas, the junction for the superbly scenic run down to the fjords at Åndalsnes. In terms of **accommodation**, roadside campgrounds are commonplace, there's a reasonable supply of HI hostels, and every town and village has at least one hotel or guesthouse.

The E6 north to Kongsvoll

Hurrying from Oslo to Trondheim and points north, the **E6** remains the most important highway in Norway, and is consequently kept in excellent condition – often with the roadworks to prove it. Inevitably, the road is used by many of the region's long-distance **buses**, and for much of its length it's also shadowed by Norway's principal **train** line. Heading out of Oslo, both the E6 and the railway thump northwards across the lowlands, clipping past the international airport at Gardermoen (see p.78) before following the north bank of Lake Mjøsa en route to **Lillehammer**, home to one of the best of Norway's open-air folk museums. Thereafter, road and rail sweep on up the **Gudbrandsdal** river valley, within sight of a string of modest little towns and villages, with the first significant attraction here being **Ringebu stave church**. The Gudbrandsdal witnessed some of the fiercest fighting of World War II when the Norwegians and their British allies tried to stem the northward German advance, a campaign remembered at the war museum in **Kvam**. Pushing on, it's just a few kilometres more to **Sjoa**, a centre for whitewater rafting, and a little further north, **Otta**, an undistinguished town but one that is within easy reach by bus of the magnificent mountains and uplands of both the **Jotunheimen** and **Rondane national parks**. Further north still is the handsome **Dovrefjell** national park, which is most pleasingly approached from tiny **Kongsvoll**. All three parks are famous for their hiking, and are networked by an extensive and well-planned system of **hiking trails**. From Kongsvoll, Trondheim is within easy striking distance; alternatively, you can detour east via either Highway 29 or 30 to **Røros**, a fascinating old iron-mining town on the mountain plateau that stretches across to Sweden.

Eidsvoll-bygningen

Some 70km from Oslo and clearly signposted off the E6, **Eidsvoll-bygningen** (May–Aug daily 10am–5pm; Sept–April Tues–Fri 10am–2pm, Sat & Sun 10am–5pm; 60kr) is a handsome and spacious old manor house that gives a real insight into the tastes of Norway's early nineteenth-century upper class. This two-storey timber house has just over thirty rooms, with what were once the owners' living areas on the first floor, beneath the servants' quarters and above the basement kitchens. The main entrance hall is in the Neoclassical style much favoured by the Dano-Norwegian elite, its columns a suitably formal introduction to the spacious suites that lie beyond. The library is well stocked, there's a billiard room and smoking room, and a string of elegant dining rooms and bedrooms. Oriental knick-knacks and English furniture appear throughout, and the occasional mural depicts Greek mythological figures. The house was owned by the Ankers family, who made their money from the local iron works – hence the splendid cast-iron stoves.

It's a delightful ensemble, but the house owes its preservation to its historical significance rather than its aesthetics. One of the Ankers, Carsten, was a close friend and ally of the Danish crown prince **Christian Frederik**, and this connection has given the house national importance. Towards the end of the Napoleonic Wars, the Russians and British insisted the Danes be punished for their alliance with the French, and proposed taking Norway from Denmark and handing it over to Sweden. In an attempt to forestall these territorial shenanigans, the Danes dispatched Christian Frederik to Norway, where he set up home in Carsten Ankers' house in 1813, and proceeded to lobby for Norwegian support. In April of the following year more than a hundred of the country's leading citizens gathered here at Eidsvoll manor house to decide whether to accept union with Sweden or go for independence with Christian Frederik on the throne. The majority of this **National Assembly** chose independence, and set about drafting a liberal constitution based on that of the United States. Predictably, the Swedes would have none of this. Four years earlier, the Swedes had picked one of Napoleon's marshals, **Jean-Baptiste Bernadotte** (see p.92), to succeed their previous king who had died without an heir. As King Karl Johan, Bernadotte was keen to flex his military muscles and, irritated by these developments, he invaded Norway in July 1814. Frederik was soon forced to abdicate and the Norwegians were pressed into union, though Karl Johan did head off much of the opposition by guaranteeing the Norwegians' new constitution and parliament, the Storting.

Carsten Ankers converted the upper storey of his home into premises for the National Assembly, comprising a handful of administrative offices plus the Room for the Constitutional Committee, where the original wooden benches have survived along with various landscape paintings. There's a rusticated modesty to it all which is really rather charming, and a statue of Venus has been put back in the room after years of being shunted up and down the adjoining corridors: after prolonged discussion, it had originally been removed because the representatives considered it an erotic distraction.

The house is in the country just to the south of the industrial town of Eidsvoll Verk: it's signed off the E6, 2km down a byroad.

Hamar

Just beyond Eidsvoll Verk, the E6 curves round the eastern shore of Norway's largest lake, **Lake Mjøsa**, a favourite retreat for Norwegian families, whose second homes dot the surrounding farmland, woods and pastures. Before the railroad arrived in the 1880s, the lake was an important transport route, crossed by boats in summer and by horse and sleigh in winter. It's also halfway country: the quiet settlements around the lake give a taste of small-town southern Norway before the E6 plunges into the wilder regions further north.

Midway round the lake, some 130km from Oslo, lies **HAMAR**, an easy-going little place of 25,000 souls, whose marinas and waterside cafés make a gallant attempt to sustain a nautical flavour. Unlikely though it may seem today, Hamar was once the seat of an important medieval bishopric, and the battered remains of its Romanesque-Gothic **Domkirke**, now protected by a striking glass and steel structure, the Hamardomen, are stuck out on the Domkirkeodden (cathedral point), a low, grassy headland about 2km west of the centre. The cathedral is thought to have been built by the "English pope" Nicholas Breakspear, who spent a couple of years in Norway as the papal legate before becoming Adrian IV in 1154, but the building, along with the surrounding episcopal complex, was ransacked during the Reformation, and local road-builders subsequently helped themselves to the stone. The ruins have now been incorporated into the **Hedmarksmuseet** (mid-May to mid-June Tues–Sun 10am–4pm; mid-June to mid-Aug daily 10am–5pm; mid-Aug to early Sept Tues–Sun 10am–4pm; 70kr, ⓦ www.hedmarksmuseet.no), which contains an archeological museum and an open-air folk museum. The latter holds around fifty buildings collected from across the region and, although it's not as comprehensive as the one in Lillehammer (see p.172), it does contain one or two particularly fine buildings, including the parsonage of Bolstad with its beautifully decorated log walls. The most scenic approach to the headland is along the pleasant lakeshore footpath that stretches 2km north from the train station.

DS Skibladner

Hamar is as good a place as any to pick up the 130-year-old **paddle steamer**, the DS *Skibladner* (ⓣ 61 14 40 80, ⓦ www.skiblander.no), which shuttles up and down Lake Mjøsa between late June and mid-August: on Tuesdays, Thursdays and Saturdays the boat makes the return trip across the lake from Hamar to Gjøvik and on up to Lillehammer; on Mondays, Wednesdays and Fridays it chugs south down to Eidsvoll and back; there's no Sunday service. Sailing times are available direct or at any local tourist office. Tickets are bought on board: return trips from Hamar to Eidsvoll cost 280kr and last two-and-a-half hours, those to Lillehammer cost 320kr and last eight hours. One-way fares cost a little over half these rates. Travellers heading north may find the trip to Lillehammer tempting at first sight, but the lake is not particularly scenic, and after four hours on the boat you may well feel like jumping overboard. The best bet is to take the shorter ride to Eidsvoll instead.

Practicalities

Hamar's **train station** is in the town centre beside the lake; **buses** stop outside. Some trains from Oslo pause here before heading up the branch line to Røros (see p.184), a fine three-and-a-half-hour ride over hills and through huge forests. The jetty for the DS *Skibladner* is about 600m to the west of the train station along the lakeshore.

There's no pressing reason to overnight in Hamar, but the town does have a fair choice of central hotel **accommodation**. The most attractive option is the *First Hotel Victoria*, a brisk modern place down by the lakeshore not far from the train station, at Strandgata 21 (ⓣ 62 02 55 00, ⓦ www.firsthotels.com; ❼, sp/r ❺); the hotel also has a competent restaurant serving Norwegian favourites. Alternatively, Hamar's all-year HI **hostel**, part of the *Vikingskipet Motel* at Åkersvikaveg 24 (ⓣ 62 52 60 60, ⓦ www.vandrerhjem.no; dorm beds 300kr, doubles ❸), occupies smart modern buildings about 2km south along the lakeshore from the train station. It's in the middle of nowhere, just across from the massive skating arena, the Vikingskipet, built for the 1994 Winter Olympics in the shape of an upturned Viking ship.

Lillehammer and around

LILLEHAMMER (literally "Little Hammer"), 50km north of Hamar and 180km from Oslo, is Lake Mjøsa's most worthwhile destination. In **winter**, it's one of the top Norwegian ski centres, a young and vibrant place whose rural lakeside setting and extensive cross-country ski trails contributed to its selection as host of the 1994 Olympic Winter Games. In preparation for the games, the Norwegian government spent a massive two billion kroner on the town's **sporting facilities**, which are now among the best in the country. Spread along the hillsides above and near the town, they include several dozen downhill ski trails catering for everyone from beginner to expert, floodlit slopes for night skiing, ski-jumping towers and multiple chair lifts, an ice hockey arena, a bobsleigh track, and several hundred kilometres of prepared cross-country skiing trails. There is even a special stadium – the Birkebeiner – where skiers can hone their skills before setting off into the local mountains, which are criss-crossed by 450km of cross-country ski trail. Several local companies, including Saga Arrangement, Gudbrandsdalsveien 203 (Ⓣ61 26 92 44, Ⓦwww.sagaarrangement.no), offer all-inclusive winter sports and activity holiday packages. As you would expect, most Norwegians arriving here in winter come fully equipped, but it's possible to rent or buy equipment locally – the tourist office (see p.173) will advise.

Lillehammer remains a popular holiday spot in **summer** too. Hundreds of Norwegians hunker down in their second homes in the hills, popping into the town centre for a drink or a meal. Cycling, walking, fishing and canoeing are popular pastimes at this time of year, with all sorts of possibilities for guided tours. Yet, however appealing the area may be to Norwegians, the countryside hereabouts has little of the wonderful wildness of other parts of Norway, and unless you're someone's guest or bring your own family, you'll probably feel rather out on a limb. That said, Lillehammer is not a bad place to break your journey, and there are a couple of attractions to keep you busy for a day or

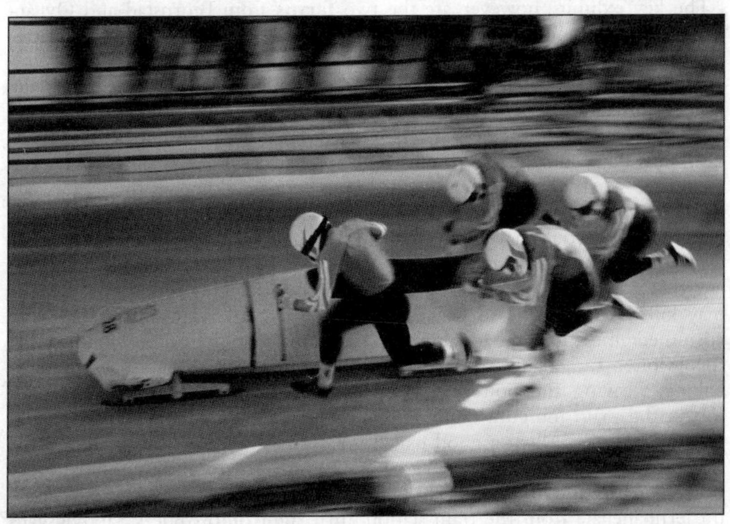

△ Lillehammer bobsleigh

two – principally the **Maihaugen** open-air museum, and the country home of Norwegian author Bjørnstjerne Bjørnson, a short drive out of town at **Aulestad**.

The town: the Kunstmuseum (Art Museum) and Maihaugen

Lillehammer's briskly efficient centre, just a few minutes' walk from one end to the other, is tucked into the hillside above the lake, the E6 and the railway. It has just one really notable attraction, the **Kunstmuseum** at Stortorget 2 (July to late Aug daily 11am–5pm; late Aug to June Tues–Sun 11am–4pm; 60kr). Housed in a flashy modern edifice, the gallery is renowned for its temporary exhibitions of contemporary art (which often carry an extra admission charge), but the small permanent collection is also very worthwhile, comprising a representative sample of the works of most major Norwegian painters, from Johan Dahl and Christian Krohg to Munch and Erik Werenskiold. In particular, look out for the striking landscapes painted by one of the less familiar Norwegian artists, **Axel Revold** (1887–1962). A student of Matisse and an admirer of Cézanne, Revold spent years working abroad before returning home and applying the techniques he had learnt to his favourite subject, northern Norway: his beautifully composed and brightly coloured *Nordland* is typical.

The much-vaunted **Maihaugen** open-air folk museum – the largest of its type in northern Europe – is located a twenty-minute walk southeast of the town centre along Anders Sandvigsgate (mid-May to Sept daily 10am–5pm; Oct to mid-May Tues–Sun 11am–4pm; 75kr, but 90kr mid-June to mid-Sept; ⓦwww.maihaugen.no). Incredibly, the whole collection represents the lifetime's work of one man, a magpie-ish dentist by the name of Anders Sandvig. Maihaugen holds 185 relocated buildings, brought here from all over the region, including a charming seventeenth-century presbytery (*prestegårdshagen*), a thirteenth-century stave church from Garmo, log storehouses and smokehouses, summer grazing huts and various workshops.

The key exhibits, however, are the two **farms** from Bjørnstad and Øygarden, dating from the late seventeenth century. Complete with their various outhouses and living areas, the two farms comprise 36 buildings, each with a specific function, such as food store, sheep-shed, hay barn, stable and bathhouse. This setup may have worked, and it certainly looks quaint, but it was, in fact, forced upon farmers by their tried-and-tested method of construction, **laft**. Based on the use of pine logs notched together at right angles, the technique strictly limited the dimensions of every building, as the usable part of the pine tree was rarely more than 8m long. Indeed, it seems likely that many farmers would have preferred to keep their winter supplies in the main farmhouse rather than in a separate store, as implied by a draconian medieval law that stated, "When a man discovers another in his storehouse… then he may kill the man if he so wishes." Outside there are farmyard animals, and costumed guides give the lowdown on traditional rural life; in the summertime there's often the chance to have a go at domestic activities such as spinning, baking, weaving and pottery – good, wholesome fun. You can spend time too in the main museum building, which features temporary exhibitions on folkloric themes. Allow a good half-day for a visit and take advantage of the free forty-minute English-language guided tour (June to mid-Aug only; every other hour, on the hour, until 2hr before closing). To get to the museum, walk up Jernbanegata from the train station, turn right onto Anders Sandvigsgate, and keep going.

For a glimpse of the countryside surrounding Lillehammer, you might want to take a ride on the antique **DS Skibladner** paddle steamer as it shuttles up and down Lake Mjøsa: catch it from the jetty about 800m south of the centre (see p.170 for further details).

Practicalities

The E6 runs along the lakeshore about 500m below the centre of Lillehammer, where the ultramodern **Skysstasjon**, on Jernbanetorget at the bottom of Jernbanegata, incorporates the **train station** and the **bus terminal**. The **tourist office** is also here (Mon–Fri 9am–4pm & Sat 10am–2pm; Ⓣ61 28 98 00, Ⓦwww.lillehammerturist.no). Staff have bucketloads of free brochures, information on local events and activities, and will help with finding accommodation. **Orientation** couldn't be easier, with all activity focused on the pedestrianized part of Storgata which runs north from Bankgata, across Jernbanegata to the tumbling River Mesnaelva; Anders Sandvigsgate and Kirkegata run parallel on either side to east and west respectively.

The tourist office can help with finding **accommodation**, or you could head straight for *Gjestebu Overnatting* (Ⓣ61 25 43 21, Ⓔgjestebu@lillehammer.online.no; mixed dorm beds 120kr, doubles ❷), which offers hostel-style accommodation in a large house-cum-lodge just north of the centre – and 800m from the train station – at Gamleveien 110. To get there, take Storgata north to Løkkegata, turn right and it is one block further on; they also have self-catering apartments here, from 550kr per night. For something rather more cosy, try *Gjestehuset Ersgaard*, Nordseterveien 201 (Ⓣ61 25 06 84, Ⓦwww.ersgaard.no; ❷), a pleasant, modern guesthouse located on a farm a couple of kilometres above town in the direction of Nordseter; they serve excellent breakfasts here and the dining room overlooks the town and lake. Back in the centre, a third recommendable option is the *First Hotell Breiseth*, across from the train station at Jernbanegata 3 (Ⓣ61 24 77 77, Ⓦwww.firsthotels.no/breiseth; ❺, sp/r ❹); the hotel dates back to the end of the nineteenth century – as evidenced by parts of the facade – and the modern interior has period touches and ninety well-appointed rooms.

Downtown Lillehammer has a good supply of **cafés** and **restaurants**. The busy *Bøndernes Hus Kafeteria*, Kirkegata 68, is a big, old-fashioned sort of place with cheap and filling self-service meals. Moving up a rung, *Blåmann*, down an alley off the pedestrianized part of Storgata at Lilletorvet 1, has a lovely leafy terrace suspended over the cascading river below and does an excellent line in steaks, grilled fish and the like. The town has an animated **nightlife**, with bars clustered around the western end of Storgata – try *Nikkers* at Elvegata 18 for lively low-key drinks, or *Brenneriet*, just over the road, a swanky nightclub and restaurant combo.

Around Lillehammer: Aulestad

Eighteen kilometres north of Lillehammer, in the village of Follebu, is **AULESTAD** (daily: late May & Sept 11am–2.30pm; June & Aug 10am–3.30pm; July 10am–5.30pm; 75kr), a good-looking villa perched on a leafy knoll, and packed with mementoes of its former owner **Bjørnstjerne Bjørnson** (1832–1910). Little known outside Norway today, Bjørnson was a major figure in the literary and cultural revival that swept the country at the end of the nineteenth century. Bjørnson made his name with the peasant tales of *Synnøve Solbakken* in 1857 and thereafter he churned out a veritable flood of novels, stories, poems and plays, many of which romanticized Norwegian country folk and, unusually for the time, were written in Norwegian, rather than the traditional Danish. He also championed all sorts of progressive causes, from Norwegian independence through to equality of the sexes and crofters' rights, albeit from a liberal viewpoint. Nowadays, however, his main claim to fame is as author of the poem that became the national anthem. Bjørnson moved to Aulestad in 1875, and an audiovisual display inside the house gives further details on the man and his times.

To get to Aulestad, head north from Lillehammer on the E6 and turn onto Highway 255 for about 10km. To get back onto the E6 heading north, follow Highway 255 from the Bjørnson house, then turn onto Highway 254: this brings you out on the E6 halfway between Lillehammer and the Ringebu church (see below).

The Gudbrandsdal

Heading north from Lillehammer, the E6 and the railway leave the shores of Lake Mjøsa to run along the **Gudbrandsdal**, a 160km-long river valley, which was for centuries the main route between Oslo and Trondheim. Enclosed by mountain ranges, the valley has a comparatively dry and mild climate, and its fertile soils have nourished a string of farming villages since Viking times – though there was some light industrialization at the beginning of the twentieth century.

Ringebu stave church

The Gudbrandsdal begins pleasantly enough, the easy sweep of its forested hills interrupted by rocky outcrops and patches of farmland dotted with brightly coloured farmhouses. After 60km, the E6 swings past the distinctive maroon spire of **Ringebu stave church** (daily: late May to mid-June & late Aug 9am–5pm; mid-June to mid-Aug 8am–8pm; 50kr), which stands on a hill 1km off the E6, and a couple of kilometres south of Ringebu village. Dating from the thirteenth century, the original church was modified and enlarged in the 1630s, reflecting both an increase in the local population and the new religious practices introduced after the Reformation. At this time, the nave was broadened, the chancel replaced and an over-large tower and spire plonked on top. The exterior is rather glum, but the western **entrance portal** sports some superb if badly weathered zoomorphic carvings from the original church. **Inside**, the highlights are mainly eighteenth-century Baroque – from the florid pulpit and altar panel through to a memorial to the Irgens family, complete with trumpeting cherubs and intricate ruffs.

Hundorp and Sygard Grytting

From the church, it's about 15km to the straggling village of **HUNDORP**, where a neat little quadrangle of old farm buildings has been tastefully turned into a roadside tourist stop, with a café, art gallery, shop and **hotel**, the *Hundorp Dale-Gudbrands gard* (Ⓣ61 29 71 11, Ⓦwww.hundorp.no; ❹). There are twelve comfortable rooms here, decorated in traditional Norwegian country style and occupying an attractive two-storey building of ancient provenance – with timber planking on top of a stone cellar. There has been a farm here since prehistoric times, its most famous owner being a Viking warrior by the name of Dalegudbrand, who became a bitter enemy of St Olav after the smashing of his picture of Thor and his enforced baptism in 1021. With a little time to spare, you could ramble down towards the river to explore the complex's immediate surroundings, where there are six small but distinct **Viking burial mounds**, as well as a rough circle of standing stones – a map in the courtyard shows how to get to them all. The stones, which date from around 700 AD, mark the spot where freemen gathered in the *allthing* to discuss issues of local importance. Presided over by the most powerful local chieftain, *allthings* were held in the open air and the assembled freemen showed their approval for any decisions taken by brandishing their weapons. There is no **train station** at Hundorp – the nearest is at Ringebu – but buses stop in front of the hotel on the E6.

A further 5km to the north, overlooking the E6, the ancient farmstead of *Sygard Grytting* (Ⓣ61 29 85 88, Ⓦwww.grytting.com; mid-June to mid-Aug) nestles amongst the orchards, providing some of the best lodgings in Norway. The eighteenth-century farm buildings are in an almost perfect state of preservation, a beautiful ensemble with the assorted barns, outhouses and main house facing onto a tiny courtyard. One of the barns – now housing bunk beds for **dormitory** accommodation (340kr per person) – dates from the fourteenth century, when its upper storey was used to shelter pilgrims on the long haul north to Trondheim cathedral (p.282). Most of the **double rooms** are in the main farmhouse (❹), which has been superbly renovated to provide extremely comfortable lodgings amidst antique furnishings, faded oil paintings and open fires. Breakfast is splendid too – the bread is baked on the premises – and dinner is available by prior arrangement.

The nearest you'll get by bus is the *Dale-Gudbrands gard* hotel in Hundorp, 5.8km away.

Kvam

Pressing on, the E6 weaves its way north following the course of the river to reach, after about 20km, **KVAM**, a modest chipboard-producing town that witnessed some of the worst fighting of World War II. Once the Germans had occupied Norway's main towns in the spring of 1940, they set about extending their control of the main roads and railways, marching up the Gudbrandsdal in quick fashion. At Kvam, they were opposed by a scratch force of Norwegian and British soldiers, who delayed their progress despite being poorly equipped – the captain in charge of the British anti-tank guns had to borrow a bicycle to patrol his defences. The battle for the Gudbrandsdal lasted for two weeks (April 14–30, 1940) and is commemorated at the **Gudbrandsdal Krigsminnesamling** (War Museum; late June to mid-Aug daily 10am–5pm; mid to late-Aug Wed–Sun 10am–4pm; 40kr), in the centre of Kvam beside the E6. In the museum, a series of first-rate multilingual displays runs through the campaign, supported by a substantial collection of military mementoes and lots of fascinating photographs. There are also informative sections on the rise of Fascism and the Norwegian resistance, plus a modest display on the role played by the villagers of Otta in the Kalmar War of 1611–13 (see p.176). Across the main street from the museum, in the **church graveyard**, is a Cross of Sacrifice, honouring the 54 British soldiers who died here while trying to halt the German advance in 1940.

Buses travel through Kvam on the E6 and there's a request stop metres from the museum; Kvam train station is about 200m south of the museum.

Sjoa

From Kvam, it's 9km further up the valley to **SJOA**, a scattered hamlet set beside the junction of the E6 and Highway 257. The latter cuts west along the

Heidal valley, where the River Sjoa boasts some of the country's most exciting **whitewater rafting**. If you want to come to grips with the river's gorges and rapids, contact the local specialists, Heidal Rafting (Ⓣ61 23 60 37, Ⓦwww.heidalrafting.no). An all-inclusive one-day rafting excursion costs around 1000kr, 700kr for half a day; a more strenuous two-day expedition inclusive of meals and lodgings will set you back around 2000kr. The season lasts from May to September and reservations are recommended, though there's a reasonably good chance of being able to sign up at the last minute. Heidal Rafting are based at Sjoa HI **hostel**, *Sjoa Vandrerhjem* (Ⓣ61 23 62 00, Ⓦwww.vandrerhjem.no; dorm beds 155–215kr, chalets ❶–❸; mid-May to Sept), which is itself worth a second look. Perched on a wooded hillside high above the river, the main building is a charming old log farmhouse dating from 1747 and, although visitors sleep in more modern quarters, this is where you eat. Breakfasts are banquet-like, and dinners (by prior arrangement only) are reasonably priced if rather less spectacular. The hostel offers two types of accommodation: there's a no-frills dormitory block at the bottom of the slope and a handful of spacious and comfortable chalets) up above. Reservations are advisable for the chalets on the weekend. The hostel is located just off Highway 257, about 1300m west of the E6. There's no train station – the nearest is at Otta 10km to the north – but buses stop on the E6 near the Highway 257 intersection.

Beyond the Heidal valley, Highway 257 continues west to meet Highway 51, the main access road to the east side of the Jotunheimen National Park at Gjendesheim (see p.181).

Otta

Just 10km beyond Sjoa lies **OTTA**, an unassuming and unexciting little town at the confluence of the rivers Otta and Lågen. It may be dull, but Otta makes a handy base for hiking in the nearby Rondane and Jotunheimen national parks (see p.177 & p.170), especially if you're reliant on public transport – though staying in one of the parks' mountain lodges is much to be preferred. In Otta, everything you need is within easy reach: the E6 passes within 500m of the town centre, sweeping along the east bank of the Lågen, while Highway 15 bisects the town from east to west with the few gridiron streets that pass for the centre lying a few metres to the south.

There are no sights as such, but the **statue** outside the Skysstasjon, just north of Highway 15, commemorates a certain **Pillarguri**, whose alertness made her an overnight sensation. During the Kalmar War of 1611–13, one of many wars between Sweden and Denmark, a band of Scottish mercenaries hired by the king of Sweden landed in the Romsdalsfjord, intent on crossing Norway to join the Swedish army. The Norwegians – Danish subjects at that time – were fearful of the Scots, and when Pillarguri spotted them nearing Otta she dashed to the top of the nearest hill and blew her birch-bark horn to sound the alarm. The locals hastily arranged an ambush at one of the narrowest points of the trail and all but wiped the Scots out – a rare victory for peasants over professionals. One of Pillarguri's rewards was to have a hill named after her, and today the stiff hike along the footpath up the forested slopes to the summit, **Pillarguritoppen** (853m), across the Otta river south of the centre, is a popular outing.

Clumped together in the Skysstasjon on the north side of Highway 15 are the **train station**, **bus terminal** and exceptionally helpful **tourist office** (July–Aug Mon–Fri 8.30am–7pm, Sat & Sun 11am–6pm; Sept–June Mon–Fri 8.30am–4pm; Ⓣ61 23 66 50, Ⓦwww.vistrondane.com), which can provide local bus timetables, book accommodation and reserve Lake Gjende boat

Moving on from Otta to the western fjords

Running west from Otta, **Highway 15** sweeps along wide river valleys bound for **Lom** (see p.247), where there's a choice of wonderful routes on into the western fjords: you can either carry on along Highway 15 towards Stryn (see p.253), or branch off north onto the nerve-jangling **Ørnevegen** (Eagle's Highway; Highway 63) to Geiranger (see p.258). Alternatively, you can turn off Highway 15 at Lom, onto the **Sognefjellsveg** (Highway 55) which climbs steeply to the south, travelling along the western flank of the Jotunheimen National Park and offering breathtaking views of its jagged peaks before careering down to Sogndal (see p.244).

The Nor-Way Bussekspress Oslo–Måløy **bus** (3 daily) runs along Highway 15 from Otta to Lom and onto Stryn. From mid-June to August, there is a once or twice daily connecting bus service from Grotli or Langvetn on Highway 15 to Geiranger, on Highway 63, and ultimately to Åndalsnes. The journey time from Otta to Lom is one hour, three hours to Stryn. From late June to mid-Sept, two or three times daily, there's a bus from Otta and Lom to Sogndal along the Sognefjellsveg, Highway 55. For fjordland bus timetables, consult Ⓦwww.fjord1.no.

tickets; they also sell DNT membership, fishing licences and a good range of hiking maps. As for **accommodation**, one of the better options is *Grand Gjestegård*, a large pension-cum-hotel with simple rooms furnished in modern style (Ⓣ61 23 12 00; ❸): it's across from the train station at the corner of Ola Dahls gate. A few metres further to the west along Ola Dahls gate, the recently revamped chain hotel *Norlandia Otta Hotell* (Ⓣ61 21 08 00, Ⓦwww.norlandia.no; ❹) makes a reasonable alternative. The nearest **campsite**, the year-round *Otta Camping* (Ⓣ61 23 03 09), lies about 1500m from the town centre on the wooded banks of the River Otta, with cabins (❷) and space for tents: to get there, cross the bridge on the south side of the centre, turn right and keep going. Otta's choice of **places to eat** is rather limited, but there is one recommendable spot, the *Pillarguri*, Storgata 7 (Ⓣ61 23 01 04), a café-restaurant, offering a good range of traditional Norwegian dishes with mains about 120kr; it's normally open daily from noon to 10pm.

Otta is within easy striking distance of the main access points to two of Norway's **national parks** – **Rondane**, just 20km or so to the east, and the **Jotunheimen**, about 90km to the southwest along highways 15 and 51. In summer, there are local **buses** (timetables on Ⓦwww.fjord1.no) from Otta bus station to both parks. To the Rondane, the bus to the sprawling chalet settlement of Mysuseter (mid-June to mid-Aug 2 daily; 30min) usually continues the 5km up to Spranghaugen car park, right on the edge of the park itself and an easy ninety-minute walk from the *Rondvassbu mountain lodge* (see p.179). The bus from Otta to Gol (late June to mid-Aug 1–2 daily; 2hr) travels along highways 15 and then 51, passing by the Gjendesheim (see p.181) in the Jotunheimen; return buses leave Gjendesheim about five hours after the arrival of the first bus of the day.

Rondane Nasjonalpark

Spreading north and east from Otta towards the Swedish border, **Rondane Nasjonalpark** was established in 1962 as Norway's first national park and is now one of the country's most popular hiking areas. Its 527 square kilometres, one third of which is in the high alpine zone, appeal to walkers of all ages and

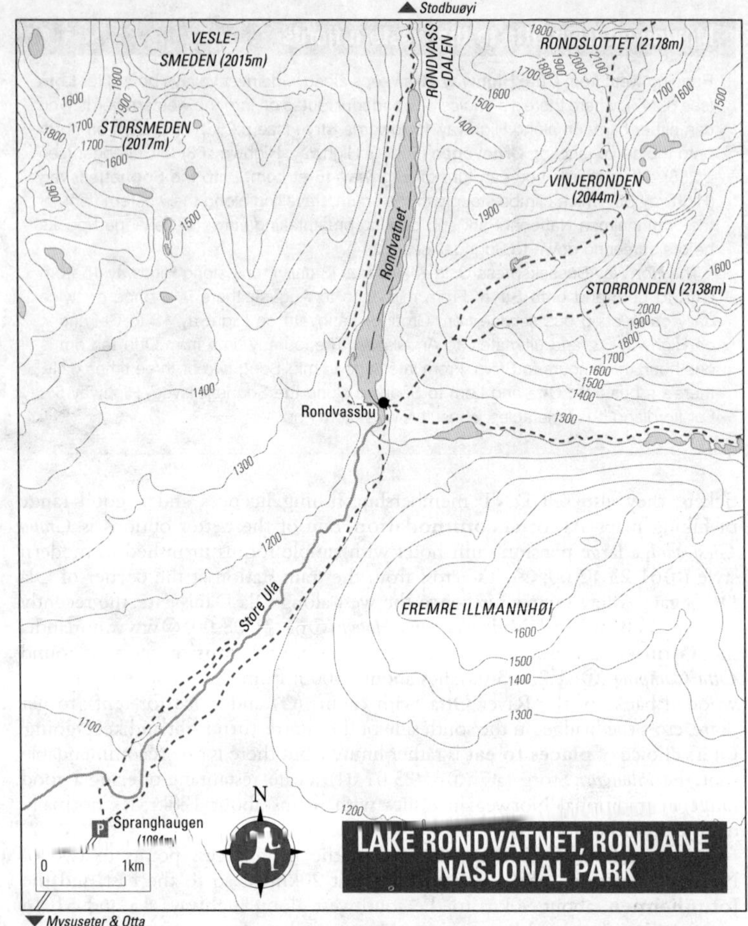

abilities. The soil is poor, so vegetation is sparse and lichens, especially reindeer moss, predominate, but the views across this bare landscape are serenely beautiful, and a handful of lakes and rivers along with patches of dwarf birch forest provide some variety. Wild mountain peaks divide the Rondane into three distinct areas. To the west of **Rondvatnet**, a centrally located lake, are the wild cirques and jagged peaks of Storsmeden (2017m), Sagtinden (2018m) and Veslesmeden (2015m), while to the east of the lake rise Rondslottet (2178m), Vinjeronden (2044m) and Storronden (2138m). Further east still, Høgronden (2115m) dominates the landscape. The mountains, ten of which exceed the 2000-metre mark, are mostly accessible to any reasonably fit and eager walker, thanks to a dense network of trails and hiking huts/lodges.

From the **Spranghaugen car park**, where the bus from Otta terminates (see p.177), it's a ninety-minute level walk northeast along the service road to the southern tip of lake **Rondvatnet** with the bleak and bare peaks of the Rondane slowly revealing themselves – a dozen peaks in all, surrounding the

△ Rondane National Park

lake's shadowy waters. At the southern tip of the lake is the DNT **Rondvassbu lodge** (late June to mid-Sept; ⓣ61 23 18 66, ⓦwww.rondvassbu.com; dorm beds for DNT members 105kr, doubles ❷), the most accessible of the park's several huts and lodges. It's a typical staffed DNT lodge, with more than one hundred beds, filling meals and pleasant service. For all but the briefest of hikes, it's best to arrive at the lodge the day before to have a chance of starting first thing the next morning. If, however, visibility is poor or you don't fancy a climb, there is a charming summer **boat service** (July–Aug 2–3 daily; 30min each way; 45kr each way, 70kr return) to the far end of Rondvatnet, from where it takes about two-and-a-half hours to walk back to *Rondvassbu* along the lake's steep western shore. Among the many other **hiking** possibilities, one popular choice is the haul up from *Rondvassbu* to the top of **Storronden** (2138m), the first peak to the right of the lake. This makes a fine excursion for the beginner, since – except for a short steep and exposed section just below the summit – there is no really difficult terrain to negotiate and the trail is clearly signed; the round trip takes about five hours – three up and two down. Neighbouring peaks involve more arduous mountain hiking, with the finest views over the range generally reckoned to be from **Vinjeronden** and nearby **Rondslottet**, both to the north of Storronden.

Jotunheimen Nasjonalpark

Norway's most celebrated hiking area, **Jotunheimen Nasjonalpark** ("Home of the Giants" National Park) lives up to its name: pointed summits and undulating glaciers dominate the skyline, soaring high above river valleys and

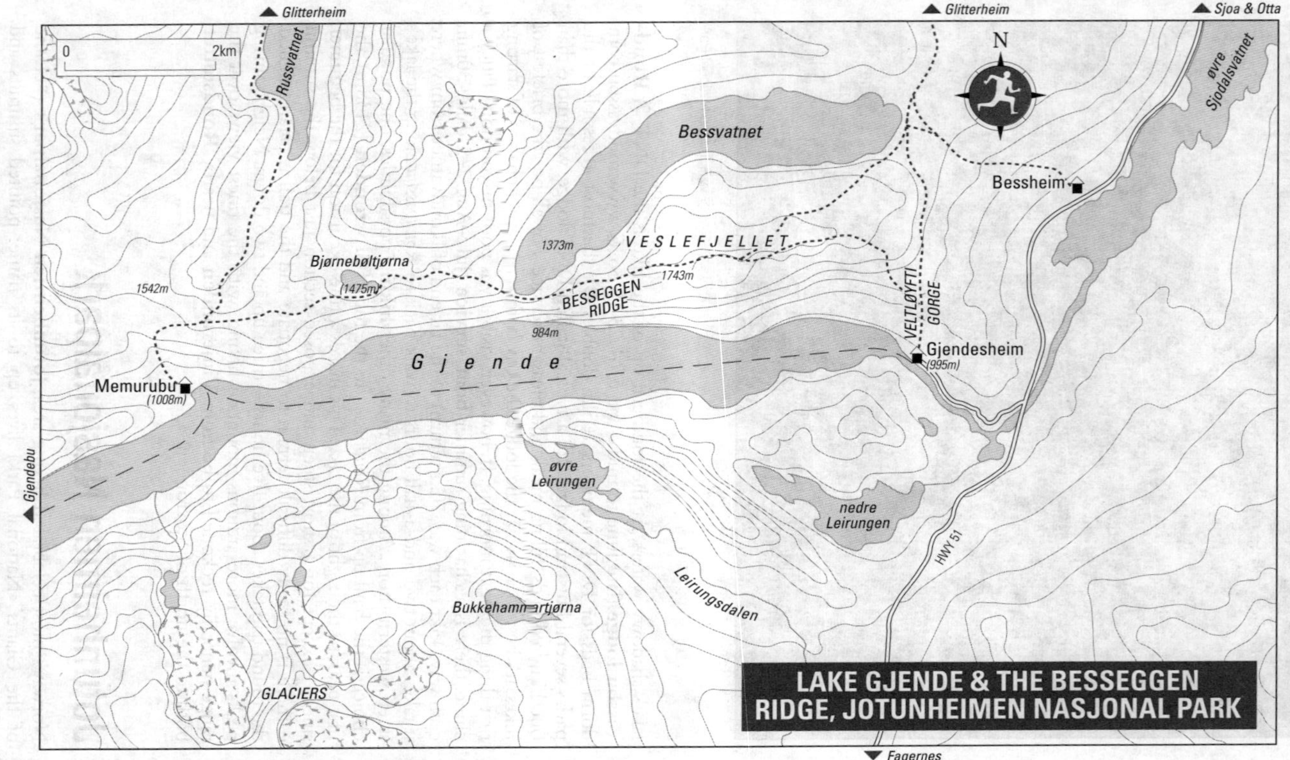
LAKE GJENDE & THE BESSEGGEN RIDGE, JOTUNHEIMEN NASJONAL PARK
Glitterheim
Glitterheim
Sjoa & Otta
Fagernes
Gjendebu
0
2km
N
Russvatnet
øvre Sjodalsvatnet
Bessvatnet
Bessheim
1373m
VESLEFJELLET
1743m
Bjørnebøltjørna
(1475m)
1542m
BESSEGGEN RIDGE
VELTLØYFTI GORGE
984m
G j e n d e
Gjendesheim
(995m)
Memurubu
(1008m)
øvre Leirungen
nedre Leirungen
HWY 51
Leirungsdalen
Bukkehammartjørna
GLACIERS

Hiking: Jotunheimen Nasjonalpark's Besseggen ridge

Start: Memurubu (1008m).
Finish: Gjendesheim (995m).
Distance: 15km.
Time: 6hr.
Highest point: Besseggen ridge (1743m).
Maps: 1617 IV Gjende (M711); 1618 III Glittertinden (M711). Jotunheimen (No. 45) 1:100,000. All produced by Statens Kartverk.
Transport: Bus from Otta to Gjendesheim (late June to Aug 1–2 daily; 2hr); boat from Gjendesheim to Memurubu (late June to mid-Sept 1–3 daily; ⓣ61 23 85 09).
Accommodation: *Gjendesheim*, full-service DNT hut (see below); *Memurubu*, full-service private hut (see p.182).

The **one-day hike** across Jotunheimen's **Besseggen ridge** high above Lake Gjende is one of Norway's most popular excursions; it takes about six hours to cover the fifteen-kilometre route, starting at Memurubu (1008m) and heading east to finish at Gjendesheim (995m), with the highest point in between being the ridge (1743m). If you do the hike in the opposite direction, you can return by boat to Gjendesheim in the evening, but you'll have to calculate your speed accurately to meet the boat at Memurubu – and that isn't easy. Whichever direction you take, be sure to confirm boat departure times before you set out, and check weather conditions too, as snow and ice can linger well into July.

Starting at the **Memurubu** jetty, the first part of the hike involves a stiff, two-and-a-half-hour haul up to the base of the **Besseggen ridge**, and this is a good spot to take a break and enjoy the views over the surrounding wilderness before tackling the ridge itself. Thereafter, the thirty-minute scramble up to the peak of the ridge is very steep, with ledges that are, on occasion, chest high; you need to be moderately fit to negotiate them. In places, the ridge narrows to 50m with a sheer drop to either side, but you can avoid straying close to the edge by following the DNT waymark "T"s. The views are superlative, but the drops disconcerting – and a head for heights is essential. Beyond the peak of the ridge, the trail is less dramatic, crossing a couple of plateaus and clambering up the slopes in between before reaching the **Veltløyfti gorge**, where a slippery scramble with steep drops requires care, though the trail is well marked and the final destination, **Gjendesheim**, is clearly visible.

lake-studded plateaux. Covering only 3900 square kilometres, the park offers an amazing concentration of high peaks, more than two hundred of which rise above 1900m, including Norway's (and Northern Europe's) two highest mountains, Galdhøpiggen (2469m) and Glittertind (2464m). Here also is Norway's highest waterfall, **Vettisfossen**, boasting a 275-metre drop and located a short walk from the Vetti lodge on the west side of the park. A network of footpaths and mountain lodges lattices the **Jotunheimen**, but be warned that the weather is very unpredictable and the winds can be bitingly cold – take care and always come well equipped.

There are no public roads into the park; visitors usually walk or ski into the interior from the Sognefjellsveg (Highway 55) in the west (see p.246) or make the slightly easier approach from the east, driving or bussing it to **Gjendesheim**, 2km off Highway 51 and some 90km from Otta; for details of buses from Otta, see p.177. Gjendesheim has long been a popular base for explorations of Jotunheimen – the first mountain hut was built here in the 1870s – but it is still no more than a ferry dock and a couple of buildings, one of which is the excellent, staffed DNT *Gjendesheim* lodge (mid-Feb to mid-April & mid-June to early

Oct; ⓣ61 23 89 10, ⓦwww.gjendesheim.no; dorm beds for DNT members 105kr, doubles ❷), at the eastern tip of long and slender **Lake Gjende**. Some 18km long and 146m deep, the lake is one of Norway's most beautiful and famous – not least because Ibsen had his Peer Gynt tumble into it on the back of a reindeer – and its glacially fed waters are tinted green on account of its myriad clay particles. Boats (mid-June to mid-Sept 1–3 daily; ⓣ61 23 85 09, ⓦwww.gjende.no) travel the length of the lake, connecting with mountain trails and dropping by two more lodges. These are the privately owned lodge at *Memurubu* (mid-June to mid-Sept; ⓣ61 23 89 99, ⓦwww.memurubu.no; ❷), halfway along the lake's north shore, and *Gjendebu*, a staffed DNT lodge (late June to mid-Sept & early March to mid-April; ⓣ61 23 89 44, ⓦwww.gjendebu.com; dorm beds for DNT members 105kr, doubles ❷), right at the lake's western end. A single fare from Gjendesheim to Memurubu costs 80kr, Gjendebu 100kr; returns are twice that unless you make the round trip on the same day, in which case fares are 110kr and 150kr respectively. It takes the boat twenty minutes to reach Memurubu, forty-five for Gjendebu. Naturally, you get to see a slice of the Jotunheimen and avoid a hike by riding the boat and sleeping at the lodges – a prudent choice in bad weather.

North along the E6 to Kongsvoll

From Otta, the E6 and the railway lead 45km north to **DOMBÅS**, a mundane crossroads settlement that does at least have a couple of good **places to stay**. The better of the two options, situated close to the train and bus station as well as the E6/E136 junction, is the *Dombås Hotell* (ⓣ61 24 10 01, ⓦwww.dombas-hotel.no; ❺, s/r ❹), whose main building, with its distinctive high gables and handsome public rooms, looks back down the Gudbrandsdal. A hotel of two halves, most of the bedrooms are tucked away in the modern annexe round the back, but the old main building holds a handsome series of long public rooms dating from the 1910s as well as a few older, more characterful rooms also offering enjoyable valley views. A cheaper choice, but also with good views, is Dombås' HI **hostel** (ⓣ61 24 09 60, ⓦwww.vandrerhjem.no; dorm beds 200kr, doubles ❸), a comfortable complex of mountain huts way up on the hillside above the E6. To get there, head north out of town along the E6 for around 1km and follow the signs up the hill (a further 0.5km).

The E136 and the Rauma branch line to Åndalsnes

Dombås is where the **E136** and the **Rauma train line** (5–6 daily; 1hr 20min) branch west for the thrilling 110-kilometre rattle down to Åndalsnes. The journey begins innocuously enough with road and rail slipping along a ridge high above a wide, grassy valley, but soon the landscape gets wilder as both nip into the hills. After 65km, they reach **Kylling bru**, an ambitious stone railway bridge, 56m high and 76m long, which spans the Rauma river. Pressing on, it's a further 20km to the shadowy hamlet of **Marstein** with the grey, cold mass of the **Trollveggen** ("Troll's Wall") rising straight ahead. At around 1100m, the Trollveggen incorporates the highest vertical overhanging mountain wall in Europe and as such is a favourite with experienced mountaineers, though it wasn't actually scaled until 1967. Somehow, the E136 and the railway manage to defile through the mountains and soon afterwards they slide down to the attractive little town of Åndalsnes (see p.262), the fjord glistening beyond.

Beyond Dombås, the E6 and the main train line head north through the mountains towards Hjerkinn, Kongsvoll (see below) and ultimately Trondheim, whilst the E136 and the dramatic Rauma branch line lead west to the port of Åndalsnes (see box opposite).

Hjerkinn

Staying on the E6 north of Dombås, it's just 30km to the outpost of **HJERKINN**, stuck out on bare and desolate moorland, its pint-sized military base battened down against the wind and snow of winter. The base overlooks the E6/Highway 29 junction, as does the adjacent **train station**, a perky wooden affair with brightly painted window frames. There's been a mountain inn here since medieval times, a staging post on the long trail to Trondheim, now just 170km away. The present inn, the *Hjerkinn Fjellstue* (ⓣ61 21 51 00, ⓦwww.hjerkinn.no; ❺), is a fitting successor, its two expansive wooden buildings featuring big open fires and breezy pine furniture. The restaurant is good, too – try the reindeer culled from local herds – and there's horse-riding from the stables next door. The inn is set on a hill overlooking the moors just over 2km from the train station beside Highway 29.

If you're travelling north bound for Røros (see p.184), then Highway 29, which branches off the E6 at Hjerkinn, is the shortest route, but Highway 30, further north (see below), is a much more scenic approach.

Kongsvoll

Beyond Hjerkinn, the E6 slices across the barren uplands before descending into a narrow ravine, the **Drivdal**. Hidden away here, just 12km from Hjerkinn, is **KONGSVOLL**, home to a tiny train station and the delightful *Kongsvold Fjeldstue* (ⓣ72 40 43 40, ⓦwww.kongsvold.no; shared facilities ❺, en suite ❻), which provides some of the most charming accommodation in the whole of Norway. As at Hjerkinn, an inn has stood here since medieval times and the present complex, a huddle of tastefully restored timber buildings with sun-bleached reindeer antlers tacked onto the outside walls, dates back to the eighteenth century. Once a farm as well as an inn, its agricultural days are recalled by several outbuildings such as the little turf-roofed storehouses (*stabbur*), the lodgings for farmhands (*karstuggu*) and the barn (*låve*), atop which is a bell that was rung to summon the hands from the fields. The main building retains many of its original features and also holds an eclectic sample of antiques. The bedrooms, dotted round the compound, are of the same high standard – and the old vagabonds' hut (*fantstuggu*), built outside the white picket fence that once defined the physical limits of social respectability, contains the cosiest family rooms imaginable. Dinner is served in the excellent **restaurant**, with mains averaging 160kr, and the complex also includes a **café** and a small Dovrefjell Nasjonalpark **information centre**. The inn makes a lovely spot to break your journey and an ideal base for hiking into the park, which extends to the east and west. If you're arriving by **train**, note that only some services stop at Kongsvoll station, 500m down the valley from the inn – and then only by prior arrangement with the conductor.

From Kongsvoll, it's about 40km to **Oppdal**, an uninspiring crossroads town where the Kristiansund road (Highway 70) meets the E6. Moving on, it's another 70km north to **Støren**, just 50km short of Trondheim, where you can turn off onto Highway 30 for the 100-kilometre drive along the picturesque **Gauldal** valley to Røros (see p.184).

Dovrefjell Nasjonalpark

Bisected by the railway and the E6, **Dovrefjell Nasjonalpark** is one of the more accessible of Norway's national parks. A comparative minnow at just 265 square kilometres, it comprises two distinct zones: spreading east from the E6 are the marshes, open moors and rounded peaks that characterize much of eastern Norway, while to the west the mountains become increasingly steep and serrated as they approach the jagged spires backing onto Åndalsnes (see p.262).

Hiking trails and **huts** are scattered across the western part of the Dovrefjell. **Kongsvoll** (see p.183) makes an ideal starting point: it's possible to hike all the way from here to the coast, but this takes all of nine or ten days. A more feasible expedition for most visitors is the two-hour circular walk up to the mountain plateau, or a two-day, round-trip hike to one of the four ice-tipped peaks of mighty **Snøhetta**, at around 2200m. There's accommodation five hours' walk west from Kongsvoll at the unstaffed **Reinheim hut** (mid-Feb to mid-Oct). On the first part of any of these hikes, you're likely to spot **musk ox**, the descendants of animals imported from Greenland in the 1950s. Conventional wisdom is that these chunky beasts will ignore you if you ignore them and keep at a distance of at least 100m. They are, however, not afraid of humans and will charge if irritated – retreat as quickly and quietly as possible if one starts snorting and scraping. Further hiking details and maps are available at the park **information centre** in the *Kongsvold Fjeldstue* (see p.183).

Røros and around

RØROS, located on a treeless mountain plateau some 160km northeast from Kongsvoll via the E6 and Highway 30, is a blustery place even on a summer's afternoon, when it's full of day-tripping tourists surveying the old part of town, little changed since its days as a copper mining centre. Røros is a unique and remarkable survivor – until the mining company went bust in 1977, mining had been the basis of life here since the seventeenth century. This dirty and dangerous work was supplemented by a little farming and hunting, and life for the average villager can't have been anything but hard. Unusually, Røros' wooden houses, some of them 300 years old, have escaped the fires that have devastated so many of Norway's timber-built towns, and as a consequence the town is on UNESCO's World Heritage list. Firm regulations now protect this rare townscape and changes to its grass-roofed cottages are strictly regulated. Film companies regularly use the town as a backdrop for their productions – it featured as a labour camp in the 1971 Anglo-Norwegian film starring Tom Courtenay called *One Day in the Life of Ivan Denisovich*, a choice of location that gives something of the flavour of the place.

The town centre

In the town centre, **Røros kirke** (early to mid-June & mid-Aug to mid-Sept Mon–Sat 11am–1pm; mid-June to mid-Aug Mon–Sat 10am–5pm, Sun 1–3pm; mid-Sept to May Sat 11am–1pm; 25kr) is the most obvious target for a stroll, its heavy tower reflecting the wealth of the early mine owners. Built in 1784, and once the only stone building in Røros, the church is more like a theatre than a religious edifice. A huge structure capable of seating 1600 people, it

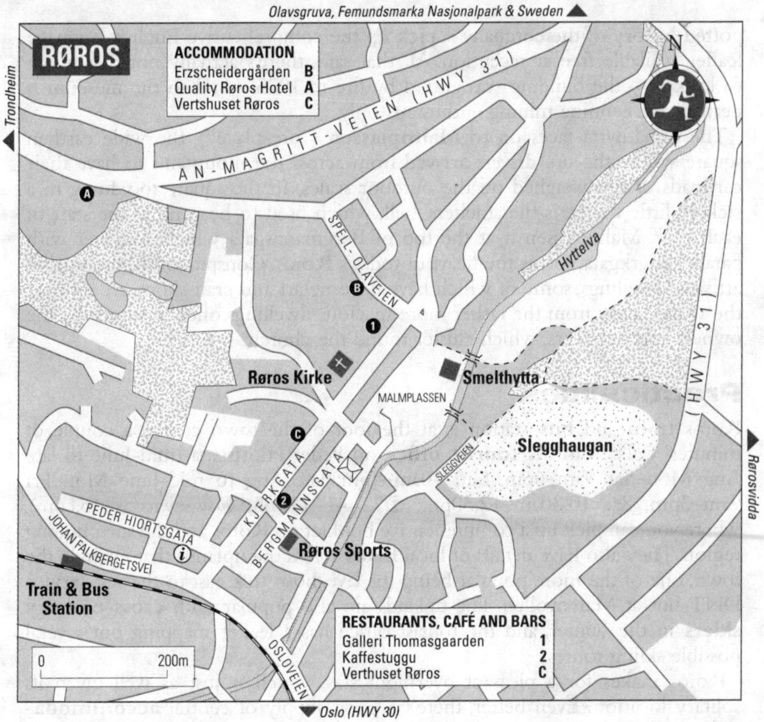

was designed, like the church at Kongsberg (see p.190), to overawe rather than inspire. Its pulpit is built directly over the altar to emphasize the importance of the priest's word, and a two-tiered gallery runs around the nave. Mine labourers were accommodated in the gallery's lower level, while "undesirables" were compelled to sit above, and even had to enter via a separate, external staircase. Down below, the nave exhibited even finer distinctions: every pew nearer the front was a step up the social ladder, while mine managers vied for the curtained boxes, each of which had a well-publicized annual rent; the monarch (or royal representative) had a private box commanding views from the back. These byzantine social arrangements are explained in depth during the **guided tour** (mid-June to mid-Aug, 1–2 daily in English), the cost of which is included in the admission fee.

Immediately below the church, on either side of the river, lies the oldest part of Røros, a huddle of sturdy cross-timbered smelters' cottages, storehouses and workshops squatting in the shadow of the **slegghaugan** (slagheaps) – more tourist attraction than eyesore, and providing fine views over the town and beyond. Here also, next to the river, are the rambling main works, the **Smelthytta** (literally "melting hut"; early to mid-June & mid-Aug to mid-Sept Mon–Fri 11am–5pm, Sat & Sun 11am–3pm; mid-June to mid-Aug daily 10am–7pm; mid-Sept to May Tues–Fri 11am–3pm, Sat & Sun 11am–2pm; 60kr), which has been tidily restored and turned into a museum. This is a large three-storey affair whose most interesting section, set in the cavernous hall that once housed the smelter, explains the intricacies of copper production. Dioramas illuminate every part of the process, and there are production charts, samples of ore and a potted history of the company – pick up the comprehensive English-language leaflet available free at reception. All that said, there's actually not that much to look at – the building was gutted by fire in 1975 – and so the museum is perhaps for genuine mining enthusiasts only.

The Smelthytta faces on to **Malmplassen** ("ore-place"), the wide earthen square where the ore drivers arrived from across the mountains to have their cartloads of ore weighed on the outdoor scales. In the square too, hung in a rickety little tower, is the smelters' bell, which used to be rung at the start of each shift. Malmplassen is at the top of Bergmannsgata which, together with parallel Kjerkgata, forms the heart of today's Røros. Conspicuously, the smaller artisans' dwellings, some of which have become art and craft shops, are set near the works, away from the rather more spacious dwellings once occupied by the owners and overseers, which cluster round the church.

Practicalities

Røros **train** and **bus** station is at the foot of the town centre, a couple of minutes' walk from the **tourist office** on Peder Hiortsgata (mid-June to late Aug Mon–Sat 9am–6pm, Sun 10am–4pm; late Aug to mid-June Mon–Fri 9am–3pm, Sat 10.30am–12.30pm; ⓣ72 41 11 65, ⓦwww.rorosinfo.com), where you can pick up a comprehensive booklet on Røros and the surrounding region. They also have details of local **hikes** across the uplands that encircle the town, one of the more popular being the five-hour trek east to the self-service DNT hut at Marenvollen. The uplands are also popular with **cross-country skiers** in the winter, and the tourist office has a leaflet mapping out several possible skiing routes.

Røros makes for a pleasant overnight stay, which is just as well given its solitary location. Even better, there's a good supply of central **accommodation** with the best deal in town being the *Erzscheidergården guesthouse*, Spell-Olaveien 6 (ⓣ72 41 11 94, ⓦwww.erzscheidergaarden.com; ❹), where there are some charming, unassuming rooms in its wooden main building. Some rooms also have fine views over town, and there's an attractive subterranean breakfast area and a cosy lounge. Also worth considering are the *Quality Røros Hotel*, An-Magritt veien (ⓣ72 40 80 00, ⓦwww.choicehotels.com; ❻, sp/r ❹), a big modern place on the northern edge of the centre, and *Vertshuset Røros*, Kjerkgata 34 (ⓣ72 41 93 50, ⓦwww.vertshusetroros.no; ❹), a guesthouse with cramped doubles that's bang in the centre of town.

When it comes to **food**, Røros is no gourmet's paradise, but there's just enough choice to get by. The unfussy homeliness of the restaurant at the *Vertshuset Røros*, Kjerkgata 34, makes it a good spot to enjoy an evening meal – choose from traditional Norwegian dishes like *kjøttkaker i brun saus* (meatballs in brown sauce) at around 100kr. For a quicker bite, *Kaffestuggu*, Kjerkgata 19, has a suntrap of a courtyard and a series of elegant little rooms where you can sample their cakes, sandwiches and reasonably priced daily specials. Finally, tucked away at Kjerkgata 48, is *Galleri Thomasgaarden*, a ceramics gallery that also houses the cosiest café in town, where you can avoid the crowds and get tasty home-cooked snacks.

Around Røros: Olavsgruva copper mine and Femundsmarka Nasjonalpark

Some 13km east of Røros off Highway 31, one of the old copper mines, the **Olavsgruva**, has been kept open as a museum, and there are daily guided tours of its workings throughout the summer (early to mid-June & late Aug to early Sept Mon–Sat 2 daily, Sun 1 daily; late June to mid-Aug 5 daily; early Sept to May Sat 1 daily; 60kr; book at Røros tourist office). The temperature down the mine is a constant 5°C, so remember to take something warm to wear – you'll need sturdy shoes too.

Further afield still, around 40km southeast of Røros and tucked in tight between the Swedish border and the elongated Lake Femund, is the remote **Femundsmarka Nasjonalpark**, whose 385 square kilometres encompass a wide variety of terrains. In the north are pine forests, marshes, lakes and rivers, which give way in the south to bare mountains and plateaux. There is no road access into the Femundsmarka, but a minor road leads from Røros to **Synnervika**, on the west side of **Lake Femund**, from where a **passenger boat**, the M/S *Fæmund* (mid-June to mid-Sept 1–6 weekly; ⓣ72 41 37 14, ⓦwww.femund.no), shuttles around the lake, stopping at several remote outposts and jetties. Among the latter, several give access to the limited network of unstaffed DNT huts and **hiking trails** that cross the park; the jetties at **Røa** (30min from Synnervika; 105kr each way) and **Haugen** (1hr 15min; 130kr each way) are perhaps the handiest. Sailing schedules are available from Røros tourist office, who also have details of connecting buses from town to the jetty. Several Røros-based operators run canoeing and fishing expeditions into the park – **Røros Sport**, at Bergmannsgata 13 (ⓣ72 41 12 18), is as good as any.

From Oslo to the western fjords

The forested dales and uplands that fill out much of central Norway between Oslo and the western fjords rarely inspire: in almost any other European country, these elongated valleys would be attractions in their own right, but here in Norway they simply can't compare with the mountains and fjords of the north and west. Almost everywhere, the architecture is routinely modern and most of the old timber buildings, which once lined the valleys, are long gone – except in the ten-a-penny open-air museums that are a feature of nearly every town. Neither does it help that the towns and villages of the region almost invariably string along the roads in long, seemingly aimless ribbons.

Of the three major trunk roads crossing the region, the **E16** is the fastest, a quick 330-kilometre haul up from Oslo to both the fjord ferry near Sogndal (see p.244) and the colossal 24km-long tunnel leading to Flåm (see p.235). Otherwise, the E16's nearest rival, the slower **Highway 7**, branches off the E16 at Hønefoss and, after a scenic wiggle across the Hardangervidda plateau, finally reaches the coast at Eidfjord near Hardangerfjord, a distance of 330km; Highway 7 also intersects with **Highway 50**, offering another possible route to Flåm. For most of its length, Highway 7 is shadowed by the **Oslo–Bergen railway**, though they part company when the train swings north for its spectacular traverse of the mountains. The third road, the **E134**, covers the 418km from Drammen near Oslo to Haugesund, passing near Odda on the Sørfjord after 323km. Again, it's a slower route, but it has the advantage of passing through the attractive town of **Kongsberg** and slipping across the southern reaches of the Hardangervidda.

Regular long-distance **buses** serve all three of the major roads.

The E16 to Leira and Borgund stave church

Clipping along the **E16** from Oslo, it's 190km up through a series of river valleys to ribbon-like **LEIRA**, where you can break your journey economically – if not exactly thrillingly – at the HI **hostel** (Ⓣ61 35 95 00, Ⓦwww.vandrerhjem.no; June to mid-Aug; dorm beds 120kr, doubles ❶), which occupies part of a roadside high-school complex. At the next village of **Fagernes**, Highway 51 branches north, to run along the eastern edge of the Jotunheimen Nasjonalpark, passing near Gjendesheim and its lodge (see p.181) before finally joining Highway 15 west of Otta (see p.176).

About 30km west of Fagernes along the E16, the scenery begins to improve as you approach the coast. The road dips and weaves from dale to dale, slip-

Stave churches

Of the 29 surviving **stave churches in the country**, the bulk are in central Norway, but taken together they represent the nation's most distinctive architectural legacy. The key feature of their design is that their timbers are placed vertically into the ground – in contrast to the log-bonding technique used by the Norwegians for everything else. Thus, a stave wall consists of vertical planks slotted into sills above and below, with the sills connected to upright posts – or **staves**, hence the name – at each corner. The general design seems to have been worked out in the twelfth century and common features include external wooden galleries, shingles and finials. There are, however, variations: in some churches, nave and chancel form a single rectangle, in others the chancel is narrower than, and tacked on to, the nave. The most fetching stave churches are those where the central section of the nave has been raised above the aisles to create – from the outside – a distinctive, almost pagoda-like effect. In virtually all the stave churches, the **door frames** (where they survive) are decorated from top to bottom with surging, intricate carvings that clearly hark back to Viking design, most memorably fantastical long-limbed dragons entwined in vine tendrils.

The **origins** of stave churches have attracted an inordinate amount of academic debate. Some scholars argue that they were originally pagan temples, converted to Christian use by the addition of a chancel, while others are convinced that they were inspired by Russian churches. In the nineteenth century, they also acquired symbolic importance as reminders of the time when Norway was independent. Many had fallen into a dreadful state of repair and were clumsily renovated – or even remodelled – by enthusiastic medievalists with a nationalist agenda. Undoing this repair work has been a major operation, and one that continues today. For most visitors, seeing one or two will suffice – and two of the finest are those at Heddal (see p.192) and Borgund (see opposite).

ping between the hills until it reaches the **Lærdal valley**, whose wooded slopes shelter the stepped roofs and angular gables of the **Borgund stave church** (daily: May to mid-June & late Aug to Sept 10am–5pm; mid-June to late Aug 8am–8pm; 65kr). One of the best-preserved stave churches in Norway, Borgund was built beside what was one of the major pack roads between east and west until bubonic plague wiped out most of the local population in the fourteenth century. Much of the church's medieval appearance has been preserved, its tiered exterior protected by shingles and decorated with finials in the shape of dragons and Christian crosses, the whole caboodle culminating in a slender ridge turret. A rickety wooden gallery runs round the outside of the church, and the doors sport an intense swirl of carved animals and foliage. Inside, the dark, pine-scented nave is framed by the upright wooden posts that define this style of church architecture, and the adjacent visitor centre fills in some of the historical and architectural background.

Beyond the church, the valley grows wilder as the E16 travels the 45km down to **Fodnes**, where a 24hr car ferry zips over to **Mannheller** (every 30min; 15min; car & driver 92kr, passengers 31kr), some 18km from Sogndal (see p.244). On the way, you'll pass the entrance to the 24km-long tunnel that extends the E16 to Flåm (see p.235) for the fastest route to Bergen and **GAMLE LÆRDALSØYRI**, a fjordside settlement that flourished up until the twentieth century. Thereafter, it went into decline, but many of its old timber buildings have survived and are now rigorously protected. The most important – and interesting – string along the main drag, Øyragata, including the old telegraph station, savings bank and general stores.

Highway 7 to Geilo and the fjords

Highway 7 branches off the E16 about 60km from Oslo at **Hønefoss**, and then cuts an unexciting course along the **Hallingdal valley**, shadowed by the main Oslo–Bergen railway. Some 180km from Hønefoss, the road forks at Hagafoss, with Highway 50 descending the dales to reach, after 100km, the Aurlandsfjord just round the coast from Flåm (see p.235). Meanwhile, Highway 7 presses on west to the winter ski resort of **GEILO**, 250km from Oslo. Frankly, Geilo is a boring town out of the skiing season, but it does have several inexpensive places to stay, including an HI **hostel** (Ⓣ32 08 70 60, Ⓦwww.vandrerhjem.no; all year; dorm beds 180kr, doubles ❷), housed in two large mountain lodge-style buildings in the town centre just off the main drag. Details of other accommodation are available from the **tourist office** (June & late Aug Mon–Fri 8.30am–5pm, Sat 9am–3pm; July to mid-Aug Mon–Fri 8.30am–8pm, Sat & Sun 9am–5pm; Sept–May Mon–Fri 8.30am–4pm & Sat 8.30am–2pm; Ⓣ32 09 59 00, Ⓦwww.geilo.no).

Just beyond Geilo, the rail line ceases to follow the road, breaking off to barrel its way over the mountains to Finse, Myrdal (where you change for the scenic branch line down to Flåm; see p.232) and points to Bergen. Highway 7, meanwhile, continues west for a further 100km, slicing across the Hardangervidda mountain plateau (see p.228). It's a lonely, handsome road that passes several places – such as **Halne** and **Dyranut** – where you can pick up the Hardangervidda's network of hiking trails. On the far side of the plateau, Highway 7 rushes down a steep valley to reach the fjords at Eidfjord (see p.227).

The E134 west to Kongsberg

Up in the hills some 80km from Oslo, **KONGSBERG** is one of the most interesting towns in the region and the main attraction along the **E134**, the third main road linking Oslo with the western fjords. A local story claims that the **silver** responsible for Kongsberg's existence was discovered by two goatherds, who stumbled across a vein of the metal laid bare by the scratchings of an ox. True or not, Christian IV (1577–1648), his eye on the main chance, was quick to exploit the find, sponsoring the development of mining here – the town's name means "King's Mountain" – at the start of a silver rush that boosted his coffers no end. In the event, it turned out that Kongsberg was the only place in the world where silver could be found in its pure form, and there was enough of it to sustain the town for a couple of centuries. By the 1750s, it

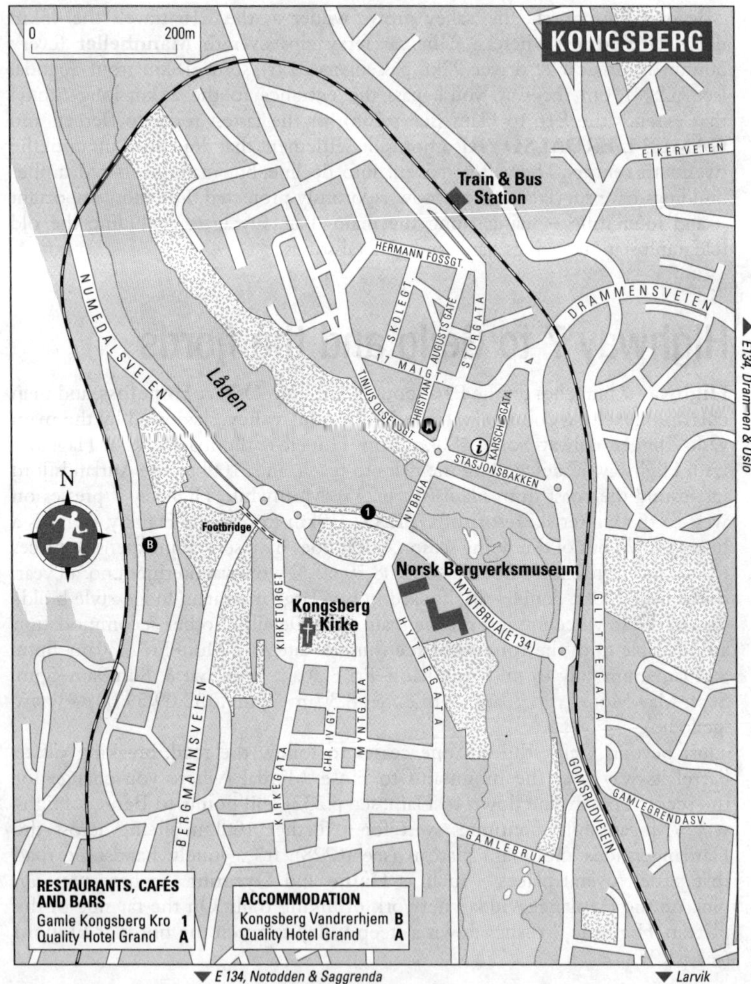

was the largest town in Norway, with half its 8000 inhabitants employed in and around the 300-odd mine shafts that littered the area. The silver works closed in 1805, but by this time Kongsberg was also the site of a royal mint and then an armaments factory, which still employs people to this day.

To appreciate the full economic and political clout of the mine owners, it's necessary to visit the church they funded – **Kongsberg kirke** (mid-May to mid-Aug Mon–Fri 10am–4pm, Sat 10am–1pm & Sun 2–4pm; mid- to late Aug Mon–Fri 10am–noon; Sept to mid-May Tues–Thurs 10am–noon; 30kr), the largest and arguably most beautiful Baroque church in Norway. It dates from 1761, when the mines were at the peak of their prosperity, and sits impressively in a square surrounded on three sides by period wooden buildings. The interior is a grand affair too, with its enormous and showy mock-marble western wall incorporating the altar, pulpit and organ. This arrangement was dictated by political considerations: the pulpit is actually above the altar, to ram home the point that the priest's stern injunctions to work harder were an expression of God's will. The **seating arrangements** were rigidly and hierarchically defined, and determined the church's principal fixtures. Facing the pulpit are the King's Box and boxes for the silver-works' managers, while other officials sat in the glass enclosures. The pews on the ground floor were reserved for their womenfolk, while the sweeping balcony was divided into three tiers to accommodate the Kongsberg petit bourgeoisie, the workers and, squeezing in at the top and the back, the lumpen proletariat.

As for the rest of Kongsberg, it's an agreeable if quiet place in summer, with plenty of green spaces. The **River Lågen** tumbles through the centre, and statues on the town bridge at the foot of Storgata commemorate various local activities, including foolhardy attempts to locate new finds of silver – one of which involved the use of divining rods. Mining enthusiasts will enjoy the **Norsk Bergverksmuseum**, Hyttegata 3 (Mining Museum; daily: mid-May to Aug 10am–5pm; Sept to mid-May noon–4pm; 60kr), housed in the old smelting works at the river's edge and sharing its premises with a tiny ski museum and coin collection, but merely wandering around the town is as enjoyable a way as any of spending time here.

One set of **silver mines**, the **Sølvgruvene**, is open for tours and makes a fine excursion, especially if you have pre-teen children to amuse. It's hidden in green surroundings 8km west of town in the hamlet of **SAGGRENDA**. To get there, drive along the E134 in the direction of Notodden and look for the sign leading off to the right. The informative ninety-minute tour includes a ride on a miniature train into the shafts through dark tunnels. There are three to six tour departures daily from mid-May to August and two weekly in September and October; the **tour** costs 130kr – 50kr for kids – and Kongsberg tourist office (see below) has the schedule; take a sweater, as it's cold underground. Back outside the mine, just 350m down the hill, the old ochre-painted workers' compound – the *Sakkerhusene* – has been restored and contains a **café** as well as some rather half-hearted displays on the history of the mines.

Kongsberg practicalities

Kongsberg **tourist office**, at Karsches gata 3 (early May to late June & late Aug to late Sept Mon–Fri 9am–4pm, Sat 10am–2pm; late June to late Aug Mon–Fri 9am–7pm, Sat & Sun 10am–4pm; late Sept to April Mon–Fri 9am–4pm; ⓣ32 29 90 50, ⓦwww.visitkongsberg.no), is a brief walk from the **train and bus station**, and can help with accommodation – not that there's much to choose from. The HI **hostel** at Vinjesgate 1 (ⓣ32 73 20 24, ⓦwww.vandrerhjem.no) is *the* place to stay, with both dorm beds (195kr) and comfortable en-suite doubles (❷) in an attractive timber lodge close to the town centre. Drivers need to follow the signs on the E134; train and bus users should walk south from the station along Storgata, cross the bridge and walk round the back of the church on the right-hand side, then head down the slope and over the footbridge – it's about a fifteen-minute walk in all. As for central **hotels**, easily the most appealing option is the *Quality Hotel Grand*, in a modern block down near the river at Christian Augusts gate 2 (ⓣ32 77 28 00, ⓦwww.choicehotels.no/hotels/no052; ❼, sp/r ❺); there are over 170 well-appointed rooms here and the hotel also has a first-class **restaurant** serving Norwegian standards with main courses averaging about 180kr. If the weather's good, head for the pleasant riverside terrace of the *Gamle Kongsberg Kro* café-restaurant, below the church.

West of Kongsberg on the E134: Heddal, Seljord and beyond

A few kilometres west of Kongsberg, the **E134** slips into **Telemark** (ⓦwww.telemarkreiser.no), a county that covers a great forested chunk of southern Norway. Just inside its borders is industrial **Notodden** and, 6km beyond that, beside the main road, is the **stave church of Heddal** (late May to late June & late Aug to mid-Sept Mon–Sat 10am–5pm, Sun 1–5pm; late June to late Aug Mon–Sat 9am–7pm, Sun 1–7pm; 35kr). Surrounded by a neat cemetery and rolling pastureland, Heddal is the largest surviving stave church in Norway, its pretty tumble of shingle-clad roofs restored to something like its medieval appearance in 1955, rectifying a heavy-handed nineteenth-century remodelling. The crosses atop the church's gables alternate with dragon-head gargoyles, a mix of Christian and pagan symbolism that is typical of many stave churches (see box on p.188). Inside, the twenty masts of the nave are decorated at the top by masks, and there's some attractive seventeenth-century wall decoration in light blues, browns and whites. Pride of place, however, goes to the ancient **bishop's chair** in the chancel. Dating from around 1250, the chair carries a relief retelling the saga of Sigurd the Dragonslayer, a pagan story that Christians turned to their advantage by recasting the Viking as Jesus and the dragon as the Devil. Across from the church, there's a **café** and a modest museum illustrating further aspects of Heddal's history.

There's another fine church around 55km further west just off the E134 (and past the first and quickest road to Rjukan; see opposite) in **SELJORD**, a small industrial town of ancient provenance that spreads between the forested hills and Lake Seljordsvatnet. Dating from the twelfth century, this **church** (open for guided tours by appointment only; ⓣ35 05 08 74) is built of stone and as such is something of a medieval rarity. The town also seems to have attracted more than its fair share of "Believe It or Not" stories: a monster is supposed to lurk in the depths of the lake; elves are alleged to gather here for some of their soirées; and the 570kg stone outside the church was, so the story goes, lifted only once, by an eighteenth-century strongman by the name of Nils Langedal, who was reared on mare's milk. Elves and sea serpents apart, there's nothing much to delay you.

Grungedal and Røldal

Beyond Seljord, it's a further 50km west along the E134 to the **Åmot crossroads** (from where roads lead to Rjukan and Dalen; see opposite), and a further 30km to the handsome **Grungedal** valley, whose string of antique farmsteads lies between lake and mountain. Pushing on, the scenery bordering the E134 becomes wilder and more dramatic as the road slips across the Hardangervidda mountain plateau (see p.228) before snaking its way on to the hamlet of **RØLDAL**, a remote little place nestled in the greenest of valleys with the mountains all around. Røldal has its own stave **church** (mid-May to mid-Sept daily 10am–5pm; 20kr), a trim, rusticated affair dating from the twelfth century but much amended. In medieval times, the church was a major point of pilgrimage on account of the crucifix with healing powers that still hangs above the altar.

Just beyond Røldal, the E134 meets the coastal Highway 13 running up from Stavanger (see p.152). For 18km, the two highways share a common stretch of road as they cut north across the western peripheries of the Hardangervidda plateau before they separate, with the E134 veering west bound for Haugesund (see p.160), 140km away, while Highway 13 continues north to pass, in 5km, the waterfalls at **Latefossen**, where two huge torrents empty into the river with a deafening roar. From the waterfall, it's a further 14km north on Highway 13 to **ODDA**, an ugly industrial centre and an unfortunate introduction to the fjords: try to allow enough time to avoid the place altogether and carry on to the much more appealing hamlet of Lofthus (see p.227).

Dalen and Rjukan

The Åmot crossroads (see opposite) is a starting point for two excursions off the E134, one south to Dalen, the other north to Rjukan, though an earlier turning off the E134 – before Seljord – is a faster route to Rjukan.

△ Telemarkskanal

From Åmot, it's just 20km south on **Highway 38** to tiny **DALEN**, the starting point for the passenger ferry that wends its way southeast along the **Telemarkskanal** to **Skien**, a journey of ten hours. No less than 105km long, the canal links the lakes and rivers of the district by means of eight locks that negotiate a difference in water levels of 72m. Completed in 1892, the canal was once an important trade route into the interior, but today it's mainly used by pleasure craft and three **passenger ferries**, which make the trip most days of the week from mid-May to early September. Ferries leave Dalen around 8.30am in the morning and the one-way fare is 400kr; contact Telemarkreiser (ⓣ35 90 00 30, ⓦwww.telemarkreiser.no) for further details and bookings. Dalen also possesses one of the region's more noteworthy country **hotels** in the comfortable *Hotel Dalen*, signposted 1km from Dalen bridge (ⓣ35 07 90 00, ⓦwww.dalenhotel.no; ❻; May–Dec). Built two years after the canal in a style influenced by stave churches, its gables are festooned with dragon heads and gargoyles, and its public rooms boast oodles of dark-stained timber, open fireplaces and stained glass.

Back at the Åmot crossroads, but this time heading north, **Highway 37** threads its way into forested hills en route to the **Vemork industrial works**, about 55km from Åmot and 7km short of Rjukan (see below), where the old hydroelectric station has been turned into the area's prime attraction, the **Norsk Industriarbeidermuseum** (Norwegian Industrial Workers' Museum; May–Sept daily 10am–4pm; mid-June to mid-Aug daily 10am–6pm; mid-Aug to Sept daily 10am–4pm; Oct–April Tues–Fri noon–3pm, Sat & Sun 11am–4pm; 60kr; ⓦwww.visitvemork.com). When it was opened in 1911, the old power station had the greatest generating capacity in the world – its ten turbines provided a combined output of 108 megawatts – and it remains a fine example of industrial architecture pretending to be something else: with its high gables and symmetrical windows it looks more like a country mansion. Inside, the museum explores the effects of industrialization on what was then a profoundly rural country, has displays on hydroelectric power and the development of the trade unions, and features a gallery of propagandist paintings about workers and the class struggle by Arne Ekeland. Yet, most foreigners come here because of the plant's role in – and excellent displays on – World War II, when it was the site chosen by the Germans for the manufacture of **heavy water** – necessary for regulating nuclear reactions in the creation of a nuclear bomb. Aware of the plant's importance, the Americans bombed it on several occasions and the Norwegian resistance mounted a string of guerrilla attacks; as a result, the Nazis decided to move the heavy water they had made to Germany. The only way they could do this was by train, and part of the journey was across Lake Tinnsjø – ingeniously the ferry was fitted with a set of railway tracks. This was the scene of one of the most spectacular escapades of the war, when the Norwegian resistance sunk ferry and train on January 20, 1944. All the heavy water was lost, but so were the fourteen Norwegian passengers – a story recounted in the 1965 film *The Heroes of Telemark*, in which Kirk Douglas played the cinematic stereotype of the Norwegian: an earnest man with an honest face, wearing a big pullover.

Just along the road east from Vemork, **RJUKAN** has a handsome river valley setting with a backdrop of harsh, rough mountains, but is itself really rather humdrum, its 4000 inhabitants sharing a modest gridiron town centre originally assembled by the Norsk Hydro power company at the start of the twentieth century. The town is, however, a useful base for hiking the Hardangervidda (see p.228), the mountain plateau whose southeast corner is above the town. Easy access to the Hardangervidda is provided by Rjukan's **Krossobanen**

cable car (all year daily 10am–4/8pm; single 40kr; ⓦwww.krossobanen.no), which carries passengers up to the plateau from a station about 2km from the tourist office, at the west end of town; for details of Hardangervidda hiking trails, enquire at the tourist office. Built in 1928, the Krossobanen was the first cable car to be built in northern Europe and Norsk Hydro stumped up the money, curiously enough because they wanted their workers to be able to see the sun in winter.

Rjukan practicalities

Long-distance **buses** to Rjukan from Oslo and Kongsberg pull in at the **bus station** on the south side of the river. The town centre is a couple of minutes' walk away, across the bridge on the north side of the river, and it's here you'll find the **tourist office**, at Torget 2 (late June to Aug Mon–Fri 9am–7pm, Sat & Sun 10am–6pm; Sept to late June Mon–Fri 9am–3.30pm; ⓣ35 09 12 90, ⓦwww.visitrjukan.no). They carry local bus timetables, sell maps and will provide advice on hiking the Hardangervidda. They also have details of local **accommodation** with one of the better bets being *Rjukan Hytteby* (ⓣ35 09 01 22, ⓦwww.rjukan-hytteby.no; 2-person cabin 650kr per night, linen an extra 90kr per person), where ten modern cottages, built in the style of the original workers' houses of the 1910s, string along the south side of the river about 800m east of the centre. There's also an HI hostel, *Rjukan Vandrerhjem* (ⓣ35 09 20 40, ⓦwww.vandrerhjem.no; early June to Sept; dorm beds 200kr, doubles ❷), in a trio of modern cabins up in the hills about 12km to the south-east of town along a wiggly mountain byroad.

As for **food**, there's a very good café-restaurant at the Norsk Industriarbeider-museum, and *Rjukan Hytteby* has a competent café.

Travel details

Trains

Dombås to: Oslo (2–4 daily; 4hr); Åndalsnes (4–6 daily; 1hr 20min).
Geilo to: Oslo (3–5 daily; 3hr 30min).
Hamar to: Oslo (3–6 daily; 1hr 20min); Røros (2–6 daily; 3hr 20min).
Hjerkinn to: Oslo (2–4 daily; 4hr 30min).
Kongsberg to: Kristiansand (3–4 daily; 3hr 20min); Oslo (3–4 daily; 1hr 10min).
Lillehammer to: Dombås (2–4 daily; 2hr); Oslo (4–8 daily; 2hr); Trondheim (2–4 daily; 4hr 30min).
Oslo to: Bergen (3–5 daily; 7–8hr); Dombås (2–4 daily; 4hr); Geilo (3–5 daily; 3hr 30min); Hamar (3–6 daily; 1hr 20min); Hjerkinn (2–4 daily; 4hr 30min); Kongsberg (3–4 daily; 1hr 10min); Kongsvoll (2–4 daily; 4hr 30min); Kristiansand (3–4 daily; 4hr 30min); Lillehammer (4–8 daily; 2hr); Myrdal (3–5 daily; 5hr); Otta (2–4 daily; 3hr 30min); Røros (2–6 daily; 5–6hr); Trondheim via Dombås (2–4 daily; 6hr 50min); Trondheim via Røros (1–2 daily; 6hr); Åndalsnes (2–4 daily; 5hr 40min).
Otta to: Oslo (2–4 daily; 3hr 30min).
Røros to: Hamar (2–6 daily; 3hr 20min); Oslo (2–6 daily; 5–6hr); Trondheim (1–3 daily; 2hr 30min).
Åndalsnes to: Dombås (4–6 daily; 1hr 20min); Oslo (2–4 daily; 5hr 40min).

Principal Nor-Way Bussekspress (ⓦwww.nor-way.no) bus services

Kongsberg to: Bergen (1–3 daily; 9hr); Oslo (3–4 daily; 1hr 20min); Rjukan (3–4 daily; 1hr 45min).
Lillehammer to: Bergen (1–2 daily; 9hr); Dombås (2–4 daily; 3hr 15min); Lom (2–3 daily; 3hr); Oslo (every 3 hours; 3 hr); Otta (2–4 daily; 2hr 30min).
Oslo to: Bergen (2–4 daily; 9–11hr); Dombås (2–4 daily, 6hr 15min); Flåm on the E16 express (3 weekly; 6hr); Hjerkinn (1–2 daily; 6hr 30min); Hundorp (2–4 daily; 4hr); Kongsberg (3–4 daily; 1hr 20min); Kongsvoll (1–2 daily; 7hr 30min); Kvam (2–4 daily; 4hr 30min); Lillehammer (every 3 hours; 3hr); Lom (2–3 daily; 6hr); Otta (3–6 daily; 5hr); Rjukan (3–4 daily; 3hr); Røros (1–2 daily; 6hr 30min); Sogndal (2–3 daily; 7hr 15min); Sjoa (9 weekly; 4hr 45min); Trondheim via Dombås

(4 weekly; 10hr); Ålesund (2 daily; 10hr 15min); Åndalsnes (2 daily; 10hr).

Otta to: Gjendesheim – for Jotunheimen National Park (late June to mid-Aug 1–2 daily; 2hr); Lillehammer (2–4 daily; 2hr 30min); Lom (3 daily; 1hr); Oslo (3–6 daily; 5hr); Spranghaugen car park – for Rondane National Park (local service; mid-June to mid-Aug 2 daily; 50min); Stryn (3 daily; 3hr); Trondheim (2–4 daily; 4hr 45min); Åndalsnes (2 daily; 4hr 45min).

Rjukan to: Kongsberg (3–4 daily; 1hr 45min); Oslo (3–4 daily; 3hr).

Røros to: Oslo (1–2 daily; 6hr 30min); Trondheim (1–4 daily; 3hr).

4

Bergen and the western fjords

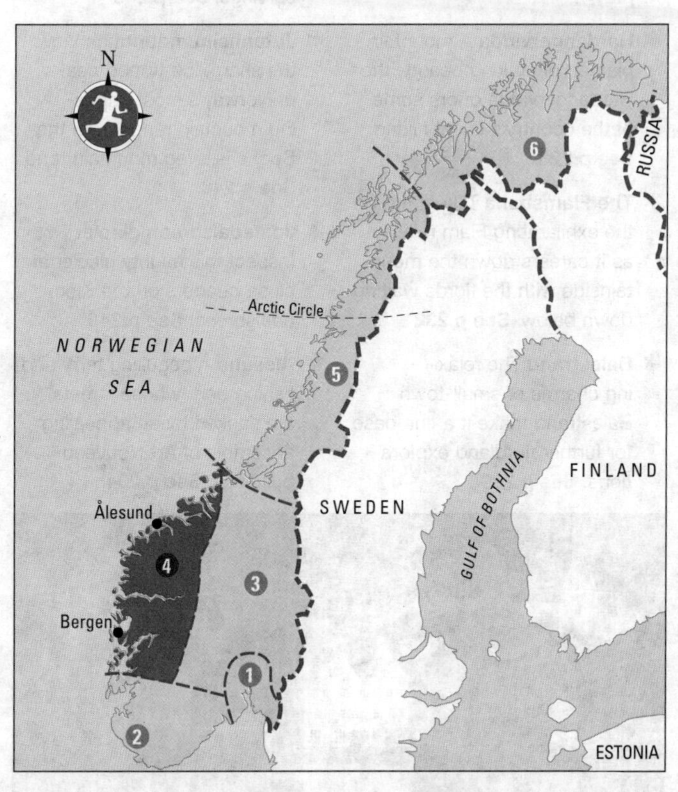

CHAPTER 4

Highlights

* **Bergen's Fløibanen** This must be Europe's quaintest funicular railway and there are wonderful views over the city at the top. **See p.209**

* **Troldhaugen** Visit the delightful fjordside home and studio of Edvard Grieg, Norway's most famous composer. **See p.214**

* **Hardangervidda** A mountain plateau of striking beauty, the Hardangervidda offers some of the country's finest hiking. **See p.228**

* **The Flåmsbana** Take a trip on the exhilarating Flåm railway as it careers down the mountainside with the fjords waiting down below. **See p.232**

* **Balestrand** The relaxing charms of small-town Balestrand make it a fine base for further fjordland explorations. **See p.239**

* **The Fjærlandsfjord** The once-remote Fjærlandsfjord offers wonderful scenery, country hikes and a couple of first-rate hotels. **See p.242**

* **Urnes stave church** The oldest stave church in Norway is renowned for its exquisite, almost frenzied Viking woodcarvings. **See p.245**

* **Jotunheim mountains** View the sharp, ice-tipped peaks of Norway's most imposing mountain range from the Sognefjellsveg mountain road. **See p.246**

* **Jostedalsbreen glacier** Inspect this mighty glacier at close quarters on the Kjenndalsbreen. **See p.249**

* **Ålesund** A beguiling ferry and fishing port, whose streets are flanked by an appealing ensemble of Art Nouveau buildings. **See p.264**

△ Bryggen, Bergen

Bergen and the western fjords

If there's one familiar and enticing image of Norway it's the **fjords**: giant clefts in the landscape running from the coast deep into the interior. Wild, rugged and serene, these huge, wedge-shaped inlets are visually stunning; indeed, the entire fjord region elicits inordinate amounts of purple prose from tourist office handouts, and for once it's rarely overstated. The fjords are undeniably beautiful, especially around early May, after the brief Norwegian spring has brought colour to the landscape, but winter, when all is unerringly quiet, has its charms too, the blue-black waters of the fjords contrasting with the blinding white of the snow that blankets the landscape. In summer, the mountains are filled with hikers and the waters patrolled by a steady flotilla of bright-white ferries, but don't let that put you off: the tourists are rarely in such numbers as to be intrusive, and even in the most popular regions, a brief walk off the beaten track will bring solitude in abundance.

The fjords run all the way up the coast to the Russian border, but are most easily – and impressively – seen on the west coast near **Bergen**, the self-proclaimed "Capital of the Fjords". Norway's second-largest city, Bergen is a welcoming place with an atmospheric old warehouse quarter, a relic of the days when it was the northernmost port of the Hanseatic trade alliance. It's also – as its tag suggests – a handy springboard for the nearby fjords, beginning with the gentle charms of the **Hardangerfjord** and the Flåmsdal valley, where the inspiring **Flamsbåna** mountain railway trundles down to the Aurlandsfjord, a small arm of the mighty **Sognefjord**. Lined with pretty village resorts, the Sognefjord is the longest and deepest of the country's fjords and is perhaps the most beguiling, rather more so than the **Nordfjord**, lying parallel to the north. Between the Sognefjord and Nordfjord lies the **Jostedalsbreen glacier**, mainland Europe's largest ice sheet, while north of the Nordfjord is the narrow, S-shaped **Geirangerfjord**, a rugged gash in the landscape that is both the most celebrated and the most visited of the fjords. Further north still, the scenery becomes even more extreme, reaching pinnacles of isolation in the splendid **Trollstigen** mountain highway, a stunning prelude to both the amenable town of **Åndalsnes** and the ferry port of **Ålesund**, with its attractive Art Nouveau buildings.

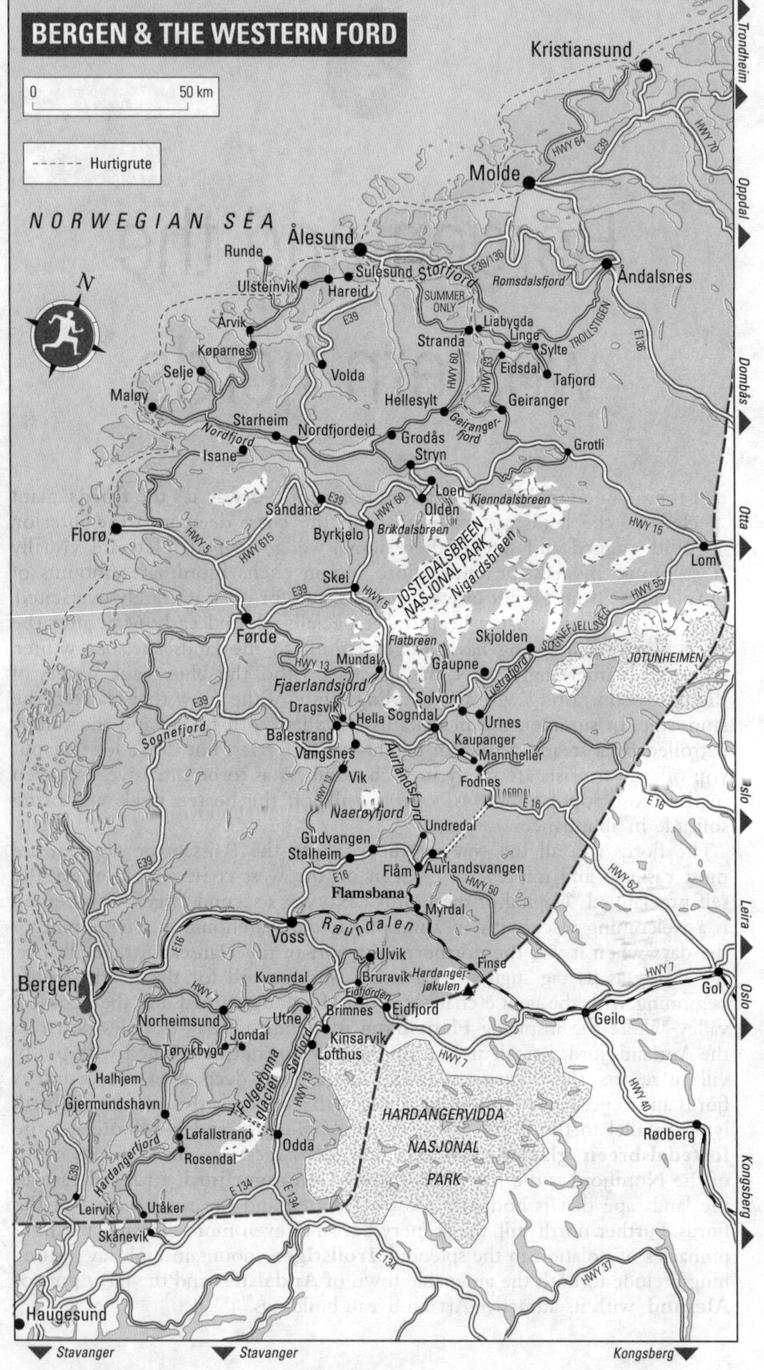
BERGEN & THE WESTERN FORD
0
50 km
Hurtigrute
NORWEGIAN SEA
N
Kristiansund
Molde
Ålesund
Runde
Sulesund
Storfjord
Ulsteinvik
Hareid
E39/136
Romsdalsfjord
Åndalsnes
SUMMER ONLY
Liabygda
Linge
Stranda
Sylte
TROLLSTIGEN
Årvik
Køparnes
Selje
Volda
Eidsdal
Tafjord
Maløy
HWY 60
HWY 63
Hellesylt
Geiranger
Starheim
Nordfjordeid
Nordfjord
Grodås
Geirangerfjord
Isane
Stryn
Grotli
Loen
Olden
Kjenndalsbreen
Sandane
Florø
Byrkjelo
Brikdalsbreen
HWY 5
HWY 615
HWY 60
HWY 15
JOSTEDALSBREEN NASJONAL PARK
Nigardsbreen
Lom
Skei
HWY 55
Førde
Flatbreen
Skjolden
SOGNEFJELLSVEG
JOTUNHEIMEN
HWY 13
Mundal
Gaupne
Fjaerlandsjord
Lustrafjord
Solvorn
Dragsvik
Hella
Sogndal
Urnes
Balestrand
Kaupanger
Sognefjord
Vangsnes
Aurlandsfjord
Mannheller
Vik
Fodnes
LAERDAL
E16
Naerøyfjord
Undredal
Gudvangen
Stalheim
Flåm
Aurlandsvangen
Flamsbana
HWY 50
HWY 62
Myrdal
Voss
Raundalen
Ulvik
Finse
Kvanndal
Bruravik
Hardangerjøkulen
HWY 7
Gol
Bergen
Eidfjorden
Brimnes
Eidfjord
Geilo
Norheimsund
Utne
Kinsarvik
Jondal
Tørvikbygd
Lofthus
Sørfjord
Folgefonna glacier
Halhjem
HARDANGERVIDDA NASJONAL PARK
HWY 40
Gjermundshavn
Løfallstrand
Odda
Rødberg
Hardangerfjord
Rosendal
E 134
Leirvik
Utåker
Skånevik
HWY 37
Haugesund
E39
Trondheim
Oppdal
Dombås
Otta
Oslo
Leira
Kongsberg
Stavanger
Stavanger
Kongsberg

Bergen

As it has been raining ever since she arrived in the city, a tourist stops a young boy and asks if it always rains here. "I don't know," he replies, "I'm only thirteen." The joke isn't brilliant, but it does contain a grain of truth. Of all the things to contend with in **BERGEN**, the weather is the most predictable: it rains on average 260 days a year, often relentlessly even in summer, and its surroundings are often shrouded in mist. Yet, despite its dampness, Bergen is one of Norway's most enjoyable cities. Its setting – amidst seven hills and sheltered to the north, south and west by a series of straggling islands – is spectacular. There's plenty to see in town too, from sturdy old stone buildings and terraces of tiny wooden houses to a veritable raft of **museums**, and just outside the city limits are Edvard Grieg's home, **Troldhaugen**, as well as the charming open-air **Gamle Bergen** (Old Bergen) museum.

More than anything else, though, it's the general flavour of the place that appeals. Although Bergen has become a major port and something of an industrial centre in recent years, it remains a laid-back, easy-going town with a nautical air. Fish and fishing may no longer be Bergen's economic lynchpins, but the bustling main harbour, **Vågen**, is still very much the focus of attention. If you stay more than a day or two – perhaps using Bergen as a base for viewing the nearer **fjords** – you'll soon discover that the city also has the region's best choice of **restaurants**, some impressive **art** galleries and a decent nightlife.

Arrival

Bergen's sturdy stone **train station** (local ⓣ55 96 69 00, national ⓣ815 00 888) is located on Strømgaten, just along the street from the entrance to the Bergen Storsenter shopping mall, within which is the **bus station**. From Strømgaten, it's a five- to ten-minute walk west to the most interesting part of the city, on and around Bergen's main harbour, **Vågen**, via the pedestrianized shopping street Marken. The **airport** is 20km south of the city at Flesland and it is connected to the centre by **Flybussen** (Mon–Fri & Sun 5am–9pm, Sat 5am–5pm, every 15–30min; 45min; 72kr one-way). These buses pull in at the bus station, the *SAS Hotel Norge*, on Ole Bulls plass, and the tourist office before proceeding to the harbourfront *SAS Royal Hotel*, on the Bryggen. **Taxis** from the rank outside the airport arrivals hall charge around 300kr for the same trip.

By boat

As well as being a hub for ferry and catamaran links with the western fjords, **Bergen** is a busy international port. Ferries from Iceland, Shetland and the Faroe Islands dock at the Skoltegrunnskaien, the quay just beyond the Bergenhus fortress, as do those from Newcastle, which call at Stavanger and Haugesund on their way here. Ferries from Denmark dock here too, with the exception of Color Line ferries from Hirsthals, which share the brand-new Hurtigruteterminalen with the Hurtigrute **coastal boat**. The Hurtigruteterminalen is on the south side of the city centre, off Nøstegaten, a five-minute walk from Engen along Jonsvollsgaten.

Hurtigbåt passenger express boats from Haugesund, Stavanger and the Hardangerfjord, as well as those from Sognefjord and Nordfjord, line up on the south side of the Vågen at the Strandkaiterminalen; local ferries from islands and fjords immediately north of Bergen mostly use this terminal too, though short excursions round the Byforden, adjoining Bergen harbour, leave from beside the Torget.

For local ferry and boat **ticket and timetable information**, see "Ferries: Domestic" under "Listings" (p.219).

By car

If you're driving into Bergen, note that a **toll** (15kr) is charged on all vehicles over 50cc entering the city centre from Monday to Friday between 6am and 10pm; pay at the tollbooths. There's no charge for driving out of the city. In an attempt to keep the city centre relatively free of traffic, there's a confusing and none-too-successful one-way system in operation, supplemented by rigorously enforced on-street parking restrictions. Outside peak periods, on-street **parking** is relatively easy and free, but during peak periods (Mon–Fri 8am–5pm, Sat 8am–10am), metered parking is available only for a maximum of two hours and costs 18kr an hour. Your best bet, therefore, is to make straight for one of the four central car parks: the largest is the 24hr Bygarasjen, a short walk from the centre, behind the Storsenter shopping mall and bus station, while the Rosenkrantz P-Hus, on Rosenkrantzgaten (Mon–Fri 7am–11pm, Sat 8am–6pm & Sun 10am–6pm), has shorter opening hours but is handier for the harbourfront. To get there, follow the international ferry signs until you pick up the car park signs. **Tariffs** vary, but reckon on 13kr per hour up to a maximum of 155kr for 24hrs.

Information

Bergen **tourist office** is pleasantly located in a large, mural-decorated hall across the road from Torget at Vågsallmenningen 1 (May & Sept daily 9am–8pm; June–Aug daily 8.30am–10pm; Oct–April Mon–Sat 9am–4pm; ⓣ55 55 20 00, ⓦwww.visitbergen.com). They supply free copies of the exhaustive *Bergen Guide*, sell the Bergen Card (see box p.204), change foreign currency, arrange car hire, and sell train, city-tour and fjord-tour tickets. They also have oodles of free information about the whole of the western fjords and operate an accommodation service, booking hotel rooms and rooms in private houses (see p.205). In high season, expect long queues. Available here too, and in many other places across the city centre, is (the Bergen version of) *Natt & Dag*, an excellent, free monthly **newssheet**, containing local news, entertainment listings and reviews. Naturally enough, it's in Norwegian, but the listings section is still easy(ish) to use.

City transport

Most of Bergen's key attractions are located in the city centre, which is compact enough to be readily explored **on foot**. For outlying sights and accommodation,

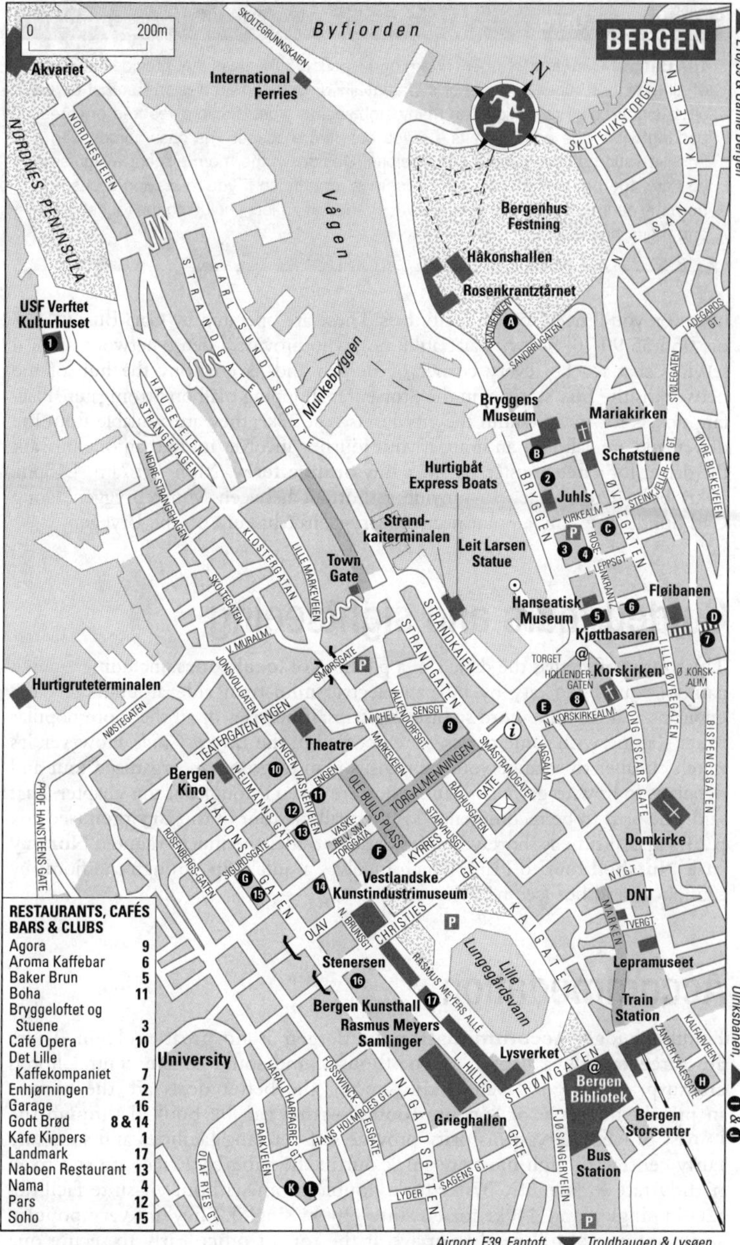

ACCOMMODATION

Bergen Vandrerhjem Montana	J	Hotel Park Pension	L	Skansen Pensjonat	D
Bergen Vandrerhjem YMCA	E	Intermission	I	Steens Hotel	K
Best Western Grand Hotel Terminus	H	Radisson SAS Hotel Norge	F	Thon Hotel Bergen Brygge	A
Crowded House	G	Radisson SAS Royal Hotel	B	Thon Hotel Rosenkrantz	C

The Bergen Card

The **Bergen Card** is a 24-hour (170kr) or 48-hour (250kr) pass that provides free use of all the city's buses and free or substantially discounted admission to most of the city's sights, plus reductions on many sightseeing trips. It also gives free on-street parking within the posted limits – if you can find a space. The pass comes with a booklet listing all the various concessions. Obviously, the more diligent a sightseer you are, the better value the card becomes, doubly so if you're staying a bus ride from the centre. The card is sold at a wide range of outlets, including the tourist office and major hotels.

however, you'll need to take a city **bus**. These are operated by Gaia Buss (Ⓣ177 or Ⓣ55 55 90 70, Ⓦwww.gaiatrafikk.no), who provide a dense network of local services that reaches every corner of Bergen and its environs; the hub of the network is the **bus station**, in the Storsenter shopping mall on Strømgaten. Flat-fare tickets for travel within the city limits cost 22kr; they are available from the driver, and are valid for an hour; if your journey involves more than one bus, ask the driver for a free transfer. Finally, a tiny **orange ferry** (Mon–Fri 7am–4.15pm; 15kr) bobs across Vågen to provide a shortcut between Munkebryggen, along Carl Sundts gate, and a point near the Bryggens Museum on the Bryggen.

Guided tours and sightseeing

The tourist office has the details of a plethora of **local tours**, including a quick gambol round the city by bus, an electric mini-train ride around the city's environs and multiple fjord sightseeing trips; itineraries of all the more popular tours – along with some prices – are detailed in the *Bergen Guide*. However, it's much cheaper to arrange your own visits than to go on an organized tour and details as to how to get where and when are given throughout this chapter. That said, one tour to be recommended is the walking tour of the **Bryggen** (see box p.207) and, if time is short, you might also consider the much-vaunted **Norway in a Nutshell** tour to Flåm, which involves a quick zip through the fjords by train, boat and bus (see p.221).

Accommodation

Finding budget **accommodation** in Bergen is no great problem. There are three hostels, a choice of guesthouses, and some of the central hotels are surprisingly good value. Also among the better deals are the **rooms** in private houses – or "private rooms" – that can be booked through the tourist office. The vast majority provide self-catering facilities and some are fairly central, though most are stuck out in the suburbs. Prices are at a fixed nightly rate – currently 370kr for a double room without en-suite facilities (260kr single), and 440kr for en suite (300kr single). They are very popular, so in summer you'll need to arrive at the tourist office early to secure one for the night. The tourist office makes a small supplementary charge (of 30kr, 50kr in advance) for making a booking, as it does for hotel and guesthouse reservations.

Hotels

Best Western Grand Hotel Terminus Zander Kaaes gate ⓣ55 21 25 00, ⓦwww.ght.no. There was a time when the tweed-jacketed visitors of prewar England headed straight for the *Grand* as soon as they arrived in Bergen – and not just because the hotel is next door to the train station. Those ritzy days are long gone, but the hotel has reinvented itself, making the most of its quasi-Baronial flourishes, notably its extensive wood panelling, chandeliers and stained glass. Breakfasts are superb and the bedrooms attractive and quiet, though some are rather pokey: if you can, have a look before you commit. ❼, sp/r ❹

Hotel Park Pension Harald Hårfagres gate 35 ⓣ55 54 44 00, ⓦwww.parkhotel.no. This excellent, family-run hotel occupies two handsome late nineteenth-century town houses on the edge of the town centre near the university. The charming interior is painted in soft pastel colours and the public areas are dotted with antiques. The bedrooms are smart, neat and appealing. It's a very popular place, so advance reservations are advised. ❺, sp/r ❹

Radisson SAS Hotel Norge Ole Bulls plass 4 ⓣ55 57 30 00, ⓦwww.bergen.radissonsas.com. Demure and reassuring top-flight hotel with a foyer of classic postwar design, whose rectangular lines are broken up by the most appealing of balconies. The rooms beyond are comfortable and engaging and there's a full range of facilities from bar to heated swimming pool. Ole Bulls plass is in the thick of things too. ❽, sp/r ❺

Radisson SAS Royal Hotel Bryggen ⓣ55 54 30 00, ⓦwww.bergen.radissonsas.com. Full marks here to the architects, who have built an extremely smart, first-rate hotel behind a brick facade that mirrors the style of the old timber buildings that surround it. All facilities – pool, health club and so forth, plus attractively appointed rooms. Popular with visiting business folk. ❽, sp/r ❺

Steens Hotel Parkveien 22 ⓣ55 30 88 88, ⓦwww.steenshotel.no. In a good-looking, late nineteenth-century villa, this well-established hotel boasts all sorts of period detail, from the bygones in the foyer through to the neo-Baronial touches – and stained-glass windows – in the dining room. The guest rooms are well-kept if a little spartan and the hotel overlooks the miniature lake and parklet that form the western tip of the green and leafy Nygardsparken. Ten minutes' walk from Vågen. ❺, sp/r ❹

Thon Hotel Bergen Brygge Bradbenken 3 ⓣ55 30 87 00, ⓦwww.thonhotels.no. Popular, budget chain hotel with plain but perfectly adequate rooms in a cumbersome modern block a stone's throw from the Bergenhus fort. The help-yourself breakfasts are very good. ❹

Thon Hotel Rosenkrantz Rosenkrantzgaten 7 ⓣ55 30 14 00, ⓦwww.thonhotels.no. Efficient, mid-range chain hotel in an old building just behind the Bryggen. Has everything you'll need, including free coffee and Internet access in the foyer, and the rooms are tidy and trim, though it's worth avoiding the ones that face the interior courtyard and insisting instead on a room that overlooks the Bryggen and, on the top floors, the harbour; there's no extra charge. Smashing buffet breakfast too. Shame about the aluminium window frames stuck in the old facade. ❻, sp/r ❹

Guesthouses

Crowded House Håkonsgaten 27 ⓣ55 90 72 00, ⓦwww.crowded-house.com. Traditionally, Bergen's guesthouses have been a tad dowdy, but this lively, appealing place is the opposite – from the pastel-painted foyer to the bright and airy, if spartan, bedrooms. There are around thirty rooms in total – singles, doubles and triples – both without bathrooms and en suite (50kr extra per person). Located halfway along Håkonsgaten, about five minutes' walk from the city centre. Singles 390kr, doubles ❷/❸

Skansen Pensjonat Vetrlidsallmenningen 29 ⓣ55 31 90 80, ⓦwww.skansen-pensjonat.no. This pleasant little guesthouse occupies a nineteenth-century stone house of elegant proportions just above – up the steps and hairpins from – the terminus of the Fløibanen funicular railway, near Torget: it's a great location, in one of the most beguiling parts of town. The pension has eleven guest rooms, four of which are en suite, and all are very homely. A real snip at ❸

Hostels

Bergen Vandrerhjem Montana Johan Blyttsveien 30, Landås ⓣ55 20 80 70, ⓦwww.montana.no. This large and comfortable HI hostel occupies lodge-like premises in the hills overlooking the city. Great views and great breakfasts, plus self-catering facilities, a laundry and Internet access. Dorm accommodation, family rooms and doubles, the pick of which are en suite in a newly added wing. The hostel is 6km east of the centre – 15min on bus #31 (stop Montana) from Nygaten. Popular with school parties, who are (usually) housed in a separate wing. Dorm beds 160–210kr, doubles ❸

Bergen Vandrerhjem YMCA Nedre Korskirkeallmenning 4 ⓣ55 60 60 55, ⓦwww.vandrerhjem.no. No-frills HI hostel in the city centre, a short walk from Torget. Has room for 170 guests, but fills up fast in summer. Facilities include a café, self-catering and a laundry. Breakfast 50kr. Dorm beds 125–170kr, doubles ❸

Intermission Kalfarveien 8 ⓣ55 30 04 00. Christian-run, private hostel in a two-storey, oldish wooden building, a five-minute walk from the train station – just beyond one of the old city gates. Open mid-June to mid-Aug. Breakfast 35kr, dorm beds 120kr.

The City

Founded in 1070 by King Olav Kyrre ("the Peaceful"), **Bergen** was the largest and most important town in medieval Norway and a regular residence of the country's kings and queens. In the fourteenth century Bergen also became an ecclesiastical centre, supporting no less than thirty churches and monasteries, and a member of the Hanseatic League, confirmation of its status as a prosperous port linked to other European cities by a vigorous trading life. The League was, however, controlled by German merchants and, after Hansa and local interests started to diverge, the Germans came to dominate the region's economy, reducing the locals to a state of dependency. Neither could the people of Bergen expect help from their kings and queens. Indeed it was the reverse: in return for easily collected taxes from the Hansa merchants, Norway's medieval monarchs compelled west-coast fishermen to sell their catch to the merchants – and at prices the merchants set themselves. As a result, the German trading station that flourished on the Bryggen, Bergen's main wharf, became wealthy and hated in equal measure, a self-regulating trading station with its own laws and an administration that was profoundly indifferent to local sentiment. In the 1550s, with Hansa power finally evaporating, a local lord – one **Kristoffer Valkendorf** – reasserted Norwegian control, but not out of the goodness of his heart. Valkendorf and his cronies simply took over the monopolies that had enriched their German predecessors, and continued to operate this iniquitous system, which so pauperized the region's fishermen, right up to the late nineteenth century. In fact, it's only after World War II that local fishermen started to receive their financial dues, a prerequisite of the economic boom that has, since the 1960s, transformed Bergen from a fish-dependent backwater to the lively city of today.

Very little of medieval Bergen has survived, although parts of the fortress, the **Bergenhus Festning** – which commands the entrance to the harbour – date from the thirteenth century. The rest of the city centre divides into several distinct parts, the most interesting being the harbourside **Bryggen**, which accommodates an attractive ensemble of stone and timber eighteenth- and nineteenth-century merchants' trading houses. The Bryggen ends at the head of the harbour, where Bergen's main square, the **Torget**, features an open-air fish market. East of here, stretching up towards the train station, is one of the older districts, a mainly nineteenth-century quarter that's at its prettiest along and around **Lille Øvregaten**. The main thoroughfare of this quarter, **Kong Oscars gate**, has been roughly treated by the developers, but it does lead to the city's most endearing museum, the **Lepramuseet** (Leprosy Museum). A stone's throw from here, the modern concrete blocks surrounding the central **lake**, Lille Lungegårdsvann, form the cultural focus of the city, holding Bergen's art galleries and main concert hall, while the chief commercial area is a few metres to the west along pedestrianized **Torgalmenningen**. The steep hill to the south of the central lake is topped by the **university**.

Most of the main sights and museums are concentrated in these areas, but no tour of the city is complete without a stroll out along the **Nordnes peninsula**, where fine timber houses pepper the bumpy terrain and the old USF sardine factory now contains a first-rate arts complex and café.

Torget

In 1890, Lilian Leland, author of *Traveling Alone: A Woman's Journey Around the World*, complained of Bergen that "Everything is fishy. You eat fish and drink fish and smell fish and breathe fish." Those days are long gone, but now that Bergen is every inch a go-ahead, modern city, tourists in search of all things piscine flock to **Torget**'s open-air **fish market** (June–Aug daily 7am–5pm, Sept–May Mon–Sat 7am–4pm). It's not a patch on the days when scores of fishing vessels crowded the quayside to empty their bulging holds, but the stalls still display mounds of prawns and crab-claws, dried cod, buckets of herring and a hundred other varieties of marine life on slabs, in tanks, under the knife, and in packets. Fruit, vegetables and flowers – as well as souvenirs – have a place in today's market too, and there's easily enough variety to assemble an excellent picnic lunch, so load up or eat up. At the end of the jetty behind Torget, also take a peek at the **statue** of Leif Andreas Larsen, one of Norway's most renowned World War II heroes; for more on the man, see p.292.

Bryggen

Spearing down the north side of Vågen, **Bryggen** is the obvious historical and cultural target after Torget. The site of the original settlement, the Bryggen's medieval provenance is recalled by a string of wooden and stone warehouses, whose distinctive gable ends face out to the waterfront. The whole area between the Bryggen and Øvregaten just behind was once known as Tyskebryggen, or "German Quay", after the **Hanseatic** merchants who operated their **trading station** here, but the name was unceremoniously dumped after World War II. Hansa influence dated back to the thirteenth century, and was derived from trading grain and beer for fish shipped here from northern Norway. Only later did the Germans come to dominate local affairs, much to the consternation of local landowners. By the middle of the sixteenth century, however, the Hanseatic League was in decline; the last German merchant hung on here till 1764, but by then economic power had long since passed to the Norwegian bourgeoisie.

The **medieval buildings** of the Bryggen were destroyed by fire in 1702, to be replaced by another set of wooden warehouses. In turn, many of these were later demolished to make way for brick and stone warehouses built in a style modelled on – and sympathetic to – that of the Hansa period. Nevertheless, a significant number of early eighteenth-century timber buildings has survived, though the first you'll come to, at the north end of Torget, has brick-and-stone neighbours. This is the **Hanseatisk Museum** (Hanseatic Museum; mid-May to mid-Sept daily 9am–5pm; mid-Sept to mid-May Tues–Sat 11am–2pm & Sun 11am–4pm; 45kr, includes Schøtstuene), a well-preserved, early eighteenth-century merchants' dwelling, kitted out in late Hansa style. Among the assorted bric-a-brac are the possessions of contemporary families, including several fine pieces of furniture and a medley of indeterminate portraits, as well as the

Guided tours of Bryggen

Informative and amusingly anecdotal English-language **guided tours** of the Bryggen start from the Bryggens Museum daily from June to August at 11am and 1pm, and take roughly an hour and a half. Tickets (80kr) are on sale at the museum, and after the tour you can reuse them to get back into the Bryggens and Hanseatic museums as well as the Schøtstuene – but only on the same day.

narrow bunk beds in which the merchants stayed away the cold. Of particular interest is the building's **painted woodwork** with broad, bold and colourful floral designs in many of the working areas and more formal, Italianate scenes in the merchants' quarters. Nonetheless, more than anything else it's the gloomy, warren-like layout of the place that impresses, not to mention the all-pervading smell of fish.

A few metres further on is the main block of old **timber buildings**, now housing souvenir shops, restaurants and bars. Despite the crowds of tourists, it's well worth nosing around here, wandering down the passageways wherever you can. Interestingly, these eighteenth-century buildings carefully follow the original building line: the governing body of the Hansa trading station stipulated the exact depth and width of each merchant's building, and the width of the passage separating them – a regularity that's actually best observed from Øvregaten (see opposite). The planning regulations didn't end there: trade had to be carried out in the front section of the building, with storage rooms at the back; above were the merchant's office, bedroom and dining room. Up above those, on the top floor, were the living quarters of the employees, grouped into rooms by rank – junior merchants, journeymen/clerks and foremen, wharf hands and, last (and least), errand boys. Every activity in this rigidly hierarchical, all-male society was tightly controlled – employees were forbidden to fraternize with the locals and stiff fines were imposed for hundreds of "offences" including swearing, waking up the master and singing at work.

The Bryggens Museum and Mariakirken

Just off the Bryggen, behind the *SAS Royal Hotel*, stands the lumpily modern **Bryggens Museum** (May–Aug daily 10am–5pm; Sept–April Mon–Fri 11am–3pm, Sat noon–3pm & Sun noon–4pm; 40kr), where a visit begins in the basement, which exhibits all manner of things dug up in the archeological excavations of the Bryggen in the 1950s. A wide range of items was unearthed, from domestic implements like combs and pots through to shoes, buckles and trade goods plus several runic sticks – perhaps surprisingly, Norwegians were laboriously carving runes onto their sticks well into medieval times. The museum displays these finds thematically both to illustrate the city's early history and provide the backcloth to a set of twelfth-century foundations at the back of the basement, left *in situ* where they were unearthed. The museum's two upper floors are given over to temporary exhibitions exploring other aspects of Bergen's past.

Behind the museum, the perky twin towers of the **Mariakirken** (St Mary's Church; late June to late Aug Mon–Fri 9.30–11.30am & 1–4pm; late Aug to late June Tues–Fri 11am–12.30pm; 20kr, free in winter) are the most distinctive feature of what is Bergen's oldest extant building, a Romanesque-Gothic church dating from the twelfth century. Still used as a place of worship, Mariakirken is now firmly Norwegian, but from 1408 to 1706 it was the church of the Hanseatic League merchants, who purchased it lock, stock and barrel. The merchants installed the church's ostentatious Baroque pulpit and its gaudy north German altarpiece, a fifteenth-century triptych, whose exquisite framing is really rather wasted on the sentimental carvings of saints and apostles it surrounds. The walls of the Mariakirken are hung with old commemorative paintings, an insipid lot for the most part with the exception of a finely detailed portrait of *Pastor Lammer, his wife and six children*, looking suitably serious in their Sunday best. The painting is by Lambert von Haven, a seventeenth-century Dutch artist, who went on to greater things at the royal court in Copenhagen; it hangs above the side door on the right-hand side of the nave.

Schøtstuene and Øvregaten

Directly opposite the Mariakirken, at Øvregaten 50, the **Schøtstuene** (mid-May to mid-Sept daily 10am–5pm; mid-Sept to mid-May Sun only, except Jan & Feb, 11am–2pm; 45kr, 25kr in winter, includes Hanseatisk Museum) comprises the old Hanseatic assembly rooms, where the merchants would meet to lay down the law or just relax – it was the only building in the whole trading post whose occupants were allowed to have heating. As you explore the comfortable rooms, it's hard not to conclude that the merchants cared not a jot for their employees shivering away nearby – though, to be fair, the wooden warehouses were a very real fire hazard.

Saving the mildly interesting Bergenhus fortress for later (see p.210), stroll east from the Schøtstuene along **Øvregaten**, an attractive cobbled street which has marked the boundary of the Bryggen for the last 800 years and was once, despite the fulminations of the Hansa merchants, the haunt of the city's prostitutes. From Øvregaten, it's still possible to discern the **layout** of the old trading station, a warren of narrow passages separating warped and crooked buildings surmounted by their hat-like, high-pitched roofs. On the upper levels, the eighteenth-century loading bays, staircases and higgledy-piggledy living quarters are still much in evidence, while the overhanging eaves of the passageways were designed to shelter trade goods.

The Fløibanen funicular railway

At the east end of Øvregaten, back near Torget, stands the lower terminus of the infinitely quaint, distinctly Ruritanian **Fløibanen funicular railway** (May–Aug Mon–Fri 7.30am–midnight, Sat 8am–midnight & Sun 9am–midnight; Sept–April same details, but only until 11pm; departures every 30min; return fare 70kr), which shuttles up to the top of **Mount Fløyen** – "The Vane" – at 320m above sea level. When the weather is fine, you get a bird's-eye view of Bergen and its surroundings from the upper terminus, and here also is a popular if rather staid café-restaurant. Afterwards, you can walk back down to the city in about 45 minutes, or push on into the woods along several well-marked, colour-coded footpaths; the shortest is the 1.6km-loop trail to Skomakerdiket lake and back.

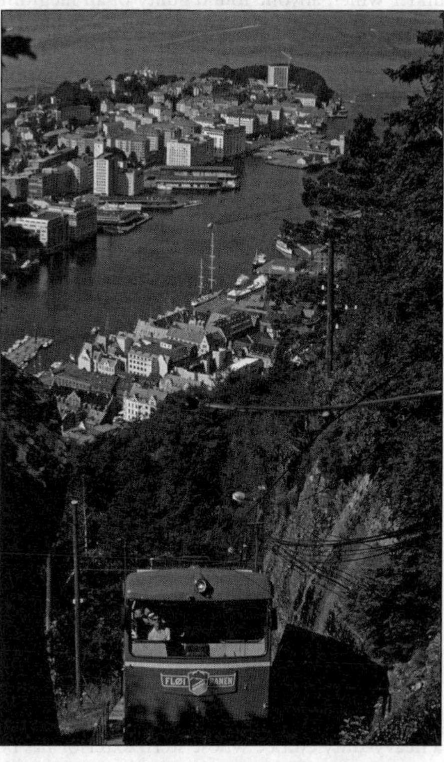

△ Bergen Fløibanen funicular railway

Back down at the funicular's lower teminus, you can either continue east along Lille Øvregaten (see p.209) or double back along Øvregaten to the Bergenhus.

Bergenhus Festning

Just to the west of the Bryggens Museum lies **Bergenhus Festning**, a large and roughly star-shaped fortification now used mostly as a park (Bergen Fortress; daily 6.30am–11pm; free). The fort's thick stone-and-earth walls date from the nineteenth century, but they enclose the remnants of earlier strongholds – or rather their copies: the Bergenhus was wrecked when a German ammunition ship exploded just below the walls in 1944. Of the two main medieval replicas, the more diverting is the forbidding **Rosenkrantztårnet** (Rosenkrantz Tower; mid-May to Aug daily 10am–4pm; Sept to mid-May Sun noon–3pm; 30kr), whose spiral staircases, medieval rooms – including Rosenkrantz's own chamber – and low rough corridors make an enjoyable gambol. It's also possible to walk out onto the rooftop battlements, from where there is a wide view over the harbour. The tower is named after a certain **Erik Rosenkrantz**, governor of Bergen from 1560 to 1568, who turned his draughty medieval quarters into a grand fortified residence, equipping his own room with fine large windows and a handsome Renaissance chimneypiece, both of which have survived in good condition. Rosenkrantz was known principally as the architect of a new law under which anyone found guilty of an illegitimate sexual affair had to confess to a priest before being fined. The law applied initially to men and women in equal measure, but by the 1590s women bore the brunt of any punishment. In Bergen, for example, women who could not pay the fine had to stand naked at the entrance to a church before being thrown out of town – the men just got exiled.

Metres from the tower is the entrance to a large cobbled courtyard, which is flanked by nineteenth-century officers' quarters and the **Håkonshallen** (mid-May to Aug daily 10am–4pm; Sept to mid-May daily except Thurs noon–3pm, Thurs 3–6pm; 30kr), a careful reconstruction of the Gothic ceremonial hall built for King Håkon Håkonsson in the middle of the thirteenth century. Surplus to requirements once Norway lost its independence, no-one knew quite what to do with the capacious hall for several centuries, but it was revamped in 1910 and rebuilt after the 1944 explosion and is now in use once again for public ceremonies.

Frequent **guided tours** of both the Rosenkrantztårnet and the Håkonshallen start in the Håkonshallen; there's no extra charge. From the fort, it's a few minutes' walk back down Bryggen to the Torget.

Lille Øvregaten to the Lepramuseet

Lille Øvregaten runs east from the Fløibanen terminal, lined by an appealing mix of expansive nineteenth-century villas and dinky timber houses, all bright-white clapboard and tiny windows. There are more old timber houses up above too, and these are, if anything, even quainter, pressing in against steep cobbled lanes that steer and veer around hunks of stone which were, at the time, simply too bothersome to move: to explore the area, take the first left up the hillside from Lille Øvregaten and follow your nose. Meanwhile, back down below, Lille Øvregaten curves round to the **Domkirke** (Cathedral; late June to late Aug Mon–Fri 11am–4pm; late Aug to late June Tues–Fri 11am–1pm; free), a heavy-duty edifice whose stern exterior has been restored and rebuilt several times since its original construction in the thirteenth century. Neither does the interior set the pulse racing, though there's a noticeable penchant for fancy wooden staircases – two leading to the organ and one to the pulpit – which can't help but seem a little flippant given the dourness of their surroundings.

More promising by far is the fascinating **Lepramuseet** (Leprosy Museum; late May to Aug daily 11am–3pm; 30kr), just up from the Domkirke at Kong Oscars gate 59. This endearingly antiquated collection is housed in the eighteenth-century buildings of **St Jørgens Hospital** (St George's Hospital), ranged around a charming cobbled courtyard, and tells the tale of the Norwegian fight against leprosy. The disease first appeared in Scandinavia in Viking times and became especially prevalent in the coastal districts of western Norway, with around three percent of the population classified as lepers in the early nineteenth century. The hospital specialized in the care of lepers, assuming a more proactive role from 1830, when a series of Norwegian medics tried to find a cure for the disease. The most successful of them was **Armauer Hansen**, who in 1873 was the first person to identify the leprosy bacillus. The last lepers left St Jørgens in 1946 and the hospital has been left untouched, the small rooms off the central gallery revealing the patients' cramped living quarters. Also on display are medical implements (including cupping glasses for drawing blood) and a few gruesome sketches and paintings of sufferers. Dating from 1702, the adjoining hospital **chapel** is delightful, its rickety, creaking timbers holding a lovely folksy pulpit and altarpiece decorated with cherubs and dainty scrollwork. The two altar paintings are crude but appropriate – *The Ten Lepers* and the *Canaanite's Daughter Healed*.

Lille Lungegårdsvann: Bergen's art galleries

Bergen's attractively landscaped central lake, **Lille Lungegårdsvann**, is a focus for summertime festivals and parades, and its southern side is flanked by the city's five main art galleries, three of which comprise the **Bergen Kunstmuseum** (Bergen Art Museum, ⓦwww.bergenartmuseum.no). These three galleries have the same opening hours and a common admission fee (50kr covers all), but the other two – one devoted to decorative art, the other to temporary exhibitions of contemporary art – are separate. Also on the southern side of the lake, behind the galleries on Lars Hilles gate, lurks the **Grieghallen** concert hall, an ugly concrete structure that serves as the main venue for the annual Bergen International Festival (see p.218).

Bergen Kunstmuseum – Lysverket

The easternmost of the five lakeside galleries, and the latest addition to the Bergen Kunstmuseum, is the **Lysverket**, Rasmus Meyers Allé 9 (mid-May to mid-Sept daily 11am–5pm; mid-Sept to mid-May Tues–Sun 11am–5pm), which occupies a distinctive Art Deco/Functionalist building, complete with its own mini-rotunda. The gallery exhibits Norwegian and international art from the seventeenth century onwards spread over three floors, one of which is usually given over to temporary exhibitions, while the other two feature a regularly rotated selection from the museum's permanent collection. It's here that the Bergen Kunstmuseum mostly chooses to display its modest selection of "Old Masters", mostly Dutch and Italian paintings, plus an engaging miscellany of medieval Greek and Russian icons. There is also a substantial selection of twentieth-century works, most notably from Picasso, Miró, Ernst, Léger and the Bauhaus painter Paul Klee. Look out also for a selection of watercolours and oils by the versatile Norwegian Jakob Weidemann (b. 1923), whose work was much influenced by French cubists during the 1940s, though he is now associated with the shimmering, pastel-painted abstracts he churned out in the 1960s. Many of these twentieth-century paintings were bequeathed to the city by **Rolf Stenersen** (1899–1978), who donated his first art collection to his hometown of Oslo in 1936 (see p.93) and was in a similar giving mood 35 years later, the beneficiary being his adopted town of Bergen. Something of a Renaissance man, Stenersen – one-time athlete, financier and chum of Munch – seems to have had a successful stab at almost everything – he even wrote some highly acclaimed short stories in the 1930s – and has a gallery named after him just along the street (see opposite). Stenersen's gift apart, the Lysverket's forte is its comprehensive collection of nineteenth-century **Norwegian paintings**. Leading the artistic charge are the stirring landscapes of Johan Christian Dahl (1788–1857) and Thomas Fearnley (1802–42), though the popularity of their grand style was short-lived, soon giving way to the romanticized peasants inhabiting the canvases of Adolph Tidemand (1814–76) and Hans Gude (1825–1903).

Bergen Kunstmuseum – Rasmus Meyers Samlinger

Just along from the Lysverket, the **Rasmus Meyers Samlinger** (Rasmus Meyer Collection; mid-May to mid-Sept daily 11am–5pm; mid-Sept to mid-May Tues–Sun 11am–5pm), in a large and distinctive building with a pagoda-like roof at Rasmus Meyers Allé 7, holds the most important part of the museum's permanent collection, a superb survey of Norwegian art from 1815 to 1915. The whole caboodle was gifted to the city by one of its old merchant families – the Meyers – and is now displayed broadly chronologically on two easily absorbed and well-organized floors. On the ground floor, the first rooms concentrate on Norwegian Romanticism, with Dahl, Fearnley and Tidemand much in evidence, followed by several period rooms, most memorably the Rococo excesses of the **Blumenthal room**, whose fancy stucco work and allegorical wall and ceiling paintings were knocked up in the 1750s for a Bergen merchant by an itinerant Danish artist by the name of Mathias Blumenthal. Up above, the first floor moves on to the Naturalist paintings of Gerhard Munthe (1849–1929), and Christian Krohg (1852–1925) and there's also a particularly good sample of the work of Erik Werenskiold (1855–1938), who is best known for his illustrations of the folk stories collected by Asbjørnsen and Moe in rural Norway. The stories had already been published several times when Werenskiold and his accomplice Theodor Kittelsen (1857–1914) got working on them, but it was they who effectively defined the appearance of the country's various folkloric figures – from trolls and up – in the popular imagination. Also of special interest are the paintings of Nikolai Astrup (1880–1929), generally regarded as the last of the Norwegian Romantics – or at least neo-Romantics: sometimes Astrup's paintings portray a benign rural idyll, at other times – as in *Kollen* – the Norwegian landscape appears dangerous and malevolent. It is, however, for its large sample of the work of **Edvard Munch** (1863–1944) that the museum is best known – if you missed out in Oslo (see p.96 & p.111), this is the place to make amends. There are examples from all Munch's major periods, with the disturbing – and disturbed – works of the 1890s inevitably stealing the spotlight, especially the searing and unsettling *Jealousy* and the fractured *Woman in Three Stages*.

Bergen Kunsthall and the Stenersen gallery

Just along the street from the Rasmus Meyer Collection is the **Bergen Kunsthall**, at Rasmus Meyers Allé 5 (Tues–Sun noon–5pm; 40kr; ⓦwww.kunsthall.no), which has developed into the city's most imaginative contemporary arts venue with up to three separate exhibitions at any one time. It's all very hit and miss – banal at worst, stunning at best – but no-one could say the exhibitions were predictable.

Next door, in a glum concrete block, the **Stenersen** (mid-May to mid-Sept daily 11am–5pm; mid-Sept to mid-May Tues–Sun 11am–5pm) specializes in temporary exhibitions of contemporary art, mostly international but with a strong Norwegian showing. The gallery occupies two smallish floors above the ground-floor shop and coffee bar.

Vestlandske Kunstindustrimuseum

Across the road from the Stenersen, the **Vestlandske Kunstindustrimuseum**, at the corner of Christies gate and Nordahl Bruns gate (West Norway Decorative Art Museum; mid-May to mid-Sept daily 11am–5pm; mid-Sept to mid-May Tues–Sun noon–4pm; 50kr), occupies the Permanenten building, a whopping neo-Gothic structure built as a cultural centre in the 1890s. A lively exhibition programme with the focus on contemporary craft and design brings in the crowds, and some of the displays are very good indeed – which is perhaps more than can be said for much of the permanent collection and its Chinese marble statues. Fans of Ole Bull (see p.216) will, however, be keen to gawp at one of the great man's violins, made in 1562 by the Italian Salò.

Torgalmenningen and the Nordnes peninsula

The broad sweep of pedestrianized **Torgalmenningen** is a suitably handsome setting for the commercial heart of modern Bergen, lined with shops and department stores and decorated at its Torget end by a vigorous large-scale sculpture celebrating figures from the city's history. At the far end is **Ole Bulls plass**, also pedestrianized and sporting a rock pool and fountain, above which stands a jaunty statue of local lad Ole Bull, the nineteenth-century virtuoso violinist and heart-throb – his island villa just outside Bergen is a popular day-trip (see p.216). Ole Bulls plass stretches up to the municipal **theatre**, Den Nationale Scene, at the top of the hill, worth the short walk for a look at the fearsome, saucer-eyed statue of Henrik Ibsen that stands guard in front. Near here too, just down Smørsgate at the back of the theatre on Strandgaten, is an old **town gate**, built in 1628 to control access to the city but soon used by the authorities to increase their revenues by the imposition of a toll.

Beyond the theatre, the hilly **Nordnes peninsula** juts out into the fjord, its western tip accommodating the large **Akvariet** (Aquarium; May–Aug daily 9am–5pm; Sept–April daily 10am–6pm; 100kr; bus #11) and a pleasant park. It takes about fifteen minutes to walk there from Ole Bulls plass – via Klostergaten/Haugeveien – but the effort is perhaps better spent in choosing a different, more southerly, route along the peninsula. This takes you past the charming timber villas of Skottegaten and Nedre Strangehagen before it cuts through the bluff leading to the old, waterside United Sardine Factories, imaginatively converted into an arts complex, the **USF Verftet Kulturhuset** (Ⓦwww.usf.no); this incorporates a groovy, harbourside café-bar, *Kafe Kippers* (see p.217).

Out from the centre

The lochs, fjords and rocky wooded hills surrounding central Bergen have channelled the city's **suburbs** into long ribbons, which trail off in every direction. These urban outskirts are not in themselves appealing, though they are extraordinarily handsome when viewed from either Mt Fløyen (see p.209) or the highest of the seven hills around town, the 642-metre **Mount Ulriken**. The **Ulriksbanen cable car** (June–Aug daily 9am–9pm; May & Sept daily 9am–5pm; Oct–April 10am–5pm or sunset; 70kr return; ⓦwww.ulriken.no) whisks up most of the mountain. Its lower terminal is behind the Haukeland Sykehus (hospital) and near the *Montana* youth hostel, about 6km east of the centre; there are walks and a café at the top too. To get to the cable car by public transport, take city bus #2 (Mon–Fri every 10–20min, Sat & Sun every 30min to 1hr) from Strandkaiterminalen.

Elsewhere, tucked away among the city's surroundings is a trio of first-rate attractions, each of which could happily occupy you for half a day. Two of them, **Troldhaugen**, Edvard Grieg's home, and **Lysøen**, Ole Bull's island villa, are south of the city, whereas the open-air **Gamle Bergen** (Old Bergen) is just to the north. A trip to the Troldhaugen is often combined with a quick visit to **Fantoft stave church**, which you can pass en route. There are organized excursions to Troldhaugen and Gamle Bergen – tickets and details from the tourist office – and all four attractions are accessible by **public transport** with varying degrees of ease, but the special bus which went direct from the city centre to Fantoft, Troldhaugen and Gamle Bergen no longer runs; there is a possibility it will be revived – check at the tourist office.

Fantoft stave church

Fantoft stave church (mid-May to mid-Sept daily 10.30am–2pm & 2.30–6pm; 30kr), just off and clearly signposted from the E39 about 5km south of downtown Bergen, was actually moved here from a tiny village on the Sognefjord in the 1880s. The first owner, a government official, had the structure revamped along the lines of the Borgund stave church (see p.189), complete with dragon finials, high-pitched roofs and an outside gallery. In fact, it's unlikely that the original version looked much like Borgund, though this is somewhat irrelevant considering that the Fantoft church got burnt to the ground in 1992. Extraordinarily, the owner didn't surrender, but had a replica of the destroyed church built instead and it stands today, a finely carved affair with disconcertingly fresh timbers, set amongst beech and pine trees just 600m from the main road.

The same buses that head to Troldhaugen (see below) pass the stop for Fantoft stave church – cross the road from the bus stop, turn right and walk up the hill behind the car park, a ten-minute stroll.

Troldhaugen

Back on the E39, it's a further 2km south to the signed turning for **Troldhaugen** (Hill of the Trolls; May–Sept daily 9am–6pm; Oct & Nov Mon–Fri 10am–2pm, Sat & Sun noon–4pm; mid-Jan to April Mon–Fri 10am–2pm, plus April Sat & Sun noon–4pm; 60kr; ⓦwww.troldhaugen.no), the lakeside home of **Edvard Grieg** (see box opposite) for the last 22 years of his life – though "home" is something of an exaggeration, as he spent several months every year touring the concert halls of Europe. Norway's only composer of world renown, Grieg has a good share of commemorative monuments in Bergen – a statue in the city park and the Grieghallen concert hall to name but two – but it's here that you get a sense of the man, an immensely likeable and much-loved figure of leftish opinions and disarming modesty: "I make no pretensions of being in

Edvard Grieg

The composer of some of the most popular works in the standard orchestral repertoire, **Edvard Grieg** (1843–1907) was born in Bergen, the son of a salt-fish merchant – which was, considering the region's historical dependence on the product, an appropriate background for a man whose romantic compositions have come to epitomize western Norway, or at least an idealized version of it. Certainly, Grieg was quite happy to accept the connection, and as late as 1903 he commented that "I am sure my music has the taste of codfish in it." In part this was sincere, but Grieg had an overt political agenda too. Norway had not been independent since 1380, and, after centuries of Danish and Swedish rule, its population lacked political and cultural self-confidence – a situation which the Norwegian nationalists of the day, including Ibsen and Grieg, were determined to change. Such was their success that they played a key preparatory role in the build-up to the dissolution of the union with Sweden, and the creation of an independent Norway in 1905.

Musically, it was Grieg's mother, a one-time professional pianist, who egged him on, and at the tender age of 15 he was packed off to the Leipzig Conservatoire to study music, much to the delight of his mentor, **Ole Bull** (see p.216). In 1863, Grieg was on the move again, transferring to Copenhagen for another three-year study stint and ultimately returning to Norway an accomplished performer and composer in 1866. The following year he married the Norwegian soprano Nina Hagerup, helped to found a musical academy in Oslo and produced the first of ten collections of folk-based *Lyric Pieces* for piano. In 1868, Grieg completed his best-known work, the *Piano Concerto in A minor*, and, in 1869, his *25 Norwegian Folk Songs and Dances*. Thereafter, the composer's output remained mainly songs and solo piano pieces with a strong folkloric influence, even incorporating snatches of traditional songs.

During the 1870s Grieg collaborated with a number of Norwegian writers, including **Bjørnstjerne Bjørnson** and **Henrik Ibsen**, one of the results being his much acclaimed *Peer Gynt Suites*, and, in 1884, he composed the *Holberg Suite*, written to commemorate the Dano-Norwegian philosopher and playwright, Ludvig Holberg. It is these orchestral suites, along with the piano concerto, for which he is best remembered today. In 1885, now well-heeled and well-known, Grieg and his family moved into **Troldhaugen** (see opposite), the house they had built for them near Bergen. By that time, Grieg had established a pattern of composing during the spring and summer, and undertaking extended performance tours around Europe with his wife during the autumn and winter. This gruelling schedule continued until – and contributed to – his death in Bergen in 1907.

the class with Bach, Mozart and Beethoven," he once wrote. "Their works are eternal, while I wrote for my day and generation."

A visit begins at the **museum**, where Grieg's life and times are exhaustively chronicled, and a short film provides yet further insights. From here, it's a brief walk to the **house** (guided tours only), a pleasant and unassuming villa built in 1885, and still pretty much as Grieg left it, with a jumble of photos, manuscripts and period furniture. Grieg didn't, in fact, compose much in the house, but preferred to walk round to a tiny **hut** he had built just along the shore. The hut has survived, but today it stands beside a modern concert hall, the **Troldsalen**, where there are **recitals** of Grieg's works from mid-June through to October. Recital tickets (160–220kr) can be bought from Bergen tourist office; free buses for these concerts leave from near the tourist office one hour before the concert begins. The bodies of Grieg and his wife – the singer Nina Hagerup – are inside a curious **tomb** blasted into a rock face overlooking the lake, and sealed with twin memorial stones; it's only a couple of minutes' walk off from the main footpath, but few people venture out to this beautiful, melancholic spot.

To get to Troldhaugen by public transport, take any **bus** from platform 20 at the city bus station (every 10–20min) and ask the driver to put you off; from the bus stop, it's a stiff and dull twenty-minute walk.

Ole Bull's villa on Lysøen

Around 25km south of Bergen, the leafy, hilly little island of **Lysøen** boasts the eccentrically ornate summer **villa** of the violinist **Ole Bull** (1810–80), which, like Grieg's home, has been turned into a museum packed with biographical bits and pieces. With its onion dome and frilly trelliswork, Bull's villa was supposed to break with what he felt to be the dour architectural traditions of Norway, but whether it works or not is difficult to say – for one thing, the arabesque columns and scrollwork of the capacious music hall-cum-main room look muddled rather than inventive. Bull may have chosen to build in a foreign style, but he was a prominent member of that group of nineteenth-century artists and writers, the **Norwegian Romanticists**, who were determined to revive the country's traditions – his special contribution being the promulgation of its folk music. He toured America and Europe for several decades, his popularity as a sort of Victorian Mantovani dented neither by his fervent utopian socialism, nor by some of his eccentric remarks: asked who taught him to play the violin, he once replied, "The mountains of Norway". Then again, people were inclined to overlook his faults because of his engaging manner and stunning good looks – smelling salts were kept on hand during his concerts to revive swooning women; they were much in use. The **guided tour** of the house (mid-May to Aug Mon–Sat noon–4pm, Sun 11am–5pm; Sept Sun noon–4pm; 30kr; Ⓦwww.lysoen.no) is a little too reverential for its own good and could do with a bit more pace, but the island's wooded footpaths, laid out by the man himself, make for some energetic walks afterwards. Maps of the island are given away free at the house, from where it's a stiff, steep but short walk over the hill to **Lysevågen**, a sheltered cove where you can go for a dip.

To reach the villa from Bergen, take the **Lysefjord-ruta bus** from the main bus station (Mon–Fri 4 daily; 110kr return), and after about fifty minutes you'll reach Buena Kai, from where a **passenger ferry** makes the ten-minute crossing to Lysøen (hourly, on the hour, when the villa is open; last ferry back from the island at 4.30pm, 5.30pm on Sun; 50kr return).

Gamle Bergen

Gamle Bergen (Old Bergen), located just off the E16/39 4km north of the city centre, is an open-air complex comprising forty wooden houses that are representative of eighteenth- and nineteenth-century Norwegian architecture. Entry to the site as well as the adjacent park, which stretches down to the water's edge, is free and there's open access, but the **buildings** can only be visited on a **guided tour** (mid-May to mid-Sept daily 9am–5pm; 50kr; tours every hour on the hour from 10am–4pm). Immaculately maintained, the interiors give a real idea of small-town life, and although the site, with its careful cobbled paths and trim gardens, is a little too cutesy, the anecdotal tour is bound to make you grin. The enduring impression is one of social claustrophobia: everyone knew everyone else's business – grim or scandalous, mundane or bizarre. It was this enforced uniformity that Ibsen loathed and William Heinesen explored in *The Black Cauldron* – see "Books", p.425.

Gamle Bergen is served by city **bus** #9 (Mon–Sat every 30min, Sun 3 daily) from Torget.

The Vikings

In a country that only became a separate kingdom in 1905, the Vikings remain a potent symbol of independence. It's all rather tongue-in-cheek – plastic Viking helmets are hardly the stuff of fervent nationalism – but it is a strong sentiment all the same, and accounts for the diligence with which the Norwegians preserve their Viking artifacts, most memorably the longships, the stave churches and the ancient burial mounds that are a magnet for visitors right across south and central Norway.

Aurlandsfjord

From raider to colonizer

Norway's **Vikings** sailed west in their longships, falling upon Scotland and Ireland with ferocious force in the ninth century. At first, the Vikings raided, robbed and then sailed away, but later they conquered and settled, creating a Norse world that at its peak stretched west to Greenland and south to Scotland, England and France. A terror to their enemies, the raiders seemed invincible, but with time they were to prove more of an historical interlude than a major turning point. Chameleon-like, the Viking settlers simply blended in with the local population in a process that only took a few generations – William the Conqueror (1027–1087), the epitome of the French baron, was the descendant of a Viking chieftain.

The sagas

Norwegian Vikings colonized Iceland in the ninth century, and it was on this remote island, between the twelfth and the fourteenth centuries, that the **sagas** were first transcribed. Written in prose, they were distilled from Norse oral tradition and mostly feature historical figures and events – albeit embroidered – revealing much about the Viking world of feuds and rivalries, superstition and magic. There are also sagas devoted to the semi-mythical heroes of the "ancient times"; the most important of these is the **Volsunga Saga**, relating the story of Sigurd the Dragonslayer. Poor old Sigurd had a terrible time: as if killing a dragon wasn't difficult enough, his foster father tried to swindle him and then the queen slipped him a magic potion, which induced Sigurd to leave the woman he loved, Brynhild, for the queen's daughter. It got worse: out of pique, Brynhild persuaded a kinsman to murder Sigurd, but immediately regretted it and threw herself on his funeral pyre. These days, of course, the Norwegians are far more amenable, but the vast majority know their sagas well and Sigurd is, for instance, still a common name. For more on sagas and folklore, see p.403.

Sigurd killing his foster father

Viking jewellery

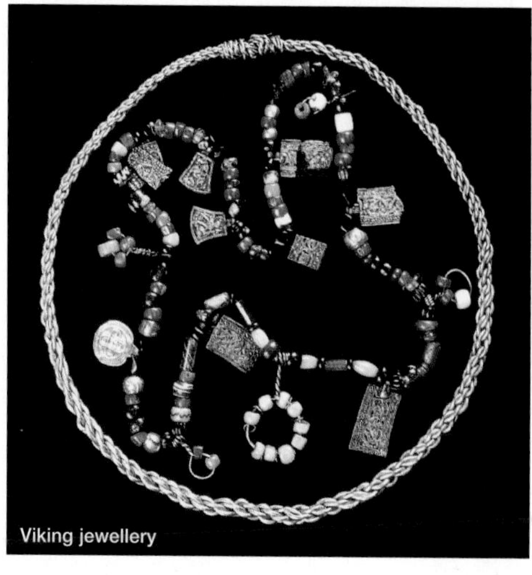
Viking jewellery

The Vikings were particularly keen on **jewellery**, both as a form of adornment and as a way of showing their wealth. The most prestigious pieces were made of gold, but throughout the Viking period this was in desperately short supply and to all intents and purposes it was replaced by silver as the prime metal of value. As for what they actually wore, the early Vikings were quite content to wear imported – or indeed looted – jewellery of pretty much any description, but by the tenth century it was the silver- and goldsmiths back home who produced the most valued pieces, decorated with a densely wrought filigree of abstract patterns. Viking gold- and silver-work is categorized into several different periods, beginning with the intricate Oseberg and Borre styles of the ninth century and culminating in the more sophisticated Jellinge and Urnes styles of the tenth. However, only the wealthier Vikings could afford gold and silver and the majority had to make do with bronze jewellery, which was mass-produced in clay moulds. The most common items were bracelets and brooches, armlets and buckles, neck rings and pendants; earrings were unknown and finger rings rare. The two finest collections of surviving Viking silverwork are both in Oslo, one at the Kulturhistorisk Museum (see p.93), the other at the Vikingskipshuset (see p.105), but there are also enjoyable displays at the Midgard Historical Centre (see p.134) and beside Borgund stave church (see p.189).

The Oseberg ship

Burying a Viking

The Vikings were not hot on theology, their paganism being a baffling hotchpotch of competing beliefs and rival gods, and neither did they have any particular rules and regulations about how to mark a **death**. Some Vikings were cremated, while others were buried in simple holes in the ground or beneath large earthen mounds. Some were buried with their treasure, others weren't; some were interred in their longships, others next to symbolic representations of their ship; and a few had their slaves killed and thrown in the tomb with them. In a few cases, the graves of Vikings who were buried in their longships have survived in good condition, preserved in mud or similar, and these have provided archeologists with a rich source of evidence. The most famous survivor is the **Oseberg ship** (see p.105), on display in Oslo and unearthed complete with a fantastic haul of treasure, including swords, daggers, fancily carved animal heads and ornate sleighs and wagons.

Borgund church

Stave churches

No less than 750 stave churches were built in Norway during the medieval period, though only 29 survive today. Though they don't date from the Viking period as such, they were all greatly influenced by Viking design and some of them, such as Urnes stave church, incorporate carved wooden panels salvaged from earlier Viking churches. Architecturally, their key feature is that the timbers are placed vertically in the ground with upright bracing posts – or staves – at each corner, but more interesting by far is the decoration: dragon finials reminiscent of longship prows protrude from their roofs, and the doorframes sport forceful and incredibly intricate carvings of men and beasts entwined in dense foliage. Among the surviving churches, the most enchanting are Borgund (see p.189) and Urnes (see p.245), though Hopperstad (see p.234), Lom (see p.247) and Heddal (see p.192) run them close. For more on the construction of stave churches, see p.188.

Eating, drinking and nightlife

Bergen has a good supply of **restaurants**, the pick of which focus on seafood – the city's main gastronomic asset. The pricier tourist haunts are concentrated on the Bryggen, but these should not be dismissed out of hand – several are first-rate. Other, marginally less expensive, restaurants dot the side streets behind the Bryggen and there's another cluster on and around Engen, but many locals tend to eat more economically and informally at the city's many **café-bars** and **coffee houses** and these are dotted all over the city centre. The busiest late-night **bars** are gathered in the vicinity of Ole Bulls plass, which is also the heart of Bergen's fairly limited club scene. As regards **opening hours**, the city's restaurants mostly open daily from noon to 10pm or 11pm, though some don't open their doors until 4pm and others close one day a week; it's a very informal scene, so reservations aren't required, though they are – of course – a good idea at the more popular places. Café-bars and coffee houses stay open much longer than restaurants, often till the early hours of the morning.

For **picnics**, the **fish market** on the Torget (June–Aug daily 7am–5pm, Sept–May Mon–Sat 7am–4pm) offers everything from dressed crab, prawn rolls and smoked-salmon sandwiches to pickled herring and canned caviar. There's also a covered market, the **Kjøttbasaren** (Mon–Fri 10am–5pm & Sat 9am–4pm), where over thirty stalls sell all manner of fresh produce and freshly baked breads. The covered market is in the long and narrow, fancily gabled building at the Torget end of the Bryggen.

Cafés, coffee houses and café-bars

Aroma Kaffebar Rosenkrantzgaten 1. Specialist coffee house with a good line in lattes and cappuccinos. Convivial atmosphere, spartan decor; also serves snacks. Mon–Thurs 11am–11.30pm, Fri & Sat 11am–12.30am & Sun 1pm–1am.

Baker Brun Kjøttbasaren. There are several *Baker Brun* café-bakery franchises in Bergen, but this is the best, serving a tasty range of sandwiches and filled rolls (on many different types of bread) inside the covered market – the Kjøttbasaren – at the Torget end of the Bryggen. Mon–Fri 10am–5pm & Sat 9am–4pm.

Café Opera Engen 24, near Ole Bulls plass. Inside a white wooden building with plant-filled windows, a fashionable crowd gathers to drink beer and good coffee. Tasty, filling snacks from as little as 60kr. DJ sounds – mostly house – at the weekend. Mon–Thurs 11am–12.30am, Fri & Sat 11am–3am & Sun noon–12.30am.

Godt Brød Nedre Korskirkealmenning 12. Eco-bakery and café (in that order), with great bread and good pastries, plus coffee and made-to-order sandwiches too. Mon–Fri 7am–6pm, Sat 7am–4.30pm & Sun 10am–5pm. Also at Vestre Torggate 2 (Mon–Fri 7am–6pm, Sat 8am–3pm & Sun 10am–5pm), though here the order is reversed – it's a café first and then a bakery.

Det Lille Kaffekompaniet Nedre Fjellsmug 2. Many locals swear by the coffee here, reckoning it to be the best in town. Great selection of teas too, and funky premises – just one medium-sized room in an old building, one flight of steps above the Fløibanen funicular terminal. Mon–Fri noon–11pm, Sat noon–6pm, Sun noon–11pm.

Kafe Kippers USF Verftet Kulturhuset, Georgernes Verft, on the Nordnes peninsula. Part of the city's leading contemporary arts complex (see p.213), this laid-back café-bar serves inexpensive, canteen-style food, with mains about 100kr, the daily special 60kr, and occasionally rustles up great barbecues. With its sea views and terrace, this is *the* place to come on a sunny evening. Puts on live music too, notably during its own jazz festival in late May. Mon–Fri 11am–12.30am, Sat & Sun noon–midnight.

Restaurants

Boha Vaskerelveien 6 ⓣ55 31 31 60. Smart and popular restaurant kitted out in attractive modern style and offering a small(ish) but very well-chosen menu. Main courses – for example chicken in pancetta with paprika – hover around 240kr. Mon–Thurs 4–10pm, Fri 4–11pm & Sat 5–11pm.

Bryggeloftet og Stuene Bryggen ⓣ55 31 06 30. A tourist favourite, this restaurant may be a tad old-fashioned – the decor is rather too traditional – but it does serve the widest range of seafood in town, delicious, plainly served meals featuring every North Atlantic fish you've ever heard of and then some. Main courses around 200kr, much less for the lunchtime specials. Mon–Sat 11am–11pm, Sun 1–11.30pm.

Enhjørningen Bryggen ⓣ55 30 69 50. Smart and fairly formal second-floor restaurant in wonderful premises – all low beams, creaking floors and old oil paintings on the walls. The prices match the decor, with most main courses approaching 300kr, but although they do a very good line in seafood, you can't help but feel you're paying over the odds. A tourist favourite. Daily 4–11pm, but closed Sun from Sept to May.

Naboen Restaurant Neumannsgate 20 ⓣ55 90 02 90. Easy-going restaurant and pub featuring a lively, inventive menu – and Swedish specialities. Offers a wide range of fish dishes, including unusual offerings such as sea bass with blood-orange sauce; the pollack is especially good. Reckon on 180–200kr for a main course. Open Sun–Thurs 4pm–1.30am, Fri & Sat 4pm–2.30am.

Nama Lodin Lepps gate 2b ⓣ55 32 20 10. Behind the Bryggen, this popular sushi and noodle restaurant is a modern affair, crisply decorated with pastel-painted walls and angular furniture. It may be popular, but it's not cheap – each piece of sushi will set you back around 30kr. Mon–Sat 3pm–midnight, Sun 2–10pm.

Pars Sigurdsgate 5 ⓣ55 56 37 22. First-rate Persian food in pleasantly kitsch surroundings. A good range of vegetarian dishes – eggplant casserole with rice, for instance, at 100kr; meat dishes in the region of 150kr. Open Tues–Thurs 4–11pm, Fri & Sat 4pm–midnight, Sun 3–10pm.

Soho Håkonsgaten 27 ⓣ55 90 19 60. Chic and ultra-modern restaurant with a creative menu. Has a great line in traditional Norwegian dishes – try the *klippfisk* (dried and salted fish), if it's on. Main courses average around 200kr. Open Mon–Sat 5–10.30pm. Attached to it is **Soho Sushi**, equally chic and with eight pieces of sushi costing 140kr (Mon–Fri 4pm till late, Sat & Sun 2.30pm till late).

Late-night bars and clubs

Agora Christian Michelsensgate 4 ⓣ55 96 08 40. Popular student hang-out with house and DJ music from Thursday through Saturday, 10pm till 3am. Regular live bands too.

Garage at the corner of Nygårdsgaten and Christies gate ⓣ55 32 19 80, ⓦwww.garage.no. Very busy place catering to a mixed crowd. Two bars on the ground floor, and a live music area in the basement – mostly rock and pop. Packed at the weekend.

Landmark Rasmus Meyers Allé 5. Club/pub with an arty atmosphere and a student scene; occasional live music and DJ sounds. In the same building as the Bergen Kunsthall gallery (see p.212). Open Tues–Thurs noon–1.30am, Fri & Sat noon–3.30am & Sun noon–6pm.

Festivals and the performing arts

Bergen takes justifiable pride in its **performing arts**, especially during the **Festspillene i Bergen** (Bergen International Festival; ⓣ55 21 06 30, ⓦwww.festspillene.no), held over twelve days from the end of May and presenting an extensive programme of music, ballet, folklore and drama. The principal venue for the festival is the **Grieghallen**, on Lars Hilles gate (ⓣ55 21 61 50, ⓦwww.grieghallen.no), where you can pick up programmes, tickets and information, as you can at the tourist office too. The city's contemporary arts centre, the **USF Verftet Kulturhuset**, down on the Nordnes peninsula (ⓣ55 31 55 70, ⓦwww.usf.no), contributes to the festival by hosting **Nattjazz** (ⓣ55 30 72 50, ⓦwww.nattjazz.no), a prestigious and long-established international jazz festival held over the same period.

The Bergen International Festival is also the main player in the wide-ranging programme of cultural events that is tabulated and promoted by the tourist office in their **Sommer Bergen** leaflet and website (ⓣ55 55 39 39, ⓦwww.sommerbergen.no). Part of this summer programme is devoted to **folk music** and **folk events** – singing, dancing and costumed goings-on of all kinds. Catch folk dancing at either the Schøtstuene (June to Aug, once weekly at 9pm; 100kr) or at **Fana Folklore**'s "country festivals" (ⓣ55 91 52 40), a mix of Norwegian music, food and dancing held on a private estate outside the city. These take place at 7pm a couple of times a week from June to August and cost 350kr per person, including meal and transport; tickets for both from the tourist office. There are also **chamber music and organ recitals** at the Mariakirken in June, July and August, and **Grieg recitals** at Grieg's home, Troldhaugen, from mid-June to October.

Outside the summer season, the **USF Verftet Kulturhuset** (see opposite) puts on an ambitious programme of concerts, art-house films and contemporary plays; the **Bergen Philharmonic** performs regularly in the Grieghallen from September to May (tickets on ⓣ81 03 31 33, ⓦwww.filharmonien.no); and Bergen's main **theatre**, Den Nationale Scene, on Engen (ⓣ55 54 97 00, ⓦwww.den-nationale-scene.no), offers a wide range of performances on three stages. Most productions are, of course, in Norwegian, but there are occasional appearances by English-speaking troupes. Finally, Bergen has one large city-centre **cinema**, Bergen Kino, Konsertpaleet, Neumanns gate 3 (premium line ⓣ82 05 00 05, ⓦwww.filmweb.no/bergenkino), a five-minute walk west of Ole Bulls plass. Predictably, American films rule the roost, so English speakers are at a linguistic advantage. **Entertainment listings** (in Norwegian) are provided in the local version of *Natt & Dag* (ⓦwww.nattogdag.no), a free monthly newssheet widely available across the city centre.

Listings

Airlines Norwegian (ⓣ815 21 815); SAS/Braathens (ⓣ815 20 400); Sterling (ⓣ815 58 810); Widerøe (ⓣ810 01 200).

Bookshop Norli (ⓦwww.norli.no), right in the city centre at Torgalmenningen 7, is easily the best bookshop in town, with a wide range of English titles as well as a comprehensive selection of Norwegian hiking and road maps. Very competitive prices also. Mon–Fri 9am–8pm, Sat 9am–4pm. There's also a smaller branch across the street at Torgalmenningen 4.

Bus enquiries Timetable information on ⓣ177; local timetables also on ⓣ555 590 70.

Car rental All the major international car rental companies have offices in town and/or at the airport, including Hertz, Nygårdsgaten 89 (ⓣ55 96 40 70) & at the airport (ⓣ55 22 60 75); Avis at Lars Hilles gate 20 (ⓣ55 55 39 55); and National, Nygårdsgaten (ⓣ55 59 97 08) & at the airport (ⓣ55 22 81 66). For the full list see under *Bilutleie* in the Yellow Pages.

Consulates Canada, Asbjørnsensgaten 20 (ⓣ55 29 71 30); Netherlands, Carl Sundts gate 29 (ⓣ55 54 42 80); UK, Øvre Ole Bulls Plass 1 (ⓣ55 36 78 10).

Emergencies Ambulance ⓣ113; Fire ⓣ110; Police ⓣ112.

Dentists Emergency dental care is available at Vestre Strømkai 19 (Mon–Fri 6–8.30pm, Sat & Sun 3.30–8.30pm; ⓣ55 56 87 17).

Exchange Bergen boasts a battery of banks willing to change foreign currency and travellers' cheques. The main post office (Mon–Fri 8am–8pm & Sat 9am–6pm), in the Xhibition shopping centre at the junction of Olav Kyrresgate and Småstrangaten, has got into the act too, but although their rates are competitive, they make a 75kr charge for each transaction. The tourist office also does foreign exchange but their rates are average, as are rates at the city's big hotels. There are ATMs dotted all over the city centre.

Ferries: Domestic: Hurtigbåt passenger express boats depart from the Strandkaiterminalen. The principal operators are HSD (south to Haugesund and Stavanger; north to Hardangerfjord; ⓣ55 23 87 80, ⓦwww.hsd.no) and Fjord1 (to Sognefjord and Nordfjord; ⓣ55 90 70 70, ⓦwww.fjord1.no). The **Hurtigrute** coastal boat sails north from Bergen daily either at 8pm (mid-April to mid-Sept) or 10.30pm (mid-Sept to mid-April); departures are from the Hurtigruteterminalen, on the south side of the city centre, about 1200m due south of the Vågen. Tickets for the Hurtigbåt services from the operators, Hurtigrute tickets from local travel agents or the operator (ⓣ55 31 59 10, ⓦwww.hurtigruten.com).

Ferries: International: Fjord Line, Skoltegrunnskaien (ⓣ815 33 500, ⓦwww.fjordline.com), operates a car ferry service from Bergen to Haugesund, Stavanger and Newcastle, and another to Haugesund, Egersund and Hantsholm in Denmark; Smyril Line, Skoltegrunnskaien (ⓣ 55 59 65 20, ⓦ www.smyril-line.com), has car-ferry sailings to Shetland, the Faroes and Iceland; and Color Line (ⓣ 810 00 811, ⓦ www.colorline.com) operates car ferries to Hirsthals in Denmark. All sailings are from Skoltegrunnskaien, except for the Color Line service to Hirsthals, which uses the Hurtigruteterminalen.

Gay scene Information on Bergen's low-key scene at the city's main gay café-bar, *Café Fincken*, Nygårdsgaten 2a (ⓣ 55 32 13 16, ⓦ www.fincken.no). Open Wed–Sun from 7pm till the wee hours, from 8pm on Saturdays.

Hiking The DNT-affiliated Bergen Turlag, Tverrgaten 4–6 (Mon–Fri 10am–4pm, Thurs till 6pm, Sat 10am–2pm; ⓣ 55 33 58 10, ⓦ www.bergen-turlag.no), will advise on hiking trails in the region, sells hiking maps and arranges guided walks.

Internet Many of Bergen's hotels and hostels now provide free Internet access for their guests and there's also free access at the main city library, Bergen bibliotek (Mon–Thurs 10am–8pm, Fri 10am–4.30pm & Sat 10am–4pm), on Strømgaten, immediately in front of the Bergen Storsenter shopping centre. Bergen has several Internet cafés as well, including the Cyber House, just back from the Torget at Hollendergaten 3 (Mon–Sat 9am–11pm & Sun noon–10pm; ⓣ 936 40 553).

Juhls' Silvergallery Bryggen 39 (ⓣ 55 32 47 40). Bergen outlet for these nationally famous, Sami-influenced jewellers, whose base is away in the north in Kautokeino (see p.358).

Laundry Coin-operated and service wash at *Jarlens Vaskoteque*, Lille Øvregate 17, near the funicular (ⓣ 55 32 55 04).

Pharmacy Apoteket Nordstjernen, in Bergen Storsenter, by the bus station (Mon–Sat 8am–11pm, Sun 10am–11pm; ⓣ 55 21 83 84).

Post office Bergen's main post office is in the Xhibition shopping centre at the junction of Olav Kyrresgate and Småstrangaten (Mon–Fri 8am–8pm & Sat 9am–6pm).

Taxi Bergen Taxi ⓣ 07000.

Trains National timetable information on ⓣ 81 50 08 88.

Vinmonopolet There is a branch of this state-owned liquor store in the Bergen Storsenter, Strømgarten (Mon–Thurs 10am–6pm, Fri 9am–6pm & Sat 9am–3pm).

The western fjords

From Bergen, it's a hop, skip and jump over the mountains to the **western fjords**. The most popular initial target is the **Hardangerfjord**, a delightful and comparatively gentle introduction to the wilder terrain that lies beyond, but similarly popular is **Voss**, inland perhaps, but still an outdoor sports centre of some renown. Voss is also a useful halfway house on the way to the **Sognefjord** by train, bus or car. By **train**, it's a short journey east to **Myrdal**, at the start of

Fjord ferries

Throughout the text there are numerous mentions of fjord **car ferries** and **Hurtigbåt passenger express boats.** The details given in parenthesis concern the frequency of operation, the duration of the crossing and the price. Hurtigbåt services are usually fairly infrequent – three a day at most – whereas many car ferries shuttle back and forth every hour or two from around 7am in the morning until 10pm at night every day of the week. **Hurtigbåt fares** are fixed individually with prices starting at around 100kr for every hour travelled: the four-hour trip from Bergen to Balestrand, for example, costs 400kr, 550kr to Flåm. Rail pass holders are often entitled to discounts of up to fifty percent and on some routes there are special excursion deals – always ask. **Car ferry fares**, on the other hand, are priced according to a nationally agreed sliding scale, with ten-minute crossings running at around 25kr per person and 60kr per car and driver, 28kr and 79kr respectively for a twenty-five minute trip.

a spectacularly dramatic train ride down the Flåmsdal valley to **Flåm**, sitting pretty against the severe shores of the **Aurlandsfjord**, one of the Sognefjord's many subsidiaries; by **road**, you can head north direct to Flåm along the E16 or stick to Highway 13 as it careers over the mountains bound for Vik and Vangsnes on the Sognefjord. It's this fjord, perhaps above all others, that captivates visitors, its stirring beauty amplified by its sheer size, stretching inland from the coast for some 200km. Beyond, and running parallel, lies the **Nordfjord**, smaller at 120km long and less intrinsically enticing, though its surroundings are more varied with hunks and chunks of the **Jostedalsbreen glacier** visible and visitable nearby. From here, it's another short journey to the splendid **Geirangerfjord** – narrow, sheer and rugged – as well as the forbidding **Norangsdal** valley, with the wild and beautiful **Hjørundfjord** beyond. Skip over a mountain range or two, via the dramatic **Trollstigen**, and you'll soon reach the town of **Åndalsnes**, which boasts an exquisite setting with rearing peaks behind and the tentacular Romsdalsfjord in front. At the western end of the Romsdalsfjord is the region's prettiest town, **Ålesund**, whose centre is liberally sprinkled with charming Art Nouveau buildings, courtesy of the Kaiser Wilhelm II.

This is not a landscape to be hurried – there's little point in dashing from fjord to fjord. Stay put for a while, go for at least one hike or cycle ride, and it's then that you'll really appreciate the western fjords in all their grandeur. The sheer size is breathtaking – but then the **geological movements** that shaped the fjords were on a grand scale. During the Ice Age, around three million years ago, the whole of Scandinavia was covered in ice, the weight of which pushed the existing river valleys deeper and deeper to depths well below that of the ocean floor – the Sognefjord, for example, descends to 1250m, ten times deeper than most of the Norwegian Sea. Later, as the ice retreated, it left huge coastal basins that filled with seawater to become the fjords, which the warm Gulf Stream keeps ice-free.

Where to stay in the fjords

Bergen advertises itself as the "Gateway to the Fjords" and the city's tourist office does indeed carry the details of a barrage of fjordland excursions – most famously the much-touted "Norway in a nutshell" tour (see below). These are, however, expensive options and you'll save money, and keep more control, if you organize your own itinerary. Also, as Bergen is in fact on the western edge of the fjords, the bulk of the day-trips from that city involve more travelling than is really comfortable. This is doubly true as the main road east from Bergen – the **E16** – is prone to congestion and possesses over twenty tunnels, many of which are horribly noxious. Avoid the E16 east of Bergen if you can, and certainly aim to branch off onto the relatively tunnel-free and much more

Norway in a Nutshell

Of all the myriad excursions organized by fjordland tour operators, the most trumpeted is the whistle-stop **Norway in a Nutshell**, which can be booked at any tourist office in the region or online at ⓦwww.norwaynutshell.com. The full trip takes seven hours, and is an exhausting but exhilarating romp that gives you a taste of the fjords in one day. The tour starts in Bergen with a train ride to Voss and Myrdal, where you change for the dramatic Flamsbåna branch line down to Flåm. Here, a two-hour cruise heads along the Aurlandsfjord and then the Nærøyfjord to Gudvangen, where you get a bus back to Voss, and the train again to Bergen. You can pick up the tour in Voss for an affordable 510kr: the full excursion from Bergen costs 790kr.

Public transport timetables

All the region's **public transport timetables** are available on the Internet. In the Hardangerfjord and the south, **HSD** (Ⓦwww.hsd.no) operates all the buses, car ferries and Hurtigbåt passenger boats, whilst **Fjord 1** (Ⓦwww.fjord1.no) provides the same services everywhere else. In addition, **Nor-way Bussekspress** (Ⓦwww.nor-way.no) handles long-distance bus routes, NSB (Ⓦwww.nsb.no) does the trains, and on the coast **Hurtigruten** (Ⓦwww.hurtigruten.com) does the Hurtigrute coastal boat. There's also a useful summary of all the region's public transport – as well as all sorts of travel tips – in the annual **Fjord Norway Travel Guide**, available for free at most tourist offices.

scenic **Highway 7** the first chance you get – about 30km east of the city. For all these reasons, the small towns that dot the fjords are far better as bases than Bergen, especially as distances once you're actually amidst the fjords are – at least by Norwegian standards – quite modest. As for specific targets, **Ulvik** and **Lofthus** are the most appealing bases in the Hardangerfjord, Sognefjord has **Mundal** and **Balestrand**, and further north the cream of the crop are **Loen**, **Åndalsnes** and **Ålesund**.

Getting around the fjords

The convoluted topography of the western fjords has produced a dense and complex public transport system that is designed to reach all the larger villages and towns at least once every weekday, whether by train, bus, car ferry, Hurtigrute coastal boat or Hurtigbåt passenger express boat. By **train**, you can reach Bergen and Flåm in the south and Åndalsnes in the north. For everything in between – the Nordfjord, Jostedalsbreen glacier and Sognefjord – you're confined to **buses** and **ferries**, although (mercifully) virtually all services connect up with each other so at least you shouldn't get stranded anywhere. General travel details for this chapter are given on p.271, and in the text itself we've detailed local connections where they are especially useful; this information should be used in conjunction with the **timetables** that are widely available across the region and on the Internet (see box above). Bear in mind also that although there may be a transport connection to the town or village you want to go to, many Norwegian settlements are scattered and you may be in for a long walk after you've arrived – a particularly dispiriting experience if it's raining.

We've covered the region **south to north** – from the Hardangerfjord to Sognefjord, Nordfjord, Geirangerfjord, Åndalsnes and Ålesund. There are certain obvious connections – from Bergen to Flåm, and from Geiranger over the Trollstigen to Åndalsnes, for example – but otherwise routes are really a matter of personal choice; the text lists the options. Note also that the **E39**, which cuts an ingenious route across the western edge of the fjord region, is potentially useful as a quick way of getting between Bergen and Ålesund, as is the Hurtigrute coastal boat.

The Hardangerfjord

To the east of Bergen, the most inviting target is the 100-kilometre **Hardangerfjord** (Ⓦwww.hardangerfjord.com), whose wide waters are overlooked by

△ Hardangerfjord

a rough, craggy shoreline and a scattering of tiny settlements. At its eastern end the Hardangerfjord divides into several lesser fjords, and it's here you'll find the district's most appealing villages, **Utne**, **Lofthus** and **Ulvik**, each of which has an attractive fjordside setting and at least one especially good place to stay. To the east of these tributary fjords rises the **Hardangervidda**, a mountain plateau of remarkable, lunar-like beauty and a favourite with Norwegian hikers. The plateau can be reached from almost any direction, but one popular starting point is **Kinsarvik**, though this approach does involve a stiff day-long climb up from the fjord.

Of the two principal **car ferries** negotiating the Hardangerfjord, one shuttles between Kvanndal, Utne and Kinsarvik, the other links Brimnes with Bruravik. There are no trains in the Hardangerfjord area, but **buses** are fairly frequent, allowing you to savour the scenery and get to the three recommended villages without too much difficulty, except possibly on Sundays when services are reduced. Both the buses and the ferries are operated by **HSD** (Ⓣ177, Ⓦwww.hsd.no). Finally, if you're planning to travel south along Highway 13 from Kinsarvik bound for either Oslo or Stavanger, be sure your itinerary does not involve an overnight stay in the eminently missable industrial town of **Odda**, at the head of the Storfjord.

East from Bergen to Norheimsund and the Kvanndal ferry

Heading east from Bergen en route to the Hardangerfjord by bus or car, the **E16** begins by travelling through a string of polluted tunnels, an unpleasant thirty-kilometre journey before you can fork off along **Highway 7**. By contrast, this is a rattlingly good trip, with the road twisting over the mountains and down the valleys, gliding past thundering waterfalls and around tight bends before racing down to **NORHEIMSUND** on the

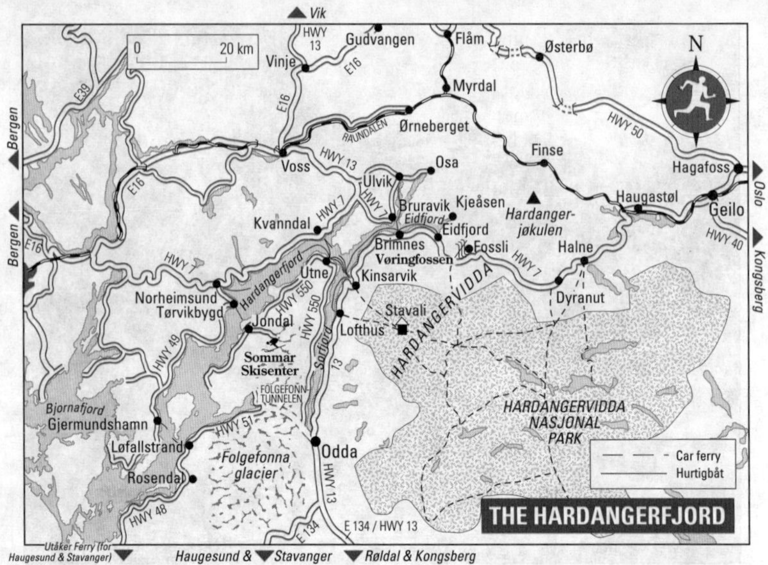

Hardangerfjord. A small-time port and furniture-making town, Norheimsund makes a gallant effort to bill itself as a gateway to the fjords, but in truth it's a modest, middling sort of place and there's precious little reason to hang around: like many fjord settlements, it's the journey to get there that is the main attraction. From June to August, Norheimsund does, however, have its uses as a minor transport hub, principally for its once daily **Hurtigbåt passenger express boat** service to Utne, Lofthus, Kinsarvik, Ulvik and Eidfjord, operated by HSD.

Leaving Norheimsund by road, Highway 7 sticks to the rugged shoreline as it travels east to the ferry dock at **Kvanndal**, another pleasant journey with every turning bringing fresh mountain and fjord views as the Hardangerfjord begins to split into its various subsidiaries. There's a choice of routes from Kvanndal: you can either press on down the northern shore of the Hardangerfjord towards Ulvik and Voss (see p.229 & p.230), or take the HSD **ferry** over from Kvanndal to Utne and/or Kinsarvik (1 or 2 hourly; 20min/40min; 25kr passenger, 65kr car & driver/33kr, 99kr). There are **buses** from Bergen to Norheimsund every couple of hours and most continue on to the Kvanndal ferry; the whole journey takes two hours and twenty minutes, ninety minutes to Norheimsund.

Utne

The tiny hamlet of **UTNE**, the Kvanndal ferry's midway point, occupies a splendid location, its huddle of houses overlooking the fjord from the tip of the rearing peninsula that divides the Hardangerfjord from the slender Sørfjord. Utne was long dependent on the orchards that still trail along the Sørfjord's sheltered slopes, its inhabitants making enough of a living to support themselves in some comfort, especially when supplemented by fishing and furniture-making: the brightly painted furniture that once hailed from the district made a popular export. Classic examples of this distinctive furniture are on display in the delightful *Utne* Hotel (Ⓣ53 66 64 00, Ⓦwww.utnehotel.no; ❸, en suite ❺), whose

27 rooms, mostly en suite, occupy an immaculately maintained old clapboard complex metres from the ferry dock. It's a lovely place – family-owned and very relaxing – and the food, traditional Norwegian cuisine at its best, is top-notch too, served amidst the ancient panelling of the dining room.

Utne's heritage is celebrated at the **Hardanger Folkemuseum** (May–June daily 10am–4pm; July–Aug daily 10am–5pm; Sept–April Mon–Fri 10am–3pm; 50kr; Ⓦwww.hardanger.museum.no), a five-minute walk along the fjord from the hotel. One of the largest and best-appointed folk museums in the region, its collection features a wide range of displays on various aspects of traditional Hardanger life, from fishing and farming through to fruit-growing and trade. A particular highlight is the large display of local **folk costume** – the women's headdresses hereabouts were amongst the most elaborate in Norway and a popular subject for the romantic painters of the nineteenth century, notably Adolph Tidemand and Hans Frederik Gude. There are also some fine examples of the Hardanger fiddle, an instrument much loved by both Ole Bull (see p.216) and Grieg (see p.215). Outside, an assortment of old wooden buildings – farmhouses, cottages, store houses and so forth – rambles over the hillside in an open-air section whose logic is hard to fathom, though in summertime, when there are demonstrations of farming and craft skills, things make much more sense. One of the more intriguing buildings is a thirteenth-century dwelling, known as an **Årestova**, whose dark and dingy interior has a central smokehole and roughly hewn log walls.

Southwest of Utne: Jondal and the Folgefonna glacier

Southwest of Utne, the peninsula separating the Hardangerfjord from the Sørfjord widens and heightens, its upper reaches dominated by the sprawling **Folgefonna** glacier. Conditions on the glacier are well-nigh perfect for **summer skiing**, both Alpine and Telemark, as well as snowboarding, and there's even a purpose-built sledge run. The place to head for is the Folgefonn Sommar Skisenter (late May to late Sept daily 9am–4pm; Ⓣ916 33 234, Ⓦwww.folgefonn.no), on the edge of the glacier at 1200m above sea level, where there is ski rental, a ski school, a café and a ski lift to the slopes. From here also, between mid-June and mid-August, Folgefonni Breførarlag (Ⓣ55 29 89 21, Ⓦwww.folgefonni-breforarlag.no) runs a programme of guided glacier hikes and climbs with the cheaper/shorter excursions beginning at about 350kr per person including equipment.

To get to the ski centre from Utne, head southwest along Highway 550 as far as Jondal, 36km away, and then turn east up the signposted, mountain toll-road for the bumpy nineteen-kilometre ride up to the glacier. From late June to July, it's also possible to do the trip by **HSD bus** (Ⓣ177, Ⓦwww.hsd.no), catching the first bus of the day from Utne to Jondal (1–3 daily; 1hr 20min), where you change for the once daily bus up to the glacier. The return bus leaves the glacier at 4pm, but there's not always a connecting bus back from Jondal to Utne – so check before you set out.

The hamlet of **JONDAL** is itself of some mild interest as the home of the Hardanger's largest **church**, a good-looking structure with a sturdy tower dating from the 1880s. It is also useful for both its **tourist office** (late June & early Aug daily 9.30am–4pm; July daily 9.30am–5.30pm; Ⓣ53 66 85 31) and its HSD **car ferry** connections over the Hardangerfjord to Tørvikbygd (hourly; 20min; passengers 25kr, driver & car 65kr), from where there are occasional connecting HSD **buses** (2–5 daily) onto Norheimsund (see p.223), just a few kilometres away along Highway 49.

South of Utne: the Baroniet Rosendal

South of Utne, Highway 550 runs along the shore of the Sørfjord bound for the unprepossessing industrial town of **ODDA**, a journey of 45km. Just before Odda, the highway passes the entrance to the 11km-long **Folgefonntunnelen** (60kr toll), which bores west beneath the Folgefonna glacier as it crosses the peninsula. When you emerge from the tunnel, it's 35km or so south along the Sildafjord to **ROSENDAL**, the location of one of Norway's few country houses – the Norwegian landowning aristocracy has always been too thin on the ground to build many of them. Dating from the seventeenth century, the house and estate, the **Baroniet Rosendal** (early May to late June & mid-Aug to mid-Sept Mon–Fri 11am–3pm, Sat & Sun 11am–5pm; late June to mid-Aug daily 10am–7pm, but Fri till 5pm; 100kr; Ⓦwww.baroniet.no), was in private hands until 1927, when the last owner bequeathed the whole lot to the University of Oslo, who are still in possession. By comparison with country houses in other European countries, the house is really quite modest, but it does hold a string of period rooms, amongst which the Baroque library and the Neoclassical "yellow room" are the most diverting, Afterwards, you can stroll out into the surrounding gardens and **park**, with its ponds, bridges and views out across the fjord. There's **B&B accommodation** (Ⓣ53 48 29 99, Ⓦwww.baroniet.no; ❸; late June to mid-Aug) here too, in one of the estate's old farmhouses, which has been pleasantly modernized to hold two dozen guest rooms; it's a popular spot, so reserve ahead.

From Rosendal, you can continue south by road and ferry to Haugesund and Stavanger or double back a handful of kilometres to **Løfallstrand** for the quick **HSD car ferry** (every 30min to 1hr; 25min; passenger 27kr, car & driver 74kr) ride over the Sidafjord to **Gjermundshamn** and Highway 49 for Norheimsund or Bergen.

Kinsarvik

From Utne, the HSD car ferry (every 1–2hr; 30min; 27kr passengers, 74kr driver & car; Ⓣ177, Ⓦwww.hsd.no) bobs over the mouth of the Sørfjord to **KINSARVIK**, a humdrum little town, which was once an important Viking marketplace. The Vikings stored their boats in the loft of the town's sturdy stone **church** (mid-May to Aug daily 10am–7pm; free), though the building was clumsily restored in the 1880s, leaving only hints of its previous appearance, most notably a series of faint chalk wall paintings dating from the thirteenth century. Kinsarvik also lies at the mouth of the forested **Husedalen valley**, with its four crashing waterfalls. The valley makes an enjoyable hike in itself, though it's mostly used as an access route up to the Hardangervidda plateau. From Kinsarvik, it takes seven hours to reach the nearest DNT hut, the self-service **Stavali** (at 1024m), but the route up to the plateau is very steep and in rainy conditions very slippery. Hiking maps can be purchased at Kinsarvik **tourist office** near the ferry jetty (late June to late Aug daily 9am–7pm; late Aug Mon–Fri 9am–5pm; Sept to late June Mon–Fri 9am–4pm; Ⓣ53 66 31 12). Although nearby Lofthus is far more enticing, Kinsarvik does have a couple of places **to stay**, with the obvious choice being the *Best Western Kinsarvik Fjord Hotel* (Ⓣ53 66 31 00, Ⓦwww.kinsarvikfjordhotel.no; ❻, sp/r ❺), in a large and reasonably attractive modern block down by the fjord not far from the ferry dock.

HSD **buses** link Kinsarvik with Lofthus, Eidfjord and Odda (2–5 daily).

Lofthus

LOFTHUS, draped beside the Sørfjord 11km to the south of Kinsarvik, with the Folgefonna glacier glinting in the distance, is an idyllic hamlet of narrow lanes and mellow stone walls, where a scattering of old grass-roofed houses sits among the orchards, pinky-white with blossom in the springtime. It's the overall impression that counts, though the **church** (May to Aug daily 10am–7pm; free), which dates from 1250, is a good-looking stone structure with immensely thick walls and several bright but crude wall paintings. A stream gushes through the village, tumbling down the steep escarpment behind Lofthus to bubble past the delightful *Ullensvang* Gjesteheim (☎53 66 12 36, ⓔullensvang.gjesteheim@c2i.net; ❸), a huddle of antique timber buildings with thirteen cosy and unassuming rooms – and great food. A second choice is the modern, plush but much less distinctive *Hotel Ullensvang* (☎53 67 00 00, ⓦwww.hotel-ullensvang.no; ❽, sp/r ❻), a massive, solitary affair plonked on the water's edge, 1km to the north of the village.

As at Kinsarvik, a steep **hiking trail** leads up from Lofthus to the Hardangervidda plateau; part of the trail includes the **Munketreppene**, stone steps laid by the monks who farmed this remote spot in medieval times. It takes about four hours to reach the plateau at Nosi (959m), and about seven or eight hours to reach the Stavali self-service DNT hut.

HSD operates a limited **bus** service between Kinsarvik and Lofthus (2–5 daily), part of a longer route from Geilo to Eidfjord and Odda.

Eidfjord and around

Heading north from Kinsarvik, **Highway 13** fidgets its way along the coastline to reach, after 19km, Brimnes, from where an HSD **car ferry** (1–2 hourly; passengers 21kr, car & driver 51kr; 10min; ☎177, ⓦwww.hsd.no) shuttles over the fjord to Bruravik, for Ulvik (see p.229) and Voss (see p.230). Beyond Brimnes, Highway 13 becomes **Highway 7**, whose first significant port of call, after another 11km, is the village of **EIDFJORD**, which struggles over a hilly neck of land between the fjord and a large and deep lake, the Eidfjordvatnet. There's been a settlement here since prehistoric times and for centuries the village prospered as a trading centre at the end of one of the main routes over the Hardangervidda – though this was very much a two-edged sword: traditionally, the villagers were obliged to build and repair foot and cart tracks up to the plateau, forced labour for which they were not paid. Nowadays, Eidfjord and its environs rustle up a trio of attractions, beginning with the **Hardangervidda Natursenter** (daily: April–May & Sept–Oct 10am–6pm; June–Aug 9am–8pm; 80kr), whose several displays focus on the plateau's natural history and geology. Secondly, a narrow byroad leads northeast from Eidfjord to reach, after about 6km, the tortuous lane that wriggles up to the **Kjeåsen mountain farm**, a lonely complex of old farm buildings, from where you'll be rewarded with spectacular views over the Simadalsfjord way down below. The road is much too narrow to take two-way traffic, but drivers can relax (a little): you can only drive up to the farm on the hour and descend on the half hour. Also within easy striking distance is the mighty, 145m-high **Vøringfossen waterfalls**, the foot of which is reached via a signposted footpath that begins beside Highway 7 about 18km east of Eidfjord; allow about ninety minutes for the hike there and back. Further views of the falls, but this time from the top, can be had from the nearby hamlet/hotel of **FOSSLI**, perched on a cliff-top, about 1km off Highway 7.

There are two recommendable **hotels** in Eidfjord, the grander of which is the fjordside *Quality Hotel & Resort Vøringfoss* (ⓣ53 67 41 00, ⓦwww.choicehotels.no; ④), a large, modern complex built in a (relatively) pleasing version of traditional style with mini-towers and decorative gable ends. The second is the *Eidfjord Hotell* (ⓣ53 66 52 64, ⓦwww.eidfjordhotel.no; ④), a crisply designed, medium-sized modern place with tastefully furnished rooms that perches on a knoll high above the fjord. The *Vøringfoss* has the better restaurant. If these hotels don't suit, the village **tourist office** (May & Sept Mon–Sat 9am–4pm; June–Aug Mon–Sat 9am–8pm & Sun noon–8pm; Oct–April Mon–Fri 10am–2pm; ⓣ53 67 34 00; ⓦwww.eidfjordinfo.com) has the details of a handful of private rooms.

HSD's Odda to Geilo **bus** service passes through Lofthus, Kinsarvik and Eidfjord (2–5 daily).

The Hardangervidda plateau

The **Hardangervidda** is Europe's largest mountain plateau, occupying a one-hundred-kilometre-square slab of land east of the Hardangerfjord and south of the Oslo–Bergen railway. The plateau is characterized by rolling fells and wide stretches of level ground, its rocky surfaces strewn with pools, ponds and rivers. The whole plateau is above the tree line, and at times has an almost lunar-like appearance, although even within this elemental landscape there are variations. To the north, in the vicinity of Finse, there are mountains and a glacier, the **Hardangerjøkulen**, while the west is wetter – and the flora somewhat richer – than the barer moorland to the east. The lichen that covers the rocks is savoured by herds of reindeer, who leave their winter grazing lands on the east side of the plateau in the spring, chewing their way west to their breeding grounds before returning east again after the autumn rutting season.

Stone Age hunters once followed the reindeer on their migrations, and traces of their presence – arrowheads, pit-traps, etc – have been discovered over much of the plateau. Later, the Hardangervidda became one of the main crossing points between east and west Norway, with horse traders, cattle drivers and Danish dignitaries all cutting across the plateau along cairned paths, many of which are still in use as part of a dense network of trails and tourist huts that has been developed by several DNT affiliates. Roughly one third of the plateau has been incorporated within the **Hardangervidda Nasjonalpark**, but much of the rest is protected too, so hikers won't notice a great deal of difference between the park and its immediate surroundings. The entire plateau is also popular for winter cross-country, hut-to-hut skiing. Many hikers and skiers are content with a day on the Hardangervidda, but some find the wide-skied, lichen-dappled scenery particularly enchanting and travel from one end of the plateau to the other, a seven- or eight-day expedition.

Access to the plateau can be gained from the **Oslo–Bergen train line** which calls at Finse (see p.283), from where hikers and skiers head off across the plateau in all directions. Finse is not, however, reachable by road, so motorists (and bus travellers) mostly use **Highway 7**, which runs across the plateau between Eidfjord (see p.227) and Geilo (see p.189). There's precious little in the way of human habitation on this lonely 100km-long stretch of road, but you can pick up the plateau's hiking trails easily enough at several points. **Dyranut** and **Halne** are two such places, respectively 39km and 47km from Eidfjord. Some hikers prefer to walk eastwards onto the Hardangervidda from Kinsarvik and Lofthus (see p.227), an arduous day-long trek up from the fjord, or from

Rjukan (see p.194), to the southeast of the plateau, where a cable car eases the uphill part of the trek.

Ulvik

Tucked away in a snug corner of the Hardangerfjord, the pocket-sized village of **ULVIK** strings prettily along the shoreline with orchards dusting the green hills behind. There's nothing specific to see – the town's main claim to fame as the place where potatoes were first grown in Norway (in 1765) just about sums things up – but it's an excellent place to unwind, a popular resort with a cluster of good hotels. **Hiking trails** lattice the rough uplands to the north of Ulvik and explore the surrounding coastline. Indeed, the local council have gone to some trouble here in their "**Kulturlandskapsplan**" (cultural landscape plan), in which four designated areas incorporate both footpaths and historic sights. The tourist office (see below) produces a detailed guide to these four areas, complete with maps, entitled the "Heritage Trails of Ulvik" (40kr), but perhaps the most enjoyable walk is the easy half-day hike up to the **Ljonakleiv crofter's farm**, an old farmstead in the hills above the village. A second option is to walk or drive along the nine-kilometre country road that leads east from Ulvik, across the adjacent promontory and up along the Osafjord to the smattering of farmsteads that constitutes **OSA**. Here, in the forested hills about 1km above the fjord, is one of the region's more unusual sights, the timber-and-brick **Stream Nest sculpture** (mid-May to mid-Aug daily 10am–4pm; 30kr), resembling a gigantic bird's nest and perched above a green river valley framed by stern hills. The sculpture was constructed by Takamasa Kuniyasu for the 1994 Lillehammer Winter Olympics, and moved here afterwards. As you near the site of the sculpture, the road passes the **Hjadlane Gallery for Samtidskunst** (Gallery of Contemporary Art; May–Sept daily 11am–6pm; free), which has a programme of temporary exhibitions.

Practicalities

Ulvik is off the main bus routes, but there is an **HSD bus** service here from Voss (3–7 daily; 1hr) and this is routed via Bruravik to pick up passengers who've arrived on the Brimnes–Bruravik ferry (see p.223). From June to August, there are also **HSD Hurtigbåt passenger express boat** services to Ulvik from Norheimsund via Utne, Lofthus and Kinsarvik (1 daily; 2hr 15min). Buses pull into the centre of the village, metres from the jetty, from where it's a couple of minutes' walk along the waterfront to the **tourist office** (mid-May to mid-Sept Mon–Sat 8.30am–5pm & Sun 1–5pm; late Sept to mid-May Mon–Fri 8.30am–1.30pm; ⓣ56 52 63 60, ⓦwww.visitulvik.com). Staff here issue all the usual information, including bus and ferry timetables, sell detailed hiking maps and rent out bikes.

Among the **hotels**, the big deal hereabouts is the *Rica Brakenes* (ⓣ56 52 61 05, ⓦwww.brakenes-hotel.no; ❻, sp/r ❹), a large and luxurious modern place occupying a lovely fjordside location in the centre of the village. If the *Brakenes* is a bit too big for your liking, the *Rica Ulvik* (ⓣ56 52 62 00, ⓦwww.rica.no; ❹/❺), five minutes' walk east along the waterfront, is a good deal less overpowering. Again, it's the setting rather than the architecture that appeals, with the fjord stretching out in front of the hotel, overlooked by the balconies of the fifty-odd modern bedrooms. Different again is the *Ulvik Fjord Pensjonat* (ⓣ56 52 61 70, ⓦwww.ulvikfjordpensjonat.no; ❹), a well-maintained and very appealing **guesthouse** situated a ten-minute walk west from the centre along the waterfront. The rooms in the main building have recently been redecorated and are very comfortable, and there's a modern annexe too. Breakfasts are first-rate and meals are also available during the day and in the evening. Otherwise, **eat** at either of the *Rica* hotels – the *Ulvik* edges it in terms of price and informality.

To Voss

Travelling east from Bergen on either the E16 or the train, you first have to clear some markedly polluted tunnels, but thereafter it's an enjoyable jaunt over the hills and round the mountains to **VOSS**, which, at 100km from Bergen, boasts an attractive lakeside setting and a splendid thirteenth-century church. Voss is, however, best known as an adventure sports and winter skiing centre, with everything from skiing and snowboarding through to summertime rafting, kayaking and horse riding. Consequently, unless you're here for a sweat, your best bet is to have a quick look round and then move on, though there is a caveat: Voss is the ideal base for a **day-trip by train** east up the Raundal valley, an especially scenic part of the Bergen–Oslo rail line. The most popular target on this stretch of the line is the Myrdal junction, where you change for the dramatic train ride down to Flåm (see box on p.232).

The Town

With the lake on one side and the River Vosso on the other, **Voss** has long been a trading centre of some importance, though you'd barely guess this from the modern appearance of the town centre. In 1023, King Olav visited to check that the population had all converted to Christianity, and stuck a big stone cross here to make his point. Two centuries later another king, Magnus Lagabøte, built a church in Voss to act as the religious focal point for the whole region.

Voss sports

Every summer, hundreds of Norwegians make a beeline for Voss on account of its **watersports**. The rivers near the town offer a wide range of conditions, suitable for everything from a quiet paddle to a finger-chewing whitewater ride. There are several operators, but **Voss Rafting Senter** (☎56 51 05 25, Ⓦwww.vossrafting.no) sets the benchmark. Their four-hour whitewater rafting trips venture out onto three rivers – the relatively placid Vosso and the much rougher Stranda and Raun; the price, including a swimming test and a snack, is 700kr, 750kr on Saturdays. Other options with the same operator and at about the same price include river-boarding (5hr), sports rafting, which is akin to canoeing (4hr), and whitewater rappelling (4hr). In addition, Nordic Ventures (☎56 51 00 17, Ⓦwww.nordicventures.com) offers all sorts of **kayaking** excursions as well as **tandem paragliding**; and Stølsheimen Fjellridning (☎56 51 91 66, Ⓦwww.fjellhest.com) specializes in mountain **horseback riding**.

In the **winter** time, **skiing** in Voss starts in late November and continues until mid-April – nothing fancy, but good for an enjoyable few days. From behind and above the train station, a **cable car** – the Hangursbanen – climbs 700m to give access to several short runs as well as the first of three chair lifts that take you up another 300m. A one-day lift pass costs 265kr (200kr per half-day), and in January and February some trails are floodlit. There's a choice of red, green and blue downhill ski routes, and amongst the latter is a long and fairly gentle route through the hills above town. Full **equipment** for both downhill and cross-country skiing can be rented by the day from Voss Ski, at the upper Hangursbanen station (☎56 51 00 32). They also offer lessons in skiing and snowboarding techniques.

The church, the **Vangskyrkja** (June–Aug daily 10am–4pm; 20kr), still stands, its eccentric octagonal spire rising above stone walls which are up to 2m thick. The interior is splendid, a surprisingly flamboyant and colourful affair with a Baroque reredos and a folksy rood screen showing a crucified Jesus attended by two cherubs. The ceiling is even more unusual, its timbers painted in 1696 with a cotton-wool cloudy sky inhabited by flying angels – and the nearer you approach the high altar, the more of them there are. That's pretty much it as far as specific sights go, though you could take a stroll along the leafy Prestegardsalléen footpath, which heads south along the shore of lake **Vangsvatnet** from opposite the church; or wander the central shops and cafés – if you've come from the hamlets and villages further north, the shopping might seem something of a treat.

Practicalities

Buses stop outside the **train station** at the western end of the town centre. From here, it's a five-minute walk to the **tourist office** (June–Aug Mon–Fri 8am–7pm, Sat 9am–7pm & Sun 2–7pm; Sept–May Mon–Fri 9am–3.30pm; Ⓣ56 52 08 00, Ⓦwww.visitvoss.no) on the main street, Uttrågata – veer right round the Vangskyrkja church and it's on the right. They have oodles of information on hiking, rafting, skiing and local touring, the bones of which are detailed in the free *Voss Guide*; they also operate an accommodation booking service.

To cater for all the visiting sportsfolk, Voss has lots of inexpensive **accommodation**, from guesthouses through to camping. The best budget bet is the excellent HI **hostel**, *Voss Vandrerhjem* (Ⓣ56 51 20 17, Ⓦwww.vandrerhjem.no; Jan–Oct), which has both double rooms (❷) and dorm beds (215kr), and is sited in a modern lodge overlooking the water about 700m from the train station. To get there, turn right outside the station building and head along the lake away from the town centre – a ten-minute walk. The hostel serves good breakfasts and large, inexpensive evening meals – though these need to be pre-booked

Moving on from Voss

When it comes to **moving on from Voss**, there are three obvious routes to choose from – one by train and two by road. **By train**, Voss is on the main Bergen–Oslo rail line and from here it's a short haul east up the Raundal valley (3–4 trains daily; Ⓦwww.nsb.no) to the **Myrdal junction**, where you change for the world-famous train ride down to Flåm on the **Flåmsbana** (see p.232). You can, however, also disembark at two isolated hiking bases – **Ørneberget** (served by slow trains only, once or twice daily) and **Finse**, both of which offer endless hiking and skiing opportunities on the Hardangervidda plateau (see p.228). Incidentally, drivers should note that although there is a mountain road east from Voss as far as Ørneberget, you can only reach Myrdal and Finse by train. Alternatively, it's a quick and easy 65km north from Voss along the **E16** to the village of **Flåm**, a pleasant and much visited little place beside the Aurlandsfjord. The E16 is the main road between Bergen and Oslo and you can, as a third possibility, dodge most of the traffic by forking off the E16 at **Vinje**, some 20km north of Voss, to take scenic **Highway 13** down the dales and over the mountains to **Vik**, where there's a fine stave church, and **Vangsnes**, on the Sognefjord. There are **buses** along both routes: **Nor-Way Bussekspress buses** (2–5 daily; Ⓦwww.nor-way.no) links Voss with Flåm and points east, and HSD's (Ⓦwww.hsd.no) Voss to Vangsnes **bus** (1–2 daily except Sat; 45min/55min) connects with the ferry over the Sognefjord to Hella and Dragsvik for Balestrand (see p.239).

– and has self-catering facilities; it also has its own sauna, laundry and Internet access, and rents out bikes and canoes. Advance booking is strongly recommended. A second inexpensive option is the rudimentary *Voss Camping* (Ⓣ56 51 15 97, Ⓦwww.vosscamping.no), located a short walk south of the Vangskyrkja church: turn left from the train station, take the right fork at the church and then turn right again, along the Prestegardsalléen footpath. It's open all year and has a few cabins (❷), an outside pool and washing machines. As for the town's **hotels**, one or two barely pass muster and easily the best bet is *Fleischer's* (Ⓣ56 52 05 05, Ⓦwww.fleischers.no; ❼, sp/r ❻), next door to the train station. Dating from the 1880s, the hotel's high-gabled and towered facade overlooks the lake and consists of the original building and a modern wing built in the same style. Parts of the hotel – and many of the bedrooms – have the whiff of real luxury, but others are more mundane. The **restaurant** serves the best food in town and there's a terrace bar as well. Their all-inclusive food-and-lodging deals offer substantial savings on the normal rate.

East from Voss: Ørneberget, Myrdal and Finse

All the trains pulling east out of Voss head up the Raundal valley, but only local trains (1–2 daily) stop – after forty minutes – at **ØRNEBERGET**, the remote mountain home of the HI *Mjølfjell Vandrerhjem* (Ⓣ56 52 31 50, Ⓦwww.mjolfjell.no; dorm beds 155–225kr, doubles ❷; March to late April & mid-June to Sept). There has been a hostel here since the 1930s, and the present version occupies a large and well-equipped lodge with oodles of pine panelling. The hostel is popular as a base for a range of sporting activities, from fishing and hiking on the Hardangervidda in the summer, to skiing in the springtime. It has self-catering facilities, a café, laundry, outdoor pool, and cycle- and canoe-rental, as well as single, double

The Flåm railway – the Flåmsbana

Lonely **Myrdal**, just forty minutes by train from Voss, is the start of one of Europe's most celebrated branch rail lines, the **Flåmsbana** (Ⓦwww.flaamsbana.no), a twenty-kilometre, 900-metre plummet down the Flåmsdal valley to **Flåm** – a fifty-minute train ride that's not to be missed under any circumstances. The track, which took four years to lay in the 1920s, spirals down the mountainside, passing through hand-dug tunnels and, at one point, actually travelling through a hairpin tunnel to drop nearly 300m. The gradient of the line is one of the steepest anywhere in the world, and as the tiny train squeals its way down the mountain, past cascading waterfalls, it's reassuring to know that it has five separate sets of brakes, each capable of bringing it to a stop. The service runs all year round, a local lifeline during the deep winter months. There are ten departures daily from mid-June to mid-September, between four and eight the rest of the year; Myrdal–Flåm fares are 175kr single, 275kr return.

In the past, the athletic have risen to the challenge and undertaken the five-hour **walk** from the railway junction at Myrdal down the old road into the valley, instead of taking the train, but much the better option is to disembark about halfway down and walk in from there. **Berekvam** station, at an altitude of 345m, will do very nicely, leaving an enthralling two- to three-hour hike through changing mountain scenery down to Flåm. **Cycling** down the valley road is also perfectly feasible, though it's too steep to be relaxing.

and family rooms, most of which are en suite; advance reservations are strongly recommended. Despite the hostel's name, it is actually 6km from Mjølfjell train station, and only 300m from **Ørneberget train station**. You can drive here, too, just about – the hostel is at the end of a narrow minor road that begins in Voss, 38km away, but you can't drive any further east to Myrdal and Finse.

Beyond Ørneberget, the higher reaches of the railway line are desolate even in good weather. All trains stop at **MYRDAL**, a remote railway junction where you change for the extraordinary train ride down to Flåm (see box opposite), and then proceed onto Finse.

Finse

Just half an hour by train from Myrdal, **FINSE** is the highest point on the Bergen–Oslo railway line, a solitary lakeside outpost on the northern periphery of the Hardangervidda plateau (see p.238). It comprises nothing more than its station and a few isolated buildings, hunkered down against the howling winds that rip across the plateau in wintertime. There's snow here from the beginning of November until well into June, and the **cross-country skiing** is particularly enthusiastic, with locals skiing off from the station in every direction. You can rent cross-country ski equipment at the *Finse 1222 Hotel* (see p.234), but you'll need to book in advance. After the snow has melted, **hiking** takes over, with one especially popular hike being the four-hour round trip to the northeast edge of the **Hardangerjøkulen glacier**. Other, longer hiking trails skirt the glacier to traverse the main body of the Hardangervidda plateau. From Finse, it's an eleven-hour hike to reach Highway 7 at Dyranut (see p.228), so most hikers overnight after around eight hours at the self-service **Kjeldebu** DNT hut (March to mid-Oct).

Cycling is similarly popular on the **Rallarvegen** ("The Navvy Road"; open July to Sept/Oct), which was originally built to allow men and materials to be brought to the railway during its construction. Now surfaced with gravel and sometimes asphalt, the Rallarvegen begins in Haugastøl beside Highway 7, runs west to Finse and then continues to Myrdal, from where you can cycle or take the Flåmsbana down to Flåm. It's 23km by bicycle from Haugastøl to Finse, 35km from Finse to Myrdal and another 22km to Flåm. The Finse to Flåm section, which passes through fine upland scenery before descending the Flåmsdal, is the most popular part of the Rallarvegen. Most cyclists travel east to west as Finse is a good deal higher than Myrdal, and the whole journey from Finse to Flåm takes around nine hours; the return trip is usually made by train, with NSB railways transporting bikes for 100kr. Note also that the highest parts of the Rallarvegen, between Finse and Myrdal, can be blocked by snow as late as July, so check conditions locally before you set out. **Mountain bike rental** is available from the *Finse 1222 Hotel* (see p.234), but advance reservations are required; bikes are picked up at the train station. Finse has scope for more specialist activities too, most notably **guided glacier walks** on the Hardangerjøkulen. These guided walks take place between July and September, last around seven hours and cost in the region of 400kr including equipment hire – contact *Finse 1222 Hotel* for further details.

If all this sounds much too energetic, you can content yourself with Finse's **Rallarmuseet** (Navvy Museum; July–Sept daily 10am–10pm; 30kr), which holds a pictorial record of the planning and construction of the Oslo–Bergen railway, whose final piece of track was laid in 1909. The old black-and-white photos are the most interesting exhibits and a well-earned tribute to the navvies, who survived such grim conditions.

Finse practicalities

Finse has two **places to stay**: both are chalet complexes, geared up for hikers, cyclists and skiers. Of the two, the *Finse 1222 Hotel* (Ⓣ56 52 71 00, Ⓦwww.finse1222.no; mid-Jan to mid-Oct; ❽ including meals) is the more comfortable, with pleasant rooms, a good restaurant and a sauna. The more frugal option is DNT's fully staffed *Finsehytta* (Ⓣ56 52 67 32, Ⓦwww.finsehytta.no; mid-March to late May & July to mid-Sept; dorm beds 135kr, doubles ❷), which sleeps up to 150. Heading east from Finse, the train takes 45 minutes to reach Geilo (see p.189), three-and-a-half hours more to Oslo.

North to Vik and Vangsnes

From Voss, it's about 20km north to **VINJE**, where **Highway 13** begins its 60km-long trek over to Vik and Vangsnes, A quintessential fjordland journey, the road begins by clambering up the Myrkdal valley, passing waterfalls and wild ravines before cutting an improbable route across the bleak and icy wastes of **Vikafjell mountain** – so improbable indeed that the highway is closed in winter, usually from late November to April, and snow is piled high on either side of the road until at least the end of May. Beyond the mountain, the road slips down into **VIK**, a rather half-hearted village that sprawls up a wide valley. The only reason to stop here is to take a peek at **Hopperstad stave church** (mid-May to mid-June & mid-Aug to mid-Sept daily 10am–5pm; mid-June to mid-Aug daily 9am–7pm; 45kr), sat on a hillock just off Highway 13, about 1500m from the fjord. In the 1880s the locals were about to knock it down, but a visiting architect and his antiquarian chum persuaded them to change their minds. The pair promptly set about repairing the place and they did a good job. Today the church is one of the best examples of its type, its angular roofing surmounted by a long and slender tower. The interior has its moments too, with a Gothic side-altar canopy, parts of which may have been swiped from France by the Vikings, and a so-called lepers' window through which the afflicted listened to church services.

From Vik, it's a straight 11km north along the fjord to **VANGSNES**, where local farmers must have had a real shock when, in 1913, Kaiser Wilhelm erected a twelve-metre high **statue** of the legendary Viking chief Fridtjof the Bold on the hilltop above their jetty. The **Fridtjovstatuen** still stands, an eccentric and vaguely unpleasant monument to the Kaiser's fascination with Nordic mythology – Fridtjof the Bold was in love with Ingebjorg, daughter of King Bele, whose statue, also commissioned by the Kaiser, is back across the fjord at Balestrand (see p.239). You can walk the 500m up from the jetty to take a closer look at Fridtjof and enjoy the fjord views from here too.

There are **car ferries** from Vangsnes north across the Sognefjord to both Hella on Highway 55 (every 40min to hourly; 15min; 23kr passengers, 60kr car & driver; Ⓦwww.fjord1.no) and Dragsvik (every 40min to hourly; 30min; 26kr passengers, 70kr car & driver; Ⓦwww.fjord1.no), just a few kilometres from Balestrand (see p.239); HSD **buses** (Ⓦwww.hsd.no) connect Voss with Vik and Vangsnes (1–2 daily except Sat; 45min/55min).

North from Voss to Flåm

Heading north along the **E16** from Voss, it's a short, scenic hop to **Flåm**, one of the region's most visited villages and justifiably famous for its railway, the

Flåmsbana (see p.232). Flåm is also an excellent base for further explorations, whether it be the ferry trip up along the **Nærøyfjord** or a day-long hike in the surrounding mountains. Nearing Flåm you'll pass through two spirited pieces of tunnelling, with stretches of 11km and 5km bored through the mountainside at colossal expense. Yet, these are but pip-squeaks when compared with the 24-kilometre-long **tunnel** that links Aurlandsdal – from a point just east of Flåm – with Lærdal and, more importantly, completes the fast road, the E16, from Bergen to Oslo. Even better, it's free. En route to Flåm, **Stalheim** boasts one of the region's finest hotels and **Undredal** is one of its quaintest villages, but Gudvangen contrives to be really dreary despite its fjordside setting.

As for public transport, **Nor-way Bussekspress** (Ⓦwww.nor-way.no) operates the **Sognebussen express bus** service, which begins in Bergen and passes through Voss bound for Flåm, Fodnes and ultimately Sogndal (2–5 daily).

Stalheim and Gudvangen

From Voss, it's 20km to Vinje and another 15km or so to **STALHEIM**, which plays host to the first-rate *Stalheim Hotel* (Ⓣ56 52 01 22, Ⓦwww.stalheim.com; ❻). The original hotel was built here in the late nineteenth century, but today's building, a large and solid-looking lodge, dates from the 1960s. Parts of the interior have been kitted out in antique Norwegian style and the modern bedrooms are very well appointed, but the highlight is the view – a simply breathtaking vista down along the Nærøyfjord. The hotel is located up a twisty byroad, just 1.5km from the E16.

From Stalheim, it's a further 10km or so to the mini-port of **GUDVANGEN**, a forlorn little place at the southern tip of the Nærøyfjord. In the summertime, hundreds of tourists pour through here partly on account of the car ferry connections to Kaupanger, but mainly because it's on the "Norway in a Nutshell" itinerary (see box on p.221). A modern complex down by the jetty incorporates souvenir shops, a café and a **hotel** of unusual design, the *Gudvangen Fjordtell* (Ⓣ57 63 39 29, Ⓦwww.gudvangen.com; May–Sept; ❹), consisting of a series of hut-like structures with turf roofs.

Undredal

Just beyond Gudvangen, the E16 disappears into an 11km-long tunnel to emerge a few kilometres short of Flåm – and a few hundred metres short of the byroad leading north to **UNDREDAL**. Just 6km long, this byroad cuts an attractive route, romping along a boulder-strewn valley to reach the village, which perches right on the edge of the Aurlandsfjord, its narrow, meandering lanes overshadowed by the severity of the surrounding mountains. There's been a settlement here since Viking times, and for much of its history the village has been reliant on the export of its goat's cheese, now produced in Undredal's two surviving diaries – there were once a dozen. The main item of interest here is the **church** (late June to mid–Aug daily 11am–6pm; 40kr), parts of which date back to the twelfth century. A tiny affair – it's one of the smallest churches in the whole of Norway – it's decorated in fine folkloric style, from the floral patterns on the walls through to the crucified Christ above the high altar and the stylized stars and naive figures on the ceiling.

Flåm and the Nærøyfjord

Fringed by meadows and orchards, **FLÅM** village sits beside the Aurlandsfjord, a slender branch of the Sognefjord, with the mountains glowering behind. It's a splendid setting, but otherwise first impressions are poor: the fjordside complex adjoining the train station is crass and commercial – souvenir trolls and the like – and on summer days the place heaves with tourists, who pour off the train, have lunch, and then promptly head out by bus and ferry. But a brief stroll is enough to leave the crowds behind at the harbourside, while out of season or in the evenings, when the day-trippers have all moved on, Flåm is a pleasant spot – and an eminently agreeable place to spend the night. If you're prepared to risk the weather, mid-September is perhaps the best time to visit: the peaks already have a covering of snow and the vegetation is just turning its autumnal golden brown.

Not only is Flåm the terminus for the Flåmsbana (see box p.232), but it's also the starting point for one of the most stupendous **ferry trips** in the fjords, the two-hour cruise up the Aurlandsfjord and down its narrow offshoot, the **Nærøyfjord** (1–4 daily; 2hr; 195kr single, 240kr return) to Gudvangen (see p.235). With high and broody cliffs keeping out the sun throughout the winter, Nærøyfjord is the narrowest fjord in Europe, and its stern beauty makes for a magnificent excursion.

Practicalities

Flåm's harbourside complex may be ugly, but it is convenient, holding a supermarket, a train station and the **tourist office** (daily: May & Sept 8.30am–4pm; June–Aug 8.30am–8pm; ⓣ57 63 21 06, ⓦwww.alr.no), where you can pick up a very useful free booklet on Aurland, Flåm and Lærdal that includes public transport timetables as well as all sorts of local information. Staff also have details on local hiking routes and sell hiking maps. If you do decide to overnight here, there's inexpensive **accommodation** at *Flåm Camping og Vandrerhjem*, which incorporates a small and well-kept HI **hostel** (May–Sept; ⓣ57 63 21 21, ⓦwww.vandrerhjem.no; dorm beds 130k, doubles ❷), plus tent spaces and cabins (❷), a couple of minutes' signposted walk from the train station. Alternatively, the *Heimly Pensjonat* (ⓣ57 63 23 00, ⓦwww.heimly.no; ❹) provides simple but perfectly adequate lodgings in a modern block about 450m east of the train station along the shore; it's a friendly, helpful place and the views down the fjord are charming. A third choice, set back from the water a couple of hundred metres from the station, is the *Fretheim Hotel* (ⓣ57 63 63 00, ⓦwww.fretheim-hotel.no; ❼, sp/r ❺), a rambling structure whose attractive older part, with high-pitched roofs and white-painted clapboard, is now flanked by a matching extension with well-appointed rooms furnished in brisk modern style. The hotel is the only good place to **eat** in town, with a banquet-like buffet every night; go early to get the pick of the buffet crop.

Moving on from Flåm

From Flåm, there are daily **Hurtigbåt passenger express boats** (ⓣ177, ⓦwww.fjord1.no) up the Aurlandsfjord and along the Sognefjord to Balestrand and Bergen. The one-way trip to Bergen takes five-and-a-half hours and costs 550kr; Balestrand is an hour and a half away and costs 190kr. By **train** (ⓣ177, ⓦwww.nsb.no), Myrdal, at the top of the Flåmsbana (see box p.232), is on the main Oslo–Bergen line, while **Nor-way Bussekspress** (ⓣ177, ⓦwww.nor-way.no) operates the **Sognebussen express bus** service, which begins in Bergen and passes through Voss, Flåm and Fodnes en route to Sogndal (2–5 daily). Heading east by car, it's tempting to use the enormous, 24km-long – and free – tunnel through to Lærdal (see p.189), but the 48km-long **mountain road** that the tunnel replaced – the **Aurlandsvegen** or **Snøvegen** (Snow Road) – has survived to provide splendid views and some hair-raising moments; it's open from the beginning of June to around the middle of October.

The Aurlandsdal valley

From Flåm, it's 6km north along the fjord to the hamlet of **AURLANDSVANGEN**, which strings along the seashore at the foot of the **Aurlandsdal valley** – and near the entrance to the whopping Lærdal tunnel. The valley was once the final part of one of Norway's most celebrated **hikes**, a classic two- or three-day expedition that began at Finse train station (see p.233), from where the trail crossed the northern peripheries of the Hardangervidda plateau before descending the Aurlandsdal, with hikers then pushing on to Flåm to get the train back again. The trail incorporated an extravagant range of scenery, from upland plateau to plunging ravines, and parts of it followed an old cattle drovers' route that once linked eastern and western Norway. The trail lost much of its allure – and some of its beauty – when **Highway 50**, which links Highway 7 near Geilo (see p.189) with Aurlandsvangen, was rammed through the Aurlandsdal as part of a hydroelectricity generation scheme in the 1970s, but sections of the old trail still provide some excellent hiking. Perhaps the most scenic section today is the 21-kilometre stretch between Østerbø (820m) and Vassbygdi (94m), which takes between six and seven hours to complete. The trails threads its way through the woods and farms of the Aurlandsdal, passing crashing waterfalls and offering handsome valley views as well as one or two tight and steep scrambles. **Østerbø**, the starting point, comprises a pair of lonely mountain lodges (see below), located about 800m off Highway 50 about 25km from Flåm; **Vassbygdi** is a dull hamlet where the trail ends at the car park and bus stop.

The **local bus** service from Aurlandsvangen to Østerbø (2–4 daily; 15min; Ⓦwww.fjord1.no) isn't great, but timetables are such that it is usually possible to catch the bus, make the hike to Vassbygdi then return to Aurlandsvangen by bus the same day. There's nowhere to stay in Aurlandsvangen, so you might end up having to walk (or catch another bus) the 6km along the main road to Flåm. However, this does mean you'll be hiking against the clock, which can be avoided by booking a taxi for the return leg or by overnighting in Østerbø at either of its two privately owned **mountain lodges** – *Østerbø Fjellstove* (Ⓣ57 63 11 77, Ⓦwww.aurlandsdalen.com; late May to Sept; dorm beds from 270kr, hotel ❺) or the adjacent and more spartan *Østerbø Turisthytte* (Ⓣ57 63 11 41, Ⓦwww.osterbo-turisthytte.no; dorm beds from 270kr; late May to Sept).

The Sognefjord

Profoundly beautiful, the **Sognefjord** (Ⓦwww.sognefjord.no) drills in from the coast for some 200km, its inner recesses splintering into half a dozen subsidiary fjords. Perhaps inevitably, none of the villages and small towns that dot the fjord quite lives up to the splendid setting, but **Balestrand** and **Mundal**, on the Fjærlandsfjord, come mighty close and are easily the best bases. Both are on the north side of the fjord which, given the lack of roads on the south side, is where you want (or pretty much have) to be – Flåm (see p.235) apart. Mundal is also near two southerly tentacles of the Jostedalsbreen glacier: **Flatbreen** and easy-to-reach **Bøyabreen**.

Highway 55 hugs the Sognefjord's north bank for almost the whole of its length, but at **Sogndal** it slices northeast to clip along the lustrous **Lustrafjord**, which boasts a top-notch attraction in **Urnes stave church**, reached via a quick ferry ride from **Solvorn**. Further north, a side road leaves Highway 55 to clamber up from the Lustrafjord to the east side of the Jostedalsbreen

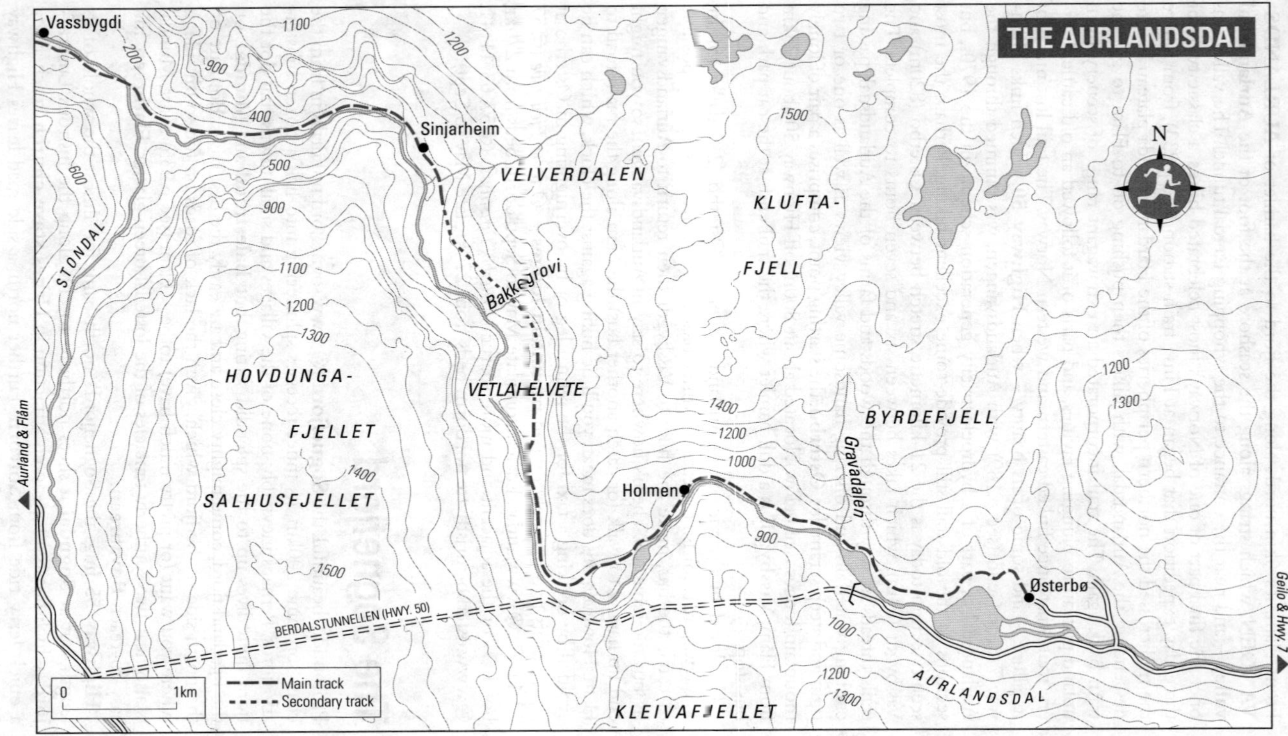
THE AURLANDSDAL
N
Vassbygdi
Sinjarheim
VEIVERDALEN
KLUFTA-
FJELL
Bakkegrovi
VETLAHELVETE
HOVDUNGA-
FJELLET
SALHUSFJELLET
BYRDEFJELL
Gravadalen
Holmen
Østerbø
STONDAL
AURLANDSDAL
KLEIVAFJELLET
BERDALSTUNNELLEN (HWY. 50)
Aurland & Flåm
Geilo & Hwy. 7
Main track
Secondary track
0
1km
200
400
500
600
900
1000
1100
1200
1300
1400
1500

△ Sognefjord

glacier at the **Nigardsbreen nodule**, arguably the glacier's finest vantage point. Thereafter Highway 55 – as the **Sognefjellsveg** – climbs steeply to run along the western side of the **Jotunheimen mountains**, an extraordinarily beautiful journey even by Norwegian standards and one which culminates with the road thumping down to **Lom** on the flatlands beside Highway 15.

Public transport (Ⓦwww.fjord1.no) to and around the Sognefjord is generally excellent. Operating about halfway along the fjord, perhaps the most useful of the **car ferries** plies between Vangsnes (see p.234), Hella and Dragsvik (for Balestrand), and in the east another useful link is the 24-hour ferry shuttle between Mannheller and Fodnes. Amongst a number of **Hurtigbåt passenger express boat** services, one handy route connects Bergen, Vik, Balestrand and Sogndal, another links Balestrand with Flåm. In addition, Nor-Way Bussekspress **long-distance buses** (Ⓦwww.nor-way.no) depart Bergen for Sogndal, arriving via Voss, Flåm and the Fodnes–Mannheller ferry, others arrive in Sogndal from Oslo and points east. Sogndal is something of a transport hub with buses leaving here to travel west along the north shore of the Sognefjord to Hella and Balestrand; northwest to Mundal and the Nordfjord (see p.249); and, in the summertime only, north to the Nigardsbreen glacier arm and Lom, which is reached along the stirring Sognefjellsveg (Highway 55).

Balestrand

An appealing first stop along the Sognefjord, **BALESTRAND** has been a tourist destination since the middle of the nineteenth century, when it was discovered by European travellers in search of cool, clear air and picturesque mountain scenery. Kaiser Wilhelm II got in on the act too, becoming a frequent visitor and sharing his holiday spot with the tweeds and hobnail boots of the British bourgeoisie. These days, the village is used as a touring base for the

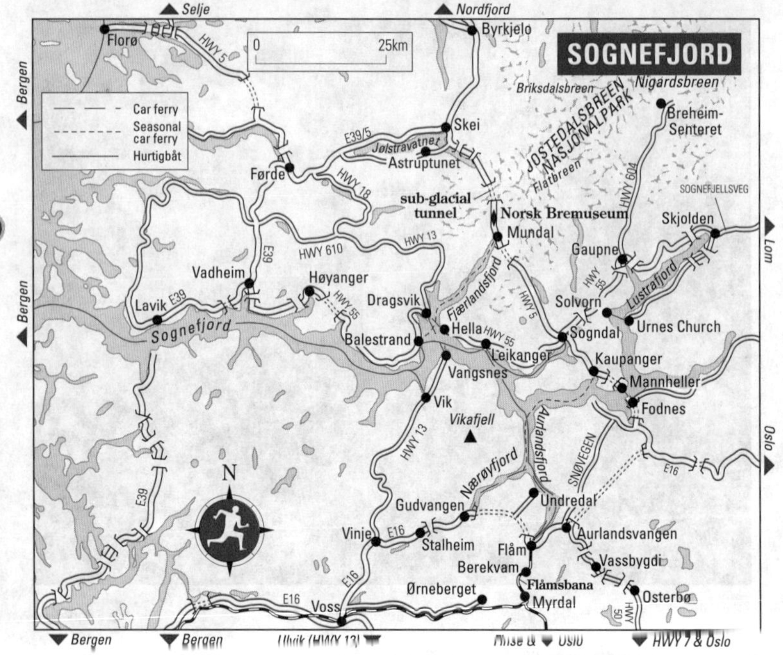

immediate area, as the battery of small hotels and restaurants above the quay testifies, but it's all very small-scale, and among the 1500-strong population farming remains the principal livelihood.

An hour or so will suffice to take a peek at Balestrand's two attractions. First up is the **English church of St Olav** (free), a spiky brown-and-beige wooden structure of 1897, built in the general style of a stave church at the behest of a British émigré, a certain Margaret Kvikne, who moved here after she married a local curate. In one of those curious hand-me-downs from Britain's imperial past, the church remains part of the Diocese of Gibraltar, which arranges English-language services during the summer. The Germans have left their mark, too. About 300m south of the church along the fjord are two humpy **Viking burial mounds**, supposedly the tombs of King Bele and his wife. On the larger of them is a statue of the king in heroic pose, plonked there by the Kaiser in 1913 to match the statue of Bele's son-in-law that stands across the fjord in Vangsnes (see p.234).

Several **hiking trails** ascend the rocky slopes immediately to the west of the village, clambering up to the peaks and lakes of the plateau beyond. None of them is easy – all begin with a short, stiff climb and pass through boggy ground, and several have steep drops too – but the scenery is splendid. Balestrand tourist office (see opposite) sells a detailed hiking map with multilingual trail descriptions, though if the weather is poor you'd be advised to leave the mountains alone, and stick to a much easier 4hr-hike (at most) along the bottom of the **Norddal valley** to the prettily situated Norddalsvatnet lake. To get to the trail head, drive west from Balestrand along Highway 55, for 24km, to **Nessane**, where a short and narrow byroad leads up the valley and past the Nessadalsvatnet lake to the car park; the trail head is just beyond. Note that after heavy rain, the trail gets far too squelchy to be much fun.

Practicalities

The only **car ferry** direct to Balestrand is the summertime service south from Mundal, on the Fjærlandsfjord (see p.242); otherwise, the nearest you'll get is Dragsvik, 9km along the fjord to the north of Balestrand, and reached by ferry from either Hella to the east or Vangsnes on the fjord's south shore (every 40min to 1hr; 15min/30min; ⓦwww.fjord1.no). The passenger **fare** from Hella to Dragsvik is 23kr, car and driver 60kr, Vangsnes to Dragsvik 26kr and 67kr. Both the Mundal ferry and **Hurtigbåt passenger express boat** services (from Bergen and Vik to the west, and Flåm and Sogndal to the east) dock at the village quayside, plumb in the centre. **Buses** stop beside the quayside too, but there are no services direct from Bergen and Voss; coming from the south it's necessary to change at Sogndal. The bus stop is in front of the Spar supermarket, and the village **tourist office** is at the back of the shop (May & Sept Mon–Fri 10am–5pm & Sat 11am–4pm; early June & late Aug Mon–Fri 10am–5pm & Sat–Sun 11am–4pm; mid-June to mid-Aug Mon–Fri 7.30am–7pm & Sat–Sun 9am–5pm; Oct–May Mon–Fri 9am–4pm; ⓣ57 69 16 17, ⓦwww.sognefjord.no). Staff hand out a wide range of fjord leaflets, sell local hiking maps, issue bus and ferry timetables and rent out bicycles.

For **accommodation**, the all-year *Midtnes Pensjonat* (ⓣ57 69 11 33, ⓦwww.midtnes.no; ❸, ❹ with fjord view), about 300m from the dock behind the English church, is a low-key, pleasantly sedate affair with a few workaday but

Moving on from Balestrand

When it comes to **moving on from Balestrand**, you're spoilt for choice. In the summertime, one especially tempting proposition is the **car ferry** (May to September 1–2 daily; 1hr 15min; passengers 160kr one-way, 240kr return; car & driver 275kr one-way, 520kr return) north up along the stunningly beautiful Fjærlandsfjord to the eminently appealing hamlet of Mundal (see p.242), from where there's the possibility of an onward bus trip to the Norsk Bremuseum and the Bøyabreen glacier arm (see p.243).

There is also a **Hurtigbåt passenger express boat** service linking Balestrand with Bergen and Vik in one direction, Sogndal in the other (1–2 daily), and another to Flåm. **Driving** north from Balestrand, **Highway 13** cuts a scenic route over the mountains on its way to its junction with the E39 (near Førde), which itself proceeds north to the Nordfjord (see p.249), but **Highway 55** to Sogndal and the eastern reaches of the Sognefjord has much more to offer – not least the wondrous Sognefjellsveg mountain road (Highway 55; see p.246). To get to Sogndal from Balestrand, it's necessary to cross the mouth of the Fjærlandsfjord by ferry from Dragsvik, 9km up along the coast to the north of Balestrand. This **Dragsvik car ferry** operates a triangular service shuttling both east across the fjord to Hella on Highway 55 (15min) and south to Vangsnes (30min), see p.234 for prices; sailings to both destinations are every forty minutes or so from mid-June to mid-August, hourly the rest of the year. The other significant cost for drivers is the 150kr toll payable as you approach Mundal from the south on Highway 5.

As for **buses**, one routing of Nor-Way Bussekspress's **Sogn og Fjordane express bus** travels west from Balestrand to Førde (1 daily; 2hr), where passengers change for Florø as well as Stryn and the Nordfjord (see p.249). This same bus also heads east (3 daily) from Balestrand to Sogndal and ultimately Oslo. At Sogndal, passengers change for Mundal and Lom (see p.247). Note, however, that connecting services can be few and far between – mostly you'll have to hang around for an hour or two (at least) between buses. All the Sognefjord's public transport timetables are **online** at ⓦwww.fjord1.no.

spacious rooms in a modern wing adjoining the original clapboard house; make sure to get a room with a fjord view. Close by, the *Balestrand Hotel* (ⓣ57 69 11 38, ⓦwww.balestrand.net; May–Sept; ❹) is very similar, with thirty unassuming rooms kitted out in modern, modest style. A third good choice, just 150m uphill from the dock, is the HI **hostel** (ⓣ57 69 13 03, ⓦwww.vandrerhjem.no; late June to mid-Aug; dorm beds 190kr, doubles ❷), which is part of the neat and trim *Kringsjå Hotell* (same number; ⓦwww.kringsja.no; ❸). This complex occupies a pleasant modern building, whose long verandah overlooks the fjord; there's a communal kitchen, a more-than-competent café-restaurant and a laundry; rowing boat rental is available, too. The big deal hereabouts, though, is *Kvikne's Hotel* (ⓣ57 69 42 00, ⓦwww.kviknes.no; ❺; May–Sept), whose various buildings dominate much of the waterfront. It's worth popping into the bar to take a look at the fancy fittings – some of which are in a sort of neo-Viking baronial style – but don't take a room without having a gander first: the best and most expensive overlook the fjord, but some are at the back of the modern annexe. Finally, the town **campsite**, *Sjøtun Camping* (ⓣ57 69 12 23, ⓦwww.sjotun.com; June to mid-Sept), occupies a treeless field just beyond the burial mounds, 1km or so south of the dock; there are cabins (❶) as well as tent and caravan pitches.

For **food**, both the *Kringsjå* and the *Midtnes* serve tasty, excellent-value dinners, and there are competent snacks and light lunches at *Gekkens Café*, upstairs in the shopping centre on the quayside. Nevertheless, the cream of the gastronomic crop is the restaurant at *Kvikne's Hotel*, which serves up a banquet-sized, help-yourself buffet (370kr) every night – go early to get the pick and be sure to leave room for the ground-moving, earth-shattering mousse.

North to the Fjærlandsfjord and Mundal

To the north of Balestrand, the **Fjærlandsfjord** is a wild place, its flanks blanketed by a thick covering of trees that extends down to the water's edge, with a succession of thundering waterfalls tumbling down vast clefts in the rock up above. The village of **MUNDAL** – sometimes inaccurately referred to as Fjærland – matches its surroundings perfectly, a gentle ribbon of old wooden houses edging the fjord, with the mountains as a backcloth. It's one of the region's most picturesque places, saved from the developers by its isolation: it was one of the last settlements on the Sognefjord to be connected to the road system, with Highway 5 from Sogndal only being completed in 1986. Moreover, Mundal has eschewed the crasser forms of commercialism to become the self-styled "Norwegian Book Town" (Den norske bokbyen), with a dozen old buildings accommodating antiquarian and second-hand **bookshops**. Naturally enough, most of the books are in Norwegian, but there's a liberal sprinkling of English editions, too. The bookselling season runs from mid-May to early September and the bookshops are mostly open daily from 10am to 6pm.

Bookshops aside, the village has two good-looking buildings, the first of which is the **Hotel Mundal** (see opposite), whose nineteenth-century turrets, verandahs and high-pitched roofs overlook the fjord from amongst the handful of buildings that amount to the village centre. Next door, the **church** (June–Aug daily 10am–6pm; free), which dates from 1861, lacks ornamentation but is immaculately maintained; its graveyard hints at the hard but healthy life of the district's farmers – most of them seem to have lived to a ripe old age. Many locals are still farmers, but in summer few herd their cattle up to the mountain pastures, as was the custom until the 1960s. The disused tracks to these summer farms (*støls*) now serve as **hiking trails** of varying length and difficulty – the tourist office (see opposite) will advise, but one of the easier routes is the two-hour (each way) jaunt west along a country lane up **Mundalsdal** to **Heimastølen**, from where a track continues up to the marshy pastures of **Mundalsfjellstølen**.

Around Mundal: Flatbreen and Bøyabreen

About 2.5km north of Mundal, along the quiet byroad that links it with Highway 5, is the **Norsk Bremuseum** (Norwegian Glacier Museum; daily: April, May, Sept & Oct 10am–4pm; June–Aug 9am–7pm; information and enquiries free but displays 80kr; Ⓣ57 69 32 88, Ⓦwww.bre.museum.no), which tells you more than you ever wanted to know about glaciers and then some. It features several lavish hands-on displays and screens films about glaciers – and package tourists turn up in droves.

The museum is one of the Jostedalsbreen Nasjonalpark's three information centres (see p.250 for details of the others), and as such has the details of all the various **guided glacier walks** on offer across the park as outlined in their *Breturar* (glacier walks) leaflet. The usual target from Mundal is the **Supphellebreen**, the Jostedalsbreen's nearest hikeable arm, or, to be precise, that part of it called **Flatbreen**, but this is a challenging albeit beautiful part of the glacier and neither is it easy to get to. Flatbreen excursions take between six and eight hours and the season runs from late July to early August. Advance reservations, at least a day beforehand, are essential on Ⓣ57 69 32 33, Ⓦwww.breogfjell.no; the cost is 650kr per person. Excursions begin at the **Øygard** car park, about 3km off Highway 5 – watch for the sign just 2km north of the Bremuseum. From the car park, it's a stiff two- to three-hour hike up the trail to the (usual) meeting point, the **Flatbrehytta**, an unstaffed DNT mountain hut. Thereafter, you spend two to three hours on the glacier. The hike up from Øygarden to the hut is a fine excursion in itself, so you might decide to dispense with the glacier walk. In this case, don't go back the way you came, but instead walk east from the Flatbrehytta along the less clearly defined trail that traverses the glacier's lateral moraine, providing superb views over the ice, and return to the car park via the next valley along.

At the other extreme, you can get close to the glacier without breaking sweat just 10km north of Mundal on Highway 5. Here, just before you enter the tunnel, look out for the signposted side road on the right, leading the 200m to the **Brævasshytta restaurant** (May–Sept daily 9am–5/8pm). This smart, modern place, a tour-package favourite, overlooks the slender glacial lake fed by the **Bøyabreen** arm of the glacier up above. It takes a couple of minutes to stroll down from the restaurant to the lake, close to the sooty shank of the glacier.

Mundal practicalities

Arriving **by car** from the south on Highway 5, there's a whopping 150kr toll to pay just before you reach the turning for Mundal. **Car ferries** from Balestrand dock in the centre of the village and connect with special excursion buses – bookable either here or in Balestrand – which take passengers on to the Bremuseum and then, after a stopoff of over an hour, to the Bøyabreen. Drivers should note that by using the ferry, they can avoid the toll providing, that is, they are continuing north from Mundal. The nearest you'll get to Mundal by regular **bus** is the Norsk Bremuseum on Highway 5, from where it's an easy 2.5-kilometre stroll south along the fjord to the village. Mundal **tourist office**, metres from the boat dock (May–Sept daily 9.30am–5.30pm; Ⓣ57 69 32 33, Ⓦwww.fjaerland.org), advises on local hiking routes, sells hiking maps and has bus and ferry timetables. **Cycle rental** is available from them too, at around 150kr per day.

There are two fjordside **hotels** in Mundal. The obvious choice is the splendid *Hotel Mundal* (Ⓣ57 69 31 01, Ⓦwww.fjordinfo.no/mundal; May–Sept; ❻), a quirky sort of place whose public rooms, which date back to 1891, display many original features, from the parquet floors and fancy wooden scrollwork through to the old-fashioned sliding doors of the cavernous dining room. The rooms are frugal and some show their age, but somehow it doesn't matter much. If you do stay, look out for the old photos on the walls of men in plus-fours and hobnail boots clambering round the glaciers – only softies bothered with gloves. Nearby, the *Fjærland Fjordstue Hotell* (ⓣ57 69 32 00, ⓦwww.fjaerland.no; May–Sept; ❹, ❺ with fjord view) is very different – a well-tended family hotel with smart modern furnishings and a conservatory overlooking the fjord. A third option is *Bøyum Camping* (ⓣ57 69 32 52) near the Bremuseum, which has huts (❸) as well as spaces for tents. Both hotels offer good, wholesome **food**.

Leaving Mundal, long-distance **buses** from beside the Norsk Bremuseum go south to Sogndal and Oslo along the E16 (3 daily) and north to Skei and Førde (3 daily). Change at Skei for onward services north to Stryn and the Nordfjord (see p.249).

East to Sogndal

From Balestrand, it's 9km north along the fjord to **Dragsvik**, where ferries shuttle over to the jetty at **Hella**, which is itself 40km from **SOGNDAL** – bigger and livelier than Balestrand, but still hardly a major metropolis, with a population of just 6600. Neither is Sogndal as appealing: it has, admittedly, a pleasant fjord setting in a broad valley, surrounded by low, green hills dotted with apple and pear trees, but its centre is a rash of modern concrete and glass. Frankly, there are other much more agreeable spots within a few kilometres' radius and your best option is to keep going.

Buses drop passengers at the **bus station** – a major interchange – on the west side of the town centre near the end of Gravensteinsgata, the long main drag. From the bus station, it's about 500m east along Gravensteinsgata to the **tourist office** (early June to late Aug Mon–Fri 9am–8pm, Sat 9am–5pm, Sun 3–8pm; late Aug to Sept Mon–Fri 9am–4pm; ⓣ57 67 30 83, ⓦwww.sognefjorden.no), housed in one of the street's flashy modern buildings. Staff issue bus and ferry timetables, and have a list of local **accommodation**, but pickings are fairly slim. The nicest place to stay – though it's no great shakes – is the *Hofslund Fjord Hotel*, a stone's throw from the tourist office at Fjøregata 37 (ⓣ57 62 76 00, ⓦwww.hofslund-hotel.no; ❹). This comprises an old wooden building and a modern annexe; ask for a room with a fjord view. Another palatable and certainly economical option is the HI **hostel** (ⓣ57 62 75 75, ⓦwww.vandrerhjem.no; mid-June to mid-Aug; dorm beds 160kr, doubles ❷), which actually manages to feel quite homely despite being housed in a residential rural high school, *Folkehøgskule*. Finding the place is straightforward too: approaching Sogndal from the southeast on Highway 5, the hostel is clearly signposted from the main drag, just beyond the bridge at the east end of town; in the opposite direction, coming from the bus station, it's about 400m beyond the roundabout at the east end of Gravensteinsgata. This same roundabout is just 50m from the tourist office and marks the start of **Fjøravegen**, the town's other main drag, which cuts through the commercial heart of Sogndal. For **food**, the restaurant of the *Quality Hotel Sogndal*, Gravensteinsgata 5 (ⓣ57 62 77 00), is reliable, offering tasty Norwegian dishes with main courses averaging around 190kr.

Around Sogndal: Kaupanger

About 10km southeast of Sogndal on Highway 5, the village of **KAUPANGER** is worth a quick detour. Here, the red and white timber houses of the old part

Moving on from Sogndal

From Sogndal, there is a **Hurtigbåt passenger express boat** service to Balestrand, Vik and Bergen (1–2 daily). Sogndal is also on the route of the **Sogn og Fjordane ekspressen** (3 daily), a long-distance express **bus** service, which – amongst several permutations – links Oslo with Gol, the Fodnes–Mannheller ferry, Kaupanger, Sogndal, Mundal on the Fjærlandsfjord, Skei (for Stryn), Førde and Florø. **Local buses** include a limited summer service north up along Highway 55, the Sognefjellsveg, the highest parts of which are closed by snow from late October to May. One bus goes to Solvorn and the Nigardsbreen glacier nodule (late June to Aug 1 daily), another to Solvorn, Turtagrø and Lom (late June to mid-Sept 1–3 daily).

Finally, **drivers** should remember that the road to Oslo is interrupted some 18km southeast of Sogndal by the round-the-clock Mannheller–Fodnes **car ferry** (every 30min; 10min; passengers 31kr, car & driver 92kr).

Public transport timetables are online at Ⓦwww.fjord1.no.

of the village slope up from the harbour towards the **stave church** (early June to late Aug daily 9.30am–5.30pm; 35kr), a much modified thirteenth-century structure whose dourness is offset by its situation: the church stands on a hillside amid buttercup meadows with views of the fjord on one side and forested hills on the other. The interior has several unusual features too, most memorably a musical score painted on one of the walls and a sad portrait of a Danish bailiff and his family with three stillborn babies. Afterwards, head down to the dock to visit the Sogn Fjordmuseum (June–Aug daily 10am–6pm; 60kr), which holds an assortment of old wooden boats. Exhibits range from sturdy inshore fishing boats and ice boats (fitted with runners for use on frozen fjord inlets) to daintier, faster craft used by Danish dignitaries. If this whets your appetite for old Norway, you might also visit the thirty-odd, mostly nineteenth-century buildings that comprise the open-air **De Heibergske Samlinger Sogn Folkemuseum** (Heiberg Collections of the Sogn Folk Museum; daily: May & Sept 10am–3pm; June–Aug 10am–5pm; 60kr), just off Highway 5 in between Kaupanger and Sogndal. Incidentally, the admission fee at either of these museums covers the other.

Northeast to Solvorn and Urnes stave church

Some 15km northeast of Sogndal on Highway 55, a steep three-kilometre turning leaves the main road to snake its way down to **SOLVORN**, an attractive little hamlet clustered beneath the mountains on the sheltered foreshore of the **Lustrafjord**. Solvorn is the site of the *Walaker Hotell* (Ⓣ57 68 20 80, Ⓦwww.walaker.com; ❺), the prettiest part of which is the old house, a comely pastel-painted building with a lovely garden and first-rate period bedrooms.

From Solvorn, a local **car ferry** (early June to Aug Mon–Fri 10am–4pm hourly, plus Sat & Sun 11am–4pm hourly; Sept to early June Mon–Fri 3–4 daily, Sun 1 daily, no Sat service; 20min; 25kr passenger, 70kr car & driver; Ⓣ917 94 211) shuttles across the Lustrafjord to the hamlet of **Ornes**, from where it's a stiff, ten-minute hike up the hill to **Urnes stave church** (early June–Aug daily 10.30am–5.30pm; 45kr). Magnificently sited with the fjord and the snow-dusted mountains as its backdrop, this is the oldest and most celebrated stave church in Norway. Parts of the building date back to the twelfth century, and its most remarkable feature is its wonderful medieval **carvings**. On the outside, incorporated into the north wall, are two exquisite door panels, the remains of an earlier church dating from around 1070 and alive with a swirling filigree of strange beasts and delicate vegetation. These forceful, superbly crafted panels bear witness to the sophistication of Viking woodcarving – indeed, the church has given its name to this distinctively Nordic art form, found in many countries where Viking influence was felt and now generally known as the "Urnes" style. Most of the interior is seventeenth-century – including some splendidly bulbous pomegranates – but there is Viking woodcarving here too, notably the strange-looking figures and beasts carved on the capitals of the staves and the sacred-heart bench-ends. A small display in the neighbouring house-cum-ticket office fills in all the details and has photographic enlargements of carvings that are hard to decipher inside the (poorly lit) church.

If you're driving, there's a choice of routes on from the church. You can head north along the minor road that tracks along the east shore of the Lustrafjord to rejoin Highway 55 at Skjolden (see below), or retrace your steps back to Highway 55 via Solvorn. The latter is the route you'll need to take if you're heading to the Nigardsbreen arm of the Jostedalsbreen glacier.

North to the Nigardsbreen

North from the Solvorn turning, it's about 15km along Highway 55 to **Gaupne**, where **Highway 604** forks north for the delightful 34-kilometre trip up the wild, forested river valley that leads to the **Breheimsenteret Jostedalsbreen Nasjonalpark information centre** (daily: May to late June & late Aug to Sept 10am–5pm; late June to late Aug 9am–7pm; displays 50kr; ⓣ57 68 32 50, ⓦwww.jostedal.com). This angular, ultramodern structure fits in well with the bare peaks that surround it and, as you sip a coffee on the terrace, you can admire the glistening glacier dead ahead – the **Nigardsbreen**, an eastern arm of the Jostedalsbreen. From the centre, it's an easy three-kilometre drive or walk along the toll road (25kr) to the shores of an icy green lake, where a tiny **boat** (mid-June to early Sept daily 10am–6pm; 30kr return) shuttles across to the bare rock slope beside the glacier, a great rumpled and seamed wall of ice that sweeps between high peaks. It's a magnificent spectacle and most visitors are satisfied with the short hike up from the jetty to the glacier's shaggy flanks, but others plump for a **guided glacier walk**. There is a plethora to choose from, beginning with a quick and easy one- to two-hour jaunt suitable for children over six (daily July to late Aug; 160kr, children 80kr), through to much tougher five-hour excursions (July to late Aug 4 weekly; 640kr). The guided glacier walk season lasts from mid-May to mid-September. Prices include equipment and the starting point is at the foot of the glacier on the far side of the lake. Tickets for the family walks can be purchased direct from the guides, but longer day-trip excursions need to be pre-booked and pre-paid at the Breheimsenteret at least one hour before departure. Advance reservations for the longer, overnight trips are essential and must be made at least four weeks beforehand. For more on the Jostedalsbreen glacier, see p.249; further information on glacier walks is given on p.250.

Along the Sognefjellsveg

Back at Gaupne, Highway 55 continues 26km northeast to **SKJOLDEN**, a dull little town that is both at the head of the Lustrafjord and at the start of the 85km-long **Sognefjellsveg** road over the mountains to Lom. Despite the difficulty of the terrain, the Sognefjellsveg – which is closed from late October to May depending on conditions – marks the course of one of the oldest trading routes in Norway, with locals transporting goods by mule or, amazingly enough, on their shoulders: salt and fish went east, hides, butter, tar and iron went west. That portion of the road that clambers over the highest part of the mountains – no less than 1434m above sea level – was only completed in 1938 under a Great Depression "make-work" scheme, which kept a couple of hundred young men busy for two years. Tourist literature hereabouts refers to the lads' "motivation and drive", but considering the harshness of the conditions and the crudeness of their equipment – pickaxes, spades and wheelbarrows – their purported enthusiasm seems unlikely.

Beyond Skjolden, the Sognefjellsveg worms its way up the Bergsdal valley to a mountain plateau which it traverses, providing absolutely stunning views of the jagged, ice-crusted Jotunheimen peaks to the east. En route are several roadside **lodges**, easily the best of which is the comfortable and very modern **Turtagrø Hotel** (Ⓣ57 68 08 00, Ⓦwww.turtagro.no; dorm bunks in the annexe 275kr, 385kr with breakfast, hotel rooms ❻; Easter–Oct), just 15km out from Skjolden. There's been a hotel here since 1888, but the present structure, a large and attractive red-timber building, was only constructed in 2001, after fire destroyed its predecessor. The interior is very Scandinavian, with spacious public rooms and even a library, and the food is first-rate, with a three-course midday meal costing about 350kr. The hotel is a favourite haunt for **mountaineers**, but it also provides ready access to the **hiking trails** that lattice the Jotunheimen National Park (see p.179), though the terrain is unforgiving and the weather unpredictable, so novice hikers beware. One tough hike from the hotel is the six-hour, round-trip haul southeast along the well-worn (but not especially well-signed) path up the **Skagastølsdal valley** to DNT's self-service **Skagastølsbu** hut, though you can of course make the hike shorter by only going some of the way. The valley is divided into a number of steps, each preceded by a short, steep ascent; the hotel is 884m above sea level, the hut, a small stone affair surrounded by a staggering confusion of ice caps, mini-glaciers and craggy ridges, is at 1758m. If you'd rather have a guide, the *Turtagrø* is a base for mountain guides, who offer an extensive programme of guided mountain and glacier walks as well as **summer cross-country skiing** – the hotel will help to sort things out; the season begins at Easter and extends until October.

On the far side of the plateau, the Sognefjellsveg clips down through forested **Leirdal**, passing the old farmstead of **ELVESETER**, some 45km from Turtagrø. Here, a complex of old timber buildings has been turned into a hotel-cum-mini-historical-theme-park, its proudest possession being a bizarre 33-metre-high plaster and cyanite column, the **Sagasøyla**. On top of the column is the figure of that redoubtable Viking Harald Hardrada and down below is carved a romantic interpretation of Norwegian history. Dating from the 1830s, the column was brought to this remote place because no one else would have it – not too surprising really. Elveseter is near the northern end of the Leirdal valley, from where it's a short hop over the hills to **Bøverdal**, which runs down into the crossroads settlement of **Lom**.

Lom

A long-time trading and transport centre, **LOM** benefits – in a modest sort of way – from the farms that dot the surrounding valleys. It also makes a comfortable living from the passing tourist trade, with motorists pausing here before the last thump down Highway 15 to the Geirangerfjord. Even so, with a population of just 700, it could hardly be described as a boom town. Lom's eighteenth-century heyday is recalled by its **stave church** (daily: late

May to mid-June & mid-Aug to mid-Sept 10am–4pm; mid-June to mid-Aug 8am–8pm; 40kr), an enormous structure perched on a grassy knoll above the river. The original church was built here about 1200, but it was remodelled and enlarged after the Reformation, when the spire and transepts were added and the flashy altar and pulpit installed. Its most attractive features are the dinky, shingle-clad roofs, adorned by dragon finials, and the Baroque acanthus vine decoration inside.

Nearby is the town's open-air museum, the **Lom Bygdamuseum Presthaugen** (late June & late Aug Tues–Sun 11am–4pm; July to mid-Aug daily 11am–5pm; 40kr), a surprisingly enjoyable collection of old log buildings in a forest setting. Norway teems with this type of museum – stay in the country long enough and the very sight of one will make you want to scream – but Lom's is better than most. It is distinguished by the **Olavsstugu**, a modest hut where St Olav is said to have spent a night, and also by what must be the biggest and ugliest *storstabburet* (large storehouse) in the country. Museum enthusiasts will also want to visit the **Norsk Fjellmuseum** (Norwegian Mountain Museum; Jan–April & Oct–Dec Mon–Fri 9am–4pm; May to mid-June & mid-Aug to Sept Mon–Fri 9am–5pm, Sat & Sun 11am–5pm; mid-June to mid-Aug Mon–Fri 9am–7pm, Sat & Sun 10am–7pm; 50kr), a modern place which focuses on the Jotunheimen mountains. It's all here in admirable detail, from the fauna and the flora to the landscapes, farmers and past mountaineers.

Practicalities

Buses to Lom pull in a few metres west of the main crossroads, and most of what you're likely to need is within easy walking distance of here. The church and the open-air museum are across the bridge on the other side of the river, as is the mountain museum, which shares its premises with the **tourist office** (Jan–April & Oct–Dec Mon–Fri 9am–4pm; May & Sept Mon–Fri 9am–4pm, Sat & Sun 10am–5pm; early June & late Aug Mon–Fri 9am–6pm, Sat & Sun 10am–5pm; mid-June to mid-Aug Mon–Fri 9am–7pm, Sat & Sun 10am–8pm; ⓣ61 21 29 90, ⓦwww.visitlom.com). The choicest **accommodation** is the *Fossheim Turisthotell* (ⓣ61 21 95 00, ⓦwww.fossheimhotel.no; ❹), about 300m east of the crossroads along Highway 15. The main lodge here is neat and smart, with an abundance of pine, and behind, trailing up the wooded hillside, are some delightful little wooden cabins (also ❹), some of which are very old and all of which are en suite. The hotel **restaurant** is excellent and reasonably

Routes on from Lom

Heading west along **Highway 15**, Lom is within comfortable striking distance of either the Geirangerfjord (see p.255) or the Nordfjord and the western flanks of the Jostedalsbreen glacier (see opposite). In the opposite direction, also along Highway 15, it's another very manageable drive to Otta (see p.176) and the main E6 highway between Oslo and Trondheim. A tantalizing choice perhaps, but, if you're after more fjord scenery, the Geirangerfjord definitely has the edge.

By **bus** from Lom, there are fast and frequent **Nor-Way Bussekspress** (ⓦwww.nor-way.no) services west to Grotli, Stryn and ultimately Bergen, and east to Otta, Lillehammer and Oslo or Trondheim. From mid-June to the end of August, you can change onto a local bus at Grotli for the Geirangerfjord – but check connections with Lom tourist office before you depart. There is also a summer bus service south along Highway 55, the Sognefjellsveg, to Turtagrø, Solvorn and Sogndal (late June to mid-Sept 1–3 daily).

priced; it specializes in traditional Norwegian cuisine. A palatable second choice is the modern *Fossberg Hotel* (☎61 21 22 50, ⓦwww.fossberg.no; ❹), a large, mostly wooden place by the crossroads. For bargain-basement lodgings, the nearest HI **hostel**, *Bøverdalen Vandrerhjem* (☎61 21 20 64, ⓦwww.vandrerhjem.no; June to late Oct; dorm beds 120kr, doubles ❶), is about 20km back down Highway 55 (the Sognefjellsveg) and occupies a series of glum modern buildings right by the roadside.

Nordfjord and the Jostedalsbreen glacier

The most direct way to get from the Sognefjord to the **Nordfjord**, the next great fjord system to the north, is to travel north from Mundal (see p.242) on Highway 5 as it tunnels beneath an arm of the vast **Jostedalsbreen glacier**, though this somehow seems a bit of a cheek – or at least environmentally dubious. With the glacier left behind, Highway 5 then presses on past the turning for the **Astruptunet**, one-time home of the artist Nikolai Astrup, before proceeding on to the inner recesses of the Nordfjord. These recesses are readily explored along **Highway 60**, which weaves a pleasant, albeit tortuous, course through a string of unexciting little towns between the fjord and the glacier's west side. Amongst them, **Loen** is the best base for further explorations, including the glacier, though humdrum **Stryn** is larger and more important. Stryn is also where Highway 60 meets **Highway 15**. The former presses on north to **Grodås**, home of the Anders Svor Museum, and Hellesylt (see p.257), while the latter runs west along the Nordfjord, with the road dipping and diving along the northern shore in between deep-green reflective waters and severe peaks. It's a handsome enough journey, but the Nordfjord doesn't have the allure of its more famous neighbours, at least in part because its roadside hamlets lack much appeal. Indeed, the main reason to head this way is to make the time-consuming trek to the solitary monastic remains of **Selja island**, about 110km from Stryn.

High up in the mountains, dominating the whole of the inner Nordfjord region, lurks the **Jostedalsbreen glacier**, a five-hundred-kilometre-square

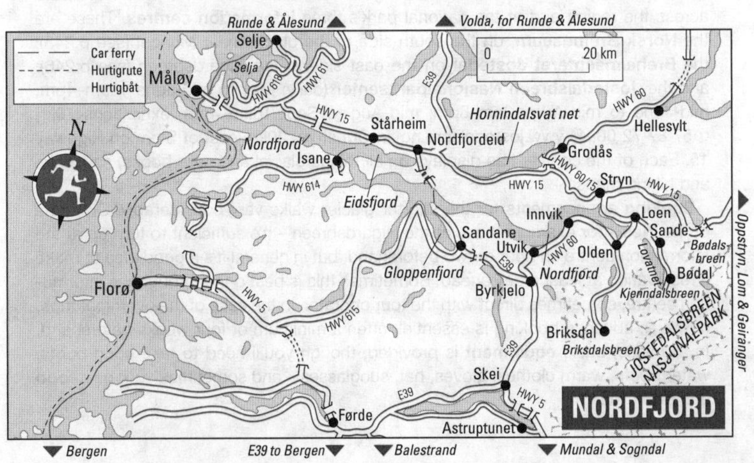

ice plateau that creaks, grumbles and moans out towards the Sognefjord, the Nordfjord and the Jotunheim mountains. The glacier stretches northeast in a lumpy mass from Highway 5, its myriad arms – or "**nodules**" – nudging down into the nearby valleys, the clay particles of its meltwater giving the local rivers and lakes their distinctive light-green colouring. Catching sight of the ice nestling between peaks and ridges can be unnerving – the overwhelming feeling being that somehow it shouldn't really be there. As the poet Norman Nicholson had it:

A malevolent, rock-crystal
Precipitate of lava,
Corroded with acid,
Inch by inch erupting
From volcanoes of cold

For centuries, the glacier presented an impenetrable east–west barrier, crossed only at certain points by determined farmers and adventurers. It's no less daunting today, but access is much freer, a corollary of the creation of the **Jostedalsbreen Nasjonalpark** in 1991. Since then, roads have been driven deep into the glacier's flanks, the comings (but mostly goings) of the ice have been closely monitored and there has been a proliferation of officially licensed **guided glacier walks** (*breturar*) on its various arms (see box below). If that sounds too energetic and all you're after is a **close look at the glacier**, then this is possible at several places, with the easiest approach being the five-minute stroll to the Bøyabreen on the south side of the glacier near Mundal (see p.242). By contrast, the east side's Nigardsbreen (see p.246) requires much more commitment – getting to the ice involves a boat ride and a short, stiff hike – as does the **Briksdalsbreen**, here on the west side of the glacier, off Highway 60. It takes about 45 minutes to walk from the end of the road to the Briksdalsbreen,

Guided glacier walks and national park information centres

Most **guided glacier walks** on the Jostedalsbreen are scheduled between late June and early September, though on some arms of the glacier the season extends from May until late September, even longer on parts of the Briksdalsbreen. The walks range from two-hour excursions to five-day expeditions. Day-trip prices start at 250–350kr per person for a two- to four-hour gambol, rising to 650kr for six to eight hours. A comprehensive leaflet detailing all the various walks is widely available across the region and at the national park's three **information centres**. These are the **Norsk Bremuseum**, on the south side of the glacier near Mundal (see p.243); the **Breheimsenteret Jostedal** on the east side at the Nigardsbreen (see p.246); and the **Jostedalsbreen Nasjonalparksenter** (daily: May to mid-June 10am–4pm; mid-June to mid-Aug 10am–6pm; mid-Aug to Sept 10am–4pm; exhibitions 70kr; ⓣ57 87 72 00, ⓦwww.jostedalsbre.no) in Oppstryn, 20km east of Stryn on Highway 15. Each of the centres has displays on all things glacial and sells books, souvenirs and hiking maps.

Booking arrangements for the shorter glacier walks vary considerably. On some of the trips – for example those at the Nigardsbreen – it's sufficient to turn up at the information centre an hour or two beforehand, but in general it's a good idea to make a reservation at least a day ahead. Sometimes this is best done through the information centre, sometimes direct with the tour operator. In the case of the overnight trips, however, advance booking is essential, often a minimum of four weeks beforehand. In all cases, basic **equipment** is provided, though you'll need to take good boots, waterproofs, warm clothes, gloves, hat, sunglasses – and sometimes your own **food** and **drink** too.

but it's still the most visited approach by a long chalk, partly on account of its pony-and-trap rides up towards the ice. Much less crowded and far prettier is the easy fifteen-minute walk to the **Kjenndalsbreen**, near Loen – a delightful way to spend a morning or afternoon.

Travelling around the Nordfjord region by **bus** presents few problems if you stick to the main highways, but services from Highway 60 to the glacier are limited. There are no buses at all to Kjenndalsbreen and an infrequent service (Mon–Fri 1–2 daily, plus June to Aug Sat & Sun 1 daily) from Stryn, Loen and Olden to Briksdalen (for Briksdalsbreen). The good news is that in the summer – from June to August – the times of the buses are coordinated so you get three hours at Briksdalsbreen between the time the first bus of the day arrives and the last one leaves.

North from Mundal to Astruptunet and Skei

Heading north from Mundal on Highway 5, it's about 30km to the Kjøsnes junction, where two long and slender lakes intersect. Turn left here, over the bridge, and it's an eleven-kilometre detour west along the southern shore of one of the lakes, Jølstravatnet, to **Astruptunet** (late May to mid-June daily 11am–5pm; mid-June to mid-Aug daily 10am–6pm; mid-Aug to mid-Sept Thurs, Sat & Sun 11am–5pm; 50kr; Ⓦwww.astruptunet.com), the one-time farmstead home and studio of Nikolai Astrup (1880–1928). On the steep slope above the lake, this huddle of old turf-roofed timber buildings looks pretty much the same as it did during the artist's lifetime, though the old barn has been replaced by a modern gallery, used for temporary exhibitions of modern art. A versatile artist, Astrup's work included paintings, sketches, prints and woodcuts, of which a good selection is on display here. However, the bulk of the collection is his landscape paintings, characteristically romanticized rural scenes in bright colours, with soft, flowing forms. Unlike many of his contemporaries, Astrup eschewed Realism in favour of Neo-Impressionism and, as such, he bridged the gap between his generation of Norwegian painters and the Matisse-inspired artists who followed.

Back on Highway 5, the Kjøsnes junction is just a couple of kilometres short of **SKEI**, where you can either head west for the hundred-kilometre journey to the coast at Florø (see p.267), or turn north for the twenty-kilometre yomp up the valley to the **Byrkjelo crossroads**. From here, it's 40km along Highway 60 to Olden, where you turn off for the Briksdalsbreen (see below), and 7km more to Loen, at the start of the road to the Kjenndalsbreen (see p.252).

Olden and the Briksdalsbreen

Hard by the Nordfjord, the hamlet of **OLDEN** doesn't have much going for it, but it is at the start of the 24km-long byroad south to **BRIKSDAL**, a scattering of mountain chalets that serves as the starting point for the easy 45-minute walk to the **Briksdalsbreen glacier arm**. The path skirts waterfalls and weaves up the river until you finally reach the glacier, surprisingly blue except for streaks of dust and dirt. It's a simple matter to get close to the ice as the only precaution is a flimsy rope barrier with a small warning sign – but do be careful. Alternatively, you can hire a **pony and trap** at the café area at the start of the trail, something that will cost you about 280kr – steep considering that you still have to hike the last bit of the path. Guided glacier walks begin at the café area, too. There are several operators to choose from; Briksdal Breføring (Ⓣ57 87 68 00, Ⓦwww.briksdalsbre.no) are as good as any.

A local **bus** service connects Stryn, Loen and Olden with Briksdal (Mon–Fri 1–2 daily, plus June to Aug Sat & Sun 1 daily); schedules between June and

August mean that passengers get about three hours at Briksdal before the departure of the return service.

Loen and the Kjenndalsbreen

LOEN spreads ribbon-like along the Nordfjord's low-lying, grassy foreshore, with ice-capped mountains breathing down its neck. The village is home to one of Norway's most famous hotels, the outstanding *Alexandra* (ⓣ57 87 50 00, ⓦwww.alexandra.no; ❼, sp/r ❺), whose exterior hardly does it justice. The hotel occupies a large and fairly undistinguished modern block overlooking the fjord, but inside the lodge-like public rooms are splendid – wide, open and extremely well appointed. There's every convenience, including a sauna and solarium, while the bedrooms are spacious, infinitely comfortable and furnished in bright modern style. Breakfasts are banquet-like, but the evening **buffets** (from 7pm; about 400kr) are even better, a wonderful selection that lays fair claim to being the best in the fjords. The *Alexandra* is, of course, fairly pricey, but across the road and right on the water's edge, the *Hotel Loenfjord* (ⓣ57 87 57 00, ⓦwww.loenfjord.no; ❻) is an excellent and less expensive second choice. A happy cross between a motel and a lodge, the *Loenfjord* comprises a long and low modern building in a vernacular version of traditional Norwegian style. The public rooms are expansive, and the evening buffet very good.

Both hotels are located on land reclaimed from the fjord and the handful of dwellings that make up the old village are located about 500m inland. Here, perched on top of a gentle ridge, is **Loen kirk**, a tidy structure dating from 1837. Its interior is unremarkable, though the folksy furnishings and fittings are pretty enough, but the views from outside over the fjord are delightful. Its churchyard also holds a couple of items of interest, namely a stone Celtic Cross that is at least a thousand years old, and a pair of **memorial plinths** to the villagers who were drowned in the disasters of 1905 and 1936. On both occasions, a great hunk of the Ramnefjell mountain fell into lake Lovatnet from the south and the ensuing tidal wave swept dozens of local farmsteads away. The second disaster was particularly tragic as the government had only just persuaded many of the villagers to return home after the first trauma.

From beside the *Hotel Alexandra*, a 21km-long byroad leads south to the **Kjenndalsbreen** arm of the Jostedalsbreen glacier. The road starts by slipping up the river valley past lush meadows, before threading along the northerly shore of **Lovatnet**, a long and thin lake of glacial blue. After 4.4km, the byroad reaches the ferry point for boat cruises along the lake (see box opposite) and then scuttles on to the hamlet of **BØDAL**, whose grassy foreshore marks the sight of the village that bore the brunt of the two tidal waves (see above): today's houses perch cautiously on the ridge well above the water. There are guided glacier walks near Bødal on the **Bødalsbreen** (June to mid-Sept; ⓣ57 87 68 00) and the meeting point is **Bødalseter**, a DNT self-service hut about 5km from Bødal up a bumpy, signposted mountain road and then a ten-minute walk from the car park. From the hut to the glacier, it's another 2.5-kilometre walk; there are no guided glacier walks on the Kjenndalsbreen itself.

Back on the Kjenndalsbreen road, it's a further 3km or so to a toll post (30kr) and a couple of hundred metres more to the **Kjenndalstova café** (May–Sept) at the very end of the Lovatnet – and the spot where the boat docks. Pushing on, it's 5km more to the car park, from where it's an easy and very pleasant fifteen-minute ramble through rocky terrain to the **ice**, whose fissured, blancmange-like blue and white folds tumble down the rock face, with a furious

Loen boat trips to the glacier

From June to August, a small **passenger boat** (1 daily; ⓣ57 87 50 50) weaves a leisurely course from one end of lake **Lovatnet** to the other, a delightful cruise through beguiling scenery. The departure point is the pint-sized **Sande jetty**, 4.4km down the Kjenndalsbreen road from the *Hotel Alexandra* in Loen, and the boat docks beside the *Kjenndalsstova* café, 5km from the Kjenndalsbreen ice face. The excursion costs 170kr, including onward transportation by bus from the café to the car park at the end of the Kjenndalsbreen road and the return journey – again by bus and boat – back to Sande; in total the round-trip takes four hours. The *Hotel Alexandra* (see opposite) issues tickets and takes bookings and will, at a pinch, give you a lift down to Sande if required.

white-green river, fed by plummeting meltwater, flowing underneath. If the weather holds, it's a lovely spot for a picnic.

There are no local **buses** to the Kjenndalsbreen.

Around Loen: Mount Skåla

Loen is also the starting point of a popular five-hour hike east up to the plateau-top of **Mount Skåla** (1848m), from where the fjord and mountain views are fantastic. The path is clearly marked, but you'll have to be in good physical condition and have proper walking gear to undertake the trek: also, check locally for snow and ice conditions at the summit before setting out. The hike back down again takes about three hours, or you can overnight in the circular stone tower at the summit, the **Skålatårnet**, which serves as a self-service DNT hut with twenty beds and a kitchen. Curiously, the tower was built in 1891 at the behest of a local doctor – one Dr Kloumann – as a recuperation centre for tuberculosis sufferers.

Stryn

STRYN, merely 12km around the fjord from Loen, is the biggest town hereabouts, though with a population of just 1200 that's hardly a major boast. For the most part, it's a humdrum modern sprawl straggling beside its long main street, but there is a pleasant pocket of antique **timber houses** huddled round the old bridge, down by the river on the west side of the centre, just to the south of the main drag; take a few moments to have a look.

The **bus station** is beside the river to the west of the town centre on Highway 15/60. From here, it's a 600m walk to the **tourist office**, bang in the centre just off the main street, Tonningsgata (early June & late Aug Mon–Fri 8.30am–6pm & Sat 9.30am–5pm; late June & early Aug Mon–Fri 8.30am–6pm, Sat & Sun 9.30am–5pm; July daily 8.30am–7pm; Sept–May Mon–Fri 8.30am–3.30pm; ⓣ57 87 40 54, ⓦwww.nordfjord.no). Staff issue free town maps, rent mountain bikes, have a wide range of local brochures and sell hiking maps. There's no strong reason to overnight here, but Stryn does possess one excellent **hotel**, the *Visnes*, Prestestegen 1 (ⓣ57 87 10 87, ⓦwww.visnes.no; ❺), an extremely comfortable, family-run place, part of which occupies a handsome – and handsomely restored – old villa with Viking-style dragon finials dating from 1896. The hotel is situated about 2km west of centre on the hilly promontory above the road to Loen (Highway 60). Stryn also has a better-than-average HI **hostel**, *Stryn Vandrerhjem* (ⓣ57 87 11 06, ⓦwww.vandrerhjem.no; June–Aug; dorm beds 200kr, doubles ❷), perched high above the centre at Geilevegen 14. This lodge-style building has self-catering facilities, a laundry and Internet access plus splendid views over Stryn and its surroundings – compensation for the lung-wrenching one-kilometre trek up here. The hostel is signposted from the main drag – north up Bøavegen – on the east side of the centre. Four-star *Stryn Camping* (Ⓣ57 87 11 36, Ⓦwww.stryn-camping.no) is handier, just a couple of hundred metres up Bøavegen; it's well equipped and has tent pitches as well as cabins (❷).

Heading west out of Stryn, highways 15 and 60 share the same stretch of road for 16km before they separate: Highway 60 then spears north to reach, after another 35km, Hellesylt, on the Geirangerfjord (see opposite), whilst Highway 15 continues west to the village of **Nordfjordeid** before travelling along the northern shore of the **Nordfjord** bound for Maløy and **Selje** (see below), just over an hour's drive away.

West from Stryn to the islet of Selja

Travelling west from **NORDFJORDEID**, it's 30km along the bare, bleak and mountainous northern shore of the **Nordfjord** to Highway 61, which leads the final 30km up and over the hills to **SELJE village**, a light scattering of houses straggling along a wide bay. Selje has a long sandy beach, but more importantly is the starting point for two-hour guided tours of the nearby **islet of Selja** (May to mid-June Sun 1 daily; mid-June to late Aug 1–3 daily; 140kr including the boat ride). The islet is the site of several medieval remains, easily the most significant of which are the ruins of **Selja Kloster**, a monastery built in the tenth century by Benedictine monks. It was originally named after the legendary St Sunniva, an Irish princess who refused to marry the pagan selected by her father. Royal blood and loyalty to the Catholic faith were prime considerations for beatification – and Sunniva got her saintly reward, but only after spending the rest of her life hidden away in a cave on this lonely island. The best-preserved part of the monastery is the church tower, but otherwise the dilapidated masonry is rather less impressive than the setting.

For details of the boat times and to make a reservation, contact the **tourist office** in Selje village (April–May & Sept Mon–Fri 8am–3pm; early June & late Aug daily 10am–4pm; late June & early Aug daily 9am–5pm; July daily 9am–7pm; Ⓣ57 85 66 06, Ⓦwww.nordfjord.no). The village has one **hotel**, the *Selje* (Ⓣ57 85 88 80, Ⓦwww.seljehotel.no; ❺), a large, modern lodge right behind the beach, which specializes in health treatments, and comes complete with indoor and outdoor pools, massage facilities and Jacuzzi.

With regard to public transport, Nor-way Bussekspress (Ⓦwww.nor-way.no) operates the **Nordfjordekspressen**, which links Stryn with Nordfjordeid and the fishing port of Måløy, at the west end of the Nordfjord, three times daily; the journey from Stryn to Måløy takes two hours. From Måløy, there's a **Hurtigbåt passenger express boat** service on to Selje (Mon–Fri 1 daily; 25min). **Driving** from Selje, you can press on north to Ålesund (see p.264), 120km away, via highways 618, 620 and 61. This involves two **car ferry** crossings, one from **Koparneset to Årvik** (every 30min to 1hr; 15min; passengers 20kr, car & driver 49kr), the other from **Hareid to Sulesund** ferry (every 30min; 25min; passengers 25kr, car & driver 71kr). On the way, you'll pass near to the bird island of Runde (see p.267).

North of Stryn to Grodås and Hellesylt

From Stryn, it's about 20km on Highway 60 to the town of **GRODÅS**, which curves round the eastern tip of **Hornindalsvaten**, at 514m Europe's deepest and Norway's clearest lake. A straggly little place, it's distinguished mainly by the **Anders Svor Museum** (mid-June to mid-Aug daily 11am–6pm; mid-May to mid-June & mid-Aug to late Sept Thurs, Sat & Sun noon–3pm; 35kr; ⓣ57 87 97 76), which occupies a comely Neoclassical structure built beside the lake in 1953. Hardly a household name today, Svor (1864–1929) was a native of Grodås who established something of an international reputation as a sculptor of those highly stylized, romantic figures that were much admired by the European bourgeoisie in the late nineteenth and early twentieth centuries. Some of the more clichéd pieces on display here, such as *Bøn* (Prayer), *Sorg* (Grief) and *Lita jente* (A Small Girl), are typical of his work, though busts of his family and friends, in particular those of his wife, Brit, and his mother, reveal much more originality and talent. Svor's career is typical of his generation, too: like other Norwegian artists, he was keen to escape the backwoods, moving to Kristiania (Oslo) in 1881 and four years later to Copenhagen, the start of an extended exile that only ended after Norway won independence in 1905.

There's no strong reason to overnight in Grodås, but the town does have a pleasant **hotel**, the *Best Western Raftevolds* (ⓣ57 87 96 05, ⓦwww.raftevold.no; ❺), a mostly modern complex that spreads out along the lakeshore. Otherwise, Highway 60 continues beyond Grodås, clipping up the valley and over the hills to reach, after 25km, the turning for the Norangsdal valley (see p.257) and shortly afterwards **Hellesylt**, on the Geirangerfjord (see below).

The Geirangerfjord and Norangsdal

The **Geirangerfjord** is one of the region's smallest fjords, but also one of its most breathtaking. A convoluted branch of the Storfjord, the Geirangerfjord cuts deep inland and is marked by impressive waterfalls, with a village at either end of its snake-like profile – **Hellesylt** in the west and **Geiranger** in the east. Of the two, Geiranger has the smarter hotels as well as the tourist crowds, Hellesylt is smaller and quieter with the added bonus of its proximity to the magnificent **Norangsdal valley**, where the hamlet of **Øye** boasts one of the region's most enjoyable hotels.

You can reach Geiranger in dramatic style from both north and south along the rip-roaring, nerve-jangling

△ Geirangerfjord

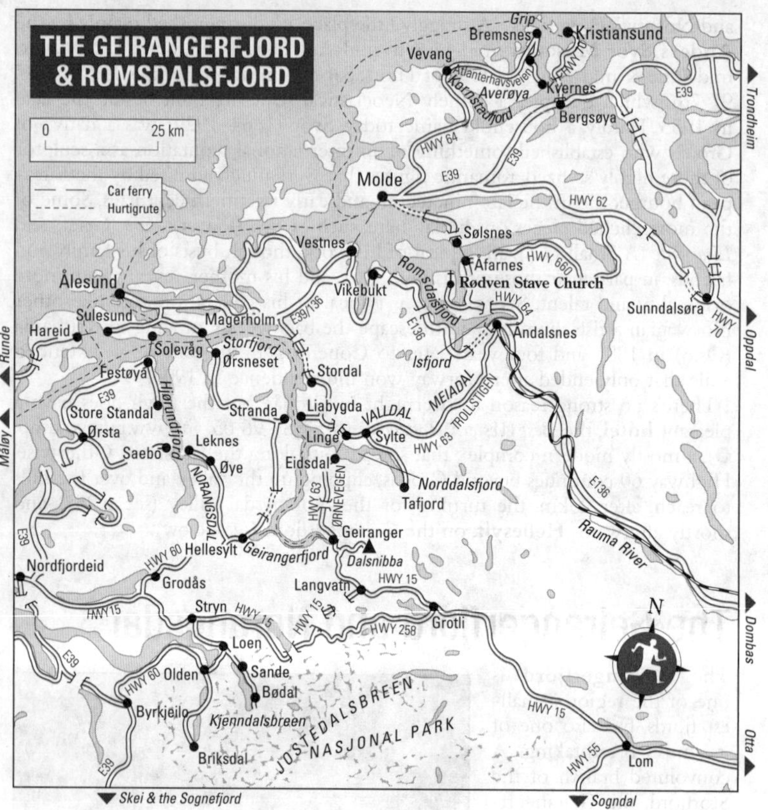

Highway 63 – the aptly named **Ørnevegen** ("Eagle's Highway"). The approach to Hellesylt along Highway 60 is comparatively demure, though taken as a whole this highway is an especially appealing route between the Nordfjord and Ålesund. In addition, **car ferries** (May–Sept 4–8 daily; 1hr; passengers 98kr one-way, car & driver 200kr) run between Hellesylt and Geiranger. This is one of the most celebrated trips in the entire region, the S-shaped waters about 300m deep and fed by a series of plunging waterfalls up to 250m in height. The falls are all named, and the multilingual commentary aboard the ferry does its best to ensure that you become familiar with every stream and rivulet. More interesting are the scattered ruins of abandoned farms, built along the fjord's sixteen-kilometre length by fanatically optimistic settlers during the eighteenth and nineteenth centuries. The cliffs backing the fjord are almost uniformly sheer, making farming of any description a short-lived and back-breaking occupation – and not much fun for the children either: when they went out to play, they were roped to the nearest boulder to stop them dropping off.

Long-distance **Nor-Way Bussekspress buses** travelling west along Highway 15 link Otta (see p.176) and Lom (see p.247) with Stryn (see p.253) via Grotli and Langvatn, at one of which – depending on the service – you change for the **local bus** north to Geiranger, though note that this onward, connecting service only operates from mid-June to August. This same local bus pushes on from

Geiranger to Åndalsnes (see p.262). Hellesylt is on the main Bergen–Ålesund bus route with **Nor-Way Bussekspress buses** linking, amongst many other places, Skei, Olden, Loen, Stryn, Grodås and Hellesylt; there are at least a couple of services daily. Finally, there's a limited **local bus** service from Hellesylt down along the Norangsdal valley to Øye and Leknes (late June to late Aug Mon–Fri 1 daily); it leaves at lunchtimes, whereas the bus from Leknes leaves mid-morning.

Hellesylt

An important and well-protected trading station since prehistoric times, **HELLESYLT** is now little more than a stopoff on tourist itineraries, with most visitors staying just long enough to catch the ferry down the fjord to Geiranger (see p.258). For daytime entertainment, there is a tiny **beach** beyond the mini-marina near the ferry quay, the prelude to some very cold swimming, or you could splash about (as many do) in the waterfall in the village centre, but by nightfall, when the day-trippers have departed, Hellesylt is quiet and peaceful.

The **tourist office** (May & Sept Sat & Sun 11am–7pm; June–Aug daily 11am–7pm; ⓣ70 26 38 80, ⓦwww.hellesylt.no) is a five-minute walk from the jetty in a modern building that doubles as an **art gallery** (same times; 50kr). On display is a set of kitsch-meets-Baroque woodcarvings illustrating Ibsen's *Peer Gynt* by a certain Oddvin Parr from Ålesund. It's all rather strange, but good fun all the same. Hellesylt has one **hotel**, the *Grand* (ⓣ70 26 51 00, ⓦwww.grandhotel-hellesylt.no; May–Sept; ❹), whose fancy wooden scrollwork and high-pitched gables have been a local landmark since 1871. However, the interior has been patchily restored and guests are put up in the modern annexe next door. The main competitor is the HI **hostel** (ⓣ70 26 51 28, ⓦwww.vandrerhjem.no; June–Aug), pleasantly positioned on the hillside above the village beside Highway 60 – and a steep 350-metre walk up the signed footpath from the jetty. They have cabins (❷) as well as both double rooms (❶) and dorm beds (125kr); facilities include self-catering and a bike store. Rowing boats can be rented at the *Grand*, which also sells fishing licences and rents out fishing equipment.

The Norangsdal valley and Øye

A century ago, pony and trap took cruise-ship tourists from Hellesylt down through the majestic **Norangsdal valley** to what was then the remote hamlet of **ØYE**, a distance of 24km. By car, it's a simple journey today, but the scene appears not to have changed at all: steep, snow-tipped peaks rise up on either side of a wide, boulder-strewn and scree-slashed valley, dented by a thousand rock falls. Near the top of the valley, the road, 8km of which is gravel, slips through mountain pastures, where local women once spent every summer with their cows. The women slept in spartan timber cabins and today roadside **plaques** at a couple of surviving cabins flesh out the details of life on these mountain pastures. Further along, the road runs besides lake **Lyngstøylvatnet**, which was created when a large rock slide dammed the valley's stream in 1908; the lake covers the remains of a group of shacks and the water is so clear that you can still make out their outlines. Pushing on, the road soon dips down into Øye, at the eastern tip of the Norangsfjord. The village's pride and joy is the splendid *Hotel Union* (ⓣ70 06 21 00, ⓦwww.unionoye.no; April–Oct; ❼), whose handsome, high-gabled exterior of 1891 was designed to appeal to touring gentry. The hotel's interior is crammed with period antiques and bygones seemingly hunted down from every corner of the globe. Each of the 27 bedrooms is individually decorated in elaborate style and most celebrate the famous people who have stayed here, like King Haakon VII and Kaiser Wilhelm II, not to mention the Danish author Karen "*Out Of Africa*" Blixen: enthusiasts might be pleased to see a pair of her lover's boots. It's a great place to spend the night – though you do have to turn a blind eye to the occasional period excesses, like the four-posters – and the food is first-rate, too. Telephones are banned, which is inducement enough to sit on the terrace and watch the weather fronts sweeping in off the glassy green **Norangsfjord**, or have a day's fishing – the hotel sells licences and dispenses advice.

No ferries dock at Øye, arriving and departing instead from **LEKNES**, just 8km away to the west. This minuscule port occupies a magnificent location at the point where the Norangsfjord meets the **Hjørundfjord**, whose blue-black waters stretch away to the north hemmed in by jagged, pyramid-shaped peaks. Only 40km long, the Hjørundfjord is one of the most visually impressive fjords in the whole of the country, a stirringly melancholic place of almost intimidating beauty. Perhaps appropriately, it takes its name from the terrible times when the Black Death swept Norway, leaving the fjord with just one inhabitant, a woman called **Hjørund**, who wandered its peaks crying at the heavens. The best way to see more of the fjord is to leave your car at Leknes and take a **round trip** on the ferry (1–3 daily) that shuttles along the shores of the Hjørundfjord, visiting several of its tiny settlements; the whole trip takes one hour and forty five minutes and costs passengers about 60kr. It's also possible to use the ferry from Leknes to go straight to the main coastal highway, the **E39**, which runs from Bergen to Ålesund. There are two possibilities: take the ferry from Leknes to **Saebo** (every 1–2hr; 15min; passengers 21kr, driver & car 53kr) and then drive 25km west to Ørsta on the E39; or catch the boat to **Store Standal** (1–3 daily; 55min; passengers 31kr, driver & car 90kr), from where it's 14km north to the **Festøya–Solevåg ferry** (every 30min; 20min; passengers 23kr, driver & car 58kr) on the E39. If you're heading north to Ålesund, the second option is a good short cut.

Geiranger

Any approach to **GEIRANGER** is spectacular. Arriving by ferry slowly reveals the village tucked away in a hollow at the eastern end of the fjord, while approaching from the north by road involves thundering along a fearsome set of switchbacks on the **Ørnevegen** (Highway 63) for a first view of the village and the fjord glinting in the distance. Similarly, the road in from Highway 15 to the south begins innocuously enough, but soon you're squirming down the zigzags to arrive in Geiranger from behind. It's a beautiful setting, one of the most magnificent in western Norway, the only fly in the ointment being the excessive number of tourists at the peak of the season. That said, the congestion is limited to the centre of the village and it's easy enough to slip away to appreciate the true character of the fjord, hemmed in by sheer rock walls interspersed with hairline waterfalls, with tiny-looking ferries and cruise ships bobbing about on its blue-green waters.

The **cruise ships** are a constant feature of the Geirangerfjord, sailing here from every part of northern Europe. The first one arrived in Geiranger in 1869, but this was packed with Quakers bearing tracts – much to the surprise of the locals, who thought they were Christians already. The Quakers may not have had much luck converting the locals, but they were certainly taken with the beauty of the Geirangerfjord and spread the word on their return home: within twenty years the village was receiving a regular supply of visitors. Seizing their chance, local farmers mortgaged, sold and borrowed anything they could to buy ponies and traps, and by the end of the century tourists were being carted up from the jetty to the mountains by the score. In 1919, the horse was usurped when a group of farmer-cum-trap owners clubbed together to import cars, which they kitted out with a municipal livery – the region's first taxi service. The present owner of the *Union Hotel* (see below) has restored a dozen or so of these **classic cars**, including a 1922 Hudson, a 1932 Studebaker and a 1931 Nash, and garaged them at the hotel: they can be admired free most afternoons – ask at the hotel reception.

Geiranger's other man-made attraction is the **Norsk Fjordsenter** (daily: mid-June to mid-Aug 10am–7pm, May to mid-June & mid-Aug to Sept 10am–5pm; 75kr; Ⓦwww.fjordsenter.info), just across from the *Union Hotel* (see below). The centre follows the usual pattern of purpose-built museums, with separate sections exploring different aspects of the region's history from communications and transportation through to fjord farms and the evolution of tourism. Perhaps the most interesting display examines the problem of fjordland avalanches – whenever there's a major rock fall into a fjord, the resulting tidal wave threatens disaster.

The Norsk Fjordsenter is, however, small beer when compared with the scenery. A network of **hiking trails** lattices the mountains that crimp and crowd Geiranger: some make their way to crashing waterfalls, yet others visit abandoned mountain farmsteads or venture up to vantage points where the views over the fjord are exhilarating if not downright scary. One popular excursion, to the mountain farm of **Skageflå**, involves both a boat ride – on one of the Geiranger Fjordservice's sightseeing boats (mid-May to mid-Sept 1–4 daily; 100kr; Ⓣ70 26 30 07) – and a stiff hour-long hike up from the fjord to the farm, followed by a three-hour trek back to Geiranger. There's also the short but precarious trail to the **Flydalsjuvet**, an overhanging rock high above the Geirangerfjord that features in a thousand leaflets. To get there, drive south up from the Geiranger jetty and watch for the sign after about 5km; the car park offers extravagant views, but the Flydalsjuvet is about 200m away, out at the end of a slippery and somewhat indistinct track.

Practicalities

Buses to Geiranger stop a stone's throw from the waterfront and a couple of hundred metres from the **ferry terminal**. The latter is used by both the ferry from Hellesylt (see p.257) and the **Hurtigrute coastal boat**, which detours from – and returns to – Ålesund on its northbound route between the middle of April and the middle of September only; it leaves Geiranger at 1.30pm. The nearby **tourist office** (mid-June to mid-Aug daily 9am–7pm; mid-May to mid-June & mid-Aug to mid-Sept 9am–5pm; Ⓣ70 26 30 99, Ⓦwww.geiranger.no) is also on the waterfront, beside the sightseeing boat dock. Staff issue bus and ferry timetables, sell hiking maps and supply free village maps, which usefully outline local hiking routes. They also promote expensive boat tours of the fjord, though the car ferry from Hellesylt is perfectly adequate.

There are several **hotels** to choose from, but advance reservations are strongly advised in July and August. Cream of the crop is the large and lavish *Union* (Ⓣ70 26 83 00, Ⓦwww.union-hotel.no; ❼, sp/r ❺; March to mid-Dec), high up the hillside but just 300m up the road from the jetty. There's been an hotel here since 1891, and although the present building, with its retro flourishes, is hardly startling, the public rooms are spacious and eminently comfortable, and there's a sauna and both indoor and outdoor pools. In addition, the bedrooms are pleasantly furnished in modern style and the best have fjord-view balconies; those on floor four are the pick. In addition, the *Union* does a first-rate buffet dinner at around 350kr – easily the best **food** around. Another good hotel option is the ultramodern timber-built *Grande Fjordhotell* (Ⓣ70 26 94 90, Ⓦwww.grandefjordhotel.com; ❹; May–Oct), which has a pleasant fjord-side location about 2km north of the centre on the road to Eidsdal. They also operate the adjacent *Geirangerfjorden Feriesenter* (Ⓣ95 10 75 27, Ⓦwww.geirangerfjorden.net; May–Sept), which has **cabins** (from ❷) and a **campsite**, which is itself next door to the very similar *Grande Hytteutleige og Camping* (Ⓣ70 26 30 68, Ⓦwww.grande-hytteutleige.no; May–Sept). The main campsite, *Geiranger Camping* (Ⓣ70 26 31 20; late May to early Sept), sprawls along the fjordside fields a couple of hundred metres to the east of the tourist office. In summer it's jam-packed with caravans, cars and motorbikes – not much fun at all.

From mid-June to August, local **buses** run north into Geiranger from Langvatn and/or Grotli on Highway 15 – it depends on the service. There are two buses daily, the one from Grotli and Langvatn going straight into Geiranger (1hr), the other, from Langvatn only, making a dramatic, one-hour detour up a rough mountain toll-road to the **Dalsnibba viewpoint**, overlooking the Geirangerfjord at 1476m. After Geiranger, both these local buses push on north bound for Åndalsnes (see p.262) via the Trollstigen (see opposite), a journey that takes three or four hours. Long-distance buses along Highway 15 connect with these local services, but check connections before you set out; Åndalsnes can also be reached by a number of other routes, including trains from Oslo.

North to Åndalsnes via the Trollstigen

Promoted as the "Golden Route", the eighty-kilometre journey **from Geiranger to Åndalsnes** along Highway 63 is famous for its mountain scenery – no wonder. Even by Norwegian standards, the route is of outstanding beauty, the road bobbing past a whole army of austere peaks whose cold severity is daunting. The journey also incorporates a ferry ride across the Norddalsfjord, a shaggy arm of the Storfjord, and can include a couple of brief but enjoyable detours – one west along the Norddalsfjord to **Stordal**, home to an especially fine church, the other east to the intriguing village of **Tafjord**. Yet, the most memorable section is undoubtedly the **Trollstigen**, a mountain road that cuts an improbable course between the Valldal valley and **Åndalsnes**, which is itself an ideal base for further fjordland explorations and has a couple of smashing places to stay. Åndalsnes is also the northern terminus of the dramatic **Rauma train line** (see p.182) from Dombås to the east.

Twice-daily from mid-June to August, a **local bus** travels the length of the Golden Route, taking the sweat out of driving round its hairpins and hairy-scary corners; the trip takes a little over three hours and includes one ferry ride. Drivers should note that the higher parts of the road are generally closed from early October to mid-May – earlier/later if the snows have been particularly heavy.

Over the Ørnevegen to Linge – and Stordal

Heading north from Geiranger, the first part of the Golden Route is the 22-kilometre, knuckle-whitening jaunt up and over the **Ørnevegen** (Highway 63) to **Eidsdal** on the Norddalsfjord. From here, a **car ferry** (every 20–45min;

10min; passengers 20kr, car & driver 50kr) shuttles over to the **Linge jetty**, from where there's a choice of routes: travel east for the Trollstigen and Tafjord (see below), or head west for the 21-kilometre detour along Highway 650 to **STORDAL**, a workaday furniture-making town in a pleasant valley setting. Stordal may not fire the soul, but it is on the way to Ålesund (see p.264) and it does possess the remarkable **Rosekyrkja** (Rose Church; late June to mid-Aug daily 11am–4pm; 30kr), standing right beside the main road. Dating from the 1780s, the church has a modest exterior, with oodles of whitewashed clapboard, but the interior is awash with floral decoration, swirling round the pillars, across the ceiling and down the walls. There's an intensity of religious feeling here that clearly demonstrates the importance of Christianity to Norway's country folk, an effect amplified by a whole series of naive, almost abstract paintings with biblical connotations.

Sylte and Tafjord

Back at the Linge jetty, it's just 3km east to **SYLTE**, a shadowy, half-hearted village that straggles along the fjord at the foot of the **Valldal valley** at the start of the Trollstigen (see below). Sylte is also where a byroad branches off Highway 63 to follow the fjord round to the remote, back-of-beyond village of **TAFJORD**, just 14km away to the east. Ignore the ugly defunct power station at the entrance to the village, but keep going over the river to the pint-sized **harbour**, notable only for its complete lack of old buildings: they were swept away in 1934, when a great hunk of mountain dropped into the Norddalsfjord, creating a sixteen-metre tidal wave that smashed into the place, killing 23 locals in the process. Safe just 400m up the slope from the harbour, the upper part of Tafjord did survive and, unlike most of its neighbours, seems to have dodged postwar development almost completely. As a result, its string of old buildings, with their thatched roofs, cairn-like chimneys and clapboard walls, demonstrates what these fjord villages looked like as late as the 1950s – and makes for a fascinating hour or so's wander.

A local **bus** makes the twenty-minute journey between Sylte and Tafjord once or twice daily on weekdays.

Over the Trollstigen

The alarming heights of the **Trollstigen** ("Troll's Ladder"), a trans-mountain route between Valldal and Åndalsnes, are equally compelling in either direction. The road negotiates the mountains by means of eleven hairpins with a maximum gradient of 1:12, but it's still a pretty straightforward drive until, that is, you meet a tour bus coming the other way – followed by a bit of nervous backing up and repositioning. Drivers (and cyclists) should also be particularly careful in wet weather.

From Sylte, the southern end of the Trollstigen starts gently enough with the road rambling up the **Valldal valley**, passing dozens of fresh strawberry stalls in June and July – many Norwegians reckon these are the best strawberries in the country, some say the world. Thereafter, the road swings north, building up a head of steam as it bowls up the **Meiadal valley** bound for the barren mountains beyond. It's here that the road starts to climb in earnest, clambering up towards the bleak and icy plateau-pass marking its high point. At the top, there are the inevitable cafés and souvenir shops, but it's all pretty low-key and a fast-flowing river muffles every untoward sound as it rushes off the plateau to barrel down the mountain below. A five-minute walk leads over to the **Utsikten** (viewing point), from where there's a magnificent panorama over the surrounding mountains and valleys. Clearly visible to the west are some of the region's most famous mountains with Bispen and Kongen (the "Bishop" and the "King") being the nearest two, at 1462m and 1614m respectively. From here also, the sheer audacity of the road becomes apparent, zigzagging across the face of the mountain and somehow managing to wriggle round the tumultuous, 180-metre **Stigfossen falls**. Furthermore, the plateau-pass is one place you can pick up the **Kløvstien**, the original drovers' track over the mountains – abandoned when the road was completed in 1936. It is not, however, an easy route to follow and parts are very steep with chains to assist. Consequently, most hikers prefer to undertake more manageable outings west to nearby peaks and mountain lakes. By contrast, the mountains to the east are part of the **Trollveggen** mountain wall and remain the preserve of climbers. As usual, prospective hikers should come properly equipped and watch for sudden weather changes.

Beyond the hairpins on the northern part of the Trollstigen, the road resumes its easy ramblings, scuttling along the **Isterdal** to meet the **E136** just 6km from Åndalsnes.

Åndalsnes

ÅNDALSNES, at the end of the splendid Rauma train line from Dombås (see p.182), is for many travellers, their first – and sometimes only – contact with the fjord country, a distinction it suits well enough. Damaged during World War II, the town centre may be modern and mundane, but it does possess a wonderful setting between lofty peaks and chill waters and, with a population of just 3500, it's small and restfully quiet. Åndalsnes is also an excellent place to start a visit to the fjordland: everything you're likely to need is near at hand, there's some first-rate accommodation, and the town is within easy reach by ferry, bus and/or car of some wonderful scenery, from the stern peaks that bump and hump away inland through to the fretted fjords that stretch towards the open sea. There's also the matter of **Rødven stave church** (late June to mid-Aug daily 11am–4pm, 30kr), just half an hour's drive away – from Åndalsnes, head east round the Isfjord and after 22km take the signed turning which covers the final 10km. In an idyllic setting amid meadows, by a stream and overlooking a slender arm of the Romsdalsfjord, the church dates from around 1300, though its distinctive wooden supports may have been added in 1712 during the first of several subsequent remodellings. Every inch a country church, the place's creaky interior holds boxed pews, a painted pulpit and a large medieval crucifix, but it's the bucolic setting that most catches the eye.

Practicalities

Buses to Åndalsnes all stop outside the **train station**, where you'll also find the **tourist office** (mid-June to mid-Aug Mon–Fri 9am–6pm, Sat & Sun 11am–6pm; mid-Aug to mid-June Mon–Fri 8am–3.30pm; ⓣ71 22 16 22, ⓦwww.visitandalsnes.com). Staff here provide bus and train timetables, issue regional guides and carry a wide range of local information geared to make you use Åndalsnes as a base. Their free *Dagsturer* (day-trips) booklet gives details of all sorts of motoring excursions in which most of their recommendations include a short hike. They also have details of local day-long hikes, fishing trips out on the fjord (300kr) and guided climbs (from 1000kr per day), not to mention fixed-rate sightseeing expeditions with Åndalsnes Taxisentral (ⓣ71 22 15 55), who charge, for example, 500kr for a brief scoot down the Trollstigen, or 450kr for the return trip to Rødven church. This is, however, hardly a bargain when you consider the special deals offered by local car hire firms. Åndal Bil (☎71 22 22 55), for instance, charge around 550kr for a 24-hour car rental. The tourist office has all the latest information on local deals. Local **hiking maps** are sold at *Romsdal Libris* (Mon–Fri 9am–5pm & Sat 9.30am–2pm), a couple of minutes' walk northwest from the tourist office in the centre of town.

The tourist office has a small supply of en-suite **private rooms** which go for 350–450kr per double per night, with self-catering facilities often provided, though most are a good walk from the town centre. Alternatively, Åndalsnes has a delightful HI **hostel** (late May to Aug; ☎71 22 13 82, ⓦwww.vandrerhjem.no; dorm beds 200kr, doubles ❷, both including breakfast), a two-kilometre hike west out of town on the E136. To get there, head up the hill out of the centre onto the E136, which you follow in the direction of Ålesund – not Dombås; cross the river and it's signed on the left-hand side. The hostel has a pleasant rural setting and its simple rooms, set in a group of antique wooden buildings, are extremely popular, making reservations pretty much essential. The buffet-style **breakfast**, with its fresh fish, is one of the best hostellers are likely to get in the whole country, but note that the hostel doesn't do evening meals, though there are self-catering facilities. There is cycle storage, cycle hire and a laundry; reception is closed from 11am to 4pm. The other excellent choice, the *Grand Hotel Bellevue*, Åndalsgata 5 (☎71 22 75 00, ⓦwww.grandhotel.no; ❺, sp/r ❹), occupies a large whitewashed block, with attractive Art Deco touches, on a hillock just up from the train station; it's the second hotel here – its predecessor was bombed to bits in 1940. The rooms on the top floors – four and five – have great views, well worth the extra 100kr or so. Among several local **campsites**, *Åndalsnes Camping og Motell* (☎71 22 16 29, ⓦwww.andalsnescamp.no) has a fine riverside setting about 3km from the town centre – follow the route to the youth hostel but turn first left immediately after the river. It's a well-equipped site with cabins (❷) and it does bicycle, boat and canoe rental.

For **food**, the *Piccolo Mama Rosa* (daily noon–11pm), a couple of minutes' walk from the station in the town centre at Vollan 5, serves filling and inexpensive pastas and pizzas from as little as 90kr per main course. Also recommendable is the evening buffet served at the *Grand Hotel Bellevue* for about 200kr – from 6pm to 9.45pm; go early to catch the best of the spread.

Moving on from Åndalsnes

Travelling on from Åndalsnes, there are regular **Nor-Way Bussekspress buses** (ⓦwww.nor-way.no) west along the E136 to Ålesund (2 daily; 2hr 10min) and northwest along Highway 64 to Molde (2 daily; 1hr 20min). The journey to Molde involves a short **ferry** trip from Åfarnes to Sølsnes (every 30min to 1hr; 15min; passengers 21kr, car & driver 53kr). Both Ålesund and Molde have good bus and ferry connections along the coast south to Bergen and north to Kristiansund and Trondheim; both are also ports of call for the **Hurtigrute coastal boat** (ⓦwww.hurtigruten.com). Heading southwest from Åndalsnes, a **local bus** (mid-June to Aug 2 daily; 3hr; ⓦwww.fjord1.no) negotiates the so-called "Golden Route" (see p.260) over the Trollstigen mountain road to Geiranger.

Incidentally, be careful to distinguish between Kristiansund (see p.269) and the southern coastal town of Kristiansand (see p.147): to save confusion, on timetables and in brochures they are often written as Kristiansund N and Kristiansand S.

Ålesund

On the coast at the end of the E136, some 120km west of Åndalsnes, the fishing and ferry port of **ÅLESUND** is immediately – and distinctively – different from any other Norwegian town. Neither old clapboard houses nor functional concrete and glass is much in evidence, but instead the centre boasts a proud conglomeration of pastel-painted facades, lavishly decorated and topped off by a forest of towers and turrets. There are dragons and human faces, Neoclassical and mock-Gothic facades, decorative flowers and even a pharaoh or two, the whole ensemble set amid the town's several harbours. These architectural eccentricities sprang from disaster: in 1904, a dreadful fire left 10,000 people homeless and the town centre destroyed, but within three years a hectic reconstruction programme saw almost the entire area rebuilt in a bizarre **Art Nouveau** style, which borrowed heavily from the German Jugendstil movement. Many of the Norwegian architects who undertook the work had been trained in Germany, so the Jugendstil influence is hardly surprising, but this was no simple act of plagiarism: the Norwegians added all sorts of whimsical, often folkloric flourishes to the Ålesund stew. The result was – and remains – an especially engaging stylistic hybrid, and Kaiser Wilhelm II, who footed the bill, was mightily pleased.

Art Nouveau aside, Ålesund has a couple of other modest attractions – the **Atlanterhavsparken**, a sort of glorified aquarium, and the old buildings of the open-air **Sunnmøre Museum** – and it also makes a good base from which to day-trip out to the bird cliffs of the island of **Runde**.

Arrival and information

From north to south, Ålesund's town centre is about 700m wide. The **bus station** is situated on the southern waterfront and from beside it **Hurtigbåt**

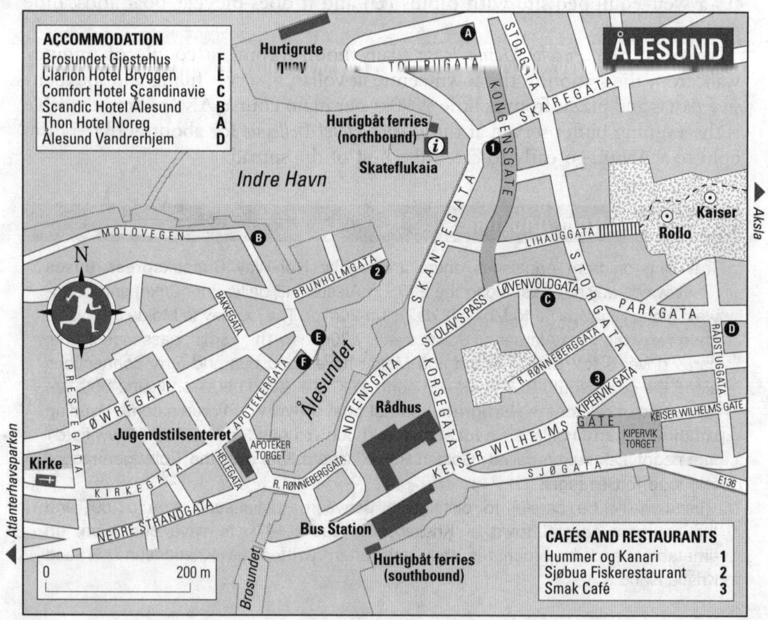

passenger express boats depart for points south on the coast; northbound Hurtigbåt services leave from the Skateflukaia quay on the other side of the town centre, just metres from the quay for the **Hurtigrute coastal boat** (Ⓦwww.hurtigruten.com), whose departure times vary with the seasons. From mid-April to mid-September, the **northbound** Hurtigrute sails daily for Geiranger at 9.30am and for Kristiansund and Trondheim at 6.45pm; from mid-September to mid-April, it does not call at Geiranger, but sails north to Kristiansund and Trondheim at 3pm. **Southbound** services are, however, the same all year, with sailings to Bergen departing at 12.45am.

Ålesund's **tourist office** is also on the Skateflukaia (June–Aug Mon–Fri 8.30am–7pm, Sat 9am–5pm & Sun 11am–5pm; Sept–May Mon–Fri 8.30am–4pm; Ⓣ70 15 76 00, Ⓦwww.visitalesund.com). They operate an accommodation booking service, supply free town maps, issue a free booklet describing Ålesund's architectural attractions and coordinate enjoyable **guided walking tours** of the centre (mid-June to mid-Aug 1 daily; 1hr 30min; 60kr).

Accommodation

One of Ålesund's real pleasures is the quality of its downtown **hotels** and **guesthouses**, but the town is equipped with other, less expensive, options too, most economically an HI **hostel**.

Brosundet Gjestehus Apotekergata 5 Ⓣ70 12 10 00, Ⓦwww.brosundet.no. An excellent guesthouse occupying an attractively converted waterside warehouse right in the centre of town. There's a sauna and self-catering facilities, but breakfast – which is included in the rate – is first-rate. ❹, sp/r ❸

Clarion Hotel Bryggen Apotekergata 1 Ⓣ70 12 64 00, Ⓦwww.choicehotels.no. Smart hotel in a carefully modernized old waterside warehouse, with good facilities and well-appointed rooms. ❼, sp/r ❹

Comfort Hotel Scandinavie Løvenvoldgata 8 Ⓣ70 15 78 00, Ⓦwww.choicehotels.no. Proficient chain hotel inhabiting a grand Art Nouveau edifice – though admittedly some of the modernization has not been very sympathetic. Brisk, uncomplicated bedrooms. ❼, sp/r ❹

Scandic Hotel Ålesund Molovegen 6 Ⓣ21 61 45 00, Ⓦwww.scandic-hotels.com. It may be one of a chain and occupy a modern block, but there's something very appealing about this relaxed and friendly hotel. The rooms are bright and cheerful, each comfortably furnished in contemporary style. Ask for a room on the top floor – they have smashing sea views. ❻, sp/r ❹

Thon Hotel Noreg Kongensgate 27 Ⓣ70 12 29 38, Ⓦwww.thonhotels.no. Suffers by comparison with its more atmospheric rivals, but the upper floors of this modern block do offer sea views and the rooms are perfectly adequate. ❻, sp/r ❹

Ålesund Vandrerhjem Parkgata 14 Ⓣ70 11 58 30, Ⓦwww.vandrerhjem.no. Small and central HI hostel in a pleasant 1920s building at the top of Rådstugata. Has a laundry, self-catering facilities and a café plus Internet access and bike rental. Open May–Aug. Dorm beds 225kr, doubles ❷

The town centre

Pedestrianized **Kongensgate**, Ålesund's main drag, features several of the town's Art Nouveau highlights, as does **Apotekergata**, just over the bridge on the other side of the harbour. The most impressive building here is the old **Apothek** (pharmacy), whose spikey tower and heavy-duty stonework lend it a decidedly neo-baronial appearance – and make it a suitable home for the newly opened **Jugendstil Senteret** (Art Nouveau Centre; June–Aug Mon–Fri 10am–6pm, Sat 10am–5pm & Sun noon–5pm; Sept Mon–Sat 11am–4pm & Sun noon–4pm; Oct–May Tues–Sat 11am–4pm & Sun noon–4pm; 50kr; Ⓦwww.jugendstilsenteret.no). In a series of well-conceived, multimedia displays, the museum examines the fire of 1904 and the rebuilding programme that followed it and there are also temporary exhibitions of Art Nouveau fine art and crafts. The Apotek itself has retained many of its original Art Nouveau fittings, most notably a splendid corkscrew staircase.

Adjoining Apotekergata is Kirkegata, probably Ålesund's most harmonious street, its long line of Art Nouveau houses decorated with playful turrets and towers reminiscent of a Ruritanian film set. Up along this street stands the town's finest building, its **kirke** (church; June–Aug Tues–Sun 10am–2pm; free), which was completed in 1909 to a decidedly Romanesque design, from the hooped windows through to the roughly dressed stone blocks and the clunky tower. Inside, the high altar is flanked by the most wonderful frescoes, a blaze of colour that fair takes the breath away. They were the work of a certain **Enevold Thømt** in the 1920s and are both keenly religious and startlingly original in their amalgamation of Art Nouveau and Arts and Crafts influences. The left-hand wall carries an image of the birth of Christ, the right the Ascension, while the vaulting of the arch above displays a variety of religious symbols – for baptism, communion, and so forth.

Apart from the nautical pleasantries of Ålesund's main harbour, the other obvious objective in the town centre is the park at the top of Lihauggata, which runs up from Kongensgata. It's a surprise to find monkey puzzle and copper beech trees here, as well as a large statue of **Rollo**, a Viking chieftain born and raised in Ålesund, who seized Normandy and became its first duke in 911; he was an ancestor of William the Conqueror. Nearby, there's also a much smaller bust of the town's benefactor, the **Kaiser**, in which – if you're used to images of him as a grizzled old man in a helmet – he looks disarmingly youthful. From the park, several hundred steps lead to the top of the **Aksla hill**, where the view out along the coast and its islands is fabulous.

Ålesund's suburbs – the Atlanterhavsparken and Sunnmøre Museum

Ålesund also possesses one of those prestige tourist attractions so beloved of development boards and local councillors. It's the **Atlanterhavsparken** (Atlantic Sea Park; June–Aug Mon–Fri & Sun 10am–7pm, Sat 10am–4pm; Sept–May daily 11am–4pm; 90kr; Ⓦwww.atlanterhavsparken.no), a large-scale recreation of the Atlantic marine environment that includes several enormous fish tanks; there's also an outside area with easy footpaths and bathing sites. The Sea Park is located on a low-lying headland 3km west of the town centre.

In the opposite direction, about 4km east of the town centre just off the E136, is one of the region's more ambitious heritage museums, the **Sunnmøre Museum**, which occupies an attractive location, spread over wooded hills by the water's edge (late May to late June Mon–Fri 11am–4pm & Sun noon–4pm; late June to late Aug Mon–Sat 11am–5pm & Sun noon–5pm; late Aug to mid-Sept Mon–Fri 11am-4pm & Sun noon–4pm; mid-Sept to late May Mon, Tues & Fri 11am–3pm & Sun noon–4pm; 65kr). Inside, a series of displays explores various aspects of local life from medieval times onwards, whilst moored outside is an assortment of old and replica **boats** typical of vessels used hereabouts from the seventh century onwards. In addition, a hiking trail heads off over the hills to thread its way past fifty-odd antique **timber buildings** moved here from other parts of the Sunnmøre district. The buildings include assorted cowsheds, storehouses, stables and dwellings, as well as a row of eighteenth-century *kyrkjebuer* (church shacks), where local country folk once holed up before attending Sunday service. By law, Norwegians had to go to church, and as this involved many of them in long and arduous journeys, *kyrkjebuer* were built next to parish churches, so the peasantry could rest and change into their Sunday best. The *kyrkjebuer* also played a romantic role: it was here that many a Norwegian caught the eye of their future wife or husband.

Eating and drinking

Ålesund has several first-rate **restaurants**. One of the best is the ✯ *Sjøbua Fiskerestaurant*, Brunholmgata 1 (Mon–Sat 2–11pm; ⓣ70 12 71 00), which serves wonderful seafood in chic surroundings and even has its own lobster tank – something of a rarity in Norway. It's expensive, with main courses hovering around 230kr, but very popular, so reservations are advised. Similarly excellent is ✯ *Hummer og Kanari*, Kongens gate 19 (Mon–Sat 11.30am–1.30am; ⓣ70 12 80 08), where a house speciality is *klippfisk* (salted and dried cod) cooked every which way and costing about 220kr. This restaurant is smart, but not as formal as the *Sjøbua*, and after the kitchen closes down – at about 9.30pm – it turns into one of the most agreeable **bars** in town. Less expensive if rather more mundane food is on offer at the hip *Smak Café*, Kipervikgata 5 (Mon–Sat 10am–1.30am & Sun 11am–1.30am); here lunches cost around 70kr, main courses in the evening about 100kr.

Around Ålesund: birdwatching on Runde

The steep and craggy cliffs on the pocket-sized island of **Runde** are the summer haunt of several hundred thousand **sea birds**. Common species include gannets,

The Hurtigrute coastal boat from Ålesund to Bergen, via Florø

If time is short and you need to fast-track south back to Bergen, the best bet is to take the **Hurtigrute coastal boat**, a thirteen-hour journey. The Hurtigrute goes via the west coast town of Florø, where, if you have some spare time, you might want to break your journey. Alternatively, you could **drive** south along the **E39 coastal highway**, a 380-kilometre journey from Ålesund to Bergen involving five ferry rides. It takes a full day's motoring to complete the trip, and you'll need to pick up ferry timetables from the tourist office at Ålesund before you set out. The route covers some fine coastal scenery, but misses almost everything of any real interest, unless you detour west from Førde, for the seventy-kilometre run along Highway 5 to Florø.

Norway's westernmost town, **FLORØ** has much in common with its west-coast neighbours: it has a blustery island setting, its economy has been boosted by the oil industry, it offers tourists sea-fishing trips and excursions to a whole string of offshore islands, and its mostly modern centre is wrapped around the traditional focus of coastal town life, the harbour. Once an important Viking centre, Florø's early days are recalled on the offshore islet of **Kinn**, where the stone **Kinnakyrkja** (church), with its intriguing carvings and Baroque altar piece, is a much modified Romanesque structure dating from the twelfth century. **Passenger boats** to Kinn leave from Florø harbour once or twice daily from mid-June to mid-August and the journey takes thirty minutes; boat timetables are available at the **tourist office**, by the harbour at Strandgata 30 (mid-June to mid-Aug Mon–Fri 8am–6pm, Sat 10am–4pm & Sun noon–4pm; mid-Aug to mid-June Mon–Fri 9am–3.30pm; ⓣ57 74 75 05; ⓦwww.vestkysten.no). They also have a list of local **accommodation**, with the best option being the waterfront *Quality Hotel Florø*, Hamnegata 7 (ⓣ57 75 75 75, ⓦwww.florahotel.no; ❺, sp/r ❹), a smart chain hotel built in the style of an old warehouse; ask for a room with a sea view. An alternative route back to Bergen from Florø is on the regular **Hurtigbåt passenger express boat**, which leaves from the main town dock (1–2 daily; 3hr 30min; 490kr).

kittiwakes, fulmars, razorbills and guillemots, but the most numerous of all is the **puffin**, whose breeding holes honeycomb the island's higher ground. Most species congregate here between late March and August, though some – like the grey heron and the velvet scoter – are all-year residents. A network of footpaths provides access to a number of birdwatching vantage points, though these invariably involve a fair climb up from the foreshore, or you can opt for a **birdwatching boat trip** from Runde harbour (May–Aug 3 daily; 2hr 30min; 150kr; ⓣ70 08 59 16). Reservations are advised, and note that the boat (which is small) does not sail in inclement weather.

The easiest way to get to Runde is to **drive** the 70km from Ålesund, a journey that involves one ferry ride: the island is itself connected to the mainland by a bridge, but you do have to catch the **car ferry** from Sulesund to Hareid (every 30min; 25min; passengers 25kr, car & driver 71kr). Runde is best visited on a day-trip from Ålesund, but there is **hostel accommodation** at the HI *Runde* Vandrerhjem (ⓣ70 08 59 16, ⓦwww.runde.no; dorm beds 150kr, doubles ❷; May–Aug), on the southeast shore of the island, 300m from the harbour; the hostel is attached to a campsite too.

North to Kristiansund

Ålesund is within easy striking distance of the next major towns up along the coast – **Molde** and **Kristiansund**, at 80km and 150km respectively. Neither is especially riveting, but Molde does put on a first-rate annual jazz festival and Kristiansund boasts a handsome coastal location plus a handful of mildly interesting sights recalling its heyday as a centre of the *klippfisk* (salted, dried cod) industry. The main road from Ålesund to Molde – the **E39** – is a pleasant coastal run culminating in a ferry crossing of the Romsdalsfjord. From Molde, there's a choice of routes to Kristiansund: the scenic **Highway 64**, incorporating the **Atlanterhavsveien**, a short but dramatic stretch of highway that hops from islet to islet on the very edge of the ocean; and the faster but more mundane continuation of the E39.

As regards public transport, **Nor-Way Bussekspress buses** (ⓦwww.nor-way.no) connect Ålesund with Molde and Trondheim (1–2 daily; 2hr/7hr 30min), and en route these buses pass through Bergsøya, where passengers change for Kristiansund, just 25km away (Mon–Sat hourly, Sun 4 daily; 40min; ⓦwww.fjord1.no); be sure to check the Bergsøya connection before you set out. The **Hurtigrute coastal boat** (ⓦwww.hurtigruten.com) also links Ålesund with Molde, Kristiansund and Trondheim, taking three hours to reach Molde, seven to Kristiansund, and thirteen-and-a-half hours to Trondheim.

Molde

From Ålesund, it's about 80km along the E39 to the **Vestnes ferry** (every 30min; 35min; passengers 31kr, car & driver 90kr), which scuttles over the Romsdalsfjord to **MOLDE**, an industrial town that sprawls along the seashore with a ridge of steep, green hills behind. Despite its modern appearance, Molde is one of the region's older towns, but it was blown to smithereens by the Luftwaffe in 1940, an act of destruction watched by King Håkon from these very same hills just weeks before he was forced into exile in England. The new town that grew up in its stead is unremarkable, but it does host the week-long **Molde Jazz Festival**, held annually in the middle of July. Programme details are widely available across the region and tickets can be purchased both online and in person from the Molde ticket office (Ⓣ71 20 31 50, Ⓦwww.moldejazz.no). Naturally enough, the big-name concerts are sold out months in advance and accommodation is impossible to find during the festival, but the authorities do operate a large official campsite, **Jazzcampen**, 3km west of the centre, for the duration. Festival apart, there's no strong reason to overnight here despite the sterling efforts of the *Rica Seilet Hotel*, which occupies a striking, sail-shaped glass tower on the fjord about 800m west of the centre at Gideonvegen 2 (Ⓣ71 11 40 00, Ⓦwww.rica.no; ❼, sp/r ❹).

All of Molde's amenities are within easy reach of each other: the Vestnes-Molde **ferry terminal** is on the east side of the centre, about 500m from the **bus station**, which is itself close to the **tourist office** at Torget 4 (mid-June to Aug Mon–Fri 9am–6pm, Sat 9am–3pm & Sun noon–5pm; Sept to mid-June Mon–Fri 8.30am–3.30pm; Ⓣ71 20 10 01, Ⓦwww.visitmolde.com).

From Molde to Kristiansund

There are two possible routes north from Molde to Kristiansund. The quicker, but less interesting, option is the **E39**, which begins with a fifty-kilometre canter northeast to a massive suspension **bridge**, which spans the straits between the mainland and the islet of **Bergsøya**. Here, **Highway 70** spears north for the 25-kilometre trip to Kristiansund via the five-kilometre Freifjord tunnel (65kr toll), while the E39 continues onto Trondheim, another 170km away to the east (see p.278).

A far more picturesque route, however, is to take **Highway 64**, which forks north off the E39 just to the east of Molde. This highway starts off by tunnelling through the mountains, before rounding the head of the slender Malmefjord. Afterwards, it rattles over the hills, down the valley and along the edge of the **Kornstadfjord** to reach the coast at the start of the **Atlanterhavsveien** (Atlantic Highway), some 50km from Molde. A spirited piece of engineering, the Atlanterhavsveien is a scenic eight-kilometre stretch of road that negotiates the mouth of the Kornstadfjord, manoeuvring from islet to islet by a sequence of bridges and causeways. In calm conditions, it's an attractive run, but in blustery weather it's exhilarating with the wind whistling round the car, the surf roaring and pounding away at the road.

Beyond, Highway 64 ploughs on across the island of **Averøy**, a twenty-kilometre run that ends at the **Bremsnes car ferry** to Kristiansund (every 30min; 20min; passengers 23kr, car & driver 58kr). On Averøy, the **Kvernes stavkirke** (mid-June to mid-Aug daily 10am–5pm; 30kr) merits a brief detour – it's 10km south of Highway 64, along the island's eastern shore. Dating from the thirteenth century, the church was built on what had previously been a pagan ceremonial site, as proved by the discovery here of a Viking phallus stone. Much modified over the centuries, the church is a simple barn-like affair distinguished by its biblical wall paintings, added in the 1630s.

Kristiansund

Despite **KRISTIANSUND**'s attractive coastal setting, straddling three rocky islets and the enormous channel-cum-harbour that they create, the town somehow manages to look quite dull. The Luftwaffe is at least partly to blame as it polished off most of the old town in 1940, and, although Kristiansund dates back to the eighteenth century, precious little remains from prewar days. One minor exception is the handful of antique clapboard houses that string along **Fosnagata**, immediately to the north of the main quay, is otherwise the gridiron of streets that now serve as the town centre, just up the slope to the west of the main quay, is resolutely modern. At the south end of the main quay is the **klippfiskkjerringa statue** of a woman carrying a fish. The statue recalls the days when salted cod was laid out along the seashore to dry, producing the *klippfisk* that was the main source of income in these parts until well into the 1950s. Appropriately, therefore, the town is also home to the **Norsk klippfiskmuseum** (mid-June to mid-Aug Mon–Sat noon–5pm, Sun 1–4pm; 30kr), housed in an old and well-worn warehouse, the **Milnbrygga**, across the harbour to the east of the main quay. The most pleasant way to reach the museum is by a small passenger boat, the **Sundbåt** (Mon–Fri 7am–5pm & Sat 10am–3.30pm; 2 hourly; 15kr single ticket, day-ticket 40kr), which leaves from beside the statue to call at each of the town's three islets. The service was once crucial for getting around Kristiansund, but the islands are now connected by bridge and the boats are, essentially, an exercise in nostalgia. The other noteworthy target is the handful of venerable timber houses that make up the **Gamle Byen** (Old Town), situated on the smallest of the three islets, **Innlandet** – south across the harbour from the main quay. Look out here also for the distinctive **Lossiusgården**, a large and handsome house that belonged to an eighteenth-century merchant; unfortunately, you can't go inside.

Around Kristiansund – Grip

Kristiansund's most popular attraction by a long chalk is **Grip**, a tiny, low-lying islet just 14km offshore. Grip is dotted with brightly painted timber homes, possesses an appealing assortment of antique boathouses, and comes complete with a much-modified medieval church where the islanders once took refuge whenever they were threatened by a storm, as they often were – indeed, when you look at the place, it's amazing anyone ever lived here at all: there's a real touch of claustrophobia here even on a calm day, and when the weather's up the effects can be quite overpowering. There are no permanent residents now – the last ones left in 1964 – but in the summertime fishermen dock in the sliver of a harbour and there are even some basic guesthouse-style **lodgings** (❷); these are bookable via the Kristiansund tourist office (see below) and advance reservations are advised.. In summer, a daily **boat** links Kristiansund with Grip (June to late Aug 1–4 daily; 30min; 170kr return), and again reservations should be made at the tourist office.

Practicalities

Buses to Kristiansund pull in beside the Nordmørskaia quay at the north end of the main **town quay**, which is where the boat for Grip (see above) and the Sundbåt city boat (see above) depart, as does the **Hurtigbåt passenger express boat** service to Trondheim (1–3 daily; 3hr 15min; Ⓦwww.fjord1.no). The **Hurtigrute** coastal boat docks at Holmakaia, a few metres to the east of the bus station. From the town quay, it's a short stroll up Kaibakken to the **tourist office** at Kongens plass 1 (mid-June to mid-Aug Mon–Fri 9am–7pm, Sat 10am–3pm & Sun 11am–4pm; mid-Aug to mid-June Mon–Fri 8.30am–3.30pm; Ⓣ71 58 54 54; Ⓦwww.visitkristiansund.com).

Kristiansund's first choice for **accommodation** is the sprightly *Quality Hotel Grand*, Bernstorrfstredet 1 (Ⓣ71 57 13 00, Ⓦwww.choicehotels.no; ❼, sp/r ❹), whose one hundred or so rooms are comfortable and well appointed; Bernstorrfstredet is just to the south of Kaibakken, the short street linking the south end of the town quay with the main square, Kongens plass. Alternatively, there's the *Rica Hotel Kristiansund*, a smart chain hotel a short walk south from the main town quay at Storgata 41 (Ⓣ71 57 12 00, Ⓦwww.rica.no; ❼, sp/r ❹). For **food**, the *Smia* restaurant, at Fosnagata 30 (Ⓣ71 67 11 70), stands head and shoulders above its competitors. Housed in a converted boat shed metres from the north end of the town quay, it serves superb fish dishes from around 190kr.

Travel details

Trains

Bergen to: Finse (3–4 daily; 2hr 15min); Geilo (3–4 daily; 3hr); Myrdal (3–4 daily; 1hr 50min); Oslo (3–4 daily; 6hr 30min); Voss (3–4 daily; 1hr 10min).
Dombås to: Trondheim (2–3 daily; 2hr 40min); Åndalsnes (3–6 daily; 1hr 20min).
Myrdal to: Flåm (mid-June to mid-Sept 10 daily; mid-Sept to mid-June 4–8 daily; 50min).
Voss to: Bergen (3–4 trains daily; 1hr 10min); Myrdal (3–4 trains daily; 40min); Oslo (3–4 trains daily; 5hr 20min).
Åndalsnes to: Dombås (3–6 daily; 1hr 20min); Oslo (2–3 daily; 5hr 30min).

Principal Nor-Way Bussekspress (®www.nor-way.no) bus services

Balestrand to: Oslo (3 daily; 8hr 15min); Sogndal (3 daily; 1hr 15min).
Bergen to: Grotli (2 daily; 8hr); Flåm (2–5 daily; 3hr); Hellesylt (1–2 daily; 7hr 40min); Loen (3 daily; 6hr 30min); Lom (2 daily; 9hr); Norheimsund (1–3 daily; 1hr 30min); Odda (1–3 daily; 3hr 30min); Oslo (express 3 weekly, 9hr; otherwise 1–4 daily; 11hr); Otta (2 daily; 10hr); Skei (3 daily; 5hr 15min); Sogndal (2–5 daily; 4hr 30min); Stavanger (3–6 daily; 5hr); Stryn (3 daily; 7hr); Trondheim (2 daily; 14hr 30min); Utne (1–3 daily; 2hr 45min); Voss (2–5 daily; 1hr 50min); Ålesund (1–2 daily; 11hr).
Kristiansund to: Oslo (1 daily; 11hr).
Molde to: Trondheim (1–2 daily; 5hr 30min); Ålesund (1–2 daily; 2hr); Åndalsnes (2 daily; 1hr 20min).
Mundal to: Oslo (3 daily; 7hr 50min); Sogndal (3 daily; 30min).
Sogndal to: Balestrand (3 daily; 1hr 15min); Bergen (2–5 daily; 4hr 30min); Mundal (3 daily; 30min); Oslo (3 daily; 7hr); Voss (2–5 daily; 3hr).
Stryn to: Bergen (3 daily; 7hr); Hellesylt (1–2 daily; 1hr); Oslo (2–3 daily; 9hr); Trondheim (2 daily; 7hr 30min).
Voss to: Bergen (2–5 daily; 1hr 50min); Flåm (2–5 daily 1hr); Gudvangen (2–5 daily; 50min); Sogndal (2–5 daily; 3hr).
Ålesund to: Bergen (1–2 daily; 11hr); Hellesylt (1–2 daily; 2hr 30min); Molde (1–2 daily; 2hr); Oslo (2 daily; 10hr); Stryn (1–2 daily; 3hr); Trondheim (1–2 daily; 7hr 30min); Åndalsnes (2 daily; 2hr 10min).
Åndalsnes to: Molde (2 daily; 1hr 20min); Ålesund (2 daily; 2hr 10min).

Principal local bus services

Geiranger to: Åndalsnes (mid-June to Aug 2 daily; 3hr).
Sogndal to: Lom (late June to mid-Sept 1–3 daily; 3hr 20min); Nigardsbreen glacier nodule (late June to Aug 1 daily; 2hr); Otta (late June to mid-Sept 1–3 daily; 4hr); Solvorn (late June to mid-Sept 1–2 daily; 20min); Turtagrø (late June to mid-Sept 1–3 daily; 1hr 50min).
Åndalsnes to: Geiranger (mid-June to Aug 2 daily; 3hr).

Principal car ferries

Balestrand to: Mundal on the Fjærlandsfjord (May to Sept 1–2 daily; 1hr 15min).
Bruravik to: Brimnes (1–2 hourly; 10min).
Dragsvik to: Hella (every 40min to hourly; 15min); Vangsnes (every 40min to hourly; 30min).
Flåm to: Gudvangen (1–4 daily; 2hr).
Fodnes to: Mannheller (every 30min; 10min).
Geiranger to: Hellesylt (May–Sept 4–8 daily; 1hr).
Gudvangen to: Flåm (1–4 daily; 2hr).
Hella to: Dragsvik (every 40min to hourly; 15min); Vangsnes (every 40min to hourly; 30min).
Kvanndal to: Kinsarvik (1 or 2 hourly; 40min); Utne (1 or 2 hourly; 20min).
Hellesylt to: Geiranger (May–Sept 4–8 daily; 1hr).
Utne to: Kinsarvik (1 or 2 hourly; 30min).

Principal Hurtigbåt passenger express boats

Bergen to: Balestrand (1–3 daily; 4hr); Florø (1–2 daily; 3hr 30min); Selje (1–2 daily; 5hr); Sogndal (1–3 daily; 5hr).
Flåm to: Balestrand (1–2 daily; 1hr 30min).
Kristiansund to: Trondheim (1–3 daily; 3hr 30min).
Norheimsund to: Eidfjord (June–Aug 1 daily; 2hr 40min); Kinsarvik (June–Aug 1 daily; 1hr 30min); Lofthus (June–Aug 1 daily; 1hr 10min); Utne (June–Aug 1 daily; 45min).

Hurtigrute coastal boat

Summertime (mid-April to mid-Sept):
Northbound departures: daily from Bergen at 8pm; Florø at 2.15am; Ålesund at 9.30am for Geiranger and 6.45pm for Molde; Geiranger at 1.30pm; Molde at 10pm; Kristiansund at 1.45am; arrives Trondheim at 8.15am.
Southbound departures: daily from Trondheim at 10am; Kristiansund at 5pm; Molde at 9.30pm;

Ålesund at 12.45am; Florø at 8.15am; arrives Bergen, where the service terminates, at 2.30pm.

Wintertime (mid-Sept to mid-April):
Northbound departures: daily from Bergen at 10.30pm; Florø at 4.45am; Ålesund at 3pm; Molde at 6.30pm; Kristiansund at 11pm; arrives Trondheim at 6am.

Southbound departures: daily from Trondheim at 10am; Kristiansund at 5pm; Molde at 9.30pm; Ålesund at 12.45am; Florø at 8.15am; arrives Bergen, where the service terminates, at 2.30pm.

Note that it's only the northbound, summertime Hurtigrute service that detours to Geiranger.

5

Trondheim to the Lofoten islands

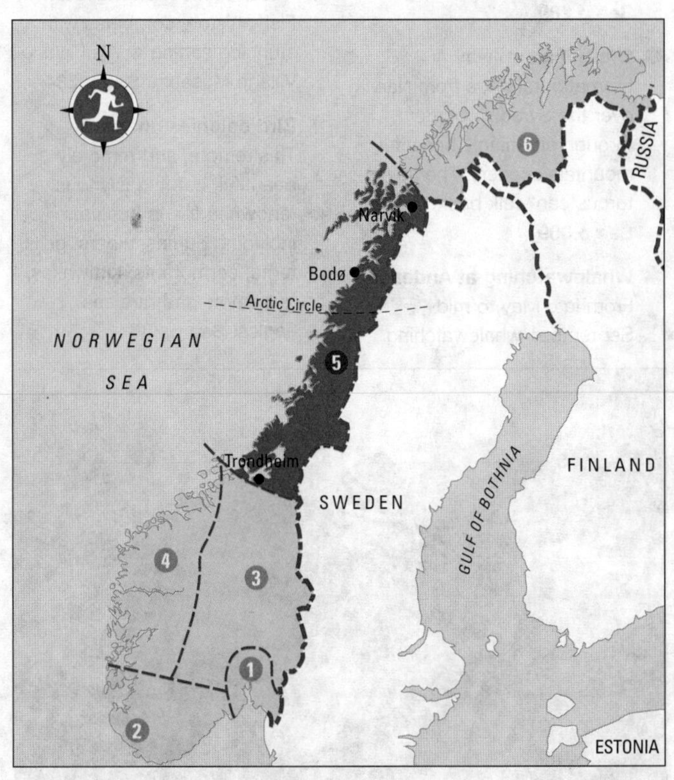

CHAPTER 5 **Highlights**

* **Trondheim Cathedral** Scandinavia's largest medieval building makes a stirring focal point for the city. See p.282

* **Bakklandet** The trendy bars and restaurants of this attractive old district in Trondheim are a great place to go for a lively/raucous night out. See p.289

* **Ofotbanen railway** A dramatic train ride from Narvik over the Swedish border through stunningly beautiful mountain scenery. The adventurous can walk back. See p.309

* **Whalewatching at Andenes** From late May to mid-September, whalewatching safaris from this remote port almost guarantee a sighting. See p.319

* **Henningsvær** One of the Lofoten islands' most picturesque fishing villages, with brightly painted wooden houses framing an attractive harbour. See p.330

* **Norsk Fiskevaersmuseum** Fishy history combines with a stunning setting at Å's Fishing Village Museum. See p.334

* **Bird colonies on Værøy** This remote, and remotely beautiful, Lofoten island is renowned for its birdlife, including puffins, eiders, gulls, terns, cormorants, kittiwakes, guillemots and rare sea eagles. See p.336

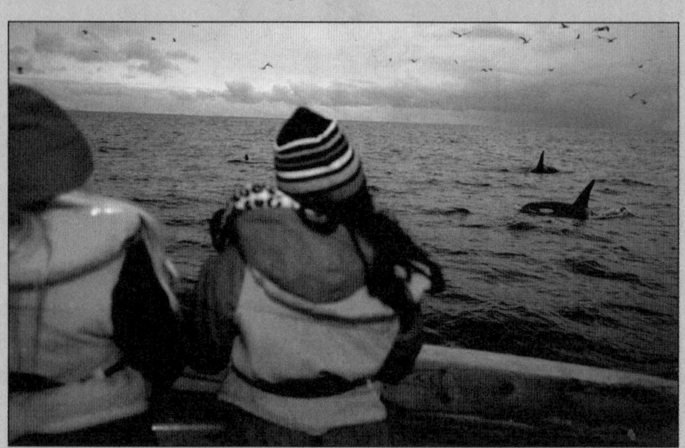

△ Whalewatching off Andenes

5

Trondheim to the Lofoten islands

Marking the transition from the rural south to the blustery north is the 900-kilometre-long stretch of Norway that extends from **Trondheim** to the island-studded coast near Narvik. Easily the biggest town hereabouts is Trondheim, a charming place of character and vitality, which boasts an imposing cathedral – the finest medieval building in the country. Trondheim is also the capital of the **Trøndelag** province, whose sweeping valleys are – by Norwegian standards at least – very fertile and is, to boot, readily accessible by train or bus from Oslo. But travel on one of the express trains that thunder further north from here, and you begin to feel far removed from the capital and the more intimate, forested south. Distances between places grow ever greater, travelling becomes more of a slog, and as Trøndelag gives way to the province of **Nordland** the scenery becomes ever wilder and more forbidding – "Arthurian", thought Evelyn Waugh.

The **E6** thrashes north from Trondheim over the hills and down the dales, but with the exception of the rugged landscape there's not much to detain you until you reach the modest little industrial town of **Mosjøen** and nearby **Mo-i-Rana**, also industrial but attractively sited beside the Ranafjord and partly rejigged to attract passing tourists. Just north of Mo-i-Rana on the E6, you cross the **Arctic Circle** – one of the principal targets for many travellers – at a point where the cruel and barren scenery seems strikingly appropriate. On the Arctic Circle, the midnight sun and 24-hour polar night occur once a year, at the summer and winter solstices respectively; the further north from here you go, the longer the period during which you can experience these two phenomena (see box, p.344).

Beyond the Arctic Circle, the mountains of the interior lead down to a fretted, craggy coastline, and even the towns, the largest of which is the port of **Bodø**, have a feral quality about them. The iron-ore port of **Narvik**, in the far north of Nordland, has perhaps the wildest setting of them all, and was the scene of some of the fiercest fighting between the Allied and Axis forces in World War II. To the west lies the offshore archipelago that makes up the **Vesterålen** and **Lofoten islands**. In the north of the Vesterålen, between **Harstad** and **Andenes**, the coastline of this island chain is mauled by massive fjords, whereas to the south, the Lofoten islands are backboned by a mighty and ravishingly beautiful mountain wall – a highlight of any itinerary. Among a handful of idyllic fishing

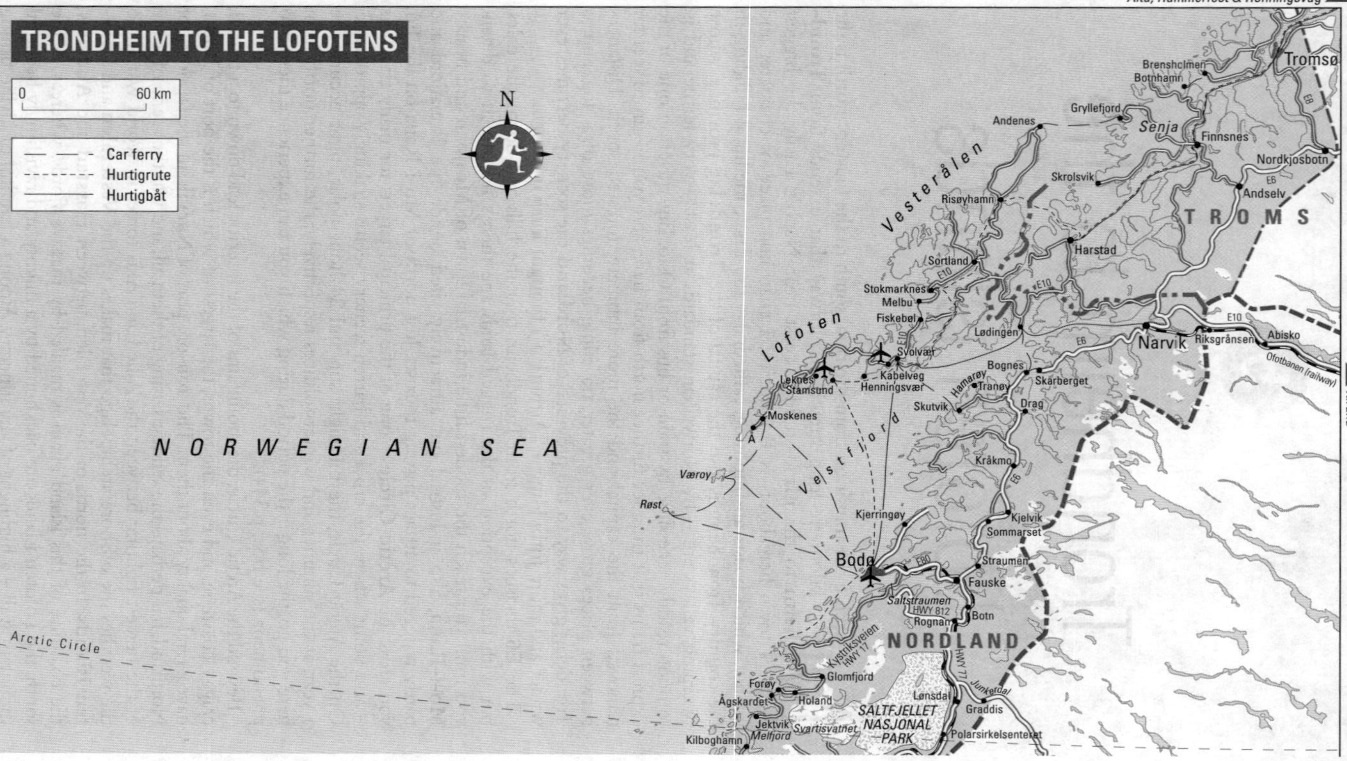
TRONDHEIM TO THE LOFOTENS
0 60 km
Car ferry
Hurtigrute
Hurtigbåt
N
Alta, Hammerfest & Honningsvåg
Kiruna
NORWEGIAN SEA
Arctic Circle
Tromsø
Brensholmen
Botnhamn
Gryllefjord
Senja
Finnsnes
Nordkjosbotn
Andenes
Skrolsvik
Andselv
TROMS
Vesterålen
Risøyhamn
Harstad
Sortland
Stokmarknes
Melbu
Fiskebøl
Lødingen
Narvik
Riksgrånsen
Abisko
Ofotbanen (railway)
Lofoten
Svolvær
Kabelveg
Henningsvær
Leknes
Stamsund
Hamarøy
Tranøy
Bognes
Skarberget
Skutvik
Drag
Moskenes
Å
Vestfjord
Kråkmo
Værøy
Røst
Kjerringøy
Kjelvik
Sommarset
Bodø
Straumen
Fauske
Saltstraumen
HWY 812
Rognan
Botn
NORDLAND
Kystriksveien
HWY 17
HWY 77
Glomfjord
Junkerdal
Lønsdal
Forøy
Ågskardet
Holand
SALTFJELLET NASJONAL PARK
Graddis
Jektvik
Svartisvatnet
Melfjord
Kilboghamn
Polarsirkelsenteret
E6
E8
E10
E80

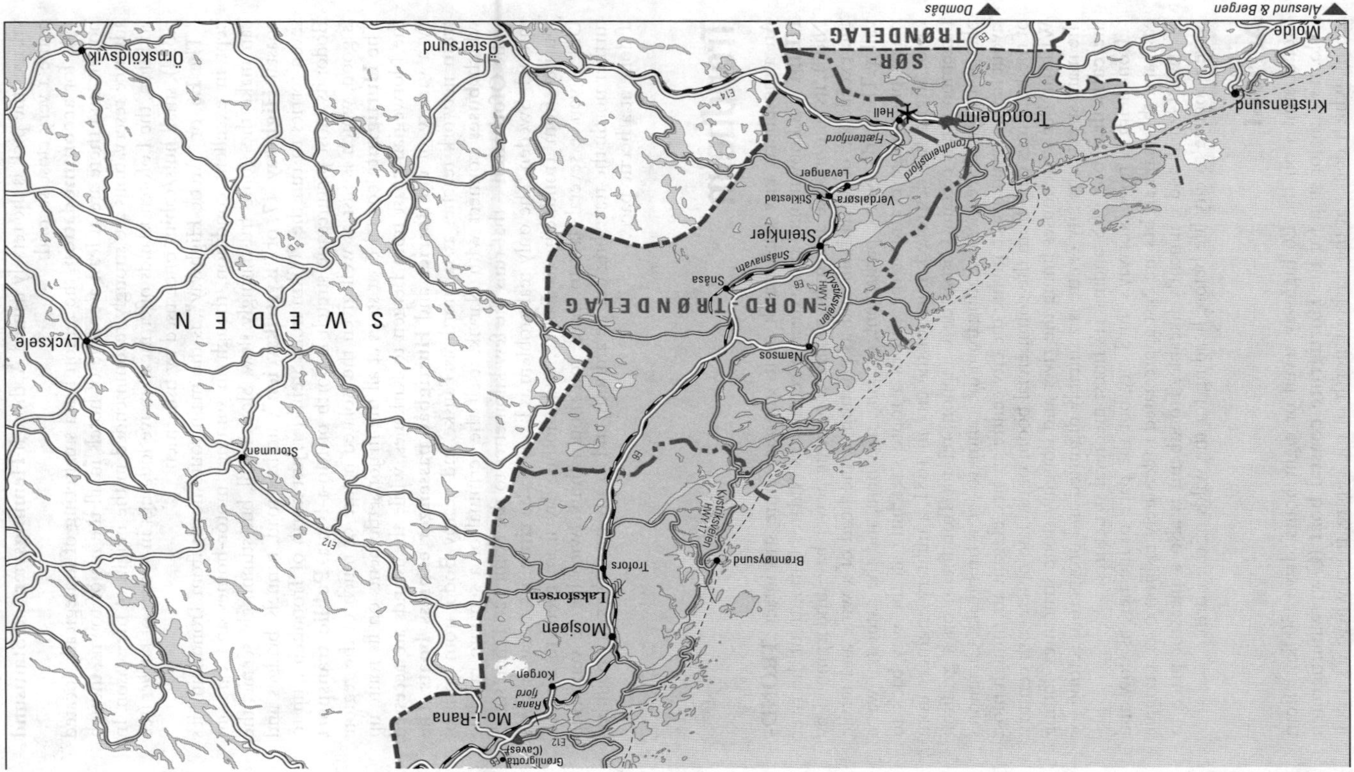

Ålesund & Bergen
Dombås
Molde
Kristiansund
Trondheim
Trondheimsfjord
Hell
Fættenfjord
Levanger
Verdalsøra
Stiklestad
Steinkjer
Snåsavatn
Snåsa
SØR-TRØNDELAG
NORD TRØNDELAG
Krystriksveien HWY 17
Namsos
Brønnøysund
Trofors
Laksforsen
Mosjøen
Korgen
Rana-fjord
Mo-i-Rana
Grønligrotta (Caves)
E6
E12
E14
SWEDEN
Östersund
Örnsköldsvik
Storuman
Lycksele

villages the pick is the tersely named **Å**, though **Henningsvær** and **Stamsund** come a very close second.

As for **accommodation**, the region has a smattering of strategically located hostels, and there are at least a couple of hotels in all the major towns, though advance reservations are strongly recommended in the height of the season. In addition, the Lofoten islands offer inexpensive lodgings in scores of *rorbuer* (see p.324), small huts/cabins once used by fishermen.

The **E6**, or "Arctic Highway", is the main route north from Trondheim: it's kept in excellent condition, though in summer motor-homes and caravans can make the going frustratingly slow. Slower still, but stunningly scenic, the coastal **Highway 17**, or "**Kystriksveien**", utilizes road, tunnels, bridges and seven ferries to run the 700km from Steinkjer, just north of Trondheim, up to Bodø: its most picturesque stretch is north of Mo-i-Rana. **Public transport** is good, which is just as well given the isolated nature of much of the region. The **Hurtigrute** coastal boat stops at all the major settlements on its route up the Norwegian coast from Bergen to Kirkenes, while the islands are accessed by a variety of **car ferries** and **Hurtigbåt passenger express boats**. The **train** network reaches as far north as Fauske and nearby Bodø, from both of which **buses** connect with Narvik, itself the terminal of a separate rail line – the **Ofotbanen** – that runs the few kilometres to the border and then south through Sweden. The only real problem is likely to be **time**: it's a day or two's journey from Trondheim to Fauske, and another day from there to Narvik. Unless you've several days to spare, you should think twice before venturing further north: the travelling can be arduous, and in any case it's pretty pointless if done at a hectic pace.

Trondheim

An atmospheric city with much of its antique centre still intact, **TRONDHEIM** was known until the sixteenth century as Nidaros ("mouth of the river Nid"), its importance as a military and economic power base underpinned by the excellence of its harbour and its position at the head of a wide and fertile valley. The early Norse parliament, or *Ting*, met here, and the cathedral was a major pilgrimage centre at the end of a route stretching all the way back to Oslo. After a fire destroyed much of the city in 1681, a military engineer from Luxembourg, a certain Caspar de Cicignon, rebuilt Trondheim on a gridiron plan, with broad avenues radiating from the centre to act as firebreaks. Cicignon's layout has survived intact, giving the city centre an airy, elegant air, though most of the buildings date from the commercial boom of the late nineteenth century. With timber warehouses lining the river and doughty stone structures dotting the main streets, the city centre is a suitably dignified and prosperous setting for the **cathedral**, one of Scandinavia's finest medieval structures.

Trondheim is now Norway's third city, but the pace of life here is slow and easy, and the main **sights** are best appreciated in leisurely fashion over a couple of days. Genial and eminently likeable, Trondheim is also a pleasant place to wave goodbye to city life before heading for the wilds of the north.

Arrival

Trondheim is on the E6 highway, seven or eight hours' drive (500km) from Oslo. It's a major stop for the **Hurtigrute coastal boat** (Ⓦ www.hurtigruten.com), which docks at the harbour north of the centre, from where it's a dull

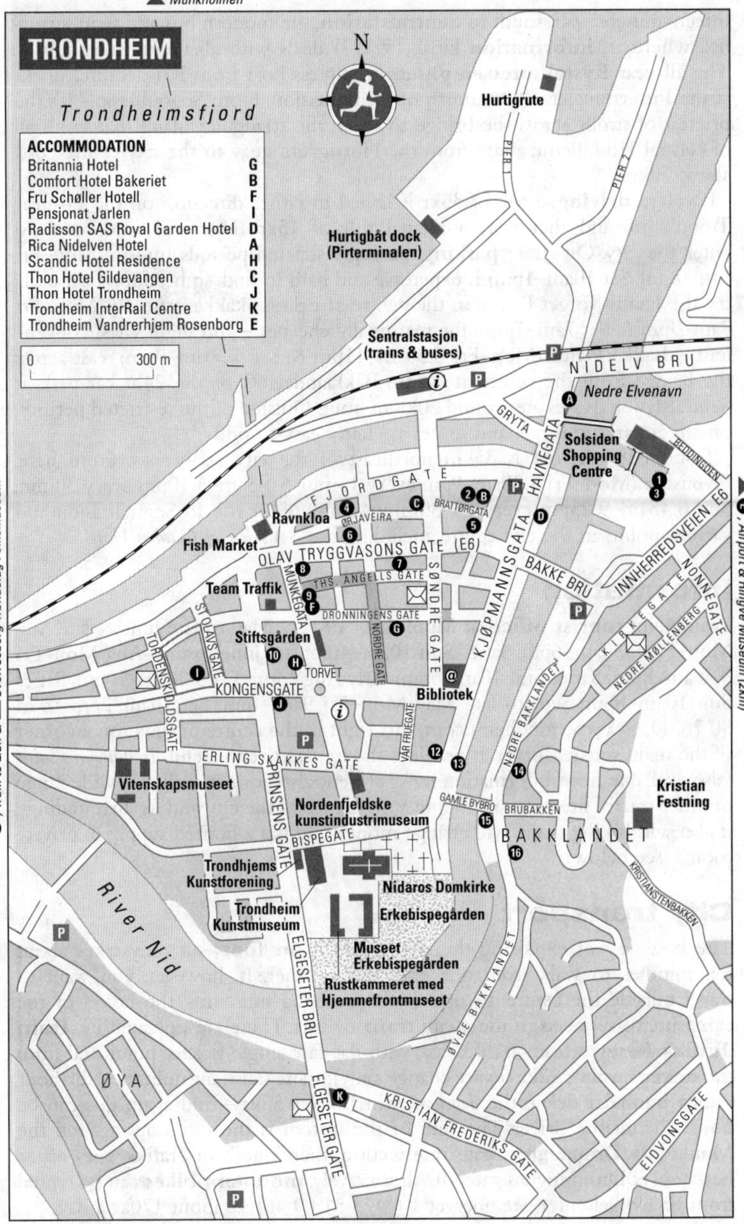

RESTAURANTS, CAFÉS & BARS

Bær & Bar	3	Café 3B	2	Frati	8	Metro	12
Baklandet Skydsstation	16	Chablis	15	Godt Brød	7	Trondheim Mikrobryggeri	10
Blau bær	1	Credo	4	Havfruen Fiskerestaurant	13	Vertshuset Tavern	11
Brukbar	9	Dromedar	14	Jadab	5		
		Erichsen	6				

fifteen-minute walk south to **Sentralstasjon**, the modern bus and train terminal, where an **information** kiosk (ⓣ177) deals with all transport enquiries. The all-year **Kystekspressen** passenger express boat from Kristiansund docks at the Pirterminalen, 300m north of Sentralstasjon. From Sentralstasjon, it's the briefest of strolls across the bridge to reach the triangular island that holds all of central Trondheim; a taxi from the Hurtigrute quay to the city centre costs about 70kr.

If you're **driving**, a toll of 35kr is levied in either direction on the E6 near Trondheim, and there's a municipal toll of 15kr (Mon–Fri 6am–6pm) to enter the city. On-street **parking** during restricted periods (mostly Mon–Fri 8am–8pm, Sat 10am–1pm) is expensive and hard to find, so head for a car park: try the handy Torget P-hus, in the centre at Erling Skakkes gate 16 (Mon–Fri 7am–9pm & Sat 7am–7pm); the marginally cheaper – and slightly less convenient – Bakke P-hus (Mon–Fri 6.30am–11pm & Sat 6.30am–9pm), east across the bridge from the centre at Nedre Bakklandet 60; or the 24hr car park at Sentralstasjon. Rates are around 20kr an hour. Outside of the restricted periods, on-street parking is free and spaces are fairly easy to find.

Trondheim **airport** is 35km northeast of the city at Værnes. From here, Flybussen (Mon–Fri 4.30am–9pm every 15min; Sat 5am–5.10pm every 30min; Sun 6.45am–9.25pm every 15–30min; 45min; 65kr) run to Sentralstasjon and various points in the city centre, including the *SAS Royal Garden Hotel*.

Information

Trondheim **tourist office**, at Munkegata 19 (late May to late June & late Aug Mon–Fri 8.30am–6pm, Sat & Sun 10am–4pm; late June to mid-Aug Mon–Fri 8.30am–8pm, Sat & Sun 10am–6pm; early Aug Mon–Fri 8.30am–10pm, Sat & Sun 10am–8pm; Sept to late May Mon–Fri 9am–4pm, Sat 10am–2pm; ⓣ73 80 76 60, ⓦwww.trondheim.com), sits right in the centre of town on a corner of the main square, Torvet. It provides the free and very useful *Trondheim Guide* (also available from information racks at Sentralstasjon) as well as a wide range of other tourist literature, including a cycle map of the city and its surroundings; it also sells hiking maps, will change money and has a limited supply of private rooms (see below).

City transport

The best way of exploring the city centre is **on foot** – it only takes about ten minutes to walk from one end to the other. If, however, you want to travel outside the centre, to one of the outlying museums, the hostel or the campsite, you'll need to use a city **tram** or **bus**. These are operated by **Team Trafikk** (ⓦwww.team-trafikk.no), with flat-fare single tickets, purchased from the driver, costing 22kr (exact change only); there's also an unlimited 24-hour public transport ticket, the *dagskort*, which costs 55kr – and again this can be bought from the driver. The hub of the system is the bus stops around the Munkegata/Dronningens gate intersection; there's a Team Trafikk sales office here too, at Dronningens gate 40. Alternatively, **mountain bikes** can be rented from Ila Sykkelsenter, Steinberget 1 (ⓣ73 51 09 40), at about 170kr a day.

Accommodation

Accommodation is plentiful in Trondheim, with a choice of private rooms, two hostels, and a selection of reasonably priced hotels and guesthouses (*pensjonater*). What's more, most of the more appealing places are dotted round the city centre, though the private rooms booked via the tourist office are usually out in the suburbs. These **private rooms** are good value, however, at a fixed rate of 400–450kr per double per night (250–340kr single), plus a small booking fee.

Hotels

Britannia Hotel Dronningens gate 5 ⓣ73 80 08 00, ⓦwww.britannia.no. Right in the middle of town, this long-established hotel has a magnificent Art Nouveau breakfast room, complete with a Moorish fountain, Egyptian-style murals and Corinthian columns. The comfortable rooms are heavily discounted in summer. ❼, sp/r ❺

Comfort Hotel Bakeriet Brattørgata 2 ⓣ73 99 10 00, ⓦwww.choicehotels.com. Competent chain hotel in a pleasantly modernized former bakery. Central location. ❼, sp/r ❻

Hotell Fru Schøller Dronningens gate 26 ⓣ73 87 08 00, ⓦwww.scholler.no. Spick-and-span hotel whose 32 rooms have slick modern furnishings and fittings. It's in a central location, above a café. ❹

Radisson SAS Royal Garden Kjøpmannsgata 73 ⓣ73 80 30 00, ⓦwww.radissonsas.com. Stylish modern hotel with sweeping architectural lines and wonderfully comfortable beds. Good summer deals make this more affordable than you might expect. Banquet-like breakfasts too. Highly recommended. ❼, sp/r ❺

Rica Nidelven Hotel Havnegata 1-3 ⓣ73 56 80 00, ⓦwww.rica.no. Shiny, spacious new hotel pushing out over the river, with lots of glass to maximize views. Smooth service and stylish touches, but not perhaps quite as distinctive as it thinks it is. ❼, sp/r ❺

Scandic Hotel Residence Torvet ⓣ21 61 47 00, ⓦwww.scandic-hotels.com. Package-tour favourite, with standard double rooms decorated in modern chain style. More expensive than most of its competitors except in summer, when there are substantial discounts. ❻, sp/r ❹

Thon Hotel Gildevangen Søndre gate 22b ⓣ73 87 01 30, ⓦwww.thonhotels.no. In a sturdy Romanesque Revival stone building, a couple of minutes' walk northeast of Torvet, this chain hotel offers one hundred or so well-appointed rooms kitted out in brisk modern style. ❻, s/r ❹

Thon Hotel Trondheim Kongens gate 15 ⓣ73 88 47 88, ⓦwww.thonhotels.no. Big, popular chain hotel in a plain and chunky modern block, right in the centre. No stars for originality, but everything is in full working order. ❻, sp/r ❹

Guesthouses, hostels and camping

Trondheim InterRail Centre Elgeseter gate 1 ⓣ73 89 95 38. Bargain-basement lodgings in the unusual, big, red and round building – the Studentersamfundet (university student centre) – that stands just over the bridge at the south end of Prinsens gate, a five-minute walk from the cathedral. Offers basic mixed-dorm accommodation at 135kr per person per night and breakfast is served in the pleasant downstairs café. No curfew, and Internet access. Open mid-June to mid-Aug only.

Pensjonat Jarlen Kongens gate 40 ⓣ73 51 32 18, ⓦwww.jarlen.st.no. Basic rooms at bargain prices, and handy for the sights, but otherwise not much fun. ❷

Trondheim Vandrerhjem Rosenborg Weidemannsvei 41 ⓣ73 87 44 50, ⓦwww.vandrerhjem.no. This large, well-equipped HI hostel is mostly parcelled up into four-bed dorm rooms. Looks more like a hospital than somewhere you'd want to stay from the outside, but the interior is pleasant enough – especially the comfortable, newer rooms. It has self-catering facilities, a laundry and a canteen. A twenty-minute, 2km hike east from the centre: cross the Bakke bru onto busy Innherredsveien (the E6) and walk uphill; turn right onto Wessels gate and it's on the left at the fourth crossroads. To save your legs, take any bus up Innherredsveien and ask the driver to let you off as close as possible. Open all year. Dorm beds 215kr, doubles ❷

The city centre

The historic **centre of Trondheim** sits on a small triangle of land bordered by a loop of the River Nid, with the curve of the long and slender Trondheimsfjord beyond. **Torvet** is the main city square, a spacious open area anchored by a statue of Olav Tryggvason, Trondheim's founder, perched on a tall stone pillar like some medieval Nelson. The broad avenues that radiate out from here were once flanked by long rows of wooden buildings, which served all the needs of a small town and administrative centre. Most of these older structures are long gone, replaced for the most part by uninspiring modern buildings, though one notable survivor is the **Stiftsgården**, a fine timber mansion erected in 1774. Nonetheless, this is small beer when compared with the **Nidaros Domkirke** (cathedral), an imposing, largely medieval structure that is the city's architectural high point. The cathedral dominates the southern part of the centre and close by is the much-restored **Erkebispegården** (Archbishop's Palace) and the pick of Trondheim's several museums, the **Nordenfjeldske Kunstindustrimuseum** (Museum of Decorative Arts) and the **Trondheim Kunstmuseum** (City Art Gallery). Near here too, on the far side of the **Gamle Bybro** – the old town bridge – is the clutter of old warehouses and timber dwellings that comprises the prettiest and most fashionable part of town, **Bakklandet**, home to some of its best bars and restaurants.

Nidaros Domkirke

The goal of Trondheim's pilgrims in times past was the colossal **Nidaros Domkirke**, Scandinavia's largest medieval building, which lords it over the south end of Munkegata (Cathedral; May to mid-June & late Aug to mid-Sept Mon–Fri 9am–3pm, Sat 9am–2pm, Sun 1–4pm; mid-June to mid-Aug Mon–Fri 9am–6pm, Sat 9am–2pm, Sun 1–4pm; mid-Sept to April Mon–Fri noon–2.30pm, Sat 11.30am–2pm, Sun 1–3pm; 50kr, also includes the Erkebispegården; Ⓦwww.nidarosdomen.no). Dedicated to Saint Olav (see box opposite), the cathedral, which is still known by the town's earlier name, is the traditional burial place of Norwegian royalty, and has been the scene of every coronation since 1814. Gloriously restored following several fires and the upheavals of the Reformation, it remains the focal point of any visit to the city and is best explored in the early morning, when it's reasonably free of tour groups.

A magnificent blue and green-grey soapstone edifice, the cathedral has a copper-green spire and roof, and a fancy set of gargoyles on the choir. At first sight, it looks homogeneous, but closer examination reveals a true amalgam of architectural styles. The Romanesque transepts, with their heavy hooped windows and dog-tooth decoration, were built by English stonemasons in the twelfth century, whilst the choir, with its pointed arches, flying buttresses and intricate tracery, is early Gothic – and clearly influenced by contemporaneous churches in England. The nave was built in the early thirteenth century, also in the early Gothic style, but was destroyed by fire in 1719; the present structure is a painstakingly accurate late nineteenth-century replica.

Inside, the gloomy half-light hides much of the lofty decorative work, but it is possible to examine the striking early twentieth-century **choir screen**, whose wooden figures are the work of Gustav Vigeland (see p.108). Vigeland was also responsible for the adjacent soapstone **font**, a superb piece of medievalism sporting four bas-reliefs depicting Adam and Eve, John the Baptist baptizing the Christ, the Resurrection and a beguiling Noah and the Ark: Noah peers apprehensively out of his boat, not realizing that the dove, with the tell-tale branch, is up above. The other item of particular interest is a famous fourteenth-century **altar frontal** (front panel of an altar painting) displayed in a chapel off the ambulatory, directly behind the high altar. At a time when few Norwegians could read or write, the cult of St Olav had to be promoted visually, and the frontal is the earliest surviving representation of Olav's life and times. In its centre, Olav looks suitably beatific holding his axe and orb; the top left-hand corner shows the dream Olav had before the battle of Stiklestad (see p.292), with Jesus dropping a ladder down to him from heaven. In the next panel down, Olav and his men are shown at prayer before the battle and, in the bottom right-hand corner, Olav meets a sticky end, speared and stabbed by

Saint Olav

Born in 995, **Olav Haraldsson** followed the traditional life of the Viking chieftain from the tender age of 12, "rousing the steel-storm" as the saga writers put it, from Finland to Ireland. He also served as a mercenary to both the duke of Normandy and King Ethelred of England, and it was during this time that he was converted to Christianity. In 1015, he invaded Norway, defeated his enemies and became king, his military success built upon the support of the more prosperous farmers of the Trøndelag, an emergent class of yeomen who were less capricious than the coastal chieftains of Viking fame. However, Olav's zealous **imposition of Christianity** – he ordered the desecration of pagan sites and the execution of those who refused baptism – alienated many of his followers and the bribes of Olav's rival Knut (Canute), King of England and Denmark, did the rest: Olav's retainers deserted him, and he was forced into exile in 1028. Two years later, he was back in the Trøndelag, but the army he had raised was far too weak to defeat his enemies, and Olav was killed near Trondheim at the **battle of Stiklestad** (see p.292).

Olav might have lost his kingdom, but the nationwide Church he founded had no intention of losing ground. Needing a local **saint** to consolidate its position, the Church carefully nurtured the myth of Olav, a sanctification assisted by the oppressive rule of the "foreigner" Knut. After the battle of Stiklestad, Olav's body had been spirited away and buried on the banks of the River Nid at what is today Trondheim. There were rumours of miracles in the vicinity of the grave, and when the bishop arrived to investigate these strange goings-on, he exhumed the body and found it, lo and behold, perfectly uncorrupted. Olav was declared a saint, his body placed in a silver casket and when, in 1066, Olav Kyrre, son of Olav's half-brother Harald the Fair-Haired, became King of Norway, he ordered work to begin on a grand church to house the remains in appropriate style. Over the years the church was altered and enlarged to accommodate the growing bands of medieval pilgrims; it achieved cathedral status in 1152, when Trondheim became the seat of an archbishopric whose authority extended as far as Orkney and the Isle of Man.

three cruel-looking soldiers. The final panel shows church officials exhuming Olav's uncorrupted body and declaring his sainthood.

At no extra charge, there are English-language **guided tours** of the cathedral during the summer (mid-June to mid-Aug 4 daily; 30min), but you won't see either the Norwegian crown jewels, which have recently been moved to the Archbishop's Palace (see below), or St Olav's silver casket-coffin: this was taken to Denmark and melted down for coinage in 1537. Before you move on, you should certainly climb the cathedral **tower** (mid-June to mid-Aug Mon–Fri 10am–5pm, Sat 10am–12.30pm, Sun 1–3.30pm, every 30min). From the top, there's a fine view of the city and the forested hills that surround it, with the fjord trailing away in one direction, the river valley in the other.

Erkebispegården

Behind the Domkirke, to the south, lies the heavily restored **Erkebispegården** (The Archbishop's Palace), a courtyard complex that was originally built in the twelfth century for the third archbishop, Øystein, though two stone-and-brick wings are all that survive of the original quadrangle – the other two wings were added later. After the archbishops were kicked out during the Reformation, the palace became the residence of the Danish governors. It was subsequently used as the city armoury, and many of the old weapons are now displayed in the **west wing** in the **Rustkammeret med Hjemmefrontmuseet** (Army and Resistance Museum; June–Aug Mon–Fri 9am–3pm, Sat & Sun 11am–4pm;

March–May & Sept–Oct Sat & Sun only 11am–4pm; free). The museum's **first floor** gives the broad details of Norway's involvement in the interminable **Dano-Swedish wars** that racked Scandinavia from the fifteenth to the nineteenth century. As part of the Danish state, Norway was frequently attacked from the east along the Halden-Oslo corridor, the most memorable incursions being by that most bellicose of Swedish kings, Karl XII. Much to the Danish king's surprise, Karl came a cropper in Norway: it was here that he was defeated for the first time and, when he came back for more, shot (possibly by one of his own men) while besieging Fredriksten fortress in 1718 (see p.131).

Of more general interest, the **second floor** describes the German invasion and occupation of **World War II**, dealing honestly with the sensitive issue of collaboration. In particular, you can hear **Vidkun Quisling**'s broadcast announcing – in a disarmingly squeaky voice – his coup d'état of April 9, 1940. There are also some intriguing displays on the daring antics of the Norwegian Resistance, notably an extraordinary – perhaps hare-brained – attempt to sink the battleship *Tirpitz* as it lay moored in an inlet of the Trondheimsfjord in 1942 (see box, p.292). This escapade, like so many others, involved **Leif Larsen**, the Resistance hero who is commemorated by a statue on the Torget in Bergen. Larsen worked closely with the Royal Navy, organizing covert operations in occupied Norway from their base in the Shetlands. Supplies and personnel were transported across the North Sea by Norwegian fishing boats – a lifeline known, in that classically understated British (and Norwegian) way, as the "Shetland bus"; the book of the same name by David Howarth (see p.419) tells the tale of this remarkable enterprise.

In the near future, the west wing will also hold the assorted baubles and bangles that comprise the Norwegian **crown jewels**, whose crowns, orbs, sceptres, robes and all-important anointing horn are a permanent fixture, as coronations were abolished by decree in 1908 and replaced with a blessing ceremony.

Moving on, the **south wing** of the palace holds the smart **Museet Erkebispegården** (Archbishop's Palace Museum; May to mid-June & mid-Aug to mid-Sept Mon–Fri 9am–3pm, Sat 9am–2pm & Sun 1–4pm; mid-June to mid-Aug Mon–Fri 9am–5pm, Sat 9am–2pm & Sun 1–4pm; mid-Sept to April Tues–Sat 11am–3pm, Sun noon–4pm; 50kr or free with cathedral ticket), which is largely devoted to a few dozen medieval statues originally retrieved and put away for safekeeping during the nineteenth-century reconstruction of the nave and west facade. Many of the statues are too battered and bruised to be engaging, but they are well displayed and several are finely carved. In particular, look out for a life-size sculpture of **St Denis**, his head in his hands (literally) in accordance with the legend that he was beheaded, but then proceeded to irritate his executioners no end by carrying his head to his grave. Downstairs, an assortment of artefacts unearthed during a lengthy 1990s archeological investigation of the palace demonstrates the economic power of the archbishops: they employed all manner of skilled artisans – from glaziers and shoemakers to ropemakers, armourers and silversmiths – and even minted their own coins.

From the back of the Erkebispegården, you can stroll out onto the grassy **lawns** beside the River Nid. A trio of rusting bastions are reminders of the military defences that once protected this side of town, but it's the setting that appeals. Footpaths snake round to the sturdy old tombs and wildflowers of the **graveyard**, just to the east of the cathedral's main entrance.

Trondheim Kunstmuseum and Trondhjems Kunstforening

Near the cathedral, at Bispegata 7b, the **Trondheim Kunstmuseum** (Trondheim Art Museum; June–Aug daily 10am–5pm; Sept–May Tues–Sun 11am–4pm; 40kr;

Ⓦwww.tkm.museum.no) is quite small, but its permanent collection features an enjoyable selection of Norwegian paintings, though these are sometimes displaced by temporary exhibitions. In particular, look out for several key works by Johan Dahl and Thomas Fearnley, the leading figures of nineteenth-century Norwegian landscape painting, as well as the romantic canvases of Hans Gude and his chum Adolph Tidemand. There's also the first overtly political work by a Norwegian artist, *The Strike* (*Streik*), painted in 1877 by the radical Theodor Kittelsen (1857–1914), better known for his illustrations of the folk tales collected by Jorgen Moe and Peder Asbjørnsen. In addition, the museum possesses a substantial selection of Munch woodcuts, sketches and lithographs, including several of those disturbing, erotically charged personifications of emotions – *Lust*, *Fear* and *Jealousy* – that are so characteristic of his oeuvre. However, all the artist's work has been removed from display for an indefinite period amid fears of the dreaded Munch art thieves who, in broad daylight, stole two Munch paintings from Oslo's Munch Museum in 2004 (see p.111).

Next door, at Bispegata 9a, the **Trondhjems Kunstforening** (Trondheim Art Society; Tues–Fri 10am–4pm, Sat & Sun noon–4pm; free; Ⓦwww.tfk.no) hosts temporary exhibitions of contemporary art, mostly Norwegian – or at least Scandinavian – but with a smattering of international works thrown in too.

The Nordenfjeldske Kunstindustrimuseum

The delightful **Nordenfjeldske Kunstindustrimuseum** is a couple of minutes' walk north from the cathedral at Munkegata 5 (Museum of Decorative Arts; June to late Aug Mon–Sat 10am–5pm, Sun noon–5pm; late Aug to May Tues–Wed & Fri–Sat 10am–3pm, Thurs 10am–5pm, Sun noon–4pm; 50kr; Ⓦwww.nkim.museum.no). The museum has a wide-ranging permanent collection, but it's too extensive to be shown in its entirety at any one time and so the exhibits are regularly rotated, especially as there is also an ambitious programme of special exhibitions: nevertheless, you can expect to see most of the pieces mentioned below. Start in the **basement**, where the historical collection illustrates bourgeois life in Trøndelag from 1500 to 1900 by means of an eclectic assemblage of furniture, faïence, glassware and silver. There are twentieth-century pieces on display here too, notably a fine selection of Art Nouveau ceramics and furniture. The domestic theme is developed on the **ground floor**, where an entire room has been kitted out with pieces by the Belgian designer and architect **Henri van de Velde** (1863–1957). On this floor also is an unusual display of folkloric **tapestries** produced in Trondheim in the early years of the twentieth century – they're modelled on original paintings by the Norwegian **Gerhard Munthe** (1849–1929), one of whose specialities was the portrayal of medieval folk tales. More modern works can be found on the **first floor**, but the highlight here is the room largely devoted to fourteen tapestries by **Hannah Ryggen**. Born in Malmø in 1894, Ryggen moved to the Trondheim area in the early 1920s and stayed until her death in 1970. Her tapestries are classically naive, the forceful colours and absence of perspective emphasizing the feeling behind them. This is committed art at its best, railing in the 1930s and 1940s against Hitler and Fascism, later moving on to more disparate targets such as the atom bomb and social conformism. But Ryggen still made time to celebrate the things she cherished: *Yes, we love this country* (tapestry no. 9) is as evocative a portrayal of her adopted land as you're likely to find.

Bakklandet and the Kristianstenfestning fortress

It's a couple of minutes' walk east of the cathedral to the **Gamle Bybro** (Old Town Bridge), an elegant wooden construction with splendid views over

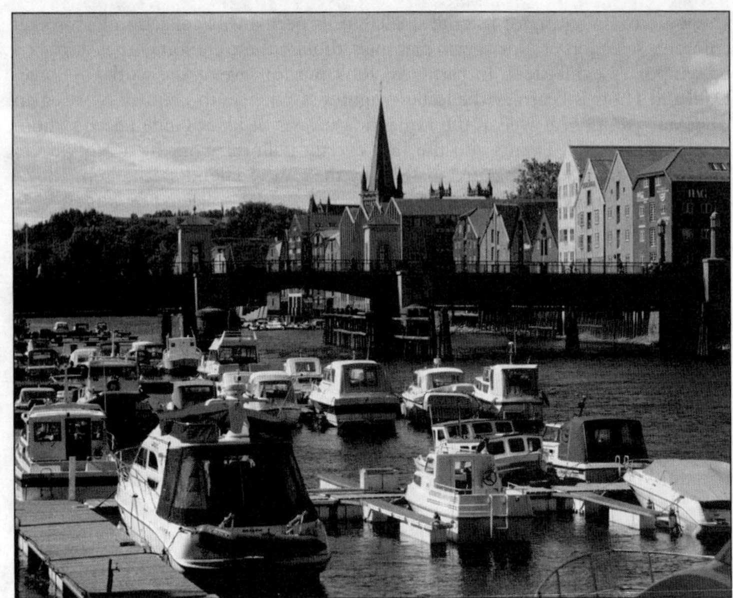

△ Trondheim

Kjøpmannsgata's early eighteenth-century gabled and timbered warehouses, now mostly restaurants and offices. There are more restaurants and a clutch of fashionable bars at the far end of the bridge in tiny **Bakklandet**, Trondheim's own "Left Bank", a one-time working-class district of brightly painted timber houses.

Up above, a stiff ten-minute walk east along Brubakken and Kristianstensbakken, is the **Kristianstenfestning** fortress (June–Aug Mon–Fri 10am–3pm, Sat & Sun 11am–4pm; free), dating from 1681 and offering wide views back over Trondheim. During the war, this was where the Germans had their revenge on members of the local resistance.

Kongens gate's medieval church ruins

Doubling back over the Gamle Bybro from Bakklandet, and following the river north along Kjøpmannsgata, you soon come to the **medieval church ruins** discovered under the **bibliotek** (library) at the east end of Kongens gate. A twelfth-century relic of the days when Trondheim had fifteen or more religious buildings, it is thought to have been a chapel dedicated to St Olav, although the evidence for this is a bit shaky. Excavations revealed nearly 500 bodies in the immediate area, which was once the church graveyard, and some skeletons are neatly displayed under glass. Entry is free and the site is accessible during library opening hours (Mon–Thurs 9am–7pm, Fri 9am–4pm & Sat 10am–3pm; also Sept–April Sun noon–4pm; free). From the library, it's just a few minutes' walk west to Torvet and the Stiftsgården.

The Stiftsgården and north to the Ravnkloa

One conspicuous remnant of old timber-town Trondheim survives in the city centre – the **Stiftsgården**, which stretches out along Munkegata just north of

Torvet (guided tours every hour on the hour till 1hr before closing: early to mid-June Mon–Sat 10am–3pm, Sun noon–5pm; late June to late Aug Mon–Sat 10am–5pm, Sun noon–5pm; 50kr). Built in 1774–78, this good-looking yellow structure is claimed to be the largest wooden building in northern Europe. These days it serves as an official royal residence, a marked social improvement on its original function as the home of the provincial governor. Inside, a long string of period rooms illustrates the genteel tastes of the mansion's late eighteenth- to early nineteenth-century occupants with a wide range of styles, from Rococo to Biedermeierstil, but it's the fanciful Italianate wall paintings that steal the decorative show. The obligatory anecdotal guided tour brings a smile or two – but not perhaps 50kr wide.

If the sight of Bakklandet's old wooden buildings has whetted your appetite, you'll enjoy the tangle of narrow alleys and pastel-painted clapboard frontages that fills out the side streets **north of Kongens gate** and west of Prinsens gate. There's nothing special to look at, but it's a pleasant area for a stroll, after which you can wander over to **Ravnkloa**, the jetty at the north end of Munkegata where the fish market is held (Mon–Fri) – and where ferries leave for Munkholmen (see below).

The Vitenskapsmuseet

Back at Torvet, it's a five- to ten-minute walk southwest to the university's **Vitenskapsmuseet** at Erling Skakkes gate 47 (Museum of Natural History and Archeology; May to mid-Sept Mon–Fri 9am–4pm, Sat & Sun 11am–4pm; mid-Sept to April Tues–Fri 9am–2pm, Sat & Sun noon–4pm; free), comprising several collections. At the front, the main building contains an assortment of forgettable stuffed animals and a largely incomprehensible ragbag of archeological finds. Don't bother with these, but instead pop into the smaller building on the left, where there's a small but enjoyable **kirkehistorie** section (church history; same hours, but Sat & Sun only from mid-Sept to April), with ecclesiastical knick-knacks from pulpits and fonts through to processional crosses and statues of the saints. Even better, in the old **suhmhuset** (hay storehouse), a low, long building at the rear, is a first-rate **middelalder** (medieval exhibition), which tracks the development of Trondheim from its foundation in the tenth century to the fire of 1681. The thoroughly researched, multilingual text is supported by an excellent range of archeological finds, and departs from the predictable "Kings and Queens" approach, investigating everything from sanitary towels and reliquary jars to popular games and attitudes to life and death.

Out from the centre

While most of Trondheim's key attractions are neatly packed within walking distance of each other, on or around the city's central island, there are a few sights to lure you out of the centre. The historic **Munkholmen Island** is an easy ten-minute ferry ride away, while a couple of museums – the **Ringve**, to the northeast of the centre, and the **Sverresborg Trøndelag Folkemuseum** in the southwest – both merit a visit.

Munkholmen island

Poking up out of the Trondheimsfjord just 2km offshore, the tiny islet of **Munkholmen** is easily reached by **boat** from the Ravnkloa jetty (late May to early Sept every hour on the hour 10am–5pm; 50kr return). The island has an eventful history. In Viking times it was used as the city's execution ground, and St Olav went to the added trouble of displaying the head of one of his enemies on a pike here, which must have made approaching mariners a tad nervous. In the eleventh century, the Benedictines founded a monastery on the island – hence its name – but it was not one of their more successful ventures: the archbishop received dozens of complaints about, of all things, the amount of noise the monks made, not to mention alleged heavy drinking and womanizing. After the Reformation, the island was converted into a prison, which doubled as a fortress designed to protect the seaward approaches to the city; later still it became a customs house. The longest-serving prisoner was the Danish count **Peder Griffenfeld** (1635–99), who spent eighteen years cooped up here until his eventual release in 1698. One of the most powerful men in Denmark, Griffenfeld played a leading role in the assumption of absolute power by King Frederick III (see p.392), but was outmanoeuvred and imprisoned by his rivals after the king's death.

Sturdy stone walls encircle almost the entire island, and behind them, sunk in a circular dip, is a set of quaint, almost cottage-like, **prison buildings** surrounding a cobbled courtyard. There are thirty-minute guided tours of the central part of the **fortress** (late May to early Sept daily 10.20am–5.20pm; 25kr), a cheerful romp through its galleries and corridors. The tour includes a visit to the spacious cell occupied by Griffenfeld, and a glimpse of the gun emplacement the Germans installed during World War II. After the tour you can wander over to the **café** or scramble along outside the walls and round the rocks beneath to either of a couple of rough, pebbly beaches.

The Ringve Museum

The **Ringve Museum** (mid-May to June & Aug to mid-Sept daily 11am–3pm; July daily 11am–5pm; mid-Sept to mid-May Sundays 11am–4pm; 75kr; Ⓦwww.ringve.com) occupies a delightful eighteenth-century country house and courtyard complex on the hilly Lade peninsula, some 4km northeast of the city centre. Devoted to musical history and to musical instruments from all over the world, the museum is divided into two sections. In the main building, the collection focuses on **antique European instruments** in period settings, with several demonstrations included in a lengthy – and obligatory – guided tour. The second section, in the old barn, contains an **international selection of musical instruments** and offers a self-guided zip through some of the key moments and movements of **musical history**. There are themes like "the invention of the piano" and "pop and rock", not to mention the real humdinger, "the marching band movement in Norway". Immaculately maintained, the surrounding **botanical gardens** (daily; free) make the most of the scenic setting. To get there, take bus #3 or #4 to Lade from Munkegata.

The Sverresborg Trøndelag Folkemuseum

Three kilometres southwest of the city centre lies one of Norway's best folk museums, the **Sverresborg Trøndelag Folkemuseum** (June–Aug daily 11am–6pm, 80kr; Sept–May Mon–Fri 11am–3pm, Sat & Sun noon–4pm, 50kr; Ⓦwww.sverresborg.no). In a pleasant rural setting, with views over the city, the museum's indoor section kicks off with some well-presented displays tracing everyday life in the Trøndelag from the eighteenth century onwards. Outside, you'll see sixty relocated Trøndelag timber buildings, including a post office, grocery store, stave church and all sorts of farmhouses and outhouses, built for a variety of purposes from curing meat to drying hay. Finally, it's worth staying for lunch here at the museum's *Vertshuset Tavern*, which serves up traditional Norwegian dishes at affordable prices. To get here, take bus #8 from the city centre.

Eating and drinking

As befits Norway's third city, Trondheim has a healthy selection of first-rate **restaurants** serving a variety of cuisines, though the Norwegian places almost always have the gastronomic edge. In particular, there's a cluster of excellent restaurants in the **Bakklandet** district, by the eastern end of Gamle Bybro, and they are joined by a string of laid-back and fashionable **café-bars**, which offer good food at more affordable prices. Elsewhere, the Brattørgata district near the west end of Bakke bru is renowned for its lively weekend bar scene, as is the **Nedre Elvehavn** district, centred around an old dock just to the east of the city centre, and accessible via the footbridge at the top of Kjøppmansgata. Finally – if needs must – the city's mobile fast-food stalls are concentrated around Sentralstasjon and along Kongens gate, on either side of Torvet.

As for **opening hours**, some restaurants open for a couple of hours at lunchtime and then in the evening, but many just stick to the evenings; some also close one day a week. Café-bars and bars almost invariably open from around 11am until the early hours of the morning – or at least until there's no-one left (standing). There's no need to book at most of the city's restaurants, but we've included the phone numbers where advance reservations are advisable.

Cafés and café-bars

Dromedar Nedre Bakklandet 3a. A modern café-bar with a laid-back atmosphere, located a few metres north of the Gamle Bybro. Arguably the best coffee in the city plus snacks and light meals – filled bagels, sandwiches etc – at bargain prices. Mon–Fri 7am–7pm, Sat 10am–7pm & Sun 11am–7pm.

Erichsen Nordre gate 7. Elegant, Viennese-style café where the cakes are as sublime as the surroundings – and the sandwiches and salads (from 55kr) are equally impressive. Mon–Fri 9am–1am & Sat 9.30am–2am.

Godt Brød Thomas Angellsgata 16. The aroma of baking bread, rolls and pastries, all organic, wafts around this cosy little café-cum-bakery, where the coffee is good and the breads and pastries even better. Daily except Sun 6am–6pm.

Restaurants

Baklandet Skydsstation Øvre Bakklandet 33 ⓣ73 92 10 44. Friendly, intimate old coaching inn with a warren of homely dining rooms and a small courtyard. A reasonably priced menu with mains from as little as 120kr features home-cooked staples such as that old Norwegian favourite bacalao (dried and salted cod fish), not to mention an earth-moving cheesecake. Mon–Fri 4pm–1am, Sat & Sun noon–1am.

Blau bær Innherredsveien 16, Nedre Elvehavn. The excellent-value, stone-baked pizzas (and blueberry tart) at this relaxed, dockside place affirm its status as one the best café-restaurants for a leisurely evening's grazing and people-watching. Mon–Thurs & Sun noon–midnight, Fri & Sat 11am–1am.

Chablis Øvre Bakklandet 66 ⓣ73 87 42 50. Just metres from the Gamle Bybro, this polished brasserie-restaurant, with its modish furnishings and fittings, serves up excellent food – Norwegian with a Mediterranean slant. A floating pontoon river terrace makes a lovely spot for a warm summer evening's meal. Main courses hover around 230kr. Open Mon–Sat 5–11pm.

Credo Restaurant & Bar Ørjaveita 4 ⓣ73 53 03 88. Smart and very popular Mediterranean/Spanish-influenced restaurant with delicious daily specials from around 180kr. The restaurant is on the ground floor, with the stylish, modern *Credo Bar* upstairs. Restaurant open Mon–Sat 6–11pm, bar Mon–Fri 4pm–2.30am & Sat 7.30pm–2.30am.

Havfruen Fiskerestaurant Kjøpmannsgata 7 ⓣ73 87 40 70. Near the cathedral, this smart and polished seafood restaurant is one of the best in town with main courses – cod, coalfish, char and so forth – averaging around 255kr. Open Mon–Sat from 6pm.

Frati Munkegata 25 ⓣ73 52 57 33. Much favoured by locals, this traditional, family-run Italian restaurant serves all the classics in plentiful and authentic portions and consequently it's always (deservedly) busy. Main courses from 120kr. Mon–Fri 3–11pm, Sat & Sun 2–11pm.

Jadab Brattørgata 3a. All the standard Indian dishes plus a few good vegetarian options in this friendly, modish restaurant. Inexpensive prices too, with mains averaging around 170kr. Mon–Sat 2pm–midnight & Sun 2–11pm.

Vertshuset Tavern Sverresborg allé 7 ⓣ73 87 80 70. In business since 1739, this restaurant-tavern used to be in the town centre, but it was moved lock, stock and barrel to the Sverresborg Folkemuseum (see p.288) several years ago. Its low-ceilinged timber rooms are furnished in appropriate period style and the food is traditional Norwegian "Husmannskost" at its best: the *Kjøttkaker i brun saus med erterstuing* (meatballs in brown gravy served with pea stew; 117kr) is hard to beat, closely followed by the *spekemat* (cured meat) at 227kr, the *rømmegrøt* (sour-cream porridge; 69kr) and the *fiskekaker* (fish cakes; 99kr). Open Mon–Fri 4pm–midnight, Sat 2pm–midnight, Sun noon–midnight.

Bars and nightclubs

Bær & Bar Innherredsveien 16. Managing to straddle that fine line between trendy and pretentious, this is the pick of the bars along the Nedre Elvehavn dockside strip. The sister of the neighbouring Blau Bær restaurant (see p.289), Bær & Bar has house and electro until 3am at the weekend, fresh fruit cocktails and outdoor seating.

Brukbar Munkegata 26 ⓦwww.brukbar.no. Interesting, colourful café and bar catering for everyone from business folk dropping in after work, to hardcore student boozers. Note the peculiar bee-shaped wall-lamps. Open daily from 11am to midnight and beyond.

Credo Bar Ørjaveita 4. Modish first-floor bar above the Credo restaurant (see p.289).

Metro Kjøpmannsgata 12 ⓦwww.gaytrondheim.com. Trondheim's only gay and lesbian bar. DJ sounds at the weekend. Open Wed 9.30pm–2am, Fri & Sat 10pm–2am.

Café 3B Brattørgata 3B. Rock 'n' roll and indie club-cum-bar, where you can drink well into the wee hours.

Trondhjem Mikrobryggeri Prinsens gate 39. Mainstream bar serving up its own microbrewery brews. Serves filling pub food too, all in a friendly atmosphere.

Listings

Airlines SAS/Braathens ⓣ054 00; Widerøe ⓣ81 00 12 00.

Banks & exchange ATMs are liberally distributed across the city centre; the main post office (see below) as well as a slew of central banks and the tourist office change currency.

Car rental Avis, Kjøpmannsgata 34 (ⓣ73 84 17 90); Hertz, Innherredsveien 103 (ⓣ73 50 35 00) and at the airport (ⓣ74 80 16 60); Europcar, at the airport (ⓣ74 82 67 00).

Consulates UK, Beddingen 8 (ⓣ73 60 02 00); Poland, TMV-kaia 23 (ⓣ73 87 69 00).

Crafts The best place to buy traditional Norwegian clothes and crafts is Husfliden, Olav Tryggvasons gate 18 (Mon–Fri 9am–5pm & Sat 9am–3pm; ⓣ73 83 32 30, ⓦwww.husfliden.no).

Dentists Dental emergencies ⓣ73 50 55 00.

DNT Trondhjems Turistforening, just west of the centre at Sandgata 30 (Mon–Fri 8am–4pm; ⓣ73 92 42 00; ⓦwww.tt.no), is the DNT's local branch, offering advice on the region's hiking trails and huts. It also organizes a variety of guided walks and cross-country skiing trips, with activities concentrated in the mountains to the south and east of the city. There are one-day excursions and longer expeditions to suit different levels of skill and fitness.

Emergencies Ambulance ⓣ113; Fire ⓣ110; Police ⓣ112.

Internet There's free Internet access at the library, Kongensgate (ⓣ72 54 75 00; Mon–Thurs 9am–7pm, Fri 9am–4pm & Sat 10am–3pm; also Sept–April Sun noon–4pm).

Pharmacy St Olav Vaktapotek, Søsiden, Beddingen 4 (Mon–Sat 8.30am–midnight, Sun 10am–midnight; ⓣ73 88 37 37); Løveapoteket Byhaven, Olav Tryggvasonsgate 28 (Mon–Fri 9am–6pm & Sat 9am–3pm; ⓣ73 83 32 83).

Police station Near Sentralstasjon at Gryta 4 (ⓣ02800); emergencies ⓣ112.

Post office Main office, with poste restante, at Dronningens gate 10 (Mon–Fri 8am–5pm & Sat 9am–2pm, though hours are reduced somewhat in the summer).

Taxis Eight ranks in and around the city centre including ranks at Torvet, Sentralstasjon, Søndre gate and the Radisson SAS Royal Garden Hotel; or call Trønder Taxi (ⓣ073 73; 24hr).

Vinmonopolet Among several city-centre branches of Vinmonopolet, the government-run liquor and wine store, there's one at Munkegata 30 (Mon–Wed 10am–5pm, Thurs & Fri 10am–6pm & Sat 9am–3pm).

North from Trondheim to Bodø

North of Trondheim, it's a long haul up the coast to the next major places of interest, Bodø, the main ferry port for the Lofoten, and the gritty but likeable port of Narvik – respectively 720km and 910km distant. The easiest way to make the bulk of the trip is by **train**, a rattling good journey with the scenery becoming wilder and bleaker the further north you go – and you usually get a blast from the whistle as you cross the Arctic Circle. The train takes nine hours to reach **Fauske**, where the line reaches its northern limit and turns west for the final 65-kilometre dash to Bodø. There's precious little to detain you in Fauske, but there are **bus** connections north to Narvik, a five-hour drive away, and many travellers take an overnight break here – though in fact nearby Bodø makes a far more pleasant stopover and there are buses to Narvik from here too.

If you're **driving**, you'll find the main highway, the **E6**, which runs all the way from Trondheim to Narvik and points north, too slow to cover more than three or four hundred kilometres comfortably in a day. Fortunately, there are several pleasant places to stop, beginning with **Steinkjer** and **Snåsa** in Trøndelag. Steinkjer is a modest little town with a couple of good hotels, Snåsa, a relaxed – and relaxing – village, again with somewhere good to stay. Further north, in Nordland, the next province up, **Mosjøen** and **Mo-i-Rana**, two rejigged and revamped former industrial towns, make pleasant pit stops, with Mo-i-Rana serving as a handy starting point for a visit to the **Svartisen glacier**, crowning the coastal peaks close by. The glacier is on the western rim of the **Saltfjellet Nasjonalpark**, a wild and windswept mountain plateau that extends east towards the Swedish border. The E6 and the railway cut through the park, giving ready access, but although this is a popular destination for experienced hikers, it's too fierce an environment for the novice or the lightly equipped.

The main alternative to the E6 is the coastal **Highway 17**, the Kystriksveien (Ⓦwww.kystriksveien.no), an ingenious and extremely scenic cobbling together of road, tunnel, bridge and car ferry that negotiates the shredded shoreline from **Steinkjer**, just north of Trondheim, all the way up to Bodø, a distance of nigh on 700km. It's a slow route – there are no less than seven ferry crossings – but if you can't spare the time to do the whole thing, you could join Highway 17 to the west of Mo-i-Rana, cutting out five ferries and the first 420km, yet still taking in the most dramatic part of the journey, including fabulous views of the **Melfjord** and the Svartisen glacier.

The E6 north to Hell and Verdalsøra

Leaving Trondheim, the **E6** tunnels and twists its way round the Trondheimsfjord to **HELL**, a busy rail junction, where one train line forks north to slice through the dales and hills of Trøndelag en route to Fauske, while the other branches east for the seventy-kilometre haul to the Swedish frontier, with Östersund beckoning beyond. Hell itself has nothing to recommend it except its name, though paradoxically *hell* in Norwegian means good fortune: don't despair, the locals still sell postcards of the train station's freight depot tagged "Hell – gods ekspedisjon" ("have a good journey"). Just beyond Hell, the road forks too, with the E6 nudging north and the E14 travelling east to Sweden. Continuing along the E6, it's about 20km to the **Fjættenfjord**, a narrow inlet of the Trondheimsfjord and one-time hideout of the battleship *Tirpitz* (see box on p.292). Beyond the Fjættenfjord, the E6 clips past the tedious little towns of **Levanger** and **Verdalsøra**, a centre for the fabrication of offshore oil platforms.

Leif Larsen and the attack on the Tirpitz

Commissioned in 1941, the German battleship **Tirpitz** spent most of its three-year existence hidden away in the **Fjættenfjord** (see p.291), where it was protected from air attack by the mountains and from naval attack by a string of coastal gun emplacements. With the fjord as its base, the *Tirpitz* was able to sally forth to attack Allied convoys bound for Russia and as such was a major irritant to the Royal Navy, who dreamt up a remarkable scheme to sink it. The navy had just perfected a submersible craft called the **Chariot**, which was 6m long, powered by electric motors, and armed with a torpedo. A crew of two volunteer divers manned the craft, sitting astride it at the rear – which must amount to some kind of definition of bravery. The plan was to transport two of these Chariots across from Shetland to Norway in a Norwegian fishing boat and then, just before the first German checkpoint, to attach them to the outside of the boat's hull. Equipped with false papers and a diversionary load of peat, the fishing boat would, it was thought, stand a good chance of slipping through the German defences. Thereafter, as soon as the boat got within reasonable striking distance, the Chariots could be launched towards the *Tirpitz* and, once they got very close to the ship, their torpedoes would be fired.

The boat selected was the *Arthur*, skippered by the redoubtable **Leif Larsen**, a modest man of extraordinary courage, who, over the course of the war, ran over fifty trips to Norway from the Shetlands. The *Arthur* had a crew of four Norwegian and six British seamen – four to pilot the Chariots and two to help them get into their diving suits. At first the trip went well. As soon as they reached Norway's coastal waters, the crew moved the Chariots from their hiding place in the hold and attached them to the hull. They then fooled the Germans and were allowed into the Trondheimsfjord, but here the weather deteriorated and the Chariots broke loose from the boat, falling to the bottom of the ocean before they could be used. There was, therefore, no choice but to abort the mission, scuttle the *Arthur* and row ashore in the hope that the crew could escape over the mountains to neutral Sweden. They divided into two parties of five, one of which made it without mishap – except for a few lost toes from frostbite – but the other group, led by Larsen, ran into a patrol. In the skirmish that ensued, one of the Englishmen, a certain A.B. Evans, was wounded and had to be left behind; the Germans polished him off.

On September 11, 1944, the *Tirpitz* was caught napping in the **Kåfjord** (see p.352) by Allied bombers, which flew in from a Russian airfield to the east, screened by the mountains edging the fjord. The *Tirpitz* was badly damaged in the attack, especially its engines, and although it managed to limp off to Tromsø the warship was finally sunk just outside that city on November 12 by a combined bombing-and-torpedo attack.

Stiklestad

From Verdalsøra, it's just 6km inland along Highway 757 to **STIKLESTAD**, one of Norway's most vaunted villages. It was here in 1030 that Olav Haraldsson, later St Olav, was killed in battle, his death now commemorated by the **Stiklestad Nasjonale Kultursenter** (Stiklestad National Culture Centre; mid-June to mid-Aug daily 9am–8pm; mid-Aug to mid-June daily 11am–5.30pm; ⓣ74 04 42 00, ⓦwww.stiklestad.no), whose assorted museums and open-air amphitheatre are spread out over a pastoral landscape. A descendant of Harald Hårfagre (the Fair-Haired), **Olav Haraldsson** (also see p.283) was one of Norway's most important medieval kings, a Viking warrior turned resolute Christian monarch whose misfortune it was to be the enemy of the powerful and shrewd King Knut of England and Denmark. It was Knut's bribes that did for Olav, persuading all but his most loyal supporters to change allegiances – as a Norse poet commented in the cautionary *Håvamål* (the Sayings of Odin), "I have never found a man so generous and hospitable that he would not take a present." Dislodged from the throne, Olav returned from exile in Sweden in 1030, but was defeated and killed here at the **Battle of Stiklestad**. His role as founder of the Norwegian Church prompted his subsequent canonization, and his cult flourished at Trondheim until the Reformation.

The government has spent millions developing the Stiklestad Nasjonale Kultursenter, one of the results being the broad-beamed **Kulturhus**, whose prime attraction is a pleasingly melodramatic **museum** (95kr) that uses shadowy dioramas and a ghoulish soundtrack to chronicle the events leading up to Olav's death. Nonetheless, the dioramas contain few artefacts of note, other than one or two bits of armour and jewellery dating from the period, and neither is the text particularly revealing, which is a pity, since something more could have been made of Olav's position in medieval Christian folklore. One such tale, passed down through the generations, relates how Olav spent the night on a remote Norwegian farm, only to discover the family praying over a pickled horse's penis. Expressing some irritation – but no surprise – at this pagan ceremony, Olav threw the phallus to the family dog and took the opportunity to explain some of the finer tenets of Christianity to his hosts. There's a second display on St Olav upstairs in the museum, focusing on his cult and how it spread across western Europe.

Across from the Kulturhus, the much modified, twelfth-century stone **kirke** (church) reputedly marks the spot where Olav was stabbed to death. Claims that the stone on which the body was first laid out had been incorporated into the church's high altar were abandoned during the Reformation, in case of damage by Protestants. Just up the hill from the Kulturhus, a five-minute walk away, is the open-air **amfiteater** (amphitheatre), where the colourful Olsokspelet (St Olav's Play), a costume drama, is performed each year as part of the **St Olav Festival**. This is held over several days either side of the anniversary of the battle, July 29, and thousands of Norwegians make the trek here; tickets need to be booked months in advance with the Kultursenter. The amphitheatre also adjoins an open-air **folkemuseum** (folk museum), containing a few indoor exhibits, and some thirty seventeenth- to nineteenth-century buildings moved here from all over rural Trøndelag.

Stiklestad is difficult to reach without your own transport, and there's nowhere to stay when you get there. A twice-daily **train** from Trondheim runs to Verdalsøra, 6km away, from where you have to walk, or use one of the taxis that usually wait outside the station. During the St Olav Festival, however, special trains and buses take visitors to the site from Trondheim – details from the Trondheim tourist office.

Steinkjer

Back on the **E6** just to the west of Stiklestad, it's a further 30km north to **STEINKJER**, a pleasant, unassuming town that sits in the shadow of wooded hills, at the point where the river that gave the place its name empties into the fjord. The Germans bombed the town to bits in 1940 because it was the site of an infantry training camp, and the modern replacement is a tidy, appealing ensemble that fans out from the long main street, Kongens gate. The E6 bypasses Steinkjer town centre, running parallel to – and about 400m to the west of – Kongens gate, with the train station in between. The E6 also passes the tourist office (mid-June to mid-Aug Mon–Fri 9am–7pm, Sat 10am–7pm & Sun noon–7pm; mid-Aug to mid-June Mon–Fri 9am–4pm; ⓣ74 16 36 17, ⓦwww.steinkjer-turist.com).

Right in the centre of town across from the train station is the *Quality Hotel Grand Steinkjer*, Kongens gate 37 (ⓣ74 16 47 00, ⓦwww.grandhotell.no; ❻, sp/r ❹), which manages to seem quite old-fashioned even though it occupies a modern tower block. The rooms on its upper floors have splendid views along the coast, and the hotel restaurant serves tasty Norwegian dishes at reasonable prices. There are several other **places to eat** nearby, the pick of these being the bright and inviting *Brod & Circus*, Kongens gate 40 (Mon–Tues 11am–5pm, Wed–Fri 11am–10pm & Sat 11am–4pm), where a range of bread, freshly baked on the premises, serves as a sound basis for a Mediterranean-inspired menu with main courses from 80kr. A good second choice is *Café Madam Brix*, Kirkegata 7 (ⓣ74 16 74 60), a cosy café-restaurant, which takes its name from the redoubtable widow who founded an inn here in 1722. There's also a year-round municipal campsite, *Guldbergaunet Camping* (ⓣ74 16 20 45, ⓔg-book@online.no), in the park on the south bank of the river, about 2km inland from the train station.

North to Snåsa

Five kilometres north of Steinkjer is the point where the Krystiksveien (Highway 17; see p.298) branches off the E6 to begin its scenic 700-kilometre journey north to Bodø. Alternatively, there's a choice of routes north to Snåsa: you can either take the E6 along the northern shore of the long and slender lake Snåsavatn, or opt for the more agreeable (and slower) Highway 763, which meanders along the southern side of the lake through farmland and wooded hills.

Taking the faster E6, it's 60km from Steinkjer to the far end of the lake and the sleepy, scattered hamlet of **SNÅSA**, a fine example of a Trøndelag rural community. It looks as if nothing much has happened here for decades, but there is one sight of note, a pretty little hilltop **church** of softly hued grey stone, dating from the Middle Ages and very much in the English style. On the west side of the village – and 6km from the E6 – is the *Snåsa Hotell* (ⓣ74 15 10 57, ⓦwww.snasahotell.no; ❹, sp/r ❸), a modern place in a lovely setting overlooking the lake; the decor is somewhat dated, but the bedrooms are comfortable and it's a peaceful spot, ideal if you want to rest after a long drive. The hotel also operates a small **campsite** (same number; all year) with huts (❷) as well as spaces for tents and caravans. There's a restaurant here too, serving humdrum but filling Norwegian staples, but if you're likely to arrive after 7pm, you should telephone ahead to check it will still be open.

Into Nordland: Mosjøen

Beyond Snåsa, the E6 leaves the wooded valleys of the Trøndelag for the wider, harsher landscapes of the province of Nordland. The road bobs across bleak plateaux and scuttles along rangy river valleys before reaching, after about 190km, the short (700m), signposted side road that leads to the **Laksforsen** waterfalls, a well-known beauty spot where the River Vefsna takes a 17-metre tumble. The café here offers a grand view of the falls, which were once much favoured by British aristocrats for their salmon-fishing.

Back on the E6 from the waterfalls, it's another 30km to the town of **MOSJØEN**, first impressions of which are not especially favourable. The setting is handsome enough, with the town wedged amid fjord, river and mountain, but a huge aluminium plant dominates, hogging the north side of the waterfront. Persevere, for Mosjøen was a small-time trading centre long before the factory arrived, and **Sjøgata**, down by the river just to the south of the plant, is lined by attractive old timber dwellings, warehouses and shops dating from the early nineteenth century. It's an appealing streetscape, especially since the buildings are still in everyday use. It only takes a few minutes to walk from one end of Sjøgata to the other, and on the way you'll encounter (the main part of) the mildly diverting **Vefsn Museum**, Sjøgata 31b (mid-Aug to May Mon–Fri 10am–3.30pm, Sat 10am–2pm; June to mid-Aug Mon–Fri 8am–3.30pm & Sun 11am–4pm; 20kr), which has displays on life in old Mosjøen and exhibits some interesting work by contemporary Nordland artists.

Mosjøen practicalities

Mosjøen train station is beside the E6 on the north side of town, in front of the aluminium plant. From here, it's about 1200m to the east end of Sjøgata – just follow the signs. The bus station is about 100m beyond the west end of Sjøgata, on Strandgata, and from here it's a few metres to the tourist office at C. M. Havigsgate 39 (late June to July Mon–Fri 9am–6pm, Sat & Sun 11am–4pm; early Aug Mon–Fri 9am–5pm; late Aug to late June Mon–Fri 9am–3.30pm; ⓣ75 11 12 40, ⓦwww.visithelgeland.com).

The pick of the town's several **hotels** is *Fru Haugans*, also metres from the tourist office at Strandgata 39 (ⓣ75 11 41 00, ⓦwww.fruhaugans.no; ❺, sp/r ❹). There's been an inn here since the eighteenth century and the present building is a well-judged amalgamation of the old and the new. Rather more unusual is the accommodation offered by the *Kulturverkstedet*, a local heritage organization that has refurbished a couple of old wooden houses at Sjøgata 22–24 and rents them out as the *Gjestehusene i Sjøgata* (ⓣ75 17 27 60; ❷–❸). They are simple but eminently appealing lodgings, with or without bed linen. *Kulturverkstedet* also operates a charming old-fashioned **café**, serving coffee and traditional Nordland pastries, but the best **restaurant** in town is *Ellenstuen*, at the *Fru Haugans Hotel*, which provides tasty, mainly Norwegian dishes from a seasonal menu that makes the most of local ingredients; main courses start at around 190kr. Otherwise, for a daytime coffee or an evening **drink**, *Lilletorget*, at Strandgata 42, is the liveliest spot in town.

Mo-i-Rana

Beyond Mosjøen, the E6 cuts inland to weave across the mountains of the interior, whilst the railway stays glued to the seashore down below. Either way, it's an enjoyable journey, though the E6 has the scenic edge, especially when it starts its long climb up the slopes of **Korgfjellet**. The road falls well short of the summit, but its highest point still offers panoramic views and is the site of a motel and a monument honouring the 550 Yugoslav prisoners of war who built this section of the road during World War II. Thereafter, the E6 hairpins down to **Korgen**, sitting pretty beneath the mountains in the bend of a river, before it slips along the fjord to Mo-i-Rana, 90km from Mosjøen.

Hugging the head of the Ranafjord, **MO-I-RANA**, or more usually "**Mo**", was a minor port and market town until World War II, after which

The Arctic Menu scheme

On and around the Arctic Circle and points north, the best Norwegian restaurants are members of the **Arctic Menu scheme**, which guarantees top-quality cooking and the use of local ingredients – from meat and fowl through to fish and seal as well as fruit and berries. A booklet, widely available at tourist offices across the north, lists all the participating restaurants, which are regularly monitored for quality and originality. Members have a common and much vaunted logo too – a black circular icon with two flashes beneath.

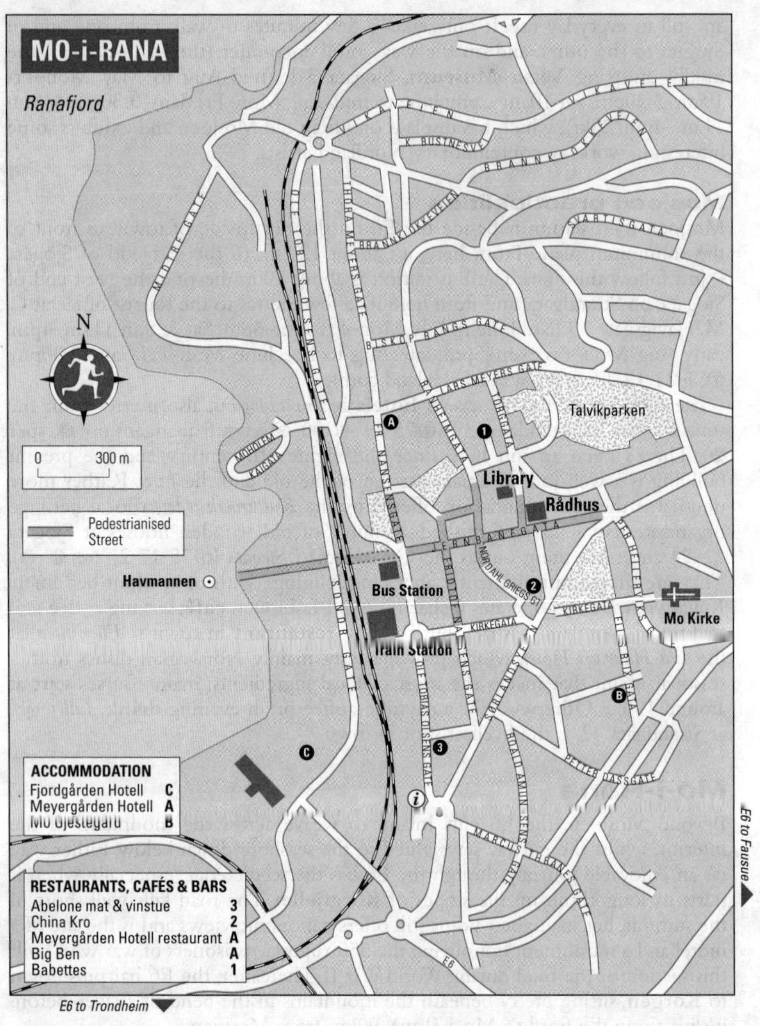

its fortunes, and appearance, were transformed by the construction of a steel plant. The plant dominated proceedings until the 1980s, when there was some economic diversification and the town began to clean itself up: the fjord shore was cleared of its industrial clutter and the E6 re-routed to create the pleasantly spacious, surprisingly leafy town centre of today. Most of Mo is resolutely modern, but look out for **Mo kirke**, a good-looking structure of 1832, with a high-pitched roof and onion dome, perched on a hill on the eastern edge of the centre. Enclosed by a mossy stone wall, the well-tended graveyard contains a communal tomb for unidentified Russian prisoners of war and the graves of six Scots Guards killed hereabouts in May 1940. In front of the church is a bust commemorating Thomas van Westen, an eighteenth-century evangelist-missionary who spearheaded early attempts to convert the Sami. Otherwise, Mo is first and foremost a handy base for visiting the east side of the **Svartisen glacier** (see p.298) and/or exploring the region's lakes, caves, fjords and mountains, though it does possess one real surprise: here, standing in the shallows, is an Antony Gormley sculpture, **Havmannen** (Man of the Sea), a large and stern-looking figure, which gazes determinedly down the fjord.

Arrival, information and transport

Mo's bus and train stations are close together, down by the fjord on Ole Tobias Olsens gate. The compact town centre lies east of this street, with the foot of the main pedestrianized drag, Jernbanegata, opposite the bus station. The tourist office is about 300m to the south of the bus and train stations, also on Ole Tobias Olsens gate (mid-June to mid-Aug Mon–Fri 9am–8pm, Sat 9am–4pm & Sun 1–7pm; mid-Aug to mid-June Mon–Fri 9am–4pm; ⓣ75 13 92 00, ⓦwww.arctic-circle.no). They have the usual local leaflets, provide free town maps and issue a free booklet detailing the Highway 17 Coastal Route (see box on p.298). Bus timetables are available too, but local services are much too patchy for any serious exploration of the town's environs without your own transport. In this regard, car rental is available from Avis, at the Esso Røssvoll gas station (ⓣ99 50 13 11), for around 750kr a day. If that looks too expensive, the tourist office rents out **bikes**, though you have to be pretty fit to reach most local points of interest – and just forget it altogether if it's raining. The tourist office can arrange a shared taxi ride to the Svartisen glacier (see p.298) and check that the boats which give access to the glacier are running. Finally, the staff will also make reservations for a wide range of guided excursions, from rafting, kayaking and fishing through to caving, climbing and trekking. A leading local operator is Rana Spesialsport, Øvre Idrettsvei 35 (ⓣ75 12 70 88 or 909 51 108, ⓦwww.spesialsport.no).

Accommodation

The pick of the town's several hotels is the excellently run and very comfortable ✱ *Meyergården Hotell*, a short walk north of the train station, off Ole Tobias Olsens gate at Fr. Nansensgate 28 (ⓣ75 13 40 00, ⓦwww.meyergarden.no; ❻, sp/r ❹). Most of the hotel is modern, but the original lodge has survived and is maintained in period style, with stuffed animal heads on the wall and elegant panelled doorways. A less expensive, but much plainer, alternative is the *Fjordgården Hotell Mo i Rana*, a tour-group favourite down by the waterfront at Søndregate 9 (ⓣ75 15 28 00, ⓦwww.fjordgarden.no; open May to Aug; ❹). A third very recommendable option is *Mo Gjestegård*, tucked into the backstreets, near the church at Elias Blix gata 5 (ⓣ75 15 22 11, ⓦwww.mo-gjestegaard.no; ❸); this family-run guesthouse is a little heavy on the pine finishings, but it's quiet and peaceful and the rooms are pleasantly homely.

Restaurants, cafés and bars

Mo's best **restaurant** is at the *Meyergården Hotell*, where you can sample an excellent range of Norwegian dishes featuring local ingredients; main courses average around 200kr. Also recommended is the *China Kro*, in the town centre at Nordahl Griegs gate 9, where the Chinese fare is surprisingly good even if the surroundings are a little drab. Alternatively, the *Abelone mat & vinstue*, Ole Tobias Olsens gate 6, serves competent pizzas and steaks, whilst *Babettes*, in the centre at Ranheimgata 2, is good for light meals and coffee. Finding a spot for a drink proves a little trickier, but *Big Ben* in the *Meyergården Hotell* has a sunny terrace that is fine for an evening drink.

Around Mo: Grønligrotta and the Svartisen glacier

The limestone and marble mountains to the northwest of Mo are pocked by caves. The most accessible is the limestone Grønligrotta (mid-June to mid-Aug daily 10am–7pm; 80kr), where an easy 35-minute guided tour follows a subterranean river and takes in a 400-metre long underground chamber. Grønligrotta is lit by electric lights – it's the only illuminated cave in Scandinavia – and it's located 25km from Mo: head north out of town along the E6 and follow the signs along the same minor road that leads to the most accessible part of the Svartisen glacier.

Norway's second largest glacier, **Svartisen** – literally "Black Ice" – covers roughly 370 square kilometres of mountain and valley between the E6 and the coast to the northwest of Mo. The glacier is actually divided into two sections – east and west – by the Vesterdal valley, though this cleft is a recent phenomenon: when it was surveyed in 1905, the glacier was one giant block, about 25 percent bigger than it is today; the reasons for this change are still obscure. The highest parts of the glacier lie at around 1500m, but its tentacles reach down to about 170m – the lowest-lying glacial arms in mainland Europe. Mo-i-Rana is within easy reach of one of the glacier's **eastern nodules**: to get there, drive north from Mo on the E6 for about 12km and then take the signed byroad to the glacier, a straightforward 23-kilometre trip running past the Grønligrotta caves (see above) and ending beside the ice-green, glacial lake **Svartisvatnet**. Here, **boats** (early June & late Aug 2 daily at 11am & 1pm; late June to

The Kystriksveien Coastal Route on Highway 17

Branching off the E6 just beyond Steinkjer (see p.293), the tortuous **Kystriksveien** (Ⓦwww.rv17.no) – the **coastal route** along Highway 17 – threads its way up the west coast, linking many villages that could formerly only be reached by sea. This is an obscure and remote corner of the country, but apart from the lovely scenery there's little of special appeal, and the seven ferry trips that interrupt the 688-kilometre drive north to Bodø (there are no through buses) make it expensive and time-consuming in equal measure. A free **booklet** describing the route can be obtained at tourist offices throughout the region – including Mo – and it contains all Highway 17's car-ferry timetables.

Conveniently, the stretch of Highway 17 between **Mo-i-Rana** and **Bodø** takes in most of the **scenic highlights**, can be negotiated in a day, and cuts out five of the ferry trips. To sample this part of the route, drive 35km west from Mo along Highway 12 to the Highway 17 crossroads, from where it's some 60km north to the **Kilboghamn–Jektvik** ferry (4–9 daily; 1hr; driver and car 127kr) and a further 30km to the ferry linking **Ågskardet** with **Forøy** (7–9 daily; 10min; driver and car 49kr). On the first ferry you cross the Arctic Circle with great views down and along the beautiful **Melfjord**, and on the second, after arriving at Forøy, you get a chance to see a westerly arm of the **Svartisen** glacier (see above), viewed across the slender Holandsfjord. For an even closer look at the glacier, stop at the information centre in **HOLAND**, 12km beyond Forøy, and catch the **passenger boat** (June to early Sept Mon–Fri 8am–9pm, Sat & Sun 10.30am–5.30pm, every 45min to 1hr 30min; 15min; 60kr return; Ⓣ94 86 55 16), which zips across the fjord to meet a connecting bus; this travels the kilometre or so up to the *Svartisen Turistsenter* (June to mid-Aug daily 10am–5pm; Ⓣ75 75 00 11, Ⓦwww.svartisen.no), from where it's another 2km to the glacier. The **Turistsenter** has a café, rents cabins (❷) and is the base for four-hour guided **glacier walks** (mid-June to mid-Aug only; prior booking is essential). From Holand, it's 140km to the Saltstraumen (see p.305) and 30km more to Bodø (see p.301).

mid-Aug hourly 10am–4pm; 20min each way; 90kr return) shuttle across the lake, though services can't begin until the ice has melted – usually by late June – so check with the tourist office in Mo before you set out. Viewed from the boat, the great convoluted folds of the glacier look rather like bluish-white custard, but close up, after a stiff three-kilometre hike past the rocky detritus left by the retreating ice, the sheer size of the glacier becomes apparent – a mighty grinding and groaning wall of ice edged by a jumble of ice chunks, columns and boulders.

The west side of the Svartisen glacier can be seen – and accessed – from the "Kystriksveien" Coastal Route, or Highway 17 (see box opposite). It can also be visited on **organized bus and ferry trips** from Bodø (see p.301).

The Arctic Circle

Given its appeal as a travellers' totem, and considering the amount of effort it takes to actually get here, crossing the Arctic Circle, about 80km north of Mo, is a bit of a disappointment. Uninhabited for the most part, the landscape is undeniably bleak, but the gleaming **Polarsirkelsenteret** (Arctic Circle Centre; May to early June & Aug daily 9am–8pm, late June to July daily 8am–10pm & early Sept daily 10am–6pm; Ⓦwww.polarsirkelsenteret.no) only serves to disfigure the scene – it's a giant lampshade of a building plonked by the roadside and stuffed with every sort of tourist bauble imaginable. You'll whizz by on the bus, the train toots its whistle, and drivers can, of course, shoot past too, though the temptation to brave the crowds is strong. Inside, you should be able to resist the Arctic exhibition (50kr), but you'll probably get snared by either the "Polarsirkelen" certificate, or the specially stamped postcards. Less tackily, there are poignant reminders of crueller times back outside, where a couple of simple stone memorials pay tribute to the Yugoslav and Soviet POWs who laboured under terrible conditions to build the Arctic railroad – the Nordlandsbanen – to Narvik for the Germans in World War II.

△ The Arctic Circle

Saltfjellet Nasjonalpark: Lønsdal and Graddis

The louring mountains in the vicinity of the Arctic Circle Centre are part of the Saltfjellet, a vast mountain plateau whose spindly pines, stern snow-tipped peaks and rippling moors extend west from the Swedish border to the Svartisen glacier. The E6 and the railway cut inland across this range between Mo-i-Rana and Rognan (see below), providing access to the cairned hiking trails that lattice the Saltfjellet, part of which – to the immediate west of the E6 – has been protected as the **Saltfjellet Nasjonalpark**. You can also reach the trails from Highway 77, which forks east off the E6 down the **Junkerdal**, a remote and rather unwelcoming river valley that leads to the Swedish border. The region is, however, largely the preserve of experienced hikers: the trails are not sufficiently clear to dispense with a compass, weather conditions can be treacherous and, although there's a good network of DNT-affiliated huts, none is staffed, nor do any of them supply provisions. Keys to these huts (most of which are owned by BOT, Bodø's hiking association; see p.303) are available locally, but clearly you have to sort this out with BOT before you set off.

Among several possible bases for venturing into the Saltfjellet, **LØNSDAL**, around 110km north of Mo and 20km beyond the Arctic Circle, is the most easily reached either on the E6 or by train from Trondheim, Mo or Bodø (1–3 daily, but some trains only stop here by request; check with the conductor). Not that there's actually much to reach: a 1km-long turning off the E6 leads first to the *Hotel Polarsirkelen Høysfjellshotell* (Ⓣ75 69 41 22; ❸), a long wooden building in a sheltered location and with a cosy modern interior, and then to the lonely train station; the hotel has the only restaurant for miles around.

From Lønsdal, **hiking trails** lead off into the Saltfjellet. One of the more manageable options is the four-hour hike east (away from the national park) to **GRADDIS**, a tiny hamlet situated beside Highway 77, 18km east of the E6. Graddis has a **guesthouse** and **camping**, the *Graddis Fjellstue og Camping* (Ⓣ75 69 43 41, Ⓔgraddis@c2i.net; late June to late Aug), which has double rooms (❸), and rudimentary cabins (❷) as well as tent pitches all on a farmstead on the wooded slopes of the Junkerdal. Despite its gloominess, the Junkerdal is a favourite spot from which to explore the Saltfjellet, not least because it's easy to reach by road from Sweden.

Botn

Some 45km north of Lønsdal, the E6 regains the coast at **Rognan**, from where it pushes along the east side of the Saltdalsfjord. About 5km from Rognan, at **BOTN**, keep your eyes peeled for the signposted, 1km-long road up to the Krigskirkegårder, truly one of Nordland's most mournful and moving places. Buried here, in a wooded glade high above the fjord, are the Yugoslav prisoners of war and their German captors who died in the district during World War II. The men are interred in two separate graveyards – both immaculately maintained, though, unlike the plainer Yugoslav cemetery, the German graveyard is entered by a sturdy granite gateway. Mostly captured Tito partisans, the Yugoslavs died in their hundreds from disease, cold and malnutrition, not to mention torture and random murder, during the construction of the **Arctic railroad** to the iron-ore port of Narvik. When the Germans occupied Norway in 1940, the railway ended at Mosjøen, but they soon decided to push it north so that their cargo ships might avoid the dangerous voyage along the coast. This line, the **Nordlandsbanen**, involved the labour of 13,000 POWs, but the

Germans failed to complete it, and it was not until 1962 that the railway finally reached Bodø.

Fauske

From Botn, it's another 30km up the E6 to **FAUSKE**, which, but for a brief stretch of line from Narvik into Sweden, marks the northernmost point of the Norwegian rail network and is, consequently, an important transport hub. Along with nearby Bodø, the town is a departure point of the twice-daily Nord-Norgeekspressen, the express **bus** service that carries passengers to Narvik, where you change for either the bus to Tromsø or the Nordkappekspressen bus, which covers the next leg of the journey up to Alta (for Honningsvåg and Nordkapp). It takes about twelve hours to get from Fauske to Tromsø, but if you are aiming for Alta, you'll have to overnight in Narvik – which is no hardship and a gorgeous five-hour run away, past fjords, peaks and snow. The Nord-Norgeekspressen leaves from beside Fauske **train station** and tickets can be purchased from the driver or in advance at any bus station. Note that there is a fifty percent discount for InterRail and Scanrail pass holders on the Narvik journey.

From Fauske's train and long-distance bus station, it's a five- to ten-minute walk down the hill and left at the T-junction to the local bus station and a few metres more to the main drag, **Storgata**, which doubles as the E6. Storgata runs parallel to the fjord and holds the handful of shops that passes for the town centre. There's no **tourist office** and there's certainly no strong reason to linger here – nearby Bodø is a much more palatable place to stay, never mind Narvik – but Fauske can still be a handy if unexciting place to break your journey. Of the town's **hotels**, the pick is the *Fauske Hotell*, Storgata 82 (Ⓣ75 60 20 00, Ⓦwww.fauskehotell.no; ❻, sp/r ❹), a chunky square block whose interior is made slightly sickly by a surfeit of salmon-coloured streaky marble. Quarried locally, the marble is exported all over the world, but is something of an acquired taste. Marble apart, the hotel rooms are comfortable enough, and the big, tasty breakfast is a real snip at 80kr. Otherwise, the most popular budget choice is the hostel-like *Seljestua*, 500m from the train station at Seljeveien 2 (Ⓣ90 73 46 96; late June to mid-Aug; ❷), but a much, much better bet is the *Lundhøgda* campsite (Ⓣ75 64 39 66, Ⓔlundhogda@c2i.net; May–Sept; cabins ❷). This occupies a splendid location about 3km west of the town centre, overlooking the mountains and the fjord: head out of town along the E80 (the Bodø road), and turn off down a signposted country lane, ablaze with wild flowers in the summertime and flanked by old timber buildings. The campsite takes caravans, has spaces for tents and also offers cabins (❷).

Bodø and around

BODØ, some 60km west of Fauske along the E80, is the terminus of the Trondheim train line and the starting point of the Nord-Norgeekspressen express bus to points north. Founded in 1816, the town struggled to survive in its early years, but was saved from insignificance by the herring boom of the 1860s, a time when the town's harbourfront was crowded with the net-menders, coopers, oilskin-makers and canneries that kept the fleet at sea. Later, it accrued several industrial plants and became an important regional centre, but was then heavily bombed during World War II and today there's precious little left of the proud, nineteenth-century buildings that once

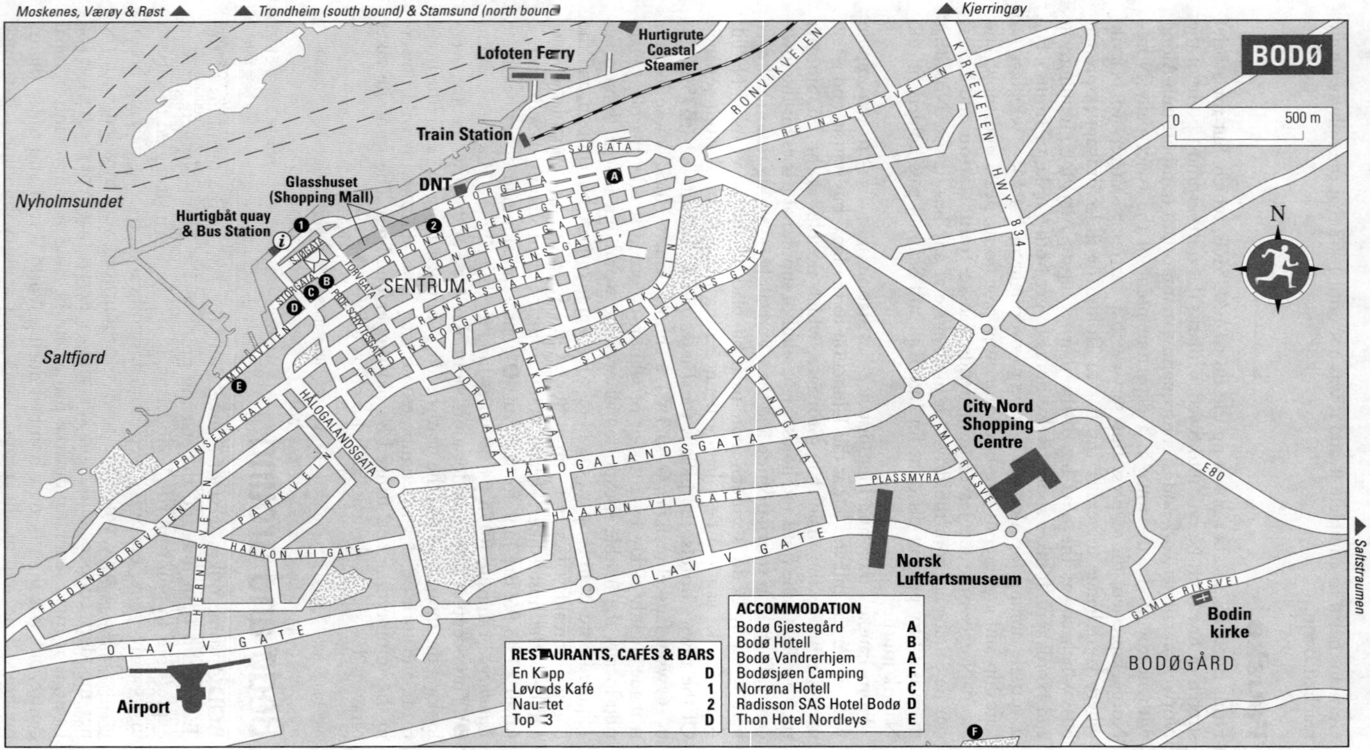

BODØ

Moskenes, Værøy & Røst
Trondheim (south bound) & Stamsund (north bound)
Kjerringøy
Saltstraumen

Lofoten Ferry
Hurtigrute Coastal Steamer
Train Station
DNT
Glasshuset (Shopping Mall)
Hurtigbåt quay & Bus Station
Nyholmsundet
Saltfjord
SENTRUM
City Nord Shopping Centre
Norsk Luftfartsmuseum
Bodin kirke
BODØGÅRD
Airport
0 500 m
N

SJØGATA, STORGATA, DRONNINGENS GATE, KONGENS GATE, PRINSENS GATE, RENSÅSGATA, FREDENSBORGVEIEN, TORVGATA, PROF. SCHYTTES GATE, MOLOVEIEN, PRINSENS GATE, HÅLOGALANDSGATA, PARKVEIEN, SIVERT NIELSENS GATE, BANKGATA, TORVGATA, BORTINDGATA, HAAKON VII GATE, OLAV V GATE, HERNESVEIEN, RONVIKVEIEN, REINSLETTVEIEN, KIRKEVEIEN HWY. 834, GAMLE RIKSVEI, PLASSMYRA, E80

ACCOMMODATION	
Bodø Gjestegård	A
Bodø Hotell	B
Bodø Vandrerhjem	A
Bodøsjøen Camping	F
Norrøna Hotell	C
Radisson SAS Hotel Bodø	D
Thon Hotel Nordleys	E

RESTAURANTS, CAFÉS & BARS	
En Kopp	D
Løvolds Kafé	1
Naustet	2
Top 3	D

flanked the waterfront. Nonetheless, Bodø manages a cheerful modernity, a bright and breezy place within comfortable striking distance of the old trading post of **Kjerringøy**, one of Nordland's most delightful spots. Bodø is also a regular stop on the Hurtigrute coastal boat route and, importantly, much the best place from which to hop over to the choicest parts of the Lofoten islands (see p.323).

Arrival and information

Bodø **airport** is just 2km south of the centre and regular local buses, marked *Sentrumsrunden,* link the airport with the central bus station (see below); a cab making the same journey costs around 90kr. The **train station** is at the eastern end of the town centre, just off the long main street, Sjøgata. The southern **Lofoten ferry** (to and from Moskenes plus the islets of Værøy and Røst) and the **Hurtigrute** coastal boat use the docks 400m and 600m respectively northeast along the waterfront from the train station. The **bus station** is 700m west along Sjøgata, in the same terminal complex as the Hurtigbåt passenger express boat dock for services to Lofoten (most usefully to and from Svolvær, see p.327). The **tourist office** is here too (late May to Aug Mon–Fri 9am–8pm, Sat 10am–6pm, Sun noon–8pm; Sept to late May Mon–Fri 9am–4pm & Sat 10am–2pm; ⓣ75 54 80 00, ⓦwww.bodoe.com). They give out information on connections to the Lofoten islands, rent out bikes and also issue an excellent town and district guide. To join the **DNT** hiking organization in Bodø, make your way to Bodø og Omegns Turistforening (BOT), Storgata 17 (Tues, Wed & Fri noon–3pm, Thurs noon–5pm; ⓣ75 52 14 13, ⓦwww.bot.no); they also dispense advice about the region's hiking trails and cabins.

Accommodation

Bodø has a reasonable supply of accommodation, including half a dozen hotels, an HI hostel, a campsite and a couple of guesthouses. In addition, the tourist office has a small supply of private rooms in the town and its environs with a fixed tariff of 400–500kr per double, plus a modest booking fee.

Bodø Gjestegård Storgata 90 ⓣ75 52 04 02, ⓔjohansst@online.no. This pleasant twenty-room guesthouse not far from the railway station offers bargain accommodation. It shares its reception with the hostel (see below). ❷

Bodø Hotell Professor Schyttes gate 5 ⓣ75 54 77 00, ⓦwww.bodohotell.no. Well-kept rooms with all the usual mod cons in this mid-sized, mid-range hotel housed in a five-storey block right in the centre of town. There's oodles of pine to admire too – all in true Scandinavian style. ❹, sp/r ❸

Bodø Vandrerhjem Storgata 90 ⓣ75 52 04 02, ⓦwww.vandrerhjem.no. This HI hostel occupies a modest, modern building with sunny balconies and a garden. It shares its reception with the *Bodø Gjestegård* (see above) and is open year-round. Dorm beds 150kr, doubles ❷

Bodøsjøen Camping Bodøsjøen ⓣ75 56 36 80. Year-round lakeside campsite located about 3.5km to the southeast of the centre, not far from the Bodin kirke. Tent pitches, caravan hook-ups and cabins (❷).

Norrøna Hotell Storgata 4b ⓣ75 51 90 60, ⓦwww.hotell-norrona.no. This standard-issue chain hotel occupies a large modern block just metres from the bus station. It's at the lower end of the market, but still reliably comfortable, and guests can enjoy the facilities of the neighbouring Radisson with whom the hotel has a special arrangement. ❹, sp/r ❸

Radisson SAS Hotel Bodø Storgata 2 ⓣ75 51 90 00, ⓦwww.bodo.radissonsas.com. The best hotel in town. Occupies an overly large, modern concrete and glass tower block, but has commodious and well-appointed rooms – and those on the upper floors have great views out to sea. ❼, sp/r ❹

Thon Hotel Nordleys Moloveien 14 ⓣ75 53 19 00, ⓦwww.thonhotels.no/nordleys. The newest hotel in Bodø, this smart, very modern hotel is right on the harbourfront, and most of the guest rooms have some kind of sea view. ❺ sp/r ❹

The Town

Bodø rambles over a low-lying peninsula that pokes out into the Saltfjord, its long and narrow centre concentrated along two parallel streets, Sjøgata and Storgata. The town is short of specific sights, but 2km southeast of the centre, on Olav V's gate, is its most popular attraction, the imaginative Norsk Luftfartsmuseum (Norwegian Aviation Museum; mid-June to mid-Aug Sun–Fri 10am–7pm & Sat 10am–5pm; mid-Aug to mid-June Mon–Fri 10am–4pm, Sat & Sun 11am–5pm; Ⓦwww.aviation-museum.com; 90kr), which tracks through the general history of Norwegian aviation. It adopts an imaginative approach to the subject and even the building is itself constructed in the shape of a two-bladed propeller: one "blade" houses air force and defence exhibits, the other civilian displays. The spot where the two blades meet straddles the ring road – Olav V's gate – and is topped by part of the old Bodø airport control tower. Among the planes to look out for are a Spitfire, a reminder that two RAF squadrons were manned by Norwegians during World War II, and a rare Norwegian-made Hønningstad C-5 Polar seaplane. Bodø was used by the US air force throughout the Cold War, and you can also see one of their U2 spy planes.

From the museum, it's a short drive east along the ring road to the Gamle riksvei roundabout, where you turn right for the one-kilometre detour to the onion-domed **Bodin kirke** (late June to mid-Aug Mon–Fri 10am–3pm; free), a pretty little stone church sitting snugly among clover meadows. Dating from the thirteenth century, the church was modified after the Reformation by the addition of a tower and the widening of its windows – the Protestants associated dark, gloomy churches with Catholic superstition. It is, however, the colourful seventeenth-century fixtures that catch the eye, plus the lovingly carved Baroque altarboard and pulpit, both painted in the eighteenth century by an itinerant German artist called Gottfried Ezechiel.

Eating and drinking

Bodø is hardly a gourmet's paradise, but there are one or two competent cafés and restaurants, kicking off with the traditional and inexpensive Norwegian menu of the canteen-style *Løvolds Kafé* (closed Sun), down by the quay at Tollbugata 9; main courses here feature local ingredients and average around 120kr, daily specials 100kr. More up-market, the *Naustet*, Storgata 11 (Ⓣ75 56 32 00), specializes in uncomplicated, excellent fish dishes from around 130kr, and the home-made chocolate ice cream is worth the visit alone. In addition, the *En Kopp* coffee bar at the *SAS Radisson Hotel* serves the best coffee in town, while the hotel's top-floor bar, *Top 13*, has the best view. A nice way to fill up cheaply is to buy a big bag of prawns (40–50kr) from one of the fishing boats along the quayside and eat al fresco at the water's edge.

Out from Bodø: Kjerringøy, Saltstraumen and the Svartisen glacier

There are three obvious excursions from Bodø: one northeast to the old trading station at Kjerringøy, another southeast to the tidal phenomenon known as the Saltstraumen, and a third, the longest, the 170-kilometre trip south to Holand (see p.298) for the Svartisen glacier. All three places can be reached by car or bike, Kjerringøy along Highway 834 and the other two via Highway 17 – the Kystriksveien – between Bodø and Mo-i-Rana (see p.298). As for **public transport**, Kjerringøy is reachable by bus and ferry, the Saltstraumen by bus, but the glacier is best seen on a guided tour. Bodø tourist office coordinates glacier tours and the most straightforward last around twelve hours, include bus and ferry transport, and cost in the region of 450kr, though that doesn't cover food. Advance booking – at least a day ahead – is advised, and be sure to have warm clothing. For longer excursions onto the glacier, contact the local specialist Nordland Turselskap direct (Ⓣ90 63 60 86, Ⓦwww.nordlandturselskap.no), though their trips are necessarily more expensive, beginning at about 600kr excluding transport.

Kjerringøy

The **KJERRINGØY trading post** (late May to late Aug daily 11am–5pm; 45kr; Ⓣ75 55 77 41, Ⓦwww.kjerringoy.no), just 40km north along the coast from Bodø by road and ferry, boasts a superbly preserved collection of nineteenth-century timber buildings set beside a slender, islet-sheltered channel. This was once the domain of the **Zahl family**, merchants who supplied the fishermen of Lofoten with everything from manufactured goods and clothes to farmyard foodstuffs in return for fish. It was not, however, an equal relationship: the Zahls, who operated a local monopoly until the 1910s, could dictate the price they paid for the fish, and many of the islanders were permanently indebted to them. This social division is still very much in evidence at the trading post, where there's a marked distinction between the guest rooms of the main house and the fishermen's bunk beds in the boat- and cookhouses. Indeed, the **family house** is remarkably fastidious, with its Italianate busts and embroidered curtains – even the medicine cabinet is well stocked with formidable Victorian remedies like the bottle of "Sicilian Hair Renewer".

There are enjoyable, hour-long **guided tours** around the main house throughout the summer (late May to late Aug, daily, every hour on the hour; 35kr), and afterwards you can nose around the reconstructed general store, drop in at the café and stroll the fine sandy beach. Taken altogether, it's a peaceful and picturesque spot and one that film-goers may recognize from the movie *I am Dina*, based on *Dina's Book*, by the Norwegian author Herbjørg Wassmo, which was filmed here.

Getting here from Bodø **by car** is easy enough – a straightforward coastal drive north along Highway 834 with the added treat of a ferry ride (Festvåg-Misten, every 30–60min, less frequently on Sun; 10min; passengers 20kr, car & driver 49kr return; Ⓣ99 28 32 09). Things are a tad more complicated **by bus**, but a day-return trip beginning at Bodø bus station is possible Monday through Friday from late June to late August; the round trip costs 92kr, including ferry – pick up a combined bus-and-ferry schedule from Bodø tourist office. More generally, there are between one and three buses daily from Bodø to Kjerringøy, where there's **accommodation** at the old parsonage, *Kjerringøy Prestegård*, about 1km north of the trading post along the main road (Ⓣ75 51 07 80, Ⓔkirkevergen@kirken.bodo.no). They have simple double rooms in the main building (❷) and slightly pleasanter ones in the renovated cowshed next door (❸).

Saltstraumen

Less interesting than Kjerringøy, but more widely publicized, is the maelstrom known as the **Saltstraumen**, 33km east of Bodø round the bay on Highway 17. Here, billions of gallons of water are forced through a narrow, 150m-wide channel four times daily, making a headlong dash between the inner and outer fjord. The whirling creamy water is at its most turbulent at high tide, and its most violent when the moon is new or full – a timetable is available from Bodø tourist office. However, although scores of tourists troop here for every high tide, you can't help but feel they wish they were somewhere else – the scenery is, in Norwegian terms at least, flat and dull, and the view from the bridge which spans the channel unexciting. That said, fishing enthusiasts will be impressed by the force of the water which pulls in all sorts of fish: cod, catfish and coley are common catches – one coley caught here weighed a remarkable 22.7 kilos (or so they say). Rods can be hired at several places, including the **Saltstraumen Opplevelsessenter** (Saltstraumen Adventure Centre; May–Aug daily 11am–6pm; Sept Sat & Sun only 11am–6pm; 65kr), housed in two adjoining buildings near the eastern end of the bridge. The centre tells you all you'd ever wanted to know about tidal currents and then some, and also has several pools where you can take a close look at local marine life.

It takes about fifty minutes to **drive** from Bodø to the Saltstraumen, or you could take local **bus** #519 (Mon–Sat 4–6 daily, Sun 1 daily; 1hr; 50kr one way), though its times rarely coincide with the high tide. In this case, you can kill a couple of hours very pleasantly at *Kafé Kjelen*, a little red house on the west side of the bridge, whose balcony offers views over the maelstrom – don't miss its *møsprumlefse*, a traditional, burrito-like pancake stuffed with a mix of sweet brown-cheese sauce, sour cream and melted butter.

North to Narvik

The 240-kilometre journey north from Fauske to Narvik is spectacular, with the **E6** rounding the fjords, twisting and tunnelling through the mountains and rushing over high, pine-dusted plateaux. The scenery is the main event hereabouts, and there's little to merit a stop, with two notable exceptions – the fascinating old farmstead at **Kjelvik**, where the hardship of rural life in Norway is revealed in idyllic surroundings, and the remote former trading post of **Tranøy**, a thirty-kilometre detour west of the E6 via Highway 81. At the end of the journey, **Narvik** is an eminently likeable industrial town that witnessed some especially fierce fighting during the German invasion of 1940. It's a good place for an overnight stop and a useful launching pad for the long haul to the far north, or a visit to the Vesterålen and Lofoten islands.

En route between Fauske and Narvik, the E6 presents two opportunities to catch a **car ferry** to Lofoten – one at Skutvik, the other at Bognes. The more southerly of the two is **Skutvik**, 35km to the west of the E6, with ferries to Svolvær. At **Bognes**, where the E6 is interrupted by the Tysfjord, there's a choice of ferries. One sails to Lødingen and the E10 on Lofoten, while a second hops across the Tysfjord to **Skarberget** to pick up the E6, just 80km south of Narvik. All these ferries are operated by OVDS (Ⓦwww.ovds.no) on a first-come, first-served basis, though in the summertime (June–Aug) the Skutvik–Svolvær ferry can be reserved ahead of time on the OVDS website or on Ⓣ76 11 82 45 (Mon–Fri 8.30am–3pm). Long-distance **buses** link Bodø, Fauske and Narvik twice daily; the bus journey from Fauske to Narvik takes five hours.

The E6 north to Bognes

Beyond Fauske, the E6 scuttles over the hills to the small industrial town of **Straumen** and then threads along the coast to **Sommarset**, an old ferry point where boats crossed the **Leirfjord** until a new stretch of road was built around the fjord in 1986. This new section is an ambitious affair that drills through the mountains with the fjord glistening below. It also passes within 250m of the old farmstead of **KJELVIK**, 58km from Fauske, where a scattering of old wooden buildings, including a cottage, woodshed, forge and mill, nestle in a green, wooded valley. It's a beautiful spot, but the tenant farmers who worked the land finally gave up the battle against their harsh isolation in 1967. There was no electricity, no water, the soil was thin, and the only contact with the outside world was by boat – supply vessels would come up the Leirfjord to the Kjelvik jetty, from where it was a steep two-kilometre hike to the farm, 200m above the fjord. Today, there's **open access** to the farm, which is kept in good condition, and wandering around is a delight: you can also follow the old footpath down to the Kjelvik jetty. **Guided tours** of Kjelvik are available in the summer (late June to late August daily 11am–5pm; 30kr; Ⓦwww.saltenmuseum.no) and, on the last Saturday of the season, the **Kjelvik festival** sees the old buildings put to their original uses. Griddle-cakes are cooked on the wood stove, and dollops of sour cream and porridge are doled out to visitors.

After Kjelvik, the E6 bores through the mountains to reach, after about 40km, the couple of houses that make up **KRÅKMO**, with the lake on one side and the domineering mass of a mighty mountain, Kråkmotind, on the other. This was once a favourite haunt of that crusty old reactionary Knut Hamsun, for more on whom see below.

From Kråkmo, it's around 50km to the point where Highway 81 branches off for Skutvik and the Svolvær car ferry (see below) and another scenic 20km or so up the E6 to **Bognes**. Here, one ferry heads west to **Lødingen** on the Vesterålen islands (mid-June to mid-Aug 10 daily, mid-Aug to mid-June 5 daily; 1hr; passenger 47kr, car & driver 150kr; Ⓣ177 in Nordland, otherwise Ⓣ75 77 24 10, Ⓦwww.ovds.no), while a second travels to **Skarberget** for the E6 and the remaining 80km to Narvik (every 1hr or 90min; 25min; passenger 28kr, car & driver 79kr; Ⓣ177, Ⓦwww.ovds.no). In summer, it's worth arriving two hours before departure to be sure of a space.

West off the E6: Tranøy, Hamsund and Skutvik (for Svolvær)

Spearing off the E6 20km before Bognes, **Highway 81** wriggles its way west across the islet-shredded coastline bound for the **Skutvik car ferry** over to Svolvær, on the Lofoten (early June to late Aug 8–10 daily; late Aug to early June 2–4 daily; 2hr; passengers 70kr, car & driver 240kr; Ⓣ177 in Nordland, otherwise Ⓣ75 77 24 10, Ⓦwww.ovds.no). The road is only 35km long, but it takes a good hour to drive and en route it threads through some dramatic scenery, all craggy shorelines and imposing peaks. About 15km from the E6, the highway spans a narrow channel to reach the island of **Hamarøy**, noteworthy as the boyhood home of the writer **Knut Hamsun** (1859–1952). Long a leading literary light, Hamsun blotted his Norwegian copybook with his admiration for Hitler and the Nazis before and during the occupation, though his culpability has been the subject of much heated debate. Whatever the truth, Hamsun remained something of a hate figure for several decades and only recently has there been a degree of rehabilitation – as witnessed by the opening of several Hamsun-related sites on this his home island.

Just after Highway 81 crosses onto **Hamarøy**, a side road cuts north to make the thirteen-kilometre journey to the old trading post of **TRANØY**, in stern and bleak surroundings on the island's northern shore. Here you'll find two art galleries celebrating Hamsun's work, beginning with the **Tranøy Galleri** (late June to mid-Aug daily 11am–6pm; free; Ⓦwww.tranoy-galleri.com), which features illustrations of Hamsun's books by Tor Arne Moen as well as the work of local artists, all for sale. Nearby, the **Hamsungalleriet på Tranøy** (Hamsun Gallery; mid-June to mid-Aug 11am–6pm, 30kr), in the old general store where

Hamsun worked as a youth, also concentrates on Hamsun-related paintings, most notably those of the Norwegian Karl Erik Harr (b. 1940).

Tranøy has a couple of excellent **places to stay**. First up is the *Edvardas hus* (ⓣ75 77 21 82, ⓦwww.edvardashus.no; ❺; mid-June to mid-Aug, rest of year by appointment only), which occupies two old buildings set a couple of hundred metres apart, one a merchant's house dating back to the 1910s, the other a former bank built a decade later; there are nine impeccably stylish, extremely comfortable bedrooms here and the food is outstanding – both at breakfast and at the pocket-sized **restaurant**, which is open to non-residents, though reservations are strongly advised. Alternatively, *Tranøy Fyr* (ⓣ91 32 80 13, ⓦwww.tranoyfyr.no; June–Aug; ❹) has a dozen straightforward rooms in the old lighthousemen's quarters, on the edge of the ocean beneath the lighthouse. *Tranøy Fyr* also has its own café-restaurant with outdoor seating in the summertime.

Doubling back to Highway 81, it's a brief drive west to the hamlet of **HAMSUND**, the site of Knut Hamsun's boyhood home, now the tiny **Hamsuns barndomshjem** (late June to late Aug daily 11am–6pm; 35kr), but there are plans to build something more substantial in his honour. From here, it's another short haul to the Skutvik ferry.

Narvik

A relatively modern town, **NARVIK** was established just a century ago as an ice-free port to handle the iron ore brought by train from the mines in northern

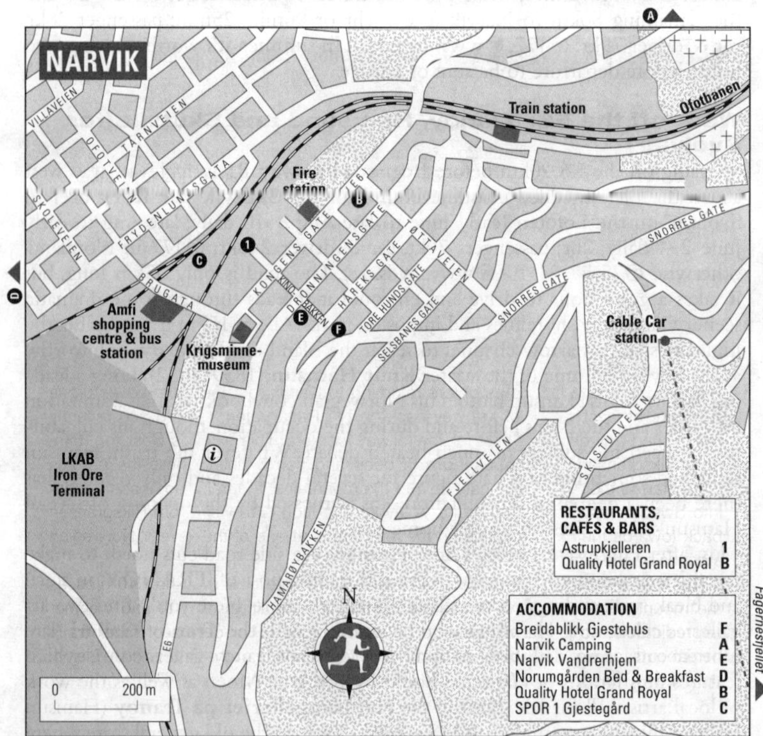

Sweden. And it doesn't make any bones about its main function either: the **iron-ore docks** are immediately conspicuous, slap-bang in the centre of town, the rust-coloured machinery overwhelming much of the waterfront. Yet, for all the mess, the industrial complex is strangely impressive, its cat's cradle of walkways, conveyor belts, cranes and funnels oddly beguiling and giving the town a frontier, very Arctic, feel. Not content with its iron, Narvik has also had a fair old stab at reinventing itself as an **outdoor sports** centre, becoming a popular destination for skiers, paraglidlers and scuba-divers – and developing a good range of guesthouses to match.

Arrival and information

Fifteen minutes' walk from one end to the other, Narvik's sloping centre straggles along the main street, **Kongens gate**, which doubles as the E6. The **train station** is at the north end of the town and from here it's a five- to ten-minute walk along Kongens gate to the **bus station**, in the basement of the Amfi shopping centre on the west side of the main drag. The **tourist office** is a little further to the south at Kongens gate 26 (early June Mon–Fri 9am–5pm, Sat 10am–5pm & Sun 11am–2pm; mid-June to mid-Aug Mon–Fri 9am–7pm, Sat 10am–7pm & Sun 11am–7pm; late Aug Mon–Fri 9am–5pm, Sat 10am–3pm; Sept–May Mon–Fri 8am–3.30pm; ⓣ76 96 56 00, ⓦwww.destinationnarvik.com). The staff issue free town maps, provide lots of information on outdoor pursuits and have the full range of bus and ferry timetables; they will also assist

The Ofotbanen

One of the real treats of a visit to Narvik is the **train ride** into the mountains that rear up behind the town and spread east across the Swedish border. Completed in 1903, this railway line – the **Ofotbanen** – was, by any standard, a remarkable achievement and the hundreds of navvies that made up the work force endured astounding hardships during its construction. The line passes through some wonderful scenery, slipping between hostile peaks before reaching the rocky, barren and loch-studded mountain plateaux beyond. **Connex** (Narvik train station ⓣ76 92 31 21, ⓦwww.connex.se), a Swedish company, now operates the **Ofotbanen** and trains arrive and depart **Narvik train station** two or three times daily, shuttling to and from Kiruna, three hours away in northern Sweden. The times of the trains mean that a short day-trip into the mountains behind Narvik is easy enough, and the obvious target is **RIKSGRÄNSEN**, a pleasant hiking and skiing centre just over the border in Sweden – so take your passport. The journey from Narvik to **Riksgränsen** takes fifty minutes and a return ticket costs 222kr, 111kr each way. Most train travellers nose around **Riksgränsen** for a few hours before returning to Narvik, but the more adventurous can **hike** at least a part of the way back on the **Rallarveien**, the old and recently refurbished trail originally built for the railway workers. This extends west for 15km from Riksgränsen to **Rombaksbotn**, a deep and narrow inlet where the navvies once started their strenuous haul up into the mountains; the trail also heads deeper into Sweden, to Abisko and Kiruna. A favourite option is to walk from Riksgränsen back towards the coast, picking up the return train at one of the several Norwegian stations on the way.

The area around the Ofotbanen isn't nearly as remote now that the **E10** crosses the mountains to the north of the railway, but the terrain is difficult and weather unpredictable, so hikers will need to be well equipped. For details of other **trails** hereabouts, as well as **cabins**, contact Narvik tourist office or the DNT affiliate Narvik og Omegn Turistforening (ⓦwww.narvikfjell.no). Hiking **maps** are available from the Narvik Libris bookshop, in the Amfi shopping centre.

with ferry and activity reservations. From the tourist office, it's another five-minute walk down along Kongens gate to the south end of the town centre and the dock for the **Hurtigbåt** passenger express boat service to Svolvær on Lofoten. The Hurtigbåt – the Arctic Fjord Express (ⓣ76 96 76 00, ⓦwww.lsbs.no) – operates once daily, takes three-and a-half hours to reach Svolvær and costs 350kr one-way.

As regards Narvik's outdoor sports, there are lots of options from hang- and para-gliding through to **mountain climbing** and guided **glacier walking** with Nord-Norsk Klatreskole (ⓣ76 07 49 11, ⓦwww.nordnorskklatreskole.no), and **scuba diving** amidst the wreck-studded waters around Narvik with Narvik Dykk & Eventyr (ⓣ99 51 22 05, ⓦwww.narvikdykaventyr.nu). Most operators rent out the appropriate specialist tackle and Narvik Dykk & Eventyr provides introductory diving lessons.

Accommodation

Narvik is a tad short of **hotels**, but it does have several very recommendable **guesthouses** and a reasonably convenient **campsite**, *Narvik Camping*, about 2km north of the centre on the E6 at Rombaksveien 75 (ⓣ76 94 58 10, ⓦwww.narvikcamping.com). It's open all year and has tent and caravan pitches, hook-ups and cabins (❷).

Breidablikk Gjestehus Tore Hunds gate 41 ⓣ76 94 14 18, ⓦwww.breidablikk.no. This pleasant, unassuming guesthouse is neat and trim, with homely en-suite rooms. Those on the upper floors have attractive views over town, and a good, hearty breakfast is included in the room rate. It's located at the top of the steps at the end of Kinobakken, a side road leading east off Kongens gate, just up from the main town square. ❷

Narvik Vandrerhjem Dronningensgate 58 ⓣ76 96 22 00, ⓦwww.narvikvendrerhjem.no. Part of a larger hotel, the hostel rooms are modern, with lots of light, and some have small balconies. Free Internet access, though this doesn't quite make up for the noise from the nightclub next door on the weekend. Take your ear plugs. Dorm beds 170kr, doubles ❷

Norumgården Bed & Breakfast Framnesveien 127 ⓣ76 94 48 57, ⓦwww.norumgaarden.narviknett.no. Lavish but good-value B&B in a 1920s timber villa. The Germans used the place as an officers' mess during the war and today, tastefully restored, it holds three large guest rooms, two of which have kitchenettes. Antiques are liberally distributed across the house and breakfast is included. ❷

Quality Hotel Grand Royal Kongens gate 64 ⓣ76 97 70 00, ⓦwww.choicehotels.com. Although some of Narvik's hotels have seen better days, the Grand, just down from the train station, is well kept; its public rooms are wood-panelled and elegant, while the bedrooms are perfectly adequate in standard chain style. ❻, sp/r ❹

SPOR 1 Gjestegård Brugata 2A ⓣ76 94 60 20, ⓦwww.spor1.no. This trim guesthouse is the pick of the budget/backpacker options with clean and comfortable rooms in a brisk, modern style. Doubles, quads and a larger dorm room plus kitchen facilities, a sauna and a bar. Occupies a creatively recycled railway building, just below the main town bridge. Dorm beds from 160kr, doubles ❷

The Town

Narvik's first modern settlers were the navvies who built the railway line, the **Ofotbanen** (see box, p.309), to the mines in Kiruna, over the border in Sweden at the end of the nineteenth century – a herculean task commemorated every March by a week of singing, dancing and drinking, when the locals dress up in period costume. The town grew steadily up until World War II, when it was demolished during ferocious fighting for control of the harbour and iron-ore supplies. Perhaps inevitably, the rebuilt town centre is rather lacking in appeal, with modern concrete buildings replacing the wooden houses that went before, but it still musters a breezy northern charm. It also possesses the fascinating **Nordland Røde Kors Krigsminnemuseum** (Red Cross War Memorial

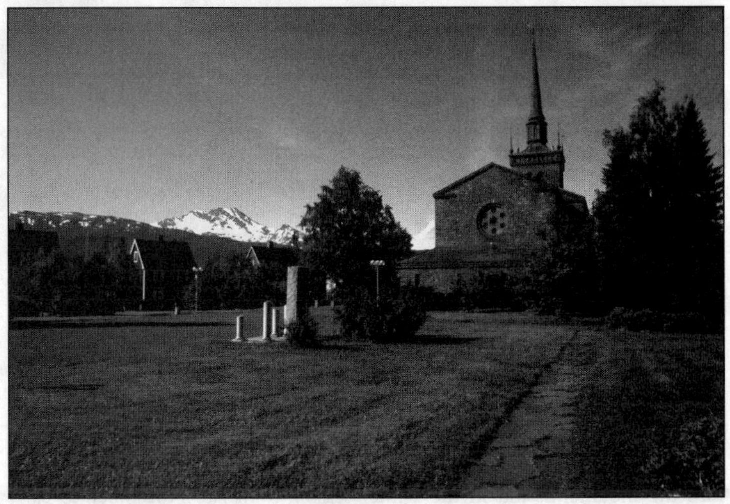

△ Narvik

Museum; April to early June & late Aug to Sept daily 11am–3pm; early June to late Aug Mon–Sat 10am–9pm & Sun noon–6pm; 50kr; Ⓦ www.warmuseum.no), just down from the tourist office. Run by the Red Cross, the museum documents the wartime German saturation bombing of the town, and the bitter and bloody sea and air battles in which hundreds of foreign servicemen died alongside a swathe of the local population. It was a complicated campaign, with the German invasion of April 1940 followed by an Allied counterattack spearheaded by the Royal Navy. The Allies actually recaptured Narvik, driving the Germans into the mountains, but were hurriedly evacuated when Hitler launched his invasion of France. The fight for Narvik lasted two months and the German commander wrote of the sea change amongst his Norwegian adversaries, who toughened up to become much more determined soldiers, and skilled ones at that: many were crack shots from their hunting days and all could ski. In the short term, this change of attitude prefigured the formation of the Resistance; in the long term it pretty much put paid to Norway's traditional isolationism. The museum gives a thoroughly moving and thoughtfully presented account of the battle for Narvik and then tracks through the German occupation of Norway until liberation in 1945.

Narvik also offers **guided tours** of the LKAB mining company's ore-terminal complex (mid-June to mid-Aug 3pm daily; 50kr), interesting if only for the opportunity to spend ninety minutes amid such giant, ore-stained contraptions. After its arrival by train, the ore is carried on the various conveyor belts to the quayside, from where some thirty million tons of it are shipped out each year. Sign up for the tours at the tourist office.

Fagernesfjellet

Narvik's **cable car** (daily: early June & Aug 1–9pm, late June 1pm–1am; 80kr single, 100kr return), located a stiff fifteen-minute walk above the town and behind the train station, is the easiest way to reach the town's mountainous environs, whisking passengers up the first 650m of the mighty **Fagernesfjellet**. There's a restaurant and viewing point at the top of the cable car, and from here,

Moving on from Narvik

There's a choice of several routes on from Narvik. The **Nordkappekspressen bus** (1 daily except Sat; 10hr) shoots north along the E6 to Alta (see p.353), whilst the **Nord-Norgeekspressen bus** (1–4 daily) makes the four-hour hop north to Tromsø (see p.344). Both trips give sight of some wonderfully wild and diverse scenery, from craggy mountains and blue-black fjords to gentle, forested valleys – though it's not perhaps quite as scenic a journey as the E6 from Fauske to Narvik. A third bus service, the **Lofoten Ekspressen** (1–2 daily) runs west from Narvik to Sortland, Stokmarknes, Svolvær and Leknes in the Lofoten islands (see p.323). On all these buses, plus the bus trips south from Narvik to Fauske (for connecting trains to Trondheim) and Bodø, most rail-pass holders are entitled to a fifty percent discount.

Narvik also has an all-year **Hurtigbåt** passenger express boat service to Svolvær (1 daily, 3hr 30min; 350kr one-way) and **Ofotbanen trains** (see box p.309) to Kiruna and Luleå in Sweden; the ride to Luleå takes around six-and-a-half hours.

on a clear day, you can see the Lofoten islands and experience the midnight sun in all its glory (end of May to mid-July). In addition, **hiking trails** delve further into the mountains, and in the winter season, from late November to early May, the cable car provides a shuttle service for **skiers and snowboarders**. The network of skiing slopes and trails includes five ski lifts, 7km of prepared courses and unlimited off-piste skiing, with some floodlit areas; for further details contact the tourist office. Finally, the cable car stops running in windy or foggy conditions, so – if you're walking there – you might want to check it's operating with the tourist office before setting out.

Eating

Things are likely to change, but at present Narvik is very short of recommendable **cafés** and **restaurants**. Probably the best option is the cellar-like *Astrupkjelleren Restaurant*, Kinobakken 1, where the mostly meaty main courses start at 170kr. Alternatively, there's the rather more formal restaurant of the *Quality Hotel Grand Royal*, which offers an all-you-can-eat buffet for around 200kr during the summer, featuring crab's claws and piles of tasty fish; for the rest of the year, it's a sit-down affair with much the same type and quality of food.

The Vesterålen islands

A raggle-taggle archipelago in the Norwegian Sea, the **Vesterålen islands**, and their southerly neighbours the Lofoten, are like western Norway in miniature: the terrain is hard and unyielding, the sea boisterous and fretful, and the main – often the only – industry is fishing. The weather is temperate but wet, and the islanders' historic isolation has bred a distinctive culture based, in equal measure, on Protestantism, the extended family and respect for the ocean.

The archipelago was first settled by semi-nomadic hunter-agriculturalists some 6000 years ago, and it was they and their Iron-Age successors who chopped down the birch and pine forests that once covered the coasts. It was boatbuilding, however, which brought prosperity: by the seventh century, the islanders were able to build ocean-going vessels, a skill that enabled the islanders to join in the Viking bonanza. Local clan leaders became important warlords, none more so than the eleventh-century chieftain **Tore Hund**, one-time liegeman of Olav Haraldsson, and one of the men selected to finish Olav off at the Battle of Stiklestad (see p.293) – the fulfilment of a blood debt incurred by Olav's execution of his nephew. In the early fourteenth century, the islanders **lost their independence** and were placed under the control of Bergen: by royal decree, all the fish the islanders caught had to be shipped to Bergen for export. This may have suited the economic interests of the Norwegian monarchy and the Danish governors who succeeded them, but it put the islanders at a terrible disadvantage. With their monopoly guaranteed, Bergen's merchants controlled both the price they paid for the fish and the prices of the goods they sold to the islanders – a **truck system** that was to survive, increasingly under the auspices of local merchants, until the early years of the twentieth century. Since World War II, improvements in fishing techniques and, more latterly, the growth in tourism and the extension of the road system have all combined to transform island life and all but end the hard times.

Somewhat confusingly, the Vesterålen archipelago is shared between the counties of **Troms** and **Nordland**: the northern Vesterålen islands are in Troms, while the southern half of the Vesterålen and all the Lofoten islands are in Nordland. The Vesterålen islands are the less rugged of the two groups – greener, gentler and less mountainous, with more of the land devoted to agriculture, though this gives way to vast tracts of peaty moorland in the far north. The villages are less immediately appealing too, often no more than narrow ribbons straggling along the coast and across any available stretch of fertile land. Consequently, many travellers simply rush through on their way to Lofoten, a mistake primarily in so far as the fishing port of **Andenes**, tucked away at the far end of the island of Andøya, has a strange but enthralling back-of-beyond charm and is a centre for **whalewatching** expeditions. In summer, Andenes also has the advantage of being linked by ferry to Gryllefjord, on the island of Senja. Other Vesterålen highlights are the magnificent but extremely narrow **Trollfjord**, where cruise ships and the Hurtigrute coastal boat perform some nifty manoeuvres, and **Harstad**, a comparative giant with a population of 22,000 and the proud possessor of a splendid medieval church.

Transport to and around the Vesterålen islands

Getting to the Vesterålen islands from the mainland by **public transport** is easy enough – indeed, the number of permutations is almost bewildering – but getting around them can be more troublesome. The **E10** is the main island road, running the 240km or so west from the E6 just north of Narvik to **Melbu**, at the southern end of the Vesterålen. A **car ferry** (see p.316) then links Melbu with Fiskebøl on the Lofoten islands (see p.324) – although this will soon be replaced by a tunnel – and thereafter the E10 proceeds without interruption to Å, at the southern tip of the Lofoten and about 160km from Fiskebøl.

If you have your own **vehicle** it's possible to drive from one end of the whole island chain to the other, catching the ferry from Gryllefjord on the mainland to Andenes and then driving south across the Vesterålen and the Lofoten islands to return to the mainland by ferry from Moskenes (see p.334). Drivers intent on a somewhat less epic trip could investigate the **car rental** outlets at Harstad, which offer special short deals from around 600kr a day. No single **itinerary** stands out, but the E6 and E10 in from Narvik has the advantage of simplicity – with Harstad, Sortland and then Andenes being an obvious approach, plus Stokmarknes if you're heading on to Lofoten. On the Vesterålen, **Andenes** has most to offer as a base, thanks to its whale- and bird-watching trips and choice of accommodation.

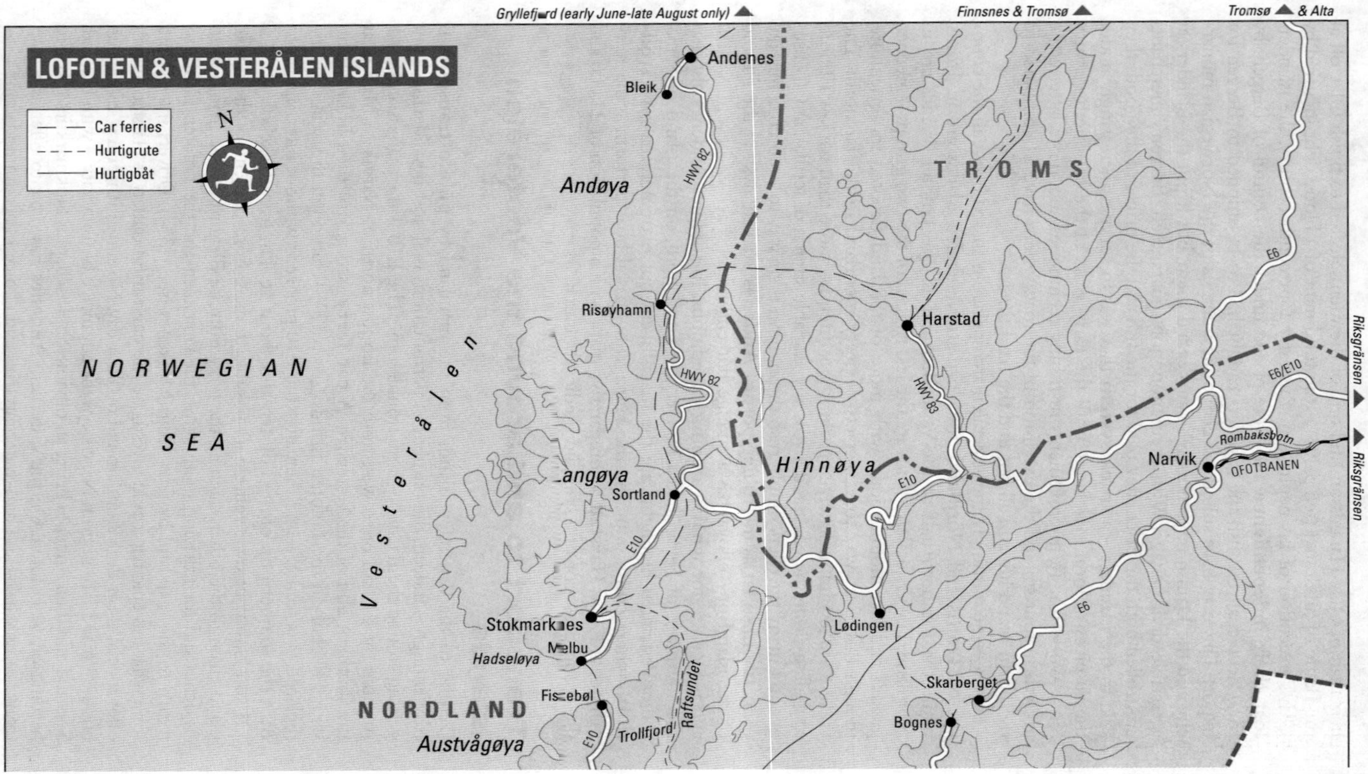

LOFOTEN & VESTERÅLEN ISLANDS

Car ferries
Hurtigrute
Hurtigbåt

N

Gryllefj■rd (early June-late August only)
Finnsnes & Tromsø
Tromsø & Alta
Riksgränsen
Riksgränsen

Andenes
Bleik
Andøya
HWY 82
Risøyhamn
TROMS
Harstad
HWY 83
E6
E6/E10
Rombaksbotn
OFOTBANEN
Narvik
NORWEGIAN
SEA
Vesterålen
Hinnøya
E10
Langøya
Sortland
Lødingen
Stokmark■es
M■lbu
Hadseløya
Skarberget
Bognes
Fis■ebøl
Raftsundet
Trollfjord
NORDLAND
Austvågøya

▶ Svartisen glacier & Kystriksveien

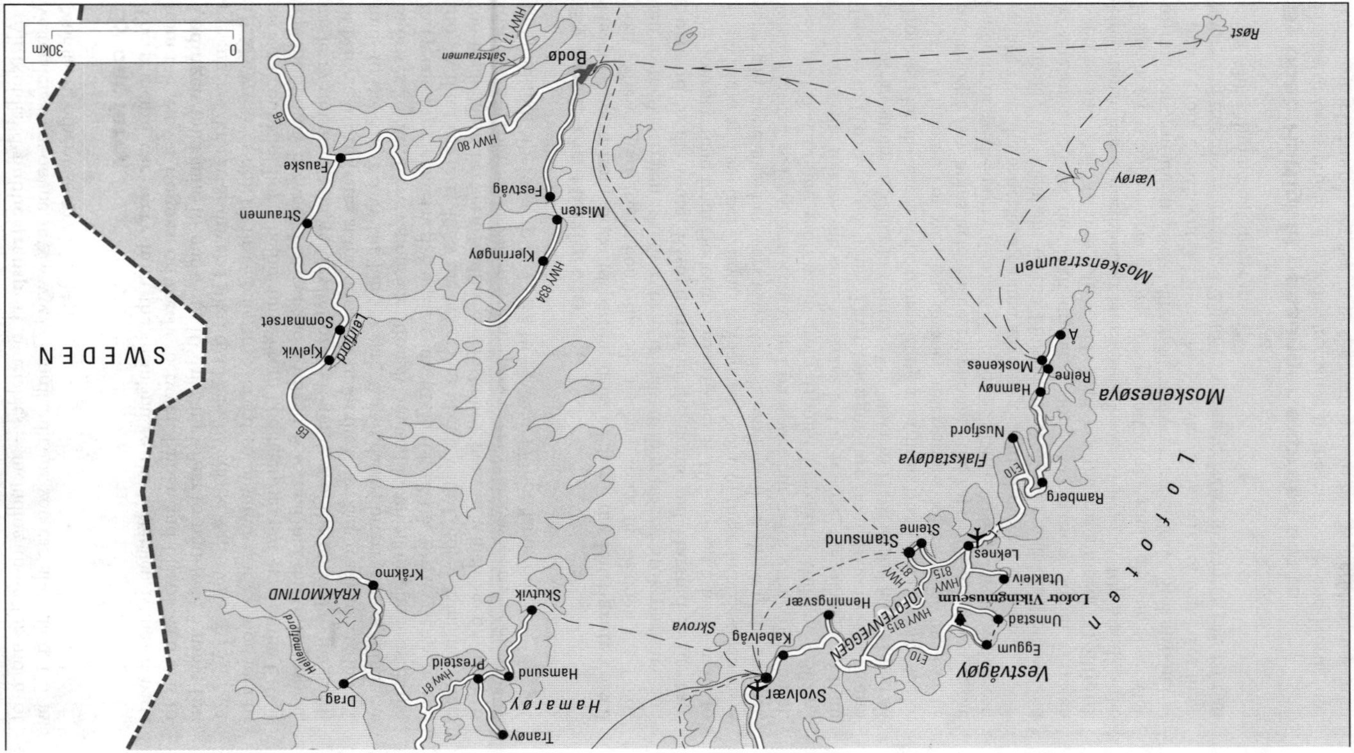

All Nordland **public transport** timetables – including those for much of Vesterålen – are online at Ⓦwww.177nordland.com; you can also call Ⓣ177 in Nordland, otherwise Ⓣ75 77 24 10.

By car ferry

The principal **car ferry** from the mainland to the Vesterålen islands departs from the jetty at **Bognes**, on the E6 between Fauske and Narvik, and sails to **Lødingen** (mid-June to mid-Aug 10 daily, mid-Aug to mid-June 5 daily; 1hr; passenger 47kr, car & driver 150kr; Ⓣ177 in Nordland, otherwise Ⓣ75 77 24 10, Ⓦwww.ovds.no). It's first-come, first-served, so in summer it's a good idea to arrive a couple of hours before time. From Lødingen, it's just 4km to the E10 at a point midway between Harstad and Sortland. A second, but this time seasonal, car ferry runs from remote **Gryllefjord**, 110km west of the E6 well to the north of Narvik, to **Andenes** at the northern tip of the Vesterålen (early to late June & mid- to late Aug 2 daily, late June to early Aug 3 daily; 2hr; passengers 130kr; car & driver 260kr). Reservations are strongly advised by email or phone with the ferry company concerned, Senjafergene (Ⓣ76 14 12 03, Ⓦwww.senjafergene .no). A third car ferry links the Vesterålen islands with Lofoten, running across the Hadselfjord between **Melbu** and **Fiskebøl**, both of which are on the E10 (daily 7am–11pm, every 90min; 30min; passengers 28kr; car & driver 68kr; Ⓣ177 in Nordland, otherwise Ⓣ75 77 24 10, Ⓦwww.177nordland.com).

By boat: the Hurtigrute

Heading north from Bodø (departing daily at 3pm), the **Hurtigrute** coastal boat (Ⓦwww.hurtigruten.com) threads a scenic route up through the Lofoten to the Vesterålen islands, where it calls at four places: **Stokmarknes** and **Sortland** in the south, **Risøyhamn** in the north and **Harstad** in the east. The journey time from Bodø to Stokmarknes is 10 hours, 3.5 hours more to Risøyhamn and another 2 hours to Harstad. None of these four destinations is especially appealing, but workaday Risøyhamn is well on the way to Andenes, while Harstad is a regional centre and transport hub with a fine old church (see p.318). Cruising southwards from Tromsø (departing daily at 1.30am), the Hurtigrute follows the same itinerary, but in reverse; the sailing time from Tromsø to Harstad is 6.5 hours. The **passenger fare** from Bodø to Risøyhamn is 743kr in summer, 520kr in winter, 558/796kr to Harstad and 805/1150kr to Tromsø. The all-year fare for transporting a car from Bodø to Harstad is 425kr, 555kr to Tromsø. For vehicles, advance reservations are essential, but can be made just a few hours beforehand by phoning the captain – ask down at the harbour or at the port's tourist office for assistance. Special deals, which can reduce costs dramatically, are often advertised at local tourist offices too.

Scenically, the highlight of the Hurtigrute cruise through the Lofoten and Vesterålen islands is the **Raftsundet**, a long and narrow sound between Svolvær and Stokmarknes, off which branches the magnificent **Trollfjord**. Unfortunately, the northbound Hurtigrute leaves Svolvær at 10pm and so the Raftsundset is only visible during the period of the midnight sun (late May to mid-July); in the opposite direction, however, boats leave Stokmarknes at a much more convenient 3.15pm. The Svolvær/Stokmarknes trip takes three hours and the passenger fare is 230kr in summer, 160kr in winter; cars cost an extra 330kr throughout the year.

By boat: Hurtigbåt passenger express boats

Hurtigbåt boats provide a speedy alternative to the car ferries and Hurtigrute. The main **Hurtigbåt** service from the mainland to the **Vesterålen** runs from

Tromsø to Harstad (2–3 daily; 2hr 45min; 380kr; Ⓦwww.tfds.no). There are also two especially useful Hurtigbåt boats to the **Lofoten**: Narvik to Svolvær in Lofoten (1 daily, 3hr 30min; 350kr; Ⓦwww.lsbs.no); and Bodø to Svolvær (1–2 daily; 3hr 30min; 260kr). In all cases, advance booking – most easily done via the local tourist office – is a good idea.

By bus

Operated by **Nor-Way Bussekspress** (Ⓦwww.nor-way.no), the long-distance **Lofoten Ekspressen** provides the main bus service from the mainland to the Vesterålen islands. There are two routings. The first leaves Narvik once or twice daily to run along the E6 and then the E10, calling at Sortland, Stokmarknes and Melbu; the bus then takes the Melbu-Fiskebøl ferry before heading onto Svolvær and ultimately Leknes on the Lofoten. The second routing (1 daily) runs north from Bodø and Fauske to the Bognes-Lødingen car ferry; from Lødingen, the bus then proceeds to Sortland, Stokmarknes and Melbu, where it takes the ferry before continuing on to Svolvær, Leknes and finally Å in Lofoten. As examples of **journey times**, Narvik to Sortland takes just over three hours, Bodø to Sortland seven.

These Nor-Way Bussekspress services are supplemented by a number of **local buses** operated by **Nordtrafikk** (Ⓣ177 in Nordland, otherwise Ⓣ75 77 24 10, Ⓦwww.177nordland.com). Two of Nordtrafikk's most useful Vesterålen services link Lødingen with Harstad (2 daily; 2hr 30min) and Sortland with Andenes (2–4 daily; 2hr).

Harstad

Readily reached by car, bus and the Hurtigrute coastal boat, **HARSTAD**, just 130km from Narvik, is easily the largest town on the Vesterålen islands. It's home to much of northern Norway's engineering industry, its sprawling docks a tangle of supply ships, repair yards and cold-storage plants spread out along the gentle slopes of the Vågsfjord. This may not sound too enticing, and it's true that Harstad wins few beauty contests, but the town does have the odd attraction, and if you're tired of sleepy Norwegian villages, it at least provides a bustling interlude.

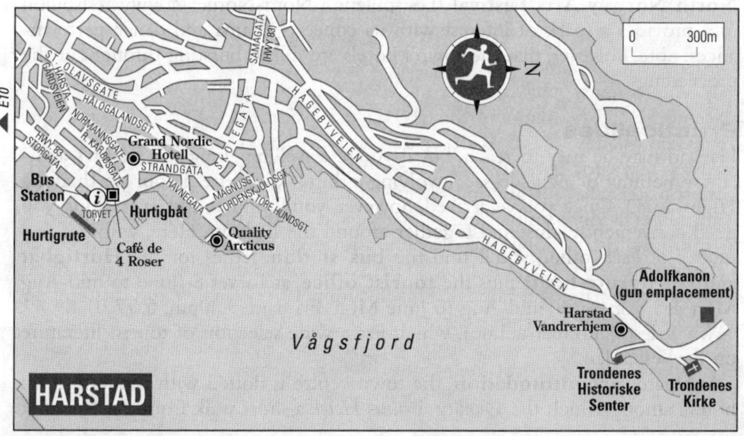

The sights

The main item of interest, the **Trondenes kirke** (opening times vary; free; guided tours early June to mid-Aug 1–3 daily except on Sat; 35kr), occupies a lovely leafy location beside the fjord 3km north of the town centre at the end of the slender Trondenes peninsula. To get there, take the local "Trondenes" **bus** (Mon–Sat 1 hourly; 10min), which leaves the bus station beside the tourist office and goes past the church – or take a taxi. By car, follow Highway 83 north from the centre and watch for the signposted turning on the right. The original wooden church was built at the behest of King Øystein (of *rorbuer* fame, see box on p.324) at the beginning of the twelfth century and had the distinction of being the northernmost church in Christendom for several centuries. The present stone church was erected in the 1300s, its thick walls and the remains of its surrounding ramparts reflecting its dual function as a church and fortress, for these were troubled, violent times. After the exterior, stern of necessity, the warm and homely **interior** comes as a surprise. Here, the dainty arches of the rood screen lead into the choir, where a late medieval, bas-relief wooden triptych surmounts each of the three altars. Of the trio, the middle triptych is the most charming: the main panel, depicting the holy family, is fairly predictable, but down below is a curiously cheerful sequence of biblical figures, each of whom wears a turban and sports a big, bushy and exquisitely carved beard.

Back outside, the **churchyard** is bordered by a dry-stone wall and holds a Soviet memorial to the eight hundred prisoners of war who died hereabouts in World War II at the hands of the Germans. There's a second reminder of the war in the form of the **Adolfkanon** (Adolf Gun), a massive artillery piece stuck on a hilltop to the north of the church in the middle of the peninsula. It's inside a military zone, and the obligatory guided tour of the **gun** and the adjacent **bunkers** (early June to mid-Aug daily at 11am, 1pm, 3pm & 5pm; late Aug daily at 3pm; 55kr), which begins at the gate of the compound, 1km from the gun, stipulates that you have to have your own vehicle to visit. The third sight on the Trondenes peninsula is the **Trondenes Historiske Senter** (Trondenes Historical Centre; early June to mid-Aug daily 10am–6pm; mid-Aug to early June daily 8am–4pm; 70kr), a plush modern complex with exhibitions on the history of the locality – dioramas, mood music, incidental Viking artefacts and the like. It's located along the fjord from the church, back towards the town centre.

As for Harstad itself, the downtown core has little appeal, though the comings and goings of the ferry boats are a diversion and in late June the ten-day **North Norway Arts Festival** (Festspillene i Nord-Norge; Ⓦwww.festspillnn.no) provides a spark of interest with its concerts, drama and dance performances; note, however, that the town's hotels are full to bursting throughout the proceedings.

Practicalities

Harstad may be easy to reach, but if you're travelling along the E10 it's actually something of a cul-de-sac, involving a thirty-kilometre detour north along Highway 83. Once you've arrived, however, you'll find almost everything you need conveniently clustered together around the harbour. Here, within a few metres of each other, you'll find the **bus station**, jetties for the **Hurtigbåt** and **Hurtigrute boats** plus the **tourist office**, at Torvet 8 (June to mid-Aug Mon–Fri 8am–6pm; mid-Aug to June Mon–Fri 8am–3.30pm; Ⓣ77 01 89 89, Ⓦwww.destinationharstad.no), which has a wide selection of tourist literature on the Vesterålen.

As regards **accommodation**, the town centre is dotted with modern chain hotels, among which the *Quality Arcticus Hotel*, a short walk from the Torvet at

Moving on from Harstad

From Harstad, the **Hurtigrute** (ⓦwww.hurtigruten.com) sails north for Tromsø at 8am and south for points in the Vesterålen and Lofoten islands at 8.30am. Alternatively, there's a **Hurtigbåt** service to Tromsø (2–3 daily; 2hr 45min; 380kr; ⓦwww.tfds.no) and frequent **buses** to Narvik, Sortland (for Andenes) and Lofoten. For **car rental**, several firms in Harstad offer short-term deals: try Europcar, Samagata 33 (ⓣ77 01 86 10), or Hertz, by the harbour (ⓣ77 06 13 46).

Havnegata 3 (ⓣ77 04 08 00, ⓦwww.arcticus-hotel.no; ❻, sp/r 4), has an attractive quayside location and perfectly adequate modern rooms. A good alternative, also occupying a modern block near the Torvet, is the neat and trim *Grand Nordic Hotell*, Strandgata 9 (ⓣ77 00 30 00, ⓦwww.nordic.no; ❻, sp/r 4). Further afield, the HI **hostel** (June to late Aug; ⓣ77 04 00 77, ⓦwww.vandrerhjem.no; dorm beds 240k, doubles ❷; reception closed 4–6pm) has the advantage of a pleasant fjordside location, near the Trondenes kirke. The hostel has self-catering facilities, washing machines and large, comfortable and pleasantly furnished double rooms, the only problem being that the building is a school for most of the year and so has a rather cold, institutional feel. The hostel is easy to reach on the local "Trondenes" bus from the station (Mon–Sat 1 hourly; 10min).

Harstad is no gastronomic nirvana, but the saving grace is *Café de 4 Roser*, Rikard Kaarbøs Plass 4 (ⓣ77 06 61 54; Mon–Sat from 6pm), which covers all the culinary bases by having a first-rate French-influenced **restaurant** upstairs and a **café-bar** down below. At the latter, they serve light meals – mussels, salads and pastas – during the day before switching to fresh-fruit cocktails after 6pm: it's the best bar in town.

On to Andenes

Back on the **E10** south of Harstad, it's 50km southwest along the fjord to the turning for the Lødingen ferry (see p.316) and 50km more to the bridge that spans the sound over to Sortland (see p.321). On the near side of this Sortland bridge, **Highway 82** begins its 100-kilometre trek north, snaking along the craggy edge of Hinnøya island before crossing a second bridge over to humdrum **Risøyhamn**, the only Hurtigrute stop on **Andøya**, the most northerly of the Vesterålen islands. Beyond Risøyhamn, the scenery is much less dramatic, as the mountains give way to hills in the west and a vast, peaty moor in the east. Highway 82 strips across this moorland and, despite offering panoramic views of the mountains back on the mainland, it's an uneventful journey on to Andenes.

At the old fishing port of **ANDENES**, lines of low-slung buildings lead up to the clutter of wooden warehouses and mini boat-repair yards that edge the harbour and its prominent breakwaters. "It is the fish, and that alone, that draws people to Andenes – the place itself has no other temptations," said the writer Poul Alm when he visited in 1944, and although this is too harsh a judgement today, the main emphasis does indeed remain firmly nautical. Among Scandinavians at least, Andenes is famous for its **Whale Safaris**, four- to five-hour cruises with a marine biologist on board to point out sperm, killer and minke whales as well as dolphins and porpoises; even better, the operators claim – with every justification– a ninety-percent chance of a whale sighting: the edge of the continental shelf, which is closer to land here than anywhere else in Norway, boasts a large stock of sperm whales, who form the basis of the tours and dawdle in these waters all year. The safari involves tracking and locating the whales with underwater microphones and then waiting for them to surface. Safaris take place once daily between late May and mid-September and there are often additional departures too, subject to demand. **Tickets** cost 765kr each (children 5–14 years, 450kr) and cover both lunch and the guided tour of the Whale Centre (see below) that precedes the boat trip. The safari isn't recommended for children under five as the sea can get rough; warm clothing and sensible shoes are essential. **Booking** (ⓣ76 11 56 00, ⓦwww.whalesafari.no) at least a day in advance is strongly advised as the trips are popular, and indeed some are booked up weeks beforehand.

The other recommended boat trip hereabouts is a **Puffin Safari** round the bird island of **Bleiksøya** (June to mid-Aug 1–2 daily; 1hr 30min; 300kr, children 150kr; bookings through the tourist office or direct ⓣ97 19 52 75, ⓦwww.puffinsafari.no), a pyramid-shaped hunk of rock populated by thousands of puffins, kittiwakes, razorbills and, sometimes, white-tailed eagles. Cruises leave from the jetty at **Bleik** (see opposite), an old and picturesque fishing hamlet around 7km southwest of Andenes that has a clear view of the islet; a local bus often makes the trip from Andenes to coincide with sailings.

Andenes sights

Andenes **Hvalsenter** (Whale Centre; late May to mid-June & mid-Aug to mid-Sept daily 8am–4pm; mid-June to mid-Aug daily 8am–7pm; 60kr), metres from the harbour, is actually a somewhat disappointing way to start a safari. The centre's incidental displays on the life and times of the animal hardly fire the imagination, and neither does the massive – and deliberately dark and gloomy – display of a whale munching its way though a herd of squid, though at least the sperm-whale skeleton, which was washed up on an Andenes beach, does give an idea of the size of the creature. Much more diverting is the **Hisnakul natural history centre** (mid-June to Aug daily 10am–6pm; Sept to mid-June daily 10am–4pm; 50kr), which explores various facets of Andøya life from its premises in a refurbished timber warehouse near the Whale Centre. The centre is short on historical artefacts, plumping instead for imaginative displays such as the two hundred facial casts of local people made in 1994 and an assortment of giant replica bird beaks. The adjacent **Nordlyssenteret** (Northern Lights Centre; late June to mid-Aug daily noon–2pm; 40kr) provides a comprehensive explanation of the northern lights (see box, p.344) – Andenes is a particularly good spot to see them – illustrated by first-class photographs and a slide show.

Close by, **Andenes fyr** (lighthouse; mid-June to Aug daily 10am–5pm; 30kr) is a 40m-high maroon structure dating from the 1850s and offering wide views over the town from the top. From here, it's a brief stroll south to the **Polarmuseet** (Polar Museum; late June to mid-Aug daily 10am–5pm; 30kr), which is located inside a modest little building with a pretty wooden porch. The interior is mostly dedicated to the Arctic knick-knacks accumulated by a certain Hilmar Nøis, an Andøy man who wintered on Svalbard no less than 38 times.

Practicalities

Bisecting the town, Andenes' long and straight main street, **Storgata**, ends abruptly at the seafront. The **bus station** is just a few metres to the east of Storgata, just back from the seafront, while the **tourist office** is on the harbour, sharing the same premises as the Northern Lights Centre (mid-June to Aug daily 10am–6pm, Sept to mid-June Mon–Fri 9am–4pm; ⓣ76 14 12 03, ⓦwww.andoyturist.no). The office has a comprehensive range of local information and can make reservations for bird-island boat trips, whale safaris and the

Moving on from Andenes – and the coastal route north to Tromsø

Operated by **Nordtrafikk** (☎177 in Nordland, otherwise ☎75 77 24 10; Ⓦwww.177nordland.com), local buses run south from Andenes to Risøyhamn and Sortland for the E10 (2–4 daily; 1hr/2hr). Heading north, it's possible to weave your way up along the coast from Andenes to Tromsø (see p.344), beginning with the seasonal **Senjafergene car ferry** (☎76 14 12 03, Ⓦwww.senjafergene.no) linking Andenes with Gryllefjord on the mainland, but note that advance reservations are strongly advised (early to late June & mid- to late Aug 2 daily, late June to early Aug 3 daily; 2hr; passengers 130kr; car & driver 260kr). From Gryllefjord, it's about 220km on to Tromsø via Highway 86 to Finnsnes, then along the scenic Highway 861 to **Botnhamn**, where a second Senjafergene car ferry crosses over to **Brensholmen** (early June to late Aug 4–7 daily; 45min; passengers 55kr, cars 140kr); from **Brensholmen** it's 70km or so on to Tromsø.

car ferry to Gryllefjord (see p.316). It also has details of local **bicycle rental** and of **hiking trails** in the surrounding district.

Andenes has a fair sprinkling of inexpensive **accommodation** and several households offer **private rooms** (❷–❹) – look out for the signs – but, considering how isolated a spot this is, you'd be well advised to make a reservation in advance. One of the nicest places to stay is a **guesthouse**, the *Sjøgata Gjestehus*, Sjøgata 4 (☎76 14 16 37, Ⓔtovekhan@online.no; May–Sept; ❷), which provides simple but inexpensive rooms in a pleasant old timber building just 200m from the tourist office. Nearby, on the seafront, is the green-timbered *Grønnbua* (☎76 14 14 99, Ⓦwww.rorbucamping.no) comprising two *sjøhus*, each of which has been parcelled up into **apartments**: one set is cosy and modern (❸), the other older and slightly shabbier (❷), though both have good views over the water. The principal **hotel** is the *Norlandia Andrikken*, a standard-issue chain hotel about 900m from the harbour at Storgata 53 (☎76 14 12 22, Ⓦwww.norlandia.no/andrikken; ❻, sp/r ❹). Finally, the town possesses a small and spartan HI **hostel**, *Andenes Vandrerhjem* (☎76 14 28 50, Ⓦwww.vandrerhjem.no; dorm beds 190kr, doubles ❶; June–Aug), in an old red building on the waterfront just to the east of the harbour. As an alternative to Andenes, you might also consider staying in tiny **BLEIK**, a much prettier place where a string of clapboard houses huddles between craggy hills and a long sandy beach. Bleik is just 7km southwest down along the coast from Andenes and it's home to the *Norlandia Bleik Apartments* (☎76 14 12 22, Ⓦwww.norlandia.no/bleik), where there are modern double rooms (❺) and apartments (❸–❺) in a handful of *sjøhus*; for more about a *sjøhus*, see p.324.

As regards **food**, the restaurant of the *Norlandia Andrikken Hotell* is easily the best place in town – the Arctic char is superb – and prices are reasonable with main courses averaging 160kr. For daytime snacks, head for *Jul. Nilsens Bakeri* (Mon–Fri 9am–3pm, Sat 9am–1pm), close to the bus station at Kong Hansgate 1.

Sortland and points south to Melbu

The small town of **SORTLAND** is little more than an unappetizing modern sprawl that straggles along the coast beside the bridge linking the islands of Hinnøya and Langøya. By virtue of its location, Sortland is also something of a **transport hub**, and bus passengers sometimes have to change here for the onward journey south to Stokmarknes and Lofoten, and always to catch the local bus north to Andenes (see p.319), which originates here. The **tourist office** at Kjøpmannsgata 2 (mid-June to late Aug Mon–Fri 10am–6pm,

Sat & Sun 11am–5pm; Sept to mid-June Mon–Fri 10am–5pm; ⓣ76 11 14 80, ⓦwww.visitvesteralen.com) is in the centre of town, a couple of hundred metres from the Hurtigrute quay and a five- to ten-minute walk from the bus station.

Stokmarknes - and the Trollfjord

Pushing southwest from Sortland, the E10 hugs the shoreline for 30km before shooting over the two bridges that span the straits between Langøya and Hadseløya; the longer bridge is equipped with a high-frequency sound device that is supposed to stop Langøya's foxes in their tracks, keeping its smaller neighbour fox-free. On the far side of the straits is **STOKMARKNES**, an unremarkable little town whose mediocrity is partly relieved by its pleasant shoreline

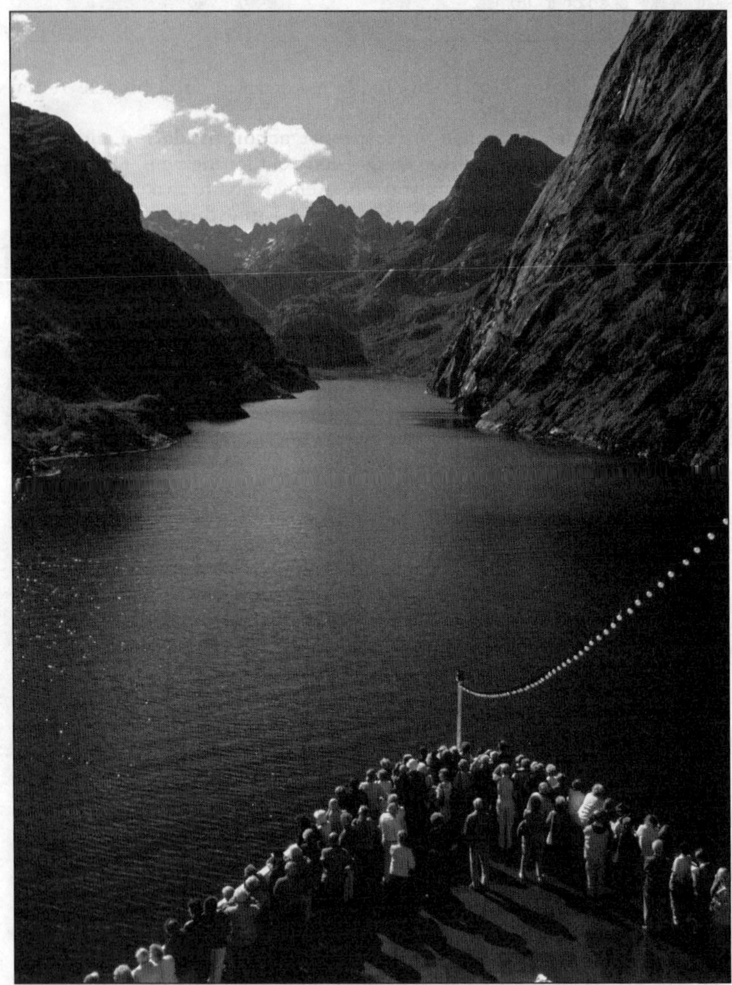

△ Trollfjord

setting. Here also you can sample the delights of the **Hurtigrutemuseet** (mid-May to mid-June & mid-Aug to mid-Sept daily noon–4pm; mid-June to mid-Aug daily 10am–6pm; mid-Sept to mid-May Mon–Fri 2–4pm, Sat noon–4pm & Sun 2–4pm; 80kr), which is entirely devoted to the history of the Hurtigrute coastal boat, with a genuine 1950s ferry, the **M/S Finnmarken**, parked up outside on the quayside. Also on the quayside is a statue of Richard With, the skipper responsible for dreaming up the coastal ferry in the 1890s.

Museum aside, the main reason to stop off in Stokmarknes is to catch the **Hurtigrute coastal boat** south to Svolvær via the Trollfjord. The boat leaves daily at 3.15pm, sailing down the **Raftsundet**, the narrow sound separating the harsh, rocky shanks of Hinnøya and Austvågøya. Towards the southern end of the sound, the ship usually makes a short detour to the **Trollfjord**, a majestic tear in the landscape just 2km long. Slowing to a gentle chug, the vessels inch up the narrow gorge, smooth stone towering high above and blocking out the light. At the head of the Trollfjord, the boats effect a nautical three-point turn and then crawl back to rejoin the main waterway. It's very atmospheric, and the effect is perhaps even more extraordinary when the weather is up. One caution: the Hurtigrute will not enter the Trollfjord when there's the danger of a rock fall, but pauses at the fjord's mouth instead. Check locally before embarkation, though you're only likely to miss out, if at all, in spring. The Hurtigrute cruise from Sortland to Svolvær takes a little over three hours and costs 160kr per passenger in winter, 230kr in summer; cars cost 330kr all year. It's all possible to visit the Trollfjord on special boat trips from Svolvær – see p.327.

As for practicalities, **buses** to Stokmarknes pull in near the harbourfront **tourist office** (mid-June to late Aug Mon–Fri 10am–5pm; Ⓣ76 16 46 60), which has details of what little local **accommodation** there is. The obvious choice is the *Hurtigrutens Hus* (Ⓣ76 15 29 99, Ⓦwww.hurtigrutenshus.com; ❻), a brassy, modern hotel-cum-conference centre plonked on the Børøya islet, about fifteen minutes' walk from the museum, at the far end of the first of two bridges back towards Sortland.

From Stokmarknes, it's 15km south along the E10 to **MELBU**, from where there is a **car ferry** over to Fiskebøl on Lofoten (daily 7am–11pm, every 90min; 30min; passengers 28kr; car & driver 68kr; Ⓣ177, Ⓦwww.177nordland.com), though this is about to be replaced by a tunnel. Melbu is also on the main **Nor-Way Bussekspress** bus routes (see p.326).

The Lofoten islands

A skeletal curve of mountainous rock stretched out across the Norwegian Sea, the **Lofoten islands** have been the focal point of northern Norway's winter fishing from time immemorial. At the turn of the year, cod migrate from the Barents Sea to spawn here, where the coldness of the water is tempered by the Gulf Stream. The season only lasts from February to April, but fishing impinges on all aspects of island life and is impossible to ignore at any time of the year. At almost every harbour stand the massed ranks of wooden racks used for drying the cod, burgeoning and odiferous in winter, empty in summer like so many abandoned climbing frames.

Sharing the same history, but better known and more beautiful than their neighbours the Vesterålen, the Lofoten islands have everything from sea-bird colonies in the south to beaches and fjords in the north. The traditional approach is by boat from Bodø and this brings visitors face to face with the islands' most striking feature, the towering peaks of the **Lofotenveggen** (Lofoten Wall), a 160-kilometre stretch of mountains, whose jagged teeth bite into the skyline, trapping a string of tiny fishing villages tight against the shore. The mountains are set so close together that on first inspection there seems to be no way through, but in fact the islands are riddled with straights, sounds and fjords.

The Lofoten have their own relaxed pace, and are perfect for a simple, uncluttered few days. For somewhere so far north, the weather can be exceptionally mild: summer days can be spent sunbathing on the rocks or hiking and biking around the superb coastline, and when it rains – as it frequently does – life focuses on the *rorbuer (*fishermen's huts*)*, where freshly caught fish are cooked over wood-burning stoves, stories are told and time gently wasted. If that sounds rather contrived, in a sense it is – the way of life here is to some extent preserved like this for tourists – but it's rare to find anyone who isn't less than completely enthralled by it all.

The **E10** weaves a scenic route across Lofoten, running the 170km from **Fiskebøl** in the north to **Å** in the south, hopping from island to island by bridge and causeway and by occasionally tunnelling through the mountains and under the sea. The highway passes through or within a few kilometres of all the islands' main villages, amongst which **Henningsvær** and **Å** are breathtakingly beautiful, with **Stamsund** coming in close behind. All three make great bases for further explorations on foot or by boat. Indeed, there's an abundance of marine activity with everything on offer from island cruises, sea-rafting and

Staying in a rorbu or sjøhus

Right across Lofoten, **rorbuer** (fishermen's shacks) are rented out to tourists for both overnight stays and longer periods. The name "rorbu" is derived from *ror*, "to row" and *bu*, literally "dwelling" – and older islanders still ask "Will you row this winter?", meaning "Will you go fishing this winter?" *Rorbuer* date back to the twelfth century, when King Øystein ordered the first of them to be built round the Lofoten coastline to provide shelter for visiting fishermen who had previously been obliged to sleep under their upturned boats. Traditionally, *rorbuer* were built on the shore, often on poles sticking out of the sea, and usually coloured with a red paint based on cod-liver oil. They consisted of two sections, a sleeping and eating room and a smaller storage area.

At the peak of the fisheries in the 1930s, some 30,000 men were accommodated in *rorbuer*, but during the 1960s fishing boats became more comfortable and since then many fishermen have preferred to sleep aboard. Most of the original *rorbuer* disappeared years ago, and, although a few have survived, visitors today are much more likely to stay in a modern version, mostly prefabricated units churned out by the dozen with the tourist trade in mind. At their best, they are comfortable and cosy seashore cabins, sometimes a well-planned conversion of an original *rorbu* with bunk beds and wood-fired stoves; at their worst, they are little better than prefabricated hutches in the middle of nowhere. Most have space for between four and six guests and the charge for a hut averages around 600kr per night – though some cost as little as 400kr, while others rise to about 1000kr. Similar rates are charged for the islands' **sjøhus** (literally sea-houses), originally the large quayside halls where the catch was processed and the workers slept. Most of the original *sjøhus* have been cleverly converted into attractive apartments with self-catering facilities, a few into dormitory-style accommodation – and again, as with the *rorbuer*, the quality varies enormously. A full list of *rorbuer* and *sjøhus* is given in the *Lofoten Info-Guide*, a free pamphlet that you can pick up at any local tourist office and on ⓦwww.lofoten-tourist.no.

fishing excursions through to birdwatching trips. Scores of places also rent out fishing boats and equipment, although, because of the strong currents, you should always seek advice about local conditions. Back on land, the islands may not have a well-developed network of huts and hiking trails, but the byroads, where you'll rarely see a car, provide mile after mile of excellent **walking** as they delve deep into the heart of the landscape. There's plenty of scope for **mountaineering** too: Austvågøya has the finest climbing, with some of the best ascents in Norway, and there's a prestigious climbing school at Henningsvær. There's more walking and yet more solitude on mountainous **Værøy** and flatter, more agricultural **Røst**, a pair of inhabited islands to the south of Å, reachable by ferry from Moskenes and Bodø.

As regards accommodation, the Lofoten islands have a sprinkling of **hotels**, a few of which are first-rate, though some are blandly modern, as well as four HI **hostels**, numerous **campsites** and the local speciality, the **rorbuer** (see box opposite). There's comprehensive tourist **information** on Ⓦwww.lofoten-tourist.no, though Ⓦwww.lofoten-info.no covers two of the more southerly islands, Moskenesøya and Flakstadøya, in greater detail.

Transport to and around the Lofoten islands

The Lofoten can be reached easily enough by car ferry, Hurtigbåt passenger express boat and the Hurtigrute coastal boat, but once you've got there you'll find **public transport** thin on the ground. What local **bus** services there are stick almost exclusively to the **E10**, the islands' only main road, and elsewhere you'll mostly have to **walk** – hardly an onerous task in such beautiful surroundings. Alternatively, **bike rental** is available at the Svolvær tourist office as well as at some hostels, hotels and guesthouses, and the detailed *Cycling in Lofoten* booklet, which includes route maps, is sold at all tourist offices.

If you have your own **vehicle**, village-hopping is easy and quick, but it's only when you leave the car and head off into the landscape that the real character of Lofoten begins to reveal itself; allow time for at least one walk or sea trip. Conversely, if you don't have a vehicle and want to reach the islands' remoter spots, it's worth considering renting a car, an inexpensive option if a few people share the cost. There are local **car rental** outlets at Svolvær, Stamsund and Svolvær and Leknes airports, where special short-term deals can bring costs down to around 650kr a day. Incidentally, speed checks are frequent, with on-the-spot fines kicking off at 1000kr.

All Nordland **public transport** timetables – including those for Lofoten – are online at Ⓦwww.177nordland.com; you can also call Ⓣ177 within Nordland, otherwise Ⓣ75 77 24 10.

By car ferry

From the mainland, the principal **car ferry** service to the Lofoten links tiny **Skutvik**, 35km west of the E6 midway between Fauske and Narvik, with **Svolvær** (early June to late Aug 8–10 daily; late Aug to early June 2–4 daily; 2hr; passengers 70kr, car & driver 240kr). A second car ferry service connects **Bodø** with three destinations on the southern peripheries of Lofoten: **Moskenes**, a tiny port just a few kilometers from the end of the E10, and the islets of **Værøy** and **Røst**. The route varies, but there's almost always one ferry a day (and sometimes more) to Moskenes throughout the year, with marginally less frequent services to the two islets; Moskenes is often the first port of call. The trip from Bodø to Moskenes takes about four hours; allow a further two hours to Værøy, and two more for Røst, and be prepared for a rough crossing. The **fare** from Bodø to Moskenes is 140kr for passengers, 520kr for a car and driver; for details of fares to the islets, see p.336.

All these ferries are operated by **OVDS** (Ⓦwww.ovds.no) on a first-come, first-served basis, so it's a good idea to turn up a couple of hours before departure. Note also that in the summertime (June–Aug) **advance reservations** are permitted – and are a very good idea: Bodø tourist office will arrange things for you or you can contact OVDS direct, either online on Ⓦwww.ovds.no, or on the company's reservation line Ⓣ76 11 82 45 (Mon–Fri 8.30am–3pm).

If you're driving to the Lofoten islands on the **E10**, which branches off the E6 north of Narvik, you'll have to use the car ferry linking **Melbu** on the Vesterålen with **Fiskebøl** on Lofoten (daily 7am–11pm, every 90min; 30min; passengers 28kr; car & driver 68kr; Ⓣ177 in Nordland, otherwise Ⓣ75 77 24 10, Ⓦwww.177nordland.com), though at some point soon it will be replaced by a tunnel.

By boat: the Hurtigrute

The northbound **Hurtigrute** leaves Bodø daily at 3pm calling at two ports in the Lofoten islands – Stamsund and Svolvær – before nudging through the Raftsundet en route to Stokmarknes, on the Vesterålen. The passenger fare for the four-and-a-half-hour cruise from Bodø to Stamsund is 370kr in summer, 261kr winter, and cars cost 330kr all year; the six-hour journey to Svolvær costs 400/280kr, cars 355kr. Advance reservations for cars are essential, though these can be made up to a few hours before departure by phoning the captain – ask down at the harbour or at the port's tourist office for assistance. Special deals, which can reduce costs dramatically, are commonly advertised at local tourist offices.

By boat: Hurtigbåt passenger express boats

Hurtigbåt passenger express boats operate from **Bodø to Svolvær** (1–2 daily; 3hr 30min; 260kr; Ⓣ177 in Nordland, otherwise Ⓣ75 77 24 10, Ⓦwww.ovds.no) and **Narvik to Svolvær** (1 daily; 3hr 30min; 350kr one-way; Ⓣ76 96 76 00, Ⓦwww.lcbc.no). In both cases, advance booking is a good idea.

By bus

The long-distance **Lofoten Ekspressen**, operated by **Nor-Way Bussekspress** (Ⓦwww.nor-way.no), provides the main bus service from the mainland to the Lofoten. There are two routings. The first leaves Narvik once or twice daily to run along the E6 and then the E10, calling at Sortland on the Vesterålen before taking the Melbu–Fiskebøl ferry to Lofoten; it then proceeds onto Svolvær, Kabelvåg and Leknes. The second routing (1 daily) leads north from Bodø and Fauske to the Bognes–Lødingen car ferry; from Lødingen, the bus then continues onto Sortland, and the Melbu–Fiskebøl ferry bound for Svolvær, Leknes and finally Å. As examples of **journey times**, Narvik–Leknes takes just seven hours, Bodø to Å fourteen.

These long-distance services are supported by a number of **local buses**, all of which are operated by **Nordtrafikk** (Ⓣ177 in Nordland, otherwise Ⓣ75 77 24 10, Ⓦwww.177nordland.com). Among a hatful of services, albeit rather intermittent, two of the most useful are Svolvær to Kabelvåg and Henningsvær (1–3 daily) and Leknes to Stamsund (Mon–Sat 3–4 daily).

By plane – and car rental

Flights leave Bodø for the Lofoten airports – or rather airstrips – at Svolvær and Leknes four to seven times a day. The operator is **Widerøe**

(Ⓦwww.wideroe.no), an SAS subsidiary, and tickets can be purchased at any travel agent or SAS agent as well as at the *Radisson SAS Hotel* in Bodø and online; **fares** from Bodø to the islands vary enormously, but a standard summer return ticket costs in the region of 900kr, half that one-way. Note also that whereas Svolvær airport is merely 5km from town, Leknes airport is miles from anywhere you might want to visit, and the onward taxi will cost an arm and a leg. There is **car rental** at both airports: Svolvær has, for instance, Avis (Ⓣ76 07 11 40) and Hertz (Ⓣ76 07 07 20) outlets, as does Leknes – Hertz (Ⓣ76 08 18 44) and Avis (Ⓣ76 08 01 04). Good-value short-term deals abound – from around 650kr per day.

Svolvær

By and large, **SVOLVÆR**, which strings over and around several headlands and bays on the southeast coast of **Austvågøya**, the largest of the islands, is a rather disappointing introduction to Lofoten. The region's administrative and transport centre, it has all the bustle but little of the charm of the other island towns, though it does have more accommodation and better restaurants than its neighbours and – to be fair – its surroundings are suitably mountainous. The only attraction of any real interest in the town itself is the **Lofoten Krigsminnemuseum**, close to the Hurtigrute quay (War Museum; June–Sept Mon–Fri 10am–4pm, Sat 11am–3pm & Sun noon–3pm; Oct–May daily 6.15–10pm; 50kr), which chronicles the British commando raids on Lofoten in 1941 (see box p.328) by means of photographs and original artefacts.

Otherwise, you're better off heading out of town to explore Svolvær's dramatic environs on one of two local **boat trips**. Every day throughout the summer several cruises (return trip 3hr; 500kr; buy tickets on board) leave Svolvær for the **Trollfjord**, an impossibly narrow, two-kilometre-long stretch of water that's also on the Hurtigrute itinerary (see p.322). Alternatively, consider a stroll on the pretty islet of **Skrova**, just offshore from Svolvær. Its only settlement trails along a slender rocky spit, attached by a causeway to the main body of island, which is dominated by the steep Mount Høgskrova (258m). The Svolvær–Skutvik ferry (see p.325 for times) usually calls at Skrova, taking just thirty minutes and costing 30kr each way; ferry times almost always make a day-trip feasible.

Svolvær also boasts one of the archipelago's most famous **climbs**, the haul up to the top of the **Svolværgeita** (the Svolvær goat), a twin-pronged peak that rises high above the E10 to the northeast of town. The lower slopes of the mountain are hard enough, but the last 40m – up the horns of the "goat" – require considerable expertise. Daring mountaineers complete the thrill by jumping from one pinnacle to the other.

Arrival and information

Ferries to Svolvær dock about 1km west of the town centre, whereas the Hurtigrute docks in the centre, a brief walk from the **bus station** and the busy **tourist office**, just off the main town square near the harbour (late May to mid-June Mon–Fri 9am–4pm & Sat 10am–2pm; mid- to late June Mon–Fri 9am–7.30pm, Sat 10am–2pm & Sun 4–7pm; late June to early Aug Mon–Fri 9am–9.30pm, Sat 9am–8pm & Sun 10am–9.30pm; early Aug to late Aug Mon–Fri 9am–7pm, Sat 10am–2pm; Sept to mid-May Mon–Fri 9am–3.30pm; Ⓣ76 06 98 00, Ⓦwww.lofoten-tourist.no). They have maps, accommodation lists and public transport details; they can also make ferry and accommodation reservations for anywhere in Lofoten, though there is a charge for this service, respectively 140kr and 50kr. Svolvær is also a good place to **rent a car**: Europcar, for example, have an outlet at Avisgaten 11 (Ⓣ76 06 83 33).

Accommodation

Svolvær's smartest **accommodation** is the gleaming *Rica Hotel Svolvær* (Ⓣ76 07 22 22, Ⓦwww.rica.no; ❻), whose various buildings, in the style of the traditional *sjøhus*, occupy a prime location on a tiny islet at the end of a causeway in the middle of the harbour. At the east end of the harbour, a longer causeway leads out to the slender islet of Svinøya, where accommodation at *Svinøya Rorbuer* (Ⓣ76 06 99 30, Ⓦwww.svinoya.no) ranges from plain and simple *rorbuer* (❸) through to deluxe en-suite cabins (❼). Back in town, you can find more modest rooms at the long-established *Svolvær Sjøhus*, by the seashore at the foot of Parkgata (Ⓣ76 07 03 36, Ⓦwww.svolver-sjohuscamp.no; ❷): to get there from the square, turn right up the hill along Vestfjordgata and it's to the right, past the library. Svolvær also has a handful of more ordinary **hotels**, for the most part surly modern blocks that hardly set the architectural pulse racing, though the *Norlandia Royal Hotell* (Ⓣ76 07 12 00, Ⓦwww.norlandia.no/royal; ❺), with its slightly confused decor, has comfortable rooms, a mini health spa, and a convenient location, a few metres up from the main square at the end of Torggata.

Restaurants and bars

Svolvær has a reasonable selection of **bars** and **restaurants**, the best you'll find on Lofoten. The *Café Bacalao*, down on the quay, is a spacious café-restaurant with snappy service and a menu that mixes Mediterranean and Norwegian cuisine with flair and imagination: lunches, and main courses in the evening, hover around 100kr. It serves excellent coffee too, and at night turns into the town's liveliest **bar**, jam-packed at the weekend. Alternatively, the restaurants of the *Rica Hotel Svolvær* and the *Svinøya Rorbuer* are both highly competent, with seafood their forte; mains from around 170kr. The classiest restaurant, however, is *Du Verden*, in the centre at J. E. Paulsens gate 12 (Ⓣ76 07 70 99), where a creative menu features the freshest of local ingredients. In the evening, prices are high but not unreasonable, with main courses averaging around 190kr, and at lunchtime the place is a snip – try the mouthwatering fish soup.

The British commando raids of 1941

The Germans occupied Norway in April 1940, but it wasn't until a year later that the British prepared their response: it took the form of a **commando raid** on Lofoten. The aims were threefold: firstly, it was thought that a successful attack would boost British morale; secondly, it was a way of tying German troops down to garrison duty along the Norwegian coast; and thirdly, the British wanted to destroy as much of Lofoten's plentiful supply of herring oil as they could, to prevent the Germans using it as a raw material in the manufacture of their explosives.

In April 1941, the first commando raid hit Svolvær, Stamsund and Henningsvær, whilst a second, a few months later, attacked Reine and nearby Sørvangen at the southern end of Lofoten. The first was the more successful, bagging 200 prisoners and destroying hundreds of barrels of oil, but the Germans extracted a bitter revenge by burning down the houses of all those Norwegians deemed to have been sympathetic to the invaders.

Kabelvåg

With its pretty wooden centre draped around the shore of a narrow and knobbly inlet, **KABELVÅG** is immediately more appealing than Svolvær, its near neighbour, just 6km away. The most important village on Lofoten from Viking times until the early years of the twentieth century, Kabelvåg was once the centre of the fishery and home to the islands' first *rorbuer*, built in 1120, as well as the first inn, which dates from 1792. The late nineteenth-century **Vågan kirke** (May–Aug Mon–Fri 9.30am–6pm, Sun noon–6pm; 20kr), a big and breezy timber church beside the E10 on the eastern edge of the village, is a reminder of those busier times, its hangar-like interior built to accommodate a congregation of over a thousand.

The village holds other attractions too, primarily the **Lofotmuseet**, located 1500m west of the centre by the seashore in the **Storvågan** neighbourhood (Lofoten Museum; May Mon–Fri 9am–3pm, Sat & Sun 11am–3pm; June–Aug daily 9am–6pm; Sept Mon–Fri 9am–3pm & Sun 11am–3pm; Sept–April Mon–Fri 9am–3pm; Ⓦwww.lofotmuseet.no; 50kr, but with a Storvågan multi-ticket including the gallery and aquarium 130kr;). This traces the history of the islands' fisheries and displays the definitive collection of fishing equipment and other cultural paraphernalia. Nearby, also in Storvågan, is the **Galleri Espolin** (May daily 11am–3pm; June to mid-Aug daily 10am–7pm; late Aug daily 10am–6pm; Sept–April Mon–Fri & Sun 11am–3pm; Ⓦwww.galleri-espolin.no; 50kr), which features paintings and sketches by Kaare Espolin Johnson (1907–94), a renowned Norwegian artist of romantic inclination, who specialized in Arctic images and imagery. Storvågan's third attraction is the **Lofotakvariet** (aquarium; same times as the Galleri; 80kr), displaying a wide variety of Atlantic species.

Kabelvåg also offers a good range of **outdoor pursuits**. The main operator is *Lofoten Aktiv*, Rødmyrveien 26 (Ⓣ99 23 11 00, Ⓦwww.lofoten-aktiv.no), who organize everything from sea-kayaking and trekking through to skiing, fishing and cycling trips, though the sea-kayaking courses are a speciality. Divers should contact *Lofotdykk*, in the centre of Kabelvåg at Kaiveien 15 (Ⓣ99 63 91 66, Ⓦwww.lofotdykk.no), for all manner of marine activities, including sea-rafting, orca-watching safaris (Oct–Dec) and, of course, diving.

Practicalities

Buses to Kabelvåg, from Svolvær and Henningsvær (1–3 daily), drop passengers right in the centre of the village, from where it's a five-minute stroll up the hill to the pleasant *Kabelvåg Hotel* (Ⓣ76 07 88 00, Ⓦwww.dvgl.no/no/2-1-3.html; ❺), which occupies an old timber building just back from the harbour. A second appealing choice is *Nyvågar Rorbuhotell* in Storvågan (Ⓣ76 06 97 00, Ⓦwww.nyvaagar.no), comprising a scattering of smart, seashore, four-bedded *rorbuer* (❻) plus a hotel (❺). The village also possesses a spartan HI **hostel**, *Kabelvåg Vandrerhjem* (Ⓣ76 06 98 98, Ⓦwww.vandrerhjem.no; dorm beds 215kr, doubles ❷; June to mid-Aug), in the school building east of the centre, 500m from the E10, but although the facilities aren't luxurious, they do serve a great big breakfast. Perhaps a better budget bet is the well-equipped house run by diving-specialists *Lofotdykk* (Ⓣ99 63 91 66, Ⓦwww.lofotdykk.no), which comes complete with a sauna and outdoor *badestamp*; basic quads here go for 180kr per person per night.

As regards **food**, the *Krambua Restaurant*, in the *Kabelvåg Hotel*, is a quiet, stylish affair with a menu that leans heavily towards quality seafood with main courses hovering around 170kr. Much livelier – in fact it's the heart of the Kabelvåg social scene – is the *Prestenbrygga Pub*, right in the centre of the village overlooking the dock. Here they serve enormous, excellent-value pizzas from 70kr, have a popular bottomless-cup-of-coffee deal, and feature a locally famous fish soup every Friday night.

Henningsvær

Heading west from Kabelvåg, it's 11km on the E10 to the 8km-long turning that leads to **HENNINGSVÆR**, the most beguiling of headland villages, a cobweb of cramped and twisting lanes lined with brightly painted wooden houses. These frame a tiny inlet that literally cuts the place in half, forming a sheltered, picture-postcard harbour. Almost inevitably, coach parties are wheeled in and out, despite the narrowness of the two high-arched bridges into the village, but for all the hustle and bustle Henningsvær is well worth an **overnight stay**.

The smartest **hotel** is the quayside *Henningsvær Bryggehotell* (☎76 07 47 50, Ⓦwww.henningsvaer.no; ❺), an attractive modern building in traditional style right on the waterfront, but the more economical choice is the frugal *Den siste Viking*, Misværveien 10 (☎76 07 49 11, Ⓦwww.nordnorskklatreskole.no; ❶), which provides unadorned lodging also right in the centre. It doubles as the home of Lofoten's best mountaineering school, Nord Norsk Klatreskole (same details), who operate a range of all-inclusive climbing holidays in the mountains near Henningsvær, catering for various degrees of fitness and experience. Prices vary depending on the trip, but a three-day, one-climb-a-day package costs in the region of 4800kr per person, including equipment, food and accommodation. Their prospectus is only printed in Norwegian, but they'll gladly discuss the various options with you in English.

Much less strenuous are **fishing trips**, a morning or afternoon's excursion for around 350kr, booked down at the harbour, or you could drop by the **Galleri Lofotens Hus**, on Hjellskjæret (daily: early to end March noon–3pm; late May to early June & mid- to late-Aug 10am–7pm; mid-June to mid-Aug daily 9am–7pm; 70kr; Ⓦwww.galleri-lofoten.no), which exhibits (and sells) the work of the contemporary Norwegian artist Karl Erik Harr. Also on display is a competent selection of late nineteenth- and twentieth-century Lofoten paintings by artists such as Einar Berge, Adelsteen Normann, Gunnar Berg and Otto Sinding – you can't miss his whopping *Funeral in Lofoten* of 1886 – plus historic and contemporary photographs and slides mostly of the islands. Henningsvær's Arctic light, plus the might of the mountains have long attracted Norwegian painters, making it something of an arts centre, and, indeed, there's more art for sale – plus ceramics and glassware – at the nearby **Engelskmannsbrygga**, on the main square (Jan to early June & mid-Aug to Dec Tues–Sun noon–4pm, mid-June to mid-Aug daily 10am–8pm; free; Ⓦwww.engelskmannsbrygga.no).

For **food**, the *Klatrekafeen*, at *Den siste Viking*, serves up a good range of Norwegian standbys from 90kr, plus soup and salads and some killer chocolate cupcakes, all washed down with first-rate coffee. Much classier, however, is the waterside *Fiskekrogen Restaurant*, Dreyersgate 19 (☎76 07 46 52), where the seafood in general, and the fish soup in particular, are simply superb; main courses from 180kr.

The Lofoten Ekspressen **bus** does not detour off the E10 to get to Henningsvær, but there is a patchy local bus service from Svolvær and Kabelvåg (13 daily).

Vestvågøy: Stamsund

It's the next large island to the southwest of Austvågøya, **Vestvågøy**, that captivates many travellers to Lofoten. This is due in no small part to the laid-back charm of **STAMSUND**, whose older buildings string along the rocky, fretted seashore in an amiable jumble of crusty port buildings, wooden houses and *rorbuer*. There have been some recent additions to the Stamsund stew, but it's all pretty low-key and the modern art gallery, Galleri 2 (June–Aug Tues–Sun noon–4pm & 6.30–9.30pm; free), about 100m from the Hurtigrute dock, is well worth a gander.

The main **bus** service to Stamsund (Mon–Sat 3–4 daily) is from Leknes, both the dull administrative centre of Vestvågøy and the site of the island's **airport**, just 15km away to the west; Leknes is reachable on the long-distance **Lofoten Ekspressen** (see p.326). Stamsund is also the first port at which the Hurtigrute **coastal boat** docks on its way north from Bodø. By **car**, the quickest way to Stamsund from Svolvær is to turn south off the E10 down Highway 815, a scenic forty-kilometre coastal drive.

As regards **accommodation**, Stamsund's HI **hostel** (Ⓣ76 08 93 34; Jan to mid-Oct; dorm beds 90kr, doubles ❷) is about 1km down the road from the port. The hostel consists of several *rorbuer* and a *sjøhus* perched over a bonny, pin-sized bay, and has a washing machine and tumble drier, and self-catering facilities. You can rent bikes here at 100kr a day, and the warden is very knowledgeable on everything about Vestvågøy, from cycling through to hiking and fishing. The **fishing** is, in fact, first-class: you can borrow the hostel's rowing boats and lines to take out on the (usually still) water, or you can take an organized fishing trip for just 200kr. Afterwards you can barbecue your catch and eat alfresco on the verandah overlooking the bay – it's this sort of laid-back atmosphere that makes the place incredibly popular. For something a little more conventionally comfortable – or just conventional – head for the stylishly decorated and intelligently revamped old rorbuer at *Skjærbrygga* (Ⓣ76 05 46 00, Ⓦwww.skjaerbrygga.no; ❺), right in the centre of Stamsund by the harbour. The old *Skjærbrygga sjøhus* has been attractively renovated too, and now contains a café and an excellent **restaurant**, which features the freshest of local ingredients; main courses at the restaurant go for around 200–250kr, much less at the café. Less pricey rorbuer can also be found 3km west along the coast from Stamsund in the minuscule hamlet of **STEINE**, where the cosy if rather spartan *Steine Rorbuer & Hytter* (Ⓣ76 08 92 83; ❸) snuggle up to the seashore.

The northwest coast of Vestvågøy

Admirers of wild scenery should consider heading out to Vestvågøy's blustery **northwest coast**, where a few hardy fishing villages hung on until they were finally abandoned to the birds, the wind and the sea in the 1950s – give or take the occasional summer resident. This coast is accessed by a series of turnings off the **E10** as it slices across Vestvågøy's drab central valley: you'll need your own car, however, as cyclists face stiff gradients and often strong winds and, although the bus service along the E10 itself is reasonable, there are no regular buses off it to the northwest coast.

Beginning in Stamsund, the first part of the excursion is the hilly fifteen-kilometre trip to Leknes, where you turn north along the E10 for the three-kilometre journey to the first signposted byroad, which leads the 10km over the hills, along the seashore and through a narrow tunnel to **UTAKLEIV**, perched on the edge of a wide and windy bay and surrounded by austere cliffs. There's more stern scenery at the end of the next turning off the E10, this time at **UNSTAD**, a huddle of houses in a diminutive river valley set beneath the mountains and with wide views out to sea. From here, a popular nine-kilometre **hiking trail** runs past mountains and lakes on one side and the surging ocean on the other, to **EGGUM**. This tiny hamlet is an especially pretty spot, its handful of houses clinging on to a precarious headland dwarfed by the mountains behind and with a whopping pebble beach in front. Eggum can also be reached by road from the E10 – it's the next turning along from the Unstad road – but before you reach the Eggum turn-off you'll pass the flashy **Lofotr Vikingmuseum**, 14km from Leknes (early to end May & early Sept daily 11am–5pm; June–Aug daily 10am–7pm; mid-Sept to early May Mon–Fri 1–3pm; 90kr; ⓦwww.lofotr.no). Inspired by the accidental discovery of the site of a Viking chieftain's house by a local farmer in 1981, the museum is housed within a reconstructed 83-metre Viking house, with flickering lights, wood tar smells and so forth adding to the atmosphere. There's also a permanent exhibition of Viking artefacts found in the vicinity, and the boathouse contains a full-size replica of the Gokstad ship displayed in Oslo (see p.105).

South to Nusfjord

By any standard the next two islands of the archipelago, **Flakstadøya** – known to the Vikings as "Vargfot", or wolf's paw, on account of its shape – and **Moskenesøya**, are extraordinarily beautiful. As the Lofoten taper towards their southerly conclusion, the rearing peaks of the Lofotenveggen crimp the sea-shredded coastline, providing a thunderously scenic backdrop to a necklace of tiny fishing villages. The E10 travels along almost all of this shoreline, leaving Leknes to tunnel west under the sound separating Vestvågøy from Flakstadøya. About 20km from Leknes, an even more improbable byroad somehow wiggles the 6km through the mountains to **NUSFJORD**, an extravagantly picturesque fishing village in a tight and forbidding cove. Unlike many *rorbuer* elsewhere in Lofoten, the ones here are the genuine nineteenth-century article, and the general store, with its wooden floors and antique appearance, fits in nicely too. Inevitably, it's tourism that keeps the local economy afloat, and the village is firmly on the day-trippers' itinerary, but it's still a beguiling place, with **accommodation** available in more than thirty comfortably refurbished – and chain-hotel owned – *rorbuer*. The one-bedroom versions hold two to four people (❷), the two-bedroom ones have space for five (❹): advance reservations are strongly advised with *Nusfjord Rorbuanlegg* (ⓣ76 09 30 20, ⓦwww.rica-lofoten.no/). There's also a **bar-restaurant**, though this gets mixed reviews.

On to Hamnøy and Reine

Back on the E10, it's a further 5km to **Flakstad kirke**, a distinctive onion-domed, red timber church built in 1780. The church's ornate pulpit was painted by the itinerant German artist Gottfried Ezechiel (see also the Bodin kirke, p.304), as was the painting above the altar, whose main motif is The Last Supper. The church announces the beginning of **RAMBERG**, the island's administrative centre – if that's what you can call the smattering of services (garage, supermarket and suchlike) that strings along the sandy beach. Pressing on, over the first of several narrow bridges, you're soon on **Moskenesøya**, where the road squirms across the mouth of the Reinefjord, hopping from islet to islet to link the fishing villages of **HAMNØY**, on the north side of the inlet, with Reine to the south. Both villages boast impossibly picturesque settings and Hamnøy also lays claim to an excellent restaurant, *Hamnøy Mat & Vinbu* (ⓣ76 09 21 45; early March to Sept), whose short menu provides traditional Norwegian cuisine

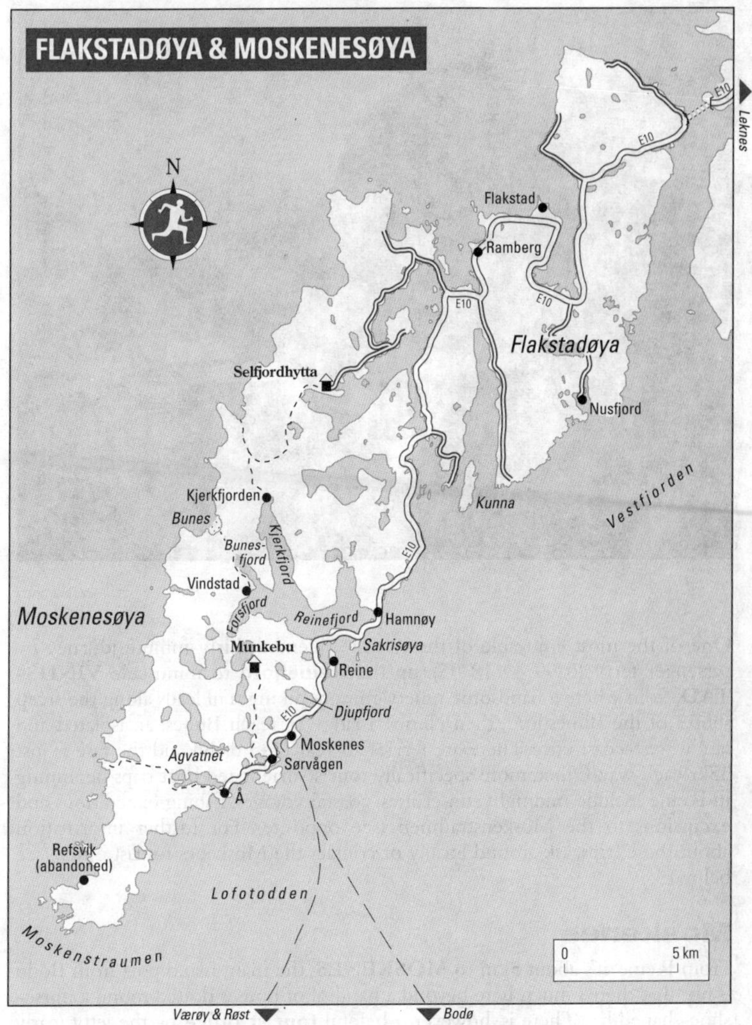

at its best: there's first-rate seafood, of course, not to mention cods' tongues – an island delicacy – and the rarely seen, but delicious, sago pudding. Hamnøy also possesses some very plain *rorbuer* – *Hamnøy Rorbuer* (Ⓣ76 09 23 20, ❷–❸), but far more appealing are those on the tiny islet of **Sakrisøya**, midway between Hamnøy and Reine, where the pretty yellow cabins of *Sakrisøy Rorbuer* (Ⓣ76 09 21 43, Ⓦwww.lofoten-info.no/sakrisoy; ❸–❺) are both well kept and cosy. The owners of the *rorbuer* also run the little fishmongers opposite, where they dish out delicious home-made fish burgers.

Despite its stunning setting, **Reine**, stuck on a promontory just off the E10 immediately to the south of Sakrisøya, is somewhat careworn and has little to recommend it other than as a useful departure point for a variety of **boat trips**.

△ Hamnøy

One of the most enjoyable of these is the splendid thirty-minute journey by passenger ferry (Ⓣ99 49 18 05), up the **Reinefjord** to minuscule **VINDSTAD**, from where a handsome ninety-minute hiking trail leads along the steep shores of the Bunesfjord, then climbs a ridge to reach Bunes, an isolated and sandy west-coast cove. There are ferries all year (2–3 daily) and the fare is just 35kr each way. Other, more specifically tourist-orientated boat trips beginning in Reine include midnight sun cruises, coastal voyages, fishing expeditions and excursions to the Moskenstraumen (see opposite). For further information about these trips, ask around locally or contact the Moskenes tourist office (see below).

Moskenes

From Reine, it's about 5km to **MOSKENES**, the main island port from Bodø – not that there's much here beyond a handful of houses dotted round a horseshoe-shaped bay. There is, however, a helpful **tourist office** by the jetty (early to late June & early to late Aug Mon–Fri 10am–5pm; late June to early Aug daily 10am–7pm; Ⓣ76 09 15 99, Ⓦwww.lofoten-info.no), and a basic **campsite** (Ⓣ99 48 94 05; June–Aug), up a gravel track a five-minute walk away.

Å

Five kilometres south of Moskenes the road ends abruptly at the tersely named **Å**, one of Lofoten's most delightful villages, its huddle of old buildings rambling along a foreshore that's wedged in tight between the grey-green mountains and the surging sea. Unusually, so much of the nineteenth-century village has survived that a good portion of Å has been incorporated into the **Norsk Fiskevaersmuseum** (Norwegian Fishing Village Museum; late June to late Aug daily 10.30am–5.30pm; late Aug to late June Mon–Fri 11am–3.30pm; 55kr), an engaging attempt to recreate life here at the end of the nineteenth century. There are about fifteen buildings to examine, including a boathouse, forge, cod-liver-oil processing plant, *rorbuer*, and the houses of both the traders who dominated things hereabouts and the fishermen who did their bidding. According to the census of 1900, Å had 91 inhabitants, of whom ten were traders and their relatives, 18 servants, and 63 fishermen and their dependants. It was a rigidly hierarchical society underpinned by terms and conditions akin to serfdom: the fishermen did not own any land and had to pay rent for the ground on which their houses stood. Payment was made in the form of unpaid labour on the merchant's farmland during the summer harvest and, to rub salt into the wound, neither could the fishermen control the price of the fish upon which they were reliant – no wonder Norwegians emigrated in their thousands. The museum has a series of **displays** detailing every aspect of village life – and very well presented it is too. Afterwards, you can extend your knowledge of all things fishy by visiting the **Tørrfiskmuseum** (Stockfish Museum; early to late June Mon–Fri 11am–4pm; late June to late Aug daily 10.30am–5.30pm; 40kr) – stockfish being the air-dried fish that was the staple diet of most Norwegians well into the twentieth century.

Å doesn't offer too much in the way of hiking trails, but there is an enyoyable route leading west from the village to the other side of the island. This begins by skirting the south shore of Lake Ågvatnet, before climbing over a steep ridge and then pushing on to the sea cliffs of the exposed west coast. The hike takes a whole day, and shouldn't be attempted in bad weather. Less energetic are the **boat trips** that leave from Å's jetty from May through to September, including day-long fishing expeditions (400kr per person), coastal cruises (3hr; 500kr), and, weather and tides permitting, cruises to the abandoned fishing village of Refsvik and the **Moskenstraumen** (5hr; 700kr), the dramatic maelstrom at the southern tip of Moskenesøya. There are other places to see similar phenomena in Norway – Bodø's Saltstraumen springs to mind – but these are the most dramatic and they were described by Edgar Allen Poe in his short story *A Descent into the Maelstrom*.

Even while I gazed, this current acquired a monstrous velocity. Each moment added to its speed – to its headlong impetuosity. In five minutes the whole sea... was lashed into ungovernable fury... Here the vast bed of the waters seamed and scarred into a thousand conflicting channels, burst suddenly into frenzied convulsion – heaving, boiling, hissing...

Practicalities

Beginning in Bodø and using the Bognes–Lødingen car ferry, the **Lofoten Ekspressen bus** runs the length of the E10 from Sortland to Å once daily; the journey time from Bodø to Å is fourteen hours, a little under four hours from Svolvær. Times do not, however, usually coincide with ferry sailings to and from Moskenes. Consequently, if you're heading from the Moskenes ferry port to Å, you'll either have to walk – it's an easy 5km – or take a taxi.

Most of the **accommodation** in Å is run by one family, who own the year-round HI hostel (singles 165kr, doubles ❶); an assortment of smart one- to eight-bedded *rorbuer* (800–1350kr per *rorbu*) surrounding the dock; and the adjacent *sjøhus*, which offers very comfortable and equally smart hotel-standard rooms (❸). The same family also runs the cosy **bar**, with seagull-egg bar snacks, and the only **restaurant**, where the seafood is excellent. Bookings for all these can be made on Ⓣ76 09 11 21, Ⓦwww.lofoten-rorbu.com. While you are here, you should also try the cinnamon buns made at the old bakery, still baking in the same oven after a hundred years.

Værøy & Røst

Værøy and **Røst** are the most southerly of the Lofoten islands, and the most time-consuming to reach: indeed, unless you're careful, the irregular ferry schedules can leave you stranded on either for a couple of days. The ferry operator is OVDS (Ⓣ76 11 82 45; Ⓦwww.ovds.no) and the gist of their timetable is that **car ferries** run from Bodø to Værøy and/or Røst once or twice a day and all of them call at Moskenes. The fare from Bodø to Værøy is 130kr per person and 480kr for a car & driver; Bodø to Røst is 160kr and 570kr; and between Værøy and Røst it's 70kr and 240kr. In the summer, from June to August, advance ferry reservations are advised, but for the rest of the year the ferries are first-come, first-served, so it's a good idea to turn up at least an hour before departure.

Both Værøy and Røst are internationally famous for their **bird colonies**, hosting a multitude of puffins, eiders and gulls, as well as cormorants, terns, kittiwakes, guillemots, rare sea eagles and more recent immigrants like the fulmar and gannet. There are lots of **bird trips** to choose from, and for a three-hour excursion you can reckon on paying between 350kr and 450kr. The weather in the islands is uncommonly mild throughout the year, potential hiking routes are ubiquitous, and the occasional beach glorious and deserted.

Værøy

Of the two islands, **Værøy**, just 8km long, is the more visually appealing, comprising a slender, lightly populated, grassy-green coastal strip that ends suddenly in the steep, bare mountains that backbone the island. Værøy's few kilometres of roads primarily connect the farmsteads of the plain, but one squeezes through the mountains to wiggle along a portion of the west coast. The island is, however, best explored on **foot**, either along the steep (and sometimes dangerous) footpaths of the mountains, or on the easier and clearer paths that lead out along the Nupsneset promontory. The most popular walk is, however, the hiking trail that leads along the west coast from the end of the road to the isolated village of **Måstad**: abandoned in the 1950s, it's a tricky walk which takes two to three hours each way. The inhabitants of Måstad varied their fishy diet by catching puffins from the neighbouring sea cliffs, a hard and difficult task in which they were assisted by specially bred dogs known as puffin dogs, or Lundehund. These small – 32–38cm high – innocuous-looking dogs have three distinctive features: they have six toes; can close their ears against dust and moisture; and can bend their heads right round on to their backs. Værøy's most important **bird cliffs** occupy the southwest corner of the island, but they are much too steep and slippery to approach on foot, so the best bet is to take a **boat trip**. There are several island operators – just ask around – and expect to pay about 350kr for a three-hour excursion.

Ferries to Værøy dock at the southeast tip of the island, about 800m from the **tourist office** (June–Oct Mon–Fri 9am–3pm; Ⓣ76 05 15 00); they can advise on boat tours and **accommodation** – though you would be foolhardy not to arrange this beforehand. The options are limited to a well-kept guesthouse at the old vicarage, the *Gamle Prestegård*, on the northern side of the island (Ⓣ76 09 54 11, Ⓦwww.prestegaarden.no; ❷), and a line of **rorbuer** (❸) belonging to the *Kornelius Kro* pub in the centre of the village (Ⓣ76 09 52 99, Ⓦwww.lofotentravel.com). There's also a basic HI **hostel** (Ⓣ76 09 53 52, Ⓦwww.vandrerhjem.no; May–Aug; dorm beds 150kr, doubles ❶), but there's no disguising the fact it used to be a police station – so try to avoid those bedrooms that used to be cells.

Finding a decent **meal** can a problem, but there are pizzas and snacks at *Kunsthavna Pub & Kafe*, the old airport at the end of the northern road. Back in the village, *Kornelius Kro* serves similar fare and they have the added benefit of a hot tub on the back terrace.

Røst

Even smaller than its neighbour, with a population of just 700, Røst is immediately different, its smattering of lonely farmsteads dotted over a flat, marshy landscape interrupted by dozens of tiny lakes. It was here in 1431 that the lifeboat of a shipwrecked Italian nobleman, Pietro Querini, was washed up after weeks at sea. Querini, and his fellow Venetians, stayed the winter and his written account is one of the few surviving records of everyday life in Nordland in the Middle Ages.

Ferries to Røst dock at the southwest corner of the island, about 3km from the main village. The **tourist office** (mid-June to mid-Aug Mon–Sat 10am–1.30pm & usually when the boat comes in; ⓣ76 09 64 11) is close to the jetty. As for **accommodation**, there are plain and inexpensive lodgings at *Kårøy Rorbucamping* (ⓣ76 09 62 38, ❸), and much more comfortable rooms at the new *Røst Bryggehotell* complex (ⓣ76 05 08 00, ⓦwww.rostbryggehotell.no; ❸). The latter organizes **boat trips** to the jagged islets that rise high above the ocean to the southwest of Røst, their steep cliffs sheltering myriad seabird colonies.

Travel details

Trains

Narvik to: Riksgränsen (2–3 daily; 50min).
Trondheim to: Bodø (3 daily; 11hr); Dombås (2–4 daily; 2hr 30min); Fauske (3 daily; 10hr 20min); Lillehammer (2–4 daily; 4hr 30min); Mo-i-Rana (3 daily; 6hr 30min); Oslo via Dombås (2–4 daily; 6hr 50min); Oslo via Røros (1–2 daily; 6hr); Otta (2–4 daily; 3hr); Røros (1–2 daily; 2hr 30min); Steinkjer (2–3 daily; 2hr); Stockholm (2 daily; 12hr).

Principal Nor-Way Bussekspress (ⓦwww.nor-way.no) bus services

Andenes to: Sortland (local bus: 2–4 daily; 2hr).
Bodø to: Fauske (2–3 daily; 1hr 10min); Kabelvåg (1 daily; 10hr 30min); Leknes (1 daily; 12hr); Lødingen (1 daily; 5hr 30min); Narvik (2 daily; 6hr 30min); Ramberg (1 daily; 12hr 30min); Reine (1 daily; 13hr 20min); Sortland (1 daily; 6hr 40min); Stokmarknes (1 daily; 8hr); Svolvær (1 daily; 10hr); Å (1 daily; 13hr 40min).
Fauske to: Bodø (2–3 daily; 1hr 10min); Kabelvåg (1 daily; 9hr); Leknes (1 daily; 10hr 30min); Lødingen (1 daily; 4hr); Narvik (2 daily; 5hr 30min); Ramberg (1 daily; 11hr); Reine (1 daily; 12hr); Sortland (1 daily; 5hr); Svolvær (1 daily; 8hr 30min); Stokmarknes (1 daily; 6hr 30min); Å (1 daily; 12hr 15min).
Harstad to: Lødingen (2–4 daily; 1hr 30min); Svolvær (local bus: 2 daily; 5hr 30min); Å (local bus: 2 daily; 8hr 30min).
Sortland to: Andenes (local bus: 2–4 daily; 2hr); Bodø (1 daily; 6hr 40min); Fauske (1 daily; 6hr 40min); Svolvær (2 daily; 2hr 15min); Å (2 daily; 6hr).
Narvik to: Alta (1–2 daily except Sat; 9hr 30min); Bodø (2 daily; 6hr 30min); Fauske (2 daily; 5hr 20min); Kabelvåg (1–2 daily; 6hr); Leknes (1–2 daily; 7hr 20min); Sortland (1–2 daily; 3hr 15min); Stokmarknes (1–2 daily; 4hr); Svolvær (1–2 daily; 5hr 40min); Tromsø (1–3 daily; 4hr).
Svolvær to: Bodø (1 daily; 10hr); Fauske (1 daily; 8hr 30min); Harstad (local bus: 2 daily; 5hr 30min); Kabelvåg (2 daily; 10min); Leknes (2 daily; 1hr 20min); Reine (1 daily; 2hr); Sortland (2 daily; 2hr 15min); Stokmarknes (2 daily; 1hr 30min); Å (1 daily; 3hr 15min).
Trondheim to: Bergen (2 daily; 14hr); Hjerkinn (2 daily; 2hr 30min); Loen (2 daily; 6hr 30min); Lom (2 daily; 5hr 30min); Oslo (1–3 daily; 8hr); Otta (2 daily; 4hr 30min); Stryn (2 daily; 7hr 30min); Røros (3 daily; 3hr); Skei (2 daily; 9hr); Ålesund (2–4 daily; 7hr).

Å to: Bodø (1 daily; 13hr 40min); Fauske (1 daily; 12hr 15min); Harstad (local bus: 2 daily; 8hr 30min); Kabelvåg (1 daily; 3hr); Leknes (1 daily; 1hr 40min); Reine (1 daily; 1hr 20min); Sortland (2 daily; 6hr); Stokmarknes (2 daily; 5hr 15min); Svolvær (1 daily; 3hr 15min).

Nord-Norgeekspressen

The **Nord-Norgeekspressen** (North Norway Express Bus) complements the railway system. It runs north from Bodø and Fauske to Alta in three segments: Bodø to Narvik via Fauske (2 daily; 6hr 30min); Narvik to Tromsø (1–3 daily; 4hr); and Tromsø to Alta (1–2 daily; 6hr 30min). Alternatively, the **Nordkappekspressen** (North Cape Express Bus) runs direct from Narvik to Alta (1 daily except Sat; 9hr 30min), where passengers overnight before picking up the second leg of the Nordkappekspressen to Honningsvåg and Nordkapp (see p.379 for details).

Car ferries

Andenes to: Gryllefjord (early to late June & mid-to late Aug 2 daily, late June to early Aug 3 daily; 2hr).
Bodø to: Moskenes (June–Aug 2–4 daily; Sept–May 1–2 daily except Sat; 4hr 15min); Røst (5 weekly; 8hr); Værøy (5 weekly; 6hr).
Bognes to: Lødingen (mid-June to mid-Aug 10 daily, mid-Aug to mid-June 5 daily; 1hr); Skarberget (every 1hr or 90min; 25min).
Botnhamn to: Brensholmen (early June to late Aug 4–7 daily; 45min).
Fiskebøl to: Melbu (daily 7am–11pm, every 90min; 30min).
Skutvik to: Svolvær (early June to late Aug 8–10 daily; late Aug to early June 2–4 daily; 2hr).
Svolvær to: Skutvik (early June to late Aug 8–10 daily; late Aug to early June 2–4 daily; 2hr).

Hurtigbåt passenger express boats

Bodø to: Svolvær (1–2 daily; 3hr 30min).
Harstad to: Tromsø (2–3 daily; 2hr 45min).
Narvik to: Svolvær (1 daily; 3hr 30min).
Trondheim to: Kristiansund (1–3 daily; 3hr 30min).

Hurtigrute coastal boat

Northbound departures: daily from Trondheim at noon; Bodø at 3pm; Stamsund at 7.30pm; Svolvær at 10pm; Stokmarknes at 1am; Sortland at 3am & Harstad at 8am.
Southbound departures: daily from Harstad at 8am; Sortland at 1pm; Stokmarknes at 3.15pm; Svolvær at 7.30pm; Stamsund at 9.30pm; Bodø at 4am & Trondheim at 10am.
Journey time Trondheim–Harstad 43hr, Trondheim–Tromsø 51hr.

6

North Norway

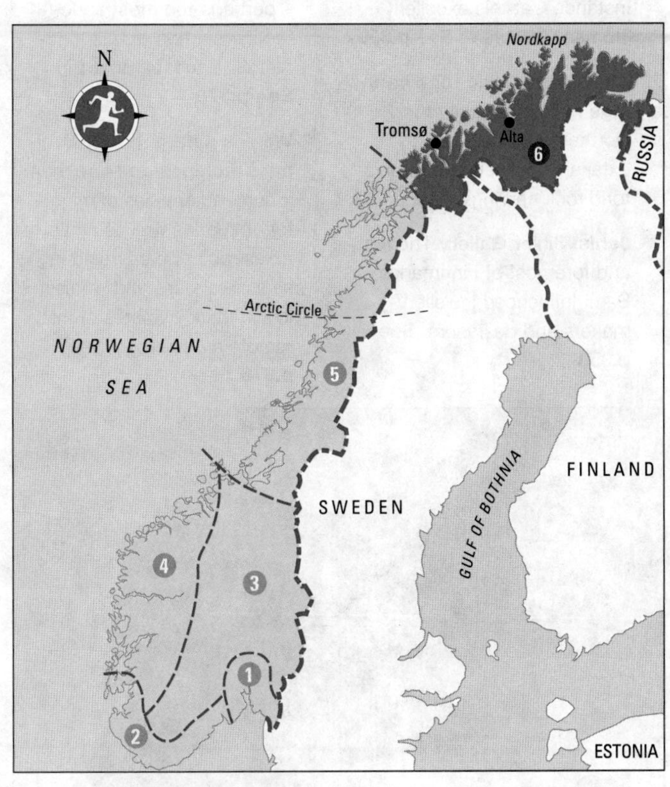

CHAPTER 6

Highlights

* **Rica Ishavshotel, Tromsø** Classy chain hotel slap-bang on the waterfront in Tromsø with all sorts of tasty little touches. See p.347

* **Sjømatrestauranten Arctandria** Try the Arctic specialities – reindeer, char and seal for instance – at this excellent Tromsø restaurant. See p.350

* **Alta's prehistoric rock carvings** Follow the trail round Northern Europe's most extensive collection of prehistoric rock carvings. See p.353

* **Juhls' Silver Gallery** The first and foremost of Finnmark's Sami-influenced jewellery-makers and designers. See p.358

* **Repvåg** An old fishing station with traditional red-painted wooden buildings on stilts, framed by a picture-postcard setting. See p.366

* **The Hurtigrute** Sail around the northern tip of Norway and across the Barents Sea – perhaps the most spectacular section of this long-distance coastal boat trip. See p.370

* **Wildlife safaris on the Svalbard archipelago** More than a hundred species of migratory birds, as well as arctic foxes, polar bears, reindeer, seals, walruses and whales, live in the icy wastes of this remote archipelago. See p.375

△ Walrus

6

North Norway

Baedeker, writing a hundred years ago about Norway's remote **northern provinces** of Troms and Finnmark, observed that they "possess attractions for the scientific traveller and the sportsman, but can hardly be recommended for the ordinary tourist" – a comment that isn't too wide of the mark even today. These are enticing lands, no question; the natural environment they offer is stunning in its extremes, with the midnight sun and polar night emphasizing the strangeness of the terrain, but the travelling can be hard, the specific sights widely separated and, when you reach them, subtle in their appeal.

Troms's intricate, fretted coastline has shaped its history since the days when powerful Viking lords operated a trading empire from its islands. Indeed, over half the population still lives offshore in dozens of tiny fishing villages, but the place to aim for is **Tromsø**, the so-called "Capital of the North" and a lively university town where King Håkon and his government proclaimed a "Free Norway" in 1940, before fleeing into exile. Beyond Tromsø, the long trek north begins in earnest as you enter **Finnmark**, a vast wilderness covering 48,000 square kilometres, but home to just two percent of the Norwegian population. Much of the land was laid waste during World War II, the combined effect of the Russian advance and the retreating German army's scorched earth policy, and it's now possible to drive for hours without coming across a building more than sixty or so years old. The first obvious target in Finnmark is **Alta**, a sprawling settlement and important crossroads that is famous for its prehistoric rock carvings. From here, most visitors head straight for the steely cliffs of **Nordkapp** (the North Cape), Europe's northernmost point, with or without a detour to the likeable port of **Hammerfest**, and leave it at that; but some doggedly press on to **Kirkenes**, the last town before the Russian border, where you feel as if you're about to drop off the end of the world. From Alta, the other main alternative is to travel inland across the eerily endless scrubland of the **Finnmarksvidda**, where winter temperatures plummet to -35°C. This high plateau is the last stronghold of the **Sami**, northern Norway's indigenous people, many of whom still live a semi-nomadic life tied to the movement of their reindeer herds. You'll spot Sami in their brightly coloured traditional gear all across the region, but especially in the remote towns of **Kautokeino** and **Karasjok**, strange, disconsolate places in the middle of the plain.

Finally, and even more adventurously, there is the **Svalbard** archipelago, whose icy mountains rise out of the Arctic Ocean 640km north of mainland Norway. Once the exclusive haunt of trappers, fishermen and coal miners, Svalbard now makes a tidy income from adventure tourism – everything from guided glacier walks to snowmobile excursions and whalewatching. You can fly

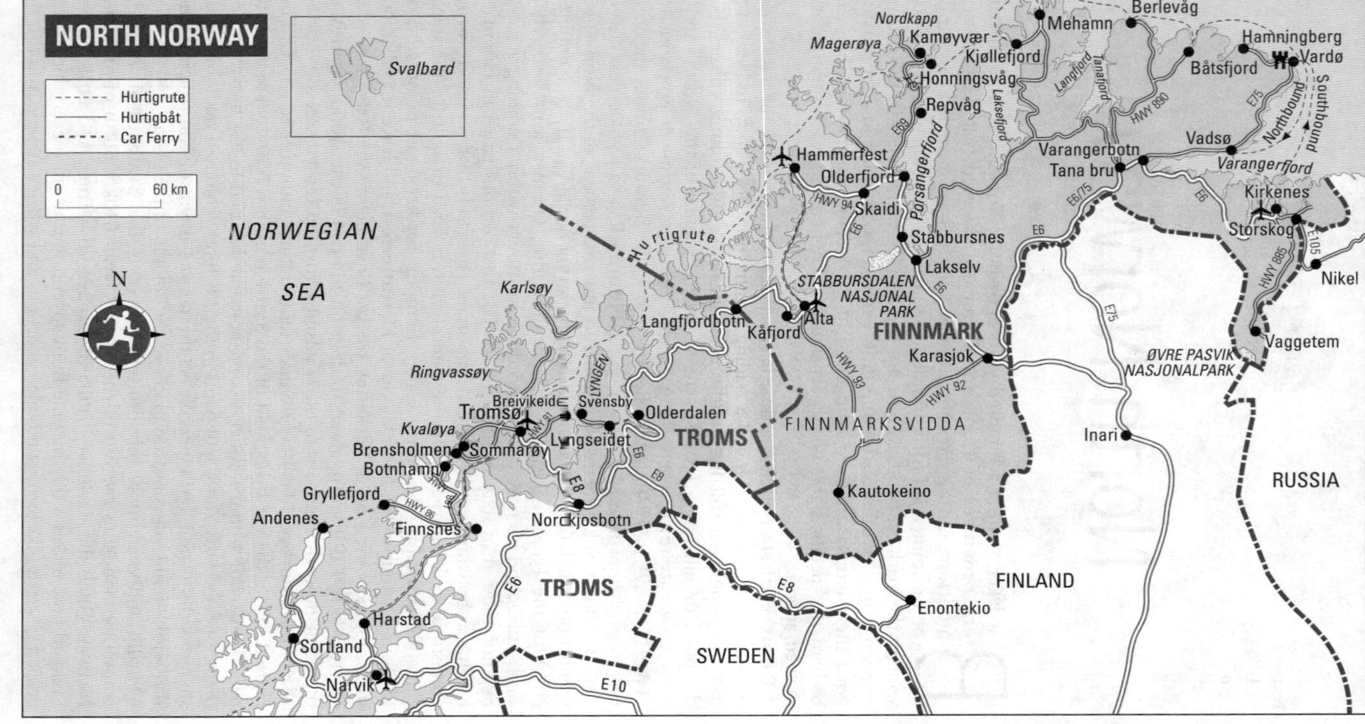

NORTH NORWAY
Svalbard
Hurtigrute
Hurtigbåt
Car Ferry
0
60 km
NORWEGIAN
SEA
N
Nordkapp
Magerøya
Kamøyvær
Kjøllefjord
Honningsvåg
Mehamn
Berlevåg
Hamningberg
Vardø
Båtsfjord
Southbound
Northbound
E75
HWY 890
Langfjord
Tanafjord
Laksefjord
Repvåg
E69
Porsangerfjord
Vadsø
Varangerbotn
Tana bru
Varangerfjord
Kirkenes
Storskog
E105
HWY 885
Nikel
Vaggetem
ØVRE PASVIK NASJONALPARK
RUSSIA
Hammerfest
Olderfjord
HWY 94
Skaidi
E6
Stabbursnes
Lakselv
STABBURSDALEN NASJONAL PARK
FINNMARK
E6/75
Hurtigrute
Karlsøy
Langfjordbotn
Kåfjord
Alta
HWY 93
Karasjok
HWY 92
FINNMARKSVIDDA
Inari
Ringvassøy
LYNGEN
Breivikeidet
Svensby
Olderdalen
Tromsø
HWY 91
Kvaløya
Lyngseidet
TROMS
Brensholmen
Sommarøy
Botnhamn
E8
Gryllefjord
HWY 86
Andenes
Finnsnes
Nordkjosbotn
Kautokeino
FINLAND
Enontekio
TROMS
Harstad
Sortland
Narvik
SWEDEN
E10

there independently from most of Norway's larger towns, including Tromsø, at bearable prices, though most people opt for a package tour.

Transport practicalities

Public transport in Troms and Finnmark is by **bus**, the **Hurtigrute** coastal boat and **plane** – there are no trains. For all but the most truncated of tours, the best idea is to pick and mix these different forms of transport – for example by flying from Tromsø to Kirkenes and then taking the Hurtigrute back, or vice versa. What you should try to avoid is endless doubling-back on the **E6**, though this is often difficult as this is the only road to run right across the region. To give an idea of the distances involved, from Tromsø it's 400km to Alta, 600km to Nordkapp and 850km to Kirkenes.

Norway's principal long-distance bus company, Nor-Way Bussekspress (Ⓦwww.nor-way.no), provides two services in the region – the **Nord-Norgeekspressen**, which links Tromsø with Alta once daily, and the **Nordkappekspressen**, linking Narvik and Alta once daily except on Saturdays. At Alta, passengers overnight before proceeding on the next leg of the Nordkappekspressen journey north to Honningsvåg, where – from late June to mid-August – they can change onto the connecting bus to Nordkapp. Alta is also where you can pick up local buses to Hammerfest, Kautokeino, Karasjok and Kirkenes, while north of Alta on the E6, the Nordkappekspressen passes through Skaidi, where you can change for the bus to Hammerfest. Bus **timetables** are available at most tourist offices and bus stations; they are also available online – Tromsbuss for Tromsø and its environs (Ⓣ177, Ⓦwww.tromsbuss.no) and FFR for the whole of Finnmark (Ⓣ177, Ⓦwww.ffr.no). On the longer rides, it's a good idea to buy **tickets** in advance, or turn up early, as buses fill up fast in the summer.

Northern Norway's main **highways** are all well maintained, but **drivers** will find the going a little slow as they have to negotiate some pretty tough terrain. You can cover 250–300km in a day without any problem, but much more and it all becomes rather wearisome. Be warned also that in July and August the E6 north of Alta can get congested with caravans and motorhomes on their way to Nordkapp. You can avoid the crush by starting early or, for that matter, by driving overnight – an eerie experience when it's bright sunlight in the wee hours of the morning. In **winter**, driving conditions can be appalling and, although the Norwegians make a spirited effort to keep the E6 open, they don't always succeed. If you're not used to driving in these sorts of conditions, don't start here – especially during the polar night. If you intend to use the region's minor, **unpaved roads**, be prepared for the worst and certainly take food and drink, warm clothes and a mobile phone. Keep an eye on the fuel indicator too, as **petrol stations** are confined to the larger settlements and they are often 100–200km apart. Car repairs can take time since workshops are scarce and parts often have to be ordered from the south.

Much more leisurely is the **Hurtigrute coastal boat**, which takes the best part of two days to cross the huge fjords between Tromsø and Kirkenes. En route, it calls at eleven ports, mostly remote fishing villages but also Hammerfest and Honningsvåg, where northbound ferries pause for three hours so that special buses can cart passengers off to Nordkapp and back. One especially appealing option, though this has more to do with comfort than speed, is to combine **car and boat** travel. Special deals on the Hurtigrute can make this surprisingly affordable and tourist offices at the Hurtigrute's ports of call will make bookings. If you are renting a car, taking your vehicle onto the Hurtigrute may well work out a lot cheaper than leaving it at your port of

Arctic phenomena

On and above the **Arctic Circle**, an imaginary line drawn round the earth at latitude 66.5 degrees north, there is a period around midsummer during which the sun never makes it below the horizon, even at midnight – hence the **midnight sun**. On the Arctic Circle itself, this only happens on one night of the year – at the summer solstice – but the further north you go, the greater the number of nights affected: in Bodø, it's from the first week of June to early July; in Alta, from the third week in May to the end of July; in Hammerfest, mid-May to late July; and in Nordkapp early May to the end of July. Obviously, the midnight sun is best experienced on a clear night, but fog or cloud can turn the sun into a glowing, red ball – a spectacle that can be wonderful but also strangely disconcerting. All the region's tourist offices have the exact dates of the midnight sun, though note that these are calculated at sea level; climb up a hill and you can extend the dates by a day or two. The converse of all this is the **polar night**, a period of constant darkness either side of the winter solstice; again the further north of the Arctic Circle you are, the longer this lasts.

The Arctic Circle also marks the typical southern limit of the **northern lights**, or Aurora Borealis, though this extraordinary phenomenon has been seen as far south as latitude 40 degrees north. Caused by the bombardment of the atmosphere by electrons, carried away from the sun by the solar wind, the northern lights take various forms and are highly mobile – either flickering in one spot or travelling across the sky. At relatively low latitudes hereabouts, the aurora is tilted at an angle and is often coloured red – the sagas tell of Vikings being half scared to death by them – but nearer the pole, they hang like gigantic luminous curtains, often tinted greenish blue. Naturally enough, there's no predicting when the northern lights will occur, but in wintertime they are not uncommon – and on a clear night they can be strangely humbling.

embarkation: car-hire drop-off charges in Norway are notoriously expensive, reaching anything up to 3500kr. At the other end of the nautical extreme, the region has two **Hurtigbåt passenger express boat** services – Alta to Hammerfest and Tromsø to Harstad.

With regard to **air travel**, the region has several **airports**, including those at Alta, Hammerfest, Honningsvåg, Kirkenes, Tromsø and Longyearbyen, on Svalbard. SAS/Braathens and its many subsidiaries – including Widerøe, which flies in and out of a string of small northern airstrips – offer summer discounts and passes (see p.30 and p.51), which can make flying an economic possibility.

As for **accommodation**, all the major settlements have at least a couple of hotels and the main roads are sprinkled with campsites. If you have a tent and a well-insulated sleeping bag, you can, in theory, bed down more or less where you like, but the hostility of the climate and the ferocity of the mosquitoes, especially in the marshy areas of the Finnmarksvidda, make most people think (at least) twice. There are HI **hostels** at Tromsø, Alta, Lakselv and Karasjok.

Tromsø

TROMSØ has been called, rather preposterously, the "Paris of the North", and though even the tourist office doesn't make any pretence to such grandiose titles today, the city is without question the effective capital of northern Norway. Easily the region's most populous town, its credentials go back to the Middle Ages and beyond, when seafarers used its sheltered harbour, and there's been a church here since the thirteenth century. Tromsø received its municipal charter in 1794, when it was primarily a fishing port and trading station, and flourished in the middle of the nineteenth century when its seamen ventured north to Svalbard to reap rich rewards hunting arctic foxes, polar bears and, most profitable of all, seals. Subsequently, Tromsø became famous as the jumping-off point for a string of Arctic expeditions, its celebrity status assured when

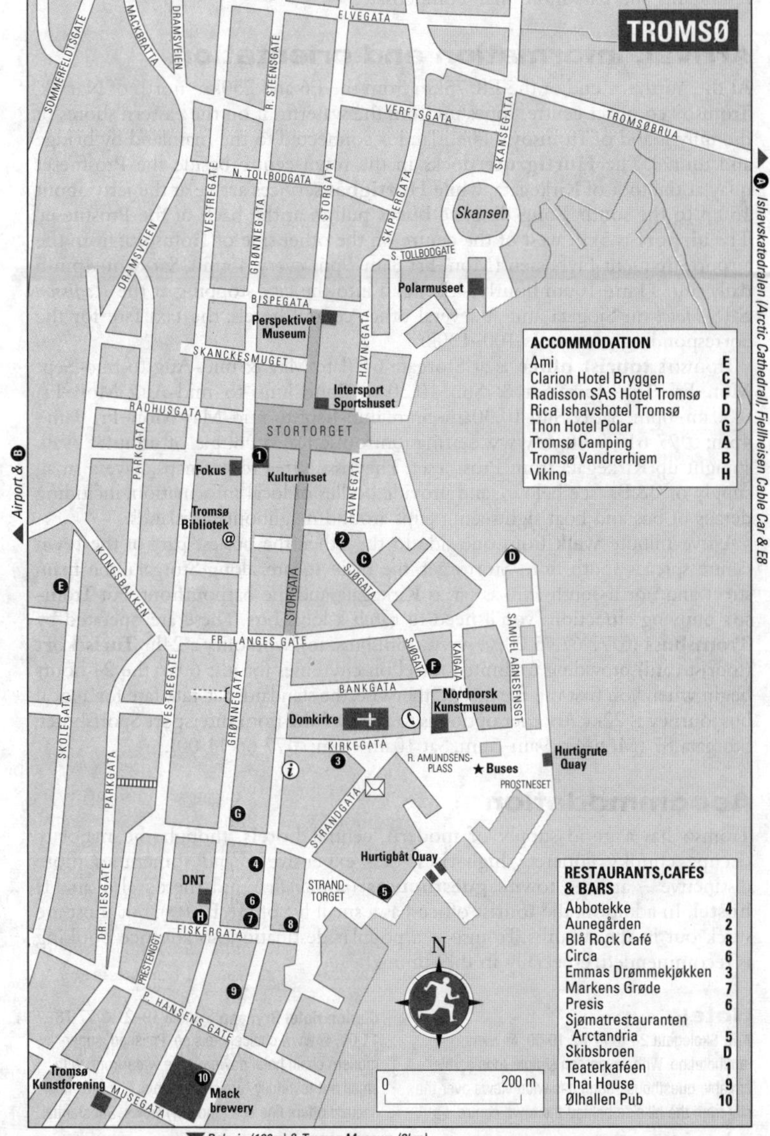

the explorer Roald Amundsen flew from here to his death somewhere on the Arctic icecap in 1928. Since those heady days, Tromsø has grown into an urbane and likeable small city with a population of 60,000 employed in a wide range of industries and at the university. It's become an important port too, for although the city is some 360km north of the Arctic Circle, its climate is moderated by the Gulf Stream, which sweeps up the Norwegian coast and keeps its harbour ice-free. Give or take the odd museum, Tromsø is short on specific **sights**, but its amiable atmosphere, fine mountain-and-fjord setting, and clutch of lively restaurants and bars more than compensate.

Arrival, information and orientation

At the northern end of the E8, 75km from the E6 and 250km north of Narvik, Tromsø's compact centre slopes up from the waterfront on the eastern shores of the hilly island of Tromsøya. The island is connected to the mainland by bridge and tunnel. The **Hurtigrute** docks in the town centre beside the Prostneset quay at the foot of Kirkegata, while **Hurtigbåt** services arrive at the jetty about 150m to the south. Long-distance **buses** pull in at the back of the Prostneset. The **airport** is 5km west of the centre on the other side of Tromsøya; from the airport, frequent Flybussen (Mon–Fri 8am–9pm every 45min, Sat 8am–4pm 5 daily, Sun 11am–10pm hourly; 45kr) run into the city, stopping at the *Radisson SAS Hotel* on Sjøgata and at several other central hotels; the taxi fare for the corresponding journey is 100–130kr.

Tromsø's **tourist office** is at Storgata 61 (late May & mid-Aug to mid-Sept Mon–Fri 9am–4pm, Sat & Sun 10.30am–2pm; June to mid-Aug Mon–Fri 8.30am–6pm, Sat & Sun 10.30am–5pm; mid-Sept to mid-May Mon–Fri 9am–4pm; ⓣ77 61 00 00, ⓦwww.destinasjontromso.no), a couple of minutes' walk straight up Kirkegata from Prostneset. They issue free town maps, have a small supply of B&Bs (see below), and provide oodles of local information, including details of bus and boat sightseeing trips around neighbouring islands.

A five-minute **walk** from one side to the other, the busiest part of the town centre spreads south from Stortorget, the main square, along Storgata, the main street and north-south axis, as far as Kirkegata and the harbourfront. For Tromsø's outlying attractions you'll need to catch a local **bus**. These are operated by **Tromsbuss** (ⓣ77 67 75 00, ⓦwww.tromsbuss.no), who offer a 24hr **Turistkort** (tourist card) providing unlimited travel on city buses for just 60kr; the 24 hours begin when you first use the card. Otherwise, the standard, flat-rate fare for a local bus journey is 22kr. Another option is to **rent a bike** from Intersport Sportshuset, Storgata 87 (Mon–Fri 9am–5pm, Sat 10am–4pm; ⓣ77 66 11 00).

Accommodation

Tromsø has a good supply of modern, central **hotels**, though the majority occupy chunky concrete high-rises. Less expensive – and sometimes more distinctive – are the town's **guesthouses** (*pensjonater*) and there's also an HI **hostel**. In addition, the tourist office has a small list of **B&Bs** (❷), but most are stuck out in the suburbs. Tromsø is a popular destination, so advance booking is recommended, especially in the summer.

Hotels

Ami Skolegata 24 ⓣ77 62 10 00, ⓦwww.amihotel.no. With seventeen simple rooms, this amiable guesthouse/hotel has wide views over the city from the hillside behind the town centre. ❷

Clarion Hotel Bryggen Sjøgata 19–21 ⓣ77 78 11 00, ⓦwww.choicehotels.no. Polished, super-modern chain hotel down on the waterfront, with small but tastefully furnished rooms. The fifth-floor Jacuzzi offers fine sea (and sky) views. Substantial weekend and summer discounts. ❼, sp/r ❹

Radisson SAS Hotel Tromsø Sjøgata 7 ⓣ77 60 00 00, ⓦwww.radissonsas.com. This plush downtown high-rise offers smart and comfortable modern rooms, and ultra-efficient service. ❺

Rica Ishavshotel Tromsø Fr. Langes gate 2 ⓣ77 66 64 00, ⓦwww.rica.no. Perched on the harbourfront, this imaginatively designed hotel is partly built in the style of a ship, complete with a sort of crow's-nest bar. Lovely rooms and unbeatable views of the waterfront make it the best place in town. ❻, sp/r ❺

Thon Hotel Polar Grønnegata 45 ⓣ77 75 17 00, ⓦwww.thonhotels.no. Small, modern rooms decorated in typical chain-hotel style, but summer and weekend discounts make this place a real bargain; central location, too. ❹, sp/r ❸

Viking Grønnegata 18 ⓣ77 64 77 30, ⓦwww.viking-hotell.no. Simple, modern and straightforward hotel-cum-guesthouse, centrally located and with very good prices. ❹

Hostels and campsites

Tromsø Camping Elvestrandvegen ⓣ77 63 80 37, ⓦwww.tromsocamping.no. Reasonably handy site about 2km east of the Arctic cathedral (Ishavskatedralen), on the mainland side of the main bridge, with cabins (❷–❹) as well as tent pitches. Open all year.

Tromsø Vandrerhjem Åsgårdsveien 9, Elverhøy ⓣ77 65 76 28, ⓦwww.vandrerhjem.no. Basic, barracks-like HI hostel located some 2km west of the centre in Elverhøy. No food is available, but there's a store close by and self-catering facilities. Reception is closed 11am–5pm. Local bus #26 runs from the centre to about 300m from the hostel, or else it's a stiff thirty-minute walk. Open mid-June to mid-Aug. Dorm beds 170kr, doubles ❷

The City

Completed in 1861, the Lutheran **Domkirke** (Cathedral; June–Aug Tues–Sat noon–4pm, Sun 10am–4pm; Sept–May Tues–Sat noon–4pm, Sun 10am–2pm; free), bang in the centre on Kirkegata, bears witness to the prosperity of the town's nineteenth-century merchants, who became rich on the back of the barter trade with Russia. They part-funded the cathedral's construction, the result being the large and handsome structure of today, whose imposing spire pokes high into the sky. Behind the church, at Sjøgata 1, stands the **Nordnorsk Kunstmuseum** (Art Museum of Northern Norway; late June to late Aug Mon–Fri noon–6pm, Sat & Sun noon–5pm; late Aug to late June Tues–Fri 10am–5pm, Sat & Sun noon–5pm; ⓦwww.museumsnett.no/nordnorsk-kunstmuseum; 30kr), comprising a well-presented collection of fine art and northern handicrafts from the 1850s onwards. It's not

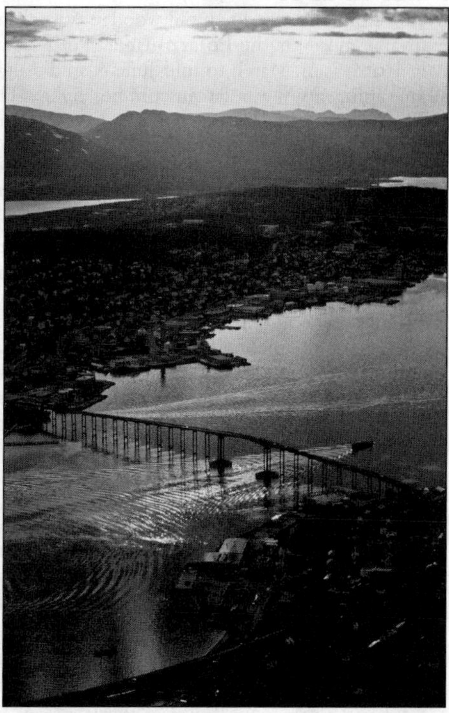

△ Tromsø

a large ensemble, but it does contain the work of many Norwegian painters, from lesser-known figures such as Axel Revold and Christian Krohg, to a handful of works by Edvard Munch (for more on whom, see p.111). There are also several Romantic peasant scenes by Adolph Tidemand and a couple of ingenious landscapes by both the talented Thomas Fearnley and Johan Dahl. The permanent collection is enhanced by frequent loans from the National Gallery in Oslo (see p.94) and by a lively programme of temporary exhibitions.

Back in front of the Domkirke, it's a gentle five-minute stroll north past the shops of Storgata to the main square, **Stortorget**, site of a daily open-air **market** selling flowers and knick-knacks. The square nudges down towards the waterfront, where fresh fish and prawns are sold direct from inshore fishing boats throughout the summer. Just beyond the square, at Storgata 95, is the **Perspektivet Museum** (mid-June to Aug Tues–Sun 11am–5pm, Sept to mid-June Tues–Fri 11am–3pm, Sat & Sun noon–4pm; 40kr), where the emphasis is on all things local, with a lively programme of temporary exhibitions concerning Tromsø and its inhabitants. The building itself, dating from 1838, is also of interest as the one-time home of the local writer Cora Sandel (1880–1974).

Follow the harbour round to the north and you're in the heart of old Tromsø: the raised ground close to the water's edge was the centre of the medieval settlement and it was here that the locals built the first fortifications. Nothing now remains of the medieval town, but you can discern the shape of a later, eighteenth-century fort in the modest knoll known as **Skansen**.

Polarmuseet

Metres from Skansen, in an old wooden waterfront warehouse, is the city's most enjoyable museum, the **Polarmuseet** (Polar Museum; daily: mid-June to mid-Aug 10am–7pm, March to mid-June & mid-Aug to Sept 11am–5pm; Oct–Feb 11am–3pm; ⓦwww.polarmuseum.no, 50kr). The collection begins with a rather unappetizing series of displays on trapping in the Arctic, but beyond is an outstanding section on Svalbard, including archeological finds recently retrieved from an eighteenth-century **Russian trapping station** – most come from graves preserved intact by the permafrost. Among many items, there are combs, leather boots, parts of a sledge, slippers and even – just to prove illicit smoking is not a recent phenomenon – a clay pipe from a period when the Russian company in charge of affairs did not allow trappers to smoke. Two other sections on the first floor focus on **seal hunting**, an important part of the local economy until the 1950s.

Upstairs, on the second floor, a further section is devoted to the polar explorer **Roald Amundsen** (1872–1928), who spent thirty years searching out the secrets of the polar regions. In 1901, he purchased a sealer, the *Gjøa*, here in Tromsø and then spent three years sailing and charting the **Northwest Passage** between the Atlantic and the Pacific. The *Gjøa* (now on display in Olso: see p.106) was the first vessel to complete this extraordinary voyage, which tested Amundsen and his crew to the very limits. Long searched-for, the Passage had for centuries been something of a nautical Holy Grail and the progress of the voyage – and at times the lack of it – was headline news right across the world. In 1910, Amundsen set out in a new ship, the *Fram* (also exhibited in Oslo; see p.106), for the Antarctic, or more specifically the **South Pole**. On December 14, 1911, Amundsen and four of his crew became the first men to reach the South Pole, famously just ahead of his British rival Captain Scott. The museum exhibits all sorts of oddments used by Amundsen and his men – from long johns and pipes through to boots and ice picks – but it's the photos that steal the show, providing a fascinating insight into the way Amundsen's polar expeditions were organized and the hardships endured. Amundsen clearly liked having his picture taken, judging from the heroic poses he struck, his derring-do emphasised by the finest set of eyebrows north of Oslo.

Finally, there's another extensive section on Amundsen's contemporary **Fridtjof Nansen** (1861–1930), a polar explorer of similar renown who, in his later years, became a leading figure in international famine relief. In 1895, Nansen and his colleague Hjalmar Johansen made an abortive effort to reach the North Pole by dog sledge after their ship was trapped by pack ice. It took them fifteen months to get back to safety, a journey of such epic proportions that tales of it captivated all of Scandinavia.

Mack, Tromsø Kunstforening and Polaria

Just to the south of the town centre, at the corner of Storgata and Musegata, the profitable **Mack brewery** proudly claims to be the world's northernmost brewery – and dreams up all sorts of bottle labels with ice and polar bears to hammer home the point. Nearby, just up Musegata, **Tromsø Kunstforening** (Tromsø Art Society; Tues–Sun noon–5pm; 30kr) occupies part of a large and attractive Neoclassical building dating from the 1890s. The art society puts on imaginative temporary exhibitions of Norwegian contemporary art with the emphasis on the work of Nordland artists.

Doubling back down Musegata, it's a couple of hundred metres south along Storgata to **Polaria** (daily: mid-May to mid-Aug 10am–7pm; mid-Aug to mid-May noon–5pm, Ⓦwww.polaria.no; 90kr), a lavish waterfront complex which deals with all things Arctic. There's an aquarium filled with Arctic species, a 180-degree cinema showing a film on Svalbard and several exhibitions on polar research. Moored outside is a 1940s sealing ship, **M/S Polstjerna** (June to mid–Aug daily 11am–6pm; 30kr, tickets at Polaria).

South of the centre: Tromsø Museum

About 3km south of the centre, near the southern tip of Tromsøya, is the **Tromsø Museum** (mid-May to mid-June & mid-Aug to mid-Sept daily 9am–6pm; mid-June to mid-Aug daily 9am–8pm; mid-Sept to mid-May Mon–Fri 9am–3.30pm, Sat & Sun 11am–5pm; 40kr), whose varied collections feature nature and the sciences downstairs, and culture and history above. Pride of place goes to the **medieval religious carvings**, naive but evocative pieces retrieved from various Nordland churches. There's also an enjoyable section on the Sami featuring displays on every aspect of Sami life – from dwellings, tools and equipment through to traditional costume and hunting techniques. To get to the museum, take bus #28 from the centre (Mon–Sat every 30min, Sun hourly).

East of the centre: Ishavskatedralen and the fjellheisen cable car

East of the town centre, over the spindly Tromsø bridge, rises the desperately modern **Ishavskatedralen** (Arctic Cathedral; June to mid-Aug Mon–Sat 9am–7pm, Sun 1–7pm; mid-Aug to May daily 4–6pm; 25kr). Completed in 1965, the church's strikingly white, glacier-like appearance is achieved by means of eleven immense triangular concrete sections, representing the eleven Apostles left after the betrayal. The entire east wall is formed by a huge stained-glass window, one of the largest in Europe, and the organ is unusual too, built to represent a ship when viewed from beneath – recalling the tradition, still seen in many a Norwegian church, of suspending a ship from the roof as a good-luck talisman for seafarers. Among several bus services, #28 (Mon–Sat every

30min, Sun every hour) comes this way, but it's only a few minutes' walk over the bridge from the centre.

From the Ishavskatedralen, it's a fifteen-minute walk – or a short ride on bus #26 – southwest to the **fjellheisen cable car** (April to late May & late Aug to Sept daily 10am–5pm; late May to late Aug daily 10am–1am; 85kr), which whisks up Mt Storsteinen. From the top, at 421m, the views of the city and its surroundings are extensive and it's a smashing spot to catch the midnight sun; there's a café at the top. Note that cable-car services are suspended during poor weather.

Eating, drinking and nightlife

With a clutch of first-rate **restaurants**, several enjoyable **cafés** and a good supply of late-night **bars**, Tromsø is as well served as any comparable Norwegian city. The best of the cafés and restaurants are concentrated in the vicinity of the tourist office, on Storgata, and most of the livelier bars – many of which sell Mack, the local brew – are in the centre, too.

The **Kulturhuset**, Grønnegata 87 (tickets ⓣ77 66 33 66, ⓦwww.kulturhuset.tr.no), is the principal venue for cultural events of all kinds, while the main **cinema**, the odd-looking Fokus, is close by at Grønnegata 100 (tickets ⓣ77 66 33 66, ⓦwww.tromsokino.no). The tourist office has details of performances.

Cafés and restaurants

Aunegården Sjøgata 29. Large(ish) café-restaurant within the old – and listed – Aunegården building. All the standard Norwegian dishes are served, at moderate prices, but these are as nothing when compared with the cakes – wonderful confections which are made at their own bakery. Weep with pleasure as you nibble at the cheesecake. Mon–Sat 10.30am–midnight, Sun noon–9.30pm.

Emmas Drømmekjøkken Kirkegata 8 ⓣ77 63 77 30. Much praised in the national press as a gourmet treat, "Emma's dream kitchen" lives up to its name, with an imaginative and wide-ranging menu focused on Norwegian produce. The grilled arctic char with chanterelle risotto is a treat and, giving reindeer a wide berth, a delicious venison dish with rowanberries is handled with finesse. Main courses are 190kr and up. Mon–Sat from 6pm, closed Sun.

Markens Grøde Storgata 30 ⓣ77 68 25 50. Classy and expensive Norwegian cuisine featuring innovative preparations of local fish and game, and lots of seasonal specialities. Main courses from 200kr. Tues–Sat 5.30–11pm.

Presis Storgata 36. Norwegian-style tapas that really works, and in super-cool surroundings too – upstairs from the *Circa* bar (see below). If you choose carefully you can fill up while keeping costs down to manageable proportions (90kr or less per tapas).

Sjømatrestauranten Arctandria Strandtorget 1 ⓣ77 60 07 20. Some of the best food in town. The upstairs restaurant serves a superb range of fish, with the emphasis on Arctic species, and there's also reindeer and seal; main courses start at around 220kr. Prices are about twenty percent less at the café-bar *Skarven*, downstairs, where there's a slightly less varied menu. Mon–Sat 4pm–midnight.

Thai House Storgata 22. Decent Thai cooking with the welcome inclusion of some excellent fish and vegetable dishes; the Thai spicy salads are especially good, and prices are moderate (mains from around 150kr). Daily 3–11pm.

Bars

Abbotekke Storgata 42. Fresh, inventive cocktails and an array of whiskies attract a classy crowd. There isn't room to swing a cat, but drinkers revel in the intimacy. Tues 6pm–midnight, Wed & Thurs 6pm–1.30am, Fri & Sat 6pm–3am, & Sun 8pm–1.30am.

Blå Rock Café Strandgata 14. Definitely the place to go for loud rock music – with and without the roll. Occasional live acts too, not to mention the best burgers in town. Mon–Thurs 11.30am–2am, Fri & Sat 11.30am–3.30am, Sun 1pm–2am.

Circa Storgata 36. With DJs Thursday to Saturday and intimate jazz concerts at least once a week, the sense of fun in this laid-back bar makes it one of the best in town. Mon–Thurs 11.30am–1.30am, Fri & Sat 11.30am–3.30am, Sun 1pm–1.30am.

Skibsbroen Fr. Langes gate 2. Inside the *Rica Ishavshotel* (see p.347), this smart little bar overlooks the waterfront from on high – it occupies the top of a slender tower with wide windows that afford sea views. Relaxed atmosphere; lots of tourists. Mon–Thurs 6pm–1.30am, Fri & Sat 3pm–3am; closed Sun.

Teaterkaféen Grønnegata 87. Inside the Kulturhus, at the corner of Stortorget, this arts-centre café-bar is long on conversation and (student) style. Daily 11am–1am.

Ølhallen Pub Storgata 4. Solid (some would say staid) pub adjoining the Mack brewery, whose various ales are its speciality. It's the first pub in town to start serving, and so pulls in the serious drinkers. Mon–Thurs 9am–5pm, Fri 9am–6pm & Sat 9am–3pm.

Listings

Airlines Norwegian ⓣ815 21 815; SAS/Braathens ⓣ05400; Widerøe ⓣ810 01 200.

Car rental Europcar, Alkeveien 5 and at the airport (ⓣ77 67 56 00); Hertz, Richard Withsplass 4 and at the airport (ⓣ77 62 44 00).

Diving and sea rafting Dykkersenteret AS, Stakkevollveien 72 (ⓣ77 69 66 00, ⓦwww.dykkersenteret.no), organizes guided diving tours to local wrecks in the surrounding fjords. Also runs fishing and midnight sun excursions plus equipment rental.

DNT Troms Turlag, Grønnegata 32 (Tues–Fri 10am–2pm; ⓣ77 68 51 75, ⓦwww.turistforeningen.no/tromsturlag). DNT affiliate

Moving on from Tromsø – Sommarøy and the coastal route to Andenes

Running up from Narvik, Nor-Way Bussekspress's (ⓦwww.nor-way.no) **Nord-Norgeekspressen bus** leaves Tromsø to push on north to Alta (1 daily; 6hr 30min); it's a fine journey that detours off the E8 to take two ferries – Breivikeide to Svensby and Lyngseidet to Olderdalen, back on the E6. At Alta, passengers change – and overnight – to catch the **Nordkappekspressen bus** onto Honningsvåg (1–3 daily; 4hr), where they change again for Nordkapp (late June to mid-Aug 1–3 daily; 45min). There are also FFR local buses (ⓣ177, ⓦwww.ffr.no) from Alta to Hammerfest, Karasjok and Kirkenes and a once daily special (read expensive) FFR bus from Honningsvåg to Nordkapp. Northbound, the **Hurtigrute** (ⓦwww.hurtigruten.com) leaves Tromsø daily at 6.30pm, taking eleven hours to reach Hammerfest; southbound it sails at 1.30am, arriving in Harstad six and a half hours later. The main **Hurtigbåt passenger express boat** service links Tromsø with **Harstad** (2–3 daily; 2hr 45min; 380kr; ⓦwww.tfds.no); there are no boats between Tromsø and Alta. For **drivers**, the quickest route from Tromsø to Alta is south along the E8 and then north on the E6, a total distance of about 420km. The shortest route – and also the prettiest – is the one followed by the Nord-Norgeekspressen bus via the Breivikeide–Svendsby and Lyngseidet–Olderdalen car ferries (see p.352).

Driving west from Tromsø past the airport, Highway 862 crosses the Sandnessundet straits to reach the mountainous island of **Kvaløya**, whose three distinct parts are joined by a couple of narrow isthmuses. On the far side of the straits, Highway 862 meanders south along the coast, offering lovely fjord and mountain views as it runs past a series of old wooden farmhouses. After about 60km, you reach **Brensholmen**, where a Senjafergene **car ferry** crosses over to **Botnhamn** (early June to late Aug 4–7 daily; 45min; passengers 55kr, cars 140kr; ⓣ76 14 12 03, ⓦwww.senjafergene.no). From here, it's a further 160km to Gryllefjord where a second Senjafergene ferry (early to late June & mid- to late Aug 2 daily, late June to early Aug 3 daily; 2hr; passengers 130kr; car & driver 260kr; reservations advised) takes you across to Andenes on Vesterålen (see p.319). If, however, you ignore the Brensholmen ferry and stay on the road, it's just 10km or so to **Sommarøy**, a tiny, treeless but grassy islet linked to Kvaløya by a causeway. Here, a holiday and conference centre, the relaxing *Sommarøy Kurs og Feriesenter* (ⓣ77 66 40 00, ⓦwww.sommaroy.no), offers hotel accommodation (❻) in the main building, plus high-quality, well-equipped seashore cabins for up to ten people; the smallest, the six-berth cabins, cost 1250kr per day. The restaurant is excellent too, particularly its Arctic specialities, and there are two traditional *badestamp* – wooden hot-tubs seating up to ten people – one inside and one outdoors, next to the ocean.

with information on local hiking trails and DNT huts.

Hiking See DNT (above) and Outdoor Pursuits (below).

Internet Free access at Tromsø Bibliotek, on Grønnegata near Stortorget (Mon–Thurs 11am–7pm, Fri 11am–5pm & Sat 11am–3pm.

Left luggage Coin-operated lockers inside the Venteromskafé, beside the Hurtigbåt quay (Mon–Fri 6.30am–8pm, Sat 10am–3pm, Sun noon–8pm); and at the bus station at the back of the Prostneset (Mon–Fri 8.30am–4pm).

Maps and books Bokhuset Libris, Storgata 86 (ⓣ77 68 30 36).

Outdoor pursuits Tromsø Villmarkssenter (Tromsø Wilderness Centre; ⓣ77 69 60 02, ⓦwww.villmarkssenter.no) at Kvaløysletta offers a wide range of activities from guided glacier walks, kayak paddling and mountain climbing in summer, to ski trips and dog-sled rides in winter. Overnight trips staying in a *lavvo* (a Sami tent) can also be arrranged. See also Diving and DNT above.

Pharmacy Svaneapoteket, Fr. Langes gate 9 (ⓣ 77 60 14 18).

Post office Main office at Strandgata 41 (Mon–Fri 8.30am–5pm, Sat 10am–2pm).

Ski rentals Intersport Sportshust, Storgata 87 (ⓣ77 66 11 00).

Taxi Tromsø Taxi ⓣ77 60 30 00 (24hr).

Vinmonopolet Grønnegata 64 (Mon–Fri 10am–6pm & Sat 10am–3pm).

Into Finnmark: from Tromsø to Alta

Beyond Tromsø, the vast sweep of the northern landscape slowly unfolds, with silent fjords cutting deep into the coastline beneath ice-tipped peaks which themselves fade into the high plateau of the interior. This forbidding, elemental terrain is interrupted by the occasional valley, where those few souls hardy enough to make a living in these parts struggle on – often by dairy farming. In summer, cut grass dries everywhere, stretched over wooden poles that form long lines on the hillsides, like so much washing hung out to dry. Curiously enough, a particular problem for the farmers hereabouts is the abundance of Siberian garlic (*Allium sibiricum*): the cows love the stuff, but if they eat a lot of it, the milk they produce tastes of onions.

Slipping along the valleys and traversing the mountains in between, the **E8** and then the **E6** follow the coast pretty much all the way from Tromsø to Alta, some 420km – and about nine hours' drive – to the north. Drivers can save around 100km (although not necessarily time and certainly not money) by turning off the E8 25km south of Tromsø onto **Highway 91** – a quieter, even more scenic route, offering extravagant fjord and mountain views. Highway 91 begins by cutting across the rocky peninsula that backs onto Tromsø to reach the **Breivikeidet–Svendsby car ferry** (every 1–2hr; Mon–Fri 6am–9pm, Sat 8am–8pm, Sun 10am–9pm; 25min; 70kr car and driver; ⓣ177, ⓦwww.bjorklid.no) over to the glaciated Lyngen peninsula. From the Svendsby ferry dock, it's just 23km over the Lyngen to the **Lyngseidet–Olderdalen car ferry** (every 1–2hr; Mon–Thurs 7am–7pm, Fri 7am–9pm, Sat 9am–7pm, Sun 10.30am–9pm; 40min; 100kr car and driver; ⓣ177, ⓦwww.bjorklid.no), by means of which you can rejoin the E6 at Olderdalen, some 220km south of Alta. This route is at its most spectacular between Svendsby and Lyngseidet, as it nudges along a narrow channel flanked by the imposing peaks of the Lyngsalpene, or Lyngen Alps.

Beyond Olderdalen, the E6 eventually enters the province of **Finnmark** as it approaches the hamlet of **LANGFJORDBOTN**, at the foot of the long and slender Langfjord. Thereafter, the road sticks tight against the coast to reach, after another 60km, the tiny village of **KÅFJORD**, whose sympathetically restored nineteenth-century church was built by the English company who operated the area's copper mines until they were abandoned as uneconomic in the 1870s. The Kåfjord itself is a narrow and sheltered arm of the Altafjord that was used as an Arctic hideaway by the *Tirpitz* and other German battleships during World War II. From here, it's just 20km further to Alta.

Alta

Despite the long haul to get here, first impressions of **ALTA** are not encouraging. With a population of just 16,000, the town comprises a string of unenticing settlements that spread along the E6 for several kilometres. The ugliest part is **Alta Sentrum**, now befuddled by a platoon of soulless concrete blocks. Alta was interesting once – for a couple of centuries not Norwegian at all but Finnish and Sami, and host to an ancient and much-visited Sami fair. World War II polished off the fair and destroyed all the old wooden buildings that once clustered together in Alta's **Bossekop** district, where Dutch whalers settled in the seventeenth century.

For all that, Alta does have one remarkable feature, the most extensive area of **prehistoric rock carvings** in northern Europe, the **Helleristningene i Hjemmeluft** (Rock Carvings in Hjemmeluft), which has been designated a UNESCO World Heritage site. The carvings are located beside the E6 as you approach Alta from the southwest, some 2.5km before the Bossekop district, and form part of the **Alta Museum** (May & Sept daily 9am–6pm; June–Aug

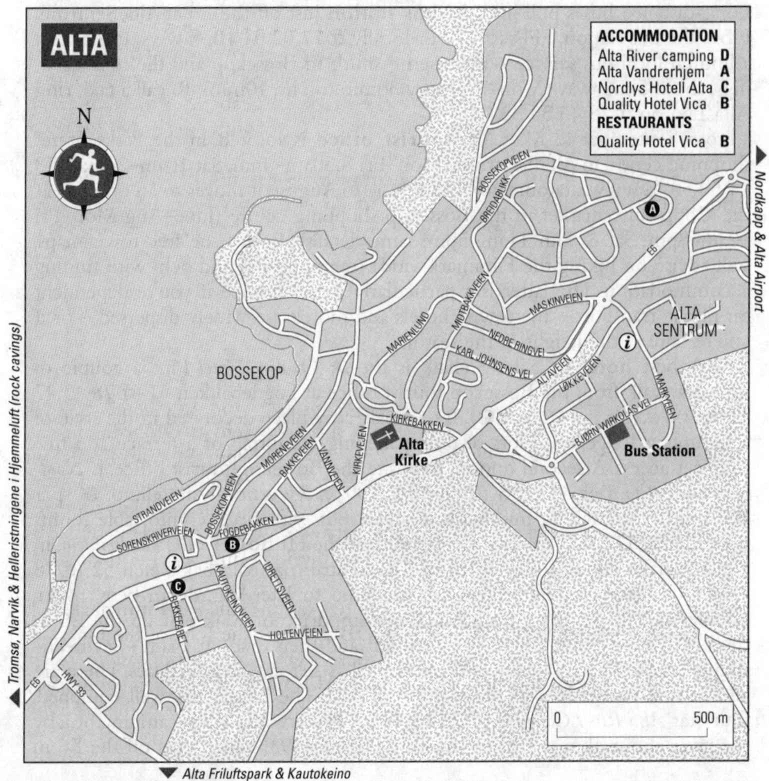

daily 8am–9pm; Oct–April Mon–Fri 9am–3pm, Sat & Sun 11am–4pm; Ⓦwww.alta.museum.no; May–Sept 80kr, Oct–April 40kr). A visit begins in the museum building, where there's a wealth of background information on the carvings in particular and on prehistoric Finnmark in general. It also offers a potted history of the Alta area, with exhibitions on the salmon-fishing industry, copper mining and so forth. The **rock carvings** themselves extend down the hill from the museum to the fjordside. A clear and easy-to-follow footpath and boardwalk circumnavigate the site, taking in all the carvings in about an hour. On the trail, there are a dozen or so **vantage points** offering close-up views of the carvings, recognizable though highly stylized representations of boats, animals and people picked out in red pigment (the colours have been retouched by researchers). They make up an extraordinarily complex tableau, whose minor variations – there are **four identifiable bands** – in subject matter and design indicate successive historical periods. The carvings were executed between 6000 and 2500 years ago, and are indisputably impressive: clear, stylish, and touching in their simplicity. They provide an insight into a prehistoric culture that was essentially settled and largely reliant on the hunting of land animals, who were killed with flint and bone implements; sealing and fishing were of lesser importance. Many experts think it unlikely that these peoples would have expended so much effort on the carvings unless they had spiritual significance, but this is the stuff of conjecture.

Practicalities

Long-distance buses pull into the **bus station** just off the E6 at Alta Sentrum. From the bus station, FFR (Ⓣ177 or locally Ⓣ77 02 04 10, Ⓦwww.ffr.no) run a limited local bus service – bybussen – south to Bossekop and the rock carvings, about 5km away (Mon–Fri every 30min to 1hr; 10min). To call a taxi, ring Alta Taxi on Ⓣ78 43 53 53.

From September to May, Alta **tourist office** is located in the Parksenteret shopping centre in Alta Sentrum (Mon–Fri 8.30am–4pm, Sat 10am–2pm; Ⓣ78 44 50 50, Ⓦwww.altatours.no). From June to August, it moves to an office near the Coop supermarket in the Bossekop shopping centre (June–Aug Mon–Fri 10am–8pm, Sat & Sun 11am–5pm; same details). Both issue free town maps, will advise on hiking the Finnmarksvidda (see opposite) and help with finding accommodation. The latter is a particularly useful service if you're dependent on public transport – the town's hotels and motels are widely dispersed – or if you're here at the height of the season.

Alta's best **hotel** by a long chalk is the *Quality Hotel Vica*, a couple of minutes' walk from the Bossekop tourist office at Fogdebakken 61 (Ⓣ78 43 47 11, Ⓦwww.vica.no; ❻, sp/r ❺). It's a small, cosy place decorated in the style of a mountain lodge, with lots of pine panelling, a suntrap of a terrace and free Internet access. A second option, opposite the Bossekop tourist office, is *Nordlys Hotell Alta*, Bekkefaret 3 (Ⓣ78 45 72 00, Ⓦwww.nordlyshotell.no; ❺, sp/r ❹), a rather uninviting mishmash of styles, but with large, comfortable rooms nonetheless. The bargain-basement choice is the HI **hostel**, *Alta Vandrerhjem*, in a plain chalet about 700m north of Alta Sentrum at Midtbakkveien 52 (Ⓣ78 43 44 09, Ⓦwww.vandrerhjem.no; late June to late Aug; dorm beds 140kr, doubles ❶). To get there from Alta Sentrum, drive or walk east up the E6 to the next roundabout, where you turn left and then first left again – a fifteen-minute stroll. There's a canteen here as well as self-catering facilities. There are also several **campsites** in the vicinity of Alta. The best is the well-equipped, four-star *Alta River Camping* (Ⓣ78 43 43 53, Ⓦwww.alta-river-camping.no), by the river about 4km out of town along Highway 93, which cuts off the E6 in

> **Moving on from Alta**
>
> Alta is something of a transport hub. The **Nordkappekspressen** (North Cape Express Bus; ⓦwww.nor-way.no) runs direct from Narvik to Alta (1 daily except Sat; 9hr 30min), where passengers overnight before picking up the second leg of the Nordkappekspressen to Honningsvåg (1–3 daily; 4hr); here they change for Nordkapp (late June to mid-Aug 1–3 daily; 45min). The Nordkappekspressen links in with the **Nord-Norgeekspressen** (North Norway Express Bus), which runs north from Bodø and Fauske to Alta in three segments: Bodø to Narvik via Fauske (2 daily; 6hr 30min); Narvik to Tromsø (1–3 daily; 4hr); and Tromsø to Alta (1–2 daily; 6hr 30min). Other long-distance routings from Alta include **FFR's bus** service (ⓣ177, or locally ⓣ77 02 04 10, ⓦwww.ffr.no) to Hammerfest (1–3 daily; 2hr 30min) and another to Kirkenes (3 weekly; 10–13hr). The same company also operates buses into the Finnmarksvidda, linking Alta with Kautokeino (Mon, Wed, Fri & Sun 1–2 daily; 2hr) and Karasjok (1–2 daily except Sat; 4hr 30min); note, however, that there are precious few buses between Kautokeino and Karasjok (Fri & Sun only 1 daily; 2hr). Finally, there is also a **Hutigbåt passenger express boat** from Alta to Hammerfest (1–2 daily; 1hr 30min; 245kr one-way).

between Bossekop and the rock paintings. They have tent spaces here as well as hotel-style rooms (❷) and cabins (❷).

Easily the best **restaurant** in town is at the *Hotel Vica*, which specializes in regional delicacies – cloudberries, reindeer and the like. Prices are very reasonable (mains around 1000kr) and traditional Sami dishes are often on the menu, too.

Around Alta: Alta Friluftspark

Aside from the rock carvings, the only reason to linger hereabouts is the **Alta Friluftspark** (ⓣ78 43 33 78, ⓦwww.alta-friluftspark.no), 20km to the south of town off Highway 93, beside the river in Storelvdalen. Here, all manner of Finnmark experiences are on offer, from snowmobile tours, dog-sled trips, ice-fishing and reindeer racing in winter, to summer fishing and boat trips along the 400m-deep Sautso canyon, Scandinavia's largest.

The Friluftspark also boasts an **Igloo Hotell** (mid-Jan to mid-April; ❼), a 100-bed, 1100-square-metre hotel built entirely out of ice and snow, including the beds and the glasses in the bar. Staying here is really fun, but the hotel is fantastically popular, so advance reservations are well-nigh essential.

The Finnmarksvidda

Venture far inland from Alta and you enter the **Finnmarksvidda**, a vast mountain plateau which spreads southeast up to and beyond the Finnish border. Rivers, lakes and marshes lattice the region, but there's barely a tree, let alone a mountain, to break the contours of a landscape whose wide skies and deep horizons are eerily beautiful. Distances are hard to gauge – a dot of a storm can soon be upon you, breaking with alarming ferocity – and the air is crystal clear, giving a whiteish lustre to the sunshine. A couple of roads cross this expanse, but for the most part it remains the preserve of the few thousand semi-nomadic **Sami** who make up the majority of the local population. Many still wear traditional dress, a brightly coloured affair of red bonnets and blue jerkins or dresses, all trimmed with red, white and yellow embroidery. You'll see permutations on

The Sami

The northernmost reaches of Norway, Sweden and Finland, plus the Kola peninsula of northwest Russia, are collectively known as **Lapland**. Traditionally, the indigenous population were called "Lapps", but in recent years this name has fallen out of favour and been replaced by the term **Sami**, although the change is by no means universal. The new name comes from the Sami word *sámpi* meaning both the land and its people, who now number around 70,000 scattered across the whole of the region. Among the oldest peoples in Europe, the Sami are probably descended from prehistoric clans who migrated here from the east by way of the Baltic. Their **language** is closely related to Finnish and Estonian, though it's somewhat misleading to speak of a "Sami language" as there are, in fact, three distinct versions, and each of these breaks down into a number of markedly different regional dialects. All three share many common features, however, including a superabundance of words and phrases to express variations in snow and ice conditions.

Originally, the Sami were a semi-nomadic people, living in small communities (*siidas*), each of which had a degree of control over the surrounding hunting grounds. They mixed hunting, fishing and trapping, preying on all the edible creatures of the north, but it was the wild reindeer that supplied most of their needs. This changed in the sixteenth century when the Sami switched over to **reindeer herding**, with communities following the seasonal movements of the animals. What little contact the early Sami had with other Scandinavians was almost always to their disadvantage – as early as the ninth century, a Norse chieftain by the name of Ottar boasted to the English king Alfred the Great of his success in imposing a fur, feather and hide tax on his Sami neighbours.

These early depredations were, however, nothing compared with the **dislocation of Sami culture** that followed the efforts of Sweden, Russia and Norway to control and colonize Sami land from the seventeenth century onwards. It took the best part of two hundred years for the competing nations finally to agree their northern frontiers – the last treaty, between Norway and Russia, was signed in 1826 – and meanwhile hundreds of farmers had settled in "Lapland", to the consternation of its indigenous population. At the same time, in the manner of many colonized peoples, Norway's Sami had accepted the **religion** of their colonizers, succumbing to the missionary endeavours of Pietist Protestants in the early eighteenth century. Predictably, the missionaries frowned upon the Sami's traditional shamanism, although the more progressive among them did support the use of Sami languages and even translated hundreds of works. Things, however, got even worse for the Norwegian

this traditional costume all over Finnmark, but especially at roadside souvenir stalls and, on Sundays, outside Sami churches.

Setting aside the slow encroachments of the tourist industry, lifestyles on the Finnmarksvidda have remained remarkably constant for centuries. The main occupation is **reindeer-herding**, supplemented by hunting and fishing, and the pattern of Sami life is mostly still dictated by the animals. During the winter, the reindeer graze the flat plains and shallow valleys of the interior, migrating towards the coast in early May as the snow begins to melt, and temperatures inland begin to climb, even reaching 30°C on occasion. By October, both people and reindeer are journeying back from their temporary summer quarters. The long, dark winter is spent in preparation for the great **Easter festivals**, when weddings and baptisms are celebrated in the region's two principal settlements, **Karasjok** and – more especially – **Kautokeino**. As neither place is particularly appealing in itself, this is without question the best time to be here, when the inhabitants celebrate the end of the polar night and the arrival of spring. There are folk-music concerts, church services and traditional sports,

Sami towards the end of the nineteenth century, when the government, influenced by the Social Darwinism of the day, embarked on an aggressive policy of "**Norwegianization**". New laws banned the use of indigenous languages in schools, and only allowed Sami to buy land if they could speak Norwegian. It was only in the 1950s that these policies were abandoned and slowly replaced by a more considerate, progressive approach.

More recently, the Sami were dealt yet another grievous blow by the **Chernobyl nuclear disaster** of 1986. This contaminated not only the lichen that feeds the reindeer in winter, but also the game, fish, berries and fungi that supplement the Sami diet. Contamination of the reindeer meat meant the collapse of the export market, and promises of compensation by the various national governments only appeared late in the day. Furthermore, the cash failed to address the fact that this wasn't just an economic disaster for the Sami, but a threat to their traditional way of life, based around reindeer herding. Partly because of the necessarily reduced role of reindeer – reindeer-herding is now the main occupation of just one-fifth of the Sami population – other expressions of Sami **culture** have expanded. Traditional arts and crafts are now widely available in all of Scandinavia's major cities and the first of several Sami films, *Veiviseren* (The Pathfinder), was released to critical acclaim in 1987. Sami music (*joik*) has also been given a hearing by world-music and jazz buffs. Although their provenance is uncertain, the rhythmic song-poems that constitute *joik* were probably devised to soothe anxious reindeer; the words are subordinated to the unaccompanied singing and at times are replaced altogether by meaningless, sung syllables.

Since the international anti-colonial struggles of the 1960s, the Norwegians have been obliged to re-evaluate their relationship with the Sami. In 1988, the country's constitution was amended by the addition of an article that read: "It is the responsibility of the authorities of the state to create conditions enabling the Sami people to preserve and develop their language, culture and way of life". The following year a Sami Parliament, the **Sameting**, was opened in Karasjok. Certain deep-seated problems do remain and, in common with other aboriginal peoples marooned in industrialized countries, there have been heated debates about land and mineral rights and the future of the Sami as a people, above and beyond one country's international borders. Neither is it clear quite how the Norwegian Sami will adjust to having something akin to dual status – as an indigenous, partly autonomous people and as citizens of a particular country – but at least Oslo is asking the right questions.

including the famed reindeer races – not, thank goodness, reindeers racing each other (they would never cooperate), but reindeer pulling passenger-laden sleds. Details of the Easter festivals are available at any Finnmark tourist office, and there's a **Kautokeino festival website** (Ⓦwww.saami-easterfestival.org). Summer visits, on the other hand, can be disappointing, since many families and their reindeer are at coastal pastures and there is precious little activity.

From Alta, the only direct route into the Finnmarksvidda is south along **Highway 93** to Kautokeino, a distance of 130km. Just short of Kautokeino, about 100km from Alta, Highway 93 connects with **Highway 92**, which travels the 100km or so northeast to Karasjok, where you can rejoin the E6 (but well beyond the turning to Nordkapp). Operated by FFR (Ⓣ177 or locally Ⓣ77 02 04 10, Ⓦwww.ffr.no), **bus** services across the Finnmarksvidda are patchy: on Monday, Wednesday, Friday and Sunday, there are one or two buses a day from Alta to Kautokeino, a journey that takes two hours, while there are only a couple of buses a week – on Fridays and Sundays – from Kautokeino to Karasjok, another two-hour haul. There's also an FFR bus service from Alta to

Karasjok along the E6, but this takes four-and-a-half hours and only runs once or twice daily except on Saturdays when it doesn't run at all. A further service links Karasjok with Hammerfest once or twice daily (except on Saturday) in just over four hours.

The best time to **hike** the Finnmarksvidda is in August and early September, after the peak mosquito season and before the weather turns cold. For the most part the plateau vegetation is scrub and open birch forest, which makes the going fairly easy, though the many marshes, rivers and lakes often impede progress. There are a handful of clearly demarcated **hiking trails** as well as a smattering of appropriately sited but unstaffed huts; for detailed information, ask at Alta tourist office.

Kautokeino

It's a two-hour drive or bus ride from Alta across the Finnmarksvidda to **KAUTOKEINO** (Guovdageaidnu in Sami), the principal winter camp of the Norwegian Sami and the site of a huge reindeer market in spring and autumn. The Sami are not, however, easy town dwellers and although Kautokeino is very useful to them as a supply base, it's still a desultory, desolate-looking place straggling along Highway 93 for a couple of kilometres, with the handful of buildings that pass for the town centre gathered at the point where the road crosses the Kautokeinoelva river. Nevertheless, the settlement has become something of a tourist draw on account of the **jewellers**, who set up their stalls here every summer, attracting Finnish day-trippers like flies. The jewellery bigwigs hereabouts are **Frank and Regine Juhls**, who braved all sorts of difficulties to set up their workshop here in 1959. It was a bold move at a time when the Sami were very much a neglected minority, but the Juhls had a keen interest in nomadic cultures and, although the Sami had no tradition of jewellery-making, they did adorn themselves with all sorts of unusual items traded in from the outside world. The Juhls were much influenced by this Sami style of self-adornment, repeating and developing it in their own work, and their business prospered – perhaps beyond their wildest dreams – and they now have shops in Oslo (see p.126) and Bergen (see p.220). As further testimony to the Juhls' commercial success, the plain and simple workshop they first built has been replaced by **Juhls' Silver Gallery** (daily: June to early Aug 8.30am–9pm; early Aug to May 9am–6pm; ring in winter to confirm hours on ⓣ78 48 43 30, ⓦwww.juhls.no), an extensive complex of low-lying showrooms and workshops, whose pagoda-like roofs are derived from the Sami. Exquisitely beautiful, high-quality silver work is made and sold here alongside a much broader range of classy craftwork. The complex's **interior** (regular, free guided tours; 30min) is intriguing in its own right, with some rooms decorated in crisp, modern pan-Scandinavian style, others done out in an elaborate version of Sami design. The gallery is located on a ridge above the west bank of the Kautokeinoelva, 2.5km south of the town centre – follow the signs.

Also south of the centre is the modern **Kautokeino kirke** (June to mid-Aug daily 9am–9pm; free), a delightful wooden building whose interior is decorated in bright, typically Sami colours – and looks particularly appealing when the Sami turn up here in their Sunday best. There are two more modest attractions on the north side of the river, beginning with the small **Kautokeino Bygdetun og Museum** (Guovdageaidnu Gilisillju or Kautokeino Parish Museum; mid-June to mid-Aug Mon–Sat 9am–7pm, Sun noon–7pm; mid-Aug to mid-June Mon–Fri 9am–3pm; 30kr), which features a history of the town inside and a number of draughty-looking Sami dwellings outside. You'll spot the same little turf huts and skin tents (known as *lavvo*) all over Finnmark – often housing souvenir stalls. Not far away, and clearly signposted to the north, is the **Kautokeino Kulturhuset** (Guovdageaidnu Kulturviessu or Cultural Centre; Ⓦwww.beaivvas.no). Winner of various architectural awards, the building houses the only state-sponsored Sami theatre in Norway.

Practicalities

Buses to Kautokeino stop beside Highway 93 in the town centre on the north side of the river – and about 350m to the north of the **tourist office** (daily: late June to early Aug 9am–4pm, July 9am–8pm; Ⓣ78 48 65 00, Ⓦwww.kautokeino.nu). The latter provides town maps and has details of local events and activities, from fishing and hiking through to "**Sami adventures**", which typically include a boat trip and a visit to a *lavvo* ("tent") where you can sample traditional Sami food and listen to *joik* (rhythmic song poems) for around 300kr. The main local tour operator is Cavzo Safari (Ⓣ78 48 75 88, Ⓦwww.samitour.no).

The only **hotel** as such is the modest and modern *Villmarkssenter* (Ⓣ78 48 76 02; ❸), across the highway from the tourist office. There are also a couple of **campsites** near the river on the southern edge of town, primarily *Kautokeino Camping og Motell* (Ⓣ78 48 54 00), with cabins (❶) and a few frugal motel rooms (❷). **Eating** establishments are thin on the ground, but there's good coffee, cakes and sandwiches at *Kaffe Galleriet*, behind the tourist office.

Karasjok

The only other settlement of any size on the Finnmarksvidda is **KARASJOK** (Kárásjohka in Sami), Norway's Sami capital, which straddles the E6 on the main route from Finland to Nordkapp – and consequently sees plenty of tourists. Spread across a wooded river valley, the town has none of the desolation of Kautokeino, yet it still conspires to be fairly mundane despite the presence

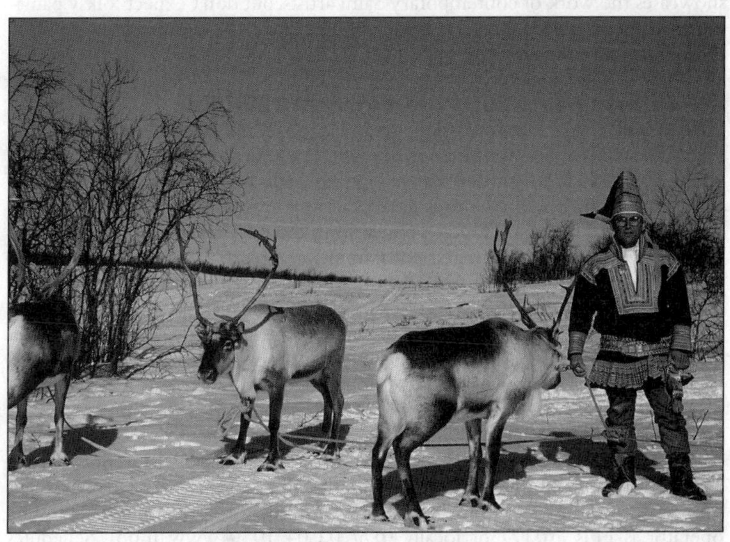

△ Sami reindeer herder

of the Sami parliament and the country's best Sami museum. The busiest place in town is the **tourist office**, Karasjok Opplevelser (early June to mid-Aug daily 9am–7pm; rest of year Mon–Fri 9am–4pm; ⓣ78 46 88 02, ⓦwww.koas.no), located on the north side of the river beside the E6 and Highway 92 crossroads, which is, to all intents and purposes, the centre of town. Staff here issue free town maps, book overnight accommodation and organize authentic(ish) Sami expeditions. The office is also incorporated within a miniature Sami theme park, **Sámpi Park** (same times; 95kr), which offers a fancy multimedia introduction to the Sami in the Stálubákti ("Magic Theatre"). Here also are examples of traditional Sami dwellings, Sami shops and a restaurant plus displays of various ancient Sami skills with the obligatory reindeer brought along as decoration or to be roped and coralled.

From the tourist office, it's a 200-metre walk north along the Nordkapp road to Museumsgata, where you turn right for **De Samiske Samlinger** (Sámi vourká dávvirat, Sami Museum; early June to late Aug Mon–Fri 9am–6pm, Sat & Sun 10am–6pm; late Aug to early June Mon–Fri 9am–3pm, Sat & Sun 10am–3pm; 30kr). This attempts an overview of Sami culture and history, with the outdoor exhibits comprising an assortment of old dwellings that illustrate the frugality of Sami life. Inside, a large and clearly presented collection of incidental bygones includes a colourful sample of folkloric Sami costumes.

On the south side of the river, just off Highway 92, you might also want to take a peek at the **Gamle kirke** (June–Aug daily 8am–9pm; free), which was the only building left standing in Karasjok at the end of World War II. Of simple design, it dates from 1807, making it easily the oldest-surviving church in Finnmark.

Carry on from the Gamle kirke along Highway 92, and the next major turning on the right leads along to the **Samisk Kunstnersenter** (Sámi daiddaguovddás, Sami Artists' Centre; early June to late Aug Mon–Sat 10am–3pm, Thurs till 7pm, & Sun noon–5pm; late Aug to early June Mon–Fri 10am–3pm, Thurs till 7pm, & Sun noon–5pm; free; ⓣ78 46 99 40). This unassuming gallery showcases the work of contemporary Sami artists, but don't expect folksy paintings – Sami artists are a diverse bunch and as likely to be influenced by postmodernism as reindeer-herding.

Hikes and tours into the Finnmarksvidda

However diverting Karasjok's sights may be, you'll only get a real feel for the Finnmarksvidda if you venture out of town. The tourist office has the details of a wide range of local **guided tours**: options include dog-sledging, a visit to a Sami camp, a boat trip on the Karasjokka river, cross-country skiing and even gold-panning. The region's most popular long-distance **hike** is the five-day haul across the heart of the Finnmarksvidda, from Karasjok to Alta via a string of strategically located huts; ask at Alta's tourist office (see p.354) for details, but note that this is not for the faint-hearted or inexperienced. A more gentle walk is the 3.5-kilometre **Åssebákti nature trail**, which passes more than a hundred Sami cultural monuments – *lavvo* and so forth – on the way. Clearly signed, the trail head is about 16km west of Karasjok along Highway 92 towards Kautokeino.

Practicalities

There's a limited **bus** service to Karasjok from Kautokeino (Fri & Sun 1 daily; 2hr) and a more frequent service from Alta along the E6 (1–2 daily except on Sat; 4hr 30min) and from Hammerfest (1–2 daily except on Sat; 4hr). The operator is FFR (ⓣ177 or locally ⓣ77 02 04 10, ⓦwww.ffr.no). Schedules mean that it's often possible to spend a couple of hours here before moving on, which is quite enough to see the sights, but not nearly long enough to get the true flavour of the place. Buses arrive at Karasjok **bus station**, on Storgata, from where it's a signposted five- to ten-minute walk west to the **tourist office** (see opposite).

The best **hotel** in town is the *Rica Hotel Karasjok* (Ⓣ78 46 74 00, Ⓦwww.rica.no; ❻, sp/r ❹), a breezy modern establishment in a large chalet-like building a short stroll north of the tourist office along the E6. More modest and less expensive accommodation is available at the year-round *Karasjok Camping*, a ten-minute walk west from the tourist office on the Kautokeino road (Ⓣ78 46 61 35), with both cabins (❷, en suite ❸) and tent spaces. Cream of the crop, however, is *Engholm Husky Vandrerhjem* (Ⓣ78 46 71 66, Ⓦwww.engholm.no), a fantastic all-year HI **hostel**, which has cosy home-made four- to six-bed **cabins** (350kr per night plus 150kr per person; dorm bed 175kr). The hostel is open all year and offers self-catering facilities, a sauna and Arctic dinners, sitting on reindeer skins around an open fire. The owner, the illustrious Sven, is an expert dog-sled racer and keeps about forty huskies; he uses them on a variety of winter guided tours – dog sledding and so forth – and in summer organizes everything from fishing trips and guided wilderness hikes to horseback riding. The hostel is 7km west out of town on the Kautokeino road (Highway 92), but that's no problem as Sven will pick up guests from Karasjok by prior arrangement. Sven hits all the gastronomic buttons, but the *Rica Hotel Karasjok* possesses the unusual *Gammen* restaurant, a set of turf-covered huts where Sami-style meals are served. It's all good fun, but the choices are pretty much limited to reindeer or salmon plus (delightful) cloudberries with sweetened cream.

From Karasjok, it's 130km west to Kautokeino; 270km north to Nordkapp; 220km northwest to Hammerfest and 330km east to Kirkenes.

Hammerfest

HAMMERFEST, some 150km north of Alta, is, as its tourist office takes great pains to point out, the world's northernmost town. It was also, they add, the first town in Europe to have electric street-lighting. Hardly fascinating facts perhaps, but both give a glimpse of the pride that the locals take in making the most of what is, indisputably, an inhospitable location. Indeed, it's a wonder the town has survived at all: a hurricane flattened the place in 1856; it was burnt to the ground in 1890; and the retreating Germans mauled it at the end of World War II. Yet, instead of being abandoned, Hammerfest was stubbornly rebuilt for a third time. Nor is it the grim industrial town you might expect from the proximity of the offshore oil wells, but a bright, cheerful port that drapes around a **horseshoe-shaped harbour** sheltered from the elements by a steep rocky hill. Hammerfest also benefits from the occasional dignified wooden building that recalls its nineteenth-century heyday as the centre of the *Pomor* trade in which Norwegian fish were traded for boat-loads of Russian flour. But don't get too carried away: Bill Bryson, in *Neither Here Nor There*, hit the nail on the head with his description of Hammerfest as "an agreeable enough town in a thank-you-God-for-not-making-me-live-here sort of way". Neither is the town's main employer, the harbourfront fish-processing plant, the stuff of Arctic romance.

The Town

Running parallel to the waterfront, **Strandgata**, the town's principal street, is a busy, 500-metre-long run of supermarkets, clothes and souvenir shops, partly

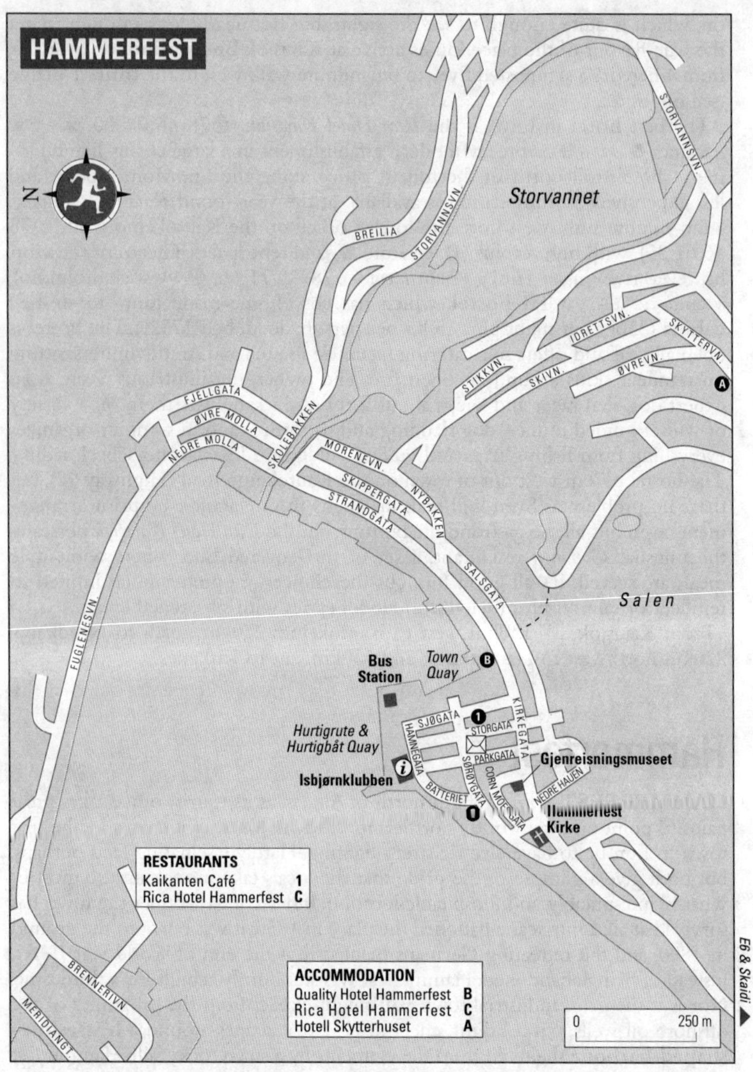

inspired by the town's role as a stop-off for cruise ships on the way to Nordkapp. However, most of the activity takes place on the **old town** quay, off Sjøgata, with tourists emerging from the liners to beetle around the harbourfront, eating shellfish from the stalls along the wharf or buying souvenirs in the small, summertime Sami market. The Hurtigrute spends a couple of hours at Hammerfest too, arriving at an unsociable 5.15am on its way north, and at a more palatable 11.15am heading south.

Beyond that, it's the general atmosphere of the place that appeals rather than any specific sight, though Hammerfest's tiny town centre does muster a couple of attractions, beginning with the **Isbjørnklubben** (Royal and Ancient Polar Bear Society; June–Aug Mon–Fri 9am–5pm, Sat & Sun 10.30am–1.30pm; Sept–May Mon–Fri 11am–1pm, Sat & Sun 10.30am–1.30pm; 40kr), in the main quayside building at Hamnegata 3. The society's pint-sized museum – filled with stuffed polar bears and seal-skin-covered furniture – tells the story of Hammerfest as a trapping centre for polar bears, eagles and arctic foxes and gives the background to the creation of the society itself in 1963. Be sure you avoid the ceremony of being "knighted" with a walrus's penis bone – not only will it set you back 250kr, but it will make you cringe with embarrassment for weeks on end.

Of more general interest is the purpose-built **Gjenreisningsmuseet** (Museum of Postwar Reconstruction; mid-June to mid-Aug Mon–Fri 9am–4pm, Sat & Sun 10am–2pm; mid-Aug to mid-June daily 11am–2pm; 40kr), a five-minute walk west of the old town quay up Kirkegata. This begins with a fascinating section on the hardships endured by the inhabitants of Finnmark during the German retreat in the face of the advancing Russians in late 1944. The Germans ordered a general evacuation and then applied a scorched earth policy, which left almost all of the region's towns and villages in ruins. Just in case any of his soldiers got the wrong idea, Hitler's orders stipulated that "Compassion for the population is out of place". Refugees in their own country, the Norwegians found shelter wherever they could and several thousand hid out in caves until May 1945, though many died from cold and malnutrition. Subsequent sections of the museum deal with postwar reconstruction, giving a sharply critical account of the central government bureaucracy initially put in charge. Under the weight of complaints, it was disbanded in 1948 and control was passed back to the municipalities. Interestingly, the left-wing Labour Party, who co-ordinated the reconstruction programme, adopted an almost evangelical stance, crusading against dirtiness, inequality and drunkenness in equal measure. As the labelling is only in Norwegian – though this may change – it's worth investing 30kr for the English-language guidebook.

For something a little more energetic, take the **footpath** that zigzags up **Salen**, the hill behind town. It takes about fifteen minutes to reach the plateau at the top, from where there are panoramic views out across the town and over to the nearby islands. The footpath begins a couple of minutes' walk from the old town quay on Salsgata, one block south of Strandgata.

Practicalities

Some 60km from the E6 along Highway 94, Hammerfest is situated on the western shore of the rugged island of Kvaløya, which is linked to the mainland by bridge. Buses pull into Hammerfest **bus station** at the foot of Sjøgata; the **Hurtigrute coastal boat** docks at the adjacent quay, as does the FFR (ⓣ177 or locally ⓣ78 41 73 50, ⓦwww.ffr.no) **Hurtigbåt passenger express boat** from Alta (1–2 daily except Sat; 1hr 30min; 245kr). The **tourist office** (mid-June to mid-Aug daily 9am–5pm; mid-Aug to mid-June daily 10am–2pm; ⓣ78 41 21 85, ⓦwww.hammerfest-turist.no) is just a few metres away at Hamnegata 3, in the same building as the Isbjørnklubben (see above). It issues free town maps and has details of local excursions, easily the most popular of which are the fishing trips and the summertime sea cruises to local bird cliffs, squawking with guillemots, gannets and kittiwakes, amongst many other types of seabird.

Hammerfest is light on places to stay, but there are two good **hotels**. First choice should be the enjoyable *Quality Hotel Hammerfest*, Strandgata 2–4 (ⓣ78 42 96 00, ⓦwww.hammerfesthotel.no; ❺, sp/r ❹), which occupies a prime spot just metres from the old town quay; it's housed in a routine modern block,

Moving on from Hammerfest

From Hammerfest, **FFR** (☎177 or locally ☎78 41 73 50, ⓦwww.ffr.no) runs **buses** to Alta (1–3 daily; 2hr 30min), Karasjok (1–2 daily except Sat; 4hr) and Kirkenes (4 weekly; 10–12hr). All pass through **Skaidi**, on the E6, where you change for the **Nordkappekspressen bus** service onto Honningsvåg (1–3 daily), changing here once again for Nordkapp (late June to mid-Aug 1–3 daily; 45min). Note that not all the Hammerfest buses make the Nordkappekspressen connection at Skaidi, so check at the bus station before you set out. FFR also operates **Hurtigbåt passenger express boats** from Hammerfest to Alta (1–2 daily; 1hr 30min; 245kr).

The **Hurtigrute** coastal boat (ⓦwww.hurtigruten.com) sails north daily from Hammerfest at 6.45am and reaches Honningsvåg at 11.45am (passengers: mid-April to mid-Sept 410kr, mid-Sept to mid-April 290kr; car, all year 350kr). At Honningsvåg, it pauses for three and a half hours, plenty enough time for special connecting buses to make the return trip to Nordkapp. Southbound, the Hurtigrute does not overlay at Honningsvåg and reaches Hammerfest at 11.15am, departing 12.45pm and taking eleven hours to reach its next major port of call, Tromsø.

Finally, Hammerfest has several **car rental** companies and they frequently offer attractive short-term deals from around 700kr a day unlimited mileage. Try Hammerfest Bilsenter, Seilmakerveien 1 (☎78 40 78 20), or Hertz, Rossmollgata 86 (☎78 41 71 66). If, however, Nordkapp is your goal, comparable rental deals are available at Honningsvåg (see p.366), 180km north from Hammerfest.

but the cosy interior has a pleasant, slightly old-fashioned air, the bedrooms equipped with chunky wooden fittings that predate the chipboard mania of today. Similarly appealing is the *Rica Hotel Hammerfest*, Sørøygata 15 (☎78 41 13 33, ⓦwww.rica.no; ❺, sp/r ❹), an attractive modern place with sea views that sits on a grassy knoll a couple of minutes' walk west of the main quay. The only budget hotel is *Hotell Skytterhuset*, Skytterveien 24 (☎78 41 15 11, ⓦwww.skytterhusetno; ❹), which, despite appearances – it's in a long, low prefabricated block originally built to house migrant fish-factory workers – has a pleasant, modern interior of pastel furnishings and laminate wooden floors. The only drawback is the location: the hotel is stuck on a windswept hillside, some 3km from and behind the town centre. To get there by car, head east from the main harbourfront along Strandgata and, after about 500m, just over the stream, turn right along Skolebakken. This leads into Storvannsveien, which circumnavigates lake Storvannet, a gloomy pool at the bottom of a steep-sided valley dotted with the houses of Hammerfest's one and only suburb; the hotel is on the hillside above the far side of the lake – the turning is clearly signed. Unless you're particularly energetic, you'll not want to walk here from the centre – it's too hilly – so take a taxi.

For **food**, the *Rica Hotel Hammerfest* possesses the best **restaurant** in town, with ocean views and delicious seafood; main courses start at around 200kr. More economical is *Kaikanten*, just up from the main quay at Sjøgata 19, where you'll find solid pub food in an amenable atmosphere.

Magerøya and Nordkapp

At the northern tip of Norway, the treeless and windswept island of **Magerøya** is mainly of interest to travellers as the location of the **Nordkapp** (North Cape), generally regarded as Europe's northernmost point – though in fact it isn't: that distinction belongs to the neighbouring headland of **Knivskjellodden**. Somehow, everyone seems to have conspired to ignore this simple latitudinal fact and now, while Nordkapp has become one of the most popular tourist destinations in the country, there isn't even a road to Knivskjellodden. Neither has the development of the Nordkapp as a tourist spot been without its critics, who argue that the large and lavish visitor centre – **Nordkapphallen** – is crass and grossly overpriced; their opponents simply point to the huge number of people who visit. Whichever side you're on, it's hard to imagine making the long trip to Magerøya without at least dropping by Nordkapp, and the island has other charms too, notably a bleak, rugged beauty that's readily seen from the **E69** as it threads across the mountainous interior from Honningsvåg, on the south coast, to Nordkapp, a distance of 34km.

The obvious base for a visit to Nordkapp is the island's main settlement, **Honningsvåg**, a middling fishing village with a clutch of chain hotels. More appealing, however, is the tiny hamlet of **Kamøyvaer**, nestling beside a narrow fjord just off the E69 between Honningsvåg and Nordkapp, and with a couple of family-run guesthouses. Bear in mind also that Nordkapp is within easy striking distance of other places back on the mainland – certainly the picturesque fishing-station-cum-hotel at **Repvåg**, and maybe even Hammerfest (see p.361) and Alta (see p.353), respectively 210km and 240km away.

Getting to Magerøya and Nordkapp

Arriving along the E6 and then the E69 from Alta and Skaidi (for Hammerfest), Nor-Way Bussekspress's **Nordkappekspressen bus** (1–3 daily) stops at Honningsvåg, where passengers change for the FFR service (Ⓣ177 or locally Ⓣ78 47 58 40, Ⓦwww.ffr.no) onto Nordkapp (mid-June to late Aug Mon–Sat 2 daily, Sun 1 daily; 45min). The schedule is such that on Mondays through Saturdays you can take the first bus from Honningsvåg to Nordkapp, spend a couple of hours there and then catch the bus back. If you catch the second bus – though this doesn't run on Sundays – you'll have two or three hours at Nordkapp from 10.15pm to 12.15am or 1.15am, which means, of course, that you can view the midnight sun. Note also that, depending on timings, you can wait for as little as fifteen minutes and as much as two-and-a-half hours between arriving at Honningsvåg on the Nordkappekspressen and leaving for Nordkapp. FFR also runs one other bus daily from Honningsvåg to Nordkapp, though this is primarily to catch Hurtigrute passengers while their ship overlays at Honningsvåg harbour; it runs all year, snow permitting, needs to be booked the day before by 3pm, and the return fare is a wallet-banging 475kr – the normal return fare is 170kr. Buses apart, the best way of proceeding from Honningsvåg to Nordkapp is to rent a car or take a taxi. Honningsvåg tourist office has the details of local **car hire** companies offering special deals – reckon on 800kr for a five-hour rental. The **taxi fare** to Nordkapp, including an hour's waiting time after you get there, is 900kr return, 500kr one-way; contact Nordkapp Taxisentral (Ⓣ78 47 22 34).

Arriving **by car**, bear in mind that the last stretch of the Honningsvåg–Nordkapp road is closed by snow in winter, roughly from November to early April, and is only open to FFR buses. To stand a chance of seeing the northern lights, try to go when the weather is clear.

North from Skaidi to Repvåg and Magerøya island

Beyond the **Skaidi** crossroads, located at the end of Highway 94 from Hammerfest, the **E6** veers east to clip across a bleak plateau that brings it,

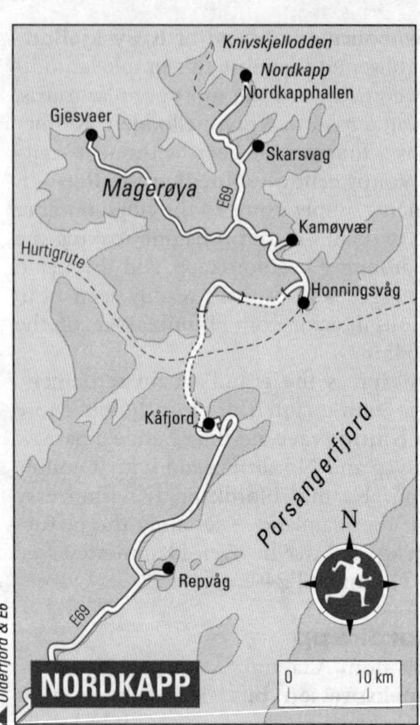

23km later, to the turning for Nordkapp. This turning, the **E69**, scuttles north along the shore of the **Porsangerfjord**, a deep and wide inlet flanked by bare, low-lying hills whose stone has been fractured and made flaky by the biting cold of winter. Here and there, the shore is interrupted by massive monoliths, but for the most part the scenery is unusually tame and the shoreline accommodates a string of fishermen's houses – plus the wooden racks used to air-dry their catch. After 48km, the E69 zips past the byroad to **REPVÅG**, an old timber fishing station on a promontory just 2km off the main highway. A rare and particularly picturesque survivor from prewar days, the station is painted red in the traditional manner and perches on stilts on the water's edge. The whole complex has been turned into the *Repvåg Fjordhotell og Rorbusenter* (ⓣ78 47 54 40, ⓦwww.repvag-fjordhotell.no; mid-April to mid-Oct), with simple, unassuming rooms (❸) in the main building, as well as a cluster of old fishermen's shacks – *rorbuer* (❷). It's a charming place to stay – solitary and scenic in equal proportions, the public areas of the hotel decked out with authentic nautical tackle and cosy furniture. Neither is tourism the only concern of the owners, as is evidenced by the split cod nailed to the outside walls to dry. Repvåg is an ideal base from which to reach Nordkapp, though once you're ensconced here, you may settle instead for one of the hotel's boat and fishing trips out on the Porsangerfjord. Almost inevitably, the hotel **restaurant** specializes in seafood – and very good it is too.

Back on the E69, it's about 25km to the ambitious – and amazingly expensive – series of tunnels and bridges (140kr toll) that spans the straits between the mainland and Honningsvåg, on the island of **Magerøya**, which you'll see long before you arrive there, a hunk of brown rock looking like an inverted blancmange.

Honningsvåg

HONNINGSVÅG, 180km from Hammerfest and just 2km off the E69, is officially classified as a village, which robs it of the title of the world's northernmost town – hard luck considering it's barely any smaller nor less hardy in the face of adversity than its neighbour. The village, largely comprising a jumble of well-worn modern buildings that reflect its role as a minor fishing- and seaport, straggles along the seashore, sheltered from the blizzards of winter by the surrounding crags – though, given the conditions, sheltered is a comparative term. Honningsvåg has accumulated several chain hotels, which make a steady living from the stream of tourists that passes through bound for the Nordkapp, and is at its prettiest at the **head of the harbour**, where an assortment of timber warehouses, dating back to the days when the village was entirely reliant on fish, make an attractive ensemble. Draped with fishing nets and tackle, these good-looking buildings perch on crusty timber stilts that jut out into the water. They have wide eaves to protect against the snow, and each has its own jetty where fishing smacks are roped in tight against the wind.

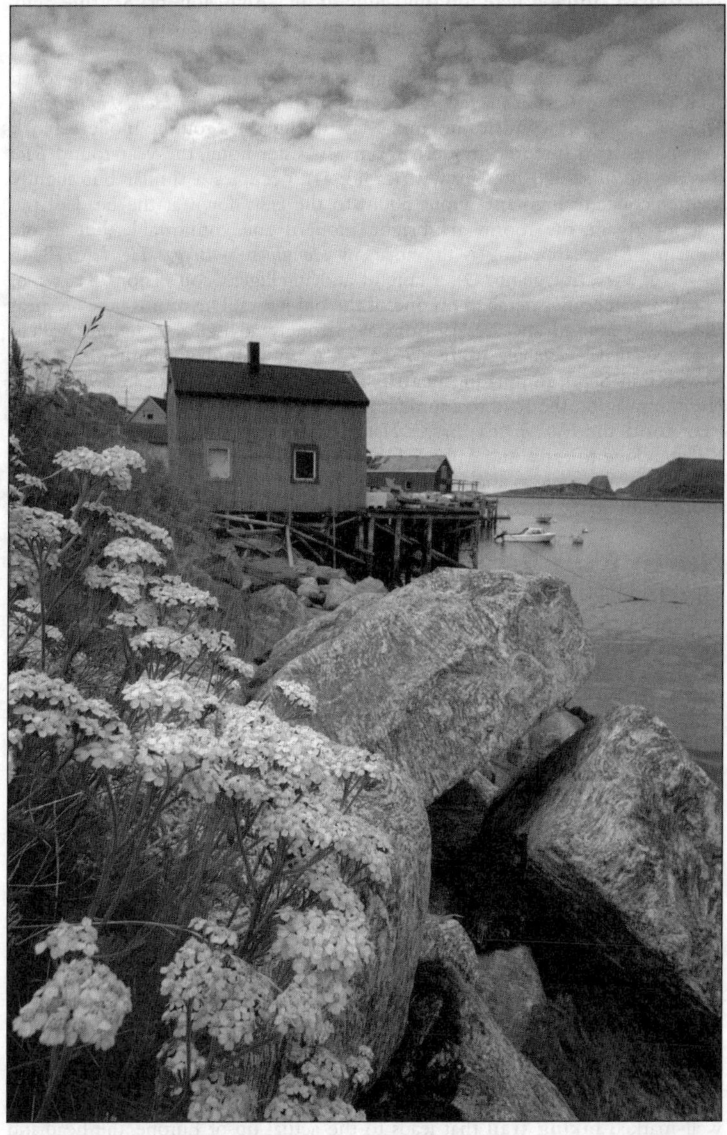

△ Honningsvåg

Practicalities

Honningsvåg strings out along its main drag for about 1km. Buses from the mainland, including the long-distance Nord-Norgeekspressen, pull into the **bus station** at its southern end. **Hurtigrute** coastal boats dock at the adjacent jetty, with northbound boats arriving at 11.45am and departing 3.15pm; southbound, the boats don't overlay here, arriving and departing at around 6.15am; the northbound service is met by special Nordkapp excursion buses. The **tourist office** is here too (mid-June to mid-Aug Mon–Fri 8.30am–8pm, Sat & Sun noon–8pm; mid-Aug to mid-June Mon–Fri 8.30am–4pm; Ⓣ78 47 70 30, Ⓦwww.northcape.no).

All of Honningsvåg's **hotels** are along or near the main street. Walking south from the bus station, it's a few metres to the first, the *Rica Hotel Honningsvåg* (Ⓣ78 47 23 33, Ⓦwww.rica.no; mid-May to Aug; ❹), a routine modern block with nearly two hundred modern rooms. Its sister hotel, the year-round *Rica Bryggen* (Ⓣ78 47 28 88, Ⓦwww.rica.no; ❺), occupies a similar but slightly smarter concrete high-rise about 500m to the east, down at the head of the harbour. Again, the rooms are bright, modern and comfortable, but hardly inspiring. More appealing is the adjacent *Honningsvåg Brygge Hotel* (Ⓣ78 47 64 64, Ⓦwww.brygge.no; ❺), a tasteful and intelligent conversion of a set of wooden warehouses perched on one of the old jetties. The rooms here are neat and cosy – and advance reservations are strongly advised. For lighter wallets, *NAF Nordkapp Camping* (Ⓣ78 47 33 77, Ⓦwww.nordkappcamping.no; late May to mid-Sept), comprising a **campsite** and **cabins** (❷), is located 9km from Honningsvåg on the road to Nordkapp.

For **food**, the *Honningsvåg Brygge Hotel* boasts the best **restaurant** by far, the *Sjøhuset* (June to early Aug daily 2–11pm; limited hours the rest of year), where the seafood is delicious and main courses hover around 190kr; reservations are strongly advised.

North from Honningsvåg

The E69 winds its way out of Honningsvåg, staying close to the shore. After 9km, just beyond the conspicuous *Rica Hotel Nordkapp*, you'll spot the turning for **KAMØYVÆR**, a pretty little village tucked in tight between the sea and the hills, just 2km from the main road. Here, right on the jetty, the old timber fishing station has been converted into the charming *Havstua* (Ⓣ78 47 51 50, Ⓦwww.havstua.no; ❸; May to mid-Sept), with five simple but smart and extraordinarily cosy rooms. It's a delightful spot and the food is also first-rate, but it's advisable to book dinner in advance. A few metres away, just back from the jetty, is the *Árran Nordkapp Gjestehus* (Ⓣ78 47 51 29, Ⓦwww.arran.as; ❹; May–Sept), not quite as appealing perhaps, but still a pleasant, family-run guesthouse in a brightly painted and well-tended house and home.

Beyond the Kamøyvær turning, the E69 twists a solitary course up through the hills to cross a high-tundra plateau, the mountains stretching away on either side. It's a fine run, with snow and ice lingering well into the summer and impressive views over the treeless and elemental Arctic terrain. From June to October this is pastureland for herds of reindeer, who graze right up to the road, paying little heed to the passing vehicles unless they wander too close. The Sami, who bring them here by boat, combine herding with souvenir selling, setting up camp at the roadside in full costume to peddle clothes, jewellery and sets of antlers, which some motorists are daft enough to attach to the front of their vehicles. About 29km from Honningsvåg, the E69 passes the start of the well-marked **hiking trail** that leads to the actual tip of Europe, the headland of **Knivskjellodden**, stretching about 1500m further north than its famous neighbour. The eighteen-kilometre hike – there and back – takes between two and three hours each way, but although the terrain isn't so severe, the climate is too unpredictable for the novice or poorly equipped hiker.

Nordkapp

Many visitors, when they finally reach **Nordkapp**, feel desperately disappointed – it is, after all, only a cliff and, at 307m, it isn't even all that high. But for others there's something about this greyish-black hunk of slate, stuck at the end of a bare, wind-battered promontory, that exhilarates the senses. Some such feeling must have inspired the prehistoric Sami to establish a sacrificial site here, and the Nordkapp certainly stirred the romantic notions of earlier generations of tourists, often inspiring them to metaphysical ruminations. In 1802, the Italian naturalist Giuseppe Acerbi, author of *Travels through Sweden, Finland and Lapland*, exclaimed, "The northern sun, creeping at midnight along the horizon, and the immeasurable ocean in apparent contact with the skies, form the grand outlines in the sublime picture presented to the astonished spectator." Quite – though the seventeenth-century traveller Francesco Negri wasn't far behind: "Here, where the world comes to an end, my curiosity does as well, and now I can return home content."

Flights of fancy apart, North Cape was named by the English explorer **Richard Chancellor** in 1553, as he drifted along the Norwegian coast in an attempt to find the Northeast Passage from the Atlantic to the Pacific. He failed, but managed to reach the White Sea, from where he and his crew travelled overland to Moscow, thereby opening a new, northern trade route to Russia. Chancellor's account, published in the geographer Richard Hakluyt's *Navigations*, brought his exploits to the attention of seamen across Europe, but it was to be another three hundred years before the Northeast Passage was finally negotiated by the Swede Nils Nordenskjøld in 1879. In the meantime, just a trickle of visitors ventured to the Nordkapp. Among them, in 1795, was the exiled Louis Philippe of Orleans (subsequently king of France), but it was the visit of the Norwegian king **Oscar II** in 1873 that opened the tourist floodgates.

Nowadays the lavish **Nordkapphallen** (North Cape Hall; daily: early May & Sept to mid-Oct noon–4pm; late May to mid-June noon–1am; mid-June to July 9am–2am; early Aug 9am–midnight; late Aug noon–midnight; mid-Oct to April 12.30–2.15pm; 190kr for 48hrs, including parking), cut into the rock of the Cape, entertains hundreds of visitors every day. Fronted by a statue of King Oscar II, the main building contains a restaurant, café, a post office where you get your letters specially stamped, and a cinema showing – you guessed it – films about the cape. There's a viewing area too, but there's not much to see except the sea – and, weather permitting, the midnight sun from May 12 to July 29. Gluttons for financial punishment can stay here too, from May to September, in **Suite 71° 10' 21"** (Ⓣ78 47 68 60) – as in Nordkapp's latitude. At the top of the building's one and only tower, the suite offers a 270-degree view through its enormous windows and is a favourite with honeymooners, though quite why this should be considered a romantic spot is hard to discern. If it's booked in advance, the suite costs around 4000kr per night, but the price tumbles to half that if it's rented on spec.

A **tunnel** runs from the main building to the cliff face. It's flanked by a couple of little side-chambers, in one of which is a chapel, where you can get married, and by a series of displays detailing past events and visitors, including the unlikely appearance of the King of Siam in 1907, who was so ill that he had to be carried up here from his boat on a stretcher. At the far end, the cavernous **Grotten Bar** offers caviar and champagne, long views out to sea through the massive glass wall and (of all things) a mock bird cliff. Alternatively, to escape the hurly-burly, you may decide to walk out onto the surrounding headland, though this is too bleak a spot to be much fun.

East to Kirkenes

East of Nordkapp the landscape is more of the same – a relentless expanse of barren plateaux, mountain and ocean. Occasionally the monotony is relieved by a determined village commanding sweeping views over the fjords that slice deep into the mainland, but generally there is little for the eyes of a tourist. Nor is there much to do in what are predominantly fishing and industrial settlements, and there are few tangible attractions beyond the sheer impossibility of the chill wilderness.

The **E6** weaves a circuitous course across this vast territory, travelling close to the Finnish border for much of its length. The only obvious target is the Sami centre of **Karasjok** (see p.359), 270km from Nordkapp and 220km from Hammerfest and easily the region's most interesting town. Frankly, there's not much reason to push on further east unless you're intent on picking up the **Hurtigrute coastal boat** as it bobs along the remote and spectacular shores of the Barents Sea. Amongst the Hurtigrute's several ports of call, perhaps the most diverting is **Kirkenes**, 320km to the east of Karasjok at the end of the E6 and near the Russian frontier: if any European town comes close to defining remoteness then this surely must be it. Kirkenes is actually the northern terminus of the Hurtigrute, from where it begins its long journey south to Bergen. Taking the boat also means that you can avoid the long haul back the way you came – and by the time you reach Kirkenes you'll certainly be heartily sick of the E6. The other shortcut is to **fly**: Kirkenes has its own airport and from here there are regular Widerøe (ⓣ81 00 12 00, ⓦwww.wideroe.no) flights to a hatful of north Norwegian towns, including Alta, Hammerfest and Tromsø; as a sample fare, a single ticket with restrictions from Kirkenes to Alta can go for as little as 500kr, though 900kr is a more usual fare. A subsidiary of SAS airlines, Widerøe flies to no less than fourteen airports – and airstrips – in Troms and Finnmark. As regards **buses**, FFR (ⓣ177, ⓦwww.ffr.no) reaches most corners of Finnmark with reasonable regularity, but its principal long-distance service links Alta (or Hammerfest) with Kirkenes along the E6, via Skaidi, Olderfjord, Karasjok and Tana Bru; the whole journey takes between ten and thirteen hours and there are three buses weekly. Many of FFR's services operate all year, as the E6 and some other main roads are kept open throughout the winter, but this does imply that **drivers** will find conditions straightforward: ice and snow can make the roads treacherous, if not temporarily impassable, at any time, and driving through the long polar darkness (late Nov to late Jan) is extremely disorientating. Note also that if you are using a **car hire**, the one-way drop-off charge in Norway is almost invariably exorbitant.

Finally, **accommodation** is very thin on the ground, being confined to a handful of the larger communities. Reservations, therefore, are strongly advised. Campsites are more frequent and usually have cabins for rent, but they are mostly stuck in the middle of nowhere.

East from Nordkapp on the E6

Beyond its junction with the E69 Nordkapp road, the **E6** bangs along the western shore of the **Porsangerfjord**, a wide inlet that slowly shelves up into the sticky marshes and mud flats at its head. After about 45km, the road reaches the hamlet of **STABBURSNES**, which is home to the small but enjoyable **Stabbursnes Naturhus og Museum** (Stabbursnes Nature House and Museum; June & Aug daily 11am–6pm; July daily 9am–8pm; Sept–May Tues & Thurs noon–3pm, Wed noon–6pm; 50kr), which provides an overview of the region's flora and fauna. There are diagrams of the elaborate heat-exchanger in the reindeer's nose that helps stop the animal from freezing to death in winter, and blow-ups of the warble fly which torments it in summer. There are also examples of traditional Sami handicrafts and a good section on Finnmark's topography, examining, for example, how and why some of the region's rivers are slow and sluggish, whilst others have cut deep gashes in the landscape. The museum is on the eastern periphery of – and acts as an information centre for – the **Stabbursdalen Nasjonalpark**, a wedge-edged chunk of land that contains the world's most northerly pine forest covering the slopes of the Stabbursdalen river valley, which runs down from the Finnmarksvidda plateau to the Porsangerfjord. The lower end of the valley is broad and marshy, but beyond lie precipitous canyons and chasms – challenging terrain, with a couple of marked hiking trails. If that sounds too much like hard work, opt instead for the easy 2.8-kilometre stroll east from the museum along the thick gravel banks of the Stabbursdalen river where it trickles into the Porsangerfjord. It's an eerily chill landscape and there's a good chance of spotting several species of **wetland bird** in spring and summer: ducks, geese and waders like the lapwing, the curlew and the arctic knot are common. Indeed, these salt marshes and mud flats are such an important resting and feeding area for migratory wetland birds that they have been protected as the Stabbursnes **nature reserve**.

From Stabbursnes, it's about 15km south to **LAKSELV**, an inconsequential fishing village at the head of the Porsangerfjord, and another 75km to Karasjok (see p.359), the best place hereabouts to spend the night. Pushing on, the **E6** weaves its way northeast along the Finnish border, joining with the **E75** from Finland long before it reaches, in 180km, **TANA BRU**, a Sami settlement clustered around a suspension bridge over the River Tana. Some 300km long, the Tana, which rattles down to the Tanafjord, an inlet of the Barents Sea, is one of Europe's best salmon rivers, but although the fishing is outstanding, it's hedged with restrictions about what you can catch and when: **Tana Tourist Information** (late June to late Aug Mon–Fri 9am–6pm, Sat & Sun 10am–5pm; rest of year Mon–Fri 8am–3.30pm; ⓣ78 92 53 99, ⓦwww.tana.kommune.no), at the *Comfort Hotel Tana*, beside the main road as you near the bridge, will advise. The only **hotel** in Tana is the very same *Comfort Hotel Tana* (ⓣ78 92 81 98, ⓦwww.choicehotels.no; ❻, sp/r ❹), a chalet-like affair with competently comfortable rooms and a restaurant; they allow camping here too.

On the east side of Tana bridge, Highway 890 branches off north bound for the coast at Berlevåg (see p.372) 140km away, while the E6/E75 pushes east for another 18km to **VARANGERBOTN**, at the head of the long and deep **Varangerfjord**. This is where the E-roads diverge: the E75 heads off to Vadsø (see p.373) and Vardø (see p.372), but the E6 continues on to Kirkenes, another 130-kilometre haul to the east. Initially, the E6 tracks along the southern shores of the Varangerfjord, a bleak, weather-beaten run with all colour and vegetation being confined to the northern shore, with its scattered farms and painted fishing boats, but then the road loops inland, clipping across the tundra, before it regains the coast for its final spurt into Kirkenes (see p.373).

East from Nordkapp on the Hurtigrute

Beyond Nordkapp, the Hurtigrute steers a fine route round the top of the country, nudging its way between tiny islets and craggy bluffs, and stopping at a series of solitary fishing villages. Amongst them the prettiest is **BERLEVÅG**, which sits amidst a landscape of eerie greenish-grey rock, splashes of colour in a land otherwise stripped by the elements. It's a tiny village, with a population of just 1200, but its cultural traditions and tight community spirit were deftly explored in Knut Jensen's documentary *Heftig og Begeistret* (Cool & Crazy), released in 2001. The **film** received rave reviews both in Norway and across Europe, a welcome fillip to Berlevåg in general and the subject matter of the film – the local men's choir, the **Berlevåg Mannsangforening** – in particular.

Berlevåg has a couple of places **to stay**, including the *Berlevåg Pensjonat og Camping*, on Havnegata (Ⓣ78 98 16 10, Ⓦwww.berlevag-pensjonat.no), with tent pitches (June–Sept) and four simple, straightforward guest rooms (all year; ❷). If you're after a room, you'd be well advised to reserve ahead of time given Berlevåg's remote location. Northbound, the Hurtigrute calls here at 10.45pm, southbound at 10.30pm; the journey time to and from Honningsvåg is 7 hours 30 minutes. FFR (Ⓣ177, Ⓦwww.ffr.no) runs buses to Berlevåg from Tana Bru (1–2 daily except Sat; 2hr 30min).

Vardø

From Berlevåg, it's just over five hours on the Hurtigrute to **VARDØ**, Norway's most easterly town and a busy fishing port of 2500 souls. Like everywhere else in Finnmark, Vardø was savaged in World War II and the modern town that grew up in the 1950s could hardly be described as beautiful, though its geography is at least unusual: Vardø spreads out over two little islets that are connected by a narrow causeway, which in turn forms the apex of the town's harbour; a tunnel connects Vardø with the mainland, just a couple of kilometres away.

Vardø's main attraction is the **Vardøhus Festning** (Vardø fortress; daily: mid-June to mid-Aug 8am–9pm; mid-Aug to mid-June 8am–6pm; 30kr), a tiny star-shaped fortress, located about 500m west of the Hurtigrute quay. The site was first fortified in 1300, but the present structure dates from the 1730s, built at the behest of King Christian VI. When this singularly unprepossessing monarch toured Finnmark he was greeted, according to one of his courtiers, with "expressions of abject flattery in atrocious verse" – and the king loved it. Christian had the fortress built to guard the northeastern approaches to his kingdom, but it has never seen active service – hence its excellent state of preservation. A small **museum** gives further details of the fort's history.

The town's main museum, however, is the **Vardø Museum**, Pers Larssengate 32 (mid-June to mid-Aug Mon–Fri 9am–6pm, Sat & Sun 11am–6pm; mid-Aug to mid-June Mon–Fri 9am–3pm; 40kr), which occupies a sturdy stone building, Lushaug, on the northwest edge of Vardø, about fifteen minutes' walk from the Hurtigrute quay. Spread over several floors, a series of well-presented displays explains Vardø's history, with sections devoted to explorers such as Willem Barents and Nansen Fridtjof; another dealing with the lucrative Pomor barter trade between northern Norway and Russia; and another examining local flora and fauna. Most interesting of all is the section on the **witch-hunting** fever that gripped Finnmark in the seventeenth century. Although the Church had long regarded the extremes of Finnmark as the realm of the devil, witch-finding only took a hold in the 1620s – half a century or so later than the rest of Europe – when, it was alleged, a coven set up shop in a cave on the edge of town. Over the next sixty years more than eighty women were burned alive in Vardø, a huge number considering the size of the population.

Around Vardø

Of Vardø's outdoor attractions, top of the list are the **boat trips** (April to mid-Oct daily; 175kr per person), which leave Vardø harbour to cruise round nearby **Hornøya**, a rocky islet and bird reserve where thousands of sea birds nest each summer. Advance bookings are essential (contact the tourist office; see below).

Alternatively, a newly completed byroad threads its way northwest from Vardø along the coast, passing through a lunar-like landscape to reach the (largely) abandoned fishing village of **Hamningberg** after 45km. It's a picturesque spot and scores of locals walk here during Vardø's main festival – Pomordagene (Pomor Days), in early July.

Vardø practicalities

The northbound **Hurtigrute** reaches Vardø at 4am and leaves just fifteen minutes later; southbound it docks at 4pm and leaves an hour later. FFR **buses** (Ⓣ177, Ⓦwww.ffr.no) run the 50km from Varangerbotn on the E6 to Vadsø (1–2 daily except Sat; 1hr 20min), where a second bus heads the 75km on to Vardø (1–2 daily; 1hr 30min); sometimes these services connect, sometimes they don't – check before you set out; the Varangerbotn–Vadsø bus starts in Kirkenes. Vardø **tourist office** is metres from the Hurtigrute quay (mid-June to late Aug Mon–Fri 10am–7pm, Sat & Sun noon–7pm; Ⓣ78 98 69 07, but late Aug to mid-June call Ⓣ78 94 48 00, Ⓦwww.varanger.com), and close by is the only **hotel** in town, the workaday *Vardo Hotell*, at Kaigata 8 (Ⓣ78 98 77 61, Ⓦwww.vardohotel.no; ❹, sp/r ❸).

Vadsø

VADSØ, four hours by **Hurtigrute** from Vardø (northbound only), used to be largely Finnish-speaking, and even now half the population of 5500 claims Finnish origins. Its main claim to fame is as the administrative centre of Finnmark, which – to be blunt – isn't much to get excited about. Russian bombers and German soldiers between them destroyed almost all the old town during World War II, the result being the mundanely modern town centre of today. There's really no reason to get off the boat here, but there are a couple of minor sights to see if you do, most notably the **Innvandrermonumentet** (the Immigration Monument), bang in the centre of town, which commemorates the many Finns who migrated here in the eighteenth and nineteenth centuries.

FFR **buses** (Ⓣ177, locally Ⓣ78 95 69 54, Ⓦwww.ffr.no) from Kirkenes/Varangerbotn (1–2 daily except Sat; 3hr 30min/1hr 20min) as well as Vardø (see opposite), pull into Vadsø **bus station** on Strandgata, which is located on a stumpy promontory – 500m by 300m – in the centre of town. From here, it's about 1km to the Hurtigrute dock, over the bridge on Vadsøya island. The best **hotel** in town is the *Rica Hotel Vadsø*, a large, modern affair in the town centre, at Oscars gate 4 (Ⓣ78 95 52 50, Ⓦwww.rica.no; ❻, sp/r ❹).

After Vadsø, the **Hurtigrute** takes a couple of hours to cross the deep blue-black waters of the **Varangerfjord** on the last stage of its journey to Kirkenes. There's snow on the mainland here even in July, which makes for a picturesque chug across the fjord, the odd fishing boat the only sign of life.

Kirkenes

During World War II, the mining town and ice-free port of **KIRKENES** was bombed more heavily than any other place in Europe apart from Malta. The retreating German army torched what was left as they fled in the face of liberating Soviet soldiers, who found 3500 locals hiding in the nearby iron-ore mines. The mines finally closed in 1996, threatening the future of this 4000-strong community, which is now desperately trying to kindle trade with Russia to keep itself afloat.

Kirkenes is almost entirely modern, with long rows of uniform houses spreading out along the Bøkfjord, a narrow arm of the Barents Sea. If that sounds dull, it's not to slight the town, which makes the most of its inhospitable surroundings with some pleasant public gardens, lakes and residential areas – it's just that it seems an awful long way to come for not very much. That said, once you've finally got here it seems churlish to leave quickly, and it's certainly worth searching out the **Grenselandmuseet** (Frontier Museum; mid-June to mid-Aug daily 10am–6pm; mid-Aug to mid-June daily 10am–3.30pm; 40kr), which focuses on the history of the region and its people, and includes a detailed account of the events of World War II, illustrated by some fascinating old photos. In the same building is a display of the work of **John Savio** (1902–38), a local Sami artist whose life was brief and tragic. Orphaned at the age of three, Savio was ill from childhood onwards and died in poverty of tuberculosis at the age of 36. This lends poignancy to his woodcuts and paintings, with their lonely evocations of the Sami way of life and the overbearing power of nature. The museum is located about 1.5km south of the main harbourfront at the end of Solheimsveien, beside one of the town's several little lakes.

The part Kirkenes played in the war is also recalled by a couple of **monuments** – one dedicated to the town's wartime women in the main square, and a second to the Red Army, plonked on Roald Amundsens gate, just to the east.

Practicalities

Kirkenes is the northern terminus of the **Hurtigrute** coastal boat, which arrives here at 10am and departs for Bergen at 12.45pm. The Hurtigrute uses the quay just over 1km east of the town centre; a local bus shuttles between the two. Kirkenes **airport** is 15km southwest of town beside the E6; regular **flybussen** (65kr one-way) connect the airport with the centre. The **bus station** is at the west end of the main harbourfront, and from here it's about 400m east along Kirkegata to the **tourist office**, at Presteveien 1 (early June to early Sept Mon–Fri 8.30am–6pm, Sat & Sun 10am–5pm; early Sept to early June Mon–Fri 8.30am–4pm; ⓣ78 99 25 44, Ⓦwww.kirkenesinfo.no).

The town's best **hotel** is the *Rica Arctic*, whose eighty well-appointed rooms occupy a smart modern block in the centre near the town square at Kongensgate 1 (ⓣ78 99 59 00, Ⓦwww.rica.no; ❻, sp/r ❹). The similarly modern *Rica Hotel Kirkenes* is less enticing, in a glum-looking, three-storey block about 800m south of the main square at Pasvikveien 63 (May–Sept; ⓣ78 99 14 91, Ⓦwww.rica.no; ❺). As for **food**, the *Rica Arctic Hotel* has a very competent restaurant, though it's slightly bettered by *Vin og Vilt*, Kirkegata 5 (ⓣ78 99 38 11), where they serve up an excellent range of Arctic specialities from reindeer to char and beyond. Main courses at both hover at around 150kr.

Around Kirkenes: Øvre Pasvik Nasjonalpark

Hidden away some 120km south of Kirkenes, where the borders of Norway, Finland and Russia intersect, is the ten-by-nine-kilometre parcel of wilderness that comprises the **Øvre Pasvik Nasjonalpark**, a western offshoot of the Siberian taiga. The park's subarctic pine forest covers a series of low-lying hills that make up about half the total area, and below lie swamps, marshes and

Crossing into Russia

From Kirkenes, it's just 16km southeast along the **E105** to **Storskog**, Norway's only official border crossing point with Russia. You can take photographs of the frontier, provided you don't snap any Russian personnel or military installations – which rather limits the options as there's little else to see. The crossing is busy for much of the year, but it's not open for casual day-trippers; in any case, the only convenient settlement nearby is the ugly Russian mining town of **Nikel**, around 40km further to the south, from where you can – extraordinarily enough – travel by train all the way to Vladivostok. Several Kirkenes travel agents organize day and weekend tours into Russia, the most worthwhile being those to the Arctic port of **Murmansk**. The trips include a visa, which takes at least ten days to arrange, so advance booking is essential. Among these travel agents, Pasvikturist, in the centre at Dr. Wesselsgate 9 (ⓣ78 99 50 80, ⓦwww.pasvikturist.no), is as good as any. They have details of trips to Murmansk, both one-night (1290kr per person) and weekend (1550kr) excursions. Incidentally, there is a Russian consulate in Kirkenes, at Arbeidergata 6 (ⓣ78 99 37 37), but they will not short-cut the visa process. If a Russian jaunt proves impossible, you'll have to be content with the reflection that if you have made it to Kirkenes and the border, you are further east than Istanbul and as far north as Alaska.

lakes. Wolverines and bears live in the forest, and there are also traces of the prehistoric Komsa culture, notably the vague remains of pit-traps beside **Lake Ødevatn**. The Kirkenes tourist office has details of guided tours to the park, which are useful as you have to be an expert wilderness hiker-cum-survivalist to delve into the park under your own steam. The absence of natural landmarks makes it easy to get lost, especially as there are no marked footpaths, nor is there any map that can be relied upon. If you're undeterred, and have your own vehicle (there's no public transport), then drive south from Kirkenes for about 100km along Highway 885 through the pine forests of the Pasvik River valley as far as **Vaggatem**. Turn off the main road 1.5km or so further on and then follow the nine-kilometre, rough forest road south to a lake, **Sortbrysttjern**, from where a footpath takes you into the park at another lake, **Ellenvatn**. If you want to **stay** hereabouts, the only option is Vaggatem's all-year *Øvre Pasvik Café and Camping* (ⓣ78 99 55 30, ⓦwww.pasvik-cafe.no), which also rents out ten simple wooden cabins (❶).

Svalbard

The **Svalbard archipelago** is one of the most hostile places on earth. Some 640km north of the Norwegian mainland (and just 1300km from the North Pole), two-thirds of its surface is covered by glaciers, the soil frozen to a depth of up to 500m. The archipelago was probably discovered in the twelfth century by Icelandic seamen, though it lay ignored until 1596 when the Dutch explorer Willem Barents named the main island, **Spitsbergen**, after its needle-like mountains. However, apart from a smattering of determined adventurers – from seventeenth-century whalers to eighteenth-century monks – few people ever lived here until, in 1899, rich **coal** deposits were discovered, the geological residue of a prehistoric tropical forest. The first coal mine was opened by an American seven years later and passed into Norwegian hands in 1916. Meanwhile, other countries, particularly Russia and Sweden, were getting into the coal-mining act, and when, in 1920, Norway's sovereignty over the

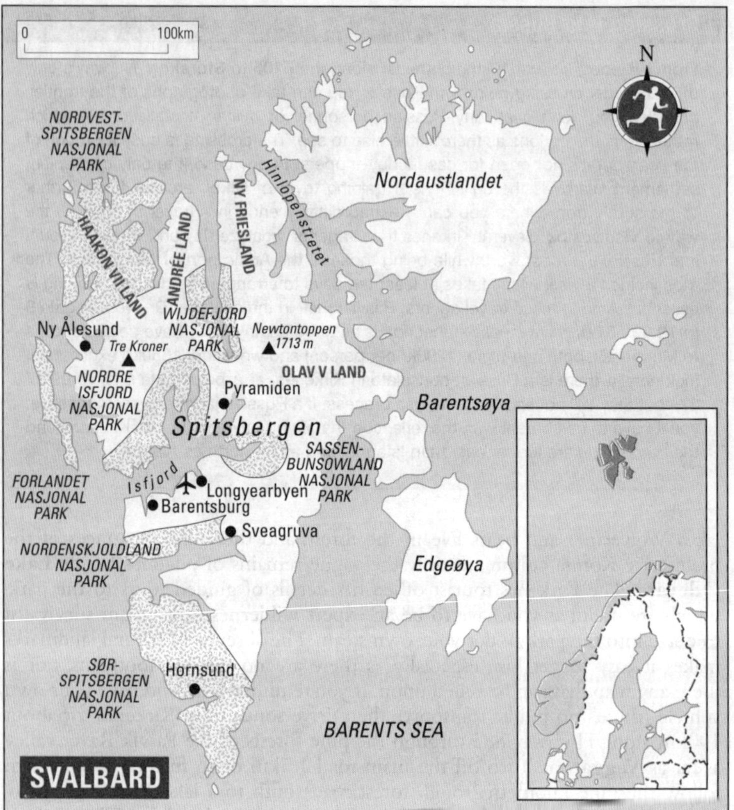

archipelago was ratified by international treaty, it was on condition that those other countries who were operating mines could continue to do so. It was also agreed that the islands would be a demilitarized zone, which made them, incidentally, sitting ducks for a German squadron, which arrived here to bombard the Norwegian coal mines during World War II.

Despite the hardships, there are convincing reasons to make a trip to this oddly fertile land, covering around 63,000 square kilometres. Between late April and late August there's continuous daylight and, with temperatures bobbing up into late teens, the snow has all but disappeared by July, leaving the valleys covered in wild flowers. And then there's the **wildlife**, an abundance of Arctic fauna, including over a hundred species of migratory birds, arctic foxes, polar bears and reindeer on land, and seals, walruses and whales offshore. In winter, it's a different story: the polar night, during which the sun never rises above the horizon, lasts from late October to mid-February, and the record low temperature is a staggering -46°C, and that's not counting the wind-chill factor.

Practicalities

The simplest way to reach Svalbard is to **fly** to the archipelago's airport at Longyearbyen on the main island, Spitsbergen. SAS/Braathens operates services there from a variety of Norwegian towns and cities, including Oslo, Bergen, Bodø, Trondheim, Alta and Tromsø, on average four or five times weekly. The Tromsø–Longyearbyen flight takes an hour and thirty minutes and a return ticket without restrictions is roughly 2500kr return, though special deals are commonplace, reducing this to 1500–1800kr. Nevertheless, before you book your flight, you'll need to reserve accommodation in Longyearbyen (see below) and – unless you're happy to be stuck in your lodgings – you'd be well-advised to pre-book **guided excursions** too.

There's a wide range on offer, from hiking and climbing through to kayaking, snowmobiling, dog sledging, glacier walking, helicopter rides, Zodiac boat trips, wildlife safaris and ice-caving, not to mention trips into a former coal mine. In the first instance, further information is available from Longyearbyen's official tourist office, **Svalbard Tourism** (Ⓣ79 02 55 50, Ⓦwww.svalbard.net), or try the excellent **Spitsbergen Travel**, also in Longyearbyen (Ⓣ79 02 61 00, Ⓦwww.spitsbergentravel.no). You can, of course, book a whole holiday with an operator back home (see Basics) or even take pot luck when you get there, but be warned that wilderness excursions are often fully booked weeks in advance. Finally, if you are determined to strike out into the wilderness independently, you first have to seek permission from, and log your itinerary with, the governor's office, Sysselmannen på Svalbard, Postboks 633, N-9171 Longyearbyen (Ⓣ79 02 43 00, Ⓦww.sysselmannen.svalbard.no) – and they will certainly expect you to carry a gun and a "shocking device" – a signal pistol or suchlike – to ward off polar bears.

Spitsbergen

The main island of the Svalbard archipelago, **Spitsbergen**, is the only one that is permanently inhabited; it has five settlements in total – three Norwegian, one Russian and one Polish – with a total population of around 3000. With just over 1700 inhabitants, the only Norwegian settlement of any size is **LONGYEARBYEN**, which huddles on the narrow coastal plain below the mountains and beside the Isfjorden, roughly in the middle of the island. It was founded in 1906, when John M. Longyear, an American mine owner, established the Arctic Coal Company here. Today, Longyearbyen is well equipped with services, including shops, cafés, a post office, bank, swimming pool, several tour companies, a campsite, a couple of guesthouses and three hotels, though advance reservations are essential for all accommodation.

Of the other Norwegian settlements, **Ny Ålesund** (40–100 inhabitants depending on the season) is a polar research centre to the northwest of Longyearbyen, and the **Sveagruva** mining community (200 day-workers) lies to the southeast. The only Russian settlement is the coal-mining township of **Barentsburg** (900) to the west of Longyearbyen. A second Russian mining settlement, Pyramiden, to the north of Longyearbyen, was abandoned in 2001 when the coal seams ran out. Since then, there have been lengthy debates as to what to do with it – the establishment of an international science station seems the most popular option. **Hornsund**, the Polish settlement, is the smallest of the five, comprising a research station with just a dozen or so scientists based here. There are no road connections between any of Svalbard's settlements, though there is about 50km of road around Longyearbyen. Public transport is limited to the airport bus, occasional cargo ships from Longyearbyen to both Barentsburg and Ny Ålesund, and a light-aircraft service from Longyearbyen to Ny Ålesund, though government employees and researchers take priority on these flights.

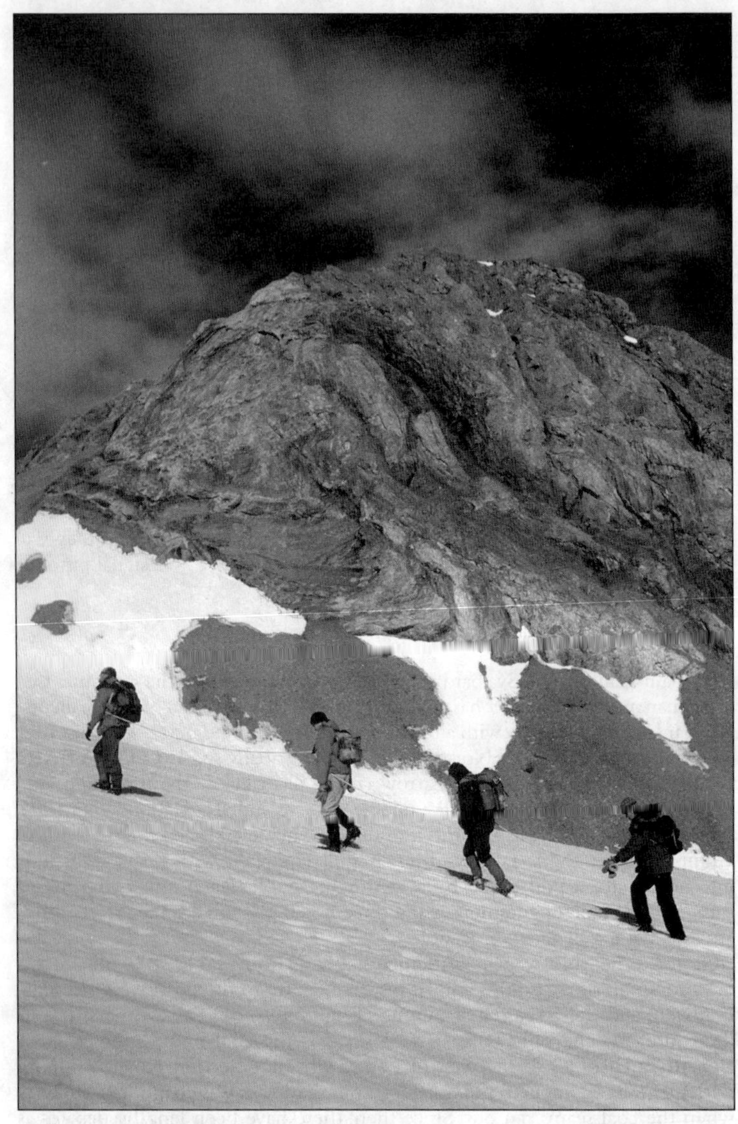

△ Hiking in Svalbard

Longyearbyen practicalities

Longyearbyen airport is 5km west of the town centre and the airport **bus** links the two, its schedule coinciding with flight arrivals and departures. The town itself trails back from the Isfjord for couple of kilometres on either side of the Longyearelva river, a ramshackle sort of place hunkered and bunkered down against the blast of winter. The few buildings that pass for the town centre are located about 500m in from the fjord just to the east of the river, and this is where you'll find the year-round **tourist office** (ⓣ79 02 55 50; ⓦwww.svalbard.net), which has information on a wide range of trips, from dog-sledging and ice-caving to snowmobile excursions and glacier walks.

Longyearbyen's smartest **hotel** is the *Radisson SAS Polar Hotel* (ⓣ79 02 34 50, ⓦwww.longyearbyen.radissonsas.com; ❼, sp/r ❻), a modern chalet-like affair with nearly one hundred rooms, the pick of which have views back over to the Isfjord; the hotel is located just to the north of the tourist office. More distinctive, albeit rather more spartan **lodgings** are to be found in several former miners' quarters, basically low-slung modern blocks parcelled up into small rooms with shared bathrooms. One of the most appealing of these is *Mary Ann's Polarrigg* (ⓣ79 02 37 02, ⓦwww.polarriggen.com; ❹), where the main block has thirty rooms with shared facilities and the newer annexe has nine en-suite rooms; it's located on the west side of the river, opposite the *SAS Polar Hotel*. For something even more classically "Arctic", there are also fifteen rooms in *Basecamp Spitzbergen* (ⓣ79 02 46 00, ⓦwww.basecampexplorer.com; ❽), a sort of enlarged mock-up of a trapper's cabin, complete with sealskins and a sauna and mostly made from old, recycled lumber; it's all a bit hoochie, but great fun all the same – and very convivial – and it's handily located just to the south of the tourist office.

The *Polar Hotel's Brasseri Nansen* is the best place **to eat** in town, serving all manner of Arctic specialities from char to reindeer, seal and (like it or not) whale. A slightly less expensive option is *Huset* (ⓣ79 02 25 00), which also specializes in Arctic dishes with main courses at around 250kr, much less if you eat at the attached **bar**; *Huset* is on the west side of the river at the southern end of town in the same building as the cinema.

Travel details

Principal FFR (ⓦwww.ffr.no) and Nor-Way Bussekspress (ⓦwww.nor-way.no) bus services

Alta to: Hammerfest (1–3 daily; 2hr 30min); Honningsvåg (1–3 daily; 4hr); Karasjok (1–2 daily except on Sat; 4hr 30min); Kautokeino (1–2 daily on 4 days a week; 2hr); Kirkenes (3 weekly; 10–13hr); Narvik (1 daily except Sat; 9hr 30min); Tromsø (1 daily; 6hr 30min).
Hammerfest to: Alta (1–3 daily; 2hr 30min); Karasjok (1–2 daily except Sat; 4hr); Kirkenes (3 weekly; 10–12hr). Note all these services are routed through Skaidi, where you change for points north and south along the E6.
Honningsvåg to: Alta (1–3 daily; 4hr); Nordkapp (late June to mid-Aug 1–3 daily; 45min).
Karasjok to: Alta (1–2 daily except on Sat; 4hr 30min); Hammerfest (1–2 daily except Sat; 4hr); Kautokeino (2 weekly; 2hr); Kirkenes (3 weekly; 5–7hr).
Kautokeino to: Alta (1–2 daily on 4 days a week; 2hr); Karasjok (2 weekly; 2hr).
Kirkenes to: Alta (3 weekly; 10–13hr); Hammerfest (3 weekly; 10–12hr); Karasjok (3 weekly; 5–7hr).
Tromsø to: Alta (1 daily; 6hr 30min); Narvik (1–3 daily; 4hr).

Nor-Way Bussekspress's Nord-Norgeekspressen and Nordkappekspressen

The **Nord-Norgeekspressen** (North Norway Express Bus) runs north from Bodø and Fauske to Alta in three segments: Bodø to Narvik via Fauske (2 daily; 6hr 30min); Narvik to Tromsø (1–3 daily; 4hr); and Tromsø to Alta (1–2 daily; 6hr 30min). Alternatively, the **Nordkappekspressen** (North Cape Express Bus) runs direct from Narvik to Alta (1 daily except Sat; 9hr 30min), where passengers overnight before picking up the second leg of the Nordkappekspressen to Honningsvåg (1–3 daily; 4hr), where you change for Nordkapp (late June to mid-Aug 1–3 daily; 45min).

Car ferries

Breivikeidet to: Svendsby (every 1–2hr; Mon–Fri 6am–9pm, Sat 8am–8pm, Sun 10am–9pm; 25min).

Brensholmen to: Botnhamn (early June to late Aug 4–7 daily; 45min).
Gryllefjord to: Andenes (early to late June & mid- to late Aug 2 daily, late June to early Aug 3 daily; 2hr).
Lyngseidet to: Olderdalen (every 1–2hr; Mon–Thurs 7am–7pm, Fri 7am–9pm, Sat 9am–7pm, Sun 10.30am–9pm; 40min).

Hurtigbåt passenger express boats

Alta to: Hammerfest (1–2 daily; 1hr 30min).
Tromsø to: Harstad (2–3 daily; 2hr 45min).

Hurtigrute coastal boat (year-round; daily)

Northbound from: Tromsø at 6.30pm; Hammerfest at 6.45am; Honningsvåg at 3.15pm; Berlevåg at 10.45pm; Vardø at 4.15am; Vadsø at 8.15am; terminates at Kirkenes at 10am.
Southbound from: Kirkenes at 12.45pm; Vardø at 5pm; (no southbound stop at Vadsø); Berlevåg at 10.30pm; Honningsvåg at 6.15am; Hammerfest at 12.45pm; Tromsø at 1.30am. The Tromsø–Kirkenes journey time is 40hrs.

Contexts

Contexts

History.. 383

Legends and folklore 403

Viking customs and rituals.. 408

Flora and fauna.. 412

Cinema.. 415

Books.. 417

Literary extracts 427

History

Despite its low contemporary profile, Norway has a fascinating past. As early as the tenth century its people had explored – and conquered – much of northern Europe, and roamed the Atlantic as far as the North American mainland. These heady days came to end, however, when Norway lost its independence in the fourteenth century, coming under the sway of first Denmark and then Sweden. Independent again from 1905, Norway was propelled into World War II by the German invasion of 1940, an act of aggression that transformed the Norwegians' attitude to the outside world. Gone was the old insular neutrality, replaced by a liberal internationalism exemplified by Norway's leading role in the environmental movement.

Early civilizations

The earliest signs of human habitation in Norway date from the end of the last Ice Age, around 10,000 BC. In the Finnmark region of north Norway, the **Komsa culture** was reliant upon sealing, whereas the peoples of the **Fosna culture**, further south near present-day Kristiansund, hunted both seals and reindeer. Both these societies were essentially static, dependent upon flint and bone implements. At Alta, the Komsa people left behind hundreds of **rock carvings and drawings**, naturalistic representations of their way of life dating from the seventh to the third millennium BC.

As the edges of the icecap retreated from the western coastline, so new migrants slowly filtered north. These new peoples, of the **Nøstvet-økser** culture, were also hunters and fishers, but they were able to manufacture stone axes, examples of which were first unearthed at Nøstvet, near Oslo. Beginning around 2700 BC, immigrants from the east, principally the semi-nomadic **Boat Axe** and **Battle-Axe peoples** – so named because of the distinctive shape of their stone weapons/tools – introduced animal husbandry and agriculture. The new arrivals did not, however, overwhelm their predecessors; the two groups coexisted, each picking up hints from the other – a reflection of the harsh infertility of the land.

These late Stone Age cultures flourished at a time when other, more southerly countries were already using metal. Norway was poor and had little to trade, but the Danes and Swedes exchanged amber for copper and tin from the bronze-making countries of central Europe. A fraction of the imported bronze subsequently passed into Norway, mostly to the Battle-Axe people, who appear to have had a comparatively prosperous aristocracy. This was the beginning of the Norwegian **Bronze Age** (1500–500 BC), which also saw a change in burial customs. In the Stone Age, the Battle-Axe peoples had dug shallow earth graves, but these were now supplanted by **burial mounds** enclosing coffins in which supplies were placed in readiness for the after-life. Building the mounds involved a substantial amount of effort, suggesting the existence of powerful chieftains who could organize the work, and who may also have been priests. Rock carvings became prevalent in southern Norway during this period too – workaday images of men ploughing with oxen, riding horses, carrying arms and using boats to navigate the coastal waters, which were supplemented by drawings of religious or symbolic significance.

In general terms, however, the Bronze Age was characterized more by the development of agriculture than by the use of metal, and stone implements remained the norm.

Around 500 BC Norway was affected by two adverse changes: the climate deteriorated, and trade relations with the Mediterranean were disrupted by the westward movement of the Celts across central Europe. The former encouraged the development of settled, communal farming in an attempt to improve winter shelter and storage, with each clan resident in a large stone, turf and timber dwelling; the latter cut the supply of tin and copper and subsequently isolated Norway from the early Iron Age. The country's isolation continued through much of the Classical period. The Greek geographer Pytheas of Marseilles, who went far enough north to note the short summer nights, probably visited southern Norway, but the regions beyond remained the subject of vague speculation. Pliny the Elder mentions "Nerigon" as the great island south of the legendary "**Ultima Thule**", the outermost region of the earth, while Tacitus, in his *Germania*, demonstrated knowledge only of the Danes and Swedes.

The expansion of the Roman Empire in the first and second centuries AD revived Norway's trading links with the Mediterranean. Evidence of these renewed contacts is provided across Scandinavia by **runes**, carved inscriptions dating from around 200 AD, whose 24-letter alphabet – the *futhark* – was clearly influenced by Greek and Latin capitals. Initially, runes were seen as having magical powers – to gain their knowledge, the god Odin hung for nine nights on *Yggdrasill*, the tree of life, with a spear in his side (see p.404) – but gradually their usage became more prosaic. Of the eight hundred or so runic inscriptions extant across southern Norway, most commemorate events and individuals: mothers and fathers, sons and slain comrades.

The renewal of trade with the Mediterranean also spread the use of **iron**. Norway's agriculture was transformed by the use of iron tools, and the pace of change accelerated in the fifth century AD, when the Norwegians learned how to smelt the brown iron ore, limonite, that lay in their bogs and lakes – hence its common name bog-iron. Clearing the forests with iron axes was relatively easy and, with more land available, the pattern of settlement became less concentrated. Family homesteads leapfrogged up the valleys, and a class of wealthy farmers emerged, their prosperity based on fields and flocks. Above them in the pecking order were local chieftains, the nature of whose authority varied considerably. Inland, the chieftains' power was based on landed wealth and constrained by feudal responsibilities, whereas the coastal lords, who had often accumulated influence from trade, piracy and military prowess, were less encumbered. Like the farmers, these seafarers had also benefited from the iron axe, which made boat-building much easier. An early seventh-century ship found at Kvalsund, near Hammerfest, was 18m long, its skilfully crafted oak hull equipped with a high prow and stern, prefiguring the vessels of the Vikings.

By the middle of the eighth century, Norway had become a country of small, independent kingships, its geography impeding the development of any central authority. In the event, it was the Yngling chieftains of southeast Norway who attempted to assert some sort of wider control. Their first leaders are listed in the Ynglinga Tal, a paean compiled by the Norwegian *skald* (court poet) Thjodolf in the ninth century. According to Thjodolf, early royal life had its ups and downs: king Domaldi was sacrificed to ensure the fertility of his land; Dag was killed by an accidental blow from a pitchfork; and Fjolnir got up in the night to take a leak, fell into a vat of mead and drowned.

The Vikings

Overpopulation, clan discord and the lure of commerce all contributed to the sudden explosion that launched the **Vikings** (from the Norse word *vik*, meaning creek, and *-ing*, frequenter of), upon an unsuspecting Europe in the ninth century. The patterns of attack and eventual settlement were dictated by the geographical position of the various Scandinavian countries. The Swedish Vikings turned eastwards, the Danes headed south and southwest, while the Norwegians sailed west, their longships landing on the Hebrides, Shetland, Orkney, the Scottish mainland and western Ireland. The Pictish population was unable to muster much resistance and the islands were quickly overrun, becoming, together with the Isle of Man, the nucleus of a new Norse kingdom that provided a base for further attacks on Scotland and Ireland.

The Norwegians founded Dublin in 836, and from Ireland turned their attention eastward to northern Britain. Elsewhere, Norwegian Vikings settled the Faroe Islands and Iceland, and even raided as far south as Moorish Spain, attacking Seville in 844. The raiders soon became settlers, sometimes colonizing the entire country – as in Iceland and the Faroes – but mostly intermingling with the local population. The speed of their assimilation is, in fact, one of the Vikings' most striking features: **William the Conqueror** (1027–87) was the epitome of the Norman baron, yet he was also the descendant of Rollo, the Viking warrior whose army had overrun Normandy just a century before.

The whole of Norway felt the stimulating effects of the Viking expeditions. The economy was boosted by the spoils of war and the population grew in physical stature as health and nutrition improved. Farmland was no longer in such short supply; cereal and dairy farming were extended into new areas in eastern Norway; new vegetables, such as cabbages and turnips, were introduced from Britain; and farming methods were improved by overseas contact – the Celts, for instance, taught the Norwegians how to thresh grain with flails.

The Vikings also rigorously exploited the hunting and fishing peoples who roamed the far north of Norway. Detailed information on Finnmark in the late ninth century comes from a surprising source, the court of **Alfred the Great**, which was visited by a Norwegian chieftain named **Ottar** in about 890. Ottar dwelt, so he claimed, "northernmost of all Norsemen", and he regaled Alfred with tales of his native land, which the king promptly incorporated within his translation of a fifth-century Latin text, the *History of the World* by Paulus Orosius. Ottar, who boasted that he owed political allegiance to no-one, had a few cows, sheep and pigs and a tiny slice of arable land, which he ploughed with horses, but his real wealth came from other sources. Fishing, whaling and walrus hunting provided both food for his retinue and exportable commodities. He also possessed a herd of six hundred tame reindeer – plus six decoy animals used to snare wild reindeer – and extracted a heavy tribute from the Sami (see p.356), payable in furs and hides.

The Vikings' brand of **paganism** (see p.404), with its wayward, unscrupulous deities, underpinned their inclination to vendettas and clan warfare. Nevertheless, institutions slowly developed which helped regulate the blood-letting. Western Norway adopted the Germanic *wergeld* system of cash-for-injury compensation; every free man was entitled to attend the local *Thing (Ting)* or parliament, while a regional *Allthing* made laws and settled disputes. Justice was class-based, however, with society divided into three main categories: the lord, the freeman, and the thrall or slave, who was worth about eight cows. The

Vikings were industrious slavers, opening slave markets wherever they went, sending thousands to work on their land back home and supplying the needs of other buyers.

Viking **decorative art** was also pan-Scandinavian, with the most distinguished work being the elaborate and often grotesque animal motifs that adorned their ships, sledges, buildings and furniture. This craftsmanship is seen to good advantage in the **ship burials** of Oseberg and Gokstad, the retrieved artifacts from which are on display in Oslo's Viking Ships Museum (p.105). The Oseberg ship is thought to be the burial ship of Åse, wife of the early ninth-century **Yngling** king, Gudrød Storlatnes. She was also the mother of Halfdan the Black, whose body had a very different fate from her own – it was chopped up, and the bits were buried across his kingdom to ensure the fertility of the land.

Norway's first kings

It was from the Ynglings of Vestfold that Norway's first widely recognized king, **Harald Hårfagri** (Fair-Hair), claimed descent. Shortly before 900 (the exact date is unclear), Harald won a decisive victory at Hafrsfjord (near modern Stavanger), which gave him control of the coastal region as far north as Trøndelag. It sparked an exodus of minor rulers, most of whom left to settle in Iceland. The thirteenth-century *Laxdaela Saga* records the departure of one such family, the Ketils of Romsdal, who would not be "forced to become Harald's vassals or be denied compensation for fallen kinsmen". Harald's long rule was based on personal pledges of fealty and, with the notable exception of the regional *Allthings*, there were no institutions to sustain it; consequently, when he died, Harald's kingdom broke up into its component parts. Harald did, however, leave a less tangible but extremely important legacy: from now on every ambitious chieftain was not content to be a local lord, but strove to be ruler of a kingdom stretching from the Trøndelag to Vestfold.

Harald's son, **Erik Bloodaxe**, struggled to hold his father's kingdom together, but was outmanoeuvred by his youngest brother, **Håkon the Good**, who secured the allegiance of the major chieftains before returning home from England where he had been raised (and Christianized) at the court of King Athelstan of Wessex. Erik fled to Northumbria to become king of Viking York. Initially, Håkon was well-received, and, although his attempts to introduce Christianity failed, he did carry out a number of far-ranging reforms. He established a common legal code for the whole of Vestfold and Trøndelag, and also introduced the system of *Leidangr*, the division of the coastal districts into areas, each of which was responsible for maintaining and manning a warship.

However, Håkon's rule was punctuated by struggles against Erik's heirs. With the backing of the Danish king Harald Bluetooth, they defeated and killed Håkon in battle in 960. Håkon's kingdom then passed to one of Erik's sons, **Harald Greycloak Eriksson**. This forceful man set about extending his territories with gusto. Indeed, he was, in Bluetooth's opinion, much too successful; keen to keep Norway within his sphere of influence, the Dane slaughtered Greycloak on the battlefield in 970 and replaced him with a Danish appointee, **Håkon Sigurdsson**, the last genuine heathen to rule Norway. But again Bluetooth seems to have got more than he bargained for. Sigurdsson based himself in Trøndelag, a decent distance from his overlord, and it's believed he soon refused

Harald Hardrada

On Magnus' death in 1047, **Harald Hardrada** (Olav's half-brother) became king, and soon consolidated his grip on the whole of Norway from the Trøndelag to the Oslofjord. The last of the Viking heroes, Hardrada was a giant of a man, reputedly almost seven feet tall with a sweeping moustache and eccentric eyebrows, and a warrior who had fought alongside Olav at Stiklestad. After the battle, he and his men had fled east, fighting as mercenaries in Russia and ultimately Byzantium, where Hardrada was appointed the commander of the Varangians, the Norse bodyguard of the Byzantine Emperor.

Back in Norway, Harald dominated the country by force of arms for over twenty years, earning the soubriquet "Hardrada" (the Hard) for his ruthless treatment of his enemies, many of whom he made "kiss the thin lips of the axe" as the saga writers put it. Neither was Hardrada satisfied with being king of just Norway. At first he tried to batter Denmark into submission through regular raiding, but the stratagem failed and he finally made peace with the Danish king, Svein, in 1064.

In 1066, the death of Edward the Confessor presented Harald with an opportunity to press his claim to the English throne. The Norwegian promptly sailed on England, landing near York with a massive fleet, but just outside the city, at Stamford Bridge, his army was surprised and trounced by Harold Godwinson, the new Saxon king of England. It was a battle of crucial importance, and one that gave rise to all sorts of legends, penned by both Norse and English writers. The two kings are supposed to have eyed each other up like prize-fighters, with Hardrada proclaiming his rival "a small king, but one that stood well in his stirrups", and Harold promising the Norwegian "seven feet of English ground, or as much more as he is taller than other men". Hardrada was defeated and killed, and the threat of a Norwegian conquest of England had – though no one realized it at the time – gone forever. Not that the victory did much good for Godwinson, whose weakened army trudged back south to be defeated by William of Normandy at the Battle of Hastings.

Medieval consolidation

Harald's son, **Olav Kyrre** (the Peaceful) – whose life had been spared after Stamford Bridge on the promise never to attack England again – went on to reign as king of Norway for the next 25 years. Peace engendered economic prosperity, and treaties with Denmark ensured Norwegian independence. Three native bishoprics were established, and cathedrals built at Nidaros, Bergen and Oslo. It's from this period, too, that Norway's surviving **stave churches** date: wooden structures resembling an upturned keel, they were lavishly decorated with dragon heads and scenes from Norse mythology, proof that the traditions of the pagan world were slow to disappear. (For more on stave churches, see p.188.)

The first decades of the twelfth century witnessed the further consolidation of Norway's position as an independent power, despite internal disorder as the descendants of Olav Kyrre competed for influence. Civil war ceased only when **Håkon IV** took the throne in 1240, ushering in what is often called "**The Period of Greatness**". Secure at home, Håkon strengthened the Norwegian hold on the Faroe and Shetland islands, and in 1262 both Iceland and Greenland accepted Norwegian sovereignty. A year later, however, the king died in the Orkneys during a campaign to assert his control over the Hebrides, and three years later the Hebrides and the Isle of Man (always the weakest links in the Norwegian empire) were sold to the Scottish crown by Håkon's successor, **Magnus the Lawmender** (1238–80).

Under Magnus, Norway prospered. Law and order were maintained, trade flourished and, in striking contrast to the rough-and-ready ways of Hardrada, the king's court even followed a code of etiquette compiled in what became known as the *Konungs skuggsja* or "King's Mirror". Neither was the power of the monarchy threatened by feudal barons as elsewhere in thirteenth-century Europe: Norway's scattered farms were not susceptible to feudal tutelage and, as a consequence, the nobility lacked both local autonomy and resources. Castles remained few and far between and instead the energies of the nobility were drawn into the centralized administration of the state, a process that only happened several centuries later in the rest of western Europe. Norwegian **Gothic art** reached its full maturity in this period, as construction began on the nave at Nidaros Cathedral and on Håkon's Hall in Bergen.

Magnus was succeeded by his sons, first the undistinguished Erik and then **Håkon V** (1270–1319), the last of medieval Norway's talented kings. Håkon continued the policy of his predecessors, making further improvements to central government and asserting royal control of Finnmark through the construction of a fortress at Vardø. His achievements, however, were soon to be swept away along with the independence of Norway itself.

Loss of sovereignty

Norway's independence was threatened from two quarters. With strongholds in Bergen and Oslo, the **Hanseatic League** and its merchants had steadily increased their influence, exerting a monopoly on imports and controlling inland trade. The power of their international trading links was felt in Norway as the royal household grew increasingly dependent on the taxes the merchants paid. The second threat was **dynastic**. When Håkon died in 1319 he left no male heir and was succeeded by his grandson, the three-year-old son of a Swedish duke. The boy, **Magnus Eriksson**, was elected Swedish king two months later, marking the virtual end of Norway as an independent country until 1905.

Magnus assumed full power over both countries in 1332, but his reign was a difficult one. When the Norwegian nobility rebelled he agreed that the monarchy should again be split: his three-year-old son, Håkon, would become Norwegian king when he came of age, while the Swedes agreed to elect his eldest son Erik to the Swedish throne. It was then, in 1349, that the **Black Death** struck, spreading quickly along the coast and up the valleys, killing almost two-thirds of the Norwegian population. It was a catastrophe of unimaginable proportions, its effects compounded by the way the country's agriculture was structured. Animal husbandry was easily the most important part of Norwegian farming, and harvesting and drying winter fodder was labour-intensive. Without the labourers, the animals died in their hundreds and famine conditions prevailed for several generations.

Many farms were abandoned and, deprived of their rents, the petty chieftains who had once dominated rural Norway were, as a class, almost entirely swept away. The vacuum was filled by royal officials, the **syslemenn**, each of whom exercised control over a large chunk of territory on behalf of a Royal Council. The collapse of local governance was compounded by dynastic toing and froing at the top of the social ladder. In 1380, Håkon died and Norway passed into Danish control with **Olav**, the son of Håkon and the Danish princess Margaret, becoming ruler of the two kingdoms.

The Kalmar Union

Despite Olav's early death in 1387, the resourceful Margaret persevered with the union. Proclaimed regent by both the Danish and (what remained of the) Norwegian nobility, she engineered a treaty with the Swedish nobles that not only recognized her as regent of Sweden but also agreed to accept any king she should nominate. Her chosen heir, **Erik of Pomerania**, was foisted on the Norwegians in 1389. When he reached the age of majority in 1397, Margaret organized a grand coronation with Erik crowned king of all three countries at Kalmar in Sweden – hence the **Kalmar Union**.

After Margaret's death in 1412, all power was concentrated in Denmark. In Norway, foreigners were preferred in both state and church, and the country became impoverished by the taxes levied to pay for Erik's various wars. Incompetent and brutal in equal measure, Erik managed to get himself deposed in all three countries at the same time, ending his days as a Baltic pirate.

Union with Denmark

In 1439, Sweden left the union, and in 1450 a Danish count, Christian of Oldenburg, was crowned king of Norway and Denmark. Thereafter, Norway simply ceased to take any meaningful part in Scandinavian affairs. Successive monarchs continued to appoint foreigners to important positions, appropriating Norwegian funds for Danish purposes and even mortgaging Orkney and Shetland in 1469 to the Scots. Danish became the official tongue, replacing **Old Norse**, which came to be regarded as the language of the ignorant and inconsequential. Only the Norwegian Church retained any power, though this was soon to be squashed by the Reformation. Only once did it look as if Norway might break the Danish stranglehold, when a Swedish-Norwegian nobleman, **Knut Alvsson**, crossed the border and overran southern Norway in 1501–2, but the Danes soon fought back and Alvsson was treacherously murdered as he sued for peace.

The Danish victor, King **Christian II**, imposed a crash programme of "Danicization" on the Norwegians and mercilessly hunted down his opponents, but his attempts to dominate the Swedes led to his forced abdication in 1523. The leaders of the Norwegian opposition rallied under the archbishop of Nidaros, Olav Engelbrektsson, but their attempt to gain terms from the new king Frederik I failed. The Danish civil war that followed the death of Frederik resulted in the victory of the **Protestant Christian III** and the loss of Norway's last independent national institution, the Catholic Church. In 1536 Christian III declared that Norway should cease to be a separate country and that the Lutheran faith should be established there. Christian even carted the silver casket that had contained the bones of St Olav back to Copenhagen, where he melted it down into coins.

Thereafter, Norway became, to all intents and purposes, simply a source of raw materials – fish, timber and iron ore – whose proceeds lined the Danish royal purse. Naturally enough, the Swedes coveted these materials too, the upshot being a long and inconclusive war (1563–70), which saw much of Norway ravaged by competing bands of mercenaries. Ironically, the Swedish attempt to capture Norway induced a change of attitude in Copenhagen: keen to keep their subjects happy, a degree of decentralization became the order of the day, and the Danes appointed a **Governor-General** (*Stattholder*) to administer justice in accordance with traditional Norwegian law.

Though slow to take root among the Norwegian peasantry, **Lutheranism** served as a powerful instrument in establishing Danish control. The Bible, catechism and hymnal were all in Danish and the bishops were all Danes too. Thus, the Norwegian **Reformation** was very much an instrument of Danish colonization rather than a reflection of widespread intellectual ferment: the urban apprentices and craftsmen who fired the movement elsewhere in Europe simply didn't exist in significant numbers here in rustic Norway. Neither had the **Renaissance** made much impact here: the first printing press wasn't established in Norway until 1643, and the reading public remained minuscule, though the country did produce a surprising number of humanist writers. Nonetheless, something of the Renaissance spirit did arrive in the form of **Christian IV** (1588–1648). Among the Danish kings of the period, he proved the most sympathetic to Norway. He visited the country often, improving the quality of its administration and founding new towns – including Kongsberg, Kristiansand and Christiania (later Oslo) – whose buildings were laid out on a spacious gridiron plan.

At last, in the late sixteenth century, the Norwegian economy began to pick up. The population grew, trade increased and, benefiting from the decline of the Hanseatic League, a native bourgeoisie began to take control of certain parts of the economy, most notably the herring industry. But Norwegian cultural self-esteem remained at a low ebb: the country's merchants spoke Danish, mimicked Danish manners and read Danish literature. What's more, Norway was a constant bone of contention between Sweden and Denmark, the result being a long series of wars in which its more easterly provinces were regularly overrun by the competing armies.

The year **1660** marked a turning point in the constitutional arrangements governing Norway. For centuries, the Danish Council of State had had the power to elect the monarch and impose limitations on his or her rule. Now, a powerful alliance of merchants and clergy swept these powers away to make **Frederik III** absolute ruler. This was, however, not a reactionary coup, but an attempt to limit the power of the conservative-minded nobility. In addition, the development of a centralized state machine would, many calculated, provide all sorts of job opportunities to the low-born but adept. As a result, Norway was incorporated into the administrative structure of Denmark with royal authority delegated to the *Stattholder*, who governed through what soon became a veritable army of professional bureaucrats.

In the event, there were indeed positive advantages for Norway: the country acquired better defences, simpler taxes, a separate High Court and further doses of Norwegian law, but once again power was exercised almost exclusively by Danes. The functionaries were allowed to charge for their services, and there was no fixed tariff – a swindler's charter for which the peasantry paid heavily. So much so, in fact, that one of the *Stattholders*, **Ulrik Gyldenløve**, launched

Hiking

Few would dispute that Norway has some of the world's most magnificent scenery. From top to bottom, the country is traversed by a sequence of wondrously rugged mountain ranges, accentuated by icy glaciers, rocky spires and deep green fjords. Great chunks of this wild terrain have been incorporated into national parks – and these have become a magnet for hikers in search of everything from easy rambles to full-scale expeditions along a multitude of clearly marked trails.

Walkers in the Aurlandsdal

Hiking trails and maps

Norway's **hiking trails** are typically marked at regular intervals by **cairns**. Most junctions are marked by **signposts**, some of which have stood for many years and are on the small side, making them hard to spot. There are also **red "T"** symbols painted on rocks – welcome route markers when the weather is poor, as they're visible from farther away than the signposts. Although waymarking is quite good, you should always purchase **hiking maps**. The entire country has been accurately mapped by the Norwegian highways department – their *Statens Kartverk M711 Norge 1:50,000* series, with red and white covers, are the most detailed, while their maroon-covered maps cover all the more popular hiking areas at the scale of 1:100,000. You can buy hiking maps at DNT outlets, the majority of tourist offices and at many bookshops.

DNT

Resting on Spitsbergen

Den Norske Turistforening (Norwegian Mountain Touring Association) plays an active part in managing all aspects of hiking in Norway. Essentially an umbrella organization, it takes care of trails and waymarking and co-ordinates more than forty local hiking associations, which run over 300 mountain lodges. DNT membership costs 455kr per annum (19–26 year olds 260kr, 13–18 years 150kr, 67-plus 340kr, under 12 100kr), and can be purchased at any of their offices or staffed mountain lodges – you don't have to be a member to stay at DNT huts, but non-members pay about fifty percent more. The association also sells maps, organizes popular all-inclusive guided tours and provides advice on equipment.

DNT's main office is in Oslo at Storgata 7 (Ⓣ22 82 28 00); its postal address is Postboks 7, Sentrum, 0101 Oslo. The website – Ⓦwww.turistforeningen.no – gives details of all its affiliated members, a full list of hiking areas with local details, and opening times and contact numbers for every DNT and affiliate hut (*hytter*), but much of the information is only in Norwegian.

Mountain lodge in Grimsdal

Mountain lodges

Staffed mountain lodges, mostly located in the southern part of the country, are often large enough to accommodate over a hundred guests, and provide a full service including meals and lodging. They are clean, friendly and well-run, usually by DNT staff – although there are some private lodges where prices are slightly higher (discounts apply for DNT members). **Self-service huts**, with twenty to forty beds, are also concentrated in the mountains of southern Norway and offer lodging with bedding, a shop selling groceries and a well equipped kitchen in which to cook. **Unstaffed huts**, often with less than twenty beds, are mostly in the north. They provide bedding, stoves for heating and cooking and all kitchen equipment, but you must bring and prepare your own food.

Reservations are accepted at staffed lodges for stays of more than two nights, though the lodges are primarily designed to cater for guests in transit. Otherwise, beds are provided on a first-come, first-served basis. During high season, lodges may sometimes be full, although this is not common. If beds are not available, you are given a mattress and blankets for sleeping in a common area. DNT members over 50 years of age are, however, always guaranteed a bed. Norwegians are proud that no one is ever turned away.

Rough camping

Rough camping is allowed freely throughout Norway, although campfires are prohibited from April 15 to September 15. You may camp freely for one night only in any one spot, so long as you are not within 150 metres of a building. In some national parks and other walking areas, these rules have been modified: you must move a bit further away from a hut, or stay near to the hut in a designated camping area. Obviously enough, the main disadvantage of camping, as opposed to staying in a lodge, is the amount of equipment you have to carry; on the other hand, the remoter regions and national parks have few – if any – lodges.

Camping by Lake Femunden

Hiking season

The **hiking season** is short and loosely defined by the opening and closing of the mountain lodges. It runs from early July (mid-June in some areas) through to late September. At this time of the year, the weather is mild and you can anticipate daytime mountain temperatures of between 20°C and 25°C: pleasant, comfortable and ideal for hiking. And, of course, it's daylight for most of the time – beyond the Arctic Circle, all the time – so you're unlikely to be searching for a mountain lodge after dark.

National parks

Jotunheimen Nasjonalpark The "Home of the Giants", Norway's most famous hiking area only covers 3900 square kilometres, but it offers an amazing concentration of towering, ice-tipped peaks, more than two hundred of them rising above 1900 metres, including northern Europe's two highest, Galdhøpiggen (2469m) and Glittertind (2464m). The park is located near the east end of the Sognefjord, about 300km from Oslo. See p.179.

Rondane Nasjonalpark The Rondane comprises both a high alpine zone, with ten peaks exceeding the 2000-metre mark, and a much gentler upland area punctuated by rounded, treeless hills. The Rondane is on the E6 between Oslo and Trondheim and is especially popular with families. See p.177.

Hardangervidda Nasjonalpark This is Europe's largest mountain plateau, stretching east in a great slab from the Hardangerfjord to Finse in the north and Rjukan in the east, and its bare, almost lunar-like rocks and myriad lakes make for some spectacular hiking. The Hardangervidda begins about 130km east of Bergen. See p.228.

Dovrefjell Nasjonalpark Bisected by the E6 and the Dombås–Trondheim railway, the Dovrefjell is one of the most accessible of Norway's national parks located about 400km north of Oslo. In the east, there are marshes and open moors with rounded ridges, but as you hike west the steep and serrated alpine peaks of the Romsdal hove into view. See p.184.

Rondane Nasjonalpark

a vigorous campaign against corruption, his efforts rewarded by a far-reaching series of reforming edicts promulgated in 1684.

The eighteenth and early nineteenth centuries

The **absolute monarchy** established by Frederik III soon came to concern itself with every aspect of Norwegian life. The ranks and duties of a host of minor officials were carefully delineated, religious observances tightly regulated and restrictions were imposed on everything from begging and dress through to the food and drink that could be consumed at weddings and funerals. This extraordinary superstructure placed a leaden hand on imagination and invention. Neither was it impartial: there were some benefits for the country's farmers and fishermen, but by and large the system worked in favour of the middle class. The merchants of every small town were allocated exclusive rights to trade in a particular area and competition between towns was forbidden. These local monopolies placed the peasantry at a dreadful disadvantage, nowhere more iniquitously than in the Lofoten islands, where fishermen not only had to buy supplies and equipment at the price set by the merchant, but had to sell their fish at the price set by him too.

The Dano-Norwegian functionaries who controlled Norway also set the **cultural** agenda, patronizing an insipid and imitative art and literature. The writings of **Petter Dass** stand out from the dross, however – heartfelt verses and descriptions of life in the Nordland where he worked as a pastor. There were liberal, vaguely nationalist stirrings too, in the foundation of the Norwegian Society in Copenhagen twelve years later.

More adventurously, there was renewed missionary interest in Norway's old colony of **Greenland**. Part of it was down to an eccentric ethnic obsession – the clergyman concerned, a certain Hans Egede, was looking for Inuit with Viking features – but Bergen's merchants footed the bill, on condition that Egede build them a fur-trading station there. In the event, it was a poor investment, as the trading monopoly was given to a Dane. There was also missionary work in Finnmark, where a determined effort was made to convert the Sami (see p.356). This was a very different undertaking from Egede's, and one that reflected the changing temperament of the Lutheran Church of Norway, which had been reinvigorated by **pietist** clergymen. One of their number, Thomas von Westen, learned the Sami language and led an extraordinarily successful mission to the far north. He was certainly a good deal more popular than many of his fellow pietists down south who persuaded **Christian VI** (1730–46) to impose draconian penalties for such crimes as not observing the Sabbath or not going to church regularly.

In the meantime, there were more wars between Denmark and Sweden. In 1700, **Frederik IV** (1699–1730) made the rash decision to attack the Swedes at the time when their king, Karl XII, was generally reckoned to be one of Europe's most brilliant military strategists. Predictably, the Danes were defeated and only the intervention of the British saved Copenhagen from falling into Swedish hands. Undeterred, Frederik tried again, and this time Karl retaliated by launching a full-scale invasion of Norway. The Swedes rapidly occupied southern Norway, but then, much to everyone's amazement, things began to go wrong. The Norwegians successfully held out in the Akershus fortress in

Christiania (Oslo) and added insult to injury by holding on to Halden too. Furthermore, a naval commander, one **Peter Tordenskiold**, became a national hero in Norway when he caught the Swedish fleet napping and ripped it to pieces off Strømstad. Karl was forced to retreat, but returned with a new army two years later. He promptly besieged the fortress at Halden for a second time, but while he was inspecting his troops someone shot him in the head – whether it was one of his own soldiers or a Norwegian has been the subject of heated debate ever since. Whatever the truth, Karl's death enabled the protagonists to agree the **Peace of Frederiksborg** (1720), which ended hostilities for the rest of the eighteenth century.

Peace favoured the growth of trade, but although Norway's economy prospered it was hampered by the increasing **centralization** of the Dano-Norwegian state. Regulations pushed more and more trade through Copenhagen, to the irritation of the majority of Norwegian merchants who were accustomed to trading direct with their customers. Increasingly, they wanted the same privileges as the Danes, and especially, given the chronic shortage of capital and credit, their own national bank. In the 1760s, Copenhagen did a dramatic U-turn, abolishing monopolies, removing trade barriers and even permitting a free press – and the Norwegian economy boomed. Nonetheless, the bulk of the population remained impoverished and prey to famine whenever the harvest was poor. The number of landless agricultural labourers rose dramatically, partly because more prosperous farmers were buying up large slices of land, and for the first time Norway had something akin to a proletariat.

Despite this, Norway was one of the few European countries little affected by the French Revolution. Instead of political action, there was a **religious revival**, with Hans Nielson Hauge emerging as an evangelical leader. The movement's characteristic hostility to officialdom caused concern, and Hauge was imprisoned, but in reality it posed little threat to the status quo. The end result was rather the foundation of a Christian fundamentalist movement that is still a force to be reckoned with in parts of west Norway.

The end of union with Denmark

Denmark-Norway had remained neutral throughout the Seven Years' War (1756–63) between England and France, and renewed that neutrality in 1792, during the period leading up to the **Napoleonic Wars**. The prewar years were good for Norway: overseas trade, especially with England, flourished, and demand for Norwegian timber, iron and cargo-space heralded a period of unparalleled prosperity at least for the bourgeoisie. However, when Napoleon implemented a trade blockade – the Continental System – against Britain, he roped in the Danes. As a result, the British fleet bombarded Copenhagen in 1807 and forced the surrender of the entire Dano-Norwegian fleet. Denmark, in retaliation, declared war on England and Sweden. The move was disastrous for the Norwegian economy, which had suffered bad harvests in 1807 and 1808, and the English blockade of its seaports ruined trade.

By 1811 it was obvious that the Danes had backed the wrong side in the war, and the idea of a union of equals with Sweden, which had supported Britain, became increasingly attractive to many Norwegians. By attaching their coat-tails to the victors, they hoped to restore the commercially vital trade with England. They also thought that the new Swedish king would be able to deal with the Danes if it came to a fight – just as the Swedes had themselves calculated when they appointed him in 1810. The man concerned, **Karl XIV Johan**, was, curiously enough, none other than Jean-Baptiste Bernadotte, formerly one of Napoleon's marshals. With perfect timing, he had helped the British defeat Napoleon at Leipzig in 1813. His reward came in the **Treaty of Kiel** the following year, when the great powers instructed the Danes to cede to Sweden all rights in Norway (although they did keep the dependencies of Iceland, Greenland and the Faroes). Four hundred years of union had ended.

Union with Sweden 1814–1905

The high-handed transfer of Norway from Denmark to Sweden did nothing to assuage the growing demands for greater independence. Furthermore, the Danish Crown Prince Christian Frederik roamed Norway stirring up fears of Swedish intentions. The prince and his supporters convened a Constituent Assembly, which met in a country house outside Eidsvoll (see p.168) in April 1814 and produced a **constitution**. Issued on May 17, 1814 (still a national holiday), this declared Norway to be a "free, independent and indivisible realm" with Christian Frederik as its king. Not surprisingly, Karl Johan would have none of this and, with the support of the great powers, he invaded Norway. Completely outgunned, Christian Frederik barely mounted any resistance. In exchange for Swedish promises to recognize the Norwegian constitution and the *Storting* (parliament), he abdicated as soon as he had signed a peace treaty – the so-called **Convention of Moss** – in August 1814.

The ensuing period was marred by struggles between the *Storting* and **Karl XIV Johan** over the nature of the union. Although the constitution emphasized Norway's independence, Johan had a suspensive veto over the *Storting*'s actions, the post of *Stattholder* in Norway could only be held by a Swede, and foreign and diplomatic matters concerning Norway remained entirely in Swedish hands. Despite this, Karl Johan proved popular in Norway, and during his reign the country enjoyed a degree of independence. The Swedes allowed all the highest offices in Norway to be filled by Norwegians and democratic local councils were established, in part due to the rise of the peasant farmers as a political force.

Under both Oscar I (1844–59) and Karl XV (1859–72), however, it was **pan-Scandinavianism** that ruled the intellectual roost. This belief in the natural solidarity of Denmark, Norway and Sweden was espoused by the leading artists of the period, but died a toothless death in 1864 when the Norwegians and the Swedes refused to help Denmark when it was attacked by Austria and Prussia; some of the loudest cries of treachery came from a young writer by the name of Henrik Ibsen, whose poetic drama, *Brand*, was a spirited indictment of Norwegian perfidy.

Domestic politics were changing too, with the rise to power in the 1850s of **Johan Sverdrup**, who started a long and ultimately successful campaign to wrest executive power from the king and transfer it to the *Storting*. By the mid-1880s, Sverdrup and his political allies had pretty much won the day, though a further bout of sabre-rattling between the supporters of Norwegian independence and the Swedish king **Oscar II** (1872–1907) was necessary before both sides would accept a plebiscite. This took place in August 1905, when there was an overwhelming vote in favour of the **dissolution of the union**, which was duly confirmed by the Treaty of Karlstad. A second plebiscite determined that independent Norway should be a monarchy rather than a republic, and, in November 1905, Prince Karl of Denmark (Edward VII of England's son-in-law) was elected to the throne as **Håkon VII**.

Meanwhile, the gradual increase in prosperity had been having important **social and cultural implications**. The layout and buildings of modern Oslo – the Royal Palace, Karl Johans gate, the university – date from this period, whilst Johan Christian Dahl, the most distinguished Scandinavian landscape painter of his day, was instrumental in the foundation of the Nasjonalgalleriet (National Gallery; see p.94) in Oslo in 1836. More importantly, Dahl and other prominent members of the bourgeoisie formed the nucleus of a **National Romantic movement** that championed all things Norwegian. The movement's serious intent was flagged up by Jens Kraft, who produced a massive six-volume topographical survey of the country, and the poet, prose writer and propagandist **Henrik Wergeland** decried the civil servant culture that had dominated Norway for so long in favour of the more sincere qualities of the peasant farmer. Indeed, the movement endowed the Norwegian peasantry with all sorts of previously unidentified qualities, while the **temperance movement** sought to bring them up to these lofty ideals by promoting laws to prohibit the use of small stills, once found on every farm. The government obliged by formally banning these stills in 1844, and by the mid-nineteenth century, consumption of spirits had dropped drastically and coffee rivalled beer as the national drink.

Similarly, the **Norwegian language** and its folklore was rediscovered by a number of academics, further restoring the country's cultural self-respect. Following on were authors like Alexander Kielland, who wrote most of his works between 1880 and 1891, and Knut Hamsun, whose most characteristic novel, *Hunger*, was published in 1890. In music, **Edvard Grieg** (1843–1907) was inspired by old Norwegian folk melodies, composing some of his most famous music for Ibsen's *Peer Gynt*, whilst the artist **Edvard Munch** completed many of his major works in the 1880s and 1890s. Finally, the internationally acclaimed dramatist **Henrik Ibsen** returned to Oslo in 1891 after a prolonged self-imposed exile.

Early Independence: 1905–39

Norway's **Independence** came at a time of further economic advance, engendered by the introduction of hydroelectric power and underpinned by a burgeoning merchant navy, the third-largest after the USA and Britain. Social reforms also saw funds being made available for unemployment relief, accident insurance schemes and a Factory Act (1909), governing safety in the workplace. An extension to the franchise gave the vote to all men over 25, and, in 1913, to women too. The education system was reorganized, and substantial sums were spent on new arms and defence. This prewar period also saw the emergence of a strong trade union movement and of a Labour Party committed to revolutionary change.

Since 1814 Norway had had little to do with European affairs, and at the outbreak of **World War I** it declared itself strictly neutral. Its sympathy, though, lay largely with the Western Allies, and the Norwegian economy boomed as its ships and timber were in great demand. By 1916, however, Norway had begun to feel the pinch as German submarine action hit both enemy and neutral shipping, and by the end of the war Norway had lost half its chartered tonnage and

2000 crew. The Norwegian economy also suffered after the USA entered the war because the Americans imposed strict trade restrictions in their attempt to prevent supplies getting to Germany, and rationing had to be introduced across Norway. Indeed, the price of neutrality turned out to be high: there was a rise in state expenditure, a soaring cost of living and, at the end of the war, no seat at the conference table. In spite of its losses, Norway got no share of confiscated German shipping, although it was partly compensated by gaining sovereignty of Spitsbergen and its coal deposits – the first extension of the Norwegian frontiers for 500 years. In 1920 Norway also entered the new League of Nations.

Later in the 1920s, the decline in world trade led to decreased demand for Norway's shipping. Bank failures and currency fluctuation were rife, and, as unemployment and industrial strife increased, a strengthening Norwegian **Labour Party** took advantage. With the franchise extended and the introduction of larger constituencies, it had a chance to win seats outside the large towns for the first time. At the 1927 election the Labour Party, together with the Social Democrats from whom they'd split, were the biggest grouping in the *Storting*. However, they had no overall majority and because many feared their revolutionary rhetoric, they were manoeuvred out of office after only fourteen days. Trade disputes and lockouts continued and troops had to be used to protect scabs.

During the war, **Prohibition** had been introduced as a temporary measure and a referendum of 1919 showed a clear majority in favour of its continuation. But the ban did little to quell – and even exacerbated – drunkenness, and it was abandoned in 1932, replaced by the government monopoly on the sale of wines and spirits that remains in force today. The **1933 election** gave the Labour Party more seats than ever. Having shed its revolutionary image, a campaigning, reformist Labour Party benefited from the growing popular conviction that state control and a centrally planned economy were the only answer to Norway's economic problems. In 1935 the Labour Party, in alliance with the Agrarian Party, took power – an unlikely combination since the Agrarians were profoundly nationalist in outlook, so much so that one of their defence spokesmen was the rabid anti-Semite **Vidkun Quisling**. Frustrated by the democratic process, Quisling had left the Agrarians in 1933 to found **Nasjonal Samling** (National Unification), a fascist movement which proposed, among other things, that both Hitler and Mussolini should be nominated for the Nobel Peace Prize. Quisling had good contacts with Nazi Germany but little support in Norway – local elections in 1937 reduced his local representation to a mere seven, and party membership fell to 1500.

The Labour government under **Johan Nygaardsvold** presided over an improving economy. By 1938 industrial production was 75 percent higher than it had been in 1914 and unemployment dropped as expenditure on roads, railways and public works increased. Social welfare reforms were implemented and trade union membership increased. When war broke out in 1939, Norway was lacking only one thing – adequate defence. A vigorous member of the League of Nations, the country had pursued disarmament- and peace-oriented policies since the end of World War I and was determined to remain neutral.

World War II

In early 1940, despite the threat posed by Hitler, the Norwegians were preoccupied with Allied mine-laying off the Norwegian coast – part of their attempt to prevent Swedish iron ore being shipped from Narvik to Germany. Indeed, such was Norwegian naivety that they made a formal protest to Britain on the day of the **German invasion**. Caught napping, the Norwegian army offered little initial resistance and the south and central regions of the country were quickly overrun. King Håkon and the *Storting* were forced into a hasty evacuation of Oslo and headed north to Elverum, evading capture by just a couple of hours. Here, at the government's temporary headquarters, the executive was granted full powers to take whatever decisions were necessary in the interests of Norway – a mandate which later formed the basis of the Norwegian government-in-exile in Britain.

The Germans contacted the king and his government in Elverum, demanding, amongst other things, that Quisling be accepted as prime minister as a condition of surrender. Though their situation was desperate, the Norwegians rejected this outright and instead chose resistance. The ensuing campaign lasted for two months and, although the Norwegians fought determinedly with the help of a few British regulars, they were no match for the German army. In June both king and government fled to Britain from Tromsø in northern Norway. The country was rapidly brought under Nazi control, Hitler sending **Josef Terboven** to take full charge of Norwegian affairs.

The fascist **Nasjonal Samling** was declared the only legal party and the media, civil servants and teachers were brought under its control. As **civil resistance** grew, a state of emergency was declared: two trade union leaders were shot, arrests increased and a concentration camp was set up outside Oslo. In February 1942 Quisling was installed as "Minister President" of Norway, but it soon became clear that his government didn't have the support of the Norwegian people. The church refused to cooperate, schoolteachers protested and trade union members and officials resigned en masse. In response, deportations increased, death sentences were announced and a compulsory labour scheme was introduced.

Military resistance escalated. A military organization (MILORG) was established as a branch of the armed forces under the control of the High Command in London. By May 1941 it had enlisted 20,000 men (32,000 by 1944) in clandestine groups all over the country. Arms and instructors came from Britain, radio stations were set up and a continuous flow of intelligence about Nazi movements sent back. Sabotage operations were legion, the most notable being the destruction of the heavy-water plant at **Rjukan**, foiling a German attempt to produce an atomic bomb. Reprisals against the resistance were severe, but only a comparative handful of Norwegians actively collaborated with the enemy.

The **government-in-exile** in London continued to represent free Norway to the world, mobilizing support on behalf of the Allies. Most of the Norwegian merchant fleet was abroad when the Nazis invaded, and by 1943 the Norwegian navy had seventy ships helping the Allied convoys. With the German position deteriorating, neutral Sweden adopted a more sympathetic policy to its Norwegian neighbours, allowing the creation of thinly disguised training grounds for resistance fighters. These camps also served to produce the police detachments that were to secure law and order after liberation.

When the Allies landed in Normandy in June 1944, overt action against the occupying Germans was temporarily discouraged, since the Allies could not safeguard against reprisals. Help was at hand, however, in the form of the **Soviets** who crossed into the far north of Norway in late October, and drove back the Germans. Unfortunately, the Germans chose to burn everything in their path as they retreated, forcing the local population into hiding. To prevent the Germans reinforcing their beleaguered Finnmark battalions, the resistance planned a campaign of mass railway sabotage, stopping three-quarters of the troop movements overnight. With their control of Norway crumbling, the Germans finally **surrendered** on May 7, 1945. King Håkon returned to Norway on June 7, five years to the day since he'd left for exile.

Terboven committed suicide and the NS collaborators were rounded up. A caretaker government took office, staffed by resistance leaders, and was replaced in October 1945 by a majority **Labour government**. The Communists won eleven seats, reflecting the efforts of Communist saboteurs in the war and the prestige that the Soviet Union enjoyed in Norway after the liberation. Quisling was shot, along with 24 other high-ranking traitors, and thousands of collaborators were punished with varying degrees of severity.

Postwar reconstruction

At the end of the war, Norway was on its knees: the far north – Finnmark – had been laid waste, half the mercantile fleet lost, and production was at a standstill. Recovery, though, fostered by a sense of national unity, was quick; it took only three years for GNP to return to its prewar level. In addition, Norway's part in the war had increased her prestige in the world. The country became one of the founding members of the **United Nations** in 1945, and the first UN Secretary-General, Tryggve Lie, was Norwegian Foreign Minister. With the failure of discussions to promote a Scandinavian defence union, the *Storting* also voted to enter **NATO** in 1949.

Domestically, there was general agreement about the form that social reconstruction should take. In 1948, the *Storting* passed the laws that introduced the Welfare State almost unanimously. The 1949 election saw the government returned with a larger majority, and Labour governments continued to be elected throughout the following decade, with the dominant political figure being **Einar Gerhardsen**. As national prosperity increased, society became ever more egalitarian, levelling up rather than down. Subsidies were paid to the agricultural and fishing industries, wages increased, and a comprehensive social security system helped to eradicate poverty. The state ran the important mining industry, was the largest shareholder in the hydroelectric company and built an enormous steel works at Mo-i-Rana to help develop the economy of the devastated northern counties. Rationing ended in 1952 and, as the demand for higher education grew, new universities were created in Bergen, Trondheim and Tromsø.

Beyond consensus: modern Norway

The political consensus began to fragment in the early 1960s. Following the restructuring of rural constituencies in the 1950s, there was a realignment in centre politics, the outmoded Agrarian Party becoming the **Centre Party**. There was change on the left too, where defence squabbles within the Labour Party led to the formation of the **Socialist People's Party** (SF), which wanted

Norway out of NATO and sought a renunciation of nuclear weapons. The Labour Party's 1961 declaration that no nuclear weapons would be stationed in Norway except under an immediate threat of war did not placate the SF, who unexpectedly took two seats at the election that year. Holding the balance of power, the SF voted with the Labour Party until 1963, when it helped bring down the government over mismanagement of state industries. A replacement coalition collapsed after only one month, but the writing was on the wall. Rising prices, dissatisfaction with high taxation and a continuing housing shortage meant that the 1965 election put a **non-socialist coalition** in power for the first time in twenty years.

Under the leadership of **Per Borten** of the Centre Party, the coalition's programme was unambitious. Nonetheless, living standards continued to rise, and although the 1969 election saw a marked increase in Labour Party support, the coalition hung on to power. Also that year, **oil and gas** were discovered beneath the North Sea and, as the vast extent of the reserves became obvious, it became clear that the Norwegians were to enjoy a magnificent bonanza – one which was destined to pay about 25 percent of the government's annual bills.

Elsewhere, Norway's politicians, who had applied twice previously for membership of the **European Economic Community** (EEC) – in 1962 and 1967 – believed that de Gaulle's fall in France presented a good opportunity for a third application, which was made in 1970. There was great concern, though, about the effect of membership on Norwegian agriculture and fisheries, and in 1971 Per Borten was forced to resign following his indiscreet handling of the negotiations. The Labour Party, the majority of its representatives in favour of EEC membership, formed a minority administration, but when the **1972 referendum** narrowly voted "No" to joining the EEC, the government resigned.

With the 1973 election producing another minority Labour government, the uncertain pattern of the previous ten years continued. Even the postwar consensus on **Norwegian security policy** broke down on various issues – primarily the question of a northern European nuclear-free zone and the stocking of Allied material in Norway – although there remained strong agreement for continued NATO membership.

In 1983, the Christian Democrats and the Centre Party joined together in a non-socialist coalition, which lasted only two years. It was replaced in 1986 by a minority Labour administration, led by **Dr Gro Harlem Brundtland**, Norway's first woman prime minister. She made sweeping changes to the way the country was run, introducing seven women into her eighteen-member cabinet, but her government was beset by problems for the three years of its life: tumbling oil prices led to a recession, unemployment rose (though only to four percent) and there was widespread dissatisfaction with Labour's high taxation policies.

At the **general election** in September 1989, Labour lost eight seats and was forced out of office – the worst result that the party had suffered since 1930. More surprising was the success of the extremist parties on both political wings – the anti-NATO leftist Socialist Party and the right-wing, anti-immigrant Progress Party both scored spectacular results, winning almost a quarter of the votes cast, and increasing their representation in the *Storting* many times over. This deprived the Conservative Party (one of whose leaders, bizarrely, was Gro Harlem Brundtland's husband) of the majority it might have expected, the result being yet another shaky minority administration – this time a **centre-right coalition** between the Conservatives, the Centre Party and the Christian Democrats, led by Jan Syse.

The new government immediately faced problems familiar to the last Labour administration. In particular, there was continuing conflict over joining the **European Community**, a policy still supported by many in the Norwegian establishment but flatly rejected by the Centre Party. It was this, in part, that signalled the end of the coalition, for after just over a year in office, the Centre Party withdrew its support and forced the downfall of Syse. In October 1990, Gro Harlem Brundtland was put back in power at the head of a **minority Labour administration**, remaining in office till her re-election for a fourth minority term in 1993. The 1993 elections saw a revival in Labour Party fortunes and, to the relief of the majority, the collapse of the Progress Party vote. However, it was also an untidy, confusing affair where the main issue, membership of the EU, cut across the traditional left-versus-right divide.

Present-day Norway

Following the 1993 election, the country tumbled into a long and fiercely conducted campaign over **membership of the EU**. Brundtland and her main political opponents wanted in, but despite the near-unanimity of the political class, the Norwegians narrowly rejected the EU in a 1994 referendum. It was a close call (52.5 percent versus 47.5 percent), but in the end farmers and fishermen afraid of the economic results of joining, as well as women's groups and environmentalists who felt that Norway's high standards of social care and "green" controls would suffer, came together to swing opinion against joining. Afterwards, and unlike the Labour government of 1972, the Brundtland administration soldiered on, wisely soothing ruffled feathers by promising to shelve the whole EU membership issue until at least 2000. Nonetheless, the **1997 election** saw a move to the right, the main beneficiaries being the Christian Democratic Party and the ultra-conservative Progress Party. In itself, this was not enough to remove the Labour-led coalition from office – indeed Labour remained comfortably the largest party – but the right was dealt a trump card by the new Labour leader, **Thorbjørn Jagland**. During the campaign Jagland had promised that the Labour Party would step down from office if it failed to elicit more than the 36.9 percent of the vote it had secured in 1993. Much to the chagrin of his colleagues, Jagland's political chickens came home to roost when Labour only received 35 percent of the vote – and they had to go, leaving power in the hands of an unwieldy right-of-centre, minority coalition. Bargaining with its rivals from a position of parliamentary weakness, the new government found it difficult to cut a clear path – or at least one very different from its predecessor – apart from managing to antagonize the women's movement by some reactionary social legislation whose none-too-hidden subtext seemed to read "A woman's place is in the home". In the spring of 2000, the government resigned and the Labour Party resumed command – but not for long: in elections the following year, they took a drubbing and the right prospered, paving the way for another ungainly centre-right administrative coalition. The coalition battled on until October 2005 when the Labour Party, along with its allies the Socialist Left Party and the Centre Party, won a general election, with the politically experienced **Jens Stoltenberg** becoming Prime Minister – as he remains at time of writing.

In the long term, quite what Norway will make of its splendid **isolation from the EU** is unclear, though the situation is mitigated by Norway's membership of the European Economic Agreement (EEA), a free-trade deal of January 1994 that covers both Norway and the EU. Whatever happens, and whether or not there is another EU referendum, it's hard to imagine that the Norwegians will suffer any permanent economic harm. They have, after all, a superabundance of natural resources and arguably the most educated workforce in the world. Which isn't to say the country doesn't collectively **fret** – a modest increase in the amount of drug addiction and street crime has produced much heart-searching, the theory being that an advanced and progressive social policy should be able to eliminate such barbarisms. This thoughtful approach, so typical of Norway, is very much to the country's credit, as is the refusal to accept a residual level of unemployment (of about 6–7 percent) that is the envy of many other Western governments. The Norwegians also fret (and argue) about **environmental** issues, with one hot potato being the country's **road building** programme. A curse afflicting prewar Norway had always been rural isolation and the Norwegians of 1945 were determined to connect (almost) all of the country's villages to the road system. Give or take the occasional hamlet, this has now been achieved and a second phase is underway, involving the upgrading of roads and the construction of innumerable tunnels. Wherever this makes conditions safer, the popular consensus for the programme survives, but there is increasing opposition to the prestige projects so beloved by status-seeking politicians – the enormous tunnel near Flåm (see p.235) being a case in point. There is, however, precious little internal argument when it comes to **whaling and sealing**, with the majority continuing to support the hunting of these animals as has been the custom for centuries – indeed, for some Norwegians whaling and sealing go some way to defining what they consider to be the national identity. This is inexplicable to many Western Europeans, who point to Norway's eminently liberal approach to most other matters, but the Norwegians see things very differently: why, many of them ask, is the culling of seals and mink seen in a different light from the mass slaughter of farmed animals?

Legends and folklore

Norway has an exceptionally rich body of **historical legend and folk tradition**, and one that plays an important part in the national consciousness. Most famous are the **sagas**, mainly written in Iceland between the twelfth and fourteenth centuries and constituting a vast collection of part-historical, part-fictionalized stories covering several centuries of Norse history. Thanks to the survival of one of these sagas, the *Poetic Edda* (see p.404), our knowledge of **Norse mythology** is far from conjectural. Much that was not recorded there survived in the oral tradition, to be revived from the 1830s onwards by the artists and writers of the National Romantic movement. Some members of this movement also set about collecting the **folk tales** and legends of the rural regions. The difficulties they experienced in rendering the Norwegian dialects into written form – there was no written Norwegian language per se – fuelled the language movement, and sent the academic Ivar Aasen roaming the countryside to assemble the material from which he formulated *Landsmål* (see p.459).

Sagas

The Norwegian Vikings settled in Iceland in the ninth century, and throughout the medieval period the Icelanders had a deep attachment to, and interest in, their original homeland. The result was a body of work that remains one of the richest sources of European medieval literature. That so much of it has survived is due to Iceland's isolation – most Norwegian sources disappeared centuries ago.

All the **sagas** feature real people and tell of events which are usually known to have happened, though the plots are embroidered to suit the tales' heroic style. They reveal much about a Norse culture in which arguments between individuals might spring from comparatively trivial disputes over horses or sheep, but where a strict code of honour and revenge meant that every insult, whether real or imagined, had to be avenged. Thus personal disputes soon turned into

△ Saga carving

clan vendettas. Plots are complex, the dialogue laconic, and the pared-down prose omits unnecessary detail. New characters are often introduced by means of tedious genealogies, necessary to explain the motivation behind their later actions (though the more adept translations render these explanations as footnotes). Personality is only revealed through speech, facial expressions and general demeanour, or the comments and gossip of others.

The earliest Icelandic work, the **Elder** or **Poetic Edda** (various English editions are available), comprises 34 lays dating from as early as the eighth century, and they combine to give a detailed insight into early Norse culture and pagan cosmogony and belief. It's not to be confused with the **Younger** or **Prose Edda**, written centuries later by Snorri Sturluson, the most distinguished of the saga writers.

Also noteworthy are *The Vinland Saga*, *Njal's Saga* and the *Laxdaela Saga*, tales of ninth- and tenth-century Icelandic derring-do; and *Harald's Saga*, a rattling good yarn celebrating the life and times of King Harald Hardrada. English translations of all the above are published by Penguin.

Norse mythology

The Vikings shared a common **pagan faith**, whose polytheistic tenets were upheld across all of Scandinavia. The deities were worshipped at a thousand village shrines, usually by means of sacrifices in which animals, weapons, boats and other artefacts, even humans, were gifted to the gods. There was very little theology to sanctify these rituals; instead the principal gods – Odin, Thor and Frey – were surrounded by mythical tales attributing to them a bewildering variety of strengths, weaknesses and powers.

Odin and Frigga

The god of war, wisdom, poetry and magic, **Odin** was untrustworthy, violent and wise in equal measure. The most powerful of the twelve Viking deities, the Aesir, who lived at Asgard, he was also lord of the **Valkyries**, women warrior-servants who tended his needs while he held court at **Valhalla**, the hall of dead heroes. As with many of the other pagan gods, he had the power to change into any form he desired. Odin's wife, **Frigga**, was the goddess protecting the home and the family.

At the beginning of time, it was Odin who made heaven and earth from the body of the giant Ymir, and created man from an ash tree, woman from an alder. However, **Yggdrasil**, the tree of life that supported the whole universe, was beyond his control; the Vikings believed that eventually the tree would die and both gods and mortals would perish in the **Ragnarok**, the twilight of the gods. Among the Anglo-Saxons, the equivalent of Odin was Woden, hence the origin of the word "Wednesday".

Thor

One of Odin's sons, **Thor** appears to have been the most worshipped of the Norse gods. A giant with superhuman strength, he was the short-tempered god of thunder, fire and lightning. He regularly fought with the evil Frost Giants in the Jotunheim mountains (see p.179), his favourite weapon being the hammer, Mjolnir, which the trolls (see p.406) had fashioned for him. His chariot was drawn by two goats – Cracktooth and Gaptooth – who could be killed and eaten at night, but would be fully recovered the next morning, providing none of their bones was broken. It's from Thor that we get "Thursday".

Loki

A negative force, **Loki** personified cunning and trickery. His treachery turned the other deities against him, and he was chained up beneath a serpent that dripped venom onto his face. His wife, **Sigyn**, remained loyal and held a bowl over his head to catch the venom, but when the bowl was full she had to turn away to empty it, and in those moments his squirmings would cause earthquakes.

Frey

The god of fertility, **Frey**'s pride and joy was Skidbladnir, a ship that was large enough to carry all the gods, but could still be folded up and put into his bag. He often lived with the elves (see p.406) in Elfheim.

Freya

Freya was the goddess of love, healing and fertility. "Friday" was named after her.

Hel

The goddess of the dead, **Hel** lived on brains and bone marrow. She presided over "Hel", where those who died of illness or old age went, living a miserable existence under the roots of Yggdrasil, the tree of life.

The Norns

Representing the past, the present and the future, the **Norns** were the three goddesses of fate, casting lots over the cradle of every new-born child.

Folk tales and legends

Norway's extensive oral folklore was first written down in the early nineteenth century, most famously by **Peter Christen Asbjørnsen** and **Jørgen Moe**, the first of whose compilations appeared to great popular acclaim in 1842. Despite all the nationalist kerfuffle regarding the Norwegianness of the tales, many of them were in fact far from unique to Norway. But while they shared many characteristics – and had the same roots – as folk tales across the whole of northern Europe, they were populated by stock characters who were recognizably Norwegian – the king, for example, was always pictured as a wealthy Norwegian farmer.

There are three types of Norwegian **folk tale**: comical tales; animal yarns, in which the beasts concerned – most frequently the wolf, fox and bear – talk and behave like human beings; and most common of all, magical stories populated by a host of supernatural creatures. The folk tale is always written matter-of-factly, no matter how fantastic the events it retells. In this respect it has much in common with the **folk legend**, though the latter purports to be factual.

Norwegian legends "explain" scores of unusual natural phenomena – the location of boulders, holes in cliffs etc – and are crammed with supernatural beings, again as is broadly familiar right across northern Europe.

The assorted **supernatural creatures** of folk tale and legend hark back to the pagan myths of the pre-Christian era, but whereas the Vikings held them of secondary importance to their gods, in Norwegian folk tales they take centre stage. In post-Christian Norwegian folk tradition, these creatures were regarded as the descendants of children that Eve hid from God. When they were discovered by him, they were assigned particular realms in which to dwell, but their illicit wanderings were legion. Towards the end of the nineteenth century, book illustrations by **Erik Werenskiold** and **Theodor Kittelsen** effectively defined what the various supernatural creatures looked like in the Norwegian public's imagination.

As mythologized in Norway, the creatures of the folk tales possess a confusing range of virtues and vices. Here's a brief guide to some of the more important.

Giants

Enormous in size and strength, the **giants** of Norwegian folklore were reputed to be rather stupid and capable both of kindly actions and great cruelty towards humans. They usually had a human appearance, but some were monsters with many heads. They were fond of carrying parts of the landscape from one place to another, dropping boulders and even islands as they went. According to the Eddic cosmogony, the first giant, Ymir, was killed by Odin and the world made from his body – his blood formed the sea, his bones the mountains and so on. Ymir was the ancestor of the evil Frost Giants, who lived in Jotunheim, and who regularly fought with Thor.

Trolls

Spirits of the underground, **trolls** were ambivalent figures, able both to hinder and help humans – and were arguably a folkloric expression of the id. The first trolls were depicted as giants, but later versions were small, strong, misshapen and of pale countenance from living underground; sunlight would turn them into stone. They worked in metals and wood and were fabulous craftsmen. They made Odin's spear and Thor's hammer, though Thor's inclination to throw the weapon at them made them hate noise; as late as the eighteenth century, Norwegian villagers would ring church bells for hours on end to drive them away. If the trolls were forced to make something for a human, they would put a secret curse on it; this would render it dangerous to the owner. Some trolls had a penchant for stealing children and others carried off women to be their wives.

Elves

Akin to fairies, **elves** were usually divided between good-hearted but mischievous white elves, and nasty black elves, who brought injury and sickness. Both lived underground in a world, Elfheim, that echoed that of humans – with farms, animals and the like – but made excursions into the glades and groves of the forests up above. At night, the white elves liked singing and dancing to the accompaniment of the harp. They were normally invisible, though you could spot their dancing places wherever the grass grew more luxuriantly in circular patterns than elsewhere. The black elves were also invisible, a good job considering they were extremely ugly and had long, filthy noses. If struck by a sunbeam, they would turn to stone. Both types of elf were prone to entice humans into their kingdom, usually for a short period – but sometimes forever.

Wights

In pre-Christian times, the Vikings believed their lands to be populated with invisible guardian spirits, the **wights** (*vetter*), who needed to be treated with respect. One result was that when a longship was approaching the shore, the fearsome figurehead at its prow was removed so as not to frighten the *vetter* away. Bad luck would follow if a *vetter* left the locality.

Draugen

Personifying all those who have died at sea, the **draugen** was a ghostly apparition who appeared as a headless fisherman in oilskins. He sailed the seas in half a boat and wailed when someone was about to drown. Other water spirits included the malicious river sprite, the **nixie**, who could assume different forms to lure the unsuspecting to a watery grave. There were also the shy and benign **mermaids** and **mermen**, half-fish and half-human, who dived into the water whenever they spied a human. However, they also liked to dress up as humans to go to market.

Witches

As with **witches** across the rest of Europe, the Scandinavian version was an old woman who had made a pact with the Devil, swapping her soul in return for special powers. The witch could inflict injury and illness, especially if she had something that the victim had touched or owned – anything from a lock of hair to an item of clothing. She could disguise herself as an animal, and had familiars – usually insects or cats – which assisted her in foul deeds. Most witches travelled through the air on broomsticks, but some rode on wolves bridled with snakes.

Viking customs and rituals

The **Vikings** have long been the subject of historical myth and legend, but accurate and unbiased contemporary accounts are few and far between. A remarkable exception is the annals of **Ibn Fadlan**, a member of a diplomatic delegation sent from the Baghdad Caliphate to Bulgar on the Volga in 921–2AD. In the following extracts Fadlan details the habits and rituals of a tribe of Swedish Vikings, the **Rus**, who dealt in furs and slaves. The first piece notes with disgust the finer points of Viking personal hygiene, the second provides a sober eyewitness account of the rituals of a Viking ship burial.

Habits and rituals

I saw the **Rus** when they arrived on their trading mission and anchored at the River Atul (Volga). Never had I seen people of more perfect physique; they are tall as date-palms, and reddish in colour. They wear neither mantle nor coat, but each man carries a cape, which covers one half of his body, leaving one hand free. Their swords are Frankish in pattern, broad, flat and fluted. Each man has (tattooed upon him) trees, figures and the like from the finger-nails to the neck. Each woman carries on her bosom a container made of iron, silver, copper or gold – its size and substance depending on her man's wealth. Attached to the container is a ring carrying her knife, which is also tied to her bosom. Round her neck she wears gold or silver rings; when a man amasses 10,000 *dirhems* he makes his wife one gold ring; when he has 20,000 he makes two; and so the woman gets a new ring for every 10,000 *dirhems* her husband acquires, and often a woman has many of these rings. Their finest ornaments are green beads made from clay. They will go to any length to get hold of these; for one *dirhem* they procure one such bead and they string these into necklaces for their women.

They are the filthiest of god's creatures. They do not wash after discharging their natural functions, neither do they wash their hands after meals. They are as stray donkeys. They arrive from their distant lands and lay their ships alongside the banks of the Atul, which is a great river, and there they build big wooden houses on its shores. Ten or twenty of them may live together in one house, and each of them has a couch of his own where he sits and diverts himself with the pretty slave-girls whom he has brought along to offer for sale. He will make love with one of them in the presence of his comrades, sometimes this develops into a communal orgy and, if a customer should turn up to buy a girl, the Rus will not let her go till he has finished with her.

Every day they wash their faces and heads, all using the same water which is as filthy as can be imagined. This is how it is done. Every morning a girl brings her master a large bowl of water in which he washes his face and hands and hair, combing it also over the bowl, then blows his nose and spits into the water. No dirt is left on him which doesn't go into the water. When he has finished the girl takes the same bowl to his neighbour – who repeats the performance – until the bowl has gone round the entire household. All have blown their noses, spat and washed their faces and hair in the water.

On anchoring their vessels, each man goes ashore carrying bread, meat, onions, milk, and *nabid* [probably a kind of beer], and these he takes to a large wooden stake with a face like that of a human being, surrounded by smaller figures, and behind them tall poles in the ground. Each man prostrates himself before the large post and recites: "O Lord, I have come from distant parts with so many girls, so many furs (and whatever other commodities he is carrying). I now bring you this offering." He then presents his gift and continues "Please send me a merchant who has many dinars and *dirhems*, and who will trade favourably with me without too much bartering." Then he retires. If, after this, business does not pick up quickly and go well, he returns to the statue to present further gifts. If results continue slow, he then presents gifts to the minor figures and begs their intercession, saying, "These are our Lord's wives, daughters and sons." Then he pleads before each figure in turn, begging them to intercede for him and humbling himself before them. Often trade picks up, and he says "My Lord has required my needs, and now it is my duty to repay him". Whereupon he sacrifices goats or cattle, some of which he distributes as alms. The rest he lays before the statues, large and small, and the heads of the beasts he plants upon the poles. After dark, of course, the dogs come and devour the lot – and the successful trader says, "My Lord is pleased with me, and has eaten my offerings."

If one of the Rus falls sick they put him in a tent by himself and leave bread and water for him. They do not visit him, however, or speak to him, especially if he is a serf. Should he recover he rejoins the others; if he dies they burn him. If he happens to be a serf, however, they leave him for the dogs and vultures to devour. If they catch a robber they hang him in a tree until he is torn to shreds by wind and weather…

The burial

…I had been told that when their chieftains died cremation was the least part of their whole **funeral procedure**, and I was, therefore, very much interested to find out more about this. One day I heard that one of their leaders had died. They laid him forthwith in a grave, which they covered up for ten days till they had finished cutting-out and sewing his costume. If the dead man is poor they make a little ship, put him in it, and burn it. If he is wealthy, however, they divide his property and goods into three parts: one for his family, one to pay for his costume, and one to make *nabid*. This they drink on the day when the slave woman of the dead man is killed and burnt together with her master. They are deeply addicted to *nabid*, drinking it day and night; and often one of them has been found dead with a beaker in his hand. When a chieftain among them has died, his family demands of his slave women and servants: "Which of you wishes to die with him?" Then one of them says "I do" – and having said that the person concerned is forced to do so, and no backing out is possible. Those who are willing are mostly the slave women.

So when this man died they said to his slave women "Which of you wants to die with him?" One of them answered "I do." From that moment she was put in the constant care of two other women servants who took care of her to the extent of washing her feet with their own hands. They began to get things ready for the dead man, to cut his costume and so on, while every day the doomed woman drank and sang as though in anticipation of a joyous event.

When the day arrived on which the chieftain and his slave woman were going to be burnt, I went to the river where his ship was moored. It had been hauled ashore and four posts were made for it of birch and other wood. Further there was arranged around it what looked like a big store of wood. Then the ship was hauled near and placed on the wood. People now began to walk about talking in a language I could not understand, and the corpse still lay in the grave; they had not taken it out. They then produced a wooden bench, placed it on the ship, and covered it with carpets of Byzantine *dibag* (painted silk) and with cushions of Byzantine *dibag*. Then came an old woman whom they called "the Angel of Death", and she spread these cushions out over the bench. She was in charge of the whole affair from dressing the corpse to the killing of the slave woman. I noticed that she was an old giant-woman, a massive and grim figure. When they came to his grave they removed the earth from the wooden frame and they also took the frame away. They then divested the corpse of the clothes in which he had died. The body, I noticed, had turned black because of the intense frost. When they first put him in the grave, they had also given him beer, fruit, and a lute, all of which they now removed. Strangely enough the corpse did not smell, nor had anything about him changed save the colour of his flesh. They now proceeded to dress him in hose, and trousers, boots, coat, and a mantle of *dibag* adorned with gold buttons; put on his head a cap of *dibag* and sable fur; and carried him to the tent on the ship, where they put him on the blanket and supported him with cushions. They then produced *nabid*, fruit, and aromatic plants, and put these round his body; and they also brought bread, meat, and onions which they flung before him. Next they took a dog, cut it in half, and flung the pieces into the ship, and after this they took all his weapons and placed them beside him.

Next they brought two horses and ran them about until they were in a sweat, after which they cut them to pieces with swords and flung their meat into the ship; this also happened to two cows. Then they produced a cock and a hen, killed them, and threw them in. Meanwhile the slave woman who wished to be killed walked up and down, going into one tent after the other, and the owner of each tent had sexual intercourse with her, saying "Tell your master I did this out of love for him."

It was now Friday afternoon and they took the slave woman away to something which they had made resembling a doorframe. Then she placed her legs on the palms of the men and reached high enough to look over the frame, and she said something in a foreign language, after which they took her down. And they lifted her agaïn and she did the same as the first time. Then they took her down and lifted her a third time and she did the same as the first and second times. Then they gave her a chicken and she cut its head off and threw it away; they took the hen and threw it into the ship. Then I asked the interpreter what she had done. He answered: "The first time they lifted her she said: "Look! I see my mother and father." The second time she said: "Look! I see all my dead relatives sitting around." The third time she said: "Look! I see my master in Paradise, and Paradise is beautiful and green and together with him are men and young boys. He calls me. Let me join him then!"

They now led her towards the ship. Then she took off two bracelets she was wearing and gave them to the old woman, "the Angel of Death", the one who was going to kill her. She next took off two anklets she was wearing and gave them to the daughters of that same woman. They then led her to the ship but did not allow her inside the tent. Then a number of men carrying wooden shield and sticks arrived, and gave her a beaker with *nabid*. She sang over it and emptied it. The interpreter then said to me, "Now with that she is bidding farewell to all her women friends." Then she was given another beaker. She took it and sang a lengthy song; but the old woman told her to hurry and drink up and enter the tent where her master was. When I looked at her she seemed completely bewildered. She wanted to enter the tent and she put her head between it and the ship. Then the woman took her head and managed to get it inside the tent, and the woman herself followed. Then the men began to beat the shields with the wooden sticks, to deaden her shouts so that the other girls would not become afraid and shrink from dying with their masters. Six men entered the tent and all of them had intercourse with her. Thereafter they laid her by the side of her dead master. Two held her hands and two her feet, and the woman called "the Angel of Death" put a cord round the girl's neck, doubled with an end at each side, and gave it to two men to pull. Then she advanced holding a small dagger with a broad blade and began to plunge it between the girl's ribs to and fro while the two men choked her with the cord till she died.

The dead man's nearest kinsman now appeared. He took a piece of wood and ignited it. Then he walked backwards, his back towards the ship and his face towards the crowd, holding the piece of wood in one hand and the other hand on his buttock; and he was naked. In this way the wood was ignited which they had placed under the ship after they had laid the slave woman, whom they had killed, beside her master. Then people came with branches and wood; each brought a burning brand and threw it on the pyre, so that the fire took hold of the wood, then the ship, then the tent and the man and the slave woman and all. Thereafter a strong and terrible wind rose so that the flame stirred and the fire blazed still more.

I heard one of the Rus folk, standing by, say something to my interpreter, and when I inquired what he had said, my interpreter answered: "He said: 'You Arabs are foolish'." "Why?" I asked. "Well, because you throw those you love and honour to the ground where the earth and the maggots and fields devour them, whereas we, on the other hand, burn them up quickly and they go to Paradise that very moment." The man burst out laughing, and on being asked why, he said: "His Lord, out of love for him, has sent this wind to take him away within the hour!" And so it proved, for within that time the ship and the pyre, the girl and the corpse had all become ashes and then dust. On the spot where the ship stood after having been hauled ashore, they built something like a round mould. In the middle of it they raised a large post of birch-wood on which they wrote the names of the dead man and the king of the Rus, and then the crowd dispersed.

Flora and fauna

There are significant differences in **climate** between the west coast of Norway, which is warmed by the Gulf Stream, and the interior, but these variations are of much less significance for the country's **flora** than altitude and latitude. With regard to its **fauna**, wild animals survive in significant numbers in the more inaccessible regions, but have been hunted extensively elsewhere, and Norway's west coast is home to dozens of enormous seabird colonies.

Flora

Much of the Norwegian landscape is dominated by vast **forests of spruce**, though these are, in fact, a relatively recent feature: the original forest cover was mainly of pine, birch and oak, and only in the last two thousand years has spruce spread across the whole of southeast and central Norway. That said, a rich variety of **deciduous trees** – notably oak, ash, lime, hazel, rowan, elm and maple – still flourishes in a wide belt along the south coast, up through the fjord country and as far north as Trondheim, but only at relatively low altitudes. For their part, **conifers** thin out at around 900m above sea level in the south, 450m in Finnmark, to be replaced by a birch zone where there are also aspen and mountain ash. Norway's deciduous trees contrive to ripen their seeds despite a short, cool summer, and can consequently be found at low altitudes almost as far north as Nordkapp (North Cape) – as can the pine, the most robust of the conifers. At around 1100m/650m, the birch fizzle out to be replaced by willow and dwarf birch, while above the timber line are bare mountain peaks and huge plateaux, the latter usually dotted with hundreds of lakes.

Norway accommodates in the region of 2000 plant species, but few of them are native. The most sought-after are the **berrying** species that grow wild all over Norway, mainly cranberries, blueberries and yellow **cloudberries**. Common in the country's peat bogs, and now also extensively cultivated, the cloudberry is a small herbaceous bramble whose fruits have a tangy flavour that is much prized in Norway. In drier situations and on the mountain plateaux, **lichens** – the favourite food of the reindeer – predominate, while in all but the thickest of spruce forests, the ground is thickly carpeted with **mosses** and **heathers**.

Everywhere, spring brings **wild flowers**, splashes of brilliant colour at their most intense on the west coast where a wide range of mountain plants is nourished by the wet conditions and a geology that varies from limestone to acidic granites. Most of these species can also be found in the Alps, but there are several rarities, notably the **alpine clematis** (*Clematis alpina*) found in the Gudbrandsdal valley, hundreds of miles from its normal homes in eastern Finland and the Carpathian Mountains. Another, larger group comprises about thirty **Canadian mountain plants**, found in Europe only in the Dovre and Jotunheim mountains; quite how they come to be there has long baffled botanists.

The mildness of the west-coast winter has allowed certain species to prosper beyond their usual northerly latitudes. Among species that can tolerate very little frost or snow are the star hyacinth (*Scilla verna*) and the purple heather

(*Erica purpurea*), while a short distance inland come varieties that can withstand only short icy spells, including the foxglove (*Digitalis purpurea*) and the holly (*Ilex aquifolium*). In the southeastern part of the country, where the winters are harder and the summers hotter, the conditions support species that can lie dormant under the snow for several months a year – for example the blue anemone (*Anemone hepatica*) and the aconite (*Aconitum septentrionale*).

In the far north, certain Siberian species have migrated west down the rivers and along the coasts to the fjords of Finnmark and Troms. The most significant is the **Siberian garlic** (*Allium sibiricum*), which grows in such abundance that farmers have to make sure their cows don't eat too much of it or else the milk becomes garlic-flavoured. Other Siberian species to look out for are the fringed pink (*Dianthus superbus*) and a large, lily-like plant, the sneezewort (*Veratrum album*).

Fauna

The larger Arctic **predators** of Norway, principally the lynx, wolf, wolverine and bear, are virtually extinct, and where they have survived they are mainly confined to the more inaccessible regions of the north. To a degree this has been caused by the timber industry, which has logged out great chunks of forest. The smaller predators – the fox, the arctic fox, the otter, the badger and the marten – have fared rather better and remain comparatively common.

In the 1930s, the **beaver** had been reduced to just 500 animals in southern Norway. A total ban on hunting has, however, led to a dramatic increase in their numbers, and the beaver has begun to recolonize its old hunting grounds right across Scandinavia. The elk has benefited from the rolling back of the forests, grazing the newly treeless areas and breeding in sufficient numbers to allow an annual cull of around 40,000 animals; the red deer of the west coast are flourishing too. Otherwise, the Norwegians own about two million sheep and around 200,000 domesticated **reindeer**, most of whom are herded by the Sami. The last wild reindeer in Europe, some 15,000 beasts, wander the Hardangervidda and its adjacent mountain areas.

Among Norway's rodents, the most interesting is the **lemming**, whose numbers vary over a four-year cycle. In the first three to four years there is a gradual increase, which is followed, in the course of a few months, by a sudden fall. The cause of these variations is not known, though theories are plentiful. In addition to this four-year fluctuation, the lemming population goes through a violent explosion every eleven to twelve years. Competition for food is so ferocious that many animals start to range over wide areas. In these so-called lemming years the mountains and surrounding areas teem with countless thousands of lemmings, and hundreds swarm to their deaths by falling off cliff edges and the like. In lemming years, predators and birds of prey have an abundant source of food and frequently give birth to twice as many young as normal – not surprising considering the lemmings are extremely easy to catch. More inexplicably, the snowy owl leaves its polar habitat in lemming years, flying south to join in the feast: quite how they know when to turn up is a mystery. The Vikings were particularly fascinated by lemmings, believing that they dropped from the sky during thunderstorms.

With the exception of the raven, the partridge and the grouse, all the **mountain birds** of Norway are **migratory**, reflecting the harshness of winter conditions. Most fly back and forth from the Mediterranean and Africa, but some winter down on the coast. **Woodland** species include the wood grouse, the black grouse, several different sorts of owl, woodpeckers and birds of prey, while the country's **lakes and marshes** are inhabited by cranes, swans, grebes, geese, ducks and many types of wader. Most dramatic of all are the coastal nesting cliffs, where millions of **seabirds**, such as kittiwakes, guillemots, puffins, cormorants and gulls, congregate. What you won't see is the great auk, a flightless, 50cm-high bird resembling a penguin that once nested in its millions along the Atlantic seaboard but is now extinct: the last Norwegian great auk was killed in the eighteenth century and the last one of all was shot near Iceland a century later.

The waters off Norway once teemed with **seals** and **whales**, but indiscriminate hunting has drastically reduced their numbers, prompting several late-in-the-day conservation measures. The commonest species of **fish** – cod, haddock, coalfish and halibut – have been overexploited too, and whereas there were once gigantic shoals of them right along the coast up to the Arctic Sea, they are now much less common. The cod, like several other species, live far out in the Barents Sea, only coming to the coast to spawn, a favourite destination being the waters round the Lofoten islands.

The only fish along Norway's coast that can survive in both salt and fresh water is the **salmon**, which grows to maturity in the sea and only swims up-river to spawn and die. In the following spring the young salmon return to the sea on the spring flood. Trout and char populate the rivers and lakes of western Norway, living on a diet of crustacea, which tints their meat pink, like the salmon. Eastern Norway and Finnmark are the domain of **whitefish**, so called because they feed on plant remains, insects and animals, which keep their flesh white. In prehistoric times, these species migrated here from the east via what was then the freshwater Baltic; the most important of them are the perch, powan, pike and grayling.

Cinema

Often overshadowed by its Nordic neighbours, **Norwegian cinema** has long struggled to make an impact on the international scene. In the last decade or so, however, a group of talented young film makers has emerged, who are responsible for a string of stylish, honest and refreshingly lucid films. Norway in general and northern Norway in particular has also developed a niche as a film location, most famously as the ice planet Hoth at the start of George Lucas' *The Empire Strikes Back* (1980).

Early Norwegian cinematic successes were few and far between, an exception being *Kon-Tiki*, a 1951 Oscar-winning documentary recording Thor Heyerdahl's journey across the Pacific on a balsa raft (see p.107), though the producer (and Oscar recipient) was a Swede, Olle Nordemar. In 1957, *Nine Lives* (*Ni Liv*), produced and directed by the Norwegian **Arne Skouen**, was widely acclaimed for its tale of a betrayed Resistance fighter, who managed to drag himself across northern Norway in winter to safety in neutral Sweden. Two years later **Erik Løchen**'s *The Hunt* (*Jakten*) was much influenced by the French New Wave in its mixture of time and space, dream and reality, as was the early work of **Anja Breien**, whose *Growing Up* (*Jostedalsrypa*) relates the story of a young girl who is the sole survivor from the Black Death in a remote fjordland village. Breien followed this up in 1975 with a successful improvised comedy *Wives* (*Hustruer*), in which three former classmates meet at a school reunion and subsequently share their life experiences. Breien developed this into a trilogy with *Wives Ten Years Later* (*Hustruer ti år efter*) in 1985 and *Wives III* in 1996. She also garnered critical success at Cannes with *Next of Kin* (*Arven*; 1979), and won prizes at the Venice film festival with *Witch Hunt* (*Forfølgelsen*; 1982), an exploration of the persecution of women in the Middle Ages.

Liv Ullmann (b. 1939) is easily the most famous Norwegian actor, but in Scandinavia she has worked mostly with Swedish and Danish producers and directors, most notably Ingmar Bergman (with whom she also had a daughter). In 1995, Ullmann brought the popular Norwegian writer Sigrid Undset's medieval epic *Kristin Lavransdatter* to the screen in a three-hour film that attracted mixed reviews. Another Norwegian writer to have had his work made into films is Knut Hamsun (see p.307 & p.424): in 1966, the Dane Henning Carlson filmed Hamsun's *Hunger* (*Sult*), and in the mid-1990s, the Swedish director Jan Troell filmed the superb biographical *Trial against Hamsun* (*Prosessen mot Hamsun*). In 1993, Oslo's **Erik Gustavson** directed *The Telegraphist* (*Telegrafisten*), based on a Hamsun story, and its success landed him the task of bringing Jostein Gaarder's extraordinarily popular novel *Sophie's World* (*Sofies Verden*; 1999) to the screen.

Nils Gaup is widely regarded as one of the most talented of Norway's current film directors. His debut film *The Pathfinder* (*Veiviseren*; 1987), an epic adventure based on a medieval Sami legend, was widely acclaimed both in Norway and abroad, not least because the dialogue was in the Sami language. Gaup followed it up with a nautical adventure, *Shipwrecked* (*Håkon Håkonsen*; 1990), and then a thriller *Head Above Water (Hodet over vannet;* 1993), which had a pretty woeful Hollywood remake starring Cameron Diaz and Harvey Keitel. Amongst other Norwegian successes in the 1990s was **Pål Sletaune**'s *Junk Mail (Budbringeren*; 1997), a darkly humorous tale of an Oslo postman who opens the mail himself, and **Erik Skjoldbjaerg**'s *Insomnia* (1997), a film noir set in the permanent summer daylight of northern Norway. Stylish and compelling, it impressed Hollywood so much that it was remade in 2002 starring Al Pacino: inevitably, though, the newer version was a big glossy film, which lacked the grittiness of the original.

Much praised, too, are **Berit Nesheim**'s *The Other Side of Sunday* (*Søndagsengler*, 1996), the story of a vicar's daughter desperate to escape from her father's oppressive control, and **Eva Isaksen**'s *Death at Oslo Central* (*Døden på Oslo S*; 1990), a moving story of drug abuse and family conflict amongst the capital's young down-and-outs. There was also Knut Erik Jensen's surprise hit, *Cool and Crazy* (*Heftig og Begeistret*; 2001), a gentle, lyrical documentary about the male voice choir of Berlevåg (see p.372), a remote community in the far north of the country. Much to Jensen's surprise, his film was picked up abroad and became a major hit on the art-house cinema circuit. Similarly successful, though in a very different cinematic vein, was **Peter Næss's** *Elling* (2001), a sort of tragic-comedy that relates the heart-warming/rending story of Elling, a fastidious and obsessive ex-mental patient who moves into an Oslo flat with one of the other former patients – an odd coupling if ever there was one. Equally idiosyncratic was **Bent Hamer**'s *Kitchen Stories* (*Salmer fra kjøkkenet*; 2003), a comic tale in which a tester for a Swedish kitchen design company is dispatched to Norway to study the culinary goings-on of Isak, a farmer who lives a solitary life deep in the countryside. The two become friends, but it's a bumpy business with each having to dispense with his prejudices against the other's country.

Books

Precious few travellers have written in English about the joys of journeying around Norway, though you might always dig out a copy of a vintage *Baedeker's Norway and Sweden*, if only for the phrasebook, from which you can learn such gems as the Norwegian for "Do you want to cheat me?", "When does the washerwoman come?" and "We must rope ourselves together to cross this glacier." Neither has Norwegian history been a major preoccupation – with the notable exception of the **Vikings**, who have attracted the attention of a veritable raft of historians and translators, whose works have focused on the surviving **Sagas**, a rich body of work mostly written in Iceland between the twelfth and fourteenth centuries. Scandinavian fiction is, however, an entirely different matter, with a flood of translations appearing on the market, a charge that has been led by the immaculate crime novels of the Swede Henning Mankell with the Norwegians following in Mankell's slipstream.

Of the **publishers**, the UK's **Norvik Press**, based at the University of East Anglia, in Norwich (@www.llt.uea.ac.uk/norvik_press), maintains an excellent back catalogue of classic Scandinavian novels and plays as well as a selection of authoritative texts on Scandinavian literary criticism. In the US, **Dufour Editions** (@www.dufoureditions.com) is strong on Scandinavia too and also recommendable is the UK's **Peter Owen** (@www.peterowen.com), an independent publishing company that produces fine new translations of modern Scandinavian novels.

Most of the books listed below are **in print and in paperback**, and those that are **out of print** (o/p) should be easy to track down either in second-hand bookshops or through Amazon's used and second-hand book service (@www.amazon.co.uk or @www.amazon.com). Note also that while we recommend all the books we've listed below, we do have favourites – and these have been marked with 🏃.

Travel and general

Anthony Dyer *Walks and Scrambles in Norway*. English-language books on Norway's hiking trails are thin on the ground. This one describes over fifty hikes and scrambles from one end of the country to the other, though the majority are in the western fjords (as in our Chapter 4). Lots of photographs and the text is detailed and thoroughly researched although the maps are only general and you'll need to buy specialist hiking ones.

Christer Elfving & Petra de Hamer *New Scandinavian Cooking*. A cook's tour through Scandinavia's capital cities mixing history, culinary trends and tips on the hottest chefs and restaurants with delicious modern recipes.

Ranulph Fiennes *Ice Fall in Norway*. A jaunt on the Jostedalsbreen glacier with Fiennes and his pals in 1970, long before he got famous. A quick and enjoyable read, though the occasional sexist comment may make you wince.

Thor Heyerdahl *The Kon-Tiki Expedition*. You may want to read this after visiting Oslo's Kon-Tiki Museum (p.107). Heyerdahl's account of the Kon-Tiki expedition aroused huge interest when it was first published, and it remains a ripping yarn – though surprisingly few people care to read it today. Heyerdahl's further exploits are related in *The Ra Expeditions* and *The Tigris Expedition*.

Roland Huntford *The Last Place on Earth*. There are dozens of books on the polar explorers Scott, Amundsen and Nansen, but this is one of the more recent, describing with flair and panache the race to the South Pole between Scott and Amundsen. Also worth a read is the same author's *Nansen*, a doorstep-sized biography of the noble explorer, academic and statesman Fridtjof Nansen.

Lucy Jago *The Northern Lights: The True Story of the Man who unlocked the Secrets of the Aurora Borealis*. Intriguing biography of Kristian Birkeland, who spent years ferreting around northern Norway bent on understanding the northern lights – a quest for which he paid a heavy personal price.

Mark Kurlansky *Cod: A Biography of the Fish that Changed the World*. This wonderful book tracks the life and times of the cod and the generations of fishermen who have lived off it. There are sections on overfishing and the fish's breeding habits, and recipes are provided too. Norwegians figure frequently – after all, cod was the staple diet of much of the country for centuries.

Sven Lindqvist *Bench Press*. Delightful little book delving into the nature of weight training – and the Swedish/Scandinavian attitude to it. Wry and perceptive cultural commentary.

Alison Raju *The Pilgrim Road to Nidaros* (o/p). The old medieval pilgrims' route from Oslo to Trondheim cathedral has recently been waymarked, and this unusual and exactingly researched book explores its every nook and cranny. Lots of helpful practical information as well as brief descriptions of every significant sight.

Ben Nimmo *In Forkbeard's Wake: Coasting Around Scandinavia*. Light and lively account of the author's sailing trip around Scandinavia, brimming with sailing mishaps and encounters with Nordic types – divers, fishermen, archeologists and a drunk Swedish dentist. An all too rare modern travel book on the region.

Christoph Ransmayr *The Terrors of Ice and Darkness*. Clever mingling of fact and fiction as the book's main character follows the route of the doomed Austro-Hungarian Arctic expedition in 1873. A story of obsession and, ultimately, insanity.

Constance Roos *Walking in Norway*. This informative guide outlines hiking routes in almost every part of Norway, with useful sections on conditions in the mountains and equipment; the descriptions of some of the hiking routes do, however, lack detail.

Roger Took *Running with Reindeer*. A thoughtful account of Took's extended visit to – and explorations of – Russia's Kola Peninsula in the 1990s, with much to say about the Sami and their current predicaments.

Paul Watkins *The Fellowship of Ghosts*. Modern-day musings as Watkins travels through the mountains and fjords of southern Norway. Easy reading, but sometimes overwritten, and if that doesn't get you the barrage of jokes probably will. There again, to be fair, there are lots of useful bits and pieces about Norway and its people.

Mary Wollstonecraft *Letters written during a Short Residence in Sweden, Norway and Denmark*. For reasons that have never been entirely clear, Wollstonecraft, the author of *A*

Vindication of the Rights of Women, and mother of Mary Shelley, travelled Scandinavia for several months in 1795. Her letters home represent a real historical curiosity, though her trenchant comments on Norway often get sidelined by her intense melancholia.

General history

Jack Adams *The Doomed Expedition.* Thorough and well-researched account of the 1940 Allied campaign in Norway in all its incompetent detail.

Martin Conway *No Man's Land* (o/p). Superb and vastly entertaining account of the history of Spitsbergen (Svalbard) from 1596 to modern times. Full of intriguing detail, such as Admiral Nelson's near-death experience (aged 14), when he set out on the ice at night to kill a polar bear. Published in Oslo, it's hard to get hold of outside of Norway.

Fredrik Dahl *Quisling: A Study in Treachery.* A comprehensive biography of the world's most famous traitor, Vidkun Quisling – the man presented in all his unpleasant fullness. Published in hardback only – by Cambridge University Press.

Rolf Danielsen (et al) *Norway: A History from the Vikings to Our Own Times.* Thoughtful and well-presented account investigating the social and economic development of Norway – a modern and well-judged book that avoids the "kings and queens" approach to its subject.

Tony Griffiths *Scandinavia: At War with Trolls – A Modern History from the Napoleonic Era to the Third Millennium.* Engaging title for an engaging, well-written and well-researched book covering its subject in a very manageable 320 pages. First published in 2004.

Thomas Kingston Derry *A History of Scandinavia* (o/p). This is a scholarly history of Scandinavia, including Iceland and Finland as part of its remit – a thorough account of the region from prehistoric times onwards. It's rather better as a reference source than as a read, however, and having been originally published in 1980, parts are out of date.

Knut Helle et al *The Cambridge History of Scandinavia.* Comprehensive history, from the Stone Age onwards, in three whopping (and expensive) volumes. No stone is left unturned, no rune unread. Published in 2003.

David Howarth *Shetland Bus.* Entertaining and fascinating in equal measure, this excellent book, written by one of the British naval officers involved, details the clandestine wartime missions that shuttled between the Shetlands and occupied Norway.

Chris Mann *Hitler's Arctic War.* A recent account of the war that raged across the Arctic wastes of Norway, Finland and the USSR from 1940–45, both on sea and land.

Alan Palmer *Bernadotte.* Biography of Napoleon's marshal, later King Karl Johan of Norway and Sweden, a fascinating if enigmatic figure whom this lively and comprehensive book presents to good effect.

Geoffrey Parker *The Thirty Years' War.* First published in the 1980s, this book provides the authoritative account of the pan-European war that so deeply affected Scandinavia in general. and Sweden in particular. Superbly written and researched.

Kathleen Stokker *Folklore Fights the Nazis: Humor in Occupied Norway 1940–1945*. A book that can't help but make you laugh, and one that also provides a real insight into Norwegian society and its subtle mores. The only problem is that Stokker adopts an encyclopedic approach, which means you have to plough through the poor jokes to get to the good ones. Published by the University of Wisconsin Press, it's rarely available in ordinary bookshops.

Raymond Strait *Queen of Ice, Queen of Shadows: The Unsuspected Life of Sonja Henie*. In-depth biography of the ice-skating gold medallist, film star and conspicuous consumer, whose art collection was bequeathed to the Oslo museum that bears her name (see p.107).

Eilert Sundt *Sexual Customs in Rural Norway: A Nineteenth-Century Study*. First published in 1857, the product of a research trip by a pioneer sociologist, this book doesn't have much sex, but does have lots about rural life – a hard existence if ever there was one. Interesting sections on diet, clothes and associated manners and mores. An Iowa State hardback, and expensive.

The Vikings, Norse mythology and folk tales

Peter Christen Asbjørnsen and Jørgen Moe *Norwegian Folk Tales*. Of all the many books on Norwegian folk tales, this is the edition you want – the illustrations by Erik Werenskiold and Theodor Kittelsen are superb. It's currently published by Pantheon.

Johannes Brøndsted *The Vikings* (o/p). Extremely readable account with fascinating sections on social and cultural life, art, religious beliefs and customs: see p.408 for an extract from this book.

H.R. Ellis Davidson *The Gods and Myths of Northern Europe*. A handy, first-rate companion to the sagas, this "who's who" of Norse mythology includes some useful reviews of the more obscure gods. Importantly, it also displaces the classical deities and their world as the most relevant mythological framework for Northern and Western Europeans.

Paddy Griffith *The Viking Art of War* (o/p). Published in 1998, this detailed text examines its chosen subject well. Excellently researched with considered if sometimes surprising conclusions.

John Haywood *The Penguin Historical Atlas of the Vikings*. Accessible and attractive sequence of maps charting the development and expansion of the Vikings as explorers, settlers, traders and mercenaries. Also the *Encyclopaedia of The Viking Age*, an easy-to-use who's who and what's what of the Viking era.

Gwyn Jones *Scandinavian Legends and Folk Tales*. The Oxford University Press commissioned this anthology, whose stories are drawn from every part of Scandinavia and cover many themes – from the heroic to the tragic – and are populated by a mixed crew of trolls, wolves, bears and princelings.

Gwyn Jones *A History of the Vikings*. Superbly crafted, erudite account of the Vikings, with excellent sections on every aspect of their history and culture. The same author wrote *Scandinavian Legends and Folk Tales*, an excellent and enjoyable analysis of its subject.

Donald Logan *The Vikings in History*. Scholarly – and radical – re-examination of the Vikings' impact on medieval Europe, indispensable for the Vikingophile.

Magnus Magnusson and Hermann Palsson (translators) *The Vinland Sagas: The Norse Discovery of America*. These two sagas tell of the Vikings' settlement of Greenland and of the "discovery" of North America in the tenth century. The introduction is a particularly interesting and acute analysis of these two colonial outposts. See also Snorri Sturluson (below).

Andrew Orchard *Cassell's Dictionary of Norse Myth and Legend*. Thorough guide to the complete cast of Scandinavian gods, trolls, heroes and monsters, complete with the social and historical background to the myths and coverage of topics such as burial rites, sacrificial practices and runes.

Else Roesdahl *The Vikings*. A clearly presented, 350-page exploration of Viking history and culture, including sections on art, burial customs, class divisions, jewellery, kingship, kinship and poetry. An excellent introduction to its subject.

Alexander Rumble (et al) *The Reign of Cnut*. Often overlooked, King Cnut (aka Canute) ruled a vast swathe of northern Europe – including England and Norway – at the beginning of the eleventh century. This academic book has several interesting chapters on aspects of his reign – for example military developments and his influence on the names of people and places in England.

Peter Sawyer *Kings and Vikings: Scandinavia and Europe AD 700–1100* (o/p). Traces the origins of Viking activity, assesses its effects on the rest of Europe and on Scandinavia itself, and follows the Vikings' gradual transformation from bands of pagan raiders into Christian farmers and merchants. Concise and to the point.

Peter Sawyer (ed) *The Oxford Illustrated History of the Vikings* (o/p). Published in 2001, this book brings together the latest historical research on the Vikings in a series of well-considered essays by leading experts. Includes sections on religion, shipbuilding and diet.

Jane Smiley et al *The Sagas of Icelanders*. Easy-to-read translations of all the main sagas – galloping tales of derring-do from medieval Iceland. The index makes it an excellent reference book too. Published by Penguin.

Snorri Sturluson *Egil's Saga, Laxdaela Saga, Njal's Saga, and King Harald's Saga*. These Icelandic sagas (for more on which, see p.403) were written in the early years of the thirteenth century, but relate tales of ninth- and tenth-century derring-do. There's clan warfare in the Laxdaela and Njal sagas, more bloodthirstiness in Egil's, and a bit more biography in King Harald's, penned to celebrate one of the last and most ferocious Viking chieftains – Harald Hardrada (see p.389). Amongst those who have worked on these English translations was the former UK TV celebrity Magnus Magnusson, who has long been a leading light in the effort to popularize the sagas: see also the *Vinland Sagas* and *The Sagas of Icelanders* above.

Architecture, film and the visual arts

Marie Bang *Johan Christian Dahl* (o/p). Authoritative and lavishly illustrated book on Norway's leading nineteenth-century landscape painter. From the Scandinavian University Press.

Ketil Bjørnstad *The Story of Edvard Munch*. Precise and detailed biography of the great artist that makes liberal use of Munch's own letters and diaries as well as contemporary newspapers and periodicals. A vivid tale indeed, just a shame that Munch isn't more likeable.

Einar Haugen and Camilla Cai *Ole Bull: Norway's Romantic Musician and Cosmopolitan Patriot* (o/p). A neglected figure, Ole Bull (see p.216), the nineteenth-century virtuoso violinist and utopian socialist, deserves a better historical fate. This biography attempts to rectify matters by delving into every facet of his life, but it's ponderously written and over-detailed. For Bull lovers only.

J.P. Hodin *Edvard Munch*. The best available general introduction to Munch's life and work, with much interesting historical detail. Beautifully illustrated, as you would expect from a Thames & Hudson publication.

Neil Kent *The Soul of the North: A Social, Architectural and Cultural History of the Nordic Countries 1770–1940*. Immaculately illustrated, erudite chronicle of Scandinavian art and architecture during its most influential periods. Highly recommended; another superb book from Thames & Hudson.

Robert Layton *Grieg*. Clear, concise and attractively illustrated book on Norway's greatest composer. Essential reading if you want to get to grips with the man and his times.

Marion Nelson (ed) *Norwegian Folk Art: The Migration of a Tradition*. Lavishly illustrated book discussing the whole range of folk art, from wood carvings through to bedspreads and traditional dress. It's particularly strong on the influence of Norwegian folk art in the US, but the text sometimes lacks focus. It's earth-shatteringly expensive too.

Sue Prideaux *Edvard Munch: Behind the Scream*. Not a classic biography perhaps, but a thorough and well-researched trawl through the life of a man who fulfilled most of the stereotypes of the alienated and tormented (drunken) artist.

Tytti Soila et al *Nordic National Cinemas* and the *Cinema of Scandinavia*. These two books are the best there is on Scandinavian cinema in general and Norwegian cinema in particular. Published in 1998, the first of the two has separate chapters on each of the Nordic countries and each chapter provides a chronological overview. The second book, published in 2005, adopts a more cinematic approach with 24 extended essays on key Scandinavian films – and an intriguing bunch they are too.

Literature and literary biography

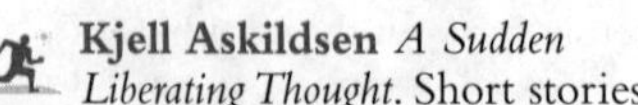

Kjell Askildsen *A Sudden Liberating Thought*. Short stories, in the Kafkaesque tradition, from one of Norway's most uncompromisingly

△ Ibsen

modernist writers: see p.437 for the title story.

Jens Bjørneboe *The Sharks*. Set at the end of the last century, this is a thrilling tale of shipwreck and mutiny by a well-known Norwegian writer, who had an enviable reputation for challenging authoritarianism of any description. Also recommended is his darker trilogy – *Moment of Freedom*, *The Powderhouse* and *The Silence* – exploring the nature of cruelty and injustice.

Johan Bojer *The Emigrants*. One of the leading Norwegian novelists of his day, Bojer (1872–1959) wrote extensively about the hardships of rural life. *The Emigrants*, perhaps his most finely crafted work, deals with a group of young Norwegians who emigrate to North Dakota in the 1880s – and the difficulties they experience. In Norway, Bojer is better known for *Last of the Vikings* (o/p), a heart-rending tale of fishermen from the tiny village of Rissa in Nordland, who are forced to row out to the Lofoten winter fishery no matter what the conditions to stop from starving. It was first published in 1921.

Lars Saabye Christensen *Herman*. Christensen made a real literary splash with *The Half Brother*, an intense tale focused on four generations of an Oslo family in the years following World War II, the narrator being Barnum, a midget, alcoholic screenplay writer. It is, however, a real doorstopper of a book and before you embark on such a long read you might want to sample Christensen's *Herman*, a lighter (and much shorter) tale of adolescence with an Oslo backdrop.

Camilla Collett *The District Governor's Daughters*. Published in 1854, this heartfelt demand for the emotional and intellectual emancipation of women is set within a bourgeois Norwegian milieu. The central character, Sophie, struggles against her conditioning and the expectations of those around her. An important early feminist novel published by the enterprising Norvik Press (see p.417).

Per Olov Enquist *The Visit of the Royal Physician*. Wonderfully entertaining and beautifully written novel, set in the Danish court in Copenhagen when Denmark governed Norway.

Knut Faldbakken *Adam's Diary*. Three former lovers describe their relationships with the same woman – an absorbing and spirited novel by one of Norway's more prolific writers.

Robert Ferguson *Enigma: the Life of Knut Hamsun*. Detailed and well-considered biography of Norway's most controversial writer (see below). The same author also wrote *Ibsen*, an in-depth biography of the playwright.

Karin Fossum *Calling out for You* and *Don't look Back*. Norway's finest crime writer, Fossum has written a string of superb thrillers in the Inspector Sejer series, and each gives the real flavour of contemporary Norway. These two novels are the best place to get started – but avoid *When the Devil holds the Candle*, which is a bit of a dud. The first chapter of *Don't look Back* is printed here on pp.444–456.

Jostein Gaarder *Sophie's World*. Hugely popular novel that deserves all the critical praise it has received. Beautifully and gently written, with puffs of whimsy all the way through, it bears comparison with Hawking's *A Brief History of Time*, though the subject matter here is philosophy, and there's an engaging mystery story tucked in too. Also try Gaarder's *Through A Glass Darkly*.

Janet Garton (ed) & **Henning Sehmsdorf** (trans) *New Norwegian Plays*. Four plays written between 1979 and 1983, including work by the feminist writer Bjørg Vik and a Brechtian analysis of Europe in the nuclear age by Edvard Hoem. Currently o/p, but contact Norvik Press or Dufour direct (see p.417) and they should be able to rustle up a copy.

Knut Hamsun *Hunger*. Norway's leading literary light in the 1920s and early 1930s, Knut Hamsun (1859–1952) was a writer of international acclaim until he disgraced himself by supporting Hitler – for which many Norwegians never forgave him. Of Hamsun's many novels, it was *Hunger* (1890) that made his name, a trip into the psyche of an alienated and angst-ridden young writer, which shocked contemporary readers. The book was to have a seminal influence on the development of the modern novel. In the latter part of his career, Hamsun advocated a return to the soil and basic rural values. He won the Nobel Prize for Literature for one of his works from this period, *Growth of the Soil*, but you have to be pretty determined to plough through its metaphysical claptrap. In recent years, Hamsun has been tentatively accepted back into the Norwegian literary fold and there has been some resurgence of interest in his works; there's also been a biographical film, *Hamsun*, starring Max von Sydow.

William Heinesen *The Black Cauldron*. It would be churlish to omit the Faroe islander William Heinesen, whose evocative novels delve into the subtleties of Faroese life – and thereby shed light on the related culture of western Norway. This particular book, arguably his best, is rigorously modernistic in approach and style – an intriguing, challenging read, with the circling forces of Faroese society set against the British occupation of the Faroes in World War II.

Sigbjørn Holmebakk *The Carriage Stone* (o/p). Evil and innocence, suffering and redemption, with death lurking in the background, make this a serious and powerful novel. These themes are explored through the character of Eilif Grotteland, a Lutheran priest who loses his faith and resigns his ministry.

Henrik Ibsen *Four Major Plays*. The key figure of Norwegian literature, Ibsen (see p.146) was a social dramatist with a keen eye for hypocrisy, repression and alienation. Ibsen's most popular plays – primarily *A Doll's House* and *Hedda Gabler* – pop up in all sorts of editions, but this particular collection, in the Oxford World Classics series, contains both these favourites as well as *Ghosts* and *The Master Builder*. What's more, it's inexpensive and translated by one of the leading Ibsen experts, James McFarlane. In print also are several editions of Ibsen's whole oeuvre – the Kessinger Publishing Company's version is currently the least expensive.

Jan Kjærstad *The Seducer*. This remarkable novel weaves and wanders, rambles and roams around the life of its protagonist, Jonas Wergeland, in a series of digressions as our hero/anti-hero sits in his flat with his murdered wife lying dead in an adjoining room. Mysterious and convoluted, pensive and whimsical, it's a truly extraordinary work that won the Nordic Prize for Literature in 2001.

Jan Kjærstad (ed, et al) *Leopard VI: The Norwegian Feeling for Real*. Promoted by the queen of Norway no less, this first-rate anthology of modern Norwegian writers hits all the literary buttons – from boozy nights out in Oslo to the loneliness of rural Norway and small-town envy. Contains 28 short stories plus potted biographies of all the writers that appear.

Björn Larsson *Long John Silver*. Larsson, a veteran Swedish sailor with an extensive knowledge of eighteenth-century British sea lore, uses his specialist knowledge to great effect in this chunky but charming novel that provides an extra twist – or two – to Stevenson's original.

Jonas Lie *The Seer & Other Norwegian Stories*. Part of the Norwegian literary and cultural revival of the late nineteenth-century, Jonas Lie is largely forgotten today, but this collection of mystical folk tales makes for intriguing reading. It is printed alongside his first great success, the novella *The Seer*, in which a teacher is saved from insanity, born of ancient (pagan) superstitions, by the power of Christianity. Also *Weird Tales from Northern Seas: Norwegian Legends*, a collection much enjoyed by no less than Roald Dahl.

Henning Mankell *Faceless Killers, Sidetracked*. Cracking yarns from Scandinavia's leading crime writer featuring Inspector Kurt Wallander, a shambolic and melancholic middle-aged police officer struggling to make sense of it all in small-town southern Sweden. Hard to beat.

Michael Meyer *Ibsen*. Lucid, immaculately researched biography of Norway's greatest playwright. Explores every nook and cranny of the man's life and times in just over 600 pages.

Christopher Moseley, ed. *From Baltic Shores*. Anthology of contemporary short stories from Denmark, Finland, Sweden, Estonia, Latvia and Lithuania. Winter and the harshness of the climate are recurring themes.

Jo Nesbø *The Devil's Star*. Part of the boom in contemporary Norwegian crime writing, this racy tale is one of the better offerings of its type, though the name of the detective involved, Harry Hole, doesn't work too well in English.

Sigbjørn Obstfelder *A Priest's Diary*. The last, uncompleted, work of a highly regarded Norwegian poet who died of consumption in 1900, aged 33. A moody, intense piece of prose-poetry, it is just a segment of an ambitious project that Obstfelder intended to be his life's major undertaking.

Per Petterson *Out Stealing Horses*. Doom and gloom, guilt and isolation deep in the Norwegian woods. Hardly cheerful fare perhaps, but stirring, unsettling stuff all the same.

Cora Sandel *Alberta and Freedom, Alberta Alone, & Alberta and Jacob*. Set in a small town in early twentieth-century Norway, the Alberta trilogy follows the attempts of a young woman to establish an independent life/identity. Characterized by sharp insights and a wealth of contemporary detail. For more on Sandel, see p.348.

Kjersti Scheen *Final Curtain*. Fast-paced detective story from one of the country's most popular crime writers. Refreshingly, the detective isn't a middle-aged man, but an Oslo-based woman.

Amalie Skram *Under Observation* and *Lucie*. Bergen's *Amalie Skram* (1846–1905) married young and went through the marital mangle before turning her experiences into several novels and a commitment to women's emancipation. For the period the novels are extraordinarily progressive, and are an enjoyable read too: see opposite for an extract from *Lucie*.

Sigrid Undset *Kristin Lavransdatter: The Cross, The Bridal Wreath, The Garland & The Mistress of Husaby*. The prolific Undset, one of the country's leading literary lights, can certainly churn it out. This historical series – arguably encapsulating her best work – is set in medieval Norway and has all the excitement of a pulp thriller, along with subtle plots and deft(ish) characterizations.

Herbjørg Wassmo *Dina's Book: A Novel*. Set in rural northern Norway in the middle of the nineteenth century, this strange but engaging tale has a plot centred on a powerful but tormented heroine: see p.433 for an extract. Also *Dina's Son*, again with a nineteenth-century setting, but with intriguing sections focused on the protagonist's move from rural Norway to the city.

Literary extracts

It was **Jostein Gaarder**'s *Sophie's World* that brought Norwegian literature to a worldwide audience in the 1990s, though in fact the Norwegians have been mining a deep, if somewhat idiosyncratic, literary seam since the middle of the nineteenth century. From Ibsen onwards, the country's authors and playwrights have been deeply influenced by Norway's unyielding geography and stern pietism, their preoccupations often focused on anxiety and alienation. **Amalie Skram**, a contemporary of Ibsen, is largely forgotten today, but her *Lucie* is a sharply observed novel and a pioneering feminist work to boot. *Lucie* provides the first of the four extracts we have included; the others are by **Herbjørg Wassmo**, **Kjell Askildsen** and the crime writer **Karin Fossum**, three of Norway's finest contemporary writers.

Amalie Skram

Born in Bergen in 1846, **Amalie Skram** was the daughter of a shopkeeper, who went bankrupt when she was seventeen – a riches to rags story reminiscent of Ibsen's early life (see p.146). She married out of poverty, but the marriage – to a sea captain – went wrong and her husband's refusal to grant a divorce brought on a nervous breakdown in 1877. Recovered, Amalie moved to Christiania (Oslo) in 1881 and here she became involved in both the political movement for an independent Norway and a number of progressive social issues, primarily attempts to regulate prostitution. Amalie also became a familiar figure on the Oslo literary scene and was well known for her controversial or, rather, progressive views. Published in 1888, *Lucie* was a coruscating attack on bourgeois morality in general, and male sexual hypocrisy in particular, with the eponymous heroine gradually ground down into submission. Inevitably, the novel created a huge furore. The extract below describes one key episode in the increasingly oppressive relationship between Lucie and her husband, Gerner.

Lucie

At the Mørks'

Dinner was over, and the women were seated around a table in the sitting room drinking coffee.

Mrs Mørk was talking about the difficulties she was having with her maids. The nursery maid had got up in the middle of the night to go to a dance, and the baby had screamed until he was blue in the face before they heard it in their bedroom.

"Oh these maids, these maids! And of course they break everything. If your purse was as deep as the ocean it still wouldn't be enough." Mrs Lunde was speaking. The wife of a sea captain, she had eight children and struggled mightily to get along on her monthly allowance.

And then they launched into stories about their housemaids' wastefulness and profligacy. When one flagged, the other started in.

Lucie listened with a stiff smile. None of the women turned to address her, but almost unconsciously left her out of the conversation. To remedy this painful situation, she feigned interest, shook her head frequently, and said at the right times, "No, you don't say. How dreadful!"

The men strolled in from the smoking room; with glowing faces and smiling eyes, they seated themselves among the women.

A young fellow with red hands and flaxen hair combed into a stiff point over his forehead struck up a conversation with Lucie.

"Has madam gone to many balls this winter?" he asked.

"No, I'm afraid not. My husband doesn't care to dance, unfortunately." Lucie smiled invitingly.

"Is that right?" the gentleman said, exposing all of his large, ugly teeth. "He really should be obliged to, when he has such a young wife, don't you think? I suppose you weren't at the carnival either?"

"An outstanding likeness of Mrs. Mørk, don't you think?" Gerner [her husband] came over to Lucie and handed her a photograph, while turning his back on the man with the teeth.

A slight shock went through Lucie. She had not seen Gerner come in with the others and thought he was still in the smoking room.

"Yes, it's a good likeness," she said, eagerly looking at the photograph.

Gerner pulled a chair over to the table and sat down.

"Don't you think so, too?" In her confusion, Lucie reached behind her husband and handed the photograph to the gentleman, who stood there smiling like an idiot.

"Can't you leave that dolt alone?" Gerner whispered. "Next you'll be asking him how many balls *he's* been to."

"What do you say, Mrs. Gerner," said Mrs. Mørk. "Do you want to play cards or sit and talk?"

"My wife likes to play whist," Gerner hurriedly replied.

"Have I done something wrong again?" Lucie muttered, looking anxiously at Theodor. "He's Mrs. Mørk's brother, you know."

"That shopkeeper," Gerner answered savagely. "Mrs. Mørk's brother, is *that* what you consider refined company? Yes, I'm coming now." Mørk had called out that the table for ombre was ready in the smoking room.

"They're dancing at Mrs. Reinertson's," Lucie said as she shuffled the cards, glancing up at the ceiling, which was actually shaking.

"Now, *there's* a widow who loves to entertain," said Mrs. Mørk. "It hasn't been a week since we were at a big party up there."

"But we didn't dance then," Lucie said with a sigh.

"No, but only the young people were invited tonight. There are loads of cousins in the family."

"It seems a bit unusual for a widow to do that kind of thing," opined Mrs. Lunde.

"Her brother, the pastor in Arendal, is very worldly too," lisped a pregnant little assistant pastor's wife with heavy blue rings under her eyes. "He's always scandalising the congregation, Jensen says."

"And she defends *Albertine* [a controversial novel of the period]," Mrs Lund went on. "Well as I always say, if you don't have any children….I'm so pleased with my eight. I'd rather have 16 than none. Your lead, Mrs. Gerner."

There was much more talking and gossiping than playing. Lucie tried to get into the conversation a couple of times, but wasn't successful. Feeling uncomfortable and out of place, she pretended to be intent on the cards. When it was finally time to eat supper she breathed a sigh of relief.

"I think that was the doorbell," Mørk said. They had finished supper and were just getting up from the table.

"It must have been the street door," his wife answered. "But what in the world is that?"

They all paused, hands on their chairs, as they were moving them back from the table. Drifting in from the next room came an intermittent muffled clamour and the tones of a violin playing a march. Mrs. Mørk went over and opened the door. The others turned around quickly with a buzz of astonishment.

The sitting room was jammed with people wearing carnival costumes and masks on their faces. It was a gaudy mixture of knights and their ladies, peasants and Italian fishermen, gypsies and dancing girls. In front of them stood a fiddler dressed as a peasant and Mrs. Reinertson in a pale grey silk dress, a gold comb in her shiny brown hair.

"Well, what do you think?" Mrs. Reinertson said laughingly to Mrs. Mørk, who had stopped in the doorway. She clapped her hands. "My guests couldn't be restrained, they're simply wild tonight. First they scared the life out of me by coming in carnival costumes, and then they absolutely insisted on coming down here. You mustn't take offence."

"How could you think that – what a fun idea they had. Come in, do come in."

"Oh now you're shy," Mrs. Reinertson laughed at her guests, who were clustered together with their arms linked, giggling in embarrassment and whispering behind their masks. "What did I say?"

"How marvellous of you to come and liven us up." With a bray of laughter Mørk walked around shaking hands with the masked guests, who bowed and curtsied and made somewhat fruitless attempts to be amusing.

"Now make yourselves at home and *act* your parts to your heart's content. By heaven, we'll have champagne! Here Lina." He handed a ring of keys through the dining room door.

"Now really Aksel," said his wife angrily, snatching the keys away from him. "The maids in the wine cellar…."

"Look, Mrs. Lund!" Lucie was so excited that she impulsively took Mrs. Lund's arm and pointed at a harlequin who was walking on his hands among the armchairs. "Oh Lord. Oh Lord, the lamp!" she cried, clinging tightly to her arm. The harlequin's feet were close to a porcelain lamp on a little marble table.

With a strained expression, Mrs. Lund moved away from Lucie. "A bit common, don't you think," she said to the assistant pastor's wife, taking her by the arm.

Champagne corks were going off explosively in the dining room and Mørk poured. "If you please, ladies and gentlemen!" he called. "People who want champagne must come in here!"

"But first take off your masks!" said Mrs. Reinertson with a clap of her hands, after which they all took off their masks and let them dangle from their arms. Then they began to laugh and talk, recognise and introduce themselves, as they all crowded around the table in the dining room to drink champagne.

There were speeches and toasts, and gradually the somewhat forced animation that had covered embarrassment gave way to a rush of good cheer.

Lucie was looking through narrowed eyes at a good-looking young man, tall and broad-shouldered, with a black moustache, red lips, and gleaming healthy teeth. He was wearing sandals on his feet and a monk's cowl over his lieutenant's uniform.

"Your health, madam," he said clinking his glass against Lucie's. "Long live celibacy!"

"Long live what?" Lucie asked, laughing heartily. "I don't know what you mean."

"You are adorable, madam!" The lieutenant threw back his head and gazed at her rapturously with brown, laughing eyes. "Should I explain it to you? Oh no, I would rather explain what celibacy is *not*. We'll take our glasses with us." He offered her his arm.

"Don't be such a flirt, Knut," Mrs. Reinertson whispered in his ear, as he and Lucie walked by. "Her husband is so jealous."

"Then we'd better cure him," Knut replied. "She's so sweet and amusing, Aunt."

"Let's sit over here." The lieutenant led Lucie to a little sofa in a corner of the sitting room beneath a tall arrangement of leafy plants, and sat down beside her. He began to chat with her in a soft, confiding tone.

Gerner observed them from the dining room, where he was talking to a knight's lady dressed in black velvet with a tall mother of pearl comb in her hair. He watched Lucie laugh and drink champagne. Occasionally she would lean back and lift her feet off the floor. Once she turned away, as if her admirer had been too forward, and the lieutenant gave her a surprised look and became earnest and intense. Gerner's half-shut eyes were narrowed more than usual and his nostrils twitched nervously.

"What are you staring at?" the knight's lady asked, turning around.

"That monk over there is amusing." – Gerner forced his mouth into a smile. – "That fop of a lieutenant in the monk's cowl."

"Oh Knut Reinertson. Knut Lionheart."

"Oh yes? Why do they call him that?" Gerner interrupted

"I don't know really, but I suppose it's because he's a heartbreaker. – Who is the lady he's talking to?"

"It's my wife," answered Gerner, looking at the knight's lady with his eyes wide open.

"Oh I see – well I'm sure we were introduced but I didn't hear the name. She is really very charming. – If only he doesn't hypnotise her."

"Hypnotise?"

"Yes, didn't you hear about that? It's quite dreadful the things he gets people to do and say. At a party the other night – papa wouldn't give me permission to try it. – What! Go up to Mrs. Reinertson's and dance? – Oh yes, let's do that!" She clapped her hands.

"What do our guests say?" cried Mrs. Mørk looking over at her husband.

"Let's go up, go up," they all answered.

"Let me lead the way," Mrs. Reinertson said, taking the fiddler by the arm.

"That's what I call hospitable," Mørk exclaimed, offering Mrs. Lund his arm.

Gerner wanted to reach Lucie to tell her they should go home, but he couldn't get past all the people and furniture. He stretched sideways over the others' shoulders in order to catch her glance, but she pretended not to notice.

"Devil take it," Gerner mumbled, when he saw her follow the others out of the door, flushed and laughing on the lieutenant's arm.

"Tonight I intend to enjoy myself," Lucie said to her escort, lifting her knees in a little dance. "It's certainly been a long time. – Imagine, I haven't gone dancing one single time since I got married."

I don't care if he kills me, I'm having a good time tonight, she thought. There'll be a scene anyway, might as well get some fun out of it.

"Do you not have a partner, Gerner?" asked Mrs. Mørk. "Then you'll have to be content with me."

He bowed silently and they left the room.

From the entryway he saw Lucie and the lieutenant turning into the bend of the staircase that led to Mrs. Reinertson's apartment. They were close together. His head was bent toward Lucie's and she was looking up at his face as he spoke.

Mrs. Mørk chattered on and on, but Gerner heard nothing; he just stared up the stairs with a white face and clenched lips.

"I wish I had a sixth sense," said the lieutenant.

"Oh, and why is that?" Lucie asked.

"So I could look into your soul and read my fate." His face was mirthful but his voice was solemn.

"Oh you," Lucie laughed, poking him in the side with her elbow.

"Every young woman's heart is an unresolved riddle, a boundless deep – an ocean of – in a word – riches and possibilities – oh, a bottomless..." he paused for a moment. "It's a sin to keep such a treasure locked away."

Lord, he's sweet, and it's so poetic, the way he talks, Lucie thought, her face alight with rapture. And he's such a gentleman.

"Oh I think you"d soon have your fill of that treasure, I do, Lieutenant Reinertson." Her voice was trembling with delight and agitation.

"Try me, madam," he begged earnestly. "Tell me what you are thinking, feeling, what delights you, makes you suffer" – he softly squeezed her arm – "especially suffer, for is there any human being who doesn't suffer?" – They had now come upstairs into rooms lit by candelabras and lamps, where the musician struck up a waltz.

And then the dancing couples whirled down the large, rectangular dining room.

Reinertson clasped Lucie firmly to his chest and danced off. She closed her eyes and leaned back against his arm. Never before had dancing felt so delicious. She felt like she was flying through the air and that her body was almost dissolving in a wonderful, tingling sensation. The furniture, the people, and everything else drifted away. She was conscious only of him and herself, and, from far away, the sound of the music. If only it never, never had to end.

"I'd surrender my soul to the pains of Hell for the key to her rooms," the lieutenant whispered after the dance, when they were sitting in an alcove off the dining room.

Blood pounded in Lucie's ears. She leaned back, fanning herself with her handkerchief. A soft smile trembled at the corners of her mouth, and her breast rose and fell. "Oh, if only I had met you before, Reinertson," she whispered back, and squeezed his hand.

This is getting amusing. She thinks I'm in love with her, thought the lieutenant.

"We can still get to know each other, of course," he said softly, squeezing her hand in return. Rubbish, I can't be bothered with this, he thought a second later, just as Lucie was about to answer. He released her hand and said. "Come, let's dance the gallop together."

They stood up and Lucie took his arm.

In the doorway, they met Gerner.

"Well here you are, finally," he said. "It's time to go home."

Lucie could tell from his voice how much it was costing him to control himself. But she didn't feel the slightest trace of fear, only a boundless joy that she was going to dance with him again.

"Just a couple of times around, counsellor," said Reinertson, "then I'll return her to you."

He danced off with her. Gerner watched them.

"Now I'll take my leave and surrender your wife to the hands of her natural guardian, as they say." The lieutenant had brought Lucie back to Gerner. "Goodnight, madam. Thank you for this evening. Goodnight, counsellor." He bowed and left.

Lucie's eyes followed him through the room with a longing expression. She seemed to have completely forgotten that Gerner was standing beside her.

"Do you hear, we're leaving." He grabbed her firmly by the wrist and walked her towards the door.

"I should say goodbye first, don't you think?" Lucie tried to free her hand.

He tightened his grip and actually pulled her past the dancing couples. "You're coming now!"

"Leave without thanking them?" Lucie said sharply, out in the front hall.

"Don't try to prolong the scandal." Gerner opened the door and pushed Lucie out through it. He could barely get his words out and his hands were shaking.

I don't care if he's in a good mood or a rotten mood, Lucie thought, as they were walking down the stairs. As long as I can see that darling Reinertson again soon.

But when they were putting on their coats in the Mørks' well-lit front hall, the sight of Theodor's pallid cheeks and clenched lips sent a chill through Lucie.

Striding down the street, Theodor took such long steps that Lucie had to trot to keep up with him. Finally she slowed and trailed along behind.

"Is it your intention to play the part of a streetwalker tonight?" Gerner had stopped by the university to wait for Lucie.

"How can anybody keep up when you run like that," Lucie answered angrily and walked past him.

"You are to conduct yourself properly." In a couple of steps Gerner was beside her. "Reminding everybody of what a trollop I married." His voice was distorted with rage.

"You're really so crude," Lucie said indifferently, walking hurriedly, almost running.

"If a man so much as looks at you, your whole body starts to tremble," Gerner went on, getting more and more agitated. "You make me look ridiculous."

"Well, that's not difficult, is it," she said with a scornful breath.

Gerner could have hit her.

"You be careful," he snarled. "You're a tart, and you'll never get that out of your blood."

"A tart! I really have to laugh. You should hear what Mrs. Reinertson has to say. I suppose you were lily-white when you married me."

"Now you start with impertinences – you've wisely refrained from that until now."

"But I won't stand for you treating me this way any more." She spoke breathlessly because of their quick pace on the slippery snow. "I won't stand for it any longer, just so you know. I suppose you think being married to you is so glorious!"

"Be quiet!" He grabbed her shoulders and shook her so violently that her little fur hat flew off her head. They had turned onto Drammensveien, and he gave her a shove that propelled her a few steps along the street.

Without uttering a sound, Lucie bent over to retrieve her hat, then took off down Drammensveien with her hat in her hand, as if she were running for her life.

Herbjørg Wassmo

Two volumes of poetry marked Herbjørg Wassmo's writing debut in 1976, at the age of 34. Shortly afterwards she switched to prose, subsequently writing two series of popular novels about contrasting women. **Dina**, the female protagonist of *Dina's bok* (Dina's Book, 1989) and *Lykkens sønn* (The Son of Fortune, 1992), is wilful to the point of ruthlessness: she eliminates her husband and takes a new lover, while the funeral is in progress elsewhere. Yet beneath her toughness is a deep sense of betrayal: rejected as a child by her father after she accidentally caused her mother's death, Dina has grown up expecting betrayal. Set in the mid-nineteenth century, the Dina stories have as their backdrop a rural community in Wassmo's native northern Norway. The extract below comes from the beginning of *Dina's Book*.

Dina's Book

The eyes of the Lord preserve knowledge, and he overthroweth the words of the transgressor.

Proverbs 22:12

Dina had to take her husband, Jacob, who had gangrene in one foot, to the doctor on the other side of the mountain. November. She was the only one who could handle the wild yearling, which was the fastest horse. And they needed to drive fast. On a rough, icy road.

Jacob's foot already stank. The smell had filled the house for a long time. The cook smelled it even in the pantry. An uneasy atmosphere pervaded every room. A feeling of anxiety.

No one at Reinsnes said anything about the smell of Jacob's foot before he left. Nor did they mention it after Blackie returned to the estate with empty shafts.

But aside from that, people talked. With disbelief and horror. On the neighbouring farms. In the parlours at Strandsted and along the sound. At the pastor's home. Quietly and confidentially.

About Dina, the young wife at Reinsnes, the only daughter of Sheriff Holm. She was like a horse-crazy boy. Even after she got married. Now she had suffered such a sad fate.

They told the story again and again. She had driven so fast that the snow crackled and spurted under the runners. Like a witch. Nevertheless, Jacob Gronelv did not get to the doctor's. Now he no longer existed. Friendly, generous Jacob, who never refused a request for help. Mother Karen's son, who came to Reinsnes when he was quite young.

Dead! No one could understand how such a terrible thing could have happened. That boats capsized, or people disappeared at sea, had to be accepted. But this was the devil's work. First getting gangrene in a fractured leg. Then dying on a sleigh that plunged into the rapids!

Dina had lost the power of speech, and old Mother Karen wept. Jacob's son from his first marriage wandered, fatherless, around Copenhagen, and Blackie could not stand the sight of sleighs.

The authorities came to the estate to conduct an inquiry into the events that had occurred up to the moment of death. Everything must be stated specifically and nothing hidden, they said.

Dina's father, the sheriff, brought two witnesses and a book for recording the proceedings. He said emphatically that he was there as one of the authorities, not as a father.

Mother Karen found it difficult to see a difference. But she did not say so.

No one brought Dina down from the second floor. Since she was so big and strong, they took no chance that she might resist and make a painful scene. They did not try to force her to come downstairs. Instead it was decided the authorities would go up to her large bedroom.

Extra chairs had been placed in the room. And the curtains on the canopy bed were thoroughly dusted. Heavy gold fabric patterned with rows of rich red flowers. Bought in Hamburg. Sewn for Dina and Jacob's wedding.

Oline and Mother Karen had tried to take the young wife in hand so she would not look completely unpresentable. Oline gave her herb tea with thick cream and plenty of sugar. It was her cure for all ills, from the scurvy to childlessness. Mother Karen assisted with praise, hair brushing, and cautious concern.

The servant girls did as they were told, while looking around with frightened glances.

The words stuck. Dina opened her mouth and formed them. But their sound was in another world. The authorities tried many different approaches.

The sheriff tried using a deep, dispassionate voice, peering into Dina's light-grey eyes. He could just as well have looked through a glass of water.

The witnesses also tried. Seated and standing. With both compassionate and commanding voices.

Finally, Dina laid her head of black, unruly hair on her arms. And she let out sounds that could have come from a half-strangled dog.

Feeling ashamed, the authorities withdrew to the downstairs rooms. In order to reach agreement about what had happened. How things had looked at the place in question. How the young woman had acted.

They decided that the whole matter was a tragedy for the community and the entire district. That Dina Grønelv was beside herself with grief. That she was not culpable and had lost her speech from the shock.

They decided that she had been racing to take her husband to the doctor. That she had taken the curve near the bridge too fast, or that the wild horse had bolted at the edge of the cliff and the shaft fastenings had pulled loose. Both of them.

This was neatly recorded in the official documents.

They did not find the body, at first. People said it had washed out to sea. But did not understand how. For the sea was nearly seven miles away through a rough, shallow riverbed. The rocks there would stop a dead body, which could do nothing itself to reach the sea.

To Mother Karen's despair, they gradually gave up the search.

A month later, an old pauper came to the estate and insisted that the body lay in Veslekulpen, a small backwater some distance below the rapids. Jacob lay crooked around a rock. Stiff as a rod. Battered and bloated, the old fellow said.

He proved to be right.

The water level had evidently subsided when the autumn rains ended. And one clear day in early December, the unfortunate body of Jacob Grønelv appeared. Right before the eyes of the old pauper, who was on his way across the mountain.

Afterward, people said the pauper was clairvoyant. And, in fact, always had been. This is why he had a quiet old age. Nobody wanted to quarrel with a clairvoyant. Even if he was a pauper.

Dina sat in her bedroom, the largest room on the second floor. With the curtains drawn. At first she did not even go to the stable to see her horse.

They left her in peace.

Mother Karen stopped crying, simply because she no longer had time for that. She had assumed the duties that the master and his wife had neglected. Both were dead, each in his or her own way.

Dina sat at the walnut table, staring. No one knew what else she did. Because she confided in no one. The sheets of music that had been piled around the bed were now stuffed away in the clothes closet. Her long dresses swept over them in the draught when she opened the door.

The shadows were deep in the bedroom. A cello stood in one corner, gathering dust. It had remained untouched since the day Jacob was carried from the house and laid on the sleigh.

The solid canopy bed with sumptuous bed curtains occupied much of the room. It was so high that one could lie on the pillows and look out through the windows at the sound. Or one could look at oneself in the large mirror with a black lacquered frame that could be tilted to different angles.

The big round stove roared all day. Behind a triple-panelled folding screen with an embroidered motif of beautiful Leda and the swan in an erotic embrace. Wings and arms. And Leda's long, blond hair spread virtuously over her lap.

A servant girl, Thea, brought wood four times a day. Even so, the supply barely lasted through the night.

No one knew when Dina slept, or if she slept. She paced back and forth in heavy shoes with metal-tipped heels, day and night. From wall to wall. Keeping the whole house awake.

Thea could report that the large family Bible, which Dina had inherited from her mother, always lay open.

Now and then the young wife laughed softly. It was an unpleasant sound. Thea did not know whether her mistress was laughing about the holy text or if she was thinking about something else.

Sometimes she angrily slammed together the thin-as-silk pages and threw the book away like the entrails from a dead fish.

Jacob was not buried until seven days after he was found. In the middle of December. There were so many arrangements to be made. So many people had to be notified. Relatives, friends, and prominent people had to be invited to the funeral. The weather stayed cold, so the battered and swollen corpse could easily remain in the barn during that time. Digging the grave, however, required the use of sledge-hammers and pickaxes.

The moon peered through the barn's tiny windows and observed Jacob's fate with its golden eye. Made no distinction between living and dead. Decorated the barn floor in silver and white. And nearby lay the hay, offering warmth and nourishment, smelling fragrantly of summer and splendour.

One morning before dawn, they dressed for the funeral. The boats were ready. Silence lay over the house like a strange piety. The moon was shining. No one waited for daylight at that time of year.

Dina leaned against the windowsill, as if steeling herself, when they entered her room to help her dress in the black clothes that had been sewn for the funeral. She had refused to try them on.

She seemed to be standing there sensing each muscle and each thought. The sombre, teary-eyed women did not see a single movement in her body.

Still, they did not give up at once. She had to change her clothes. She had to be part of the funeral procession. Anything else was unthinkable. But finally, they did think that thought. For with her guttural, animal-like sounds, she convinced everyone that she was not ready to be the widow at a funeral. At least not this particular day.

Terrified, the women fled the room. One after another. Mother Karen was the last to leave. She gave excuses and soothing explanations. To the aunts, the wives, the other women, and, not least of all, to Dina's father, the sheriff.

He was the hardest to convince. Bellowing loudly, he burst into Dina's room without knocking. Shook her and commanded her, slapped her cheeks with fatherly firmness while his words swarmed around her like angry bees.

Mother Karen had to intervene. The few who stood by kept their eyes lowered.

Then Dina let out the bestial sounds again. While she flailed her arms and tore her hair. The room was charged with something they did not understand. There was an aura of madness and power surrounding the young, half-dressed woman with dishevelled hair and crazed eyes.

Her screams reminded the sheriff of an event he carried with him always. Day and night. In his dreams and in his daily tasks. An event that still, after thirteen years, could make him wander restlessly around the estate. Looking for someone, or something, that could unburden him of his thoughts and feelings.

The people in the room thought Dina Grønelv had a harsh father. But on the other hand, it was not right that such a young woman refused to do what was expected of her.

She tired them out. People decided she was too sick to attend her husband's funeral. Mother Karen explained, loudly and clearly, to everyone she met:

"Dina is so distraught and ill she can't stand on her feet. She does nothing but weep. And the terrible thing is, she's not able to speak."

First came the muffled shouts from the people who were going in the boats. Then came the scraping of wood against iron as the coffin was loaded onto the longboat with its juniper decorations and its weeping, black-clad women. Then the sounds and voices stiffened over the water like a thin crusting of beach ice. And disappeared between the sea and the mountains. Afterward, silence settled over the estate as though this were the true funeral procession. The house held its breath. Merely let out a small sigh among the rafters now and then. A sad, pitiful final honour to Jacob.

The pink waxed-paper carnations fluttered amid the pine and juniper boughs across the sound in a light breeze. There was no point in travelling quickly with such a burden. Death and its detached supporting cast took their time. It was not Blackie who pulled them. And it was not Dina who set the pace. The coffin was heavy. Those who bore it felt the weight. This was the only way to the church with such a burden.

Now five pairs of oars creaked in the oarlocks. The sail flapped idly against the mast, refusing to unfurl. There was no sun. Grey clouds drifted across the sky. The raw air gradually became still.

The boats followed one another. A triumphal procession for Jacob Grønelv. Masts and oars pointed toward ocean and heaven. The ribbons on the wreaths fluttered restlessly. They had only a short time to be seen.

Mother Karen was a yellowed rag. Edged with lace, it is true.

The servant girls were wet balls of wool in the wind.

The men rowed, sweating behind their beards and moustaches. Rowing in rhythm.

At Reinsnes everything was prepared. The sandwiches were arranged on large platters. On the cellar floor and on shelves in the large entry were pewter plates filled with cakes and covered by cloths.

Under Oline's exacting supervision, the glasses had been rubbed to a glistening shine. Now the cups and glasses were arranged neatly in rows on the tables and in the pantry, protected by white linen towels bearing the monograms of Ingeborg Grønelv and Dina Grønelv. They had to use the linen belonging to both of Jacob's wives today.

Many guests were expected after the burial.

Dina stoked the fire like a madwoman, although there was not even frost on the windows. Her face, which had been grey that morning, began slowly to regain its colour.

She paced restlessly back and forth across the floor with a little smile on her lips. When the clock struck, she raised her head like an animal listening for enemies.

Kjell Askildsen

Born in Mandal in southern Norway in 1929, **Kjell Askildsen** came to literary prominence in the 1950s with his Kafkaesque accounts of alienated individuals. Subsequent stories adopted a more political tone, and although his output has been far from prolific he is widely regarded as one of Scandinavia's finest writers. In recent years, Askildsen has chosen to express himself through the **monologues** of old men, whose ordinary, everyday struggles hold loneliness and despair at bay, though these are themselves just manifestations of the abyss – the metaphysical nothingness of existence. These are not, however, dreary, self-indulgent monologues, for each is underpinned by a steel-like spirit of endurance and illuminated with sharp flashes of dry humour. Nor are they devoid of human values, such as the desire for justice, human dignity and common decency, upheld in spite of the cool knowledge of life's futility and the quirky frailty of old age. *A Sudden Liberating Thought* was published in 1987.

A Sudden Liberating Thought

I live in a basement; it's due to the fact that my life has been going downhill, in every sense of the word.

My room has only one window, and only its upper portion is above the sidewalk; this causes me to see the outside world from below. It's not a very big world, but it often feels big enough.

I can only see the legs and the lower part of the body of those who walk by on the sidewalk on my side of the street, but after living here for four years I mostly know to whom they belong. This is because there's little traffic; I live far up a dead end street.

I am a taciturn person, but sometimes I talk to myself. The things I say then have to be said, it seems to me.

One day, having just seen the lower part of the landlord's wife pass by as I stood by the window, I felt suddenly so lonely that I decided to go out.

I put on my shoes and coat and stuck my reading glasses in my coat pocket, just in case. Then I left. The advantage of living in a basement is that you walk up when you are rested and down when you come home tired. That's the only advantage, I guess.

It was a warm summer day. I went to the park beside the abandoned firehouse, where I can usually sit undisturbed. But I had scarcely sat down when some old fellow my own age came along and sat down beside me, though there were plenty of vacant benches. I had gone out because I felt lonely, to be sure, but not to talk; just for a change. I was becoming more and more nervous that he would say something, and I even thought of getting up and leaving, but where was I to go, this being the place I'd set my mind on. But he remained silent, and that struck me as being so sympathetic that I felt quite well-disposed toward him. I even tried to look at him, without attracting his attention, of course. But he noticed it, because he said, "You will excuse me for saying so, but I sat down here because I thought I wouldn't be disturbed. I can move if you wish, no trouble."

"Sit," I said, somewhat bewildered. Naturally, I didn't make any further attempt to observe him, he had my deepest respect. Naturally too, even more so, I did not speak to him. I felt something strange inside me, something not-lonely, simply a kind of well-being.

He sat there for about half an hour; then he got up, with a bit of difficulty, turned to me and said, "Thanks. Goodbye."

"Goodbye."

He left, taking remarkably long steps and flailing his arms, as though sleep-walking.

The following day at the same time, or a little earlier, I went again to the park. After all the thoughts and speculations he had evoked in me, it seemed somehow the natural thing to do; it was hardly a free choice, whatever that may be.

He came. I saw him from afar and recognized him by his gait. That day too there were vacant benches, and I was curious to know whether he would choose to sit with me. I looked in another direction naturally, pretending I hadn't even seen him, and when he sat down I made as though I didn't notice him. He didn't seem to take any notice of me either; it was a somewhat unusual situation – a sort of unplanned non-meeting. I must admit I felt uncertain whether or not I wanted him to say something, and after half an hour or so I felt just as uncertain whether to leave first or wait till he had gone. Actually, it wasn't an unpleasant uncertainty – I could go on sitting there in any case. But suddenly it occurred to me for some reason or other that he had gotten an edge on me, and then my decision came easily. I stood up, looked at him for the first time and said, "Goodbye."

"Goodbye," he answered, looking me straight in the eye. One couldn't find fault with his glance in any way.

I left. As I was walking away, I couldn't help wondering how he would characterize my gait, and suddenly I felt my body jam up and my steps turn stiff and awkward. I was annoyed, no use denying it.

That evening as I stood beneath the window looking out – there wasn't very much to see – I thought that if he came the following day I would say something. I even figured out what I was going to say, how I would introduce what might turn out to be a conversation. I would wait a quarter of an hour and then I would say, without looking at him, "It's about time we start talking." No more, just that. Then he could answer or not answer, and if he didn't answer I would get up and say, "In the future I would prefer that you sit on another bench."

I also came up with many other things that evening, things I would say if a conversation should develop, but I rejected most of them as uninteresting and too commonplace.

The following morning I was excited and uncertain, even wondering whether I shouldn't stay home. I resolutely pushed aside the decision of the evening before; if I did go, I certainly wouldn't say anything.

I went, and he came. I didn't look his way. Suddenly it occurred to me how odd it was that he always came less than five minutes after I myself had turned up – as if he had been standing somewhere nearby and seen me coming. Sure, I thought, of course he lives in one of those buildings beside the firehouse, he can see me from one of the windows.

There was no time to speculate any further on this, for he suddenly began talking. I have to admit that what he said made me feel pretty uneasy.

"Excuse me," he said, "but if you don't mind, perhaps it's about time we start talking."

I didn't answer right away; then I said, "Perhaps. If there's something to say."

"You aren't sure there's anything to say?"

"I'm probably older than you."

"That's not impossible."

I didn't say any more. I felt a disagreeable uneasiness, on account of the peculiar exchange of roles that had taken place. He was the one who had started the conversation, and very nearly with my own words, and it fell to me to answer as I had imagined he might answer. It was as if I could just as well be him and he just as well be me. It was disagreeable. I wanted to leave. But having, so to speak, been forced to identify with him, I found it difficult to hurt or even offend him.

A minute may have gone by before he said, "I'm eighty-three."

"Then I was right."

Another minute passed.

"Do you play chess?" he asked.

"A long time ago."

"Almost nobody plays chess any more. All those I've played chess with have died."

"It's been at least fifteen years," I said.

"The most recent one died last winter. No great loss actually, he didn't have his wits about him any more. I would always beat him after less than twenty moves. But he did get a certain pleasure from it, presumably the last pleasure that remained to him. Maybe you knew him."

"No," I said quickly, "I didn't know him."

"How can you be so… Well, that's your business."

He was certainly right about that and I felt like saying so, but gave him credit for not completing his question.

Then I saw him turn his face to look at me. He sat like this for quite a while. It was anything but pleasant, so I got my eyeglasses from my coat pocket and put them on. Everything in front of me – trees, houses, benches – disappeared in a fog.

"You're nearsighted?" he said after a while.

"No," I said, "quite the contrary."

"I mean – you need glasses to see what's far away."

"No, quite the contrary. It's the things nearby I have problems with."

"I see."

I didn't say any more. When I noticed that he turned his face away again, I removed my glasses and put them back in my pocket. He said nothing more either, so when I thought a suitable amount of time had passed, I got up and said courteously, "Thanks for the chat. So long."

"So long."

I walked away with firmer steps that day, but when I got home and had calmed down, I started again making hasty plans for my next meeting with him. Pacing the floor, I came up with many absurdities, a subtlety or two as well; I wasn't above triumphing over him a bit, but that was simply because I looked upon him as my equal, in spite of everything.

I didn't sleep well that night. When I was still young enough to believe that the future could offer surprises, it often happened that I slept poorly, but that was long ago, before it became clear to me, I mean absolutely clear, that the day you die it doesn't matter whether you've had a good or a miserable life. So the fact that I slept poorly that night both surprised and upset me. Nor had I eaten anything that could've caused it, only a couple of boiled potatoes and a tin of sardines; I had slept soundly on that many times before.

The following day he didn't come until almost a quarter of an hour had gone by. I had started giving up hope – it was an unaccustomed feeling: having a hope to give up. But then he came.

"Good morning," he said.

"Good morning."

Then we said nothing more for a while. I knew very well what I would say if the pause grew too long, but I preferred that he talk first, and he did.

"Your wife ... is she still alive?"

"No, she isn't, it's been a long time, I've mostly forgotten her. And yours?"

"Two years ago. Today."

"Oh. Then it is a day of mourning of sorts."

"Well, yes. You can't help feeling the loss, of course. But I don't celebrate it by visiting her grave, if that's what you mean. Graves are a damn nuisance. Beg pardon. I didn't choose my words very well."

I didn't answer.

"Beg pardon," he said, "if I've hurt your feelings, I didn't mean it that way."

"You haven't."

"Good. For all I knew you might even be religious. I had a sister who believed in eternal life! What conceit!"

I was again struck by the fact that he actually sat there speaking my lines, and for a moment I was foolish enough to think that it was nothing but my imagination, that he didn't even exist, that in reality I sat there talking to myself. And it was probably this piece of folly that made me ask a completely unpremeditated question, "Who are you really?"

Fortunately he didn't answer immediately, so I managed to edge away somewhat from a rather awkward situation.

"Don't misunderstand me. I wasn't really speaking to you. It was simply that I came to think of something."

I noticed how he turned his face to look at me, but this time I didn't take out my glasses. I said, "Besides, I would rather not leave the impression that I am in the habit of asking about things to which there are no answers."

Afterward we sat in silence. It wasn't a restful silence; I would have preferred to leave. In a couple of minutes, I thought – if he hasn't said anything in two minutes I'll leave. And I began to count the seconds in my mind. He didn't say anything, and I got up, to the second. He also got up, the very same moment.

"Thanks for the chat," I said.

"The same to you. Too bad you won't play chess."

"I don't think you would enjoy it very much. Besides, your partners seem to be in the habit of dying."

"Yes indeed," he said, suddenly seeming absent-minded.

"So long," I said.

"So long."

That day I was more tired than usual when I got home; I had to lie down a few moments. After a while I said aloud, "I'm old. And life is very long."

When I woke up the next morning it was raining. To say I was disappointed would be putting it mildly. But as the day wore on and the rain didn't let up,

I realized I would go to the park no matter what. I wouldn't be able not to. It wasn't important to me that he should show up as well, that wasn't the point. It was only that, if he came, I wanted to – had to – be there. As I found myself sitting on that wet bench in the rain, I even hoped he wouldn't come. There was an element of exposure, of indecency, in sitting so completely alone in a rain-soaked park.

But he came all right – didn't I know it! By contrast with me, he wore a black raincoat that reached almost to the ground. He sat down.

"You defy the weather," he said.

It was obviously meant just as an observation, but because of what I had been thinking immediately before he turned up, it seemed to me somewhat tactless, so I didn't answer. I noticed I had become ill-humoured and that I regretted having come. Besides, I was starting to get wet and my coat felt heavy, it seemed almost ludicrous to go on sitting there, so I said, "I just went out for some fresh air, but then I got tired. I'm an old man."

And to forestall any speculations on his part, I added, "Old habit, you know."

He didn't say anything, which struck me, quite absurdly, as being provocative. And what he said finally, after a long pause, didn't make me feel any more well-disposed toward him.

"You don't like people very much, do you, or am I mistaken?"

"Like people?" I answered. "What do you mean?"

"Well, you know, it's only the sort of thing one says. I didn't mean to be intrusive."

"Of course I don't like people. And of course I like people. If you asked me if I liked cats or goats, or butterflies for that matter, but people. Besides, I hardly know anybody."

I regretted my last remark at once, but luckily that was not what he latched on to.

"That was quite something," he said. "Goats and butterflies!"

I could hear him smiling. I had to admit I had been unduly dismissive, so I said, "If you want a general answer to a general question, I do like both goats and butterflies more unconditionally than I like people."

"Thanks, I got the point long ago. I'll remember to be more precise the next time I presume to ask you something."

He said this in a friendly way, and it is no exaggeration to say that I felt sorry, even though my being difficult was simply due to my low spirits. And because I felt sorry, I said something I at once felt sorry having said; "Beg pardon, but words are almost the only things still left to me. Beg pardon."

"By all means. It was my fault. I ought to have considered who you are."

My heart sank – did he know who I was? Did he come here every day because he knew who I was? I couldn't help feeling both uneasy and insecure, so much so that I acted almost automatically, sticking my hand into my coat pocket in search of my glasses.

"What do you mean?" I said. "Do you know me?"

"Yes. If that's the right word. We have met before. I didn't realize it when I first sat down on this bench. It gradually dawned on me that I'd seen you before, I just wasn't able to place you, not till yesterday. It was something you said, and suddenly I knew what my connection with you was. You don't remember me, do you?"

I stood up.

"No."

I looked straight at him. I was quite unaware of ever having seen him.

"I am… I was your judge."

"You, you –"

I couldn't think of anything more to say.

"Sit down, please."

"I'm wet. Indeed! You were… so it was you. Indeed! Well, goodbye, I have to go."

I left. It wasn't a dignified exit, but I was upset, and I walked faster than I'd done in many years. When I got home I had barely the strength to rid myself of my soaked overcoat before tumbling into bed. I had violent palpitations, and I was firmly determined never to set foot in the park again.

But after a few moments, when my pulse functioned normally again, my thoughts began to do so as well. I accepted my reaction: something hidden had emerged into the light again and I'd been caught off guard, that was all. There was no mystery about it.

I got up from the bed. It gives me a certain satisfaction to state that I was my old self once more, completely. I planted myself underneath the window and said aloud, "He shall see me again."

The following day the nice weather was back, which was a relief, and my coat was practically dry. I went to the park at the usual time; he wasn't going to notice anything irregular about me, or imagine he'd got an edge on me.

But when I approached the bench he was already there, so he was the one who was behaving irregularly.

"Good morning," he said.

"Good morning," I answered, taking my seat, and so as to take the bull by the horns I added at once, "I thought you might not show up today."

"Bravo," he said. "Zero for you."

That was an answer I couldn't find fault with. He was, indeed, my equal.

"Did you often feel guilty?" I asked.

"I don't understand."

"As a judge, did you often feel guilty? After all, it was your profession to assign to others the required amount of guilt."

"It was my profession to define the law on the basis of other people's assessment of guilt."

"Are you trying to excuse yourself? It isn't necessary."

"I didn't feel guilty. On the other hand, I often felt at the mercy of the law's rigidity. As in your own case."

"Yes. Because you're not superstitious, after all."

He gave me a quick glance.

"What do you mean by that?" he said.

"It is only superstitious people who think it is a doctor's business to prolong the suffering of those who are doomed."

"Aha, I understand. But aren't you afraid that legalization of euthanasia could be misused?"

"Of course it couldn't be misused. For then euthanasia would no longer be euthanasia but murder."

He didn't answer; I cast a sidelong glance at him: he had a sullen, impassive expression. That was okay by me, though I didn't know whether his sullenness was due to what I had said, or whether he simply looked like that habitually; it was hard to tell, since I had practically never looked at him. Now I felt like making up for lost time and inspecting him thoroughly, and so I did, openly, turning my face and staring at his profile. It was the least I could permit myself in the presence of the man who had sentenced me to prison for several years. I even fished out my glasses and placed them on my nose. It wasn't at all necessary, I could see him clearly without, but I felt a sudden desire to provoke him. It was so unlike me to stare directly at a person that I felt alien to myself for a moment; it was a strange and not at all disagreeable sensation. And the fact that I committed this one breach of my usual behaviour turned out to be surprisingly infectious. For the first time in many years, I laughed; it must have sounded quite ugly. Anyway, without looking at me, he said in a brusque tone, "I don't care what you're laughing at, but it doesn't sound like you're enjoying yourself. And that's a pity. For in other respects you are a sensible person."

I immediately felt mollified, as well as a little ashamed, and I withdrew my eyes from his angry profile, saying, "You're right. It wasn't much of a laugh."

More than that I didn't want to give him.

We sat in silence. I thought about my wretched life and grew melancholy. I visualized the judge's home, with good chairs and big bookshelves.

"You probably have a housekeeper?" I said.

"Yes. Why do you ask about that?"

"I'm merely trying to imagine the existence of a retired judge."

"Oh, it's nothing to brag about. You know, the inactivity, all those idle days."

"Yes, time refuses to pass."

"And it's the only thing that's left."

"Time that gets to feel too slow, full of illness to boot perhaps, which slows it even more – then it's over. And when the moment finally comes, we think: what a meaningless life.

"Well, meaningless – "

"Meaningless."

He didn't answer. Neither of us said another word. After a while I got up; however lonely I felt, I didn't want to share my depression with him.

"Goodbye," I said.

"Goodbye, doctor."

Depression breeds sentimentality, and the word "doctor", spoken without a tinge of irony, sent a warm wave through me. I turned abruptly and hurried off. And right there and then, before I was out of the park, I knew I wanted to die. I wasn't surprised; at most I was surprised that I wasn't. All at once both my depression and my sentimentality seemed to have vanished. I slowed my pace, feeling an inward calm that called for slowness.

When I got home, still feeling a lucid calm inside me, I took out writing paper and an envelope. On the envelope I wrote: "To the judge who sentenced me." Then I sat down at the little table where I usually eat and began to write this story.

Today I went to the park for the last time. I was in a strange, almost audacious mood, due perhaps to the unaccustomed joy I had felt in putting my previous meetings with the judge into words or, more likely, to the fact that I hadn't wavered in my decision, not for a moment.

Today, too, he was sitting there when I came. I thought he looked troubled. I greeted him more amicably than usual, it came quite naturally to me. He gave me a quick glance, as if to ascertain whether I really meant it.

"Well," he said, "you're having one of your better days today?"

"I'm having my good day, yes. And you?"

"Reasonably good, thanks. So you don't believe any more that life is meaningless?"

"Oh yes, completely."

"Hmm. I wouldn't be able to live with such a realization."

"You're forgetting the instinct of self-preservation, aren't you? It's very tenacious and has been the bane of many a rational decision."

He didn't answer. I hadn't intended to sit there long, so after a brief pause I said, "We won't be seeing each other any more. Today I've come to say goodbye."

"Is that so? What a pity. Are you going away?"

"Yes."

"And you won't be back?"

"No."

"Hmm. Really. I hope you won't think me too familiar when I tell you I'll miss our meetings."

"Nice of you to say so."

"Time will drag even more."

"There are lonely men sitting on many other benches."

"Oh, you don't understand what I mean. May I ask where you're going?"

Some have maintained that he who knows he's going to die within twenty-four hours feels free to do whatever he wants. It isn't true; one is, even then, incapable of acting contrary to one's nature, one's self. To be sure, giving him an open and honest answer wouldn't have been to behave contrary to my nature, but I had decided in advance not to reveal my destination to him, seeing no reason why I should upset him – he was, in spite of everything, the only person who would be bereaved by my passing, if I may say so. But what should I answer?

"You will be informed," I said at last.

I noticed he was taken aback, but he didn't say anything. Instead he put his hand in his inside pocket and took out his wallet. After looking around in it for a moment, he held out his card to me.

"Thanks," I said, putting it in my coat pocket. I felt I should go. I got up. He too got up. He held out his hand. I took it.

"Take care," he said.

"Thanks, you too. Goodbye."

"Goodbye."

I left. I had a feeling he didn't sit down again, but I didn't turn around to check. I walked calmly homeward, thinking about nothing in particular. Something inside me was smiling. After reaching the basement I stood awhile underneath the window and looked out at the empty street, before sitting down at the table to finish this story. I'm going to put the judge's card on top of the envelope.

It's done. In a moment I'll fold the sheets and place them in the envelope. And now, just before it's going to happen, as I am about to undertake the only definitive act a human being is capable of executing, there is one thought that overshadows all the others: Why didn't I do this long ago?

Translated by Sverre Lyngstad; reprinted by permission of Norvik Press.

Karin Fossum

Born in Sandefjord in southern Norway in 1954, **Karin Fossum** began her literary career in the early 1970s with the publication of a collection of poetry. Yet it was not poetry that made her name, but the sharp brilliance of her crime writing in the **Detective Inspector Konrad Sejer** series. In the last decade, Norway has produced an abundance of crime writers, but Fossum is generally regarded as the most talented, her taut and tight tales gripping and unpredictable in equal measure. To the non-Norwegian, they are also appealing in so far as they give the real flavour of that country and an insight into the collective mind of its people (in so far as this exists). The extract below comes from the beginning of *Don't Look Back*, which first appeared in English translation in 2002.

Ragnhild opened the door cautiously and peered out. Up on the road everything was quiet, and a breeze that had been playing amongst the buildings during the night had finally died down. She turned and pulled the doll's pram over the threshold.

"We haven't even eaten yet," Marthe complained.

She helped push the pram.

"I have to go home. We're going out shopping," Ragnhild said.

"Shall I come over later?"

"You can if you like. After we've done the shopping."

She was on the gravel now and began to push the pram towards the front gate. It was heavy going, so she turned it around and pulled it instead.

"See you later, Ragnhild."

The door closed behind her – a sharp slam of wood and metal.

Ragnhild struggled with the gate, but she mustn't be careless. Marthe's dog might get out. He was watching her intently from beneath the garden table. When she was sure that the gate was properly closed, she started off across the street in the direction of the garages. She could have taken the short-cut between the buildings, but she had discovered that it was too difficult with the pram. Just then a neighbour closed his garage door. He smiled to her and buttoned up his coat, a little awkwardly, with one hand. A big black Volvo stood in the driveway, rumbling pleasantly.

"Well, Ragnhild, you're out early, aren't you? Hasn't Marthe got up yet?"

"I slept over last night," she said. "On a mattress on the floor."

"I see."

He locked the garage door and glanced at his watch; it was 8.06 am. A moment later he turned the car into the street and drove off.

Ragnhild pushed the pram with both hands. She had reached the downhill stretch, which was rather steep, and she had to hold on tight so as not to lose her grip. Her doll, who was named Elise – after herself, because her name was Ragnhild Elise – slid down to the front of the pram. That didn't look good, so she let go with one hand and put the doll back in place, patted down the blanket, and continued on her way. She was wearing sneakers: one was red with green laces, the other was green with red laces, and that's how it had to be. She had on a red tracksuit with Simba the Lion across the chest and a green anorak over it. Her hair was extraordinarily thin and blond, and not very long, but she had managed to pull it into a topknot with an elastic band. Bright plastic fruit dangled from the band, with her sprout of hair sticking up in the middle like a tiny, neglected palm tree. She was six and a half, but small for her age. Not until she spoke would one guess that she was already at school.

She met no one on the hill, but as she approached the intersection she heard a car. So she stopped, squeezed over to the side, and waited as a van with its paint peeling off wobbled over a speed bump. It slowed even more when the girl in the red outfit came into view. Ragnhild wanted to cross the street. There was a pavement on the other side, and her mother had told her always to walk on the pavement. She waited for the van to pass, but it stopped instead, and the driver rolled down his window.

"You go first, I'll wait," he said.

She hesitated a moment, then crossed the street, turning around again to tug the pram up onto the pavement. The van slid forward a bit, then stopped again. The window on the opposite side was rolled down. His eyes are funny, she thought, really big and round as a ball. They were set wide apart and were pale blue, like thin ice. His mouth was small with full lips, and it pointed down like the mouth of a fish. He stared at her.

"Are you going up Skiferbakken with that pram?"

She nodded. "I live in Granittveien."

"It'll be awfully heavy. What have you got in it, then?"

"Elise," she replied, lifting up the doll.

"Excellent," he said with a broad smile. His mouth looked nicer now.

He scratched his head. His hair was dishevelled, and grew in thick clumps straight from his head like the leaves of a pineapple.

Now it looked even worse.

"I can drive you up there," he said. There's room for your pram in the back."

Ragnhild thought for a moment. She starred up Skiferbakken, which was long and steep. The man pulled on the handbrake and glanced in the back of the van.

"Mama's waiting for me," Ragnhild said.

A bell seemed to ring in the back of her mind, but she couldn't remember what it was for.

"You'll get home sooner if I drive you," he said.

That decided it. Ragnhild was a practical little girl. She wheeled the pram behind the van and the man hopped out. He opened the back door and lifted the pram in with one hand.

"You'll have to sit in the back and hold on to the pram. Otherwise it'll roll about," he said, and lifted in Ragnhild too.

He shut the back doors, climbed into the driver's seat, and released the brake.

"Do you go up this hill every day?" He looked at her in the mirror.

"Only when I've been at Marthe's. I stayed over."

She opened a flowered overnight bag from under the doll's blanket and opened it, checking that everything was in place: her nightgown with the picture of Nala on it, her toothbrush and hairbrush. The van lumbered over another speed bump. The man was still looking at her in the mirror.

"Have you ever seen a toothbrush like this?" Ragnhild said, holding it up for him. It had feet.

"No!" he said. "Where did you get it?"

"Papa bought it for me. You don't have one like it?"

"No, but I'll ask for one for Christmas."

He was finally over the last bump, and he shifted to second gear.

It made an awful grinding noise. The little girl sat on the floor of the van steadying the pram. A very sweet little girl, he thought, red and cute in her tracksuit, like a ripe little berry. He whistled a tune and felt on top of the world, enthroned behind the wheel in the big van with the little girl in the back. Really on top of the world.

The village lay in the bottom of the valley, at the end of the fjord, at the foot of a mountain. Like a pool in a river, where the water was much too still. And everyone knows that only running water is fresh. The village was a stepchild of the municipality, and the roads that led there were indescribably bad. Once in a while a bus deigned to stop by the abandoned dairy and pick up people to take them to town. There were no night buses back to the village.

Kollen, the mountain, was a grey, rounded peak, virtually neglected by those who lived there, but eagerly visited by people from far-off places. This was because of the mountain's unusual minerals and its flora, which was exceptionally rare. On calm days a faint tinkling could be heard from the mountaintop; one might almost believe it was haunted. In fact, the sound was from sheep grazing up there. The ridges around the mountain looked blue and airy through the haze, like soft felt with scattered woollen veils of fog.

Konrad Sejer traced the main highway in the road atlas with a fingertip. They were approaching a roundabout. Police Officer Karlsen was at the wheel, keeping an attentive eye on the fields while following the directions.

"Now you have to turn right on to Gneisveien, then up Skiferbakken, then left at Feltspatveien. Granittveien goes off to the right. A cul-de-sac," Sejer said pensively. "Number 5 should be the third house on the left."

He was tense. His voice was even more brusque than usual.

Karlsen manoeuvred the car into the housing estate and over the speed bumps. As in so many places, the new arrivals had taken up residence in clusters, some distance from the rest of the local community. Apart from giving directions, the two policemen didn't talk much. They approached the house, trying to steel themselves, thinking that perhaps the child might even be back home by now. Perhaps she was sitting on her mother's lap, surprised and embarrassed by all the fuss. It was 1pm, so the girl had been missing for five hours. Two would have been within a reasonable margin, five was definitely too long. Their unease was growing steadily, like a dead spot in the chest where the blood refused to flow. Both of them had children of their own; Karlsen's daughter was eight, Sejer had a grandson of four. The silence was filled with images, which might turn out to be correct – this is what struck Sejer as they drew up in front of the house.

Number 5 was a low, white house with dark blue trim. A typical prefab house with no personality, but embellished like a playroom with decorative shutters and scalloped edges on the gables. The yard was well kept. A large veranda with a prettily turned railing ran around the entire building. The house sat almost at the top of the ridge, with a view over the whole village, a small village, quite lovely, surrounded by farms and fields. A patrol car that had come on ahead of them was parked next to the letterbox.

Sejer went first, wiping his shoes carefully on the mat, and ducking his head as he entered the living room. It only took them a second to see what was happening. She was still missing, and the panic was palpable. On the sofa sat the mother, a stocky woman in a gingham dress. Next to her, with a hand on the mother's arm, sat a woman officer. Sejer could almost smell the terror in the room. The mother was using what little strength she had to hold back her tears, or perhaps even a piercing shriek of terror. The slightest effort made her breathe hard, as was evident when she stood up to shake hands with Sejer.

"Mrs Album," he said. "Someone is out searching, is that correct?"

"Some of the neighbours. They have a dog with them."

She sank back on the sofa.

"We have to help each other."

He sat down in the armchair facing her and leaned forward, keeping his eyes fixed on hers.

"We'll send out a dog patrol. Now, you have to tell me all about Ragnhild. Who she is, what she looks like, what she's wearing."

No reply, just persistent nodding. Her mouth looked stiff and frozen.

"Have you called every possible place where she could be?"

"There aren't many," she murmured. "I've called them all."

"Do you have relatives anywhere else in the village?"

"No, none. We're not from round here."
"Does Ragnhild go to kindergarten or nursery school?"
"There weren't any openings."
"Does she have any brothers or sisters?"
"She's our only child."

He tried to breathe without making a sound.

"First of all," he said, "what was she wearing? Be as precise as you can."

"A red tracksuit," she stammered, "with a lion on the front. Green anorak with a hood. One red shoe and one green shoe."

She spoke in fits and starts. Her voice threatening to break.

"And Ragnhild herself? Describe her for me."

"About four foot tall. Two and a half stone. Very fair hair. We just took her for her sixth-year check-up."

She went to the wall by the TV, where a number of photos were hanging. Most of them were of Ragnhild, one was of Mrs Album in national costume, and one of a man in a field uniform of the Home Guard, presumably the father. She chose one in which the girl was smiling and handed it to him. Her hair was almost white. The mother's was jet-black, but the father was blond. Some of his hair was visible under his service cap.

"What sort of girl is she?"

"Trusting," she gasped. "Talks to everybody." This admission made her shiver.

"That's just the kind of child that gets along best in this world," he said firmly. "We'll have to take the picture with us."

"I realise that."

"Tell me," he said, sitting back down, "where do the children in the village go walking?"

"Down to the fjord. To Prestegårds Strand or to Horgen. Or to the top of Kollen. Some go up to the reservoir, or they go walking in the woods."

He looked out the window and saw the black firs.

"Has anyone at all seen Ragnhild since she left?"

"Marthe's neighbour met her by his garage when he was leaving for work. I know because I rang his wife."

"Where does Marthe live?"

"In Krystallen, just a few minutes from here."

"She had her doll's pram with her?"

"Yes. A pink Brio."

"What's the neighbour's name?"

"Walther," she said, surprised. "Walther Isaksen."

"Where can I find him?"

"He works at Dyno Industries, in the personnel department."

Sejer stood up, went over to the telephone and called information, then punched in the number, and waited.

"I need to speak to one of your employees immediately. The name is Walther Isaksen."

Mrs Album gave him a worried look from the sofa. Karlsen was studying the view from the window, the blue ridges, the fields, and a white steeple church in the distance.

"Konrad Sejer of the police," Sejer said curtly. "I'm calling from 5 Granittveien and you probably know why."

"Is Ragnhild still missing?"

"Yes. But I understood that you saw her when she left Marthe's house this morning."

"I was shutting my garage door."

"Did you notice the time?"

"It was 8.06am. I was running a little late."

"Are you sure of the time?"

"I have a digital watch."

Sejer was silent, trying to recall the way they had driven.

"So you left at 8.06am by the garage and drove straight to work?"

"Yes."

"Down Gneisveien and out to the main highway?"

"That's correct."

"I would think," Sejer said, "that at that time of day most people are driving towards town and there's probably little traffic going the other way."

"Yes, that's right. There are no main roads going through the village, and no jobs, either."

"Did you pass any cars on the way that were driving towards the village?"

The man was silent for a moment. Sejer waited. The room was as quiet as a tomb.

"Yes, actually, I did pass one, down by the flats, just before the roundabout. A van, I think, ugly and with peeling paint. Driving quite slowly."

"Who was driving it?"

"A man," he said hesitantly. "One man."

"My name is Raymond." He smiled.

Ragnhild looked up, saw the smiling face in the mirror, and Kollen Mountain bathed in the morning light.

"Would you like to go for a drive?"

"Mama's waiting for me."

She said it in a sort of stuck-up voice.

"Have you ever been to the top of Kollen?"

"One time, with Papa. We had a picnic."

"It's possible to drive up there," he explained. "From the back side, that is. Shall we drive up to the top?"

"I want to go home," she said, a bit uncertain now.

He shifted down and stopped.

"Just a short ride?" he asked.

His voice was thin. Ragnhild thought he sounded so sad. And she wasn't used to disappointing the wishes of grown-ups. She got up, walked forward to the front seat and leaned over.

"Just a short ride," she repeated. "Up to the top and then back home right away."

He backed into Feldspatveien and drove back downhill.

"What's your name?" he asked.

"Ragnhild Elise."

He rocked a little from side to side and cleared his throat, as if to admonish her.

"Ragnhild Elise. You can't go shopping so early in the morning. It's only 8.15am. The shops are closed."

She didn't answer. Instead she lifted Elise out of the pram, put her on her lap and straightened her dress. Then she pulled the dummy out of the doll's mouth. Instantly the doll began to scream, a thin, metallic baby cry.

"What's that?" he braked hard and looked in the mirror.

"That's just Elise. She cries when I take her dummy out."

"I don't like that noise! Put it back in!"

He was restless at the wheel now, and the van weaved back and forth.

"Papa is a better driver than you are," she said.

"I had to teach myself," he said sulkily. "Nobody wanted to teach me."

"Why not?"

He didn't reply, just tossed his head. The van was out on the main highway now; he drove in second gear down to the roundabout and passed through the intersection with a hoarse roar.

"Now we're coming to Horgen," she said, delighted.

He didn't reply. Ten minutes later he turned left, up into the wooded mountainside. On the way they passed a couple of farms with red barns and tractors parked here and there. They saw no-one. The road grew narrower and peppered with holes. Ragnhild's arms were starting to grow tired from holding onto the pram, so she laid the doll on the floor and put her foot between the wheels as a brake.

"This is where I live," he said suddenly and stopped.

"With your wife?"

"No, with my father. But he's in bed."

"Hasn't he got up?"

"He's always in bed."

She peered cautiously out of the window and saw a peculiar house. It had been a hut once, and someone had added onto it, first once, then again. The separate parts were all different colours. Next to it stood a garage of corrugated iron. The courtyard was overgrown. A rusty old trowel was being slowly strangled by stinging nettles and dandelions. But Ragnhild wasn't interested in the house; she had her eye on something else.

"Bunnies!" she said faintly.

"Yes," he said "Do you want to look at them?"

He hopped out, opened the back, and lifted her down. He had a peculiar way of walking; his legs were almost unnaturally short and he was severely bowlegged. His feet were small. His wide nose nearly touched his lower lip, which stuck out a bit. Under his nose hung a big, clear drop. Ragnhild thought he wasn't that old, although when he walked he swayed like an old man. But it was funny too. A boy's face on an old body. He wobbled over to the rabbit hutches and opened them. Ragnhild stood spellbound.

"Can I hold one?"

"Yes. Take your pick."

"The little brown one," she said, entranced.

"That's Påsan. He's the nicest."

He opened the hutch and lifted out the rabbit. A chubby, lop-eared rabbit, the colour of coffee with a lot of cream. It kicked its legs vigorously but calmed down as soon as Ragnhild took it in her arms. For a moment she was utterly still. She could feel its heart pounding against her hand, as she stroked one of its ears cautiously. It was like a piece of velvet between her fingers. Its nose shone black and moist like a liquorice drop. Raymond stood next to her and watched. He had a little girl all to himself, and no-one had seen them.

"The picture," Sejer said, "Along with the description, will be sent to the newspapers. Unless they hear otherwise, they'll print it tonight."

Irene Album fell across the table sobbing. The others stared wordlessly at their hands, and at her shaking back. The woman officer sat ready with a handkerchief. Karlsen scraped his chair a bit and glanced at his watch.

"Is Ragnhild afraid of dogs?" Sejer said.

"Why do you ask?" she said with surprise.

'Sometimes when we're searching for children with the dog patrol, they hide when they hear our German shepherds."

"No, she's not afraid of dogs."

The words reverberated in his head. *She's not afraid of dogs.*

"Have you had any luck getting hold of your husband?"

"He's in Narvik on manoeuvres," she whispered. "On the plateau somewhere."

"Don't they use mobile phones?"

"They're out of range."

"The people who are looking for her now, who are they?"

"Boys from the neighbourhood who are home in the daytime. One of them has a phone with him."

"How long have they been gone?"

She looked up at the clock on the wall. "More than two hours."

Her voice was no longer quavering. Now she sounded doped, almost lethargic, as if she were half asleep. Sejer leaned forward and spoke to her as softly and as clearly as he could.

"What you fear most has probably *not* happened. Do you realise that? Usually, children disappear for all sorts of trivial reasons. And it's a fact that children get lost all the time, just because they're children. They have no sense of time or responsibility, and they're so maddeningly curious that they follow any impulse that comes into their head. That's what it's like to be a child, and that's why they get lost. But as a rule they turn up just as suddenly as they disappeared. Often they don't have a good explanation for where they've been or what they were doing. But generally" – he took a breath – "they're quite all right."

"I know!" she said, staring at him. "But she's never gone off like this before!"

"She's growing up and getting bigger," he said persuasively.

"She's becoming more adventurous."

God help me, he thought, I've got an answer for everything. He got up and dialled another number, repressing an urge to look at his watch again – it would be a reminder that time was passing, and they didn't need that. He reached the Duty Officer, gave him a brief summary of the situation and asked him to contact a volunteer rescue group. He gave him the address in Granittveien and gave a quick description of the girl: dressed in red, almost white hair, pink doll's pram. Asked whether any messages had come in, and was told none had been received. He sat down again.

"Has Ragnhild mentioned or named anyone lately whom you didn't know yourself?"

"No."

"Did she have any money? Could she have been looking for a shop?"

"She had no money."

"This is a small village," he went on. "Has she ever been out walking and been given a ride by one of the neighbours?"

"Yes, that happens sometimes. There are about a hundred houses on this ridge, and she knows almost everyone, and she knows their cars. Sometimes she and Marthe have walked down to the church with their prams, and they've been given a ride home with one of the neighbours."

"Is there any special reason why they go to the church?"

"There's a little boy they know buried there. They pick flowers for his grave, and then they come back up here. I think it seems exciting to them."

"You've searched the church?"

"I rang for Ragnhild at ten o'clock. When they told me she had left at eight, I jumped in the car. I left the front door unlocked in case she came back while I was out searching. I drove to the church and down to the Fina petrol station, I looked in the auto workshop and behind the dairy, and then I drove over to the school to look in the schoolyard, because they have jungle gyms and things there. And then I checked the kindergarten. She was so keen on starting school, she…"

Another bout of sobbing took hold. As she wept, the others sat still and waited. Her eyes were puffy now, and she was crumpling her skirt in her fingers in despair. After a while her sobs died away and the lethargy returned – a shield to keep the terrible possibilities at bay.

The phone rang. A sudden ominous jangle. She gave a start and got up to answer it, but caught sight of Sejer's hand held up to stop her. He lifted the receiver.

"Hello, is Irene there?"

It sounded like a boy. "Who's calling?"

"Thorbjørn Haugen. We're looking for Ragnhild."

"You're speaking with the police. Do you have any news?"

"We've been to all the houses on the whole ridge. Every single one. A lot of people weren't home, though we did meet a lady in Feltspatveien. A lorry had backed into her farmyard and turned around, she lives in number 1. A kind of van, she thought. And inside the van she saw a girl with a green jacket and white hair pulled into a topknot on her head. Ragnhild often wears her hair in a topknot."

"Go on."

"It turned halfway up the hill and drove back down. Disappeared around the curve."

"Do you know what time it was?"

"It was 8.15 am."

"Can you come over to Granittveien?"

"We'll be right there, we're at the roundabout now."

He hung up. Irene Album was still standing.

"What was it?" she whispered. "What did they say?"

"Someone saw her," he said slowly. "She got into a van."

Irene Album's scream finally came. It was as if the sound penetrated through the tight forest and created a faint movement in Ragnhild's mind.

"I'm hungry," she said suddenly. "I have to go home."

Raymond looked up. Påsan was shuffling about on the kitchen table and licking up the seeds they had scattered over it. They had forgotten both time and place. They had fed all the rabbits, Raymond had shown her his pictures, cut out of magazines and carefully pasted into a big album. Ragnhild kept roaring with laughter at his funny face. Now she realised it was getting late.

"You can have a slice of bread."

"I have to go home. We're going shopping."

"We'll go up to Kollen first, then I'll drive you home afterwards."

"Now!" she said firmly. "I want to go home now."

Raymond thought desperately for a way to stall her.

"All right. But first I have to go out and buy some milk for Papa, down at Horgen's shop. You can wait here, then it won't take as long."

He stood up and looked at her. Her bright face, with the little heart-shaped mouth that made him think of heart-shaped cinnamon sweets. Her eyes were clear and blue and her eyebrows dark, surprising beneath her white fringe. He sighed heavily, walked over to the back door and opened it.

Ragnhild really wanted to leave but she didn't know the way home so she would have to wait. She padded into the little living room with the rabbit in her arms and curled up in a corner of the sofa. They hadn't slept much last night, she and Marthe, and with the warm animal in the hollow of her throat she quickly grew sleepy. Soon her eyes closed.

It was a while before he came back. For a long time he sat and looked at her, amazed at how quietly she slept. Not a movement, not a single little sigh. He thought she had expanded a bit, become larger and warmer, like a loaf in the oven. After a while he grew uneasy and didn't know what to do with his hands, so he put them in his pockets and rocked a little in his chair. Started kneading the fabric of his trousers between his hands as he rocked and rocked, faster and faster. He looked anxiously out the windows and down the hall to his father's bedroom. His hands worked and worked. The whole time he stared at her hair, which was shiny as silk, almost like rabbit fur. Then he gave a low moan and stopped himself. Stood up and poked her lightly on the shoulder.

"We can go now. Give me Påsan."

For a moment Ragnhild was completely bewildered. She got up slowly and stared at Raymond, then followed him out to the kitchen and pulled on her anorak, and padded out of the house as the little brown ball of fur vanished back into its cage. The pram was still in the back of the van. Raymond looked sad, but he helped her climb in, then got into the driver's seat and turned the key. Nothing happened.

"It won't start." He said, annoyed. "I don't understand. It was running a minute ago. This piece of junk!"

"I have to go home!" Ragnhild said loudly, as if it would help the situation. He kept trying the ignition and stepping on the accelerator; he could hear the starter motor turning, but it kept up a complaining whine and refused to catch.

"We'll have to walk."

"It's much too far!" she whined.

"No, not from here. We're on the side of Kollen now, we're almost at the top, and from there you can look straight down on your house. I'll pull your pram for you."

He put on a jacket that lay on the front seat, got out and opened the door for her. Ragnhild carried her doll and he pulled the pram behind him. It bumped a little on the pot-holed road. Ragnhild could see Kollen looming farther ahead, ringed by dark woods. For a moment they had to pull off to the side of the road as a car passed them noisily at high speed. The dust hung like a thick fog behind it. Raymond knew the way, and he wasn't very fit, so it was no problem for Ragnhild to keep up. After a while the road grew steeper, ending in a turning space, and the path, which went round to the right of Kollen, was soft and dusty. The sheep had widened the path, and their droppings lay as thick as hail. Ragnhild amused herself by treading on them, they were dry and powdery. After a few minutes there was a lovely glistening visible through the trees.

"Serpent Tarn," Raymond said.

She stopped next to him, stared out across the lake and saw the water-lilies, and a little boat that lay upside down on the shore.

"Don't go down to the water," said Raymond. "It's dangerous. You can't swim here, you"d just sink into the sand and disappear. Quicksand," he added, with a serious expression. Ragnhild shuddered. She followed the bank of the tarn with her eyes, a wavy yellow line of rushes, except for one place where what might be called a beach broke the line like a dark indentation. That's what they were staring at. Raymond let go of the pram, and Ragnhild stuck a finger in her mouth.

Thorbjørn stood fiddling with the mobile phone. He was about 16, and had dark shoulder-length hair with a hint of dandruff, held in place with a patterned bandana. The ends stuck out at the knots at his temples like two red feathers, making him look like a pale Indian. He avoided looking at Ragnhild's mother, staring hard at Sejer instead, licking his lips constantly.

"What you have discovered is important," Sejer said. "Please write down her address. Do you remember the name?"

"Helga Moen, in number 1. A grey house with a kennel outside."

He almost spoke in a whisper as he printed the words in big letters on the pad that Sejer gave him.

"Your boys have been over most of the area?" Sejer asked.

"We were up on the Kollen first, then we went down to Serpent Tarn and went over the paths there. We went to the high tarn, Horgens Store and Prestegårds Strand. And the church. Last, we looked at a couple of farms, at Bjerkerud and at the Equestrian Sports Centre. Ragnhild was, uh, I mean *is* very interested in animals."

The slip of the tongue made him blush. Sejer patted him lightly on the shoulder.

"Sit down, Thorbjørn."

He nodded to the sofa where there was room next to Mrs Album. She had graduated to another phase, and was now contemplating the dizzying possibility that Ragnhild might never come home again, and she might have to live the rest of her life without her little girl and her big blue eyes. This realisation came in small stabs of pain. Her whole body was rigid, as if she had a steel rod running up her spine. The woman officer, who had hardly said a word the whole time they had been there, stood up slowly. For the first time she ventured to make a suggestion.

"Mrs Album," she asked quietly, "why don't we make everyone some coffee?"

The woman nodded weakly, got up and followed the officer out to the kitchen. A tap was turned on and there was the sound of cups clattering. Sejer motioned Karlsen over towards the hallway. They stood there muttering to one another. Thorbjørn could just see Sejer's head and the tip of Karlsen's shoe, which was shiny and black. In the dim light they could check their watches without being observed. They did so and nodded in agreement. Ragnhild's disappearance had become a serious matter, all the department's resources would have to be utilised. Sejer scratched his elbow through his shirt.

"I can't face the thought of finding her in a ditch."

He opened the door to get some fresh air. And there she stood. In her red jogging suit, on the bottom step, with a tiny white hand on the railing.

"Ragnhild?" he said in astonishment.

A happy half-hour later, as the car sped down Skiferbakken, Sejer ran his fingers through his hair with satisfaction. Karlsen thought his hair looked like a steel brush now that it was cut shorter than ever. The kind of brush used to clean off old paint. Sejer's lined face looked peaceful, not closed and serious as it usually did. Halfway down the hill they passed the grey house. They saw the kennel and a face at the window. If Helga Moen was hoping for a visit from the police, she would be disappointed. Ragnhild was sitting safely on her mother's lap with two thick slices of bread in her hand.

The moment when the little girl stepped into the living room was etched into the minds of both officers. The mother, hearing her thin little voice, rushed in from the kitchen and threw herself at Ragnhild, lightning fast, like a beast of prey grasping its victim and never wanting to let it go. Ragnhild's thin limbs and the white sprout of hair stuck out through her mother's powerful arms. And there they stood. Not a sound was heard, not a single cry from either of them. Thorbjørn was practically crushing the phone in his hand, the woman officer was making a clatter with the cups, and Karlsen kept twisting his moustache with a blissful grin on his face. The room brightened up as though the sun had suddenly shot a beam through the window. And then finally, with a sobbing laugh:

"YOU TERRIBLE CHILD!"

"I've been thinking," Sejer cleared his throat, "about taking a week's holiday. I have some time off due to me."

Karlsen crossed a speed bump.

"What will you do with it? Go skydiving in Florida?"

"I thought I'd air out my cabin."

"Near Brevik, isn't that where it is?"

"Sand Island."

They turned onto the main road and picked up speed.

"I have to go to Legoland this year," Karlsen muttered. "Can't avoid it any longer. My daughter is pestering me."

"You make it sound like a punishment," Sejer said. "Legoland is beautiful. When you leave I guarantee you'll be weighed down with boxes of Lego and you'll be bitten by the bug. Do go, you won't regret it."

"So, you've been there, have you?"

"I went there with Matteus. Do you know that they've built a statue of Sitting Bull out of nothing but pieces of Lego? One point four million pieces with special colouring. It's unbelievable."

He fell silent as he caught sight of the church off to the left, a little white wooden church a bit off the road between green and yellow fields, surrounded by lush trees. A beautiful little church, he thought; he should have buried his wife in a spot like that, even though it would have been a long way to come. Of course, it was too late now. She had been dead more than eight years and her grave was in the cemetery in the middle of town, right by the busy high street surrounded by exhaust fumes and traffic noise.

"Do you think the girl was all right?"

"She seemed to be. I've asked the mother to ring us when things calm down a bit. She"ll probably want to talk about it eventually. Six hours," he said thoughtfully, "that's quite a while. Must have been a charming lone wolf."

"He evidently had a driver's licence, at least. So he isn't a total hermit."

"We don't know that, do we? That he has a driver's licence?"

"No, damn it, you're right," Karlsen said. He braked abruptly and turned into the petrol station in what they called "downtown", with a post office, bank, hairdresser, and the Fina station. A poster bearing the words "sale on medicine" was displayed in the window of the low-price Kiwi grocery, and the hairdresser had a tempting offer for a new tanning bed.

"I need something to eat. Are you coming?"

They went in and Sejer bought a newspaper and some chocolate.

He peered out the window and down to the fjord.

"Excuse me," said the girl behind the counter, staring nervously at Karlsen's uniform. "Nothing has happened to Ragnhild, has it?"

"Do you know her?" Sejer put some coins on the counter.

"No, I don't know her, but I know who they are. Her mother was here this morning looking for her."

"Ragnhild is all right. She's back at home."

She smiled with relief and gave him his change.

"Are you from round here?" Sejer asked. "Do you know most people?"

"I certainly do. There aren't many of us."

"If I ask you whether you know a man, maybe a little odd, who drives a van, an old, ugly van with its paint peeling off, does that ring a bell?"

"That sounds like Raymond," she said, nodding. "Raymond Lake."

"What do you know about him?"

"He works at the Employment centre. Lives in a cabin on the far side of Kollen

C CONTEXTS | Literary extracts

with his father. Raymond has Down's syndrome. About 30, and very nice. His father used to run this station, by the way, before he retired."

"Does Raymond have a driver's licence?"

"No, but he drives anyway. It's his father's van. He's an invalid so he probably doesn't have much control over what Raymond does. The sheriff knows about it and pulls him over now and then, but it doesn't do much good. He never drives above second gear. Did he pick up Ragnhild?"

"Yes."

"Then she couldn't have been safer," she smiled. "Raymond would stop to let a ladybird cross the road."

The both grinned and went back outside. Karlsen bit into his chocolate and looked around.

"Nice town," he said, chewing.

Sejer, who had bought an old-fashioned marzipan loaf, followed his gaze. "That fjord is deep, more than 300 metres. Never gets above 17 degrees Celsius."

"Do you know anyone here?"

"I don't, but my daughter Ingrid does. She's been here on a folklore walk, the kind of thing they organise in the autumn. "Know your district." She loves stuff like that."

He rolled the candy wrapper into a thin strip and stuck it into his shirt pocket. "Do you think someone with Down's syndrome can be a good driver?"

"No idea," Karlsen said. "But there's nothing wrong with them except for having one chromosome too many. I think their biggest problem is that they take longer to learn something than other people do. They also have bad hearts. They don't live to be very old. And there's something about their hands."

"What's that?"

"They're missing a line on their palm or something."

Sejer gave him a surprised look. "Anyway, Ragnhild certainly let herself be charmed."

"I think the rabbits helped."

Karlsen found a handkerchief in his inside pocket and wiped the chocolate from the corners of his mouth. "I grew up with a Down's syndrome child. We called him "Crazy Gunnar". Now that I think of it, we actually seemed to believe that he came from another planet. He's dead now – only lived to be 35."

They got into the car and drove on. Sejer prepared a simple little speech that he would serve up to the department chief when they were back at headquarters. A few days off to go up to his cabin seemed tremendously important all of a sudden. The timing was right, the long-term prospects were promising, and the girl showing up safe and sound at home had put him in a good mood. He stared over fields and meadows, registered that they had slowed down, and saw the tractor in front of them. A green John Deere with butter-yellow wheel rims was crawling at a snail's pace. They had no chance to overtake it; each time they came to a straight stretch, it proved to be too short. The farmer, who was wearing a gardener's cap and earmuffs, sat like a tree stump, as though he was growing straight up out of the seat. Karlsen changed gears and sighed.

"He's carrying Brussels sprouts. Can't you reach out and grab a box? We could cook them in the kitchen at the canteen."

"Now we're going as fast as Raymond does," muttered Sejer.

"Life in second gear. That really would be something, don't you think?"

He settled his grey head against the head-rest and closed his eyes.

From *Don't Look Back* by Karin Fossum, published by Harvill Press. Reprinted by permission of The Random House Group Ltd.

Language

Language

Pronunciation 459

Words and phrases 460

Menu reader 462

Glossary of Norwegian terms 465

Glossary of art and architectural terms 466

Language

There are two official Norwegian languages: **Riksmål** or **Bokmål** (book language), a modification of the old Dano-Norwegian tongue left over from the days of Danish dominance; and **Landsmål** or **Nynorsk**, which was codified during the nineteenth-century upsurge of Norwegian nationalism and is based on rural dialects of Old Norse provenance. Roughly eighty-five percent of schoolchildren have *Bokmål* as their primary language, and the remaining fifteen percent are *Nynorsk* speakers, concentrated in the fjord country of the west coast and the mountain districts of central Norway. Despite the best efforts of the government, *Nynorsk* is in decline – in 1944 fully one-third of the population used it. As the more common of the two languages, *Bokmål* is what we use here.

You don't really need to know any Norwegian to get by in Norway. Almost everyone speaks some English, and in any case many words are not too far removed from their English equivalents; there's also plenty of English (or American) on billboards, the TV and at the cinema. Mastering "hello" or "thank you" will, however, be greatly appreciated, while if you speak either Danish or Swedish you should have few problems being understood. Incidentally, Norwegians find Danish easier to read than Swedish, but orally it's the other way round.

Phrasebooks are fairly thin on the ground, but Berlitz's *Norwegian Phrasebook with Dictionary* has – as you would expect from the title – a mini-dictionary, not to mention a useful grammar section and a menu reader; Dorling Kindersley's *Norwegian Phrasebook* is comparable. There are several **dictionaries** to choose from, all of which include pronunciation tips and so forth. The best is generally considered to be the Collins *English-Norwegian Dictionary*, though this is currently out of print and you might decide to opt for the Berlitz *Norwegian Dictionary* instead. As for learning the language, the *Teach Yourself Norwegian course*, by Margaretha Danbolt Simons, is recommended and comprises tapes and books.

Pronunciation

Pronunciation can be tricky. A **vowel** is usually long when it's the final syllable or followed by only one consonant; followed by two it's generally short. Unfamiliar ones are:

ae before an r, as in **bad**; otherwise as in **say**

ø as in **fur** but without pronouncing the r

å usually as in **saw**

øy between the **ø** sound and **boy**

ei as in **say**

Consonants

are pronounced as in English except:

c, **q**, **w**, **z** found only in foreign words and pronounced as in the original language

g before i, y or ei, as in **yet**; otherwise hard

hv as in **view**

j, gj, hj, lj as in **y**et
rs almost always as in **sh**ut
k before i, y or j, like the Scottish lo**ch**; otherwise hard
sj, sk before i, y, ø or øy, as in **sh**ut

Words and phrases

Basic phrases

snakker du engelsk?	do you speak English?
ja	yes
nei	no
forstår du?	do you understand?
jeg forstår ikke	I don't understand
jeg forstår	I understand
vær så god	please (is near enough,though there's no direct equivalent)
takk (tusen takk)	thank you (very much)
vær så god	you're welcome
unnskyld	excuse me
god morgen	good morning
god dag	good afternoon
god natt	good night
adjø	goodbye
i dag	today
i morgen	tomorrow
i overmorgen	day after tomorrow
om morgenen	in the morning
om ettermiddagen	in the afternoon
om kvelden	in the evening

Some signs

inngang	entrance
utgang	exit
herrer/menn	gentlemen
damer/kvinner	ladies
åpen	open
stengt	closed
ankomst	arrival
politi	police
sykehus	hospital
sykkelsti	cycle path
røyking forbudt	no smoking
camping forbudt	no camping
uvedkommende forbudt	no trespassing
ingen adgang	no entry
trekk/trykk	pull/push
avgang	departure
avgift	parking fees

Questions and directions

hvor? (hvor er?)	where? (where is/are?)
når?	when?
hva?	what?
hvor mye/hvor mange?	how much/many?
hvorfor?	why?
hvilket?	which?
hva kaller man det på norsk?	what's that called in Norwegian?
kan de vise meg veien til ...?	can you direct me to ...?
det er (er det?)	it is/there is (is it/is there)
hvor mange er klokken?	what time is it?
stor/liten	big/small
billig/dyrt	cheap/expensive
tidlig/sent	early/late
varm/kald	hot/cold
i nærheten/langt borte	near/far
god/dårlig	good/bad
ledig/opptatt	vacant/occupied
litt/mye	a little/a lot
mer/mindre	more/less
kan vi campe her?	can we camp here?

er det et vandrerhjem i nærheten?	is there a youth hostel near here?
hvordan kommer jeg til ...?	how do I get to ...?
hvor langt er det til ...?	how far is it to ...?
billett	ticket
en vei/tur-retur	single/return
kan jeg få sitte på til ...?	can you give me a lift to ...?
venstre/høyre	left/right
kjør rett frem	go straight ahead

Numbers

null	0
en	1
to	2
tre	3
fire	4
fem	5
seks	6
sju	7
åtte	8
ni	9
ti	10
elleve	11
tolv	12
tretten	13
fjorten	14
femten	15
seksten	16
sytten	17
atten	18
nitten	19
tjue	20
tjueen	21
tjueto	22
tretti	30
førti	40
femti	50
seksti	60
sytti	70
åtti	80
nitti	90
hundre	100
hundreogen	101
to hundre	200
tusen	1000

Days

søndag	Sunday
mandag	Monday
tirsdag	Tuesday
onsdag	Wednesday
torsdag	Thursday
fredag	Friday
lørdag	Saturday

Months

januar	January
februar	February
mars	March
april	April
mai	May
juni	June
juli	July
august	August
september	September
oktober	October
november	November
desember	December

(Note: days and months are never capitalized)

Menu reader

Basics and snacks

appelsin, marmelade	marmalade
brød	bread
eddik	vinegar
egg	egg
eggerøre	scrambled eggs
flatbrød	crispbread
fløte	cream
grønsaker	vegetables
grøt	porridge
iskrem	ice cream
kaffefløte	single cream for coffee
kake	cake
kaviar	caviar
kjeks	biscuits
krem	whipped cream
melk	milk
mineralvann	mineral water
nøtter	nuts
olje	oil
omelett	omelette
ost	cheese
pannekake	pancakes
pepper	pepper
potetchips	crisps (potato chips)
pommes-frites	chips (French fries)
ris	rice
rundstykker	bread roll
salat	salad

Norwegian specialities

brun saus – gravy served with most meats, rissoles, fishcakes and sausages.
fenalår – marinated mutton that is smoked, sliced, salted, dried and served with crispbread, scrambled egg and beer.
fiskeboller – fish balls, served under a white sauce or on open sandwiches.
fiskekabaret – shrimps, fish and vegetables in aspic.
fiskesuppe – fish soup.
flatbrød – a flat unleavened cracker, half barley, half wheat.
gammelost – a hard, strong smelling, yellow-brown cheese with veins.
geitost/gjetost – goat's cheese, slightly sweet and fudge-coloured. Similar cheeses have different ratios of goat's milk to cow's milk.
gravetlaks – salmon marinated in salt, sugar, dill and brandy.
juleskinke – marinated boiled ham, served at Christmas.
kjøttkaker med – homemade burgers with **surkål** – cabbage and a sweet and sour sauce.
koldtbord – a midday buffet with cold meats, herrings, salads, bread and perhaps soup, eggs or hot meats.
lapskaus – pork, venison (or other meats) and vegetable stew, common in the south and east, using salted or fresh meat, or leftovers, in a thick brown gravy.
lutefisk – fish (usually cod) preserved in an alkali solution and seasoned; an acquired taste.
multer – cloudberries – wild berries mostly found north of the Arctic Circle and served with cream (med krem).
mysost – brown whey cheese, made from cow's milk.
nedlagtsild – marinated herring.
pinnekjøtt – western Norwegian Christmas dish of smoked mutton steamed over shredded birch bark, served with cabbage; or accompanied by boiled potatoes and mashed swedes (kålrabistappe).
reinsdyrstek – reindeer steak, usually served with boiled potatoes and cranberry sauce.
rekesalat – shrimp salad in mayonnaise.
ribbe, julepølse – eastern Norwegian Christmas medisterkake dish of pork ribs, sausage and dumplings.
spekemat – various types of smoked, dried meat.
Trondhjemsuppea – kind of milk broth with raisins, rice, cinnamon and sugar.

salt	salt	**suppe**	soup
sennep	mustard	**syltetøy**	jam
smør	butter	**varm pølse**	hot dog
smørbrød	open sandwich	**yoghurt**	yoghurt
sukker	sugar		

Meat (kjøtt) and game (vilt)

dyrestek	venison	**postei**	pâté
elg	elk	**pølser**	sausages
kalkun	turkey	**reinsdyr**	reindeer
kjøttboller	meatballs	**ribbe**	pork rib
kjøttkaker	rissoles	**skinke**	ham
kylling	chicken	**spekemat**	dried meat
lammekjøtt	lamb	**stek**	steak
lever	liver	**svinekjøtt**	pork
oksekjøtt	beef	**varm pølse**	frankfurter/hot-dog

Fish (fisk) and shellfish (skalldyr)

ansjos	anchovies (brisling)	**rødspette**	plaice
blåskjell	mussels	**røkelaks**	smoked salmon
brisling	sprats	**sardiner**	sardines (brisling)
hummer	lobster	**sei**	coalfish
hvitting	whiting	**sild**	herring
kaviar	caviar	**sjøtunge**	sole
krabbe	crab	**småfisk**	whitebait
kreps	crayfish	**steinbit**	catfish
laks	salmon	**torsk**	cod
makrell	mackerel	**tunfisk**	tuna
piggvar	turbot	**ørret**	trout
reker	shrimps	**ål**	eel

Vegetables (grønsaker)

agurk	cucumber/gherkin/ pickle	**løk**	onion
		mais	sweetcorn
blomkål	cauliflower	**nepe**	turnip
bønner	beans	**paprika**	peppers
erter	peas	**poteter**	potatoes
gulrøtter	carrots	**rosenkål**	Brussels sprouts
hodesalat	lettuce	**selleri**	celery
hvitløk	garlic	**sopp**	mushrooms
kål	cabbage	**spinat**	spinach
linser	lentils	**tomater**	tomatoes

Fruit (frukt)

ananas	pineapple
appelsin	orange
aprikos	apricot
banan	banana
blåbær	blueberries
druer	grapes
eple	apple
fersken	peach
fruktsalat	fruit salad
grapefrukt	grapefruit
jordbær	strawberries
multer	cloudberries
plommer	plums
pærer	pears
sitron	lemon
solbær	blackcurrants
tyttbær	cranberries

Cooking terms

blodig	rare, underdone
godt stekt	well done
grillet	grilled
grytestekt	braised
kokt	boiled
marinert	marinated
ovnstekt	baked/roasted
røkt	smoked
stekt	fried
stuet	stewed
sur	sour, pickled
syltet	pickled
saltet	cured

Bread, cake and desserts

bløtkake – cream cake with fruit

fløtelapper – pancakes made with cream, served with sugar and jam

havrekjeks – oatmeal biscuits, eaten with goat's cheese

knekkebrød – crispbread

kransekake – cake made from almonds, sugar and eggs, served at celebrations

lomper – potato scones-cum-tortillas

riskrem – rice pudding with whipped cream and sugar, usually served with frukt saus, a slighly thickened fruit sauce

tilslørtbondepiker – stewed apples and breadcrumbs, served with cream

trollkrem – beaten egg whites (or whipped cream) and sugar mixed with cloudberries (or cranberries)

vafle – waffles

Drinks

akevitt	aquavit
appelsin	orange squash
saft/juice	juice
brus	fizzy soft drink
eplesider	cider
fruktsaft	sweetened fruit juice
kaffe	coffee
melk	milk
mineralvann	mineral water
øl	beer
sitronbrus	lemonade
te med melk/sitron	tea with milk/lemon
vann	water
varm sjokolade	hot chocolate
vin	wine
søt	sweet
tørr	dry
rød	red
hvit	white
rosé	rosé
skål	cheers

Glossary of Norwegian terms

apotek chemist

bakke hill

bokhandel bookshop

bre glacier

bro/bru bridge

brygge quay or wharf

dal valley/dale

DNT (Den Norske Turistforening) Nationwide hiking organization whose local affiliates maintain hiking paths across almost all the country

Domkirke Cathedral

drosje taxi

E.kr AD

elv/bekk river/stream

ferje/ferge ferry

fjell/berg mountain

Flybussen Airport bus (literally "plane bus")

F.kr BC

foss waterfall

gågate urban pedestrianized area

gate (gt.) street

Gamle byen Literally "Old Town"; used wherever the old part of town has remained distinct from the rest (eg Fredrikstad, p.129). Also spelt as one word.

hav ocean

havn harbour

Hurtigbåt Passenger express boat; usually a catamaran

Hurtigrute Literally "quick route", but familiar as the name of the boat service along the west coast from Bergen to Kirkenes

hytte cottage, cabin

innsjø lake

jernbanestasjon railway station

kirke/kjerke church

Kfum/kfuk Norwegian YMCA/YWCA

klokken/kl. o'clock

klippfisk salted whitefish, usually cod

moderasjon discount or price reduction

Moms or mva Sales tax – applied to almost all consumables

museet museum

NAF Nationwide Norwegian automobile association. Membership covers rescue and repair

rabatt discount or price reduction

rådhus town hall

rorbu originally a simple wooden cabin built near the fishing grounds for incoming (ie non-local) fishermen. Many cabins are now used as tourist accommodation, especially in the Lofoten (see pp.323–337)

Sami Formerly called Lapps, the Sami inhabit the northern reaches of Norway, Finland and Sweden – Lapland

sentrum city or town centre

sjø sea

sjøhus harbourside building where the catch was sorted, salted, filleted and iced. many are now redundant and some have been turned into tourist accommodation

skog forest

slott castle, palace

Stavkirke Stave church

Storting Parliament

tilbud special offer

torget main town square, often home to an outdoor market; sometimes spelt Torvet

Vandrerhjem Youth hostel

vann/vatn water or lake

vei/veg/vn. road

øy/øya islet

Glossary of English art and architectural terms

Ambulatory Covered passage around the outer edge of the choir in the chancel of a church.

Art Deco Geometrical style of art and architecture popular in the 1930s.

Art Nouveau Style of art, architecture and design based on highly stylized vegetal forms. Particularly popular in the early part of the twentieth century.

Baroque The art and architecture of the Counter-Reformation, dating from around 1600 onwards, and distinguished by extreme ornateness, exuberance and the complex but harmonious spatial arrangement of interiors.

Classical Architectural style incorporating Greek and Roman elements – pillars, domes, colonnades, etc – at its height in the seventeenth century and revived, as Neoclassical, in the nineteenth century.

Fresco Wall painting – made durable through applying paint to wet plaster.

Gothic Architectural style of the thirteenth to sixteenth centuries, characterized by pointed arches, rib vaulting, flying buttresses and a general emphasis on verticality.

Misericord Ledge on a choir stall on which the occupant can be supported while standing; often carved with secular subjects (bottoms were not thought worthy of religious ones).

Nave Main body of a church.

Neoclassical Architectural style derived from Greek and Roman elements – pillars, domes, colonnades, etc – popular in Norway throughout the nineteenth century.

Renaissance Movement in art and architecture developed in fifteenth-century Italy.

Rococo Highly florid, light and graceful eighteenth-century style of architecture, painting and interior design, forming the last phase of Baroque.

Rood screen Decorative screen separating the nave from the chancel.

Romanesque Early medieval architecture distinguished by squat forms, rounded arches and naive sculpture.

Stucco Marble-based plaster used to embellish ceilings, etc.

Transept Arms of a cross-shaped church, placed at ninety degrees to nave and chancel.

Triptych Carved or painted work on three panels. Often used as an altarpiece.

Vault An arched ceiling or roof.

Travel store

Travel Specials
First-Time Around the World
First-Time Asia
First-Time Europe
First-Time Latin America
Travel Online
Travel Health
Travel Survival
Walks in London & SE England
Women Travel

Maps
Algarve
Amsterdam
Andalucia & Costa del Sol
Argentina
Athens
Australia
Barcelona
Berlin
Boston
Brittany
Brussels
California
Chicago
Corsica
Costa Rica & Panama
Crete
Croatia
Cuba
Cyprus
Czech Republic
Dominican Republic
Dubai & UAE
Dublin
Egypt
Florence & Siena
Florida
France
Frankfurt
Germany
Greece
Guatemala & Belize
Hong Kong
Iceland
Ireland
Kenya & Northern Tanzania
Lisbon
London
Los Angeles
Madrid
Mallorca
Malaysia
Marrakesh
Mexico
Miami & Key West
Morocco
New England
New York City
New Zealand
Northern Spain
Paris
Peru
Portugal
Prague
The Pyrenees
Rome
San Francisco
Sicily
South Africa
South India
Spain & Portugal
Sri Lanka
Tenerife
Thailand
Toronto
Trinidad & Tobago
Tuscany
Venice
Vietnam, Laos & Cambodia
Washington DC
Yucatán Peninsula

Dictionary Phrasebooks
Croatian
Czech
Dutch
Egyptian Arabic
French
German
Greek
Hindi & Urdu
Italian
Japanese
Latin American Spanish
Mandarin Chinese
Mexican Spanish
Polish
Portuguese
Russian
Spanish
Swahili
Thai
Turkish
Vietnamese

Computers
Blogging
iPods, iTunes & music online
The Internet
Macs & OS X
PCs and Windows
Playstation Portable
Website Directory

Film & TV
American Independent Film
British Cult Comedy
Chick Flicks
Comedy Movies
Cult Movies
Gangster Movies
Horror Movies
James Bond
Kids' Movies
Sci-Fi Movies
Westerns

Lifestyle
eBay
Ethical Shopping
Babies
Pregnancy & Birth

Music Guides
The Beatles
Bob Dylan
Classical Music
Elvis
Frank Sinatra
Heavy Metal
Hip-Hop
Jazz
Music Playlists
Opera
Pink Floyd
Punk
Reggae
Rock
The Rolling Stones
Soul and R&B
World Music (2 vols)

Popular Culture
Books for Teenagers
Children's Books, 0-5
Children's Books, 5-11
Conspiracy Theories
Cult Fiction
The Da Vinci Code
Lord of the Rings
Shakespeare
Superheroes
Unexplained Phenomena

Sport
Arsenal 11s
Celtic 11s
Chelsea 11s
Liverpool 11s
Man United 11s
Newcastle 11s
Rangers 11s
Tottenham 11s
Poker

Science
Climate Change
The Universe
Weather

NOTES

Small print and Index

A Rough Guide to Rough Guides

Published in 1982, the first Rough Guide – to Greece – was a student scheme that became a publishing phenomenon. Mark Ellingham, a recent graduate in English from Bristol University, had been travelling in Greece the previous summer and couldn't find the right guidebook. With a small group of friends he wrote his own guide, combining a highly contemporary, journalistic style with a thoroughly practical approach to travellers' needs.

The immediate success of the book spawned a series that rapidly covered dozens of destinations. And, in addition to impecunious backpackers, Rough Guides soon acquired a much broader and older readership that relished the guides' wit and inquisitiveness as much as their enthusiastic, critical approach and value-for-money ethos.

These days, Rough Guides include recommendations from shoestring to luxury and cover more than 200 destinations around the globe, including almost every country in the Americas and Europe, more than half of Africa and most of Asia and Australasia. Our ever-growing team of authors and photographers is spread all over the world, particularly in Europe, the USA and Australia.

In the early 1990s, Rough Guides branched out of travel, with the publication of Rough Guides to World Music, Classical Music and the Internet. All three have become benchmark titles in their fields, spearheading the publication of a wide range of books under the Rough Guide name.

Including the travel series, Rough Guides now number more than 350 titles, covering: phrasebooks, waterproof maps, music guides from Opera to Heavy Metal, reference works as diverse as Conspiracy Theories and Shakespeare, and popular culture books from iPods to Poker. Rough Guides also produce a series of more than 120 World Music CDs in partnership with World Music Network.

Visit www.roughguides.com to see our latest publications.

Rough Guide travel images are available for commercial licensing at www.roughguidespictures.com

Rough Guide credits

Text editors: Lucy Ratcliffe and Polly Thomas
Layout: Ajay Verma
Cartography: Jai Prakash Mishra
Picture editor: Mark Thomas
Production: Aimee Hampson
Proofreader: Jan McCann
Cover design: Mark Thomas
Editorial: London Kate Berens, Claire Saunders, Geoff Howard, Ruth Blackmore, Richard Lim, Clifton Wilkinson, Alison Murchie, Karoline Densley, Andy Turner, Keith Drew, Edward Aves, Nikki Birrell, Helen Marsden, Alice Park, Sarah Eno, Joe Staines, Duncan Clark, Peter Buckley, Matthew Milton, Tracy Hopkins, David Paul, Lucy White, Ruth Tidball; **New York** Andrew Rosenberg, Steven Horak, AnneLise Sorensen, Amy Hegarty, Hunter Slaton, April Isaacs, Sean Mahoney, Ella Steim
Design & Pictures: London Simon Bracken, Dan May, Diana Jarvis, Jj Luck, Harriet Mills, Chloë Roberts; **Delhi** Madhulita Mohapatra, Umesh Aggarwal, Jessica Subramanian, Ankur Guha, Pradeep Thapliyal, Sachin Tanwar
Production: Sophie Hewat, Katherine Owers
Cartography: London Maxine Repath, Ed Wright, Katie Lloyd-Jones; **Delhi** Manish Chandra, Rajesh Chhibber, Ashutosh Bharti, Rajesh Mishra, Animesh Pathak, Jasbir Sandhu, Karobi Gogoi
Online: New York Jennifer Gold, Suzanne Welles, Kristin Mingrone; **Delhi** Manik Chauhan, Narender Kumar, Manish Shekhar Jha, Rakesh Kumar, Chhandita Chakravarty, Amit Verma
Marketing & Publicity: London Richard Trillo, Niki Hanmer, David Wearn, Demelza Dallow, Louise Maher, Jess Carter; **New York** Geoff Colquitt, Megan Kennedy, Katy Ball; **Delhi** Reem Khokhar
Custom publishing and foreign rights: Philippa Hopkins
Manager India: Punita Singh
Series editor: Mark Ellingham
Reference Director: Andrew Lockett
PA to Publishing Director: Megan McIntyre
Publishing Director: Martin Dunford

SMALL PRINT

Publishing information

This fourth edition published July 2006 by **Rough Guides Ltd**,
80 Strand, London WC2R 0RL
345 Hudson St, 4th Floor,
New York, NY 10014, USA
14 Local Shopping Centre, Panchsheel Park,
New Delhi 110017, India
Distributed by the Penguin Group
Penguin Books Ltd,
80 Strand, London WC2R 0RL
Penguin Putnam, Inc.
375 Hudson Street, NY 10014, USA
Penguin Group (Australia)
250 Camberwell Road, Camberwell,
Victoria 3124, Australia
Penguin Books Canada Ltd,
10 Alcorn Avenue, Toronto, Ontario,
Canada M4V 1E4
Penguin Group (New Zealand)
Cnr Rosedale and Airborne Roads
Albany, Auckland, New Zealand
Cover concept by Peter Dyer.

Typeset in Bembo and Helvetica to an original design by Henry Iles.
Printed and bound in China

488pp includes index
A catalogue record for this book is available from the British Library
ISBN 1-84353-660-9
ISBN 13: 9-78184-353-660-4
The publishers and authors have done their best to ensure the accuracy and currency of all the information in **The Rough Guide to Norway**, however, they can accept no responsibility for any loss, injury, or inconvenience sustained by any traveller as a result of information or advice contained in the guide.
1 3 5 7 9 8 6 4 2

Help us update

We've gone to a lot of effort to ensure that the fourth edition of **The Rough Guide to Norway** is accurate and up to date. However, things change – places get "discovered", opening hours are notoriously fickle, restaurants and rooms raise prices or lower standards. If you feel we've got it wrong or left something out, we'd like to know, and if you can remember the address, the price, the time and the phone number, so much the better. We'll credit all contributions, and send a copy of the next edition (or any other Rough Guide if you prefer) for the best letters. Everyone who writes to us and isn't already a subscriber will receive a copy of our full-colour thrice-yearly newsletter. Please mark letters: **"Rough Guide to Norway Update"** and send to: Rough Guides, 80 Strand, London WC2R 0RL, or Rough Guides, 4th Floor, 345 Hudson St, New York, NY 10014. Or send an email to **mail@roughguides.com**

Have your questions answered and tell others about your trip at
www.roughguides.atinfopop.com

Acknowledgements

Phil Lee would like to thank his editor, Lucy Ratcliffe, for her patient and good-humoured work on this new edition of Norway – it was much appreciated. He would also like to thank his stepdaughter, Emma Rose Rees, for her timely contributions.

Readers' letters

Thanks to all the readers who took the trouble to write in with their comments and suggestions. In particular, thanks to

Jon Alcock; Tom Andrews; Henning Arp; Geir Benden; Philip Borg-Wheeler; Graeme Brock; Ross Brown; Dora Caldwell; Peggy Chen; Heidi Dahl; K. Everett; Silje Figenschou; Melanie Francis; Adrian Enok Friis; Sarah Fuller; Heather & Martin Gill; Lewis Graham; Joe Gumino; Isebaert Gustaaf; Lars Gustavsen; Øyvind Heen; Louse Wies & Dennis Hesseling; A.E.W. Hudson; Kari Jorgensen; John Joyner; Brent Knoll; Per Krogsrud; Anh Le; Jeffrey Mahn; Charlotte Marceau; Richard McDonough; Marie Massa; Core Minnema; Andre Moreira; Lupe Moreno; Colin Nachenius; Luke Nicolaides; David & Win Normington; Jessica Osborn; Trine Pedersen; Piergiorgio Pescali; Helge Dahl Pettersen; Michael Plunkett; Jane Rackley; Tarmo Rajasaari; Paul Richards; Harry Saltzman; H. Sefi; Elly Shepherd; Jan Skotheim; A. Sorensen; Blaine Stothard; Nick Williamson; Tom Wolfenden; Gemma Woodhouse; Jasmin Wyler; Peter Zombori.

Photo credits

Title page
House on Lyngenfjord © blickwinkle/Alamy

Full page
Hamnøy © Gavin Hellierx

Introduction
Arctic tern © Louise Murray/Getty Images
Passenger ferry on Sognefjorden © Arnulf Husmo/Getty Images
The northern lights © Orion Press/Getty Images
Puffin © Per Eide/NTR
Roald Amundsen © Corbis
Bergen © BL Images/Alamy
Liberty Day parade © Arnulf Husmo/Getty Images
Dog sledging © Staffan Wildstrand/Corbis
Dried cod © Arco Images/Alamy
Jostedalsbreen glacier © Corbis
People in the midnight sun © Kim Heart/Robert Harding Picture Library/Alamy
Shellfish, Bergen fish market © Sophie Morris/Hutchison Library
Oslo © Altrendo Panoramic/Getty Images

Things not to miss
01 Jotunheimen National Park © A.Tovy/Trip
02 Midnight sun at Nordkapp © Bruce Adams/Eye Ubiquitous/Alamy
03 Polar bear © Bryan Knox/Papilio/Alamy
04 Vigelandsparken © Danita Delimont/Alamy
05 Flåm mountain railway © Chris Coe/Axiom
06 Art Nouveau building in Kongensgate, Ålesund © Leslie Garland Picture Library/Alamy
07 Swimming in the Oslofjord © Paul A. Souders/Corbis
08 Hørundfjord © Phil Lee
09 Norwegian Fishing Village Museum © Stig Einarsen/Lofoten
10 Edvard Greig's house © Robert Harding Picture Library
11 Union Hotel © Phil Lee
12 Bergen © Robert Harding Picture Library/Alamy
13 Whalewatching © George McCallum Photography/Alamy
14 Urnes stave church © Phil Lee
15 The Josteldalsbreen glacier © Chris Coe/Axiom
16 Oseberg ship © John Henshall/Alamy
17 Trondheim cathedral © WorldFoto/Alamy
18 Geirangerfjord © E. Simanor/Robert Harding Picture Library
19 Alta rock carvings © Phil Lee
20 Seabird colony on Vaerey © Stig Einarsen/Lofoten Fotogalleri

21 Svalbard © N. Price/Trip
22 Henningsvar © Terje Rakke/NTR
23 Mandal © Phil Lee
24 Summer night at the shore (oil on canvas) by Edvard Munch © Kunsthistorisches Museum, Vienna, Austria/ The Bridgeman Art Library
25 Kjerringoy trading station © Eepen Mortensen/ Destinations Bodo

Colour insert: The Vikings
Wooden Viking figurehead © Corbis
Aurlandsfjord © Gavin Hellier, Jon Arnold Images/ Alamy
Saga carving © Corbis
Viking jewellery © Ted Spiegel/Corbis
Oseberg ship © Richard T. Nowitz/Corbis
Borgund church © eye35.com/Alamy

Colour insert: Hiking
Mountains in Fjordane © Vincent Lowe, Leslie Garland Picture Library/Alamy
Hikers in the Aurland Valley © Nick Hanna/Alamy
Trekkers resting in Spitsbergen © Bo Jansson, Pixonnet/Alamy
Mountain lodge © Mikael Utterstrom/Alamy
Camping by Lake Femunden © Mikael Svensson/ Alamy
Rondane National Park © Mikael Utterstrom/ Alamy

Black and whites
p.74 Vigelandsparken statues, Oslo © Walter Bibikow/Jon Arnold Images/Alamy
p.92 Liberty Day Parade © Arnulf Husmo/Getty Images
p.106 Gjoa ship © Leslie Garland Picture Library/ Alamy
p.115 People outside restaurant in Oslo © Chad Ehlers/Alamy
p.130 Frederikstad © WorldFoto/Alamy
p.138 View from Pulpit Rock © Loetscher Martin/ Alamy
p.142 Arendal Harbour © Leslie Garland Picture Library/Alamy
p.156 Stavanger © D. Saunders/Trip
p.164 Jotunheimen National Park © Armands Punders/Alamy
p.171 Bob-sleigh team in Lillehammer © Daikusan/Getty Images
p.179 Rondane National Park © Dagfinn Skjelle/ Alamy
p.193 Telemarkskanal © John Peter Photography/ Alamy
p.198 Bergen © Alamy
p.209 Bergen Funicular © WorldFoto/Alamy
p.223 Hardangervidda National Park © Chris Lisle/Corbis
p.238 Sognefjord © Leslie Garland Picture Library
p.255 Ferry on Geirangerfjord © Chad Ehlers/ Alamy
p.274 Whalewatchers © Staffan Widstrand/Corbis
p.286 Trondheim © Oldrick Karasek/Alamy
p.299 Arctic Circle marker stone © Dave and Sigrun Tollerton/Alamy
p.311 Narvik Church © Ian Simpson/Alamy
p.322 Trollfjord © Rolf Richardson/Alamy
p. 334 Lofoten Islands © nagelestock.com
p.340 Bearded seal © blickwinkel/Alamy
p.347 Tromso © John Cleare/Alamy
p.359 Sami man with reindeer © Arco Images/ Alamy
p.367 Honningsvag © Gary Cook/Alamy
p.378 Svalbard © Pixonnet.com/Alamy
p.387 Statue of Olav Tryggvasaon © MedioImages/Alamy
p.403 Saga carving © Corbis
p.423 Ibsen statue © Rolf Richardson/Alamy

Index

Note that in the Norwegian alphabet entries beginning with the letters Ø and Å come after “y” at the end of the alphabet; here we have also listed them under O and A. Map entries are in colour.

A

Å 334
accommodation 54–57
air passes 30, 51
airlines and flight routings
- from Australia and New Zealand 33
- from Ireland 31
- from North America 31
- from South Africa 33
- from the UK 30

airports (international)
- Bergen 201
- Gardermoen (Oslo) 78
- Stavanger 154
- Torp (Sandefjord) 79, (Oslo) 141

Ålesund 264
Ålesund 264–267
Alfred the Great 385
alphabet, Norwegian 69
Alta 353
Alta 353–355
Åmot 192
Amundsen, Roald 10, 106, 348
Åndalsnes 262
Andenes 319
Andøya 319
Arctic Circle Centre 299
Arctic Menu scheme 295
arctic phenomena 344
Arendal 142
Åsgårdstrand 134
Askildsen, Kjell 437
Astrup, Nikolai 212, 251
Astruptunet 251
Atlanterhavsveien 269
ATMs 45
Aulestad 173
Aurlandsdal valley 238
Aurlandsdal valley 237
Aurlandsfjord 235
Aurlandsvangen 237
Aurlandsvegen 236
aurora borealis 344

B

Balestrand 239
banks 45
Barentsburg 377
Baroniet Rosendal 226
Berekvam 232
Bergen 203
Bergen & the western fjords 200
Bergen 201–220
- accommodation 204
- Akvariet 213
- arrival 201
- art galleries 211
- bars 218
- Bergen Card 204
- Bergenhus Festning 210
- Bryggen 207
- Bryggens Museum 208
- Bull, Ole 216
- café-bars 217
- cafés 217
- clubs 218
- coffee houses 217
- consulates 219
- Domkirke 210
- eating and drinking 217
- Fantoft stave church 214
- festivals 219
- Fløibanen 209
- folk music & dancing 218
- funicular railway 209
- Gamle Bergen 216
- gay Bergen 220
- Grieg, Edvard 214–216
- Grieghallen 211, 218
- guesthouses 205
- guided tours 204
- Hanseatisk Museum 207
- hostels 205
- hotels 205
- information 202
- Kunsthall 212
- Kunstmuseum 211
- Lepramuseet 211
- listings 219
- Lysøen 216
- Lysverket 211
- Mariakirken 208
- markets 217
- Mount Fløyen 209
- Mount Ulriken 214
- nightlife 217
- Nordnes peninsula 213
- Øvregaten 209
- parking 202
- performing arts 218
- Rasmus Meyers Samlinger 212
- restaurants 217
- Schøtstuene 209
- Stenersen gallery 213
- Torgalmenningen 213
- Torget 207
- transport, city 202
- Troldhaugen 214
- USF Verftet 213, 218
- Vestlandske Kunstindustrimuseum 213

Bergsøya 269
Berlevåg 372
Bernadotte, Jean-Baptiste 92
Besseggen ridge 181
bibliography 417–426
bicycles 53
Birkebeinerrennet, the 65
Bjørnson, Bjørnstjerne 173
Black Death, the 390
Bleik 320, 321
Bleiksøya 320
Bødal 252
Bødalsbreen glacier arm 252
Bodø 302
Bodø 301–304
Bugøynes 307, 316
Bokmål 459
Boknafjord 160
books on Norway 417–426
border controls 40
border crossings 69
Borgund stave church 189
Borre 134
Botn 300
Botnhamn 321, 351
Bøverdal valley 247
Bøyabreen glacier arm 243
Breivik, Bård 101
Breivikeidet 352
Brensholmen 321, 351
Briksdal 251
Briksdalsbreen glacier arm 251
British commando raids 328
Brundtland, Dr Gro Harlem 400
Bull, Ole 216
burial mounds
- Bronze Age 383
- Viking 134, 175

burial, Viking ship 408–411
buses
- to Norway from the rest of Scandinavia 39

to Norway from the UK...... 35
within Norway 48
Bussekspress, Nor-Way 48
Byrkjelo..........................251

C

cabins 57
camping..........................57
Camping Card, Scandinavia 57
car rental 53
Carlsen, Bjørn..........................101
cell phones 63
Central Norway.... 166–167
changing money 45
Chernobyl 357
cinema, Norwegian 415
climate 16
climate change 29
cloudberries..........................412
coaches to Norway
from the rest of Scandinavia 39
from the UK..................... 35
Coastal Route (Highway 17)..........................298
commando raids 328
consulates, Norwegian 40
costs, average..........................44
credit cards 45
crime..........................64
cross-country skiing.......66
cruise operators to Norway from the UK..........................37
currency..........................45
cycling 53

D

Dahl, Johan Christian....95, 212
Dahl, Roald..........................127
Dalen 194
Dalsnibba 260
debit cards 45
Den Norske Turistforening see DNT
dental treatment 42
dialling codes, international..........................62
disabilities, travellers with..........................67
distance chart..........................13
DNT ......57, 65, 110, Hiking colour section
doctors 42
Dombås..........................182
Douglas, Kirk..........................194
Dovrefjell Nasjonalpark (national park)...........184
Dragsvik..........................234, 244
Drammen..........................132
draugen 407
drink..........................59
driving within Norway 51–53
Drøbak..........................128
Dyranut..........................189, 228

E

Egedius, Halfdan 96
Egersund 153
Eggum 332
EHIC 43
Eidfjord 227
Eidsdal..........................260
Eidsvoll Verk 169
Eidsvoll-bygningen.......168
Ekeland, Arne 96
elves 406
Elveseter..........................247
email 63
embassies, Norwegian...40
emergencies, medical 43
emergency numbers..........62
Enger, Erling 96
Eurail pass..........................35
exchange rates..........................45
Explore Norway air pass..........................51

F

Fadlan, Ibn 408
Fagernes..........................188
Fantoft stave church ...214
fauna and flora 412–414
Fauske..........................301
Fearnley, Thomas...95, 212
Fedafjord 153
Femund, Lake 187
Femundsmarka Nasjonalpark (national park)..........................186
ferries
to Norway from the rest of Scandinavia 39
to Norway from the UK...... 36
within Norway 49
festivals and events........61
Festøya..........................258
film, Norwegian 415
Finnmark..........................352
Finnmarksvidda..........................355
Finse..........................233
fishermen's shacks.......324
fishing..........................66
Fiskebol........316, 323, 326
Fjærlandsfjord 242
Fjættenfjord 291
fjords, the western 220–270
Flakstadøya & Moskenesøya..........................333
Flakstadøya 332
Flåm..........................235
Flåm railway (Flåmsbana) 232
Flatbreen glacier arm 243
Flatbrehytta 243
Flekkefjord..........................151
Flights to Norway
from Australia and New Zealand..................... 32
from Ireland..................... 31
from North America 31
from the rest of Scandinavia 39
from South Africa............. 33
from the UK..................... 29
flights
within Norway 50
online booking 27
flora and fauna 412–414
Florø..........................267
Fly Norway air pass.........51
Flydalsjuvet..........................259
Fodnes..........................189
Folgefonna glacier........225
Folgefonntunnelen........226
folk music & dancing....218
folklore, legends and 403–407
food 58–59
Fossli 227
Fossum, Karin 444
Fredrikstad..........................129
Fredrikstad 129–131
Frigga 404
Friluftspark, Alta 355

G

Gamle Lærdalsøyri 189
Gardermoen airport (Oslo) 78
Gaupne..........................246
gay Norway 69
Geilo 189
Geiranger..........................258
Geirangerfjord & Romdalsfjord 256
Geirangerfjord..... 255–260
giants..........................406
Gjende, Lake..........................182
Gjendebu..........................182
Gjendesheim 181
Gjermundshamn..........226

INDEX

glacier arms
- Bødalsbreen........................252
- Bøyabreen...........................243
- Briksdalsbreen 251
- Flatbreen.............................243
- Kjenndalsbreen 252
- Nigardsbreen.......................246
- Supphellebreen 243

glaciers
- Folgefonna 225
- Hardangerjøkulen.................233
- Jostedalsbreen....... 243, 246, 249–253
- Svartisen 298

glossaries 465–466
Gokstad Viking longship.....................105
Gormley, Antony..........297
Graddis.........................300
Grieg, Edvard 214–216
Grimstad.......................144
Grip..............................270
Grodås...........................254
Grønligrotta 298
Grungedal valley...........193
Gryllefjord............316, 321
Gudbrandsdal....... 174–177
Gude, Hans Frederik.....95, 212
Gudvangen....................235
guesthouses 55

H

Hagafoss 189
Halden 131
Hallingdal valley 189
Halne 189, 228
Hamar...........................169
Hammerfest 362
Hammerfest 361–364
Hamningberg.................373
Hamnøy 332
Hamsun, Knut 307, 424
Hamsund.......................308
Hanseatic League.......206, 207, 390
Hansen, Armauer 211
Haraldsson, Olav (St) 283, 292, 388
Hardangerfjord............224
Hardangerfjord, the 222–230
Hardangerjøkulen glacier 233
Hardangervidda Nasjonalpark (national park).........................228
Hardangervidda plateau.........................228
Hardrada, Harald.........389
Harstad 317
Harstad..........................317
Haugen 187
Haugesund 160
health.............................42
Heddal stave church..........................192
Heidal valley 176
Heinesen, William.........425
Heli...............................291
Hella 234, 244
Hellesylt........................257
Henie, Sonja 108
Henningsvær 330
Heroes of Telemark, the..............................194
Heyerdahl, Thor 107, 417
hiking.......65, Hiking colour section
history of Norway 383–402
Hjerkinn........................183
Hjørundfjord.................258
Holand 298
holidays, public 60
Holmenkollen................110
Hønefoss 189
Honningsvåg ....[illegible]
Hopperstad stave church.........................234
Hornindalsvaten 254
Hornøya........................373
Horten...........................132
hostels 56
hotel discount passes 55
hotels.............................54
Hundorp 174
Hurtigbåt passenger express boats.............49
Hurtigrute coastal boat 49, 50
Husedalen valley 226
hytter 57

I

Ibn Fadlan 408
Ibsen, Henrik........93, 144, 146, 425
Igloo Hotell 355
inns...............................55
insurance.......................43
international airports see airports
Internet
- access 63
- sites.................................41

InterRail pass................35

J

Jomfruland 142
Jondal...........................225
Jossingfjord..................153
Jostedalsbreen glacier 243, 246, 249–253
Jotunheimen Nasjonalpark (national park) 180
Jotunheimen Nasjonalpark (national park)............179
Juhl's Silver Gallery, Kautokeino 358
Junkerdal......................300

K

Kabakov, Ilya 100
Kabelvåg.......................329
Kåfjord..........................352
Kalmar Union...............391
Kamøyvær 368
Karasjok........................359
Karl XIV Johan, King 92, 392
Kaupanger...........244, 245
Kautokeino 358
kilometre chart 13
[illegible] 207
Kinsarvik......................226
Kirkenes.......................373
Kittelsen, Theodor 95, 142, 212, 285, 406
Kjeåsen........................227
Kjeldebu 233
Kjelvik 306
Kjenndalsbreen glacier arm 252
Kjeragbolten 159
Kjerringøy 305
klippfisk 12, 270
Knivskjellodden 369
Kongsberg 190
Kongsberg.........190–192
Kongsvoll......................183
Korgen..........................295
Korgfjellet 295
Kragerø........................141
Kråkmo.........................307
Kristiansand 147
Kristiansand 147–150
Kristiansund.................269
Krohg, Christian 95, 212
Kvam 175
Kvanndal......................224
Kvernes stave church...269
Kylling bru 182
Kystriksveien (Highway 17).............298
Kystvegen, the 160

INDEX

L

Lærdal valley 189
Lærdalsøyri, Gamle 189
Lake Femund 187
Lake Gjende 182
Lake Mjøsa 169
Lakselv 371
Laksforsen 293
Landsmål 459
Langfjordbotn 352
language 459–465
Lapps 356–357
Larsen, Leif 207, 292
Larvik 141
Latefossen 193
left luggage 70
legends and folklore 403–407
Leira 188
Leirdal 247
Leknes (Norangsdal) 258
lemmings 413
leprosy, in Bergen 211
lesbian Norway 69
Levanger 291
Liknes 153
Lillehammer 171–173
Lillesand 145
Lindesnes 151
Linge 261
Lødingen 307, 316
Loen 252
Løfallstrand 226
Lofoten & Vesterålen Islands 314–315
Lofoten Islands ... 323–337
Lofoten Islands, Trondheim to the 276–277
Lofotenveggen 324
Lofthus 227
Lom 247
Longyearbyen 377
Lønsdal 300
Lovatnet 252, 253
Lustrafjord 245
Lutheranism 392
Lyngdal 153
Lyngseidet 352
Lysebotn 159
Lysefjord 159
Lysøen 216

M

Magerøya 364, 366
Magnusson, Magnus 421
Maihaugen, Lillehammer 172
mail 62
Mandal 150
Manheller 189
maps 42
Marstein 182
media 64
medical treatment 42
Meiadal valley 261
Melbu 316, 323, 326
Melfjord 298
Memurubu 181, 182
menu reader 462–464
Menu, Arctic scheme ... 295
Merdø 143
Midgard Historisk Senter, Borre 134
midnight sun 15, 344
mileage chart 13
Mjøsa, Lake 169
mobile phones 63
Mo-i-Rana 296
Mo-i-Rana 295
Molde 268
Monroe, Marilyn 160
Mosjøen 293
Moskenes 334
Moskenesøya 332
Moskenstraumen 335
mosquitoes 70
Moss 127
Mount Skåla 243
mountain huts 57
Møvik 149
Munch, Edvard 92, 96, 111, 134, 212, 285, 422
Munch-museet, ... Oslo (Munch Museum) 111
Mundal 242
Munthe, Gerhard 95, 285
Murmansk (Russia) 375
musk ox 184
Myrdal 232, 233

N

Nærøyfjord 236
Nansen, Fridtjof 349
Narvik 308
Narvik 308–312
national parks
  Dovrefjell 184
  Femundsmarka 186
  Hardangervidda 228
  Jotunheimen 179, 180
  Øvre Pasvik 374
  Rondane 177, 178
  Saltfjellet 300
  Stabbursdalen 371
Nerdrum, Odd 101
Nessane 240
Nigardsbreen glacier arm 246
Nikel (Russia) 375
Nobel Fredssenter (Peace Centre) 99
Nobel, Alfred 99
Norangsdal valley 257
Norangsfjord 258
Norddal valley 240
Nordfjord 249
Nordfjord 249–254
Nordfjordeid 254
Nordkapp 366
Nordkapp 369
Norheimsund 223
Norse mythology 404
Norske Vandrerhjem 56
North Cape 369
North Norway 342
northern lights 344
Northwest Passage 348
Nor-Way Bussekspress 48
Norway in a Nutshell 221
Norway Rail Pass 48
Norway, Central ... 166–167
Norway, North 342
Norway, South 140
Norwegian (language) 459–465
Norwegian consulates 40
Norwegian embassies 40
Norwegian Emigration Centre 157
Norwegian Tourist Board 41
Norwegian tourist offices abroad 41
Norwegian Wood music festival 121
Notodden 192
Nusfjord 332
Nutshell, Norway in a ... 221
Nynorsk 459

O

Odda 193, 226
Odin 404
Ofotbanen, the 309
Olav, St 283, 292, 388
Olavsgruva 186
Olden 251
Olderdalen 352
online booking 27
opening hours 60
Oppdal 183
Ørneberget 232
Ornes 245
Ørnevegen 256, 258
Osa 229
Oseberg Viking longship 105

INDEX

Oslo 75–127
Oslo 80–81
Oslo and the Oslofjord ... 76
Oslo, Central – cafés, restaurants & bars 116–117
Oslo, Central 90–91
accommodation 85–88
airport, Gardermoen 78
airport, Torp 79, 141
Aker Brygge 99
Akershus 102
Akershus Slott (castle) 103
Ankerbrua......................... 98
Arkitekturmuseet (Architecture) 100
arrival 78
Astrup Fearnley Museet (Modern Art).................. 101
Aula 91
B&Bs 87
Bankplassen 100
Barnekunstmuseet (Children's Art) 124
bars 119
beaches 114
Bygdøy Peninsula 103–107
café-bars......................... 115
cafés 115
camping 88
Central Oslo 88–103
children's attractions .... [illegible]
cinema 123
classical music................. 122
coffee houses 115
Damstredet 98
DNT 110
Domkirke 89
eating and drinking ...114–120
embassies 126
entertainment 120
festivals, music 121
fishing............................. 123
Forsvarsmuseet (Armed Forces) 103
Frammuseet 106
Frogner Manor 109
Frognerparken.................. 108
Frognerseteren................. 110
Gamle Aker Kirke 98
Gamlebyen 113
gay Oslo 126
Grünerløkka....................... 98
guesthouses 87
Henie-Onstad Kunstsenter (Art Centre) 107
Hjemmefrontmuseum (Resistance Museum) ... 102
Holmenkollen 110
hostels 87
hotels 86
Hovedøya 114
Ibsen, Henrik 93
Ibsen-museet 93
information 82
islands 114
Jakob Kulturkirke 98
jazz 122
jewellery 126
Karl Johans gate 89
Kongelige Slott (Royal Palace) 92
Kon-Tiki Museet 107
Kulturhistorisk Museum 93
Kunstindustrimuseet (Applied Art) 97
Ladegård 113
Langøyene 114
Listings 125
Munch, Edvard..... 92, 96, 111
Munch-museet (Munch Museum) 111
music festivals 121
music, classical 122
music, live 121
Nasjonalgalleriet (National Gallery) 94
Nasjonalmuseet 89
nightclubs 121
nightlife............................ 120
Nobel Fredssenter (Peace Centre) 99
Nobel, Alfred 99
Nordmarka 110
Norsk Teknisk Museum (Technology) 124
Norsk Folkemuseum (Folk Museum) 104
Norsk Sjøfartsmuseum (Maritime) 107
opera 122
Oseberg Viking longship 105
Oslo Bymuseum (City Museum) 109
Oslo Pass 83
parking 82
Rådhus 98
restaurants 118
Royal Palace 92
Samtidskunst, Museet for (Contemporary Art) 100
Sjømannsskolen 113
skating, ice 124
skiing 123
Skimuseet (Ski Museum) 110
sleigh rides 124
Sognsvannet 111
sports 123
St Olav Domkirke 97
Stenersenmuseet 93
Stortinget (Parliament) 89
Teatermuseet (Theatre Museum) 100
theatre 123
Trafikanten 83
transport, city 83
Tryvannstårnet TV tower 110
Ullevålseter 110
Unginfo...................... 83, 127
University 91
Use-It 83, 127
Vigelandsparken (Vigeland Sculpture Park).............. 108
Vikingskipshuset (Viking Ships Museum) 105
youth hostels 87
Oslofjord 128
Oslofjord 127–134
Østerbø............................ 237
Otta................................. 176
outdoor pursuits 65–67
Øvre Pasvik Nasjonalpark (national park).............. 374
Øye 257
Øygardstøl 159

P

package tours 36
from Australia 38
from Ireland 37
from New Zealand 38
from North America 38
from the UK........................ 37
paragliding...................... 230
passes, air 30
passes, hotel 55
passports.......................... 40
pensions .... [illegible]
permits, work & residence 40
phones.............................. 62
phrases in Norwegian ... 460
Pietism............................ 393
polar night 344
Polarsirkelsenteret 299
population of Norway 8
Porsangerfjord 366, 371
Porsgrunn 141
post 62
prehistoric rock carvings (Alta)............................ 353
Preikestolen (Pulpit rock) 159
private rooms 56
public holidays 60
puffin safari 320
Pulpit rock (Preikestolen) 159

Q

Quisling, Vidkun 102, 149, 284, 397

R

radio 64
rafting 67, 176, 230
Raftsundet 316, 323

Ragnarok 404
rail
contact numbers 34
passes 34, 48
to Norway from the rest of Scandinavia 39
to Norway from the UK 34
railway timetables (international) 35
railways, Norwegian 46
rainfall, average daily 16
Rallarvegen 233
Rallarveien (Narvik) 309
Ramberg 332
Rauma (train line) 182
Reformation, the 392
Refsa 159
Refsvatn 159
Reine 333
Reinefjord 334
Repvåg 366
residence permits 40
Revold, Axel 93, 96, 172
Riksgränsen (Sweden) 309
Riksmål 459
Ringebu 174
Risøyhamn 319
river rafting 67
Rjukan 194, 398
rock carvings, prehistoric (Alta) 353
Rødven stave church 262
Rognan 300
Røldal stave church 193
Rombaksbotn 309
Romdalsfjord & Geirangerfjord 256
Rondane Nasjonalpark (national park) 178
Rondane Nasjonalpark (national park) 177
Rondvassbu 179
Rondvatnet 178
rorbuer (fishermen's shacks, Lofoten) 324
Røros 185
Røros 184–187
Rose, Knut 101
Rosekyrkja church, Stordal 261
Rosendal 226
Røst 337
Runde 267
runes 384
Russian border 375
Ryggen, Hannah 285

S

Saebo 258
sagas 403
Saggrenda 191
St Olav 283, 292, 388
Sakrisøya 333
Saltfjellet Nasjonalpark 300
Saltstraumen 305
Sami 356–357
Sandefjord 141
Sandel, Cora 348
Savio, John 374
ScanRail pass 34
Selja island 254
Selje 254
Seljord 192
Setsedal 150
sexual harassment 65
short stories 427–456
Sjoa 175
sjøhus (sea-houses, Lofoten) 324
Skagastølsbu 247
Skageflå 259
Skaidi 364, 365
Skåla, Mount 253
Skarberget 307
Skaurøya 145
Skei 251
Skibladner, DS 170
Skien 194
skiing 65
cross-country 66
summer 66, 225
Skjærgårdspark 145
Skjolden 246
Skram, Amalie 427
Skrova 327
Skutvik 307, 325
smoking 70
Snåsa 293
snowboarding 65
Sogndal 244
Sognefjellsveg 246
Sognefjord 240
Sognefjord 237–246
Sohlberg, Harald 96
Solevåg 258
Solvorn 245
Sommarøy 351
Sommarset 306
Sørensen, Henrik 96
Sortland 321
South Norway 140
Spitsbergen 377
Stabbursdalen Nasjonalpark (national park) 371
Stabbursnes 371
Stalheim 235
Stamsund 331
Stavali 226
Stavanger 153
Stavanger 152–158
stave churches 188
Borgund 189
Fantoft 214
Heddal 192
Hopperstad 234
Kaupanger 245
Kvernes 269
Lom 247
Ringebu 174
Rødven 262
Røldal 193
Urnes 245
Steine 331
Steinkjer 293
Stigfossen falls 262
Stiklestad 292
stokfisk 12
Stokmarknes 322
Stordal 261
Store Standal 258
Støren 183
stories, short 427–456
Storskog 375
Straumen 306
Stryn 253
Supphellebreen glacier arm 243
Svalbard 376
Svalbard 375–379
Svartisen glacier 298
Svendsby 352
Svolvær 327
Svolværgeita 327
Svor, Anders 255
Sygard Grytting 175
Sylte 261
Synnervika 187

T

Tafjord 261
Tana Bru 371
Tau 159
tax-free shopping 45
Telemark 192
Telemarking 66
Telemarkskanal 194
telephones 62
television 64
temperatures, average daily 16
Thor 404

Tidemand, Adolph..95, 212
time zones.....................70
timetables, train
(international)..............35
tipping 70
Tirpitz...................292, 353
Tønsberg 132
Torp airport
(Sandefjord) 79, 141
Torsnes 159
tourist offices abroad,
Norwegian 41
trains
contact numbers..............34
passes.........................34, 48
timetables
(international).................35
to Norway from the rest of
Scandinavia....................39
to Norway from
the UK..............................34
within Norway....................46
Tranøy...........................307
travel agents
in Australia 33
in Ireland 31
in New Zealand..................33
in North America................32
in the UK............................30
Troldhaugen..................214
Trollfjord........316, 323, 327
trolls..............................406
Trollstigen 261
Trollveggen 182
Tromsø 345
Tromsø.................344–351
Trondheim 279
Trondheim 278–299
Trondheim to the
Lofoten
Islands..................276–277
Tufta, Bjørn Sigurd 101
Turtagrø 247
TV 64

U

Ullman, Liv....................415
Ulvik..............................229
Undredal........................235
Unstad...........................332
Urnes stave
church........................245
Utakleiv..........................331
Utne...............................224

V

Vadsø.............................373
Værøy 336
Vaggatem 375
Valhalla 404
Valkyries 404
Valldal valley 261
Vandrerhjem, Norske......56
Vangsnes.......................234
Varangerbotn.................371
Varangerfjord.................371
Vardø 372
Vassbygdi 237
vegan food 59
vegetarian food 59
Vemork 194
Verdalsøra.....................291
Verdens Ende 133
Vesterålen and Lofoten
Islands..............314–315
Vesterålen
Islands...............312–333
Vestvågøy......................331
Vigeland, Emanuel........109
Vigeland, Gustav 108
Vigelandsparken (Vigeland
Sculpture Park)..........108
Vik..................................234
Viking
burial mounds.........134, 175,
Vikings Colour Section
customs and rituals...408–411
longships.........................105
ship burial ...408–411, Vikings
Colour Section
Vikings in North America
(Vinland)....................387
Vikings, the..... 385, Vikings
Colour Section
Vindstad 334
Vinje..............................234
Vinland sagas 387
visas 40
Visit Scandinavia
air pass.........................30
Vøringfossen.................227
Voss..............................230

W

Wassmo, Herbjørg........433
weather...........................16
websites 41
Weidemann, Jakob.......211
Werenskiold, Erik...95, 212,
406
Wergeland, Henrik 103, 396
western fjords,
the 220–270
whale safaris 319
white-water rafting 67,
176, 230
wights 407
wiring money 45
witches 407, 372
work permits 40
World War I...................396
World War II..................397

Y

Yggdrasil 404
youth hostels...................56

Ø

Øygardstøl....................159
Øvre Pasvik Nasjonalpark
(national park)............374
Øye 257
Ørnevegen....................256
Østerbø.........................237
Ørneberget 232

Å

Å 334
Ålesund 264
Ålesund...............264–267
Åndalsnes.....................262
Åmot.............................192
Åsgårdstrand................134